WEST GERMANY, COLD WAR EUROPE AND THE ALGERIAN WAR

This book is an illuminating and provocative account of Germany's role as sanctuary for Algerian nationalists during their fight for independence from France between 1954 and 1962. It explores key issues such as the impact of external sanctuaries on French counter-insurgency efforts; the part played by security and intelligence services while attempting to eliminate these sanctuaries; the Algerian war's influence on West German foreign and security policy; and, finally, the emergence of West German civic engagement in support of Algeria's independence struggle. Mathilde von Bülow sheds new light on how FLN activities in West Germany shaped the newly independent country's perception of its place in international society, on how the role of anti-colonial movements and insurgencies in the developing world shaped the dynamics of the Cold War and on how the Algerian war was fought and won.

MATHILDE VON BÜLOW is Lecturer in History at the University of Glasgow, where she is also co-Director of the Scottish Centre for War Studies.

NEW STUDIES IN EUROPEAN HISTORY

The aim of this series in early modern and modern European history is to publish outstanding works of research, addressed to important themes across a wide geographical range, from southern and central Europe, to Scandinavia and Russia, from the time of the Renaissance to the present. As it develops, the series will comprise focused works of wide contextual range and intellectual ambition.

A full list of titles published in the series can be found at:
www.cambridge.org/newstudiesineuropeanhistory

WEST GERMANY, COLD WAR EUROPE AND THE ALGERIAN WAR

MATHILDE VON BÜLOW

University of Glasgow

CAMBRIDGE
UNIVERSITY PRESS

CAMBRIDGE
UNIVERSITY PRESS

University Printing House, Cambridge CB2 8BS, United Kingdom

Cambridge University Press is part of the University of Cambridge.

It furthers the University's mission by disseminating knowledge in the pursuit of education, learning and research at the highest international levels of excellence.

www.cambridge.org
Information on this title: www.cambridge.org/9781107088597

First published 2016

Printed in the United States of America by Sheridan Books, Inc.

A catalogue record for this publication is available from the British Library

Library of Congress Cataloging-in-Publication data
Von Bulow, Mathilde, 1977–
West Germany, Cold War Europe and the Algerian War / Mathilde Von Bulow (University of Glasgow).
Cambridge, United Kingdom ; New York : Cambridge University Press, 2016. | Series: New studies in European history | Includes bibliographical references and index.
LCCN 2016001751 | ISBN 9781107088597 (hardback)
LCSH: Algeria – History – Revolution, 1954–1962 – Diplomatic history. | Algeria – Foreign relations – Germany (West) | Germany (West) – Foreign relations – Algeria. | Nationalists – Algeria – History – 20th century. | Algerians – Germany (West) – History – 20th century. | Asylum, Right of – Germany (West) – History – 20th century. | Jabhat al-Taḥrīr al-Qawmī – History. | Algeria – Colonial influence – History – 20th century. | France – Colonies – History – 20th century. | Cold War – Political aspects – Europe.
LCC DT295 .V66 2016 | DDC 965/.0462–dc23
LC record available at http://lccn.loc.gov/2016001751

ISBN 978-1-107-08859-7 Hardback

Contents

Acknowledgements

This book originated as a PhD submitted to the Faculty of History at the University of Cambridge, where I benefited from the support of many friends and scholars. I owe a tremendous gratitude to my former supervisor, Christopher Andrew. His encouragement and assistance gave me the confidence to see this project through, and he still inspires me to become a better historian. I am equally thankful to the convenors of the Intelligence, International History and Modern European History Seminars, especially David Reynolds, Robert Tombs and Kristina Spohr. These seminars provided me a wonderful opportunity to learn and test some of my own ideas in an intellectually rigorous yet always friendly setting. My housemates at Selwyn Gardens and friends at Leckhamptom, meanwhile, provided cheer and companionship and reminded me that there are other things in this world than my PhD; Liz Chambers, Lila Koumandou, Peter Stokes, Alain Tschudin, and Khaled El Rouayheb – I thank you in particular. Chantal Aubin, Heather Jones and Andrew Webster, for their part, were excellent archive companions in Paris. A special mention should also go to Naila and her father, whom I was privileged to meet, and whose experience of the Algerian war helped inspire this story.

The research for this book could not have been completed without the financial support of Corpus Christi College, the Cambridge Commonwealth Trust, the Overseas Research Students Award Scheme, Cambridge's Faculty of History, the Royal Historical Society, the Social Sciences and Humanities Research Council of Canada, the German Historical Institute in Paris, the Institute for European History in Mainz and the Dean's Fund at the University of Nottingham. The generous funding I received from these bodies enabled prolonged research trips to France and Germany as well as numerous conference trips to present my findings. I am particularly grateful to the community of scholars and students I encountered at the German Historical Institute and Institute for European History, especially Werner Paravicini, Corinna Franz, Stefan

Martens, Heinz Duchhardt and Ralph Melville, who not only imparted valuable advice and constructive criticism but also demonstrated compassion at a time of difficulty. It was a privilege to participate in the life and work of both Institutes. The moral and material support I received over the years also enabled me to seek out publication opportunities for articles and book chapters, efforts that ultimately culminated in this manuscript.

A particular debt of gratitude goes to the School (then Department) of History at the University of Nottingham for helping me transform my PhD with its narrow focus into a manuscript for publication. John Young, Elizabeth Harvey, Colin Heywood and Maiken Umbach not only ensured I had the institutional support I needed to pursue my research, they also offered valuable intellectual and professional insights for which I am very grateful. I also wish to thank my many wonderful colleagues, especially Karen Adler, Dave Appleby, Sarah Badcock, Gwilym Dodd, Andrew Cobbing, Sheryllynne Haggerty, Dan Hucker, David Laven, Rob Lutton, Spencer Mawby, Joe Merton, Liudmyla Sharipova, Claire Taylor and Sue Townsend. Their collegiality and spirit are inspirational and infectious; their knowledge profound. I consider myself fortunate to count many of them as friends. My students, too, deserve a mention. Their inquisitiveness and eagerness to learn was stimulating and helped me work through many a conundrum during the writing of this book.

My new colleagues at the University of Glasgow, meanwhile, provided vital assistance and encouragement as I raced to submit my manuscript and turn around proofs. Lynn Abrams and Callum Brown have been excellent mentors, and I am grateful for the friendship and support of Stuart Airlie, Alex Marshall, Marina Moskowitz, Simon Newman, May Rosenthal-Sloan, Matthew Strickland and Jochen (and Kirsten) Schenk. I owe a particular gratitude to Peter Jackson, who, long before becoming my friend and colleague, offered constructive criticism and provided me with opportunities to present and publish early findings. Without his cajoling I would not have had the courage to submit my book proposal to Cambridge University Press. I am glad I listened to him.

Whether I met them at conferences, seminars, workshops, or in archives, there have been many other excellent scholars who have provided helpful feedback and tips or simply inspiration. Through them, I was exposed to stimulating discussion, new ideas and alternative perspectives. Wolfgang Krieger, Jean-Paul Cahn and the late Klaus-Jürgen Müller, Fritz Taubert, Wolfram Kaiser, Jessica Gienow-Hecht, Arne Westad, Andrew Webster, Andrew Barros, Lorne Breitenlohner and Theo Pronk provided valuable advice and feedback during the early stages of this project. Further aiding the development of this project were discussions with Raphaëlle Branche, Sylvie Thénault, Maurice Vaïsse, Niek Pas, Daho Djerbal, Martin Evans, Martin Alexander, Martin Shipway, Linda Amiri, Mohamed Boukechour, Amar Mohand-Amer, Fabian Klose, Jennifer Onyedum, Levent Işyar, Helene von Bismarck, Paul McGarr, Rana Barakat, Kim Wagner, Alex Keese, Sam Kalman, Claire Eldridge, Jennifer Sessions and Mairi MacDonald, whether at conferences or in private. I also owe a tremendous gratitude to William Roger Louis and Philippa Levine, who commented on portions of the manuscript. As leaders of the National History Centre's fifth International Seminar on Decolonization, they, alongside Dane Kennedy, Jason Parker and Pillarisetti Sudhir, were responsible for many animated and stimulating discussions about the nature of imperialism and decolonisation. Above all, I sincerely thank Martin Thomas for sharing with me his immense knowledge and expertise, for his tireless assistance and encouragement, and for providing me with opportunities to present and publish some of my early findings.

Equally important for the completion of this book was the generous assistance I received from archivists and librarians. In France, the staff at the *Archives Diplomatiques* of the *Quai d'Orsay*, as it was then, as well as the *Service Historique de la Défense*, the *Service d'Histoire Contemporaine*, the *Archives Nationales* and the *Service des Archives et du Musée de la Préfecture de Police de Paris* helped me navigate finding aids and deal with countless 'demandes de dérotations'. In Germany, too, I was able to rely on expert guidance and assistance in the *Bundesarchiv* in Koblenz, the *Politische Archiv des Auswärtigen Amts*, the *Archiv der sozialen Demokratie*, as well as the archives of the *Deutsche Rote Kreuz*, the *Evangelische Werk für Diakonie und Entwicklung* and the *Deutsche Caritasverband*. Much of the writing of this manuscript, meanwhile, was done at the African Studies Centre at Leiden University, *Koninklijke Bibliotheek* in Den Haag and *Staatsbibliothek zu Berlin*, whose librarians handled my many requests with great patience, and whose cafeterias sustained me with a constant flow of bad but much-needed coffee.

My sincere thanks also go to Michael Watson, Amanda George and everyone at Cambridge University Press for their supreme patience, effort and professionalism. This includes the anonymous readers, who provided extremely valuable feedback for which I am grateful. Chapters 3 and 7 incorporate and expand on material that appeared previously in the following articles and book chapters: Mathilde von Bülow, 'Franco-German Intelligence Cooperation and the Internationalization of Algeria's War of Independence (1954–62)', *Intelligence and National Security* 28/3 (2013), pp. 397–419 (www.tandfonline.com/doi/abs/10.1080/02684527.2013.789638); Ibid., 'Exposing the "Paradoxical Citizenship": French Authorities' Responses to the Algerian Presence in Federal Germany during the Algerian War, 1954–1962', in *The French Colonial Mind. Vol.2: Violence, Military Encounters, and Colonialism* (ed.) Martin Thomas (Lincoln NB, 2011), pp. 304–33; Ibid., 'Hôtes importuns. Des Algériens en République fédérale pendant la guerre d'Algérie', in *Migrations et identités. L'exemple de l'Allemagne aux XIXe et XXe siècles* (eds.) Jean-Paul Cahn and Bernard Poloni (Villeneuve d'Ascq, 2009), pp. 119–29. Chapters 5 and 9 include material first published in Mathilde von Bülow, 'Myth or Reality? The Red Hand and French Covert Action in Federal Germany during the Algerian War, 1956–61', *Intelligence and National Security* 22/6 (2007), pp. 787–820 (www.tandfonline.com/doi/abs/10.1080/02684520701770626). I thank the editors and publishers for their permission to use this material. I also take full responsibility for any errors and omissions found in this work and would be grateful for notice of such for future corrections.

Finally, my heartfelt gratitude goes to my friends and family, who supported me through this project. Nadine, Ali, Niko and Inez, Andreas and Änne, Sue and Paul generously opened their homes to me on my archive trips, providing good cheer, conversation and companionship. Alex and Bea, too, provided moral support and good company. Denis Smyth, my mentor, gave me encouragement and guidance without which I might never have become a historian. Phil O'Brien's love and support, his deep knowledge and experience as well as common sense have kept me grounded and calm. I am also grateful to my three brothers – Karl, Alex and Götz – and their families, for being there for me and spurring me on. Most of all, I thank my loving parents, Hans and Katharina, who have always supported me, unreservedly. Their life experiences, courage, passion and spirit of adventure inspired me to study the historical encounters of peoples of different nationalities and cultures. This book is dedicated to them.

Abbreviations

Text and notes

ALN	*Armée de libération nationale* – Algerian National Liberation Army
ARD	*Arbeitsgemeinschaft der öffentlich-rechtlichen Rundfunksender der Bundesrepublik Deutschland* – West German (first) public broadcasting corporation
ASVD	*Arabischer Studentenverband in Deutschland* – Arab Student Union in (West) Germany
AUMA	*Association des 'ulamā musulmans algériens* – Association of Muslim Algerian Scholars
AWO	*Arbeiterwohlfahrt* – Workers' Welfare Organisation
BdI	*Bundesverband der deutschen Industrie* – Federation of (West) German Industries
BfV	*Bundesamt für Verfassungsschutz* – Federal Office for the Protection of the Constitution
BKA	*Bundeskriminalamt* – Federal Criminal Police Office
BND	*Bundesnachrichtendienst* – Federal Intelligence Service
CCE	*Comité de Coordination et d'Exécution* – Coordination and Execution Committee of the FLN
CDU	*Christlich Demokratische Union* – Christian-democratic Union
CNRA	*Conseil National de la Révolution Algérienne* – National Council of the Algerian Revolution
COCOM	NATO Coordinating Committee for East-West Trade Policy
COSEC	Coordinating Secretariat of National Unions of Students, Leiden
CRA	*Croissant Rouge Algérien* – Algerian Red Crescent
CSU	*Christlich Soziale Union* – Christian-social Union

DGB	*Deutscher Gewerkschaftsbund* – Confederation of (West) German Trade Unions
DPA	*Deutsche Presse-Agentur* – West German Press Agency
DRK	*Deutsches Rotes Kreuz* – West German Red Cross
DST	*Direction de la Surveillance du Territoire* – Directorate for Territorial Surveillance
EDF	European Development Fund
EPU	European Payments Union
Euratom	European Atomic Energy Community
FAZ	*Frankfurter Allgemeine Zeitung* – Frankfurt General Newspaper
FDGB	*Freier Deutscher Gewerkschaftsbund* – Free German Trade Union Federation, GDR
FLN	*Front de libération nationale* – Algerian National Liberation Front
FRG	Federal Republic of Germany
GDR	German Democratic Republic
GPRA	*Gouvernement provisoire de la République algérienne* – Provisional Government of the Algerian Republic
ICFTU	International Confederation of Free Trade Unions
ICRC	International Committee of the Red Cross
IGM	*Industriegewerkschaft Metall* – Industrial Union of Metalworkers
KAAD	*Katholischer Akademischer Austausch Dienst* – Catholic Academic Exchange Service
MALG	*Ministère de l'Armement et des Liaisons Générales*, GPRA – Ministry for Armaments and General Relations
MNA	*Mouvement national algérien* – Algerian National Movement
NATO	North Atlantic Treaty Organization
OAS	*Organisation de l'armée secrète* – Secret Army Organisation
OS	*Organisation Spéciale* – Special Organisation (the armed wing of the PPA-MTLD and later of the *Fédération de France du* FLN)
PCF	*Parti Communiste Français* – French Communist Party
PPA-MTLD	*Parti populaire algérien – Mouvement pour le triomphe des libertés démocratiques* – Algerian Popular Party – Movement for the Triumph of Democratic Liberties

RG	*Renseignements Généraux* – General Intelligence Directorate
SDECE	*Service de documentation extérieure et de contre-espionnage* – External Documentation and Counter-Espionage Service
SDS	*Sozialistischer deutscher Studentenbund* – Socialist (West) German Student Union
SFIO	*Section Française de l'Internationale Ouvrière* – French Section of the Workers' International
SPD	*Sozialdemokratische Partei Deutschlands* – Social-Democratic Party of Germany
UAR	United Arab Republic
UDMA	*Union démocratique du manifeste algérien* – Democratic Union of the Algerian Manifesto
UGEMA	*Union générale des étudiants musulmans algériens* – General Union of Muslim Algerian Students
UGTA	*Union générale des travailleurs algériens* – General Union of Algerian Workers
UN	United Nations
UNHCR	United Nations High Commission for Refugees
US	United States (of America)
VdR	*Verband deutscher Reeder* – Association of (West) German Shipowners
VdS	*Verband deutscher Studentenschaften* – Association of (West) German Student Unions
ZDF	*Zweites Deutsches Fernsehen* – Second (West) German Television Station

Notes only

10.RM	*Dixième Région Militaire* – 10th Military Region (Algeria)
AA	*Auswärtiges Amt* – West German Foreign Office
ADCV	*Archiv des Deutschen Caritasverbandes*, Freiburg
ADN	*Allgemeiner Deutscher Nachrichtendienst* – East German news service
ADRK	*Archiv des Deutschen Roten Kreuzes*, Berlin
AdsD	*Archiv der sozialen Demokratie*, Bonn
AEWDE	*Archiv des Evangelischen Werks für Diakonie und Entwicklung*, Berlin

AHC	*Archives d'histoire contemporaine*, SciencesPo, Paris
AL/ALG	*Afrique-Levant/Algérie* – Africa-Near East Division/ Algeria
AL/MAR	*Afrique-Levant/Maroc* – Africa-Near East Division/ Morocco
AM/EUA	*Amérique/États-Unis de l'Amérique* – Americas Division/USA
AN	*Archives Nationales*, Paris
AstA	*Allgemeiner Studentenausschuss* – General Student Committee
BA/K	*Bundesarchiv*, Koblenz
BAgW	*Bundesamt für gewerbliche Wirtschaft* – Federal Office for Trade and Industry
BDFD	*Die Bundesrepublik Deutschland und Frankreich: Dokumente, 1949–1963*
BfdW	*Brot für die Welt* – 'Bread for the World'
BMA	*Bundesministerium für Arbeit* – Federal Ministry for Labour
BMF	*Bundesministerium der Finanzen* – Federal Ministry of Finance
BMI	*Bundesministerium des Innern* – Federal Ministry of the Interior
BMJ	*Bundesministerium der Justiz* – Federal Ministry of Justice
BMV	*Bundesministerium für Verkehr* – Federal Ministry for Transport
BMVg	*Bundesministerium für Verteidigung* – Federal Ministry for Defence
BMWi	*Bundesministerium für Wirtschaft* – Federal Ministry for Economic Affairs
BPA	*Bundespresseamt* – Federal Press Office
CCFFA/2	*Commendement en chef des forces françaises en Allemagne/ Deuxième bureau* – High Command of the French Forces in Germany/Military Intelligence
DDF	*Documents Diplomatiques Français*
DGGA/BE	*Délégation générale du gouvernement en Algérie/Bureau d'études* – General Delegation of the French Government in Algeria/Office of General Studies
EM(I)/2	*État-major (interarmées)/Deuxième bureau* – (Joint) General Staff/Military Intelligence

EMA/2	*État-major des forces armées/Deuxième bureau* – General Staff of the Armed Forces, Military Intelligence
EMGDN/2	*État-major général de la Défense Nationale/ Renseignements* – General Staff of the Ministry for National Defence/Military Intelligence
EMI/2	*État-major interarmées des Forces en Algérie/Deuxième bureau* – Joint General Staff of French Forces in Algeria/Military Intelligence
EU/RFA	*Europe/République Fédérale d'Allemagne* – Europe Division/FRG
FDP	*Freie Demokratische Partei Deutschlands* – Free-Democratic Party
INS/AFN	*Inspection générale des Forces terrestres, maritimes et aériennes de l'Afrique française du Nord* – General Inspectorate of Land, Sea and Air Forces in French North Africa
JSS	*Journal of Strategic Studies*
LfV	*Landesamt für Verfassungsschutz* – State Office for the Protection of the Constitution
LKA	*Landeskriminalamt* – State Criminal Police Office
LMI	*Landesministerium des Innern* – State Ministry of the Interior
MAE	*Ministère des Affaires Etrangères (French Foreign Ministry) & Archives diplomatiques*, Paris
MLA	*Mission de liaison pour les affaires algériennes* – Liaison Mission for Algerian Affairs
NL	*Nachlass* – Personal Papers
PA/AA	*Politisches Archiv des Auswärtigen Amts*, Berlin
RA	*Revue d'Allemagne et des Pays de langue allemande*
SAMPP/P	*Service des Archives et du Musée de la Préfecture de Police*, Paris
SBZ	*Sowjetische Besatzungszone* – Soviet Occupation Zone in Germany
SEAA	*Secrétariat d'etat aux affaires algériennes* – State Secretariat for Algerian Affairs
SG-Bonn	*Sicherungsgruppe Bonn* – Federal security and protection service of the BKA
SHD-T	*Service Historique de la Défense – Armée de Terre*, Vincennes

SSDN(F)A	*Service de sécurité de la Défense nationale et des (Forces) Armées* – Armed Forces Security Service
STR	*Service technique de recherche* – Signals intelligence service
StS	*Staatssekretär* – State Secretary
VdDBT/D	*Verhandlungen des Deutschen Bundestages. Drucksachen*
VdDBT/StB	*Verhandlungen des Deutschen Bundestages. Stenographische Berichte*

Introduction

On the morning of 5 November 1958, while a young man and woman were about to enter the Tunisian Embassy in the West German capital, Bonn, they came under fire from a speeding Mercedes. The woman escaped unharmed and disappeared from the scene, never to be located by the arriving police. Her companion, gravely injured in the attack, collapsed on the spot. He was identified as Améziane Aït Ahcène, an Egyptian lawyer who ostensibly worked for the Tunisian embassy. Améziane Aït Ahcène's true identity was in fact Algerian, and as the front pages of the major West German newspapers soon reported, he was the unaccredited representative of the *Gouvernement provisoire de la République algérienne* (GPRA) in Bonn. This government-in-exile had been created two months earlier by Algerian nationalists engaged, since 1 November 1954, in a brutal struggle for independence from France. With the victim identified as an allegedly senior member of the *Front de libération nationale* (FLN), the movement behind the GPRA, the gangster-style assassination attempt on Aït Ahcène led to extensive press speculation. Was his attempted murder related to the savage Algerian war? If that were the case – and this seemed to be the most likely explanation to most observers – then who was behind this attempt at public execution? Were the perpetrators rivals within the FLN, as the French authorities and media implied, or were they members of the *Mouvement national algérien* (MNA), the only remaining nationalist group challenging the FLN's claim to be the sole legitimate representative of the Algerian people? Did they perhaps belong to the group of European reactionaries, or *ultras*, who fought so bitterly for the preservation of *l'Algérie française*? Or were Arab diplomats in Bonn right to accuse the French secret services of carrying out the attack?[1]

Whoever the perpetrators were, the assassination attempt on Améziane Aït Ahcène seemed to confirm rumours that had been circulating for

[1] For a graphic description of the event and the ensuing debate, see: 'Der Tod kommt mit der Post. Spiegel-Serie über Frankreichs "Rote Hand"', *Der Spiegel* 14/10 (2 March 1960), pp. 38–50.

months: namely, that the Federal Republic of Germany (FRG) had become a refuge and operational base for Algerians seeking to evade the French authorities.[2] One West German newspaper had spoken as early as January 1958 of an 'Algerian invasion', and by February and March, national dailies such as the *Frankfurter Allgemeine Zeitung* (FAZ) and *Die Welt* had begun to draw attention not only to the plight of Algerian refugees in the Federal Republic but also to the increasingly brazen activities of the FLN there.[3] In August, the French newspaper *Paris-Journal* alleged that the FLN had established its European headquarters in West Germany in order to camouflage 'the principal organisms of Algerian terrorism in France'.[4] Coming just one day after the FLN had launched the second front of its independence struggle through a series of terrorist attacks on police stations and petrol plants across France, the assertion caused a sensation. Ever more newspapers remarked on the influx of Algerians and the FLN's mounting activity east of the Rhine, including foreign newspapers such as the Dutch *Maasbode*, the Swiss *St. Galler Tagblatt* and the *Luxemburger Wort*.[5] By the time of the attempt on Aït Ahcène's life, the steady stream of speculation had turned into a flood. The shooting prompted popular tabloids, such as Hamburg's *Bild*, to wonder 'whether the dirty war' between France and the FLN had arrived in West Germany, while Bonn's *Rheinischer Merkur* warned that if federal authorities failed to stem the surging tide of refugees and rebels entering the country, the FRG would soon face an 'Algerian plague à la Paris and Marseille'. In other words, unless the government reacted quickly, the Algerian war of independence would spread across the French border into West Germany itself.[6]

[2] Unless specified otherwise, the term 'Algerian' is used throughout this study to denote Muslim Algerians, who were Arab or Berber. Their official status will be discussed further in Chapter 3.

[3] 'Algerische Invasion? Die Ausstrahlung des französisch-algerischen Konfliktes auf die Bundesrepublik', *Rheinischer Merkur* (Bonn), 31 January 1958; 'Algerier flüchten in die Bundesrepublik', *Frankfurter Allgemeine Zeitung* (*FAZ*), 25 February 1958; 'Wie steht es mit dem Asylrecht?' *Die Welt* (Hamburg), 21 March 1958; 'Algerier suchen in der Bundesrepublik Zuflucht', *Neue Rhein Zeitung* (Essen), 1 March 1958.

[4] 'Les chefs FLN de France ont leur quartier général en Allemagne', *Paris-Journal*, 26 August 1958.

[5] 'Die algerischen Nationalisten organisieren sich in West Deutschland. Bis jetzt 2,000 Flüchtlinge auf dem Bundesgebiet', *St. Galler Tagblatt*, 23 September 1958; 'Die algerischen Nationalisten organisieren sich in Bonn: Bundesregierung in einer peinlichen Situation', *Luxemburger Wort*, 24 September 1958; the *Maasbode* article, dated 26 September 1958, is cited in: Dépêche no.804 de l'ambassade de France à La Haye, 1 October 1958, Ministère des Affaires Etrangères (MAE), Paris, Mission de liaison pour les affaires algériennes (MLA)/2. See also: 'Vom Regen in die Traufe des Asyls', *Aachener Nachrichten*, 7 June 1958; 'Algerische Flüchtlinge in der Bundesrepublik', *FAZ*, 16 September 1958.

[6] 'Algerische Aktivität', *Rheinischer Merkur*, 14 November 1958. The *Bild* is cited in: Télégramme no.2662/65 de l'ambassade de France à Bonn, 7 November 1958, MAE, MLA/2.

In 1958, sinister scenarios such as those depicted by the *Bild* or *Rheinische Merkur* appeared all too real to the authorities in Paris and Bonn. After all, Aït Ahcène was neither the first nor the last Algerian – or German, for that matter – to fall prey to an assassination attempt in West Germany during Algeria's independence struggle. In fact, the attempted execution of Aït Ahcène constituted a seminal moment in a complex process that came to entwine the Franco-Algerian struggle with the Franco-German rapprochement within the wider context of the Cold War, decolonisation, and the FRG's efforts at moral and political rehabilitation. This book seeks to unravel that process and explain its meaning and consequences. At its heart are a series of pivotal relationships usually treated as discrete and unrelated. On the one hand is the Franco-Algerian relationship that manifested itself in an increasingly bitter struggle over the fate of colonial Algeria at a time of rapid decolonisation and rising Cold War tensions. On the other hand is the Franco-German relationship, which experienced an unprecedented rapprochement at the precise moment the French nation had to come to terms with the loss of its colonial empire in Algeria and elsewhere. Lastly, there is the relationship that the newly sovereign Bonn Republic sought to establish not just to its European and Atlantic partners but also to the emerging nations of what at that time was termed the Third World.[7] By focusing on the intricate linkages between these relationships, this book will cast important fresh light on all three.

The passions and anxieties aroused by the Algerian war's spillover into the Bonn Republic, so manifest in the French and West German press in 1958, have received little attention from scholars working on West German foreign relations and security policy or on Algeria's decolonisation. This tendency is not altogether surprising. For decades, French politicians and historians perpetuated the myth of the Franco-Algerian struggle as an internal affair. In November 1954, Prime Minister Pierre Mendès-France famously stipulated, one 'does not compromise when it comes to defending the internal peace of the nation, the unity and the integrity of the Republic'. His interior minister, François Mitterrand, added that while the response to the FLN's insurrection would be fierce, France 'will avoid

[7] Coined by French demographer Alfred Sauvy in 1952, the term 'Third World' was used to mark the distinct position of formerly colonised states in Africa, Asia and Latin America, which refused to side with the Western or Eastern blocs, representing a 'third force' in the Cold War. The Third World, or South, also connoted a global 'third estate', whose demographic and socio-economic realities and underdevelopment challenged both the capitalist and communist powers of the northern hemisphere. See: B.R. Tomlinson, 'What Is the Third World?' *Journal of Contemporary History* 38/2 (2003), pp. 309–311.

everything that could appear like a kind of state of war'. Every successive French cabinet adhered to this rhetorical formula, for constitutionally Algeria was part of France. Not even General Charles de Gaulle, the man who eventually conceded Algerian independence, strayed from the line that the 'events' in Algeria constituted a domestic emergency of purely French concern.[8] In fact, only in 1999 did the French National Assembly pass a decree explicitly and officially referring to the hitherto unnamed 'events' of 1954 to 1962 as *la guerre d'Algérie*, thereby acknowledging that France had in fact waged war against the FLN.[9] According to the official rhetoric, then, this last and most brutal chapter in the history of France's colonial disengagement should have concerned the Federal Republic no more or less than any other member of the international community.[10]

A similar logic can be observed in Algerian historiography and commemorative practices. Here, too, emphasis has rested predominantly on the war's internal dimension. According to historian Mohammed Harbi, a former high-ranking member of the FLN forced into exile in the early 1970s, the autocratic regime that emerged under President Houari Boumediène in 1965 deliberately constructed the myth of the year 1954 as a *tabula rasa*: it was then, with the foundation of the FLN, that Algerian nationalism was born as a united, homogenous movement leading a peasant revolution to victory and independence.[11] The state embarked on what historian Hassan Remaoun has called a 'policy of writing and

[8] Citations from Alistair Horne, *A Savage War of Peace: Algeria, 1954–1962*, 4th edn (London, 2002), p. 98, and Benjamin Stora, *La gangrène et l'oubli. La mémoire de la guerre d'Algérie*, 2nd edn (Paris, 1998), pp. 15–16.

[9] On French politics of commemoration of the Algerian war, see: Stora, *Gangrène*; Raphaëlle Branche, *La guerre d'Algérie: une histoire apaisée?* (Paris, 2005); Jo McCormack, *Collective Memory: France and the Algerian War* (Lanham MD, 2007); Mohammed Harbi and Benjamin Stora, 'La guerre d'Algérie: de la mémoire à l'Histoire', in *La guerre d'Algérie 1954–2004. La fin de l'amnésie* (eds.) Mohammed Harbi and Benjamin Stora (Paris, 2004), pp. 9–16; Christiane Kohser-Spohn and Frank Renken (eds.), *Trauma Algerienkrieg. Zur Geschichte und Aufarbeitung eines tabuisierten Konflikts* (Frankfurt/Main, 2005); Frank Renken, *Frankreich im Schatten des Algerienkrieges. Die Fünfte Republik und die Erinnerung an den letzten großen Kolonialkonflikt* (Göttingen, 2006); Todd Shepard, *The Invention of Decolonization. The Algerian War and the Remaking of France* (Ithaca NY; London, 2006).

[10] Arnold Fraleigh, 'The Algerian Revolution as a Case Study in International Law', in *The International Law of Civil War* (ed.) Richard Falk (Baltimore ML, 1971), p. 191.

[11] Gilbert Meynier maintains that the word 'revolution' is theoretically a misnomer for the Algerian war. Notwithstanding the socialist turn that followed its resolution, the conflict produced neither a Marxist-type revolution nor any other fundamental transformation of socio-economic, political or cultural institutions. To Meynier, the term only applies in its Arabic form – *tharwa*, which translates more precisely as 'revolt' or 'insurrection' – and only insofar as the war resulted in an overthrow of the colonial order. See his *Histoire intérieure du FLN, 1954–1962* (Paris, 2002), pp. 157–63; his essay in *Trauma Algerienkrieg*, pp. 153–73; or his 'Problématique historique de la nation algérienne', *NAQD. Revue d'études et de critique sociale* 14/15 (2001), p. 31.

rewriting History'. On the one hand, this policy rightly sought to rectify 'the falsifications that were supposed to have been made by colonial history', for only by 'decolonising history' – as historian Mohamed Sahli wrote in 1965 – could Algerians recover their own voice in the production of historical knowledge.[12] On the other hand, the policy also pursued a political agenda, for it deliberately obscured the role of nationalist leaders other than those who rose to power and prominence post-independence. By favouring and indeed overstating the role played by the internal armed struggle of the *mujâhideen*, as the *Armée de libération nationale*'s (ALN) combatants referred to themselves, this interpretation left little room for rival movements such as the MNA and other political parties like Ferhat Abbas's *Union démocratique du manifeste algérien* (UDMA) and Abd al-Hamid Ben Badis's *Association des 'ulamā musulmans algériens* (AUMA), or even the FLN's precursor, the *Parti du peuple algérien – Mouvement pour le triomphe des libertés démocratiques* (PPA-MTLD). It also left little room for the FLN's external organisation, especially the movement's diplomats or its metropolitan branch, the *Fédération de France*.[13]

The FLN's 'official history' of Algerian decolonisation, like its French counterpart, have been, and are being, challenged from multiple directions, of course, including the international dimension. Even when viewed from the perspective of what historian Matthew Connelly has called the 'foreign policy of national liberation', however, the connection between West Germany and the Algerian war does not become immediately apparent.[14] When the FLN launched its insurrection on 1 November 1954, Germany was still a divided and militarily occupied country. The abrogation of the Occupation Statute on 5 May 1955 restored the Federal Republic's independence, yet it did so within the structural framework of Western integration. Ultimately, the country's sovereignty would remain constrained until the four wartime allies agreed on the terms of

[12] Mohamed Sahli, *Décoloniser l'histoire* (Paris, 1965).

[13] Mohammed Harbi, 1954. *La guerre commence en Algérie* (Brussels, 1984), pp. 152–73; Hassan Remaoun, 'L'intervention institutionnelle et son impact sur la pratique historiographique en Algérie: la politique "d'Écriture et de Réécriture de l'histoire"', *Insaniyat. Revue algérienne d'anthropologie et de sciences sociales* 19/20 (2003), pp. 7–40, esp. p. 27. Refer also to Stora, *Gangrène*, parts II–IV, and to the contributions by Daho Djerbal, Hassan Remaoun, Guy Pervillé, Gilbert Meynier, Tayeb Chenntouf, Fouad Soufi and Werner Ruf in *Trauma Algerienkrieg*.

[14] Matthew Connelly, 'Rethinking the Cold War and Decolonization: The Grant Strategy of the Algerian War of Independence', *International Journal of Middle East Studies* 33/2 (2001), p. 223. On the FLN's foreign policy, see also Connelly's *A Diplomatic Revolution: Algeria's Fight for Independence and the Origins of the Post-Cold War Era* (Oxford, 2002); Slimane Chikh, *L'Algérie en armes ou le temps des certitudes* (Paris, 1981), part 4; Meynier, *Histoire*, part 6; Guy Pervillé, 'L'insertion internationale du FLN algérien', *Relations internationales* 31 (1982), pp. 373–86.

a final peace treaty.[15] Reliant on the goodwill and protection of its western allies, including France, the Bonn government's ability to pursue an independent foreign policy remained limited.[16] After the horrors wrought by the Nazi regime, the abrogation of the Occupation Statute did not result in the FRG's immediate and full return into the fold of the international community, nor did its remarkable, export-driven economic growth (the so-called *Wirtschaftswunder*) guarantee the country an automatic place among the great powers. Together with its eastern counterpart, the German Democratic Republic (GDR), the country only became a voting member of the United Nations (UN) a full decade after Algeria's independence, once the Basic Treaty of 21 December 1972 permitted a normalisation of German–German relations. As such, the Federal Republic had no voice in the FLN's annual campaigns to gain the UN General Assembly's support for Algerian independence.[17] Nor would it have been likely to endorse that cause, for the Bonn government made no secret of the importance it attached to Franco-German reconciliation. Between 1954 and 1962, the two neighbours moved from a 'hereditary enmity', stretching far beyond the Franco-Prussian war, towards what historian Ulrich Lappenküper has called an '*entente élémentaire*'.[18] The emergent partnership, which culminated in the historic Elysée Treaty of Franco-German friendship of January 1963, evolved into the driving motor of European integration and formed the core of de Gaulle's 'grand design' for a French-led European third force between the two superpowers.[19] Diplomatically, therefore, the FRG would have made an unlikely supporter of the FLN's cause.

[15] Full sovereignty was not restored until the 'Two Plus Four Agreement', or Treaty on the Final Settlement with Respect to Germany of 12 September 1990, one of the treaties enabling Germany's reunification. See: Ulrich Lappenküper, *Die Außenpolitik der Bundesrepublik Deutschland 1949 bis 1990* (Munich, 2008).

[16] Georges-Henri Soutou, *L'Alliance incertaine: les rapports politico-stratégiques franco-allemands, 1954–1996* (Paris, 1996), p. 22.

[17] On FLN policy towards the UN, see: Martin Thomas, 'France Accused: French North Africa before the United Nations, 1952–1962', *Contemporary European History* 10/1 (2001), pp. 91–121; Maurice Vaïsse, 'La guerre perdue à l'ONU?', in *La Guerre d'Algérie et les français* (ed.) Jean-Pierre Rioux (Paris, 1990), pp. 541–62; Hal V. Cartwright, 'Revolutionary Algeria and the UN: a study in agenda politics', PhD thesis (University of Maryland, 1974); Khalfa Mameri, *Les Nations Unies face à la question algérienne* (Alger, 1970); Mohamed Alwan, *Algeria before the United Nations* (New York, 1959).

[18] On the role of Franco-German enmity in the construction of modern French and German nationalism, see: Michael Jeismann, *Das Vaterland der Feinde: Studien zum nationalen Feindbegriff und Selbstverständnis in Deutschland und Frankreich, 1792–1918* (Stuttgart, 1992).

[19] Ulrich Lappenküper, *Die deutsch-französischen Beziehungen, 1949–1963. Von der ‚Erbfeindschaft' zur ‚Entente élémentaire'*, Bd. 1–2 (Munich, 2001). Other important studies of Franco-German relations include: Eckart Conze, *Die gaullistische Herausforderung. Die deutsch-französischen Beziehungen in der amerikanischen Europapolitik 1958–1963* (Munich, 1995); Martin Koopmann, *Das schwierige*

From a West German perspective, too, the Algerian war should have been of little consequence. Occupied and partitioned since the end of World War II, the two German states that emerged in 1949 were preoccupied by matters closer to home, whether economic reconstruction and political as well as moral rehabilitation, the attainment of full sovereignty and equality within the international community, or the questions of rearmament and national reunification. The Bonn Republic sought to accomplish these goals as well as security from Soviet-bloc aggression within the framework of Chancellor Konrad Adenauer's *Westpolitik*, a policy that stipulated a close integration or binding (*Bindung*) with western Europe and the Atlantic alliance. During the early years of the Algerian war, this policy produced some momentous breakthroughs: the October 1954 Paris Accords paved the way for the termination of the Occupation Statute, granting the FRG membership in NATO and the Brussels Pact; the October 1956 Treaty of Luxemburg ended the French protectorate over Saarland; and the historic Treaties of Rome of March 1957 established the European Common Market and Atomic Energy Community (Euratom).[20] Although the early years of the Algerian war witnessed a consolidation of the Bonn Republic's position in the Western alliance, the later years of the conflict coincided with the second Berlin crisis of 1958 to 1962, one of the worst episodes of the European Cold War. This serious escalation of tensions between the two opposing power blocs, which saw the construction of the Berlin Wall in August 1961, placed considerable strain on the Western alliance and threatened West Germany's very survival.[21]

Bündnis. Die deutsch-französischen Beziehungen und die Außenpolitik der Bundesrepublik Deutschland 1958–1965 (Baden-Baden, 2000); Hermann Kusterer, *Der Kanzler und der General* (Stuttgart, 1995); Wilfried Loth and Robert Picht (eds.), *De Gaulle, Deutschland und Europa* (Opladen, 1991); Reiner Marcowitz, *Option für Paris? Unionsparteien, SPD und Charles de Gaulle 1958–1969* (Munich, 1996); Raymond Poidevin and Jacques Bariéty, *Les Relations franco-allemandes 1815–1975* (Paris, 1977); Gilbert Ziebura, *Die deutsch-französischen Beziehungen seit 1945: Mythen und Realitäten* (Pfullingen, 1970).

20 The literature on West German foreign policy during the Adenauer era is vast. Some of the standard studies include: Wolfram F. Hanrieder, *Deutschland, Europa, Amerika. Die Außenpolitik der Bundesrepublik Deutschland 1949–1994*, 2nd edn (Paderborn, 1995); Klaus Hildebrand, *Integration und Souveränität: die Außenpolitik der Bundesrepublik Deutschland, 1949–1982* (Bonn, 1991); Ludolf Herbst, *Option für den Westen: vom Marshallplan bis zum deutsch-französischen Vertrag* (München, 1989); Christian Hacke, *Weltmacht wider Willen: die Außenpolitik der Bundesrepublik Deutschland* (Stuttgart, 1988); Helga Haftendorn, *Sicherheit und Entspannung: zur Außenpolitik der Bundesrepublik Deutschland, 1955–1982* (Baden-Baden, 1983); Hans-Peter Schwarz, *Die Ära Adenauer. Gründerjahre der Republik, 1949–1957* (Stuttgart, 1981); Hans-Peter Schwarz, *Die Ära Adenauer. Epochenwechsel, 1957–1963* (Stuttgart, 1983); Waldemar Besson, *Die Außenpolitik der Bundesrepublik. Erfahrungen und Maßstäbe* (Munich, 1970); Arnulf Baring, *Außenpolitik in Adenauers Kanzlerdemokratie* (Munich, 1969).

21 On the Berlin crisis, see: John P. S. Gearson and Kori Schake (eds.), *The Berlin Wall Crisis: Perspectives on Cold War Alliances* (New York, 2002); Rolf Steininger, *Der Mauerbau. Die Westmächte und Adenauer in der Berlinkrise 1958–1963* (Munich, 2001); Marc Trachtenberg,

To most historians, the European Cold War and imperative of Western integration absorbed all of the Bonn government's energies, leaving little room for attention to faraway colonial conflicts. Having forcibly lost its colonies in Africa, Asia and the Pacific through the Treaty of Versailles of 1919, Germany was never directly involved in the process of decolonisation that gathered pace after World War II. After the defeat of the Third Reich, references to colonial revisionism and military expansionism disappeared from public discourse. If anything, the Bonn Republic's 'postcolonial, post-Nazi identity include[d] a repudiation or at least a forgetting of Germans' older imperial reach or [overseas] ambition', so much so that it became 'insular, even self-consciously provincial'.[22] Forgotten was the genocidal violence inflicted during the Herero and Nama wars of 1904–1907 or the Maji-Maji war of 1905–1908, which were now overshadowed by the Holocaust. When the colonial past was invoked, a selective reinterpretation occurred and a legend was formed of Germans as 'benevolent colonisers' who built roads, railway lines and schools. This legend survived precisely because the German colonial period was cut short and Germans never experienced the 'empire strikes back' effects of anti-colonial nationalism and postcolonial migration.[23] According to the West German novelist Uwe Timm, the legend also persisted because, 'after the horrors of German fascism – Germans thought [or wanted to think] that in this area at least they had an edge on other peoples'.[24]

By now, of course, that legend has been thoroughly debunked.[25] The cultural and political history of the short-lived German colonial empire has witnessed a dramatic revival in recent decades. So has the history of German encounters with colonialism and imperialism more

A Constructed Peace. The Making of the European Settlement, 1945–1963 (Princeton NJ, 1999), chs. 7–9; Ann Tusa, *The Last Division: A History of Berlin, 1945–1989* (Reading MA, 1997).

22 Lora Wildenthal, 'Notes on a History of "Imperial Turns" in Modern Germany', in *After the Imperial Turn* (ed.) Antoinette Burton (Durham NC, 2003), pp. 145, 144.

23 Monika Albrecht, 'Postcolonialism and Migration into Germany's Colonial Past', *German Life and Letters* 65/3 (2012), pp. 363–77; Britta Schilling, *Postcolonial Germany: Memories of Empire in a Decolonized Nation* (Oxford, 2014), p. 5.

24 In popular memory, the Third Reich's quest for *Lebensraum* in Eastern Europe was not associated with German overseas colonialism. Timm is cited in: Sara Friedrichsmeyer, Sara Lennox and Susanne Zantop (eds.), 'Introduction', in *The Imperialist Imagination: German Colonialism and its Legacy* (Ann Arbor, 1998), pp. 24–5; and in Uta G. Poiger, 'Imperialism and Empire in Twentieth-Century Germany', *History and Memory* 17/1–2 (2005), p. 124.

25 In July 2015, the German government formally acknowledged that the repression exacted against the Herero and Nama constituted genocide and a war crime. See: 'Berlin nennt Herero-Massaker erstmals "Völkermord"', *Süddeutsche Zeitung* (Munich), 10 July 2015; 'Regierung bekennt sich zu Völkermord', ARD tagesschau.de, 10 July 2015 (www.tagesschau.de/inland/voelkermord-herero-103.html).

generally, including those with other colonial empires. Much of the resultant scholarship focuses on the period before 1945.[26] Only recently have scholars started to interrogate the manner in which Germany's colonial past, or its encounters with other European colonialisms, continued to permeate East and West German political, literary and memory cultures post-1945. Scholars are therefore beginning to answer Uta Poiger's call for a deeper examination of how the legacy and persistence of empire helped shape the manner in which the two Germanys interacted with the non-European world.[27]

Meanwhile, much of the literature on West German foreign and security policy continues to depict the process of decolonisation that gathered pace during the 1950s as a tangential and marginal issue.[28] For Adenauer,

[26] This is by no means a complete overview, but see: Eric Ames, Marcia Klotz and Lora Wildenthal (eds.), *Germany's Colonial Past* (Lincoln NE, 2005); Shelley Baranowski, *Nazi Empire: German Colonialism and Imperialism from Bismarck to Hitler* (Cambridge, 2011); Russell A. Berman, 'German Colonialism: Another *Sonderweg?*' *European Studies Journal* 16/2 (1999), pp. 25–36 (the article is part of a special issue edited by Marcia Klotz entitled *German Colonialism*); Ibid., *Enlightenment or Empire: Colonial Discourse in German Culture* (Lincoln NE, 1998); Sebastian Conrad, *Deutsche Kolonialgeschichte* (Munich, 2008); Pascal Grosse, *Kolonialismus, Eugenik und bürgerliche Gesellschaft in Deutschland, 1850–1914* (Frankfurt/Main, 2000); Isabel Hull, *Absolute Destruction: Military Culture and the Practice of War in Imperial Germany* (Ithaca NY, 2005); Volker Langbehn and Mohammed Salama (eds.), *German Colonialism: Race, the Holocaust, and Postwar Germany* (New York, 2011); Michael Perraudin and Jürgen Zimmerer (eds.), *German Colonialism and National Identity* (New York, 2011); Jared Poley, *Decolonization in Germany: Weimar Narratives of Colonial Loss and Foreign Occupation* (Bern, 2005); Felicity J. Rash, *German Images of the Self and the Other: Nationalist, Colonialist and Anti-Semitic Discourse, 1871–1918* (Basingstoke, 2012); Lora Wildenthal, *German Women for Empire, 1884–1945* (Durham NC, 2002); Susanne Zantop, *Colonial Fantasies: Conquest, Family, and Nation in Precolonial Germany, 1770–1870* (Durham NC, 1997); Jürgen Zimmerer, *Von Windhoek nach Auschwitz. Beiträge zum Verhältnis von Kolonialismus und Holocaust* (Münster, 2007). For good introductions and surveys of the existing literature, see: Edward R. Dickinson, 'The German Empire: An Empire?' *History Workshop Journal* 66 (2008), pp. 129–62; Robert Gerwarth and Stephan Malinowski, 'Hannah Arendt's Ghosts: Reflections on the Disputable Path from Windhoek to Auschwitz', *Central European History* 42/2 (2009), pp. 279–300; Philipp Ther, 'Imperial instead of National History: Positioning Modern German History on the Map of European Empires', in *Imperial Rule* (eds.) Alexei Miller and Alfred J. Rieber (Budapest, 2004), pp. 47–66.

[27] Poiger, 'Imperialism', pp. 117–43. See: Monika Albrecht, *'Europa ist nicht die Welt': (Post) Kolonialismus in Literatur und Geschichte der westdeutschen Nachkriegszeit* (Bielefeld, 2008); Dirk Göttsche, *Remembering Africa: The Rediscovery of Colonialism in Contemporary German Literature* (Rochester NY; Woodbridge, 2013); Young-Sun Hong, *Cold War Germany, the Third World, and the Global Humanitarian Regime* (Cambridge, 2015); Sandra Maß, *Weiße Helden, schwarze Krieger. Zur Geschichte kolonialer Männlichkeit in Deutschland, 1918–1964* (Cologne, 2006); Schilling, *Postcolonial Germany*; Jason Verber, 'The Conundrum of Colonialism in Postwar Germany', PhD thesis (University of Iowa, 2010); Joachim Zeller, *Kolonialdenkmäler und Geschichtsbewußtsein. Eine Untersuchung der kolonialdeutschen Erinnerungskultur* (Berlin, 1999).

[28] It is worth pointing out some recent exceptions, which include: Verber, 'Conundrum', especially his ch. 2; Katrina M. Hagen, 'Internationalism in Cold War Germany', PhD thesis (University of Washington, 2008).

who remained the most important architect and arbiter of West German foreign relations until his retirement in October 1963, decolonisation only assumed significance in a Cold War context.[29] The end of European colonial rule turned Africa and Asia into an 'insecurity factor' in West German foreign and national security policy, one that at times came to jeopardise Bonn's efforts to prevent the diplomatic recognition of the communist GDR and impede the legitimation and institutionalisation of Germany's post-war division.[30] This policy, known as the Hallstein doctrine, combined with the ideological prism of the Cold War, is essential to any examination of West German foreign policy in the context of decolonisation. Even so, most historians contend that Bonn's 'personal' Cold War to isolate the GDR in the nascent Third World rarely assumed centre stage.[31]

Considering these historiographical tendencies, one can understand why scholars have overlooked the relationship between the Algerian war and West German foreign and security policy, including the Franco-German rapprochement. Yet when one reads through the files of French and German diplomacy or those of the security and intelligence services, a very different picture emerges, one that confirms the sinister scenarios that, by 1958, were being described in the press. In October of that year, for instance, the French *Service de documentation extérieure et de contre-espionnage* (SDECE), or foreign intelligence service, alerted the authorities to the fact that 'Algerian terrorists were arriving in the Federal Republic in droves'.[32] Five months later, another intelligence report concluded dramatically that

> [a]lthough the federal government carries no responsibility for it, West Germany has become the theatre of manifold intrigues, where Soviet agents, neo-Nazis, FLN delegates and Arab diplomats mingle their tracks.[33]

As will be seen, such conspiratorial statements were somewhat hyperbolic. Yet in the months and years that followed, French military and intelligence

[29] Hans-Peter Schwarz, *Adenauer: Der Staatsmann, 1952–1967* (Stuttgart, 1991), p. 316.

[30] Heinrich End, *Zweimal deutsche Außenpolitik. Internationale Dimensionen des innerdeutschen Konflikts 1949–72* (Cologne, 1973), p. 47.

[31] The doctrine was named after State-Secretary Walter Hallstein, who became President of the European Commission in 1958. See: William G. Gray, *Germany's Cold War. The Global Campaign to Isolate East Germany, 1949–1969* (Chapel Hill and London, 2003); Rüdiger Marco Booz, *'Hallsteinzeit' Deutsche Außenpolitik 1955–1972* (Bonn, 1995); End, *Zweimal*; Ulf Engel and Hans-Georg Schleicher, *Die beiden deutschen Staaten in Afrika: Zwischen Konkurrenz und Koexistenz 1949–1990* (Hamburg, 1998); Werner Kilian, *Die Hallstein-Doktrin. Der diplomatische Krieg zwischen der BRD und der DDR 1955–1972* (Berlin, 2001).

[32] Notice d'information no. 11836/IIB/SDECE, 14 October 1958, Service Historique de la Défense – Terre (SHD-T), Vincennes, 10T/262* (documents marked by an asterisk are accessible *sur dérogation*).

[33] Bulletin d'information, anon., March 1959, SHD-T, 1H/1164/D (Dossier) 2.

authorities often expressed similar sentiments. The *deuxième bureau* (military intelligence) consistently referred to West Germany as a '*terrain de repli*' (field of retreat), '*plaque tournante*' (turntable) and '*base logistique*' (logistical base) for FLN militants. The French intelligence services produced reams of evidence allegedly proving that Algerian nationalists engaged in a whole range of 'rebel activities' east of the Rhine, from propaganda and fundraising to terrorism and arms trafficking. Falling under the auspices of what French authorities called the FLN's external organisation, these activities were considered to be the very lifeline of the Algerian rebellion.[34] As the *deuxième bureau* of French forces in Algeria stated in 1961: 'It is certainly the [external] organisation, once of secondary but today of prime importance, which constitutes the rebels' principal force' as well as its most 'coherent machine of war'.[35] While most of this organisation was situated in sanctuaries across the Arab world, particularly in Tunisia and Morocco, the French military and intelligence services concluded that the Bonn Republic had become the FLN's headquarters in Europe.

It therefore seems unrealistic to suggest that France's eastern neighbour remained disengaged and unaffected by Algeria's independence struggle. The Federal Republic was certainly perceived to be much more deeply entangled in the bitter colonial conflict than has hitherto been recognised in most of the scholarly literature. Clearly, there was a reason why the press and the French security and intelligence services began referring to an 'Algerian invasion' of the country. Something had to explain the fact that Algerian 'terrorists' were arriving there 'in droves'. West Germany must have held some significance to the FLN, whether as an external base, refuge or headquarters: why else would Améziane Aït Ahcène have been stationed there? The assassination attempt on the FLN's first representative in Bonn was itself neither a rogue nor an isolated event. Rather, it was symptomatic of a much broader development, one that transformed West Germany from neutral territory into an external sanctuary and site of contestation in the Franco-Algerian conflict. Lastly, if the French intelligence services and European press were right in their assessments of these developments, if the

[34] For examples, see: Notice d'information no. 11838/SDECE, 20 October 1958, SHD-T, 10T/525*; Notice d'information no. 29648/SDECE, 5.4.1960, SHD-T, 10T/528/D2*; Note no. 3450 du deuxième bureau de l'État-major interarmées des forces en Algérie (EMI/2), 23 June 1960; Mémento no. 1878, Bureau d'Études, Délégation Générale du Gouvernement en Algérie (DGGA/BE), 22 August 1960; Note d'information, anon., January 1961; Mémento no.40/DGGA/BE, January 1962, SHD-T 1H/1743/D1.

[35] Note no. 1937/EMI/2, 1 June 1961; Fiche, EMI/2, 17 May 1960, SHD-T, 1H/1743/D1.

'savage war of peace' did indeed spill across the Rhine, then what exactly did this mean both for the Algerian war and for West Germany?

These questions are at the heart of the analysis in this book. Its fundamental thesis is encapsulated in two contentions. First, the book argues that the FRG served as an important external sanctuary and rear base for the FLN and reveals for the first time the fundamental challenges this development posed to French counterinsurgency efforts. Second, the book contends that Algeria's independence struggle came to exert decisive and powerful influence on West German foreign and security policy as conceived not just by governmental actors but also by civil-society ones. These two arguments cannot be separated from one another; they are mutually reinforcing and inherently intertwined. After all, it was the Algerian presence in West Germany that ultimately implicated the country in the Franco-Algerian conflict. The FLN's use of federal territory as an external *sanctuary* not only posed a direct challenge to West German foreign and security policy, it also threatened the Bonn Republic's recently acquired *sovereignty.* In combining these two arguments, the book seeks to shed important fresh light not just on the role of extraterritorial sanctuaries in late colonial and irregular warfare but also on the early efforts of West German state and non-state actors to forge for their young country a new identity and role in international affairs.

Sanctuary

The FLN's exterior organisation, historian Guy Pervillé once noted, 'always comprised more than a simple diplomatic apparatus', and its action 'was never the prerogative of a corps of [diplomatic] specialists'.[36] This contention might appear obvious. After all, as a movement engaged in an armed and revolutionary struggle to overthrow the colonial status quo, the FLN understood the fundamental importance of sanctuaries, or base areas, whether active or passive, internal or external. According to Chinese communist leader Mao Zedong, 'guerrilla warfare could not last long or grow without base areas'.[37] Sanctuaries mattered because they provided insurgent forces the time, space, and security required to build up troops and resources and develop effective and durable politico-administrative

[36] Pervillé, 'L'insertion internationale', p. 374.

[37] Mao Tse-Tung, 'Problems of Strategy in Guerrilla War against Japan, May 1938', in *Selected Military Writings* (Peking, 1967), p. 167–8.

structures, including an 'insurgent-state-in-waiting'.[38] Based in secure, often inaccessible terrain, sanctuaries made it possible for insurgent groups to train military recruits as well as political cadres, organise logistical networks, establish stable communications, plan and launch operations against the enemy, and expand links so as to win over local populations. Sanctuaries and base areas thus constituted 'force multipliers' in guerrilla warfare; they made it possible for insurgents to engage a more powerful and territorially entrenched state.[39] Their creation constituted one of Mao's seven fundamental steps to winning a revolutionary war, a view also shared by the Vietnamese military leader Võ Nguyên Giáp, who famously defeated France at the 1954 battle of Dien Bien Phu.[40] As shall be seen, the FLN, too, put great effort into the creation of base areas, including sanctuaries in foreign and non-belligerent countries such as the FRG.

Notwithstanding their importance, sanctuaries remain an understudied aspect of the Algerian war.[41] This reflects a wider trend in the historiography of the wars of national liberation that occurred post-1945. On the one hand, much of the theoretical, conceptual and historical literature on modern guerrilla warfare agrees that an insurgent movement's ability to secure safe havens and base areas has a significant impact on the duration, scope and intensity of a war as well as on its outcome.[42] As such, counter-insurgency strategies and manuals have often emphasised the need for combating, undermining and denying an insurgency territorial and other forms of sanctuary.[43] On the other hand, the current literature on sanctuary focuses either on the ethnic and identity conflicts that came to dominate the post-Cold War era, for instance in Africa, where civil wars

[38] Rex Brynen, *Sanctuary and Survival: The PLO in Lebanon* (Boulder CO, 1990), http://prrn.mcgill.ca/research/papers/brynen2_01.htm (accessed 25 November 2014).

[39] Rem Korteweg, 'Black Holes: On Terrorist Sanctuaries and Governmental Weakness', *Civil Wars* 10/1 (2008), p. 66.

[40] Ibid.; Mao Tse-Tung, *On Guerrilla Warfare* (trans.) S.B. Griffith (New York, 1961), p. 107; Võ Nguyên Giáp, *The Military Art of People's War* (trans.) R. Stetler (New York, 1971), pp. 87–92, 96, 160, 179–81. See also: Michael A. Innes, 'Deconstructing Political Orthodoxies on Insurgent and Terrorist Sanctuaries', *Studies in Conflict & Terrorism* 31 (2008), pp. 255, 262; David Kilcullen, 'Counter-insurgency Redux', *Survival: Global Politics and Strategy* 48/4 (2006), p. 118.

[41] The most thorough study to date of the FLN's relations to its Arab sanctuary states is in Meynier's magisterial *Histoire*, pp. 557–80. See also: Amira Aleya-Sghaier, 'La Tunisie: base-arrière de la révolution algérienne', *Revue d'Histoire Maghrébine* 118 (2005), pp. 155–60.

[42] For a good overview of the existing literature and its treatment of sanctuary, see: Bruce J. Reider, 'External Support to Insurgencies', *Small Wars Journal* 10/10 (2014), http://smallwarsjournal.com/jrnl/art/external-support-to-insurgencies (accessed 10 July 2015).

[43] One of the latest examples is the updated US Army Field Manual FM3–24, published May 2014: http://armypubs.army.mil/doctrine/DR_pubs/dr_a/pdf/fm3_24.pdf (accessed 10 July 2015). See also: Hannes Artens, 'Sanctuary State – Insurgency Relations in Ethnic Conflicts: A New Explanatory Model', *Oficina do CES* 392 (November 2012), p. 1.

so frequently spilled over territorial frontiers into neighbouring countries and regions, or on the US-led wars in Afghanistan and Iraq as well as the Global War on Terrorism of which they were a part. The transnational nature of these conflicts has shifted scholarly attention to the vital importance of external sanctuaries – those located beyond the territorial confines of the state against which an insurgent force or terrorist group is fighting. Notions of external sanctuary are therefore closely bound up with conceptions of the sovereign power of the state and its role in harbouring third parties. Many sanctuary-states are considered to be ideological and political allies of the foreign insurgent force or terrorist group they host. Failing or failed states, meanwhile, are too weak to prevent an insurgent force or terrorist group from operating on their territory. Much of the literature has focused on the attendant opportunities and challenges these two types of external sanctuary have posed to counterinsurgent strategies, especially in the context of the Global War on Terrorism.[44]

[44] Examples include: Daniel Byman, *Deadly Connections: States that Sponsor Terrorism* (Cambridge, 2005); Ibid., Peter Chalk, Bruce Hoffman, William Rosenau, *Trends in Outside Support for Insurgent Movements* (Santa Monica CA, 2001); Mark A. Carlson, 'The Pakistan Safe Haven: Feeding the Fight in Afghanistan', PhD thesis (Air University, 2008); Joseph D. Celeski, 'Attacking Insurgent Space: Sanctuary Denial and Border Interdiction', *Military Review* (2006), pp. 51–7; Jeffrey T. Checkel (ed.), *Transnational Dynamics of Civil War* (Cambridge, 2013); Kristian S. Gleditsch, 'Transnational Dimensions of Civil War', *Journal of Peace Research* 44/3 (2007), pp. 293–309; Eric J. Haas, 'Operations at the Border: Efforts to Disrupt Insurgent Safe-Havens', *Art of War Papers* (Fort Leavenworth KA: US Army Command and General Staff College, 2011); Jennifer M. Hazen, *What Rebels Want: Resources and Supply Networks in Wartime* (Ithaca NY, 2013); Bruce Hoffman, *Inside Terrorism*, rev. edn (New York, 2006); Michael A. Innes (ed.), *Denial of Sanctuary: Understanding Terrorist Safe Havens* (Westport CT, 2007); Ibid. (ed.), 'Protected Status, Sacred Sites, Black Holes and Human Agents', Special Issue of *Civil Wars* 10/1 (2008), pp. 1–6; Ali Ahmad Jalali and Lester Grau, *The Other Side of the Mountain: Mujahideen Tactics in the Soviet-Afghan War* (Fort Leavenworth KS, 1995); Mary Kaldor, *New and Old Wars: Organized Violence in a Global Era*, 3rd edn (Stanford CA, 2012); David Kilcullen, 'Countering Global Insurgency', *Journal of Strategic Studies* 28/4 (2005), pp. 597–617; Randy J. Kolton, *Isolating the Theatre of War: Operational Implications of Border Sanctuaries in Limited War* (Fort Leavenworth KA, 2014); David A. Lake and Donald Rothchild (eds.), *The International Spread of Ethnic Conflict: Fear, Diffusion, and Escalation* (Princeton NJ, 1998); Sarah K. Lischer, *Dangerous Sanctuaries: Refugee Camps, Civil War, and the Dilemmas of Humanitarian Aid* (Ithaca NY, 2005); Robert M. Monarch, 'Denying Sanctuary: Rejecting Safe Havens in Counterinsurgency Operations', *Strategy Research Project* (US Army War College, 2009); James A. Piazza, 'Incubators of Terror: Do Failed and Failing States Promote Transnational Terrorism?' *International Studies Quarterly* 52 (2008), pp. 469–88; Jeffrey Record, 'External Assistance: Enabler of Insurgent Success', *Parameters* (Autumn 2006), pp. 36–49; Ibid., *Beating Goliath: Why Insurgencies Win* (Washington DC, 2007), ch. 2; Idean Salehyan, *Rebels without Borders: Transnational Insurgencies in World Politics* (Ithaca NY, 2009); Ibid., 'Transnational Rebels: Neighboring States as Sanctuary for Rebel Groups', *World Politics* 59/2 (2007), pp. 217–42; Paul Staniland, 'Defeating Transnational Insurgencies: The Best Offense Is a Good Fence', *The Washington Quarterly* 29/1 (2005–6), pp. 21–40; Ibid., 'Organizing Insurgency: Networks, Resources, and Rebellion in South Asia', *International Security* 37/1 (2012), pp. 142–77.

External sanctuaries are hardly new to irregular warfare, however, nor are they inherently entwined with the phenomena of state-failure or fragmentation. They played an equally pivotal role in many of the wars of national liberation of the post-1945 era. As such, they also contributed to the process of state-building, especially in the context of decolonisation. The FLN's liberation war was certainly not unique in this respect. Well before it, the communist-led Vietminh made effective use of external bases and supply lines to sustain its fight against French colonialism. Its successor, the National Front for the Liberation of South Vietnam ('Vietcong') equally relied on foreign territory to shift manpower and materiel during the Vietnam War. Other examples include the African National Congress, which for decades orchestrated its struggle against Apartheid from exile in Zambia and Tanzania, with additional bases at various points in Angola, Uganda, Botswana, Mozambique, Lesotho, Swaziland and even the United Kingdom. The Zimbabwe African National Union and its Liberation Army operated from bases in Zambia and, later, in Mozambique, whose own Liberation Front (FRELIMO) had relied on external sanctuaries not just in Zambia but also in Tanzania. External safe havens in the Congo, Zambia and Namibia also helped sustain the various insurgent groups fighting to liberate Angola from Portuguese colonial rule. Likewise, the highly successful African Party for the Independence of [Portuguese] Guinea and Cape Verde operated from sanctuaries in neighbouring Guinea and Senegal. The Palestine Liberation Organization (PLO), too, initiated and conducted its liberation struggle from bases outside of Israeli control. As the Palestinian intellectual and statesman Ibrahim Abu-Lughod argued, 'It is imperative for the population engaged in a war of national liberation to have the full material and political support of an external state'.[45]

Considering their real and perceived importance, it is remarkable that the role of external sanctuaries during the wars of national liberation has not received more scholarly attention. Relatively little has been written about the modalities or impact of French efforts at sanctuary denial and border interdiction during the Indochina War, for instance, perhaps because scholars have tended to focus on the American experience during the Vietnam War instead, especially in relation to the Ho Chi Minh trail.[46]

[45] Ibrahim Abu-Lughod, 'Lebanon and Palestine: Some Contrasts in the Application of the Principles of National Liberation', *Arab Studies Quarterly* 7/4 (1985), p. 83.

[46] On the Indochina War, see: Christopher E. Goscha, *Thailand and the Southeast Asian Networks of the Vietnamese Revolution, 1885–1954* (Richmond, 1999); Michel Lux, *La guerre d'Indochine, au 3e escadron monté du Cambodge, 1949–1951* (Nantes, 2009); J.J. Zasloff, 'The Role of the Sanctuary in Insurgency: Communist China's Support to the Vietminh, 1946–1954', *RAND Memorandum* (May

Likewise, Henry Patterson points out that the academic literature on the Troubles in Northern Ireland has almost completely ignored the role of the Republic of Ireland as an external sanctuary and base for the Provisional Irish Republican Army.[47] In his 1990 study of the PLO in Lebanon, Rex Brynen argued that this oversight had two explanations: first, the principal theoreticians of revolutionary warfare – Mao and Giáp – wrote mainly about internal sanctuaries; second, and contrary to Abu-Lughod's assertion, insurgent movements have themselves preferred to downplay the external dimensions to their struggles, emphasising instead their self-reliance and resilience.[48] Although scholarly interest in the international and transnational dimensions of late colonial conflicts has certainly grown, the existing literature still largely ignores extraterritorial safe havens.[49] External sanctuaries on non-belligerent territory constitute such a vital complement to, and precondition for, the waging of internal armed struggle, the pursuit of diplomatic initiatives and the launching of internal and external propaganda campaigns that they seem to have been taken for granted. Only recently have scholars begun to examine the manner in which external sanctuaries impacted upon the various liberation struggles outlined earlier.[50]

1967). On the Vietnam War, see: Thomas Briggs, *Cash on Delivery: CIA Special Operations during the Secret War in Laos* (Rockville MD, 2009); Thomas A. Bruscino Jr., 'Out of Bounds: Transnational Sanctuary in Irregular Warfare', *Global War on Terrorism Occasional Paper* 17 (Fort Leavenworth KA, 2006); Bernard Nalty, *The War against Trucks: Aerial Interdiction in Southern Laos, 1968–1972* (Washington DC, 2005); John Prados, *The Blood Road: The Ho Chi Minh Trail and the Vietnam War* (New York, 1999); Richard L. Stevens, *Mission on the Ho Chi Minh Trail: Nature, Myth, and War in Viet Nam* (Norman OK, 1995); William Shawcross, *Sideshow: Kissinger, Nixon, and the Destruction of Cambodia*, 3rd edn (New York, 1987); Robert Thompson, 'Rear Bases and Sanctuaries', in *The Lessons of Vietnam* (eds.) W. Scott Thompson and D. Frizzell (New York, 1977), pp. 73–85; Roger Warner, *Back Fire: The CIA's Secret War in Laos and Its Link to the War in Vietnam* (New York, 1995).

47 Henry Patterson, *Ireland's Violent Frontier: The Border and Anglo-Irish Relations during the Troubles* (Basingstoke, 2013), p. 2.

48 Brynen, *Sanctuary*.

49 Examples of scholarly work on the international dimensions of decolonisation include: Mark Philip Bradley, 'Decolonization, the Global South, and the Cold War, 1919–1962', in *The Cambridge History of the Cold War*, vol. I (eds.) M.P. Leffler and O.A. Westad (Cambridge, 2010), pp. 464–85; Roland Burke, *Decolonization and the Evolution of International Human Rights* (Philadelphia, 2010); Connelly, *Diplomatic Revolution*; K. Fedorowich and M. Thomas (eds.), *International Diplomacy and Colonial Retreat* (London, 2001); Cary Fraser, 'Decolonization and the Cold War', in *The Oxford Handbook of the Cold War* (eds.) R.H. Immerman and P. Goedde (Oxford, 2013), pp. 469–85; Marc Frey, R.W. Pruessen, T.T. Yong (eds.), *The Transformation of Southeast Asia: International Perspectives on Decolonization* (New York, 2003); C.E. Goscha and C. Ostermann (eds.), *Connecting Histories: Decolonization and the Cold War in Southeast Asia* (Stanford CA, 2009); Leslie James and Elisabeth Leake (eds.), *Decolonization and the Cold War. Negotiating Independence* (London, 2015); M.A. Lawrence and F. Logevall (eds.), *The First Vietnam War: Colonial Conflict and Cold War Crisis* (Cambridge MA, 2007).

50 Examples include: John P. Cann, 'Securing the Borders of Angola, 1961–1974', *Revista Militar* 2495 (2009), www.revistamilitar.pt/artigo.php?art_id=531 (accessed 12 December 2014); Yong

This book contributes to the growing literature seeking to redress this gap. It does so by focusing not only on the one movement and conflict that became the trendsetter and inspiration for national liberation movements emerging in its wake but also on a sanctuary-state – West Germany – whose role remains most obscured.[51] The Algerian war's overspill beyond the territorial confines of the imperial heartland was in many ways unparalleled. After all, as Jim House and Neil MacMaster remind us, colonial wars were usually geographically contained events that rarely impinged on the metropoles fighting them. Overspill, when it occurred, generally affected only faraway territories neighbouring a restive colony.[52] In the context of the Algerian war, however, a combination of geographical proximity, lax border controls, lenient immigration and asylum policies, federalist state-structures, a free press and liberal economy all helped turn West Germany into a preferred safe haven and logistical-operational base for the FLN.

By using the FRG as a safe haven and base area from whence to pursue diplomatic initiatives, propaganda campaigns and subversive activities, including gunrunning, fundraising, recruitment and planning for armed action, the FLN set a precedent. Never before had a colonial liberation movement established such a large and well-defined sanctuary in Europe

Mun Cheong, *The Indonesian Revolution and the Singapore Connection, 1945–1949* (Singapore, 2004); Stephen Ellis, *External Mission: The ANC in Exile, 1960–1990* (New York, 2013); Daniel Kaiser, 'Transnationale Dimensionen antikolonialen Widerstands in Mosambik', *Forschungsjournal Soziale Bewegungen* 27/3 (2014), pp. 38–45; Kersti Larsdotter, 'Fighting Transnational Insurgents: The South African Defense Force in Namibia, 1966–1989', *Studies in Conflict and Terrorism* 37/12 (2014), pp. 1024–38; Tom Lodge, 'State of Exile: The African National Congress of South Africa, 1976–86', *Third World Quarterly* 9/1 (1987), pp. 1–27; Hugh Macmillan, *The Lusaka Years: The ANC in Exile in Zambia, 1963–1994* (Jacana Media, 2013); Filipe Ribeiro de Meneses and Robert McNamara, 'The Last Throw of the Dice: Portugal, Rhodesia and South Africa, 1970–74', *Portuguese Studies* 28/2 (2012), pp. 201–15; Washa G. Morapedi, 'The Dilemmas of Liberation in Southern Africa: The Case of Zimbabwean Liberation Movements and Botswana, 1960–1979', *Journal of Southern African Studies* 38/1 (2012), pp. 73–90; Michael G. Panzer, 'Building a Revolutionary Constituency: Mozambican Refugees and the Development of the FRELIMO Proto-State, 1963–1968', *Social Dynamics* 39/1 (2013), pp. 5–23; Jeffrey Treistman, 'Home Away from Home: Dynamics of Counterinsurgency Warfare', *Comparative Strategy* 31/3 (2012), pp. 235–52.

51 Abu-Lughod, 'Lebanon and Palestine', p. 78; Odd Arne Westad, *The Global Cold War: Third World Interventions and the Making of Our Times* (Cambridge, 2007), pp. 105–6. On the Algerian war's reverberations, see Jeffrey J. Byrne's *Mecca of Revolution: Algeria, Decolonization, and the Third World Order* (Oxford, 2016).

52 Jim House and Neil MacMaster, *Paris 1961: Algerians, State Terror and Post-Colonial Memories* (Oxford, 2006), pp. 5, 15, 25. Actually, radical nationalists such as the Fenians and Indian revolutionaries posed security threats to metropolitan Britain in the late nineteenth century already. See: Niall Whelehan, *The Dynamiters: Irish Nationalism and Political Violence in the Wider World, 1867–1900* (Cambridge, 2012); Harald Fischer-Tiné, 'Indian Nationalism and the "World Forces": Transnational and Diasporic Dimensions of the Indian Freedom Movement on the Eve of the First World War', *Journal of Global History* 2/3 (2007), pp. 325–44.

itself, with smaller bases also in Belgium and Switzerland. The closest analogy at the time was the Irish Republican Army's use of the Republic of Ireland as an operational base against British-controlled Northern Ireland.[53] Without external sanctuaries the FLN would have been hard-pressed to sustain either its armed struggle or its diplomatic initiatives and propaganda campaigns. In view of the *mujâhideen*'s manifold weaknesses vis-à-vis their adversary, the FLN had to find alternative modes of operation and organisation. The movement needed ways to protect and develop not only its military and political cadres but also its material resources and capabilities. Just like Tunisia, Morocco or Egypt, West Germany offered Algerian militants refuge from political persecution, police repression and physical annihilation. The country provided them with secure bases from which to plan, direct and execute both violent and non-violent operations, and it became an essential platform for the diverse logistical efforts that sustained and underpinned the movement's armed struggle both in Algeria and in metropolitan France, including the procurement of arms, munitions and other supplies.

As an extraterritorial sanctuary beyond the confines of French sovereignty, West Germany limited the asymmetry of power between the FLN and France. The development, nature and role of this safe haven consequently deserves closer study, for it can tell us much about the movement's ability to defeat an adversary so much more powerful than itself. It can also help us understand the different processes driving the internationalisation of insurgency warfare in the era of decolonisation. The Algerian presence in West Germany provides us with an opportunity to merge these lines of enquiry. It also represents an important case apart, one that differs from the states or territories usually associated with rebel or terrorist sanctuaries. After all, unlike its Moroccan or Tunisian counterparts, the Bonn government was never a willing host to the FLN that shared the movement's ideological outlook or political goals. Nor was the country a weak, failing or failed state in which the FLN could operate with impunity. The FRG also shared none of the ethnic or cultural affinities that made Algeria's neighbours such natural sponsors of the FLN's cause, or that linked the Irish Republic to the IRA.[54] And yet the country still

[53] Patterson, *Ireland's Violent Frontier*; Richard English, *Armed Struggle: A History of the IRA* (Basingstoke, 2004); Toby Harnden, *Bandit Country: The IRA and South Armagh* (London, 1999); or for personal accounts: Kieran Conway, *Southside Provisional: From Freedom Fighter to the Four Courts* (Dublin, 2014); Sean O'Callaghan, *The Informer* (London, 1998). I am indebted to Professor Richard English for these references.

[54] On typologies of sanctuary, see: Artens, 'Sanctuary State – Insurgency Relations'; A. Campana and B. Ducol, 'Rethinking Terrorist Safe Havens: Beyond a State-Centric Approach', *Civil Wars* 13/4 (2011), pp. 396–413; Innes, 'Deconstructing', pp. 251–67; Korteweg, 'Black Holes', pp. 60–71; Piazza,

became an important host to the movement's external organisation. As the FLN's logistical and operational headquarters in Europe, it played a key role in sustaining the Algerian fight for independence, particularly in the metropole. Situated in the prosperous and politically open heartland of Western Europe, the FRG also provided opportunities in the realm of logistics, procurement and public diplomacy that could not be had in developing countries such as Tunisia, Morocco or Egypt. This made the country an important lifeline for the FLN's cause.

Algerian activity in West Germany also casts novel light on the French struggle to defeat the FLN. Since a state's authority and ability to act are territorially defined, insurgent groups with access to external sanctuaries raise the costs of counterinsurgency and diminish its effectiveness.[55] As this book will show, the FLN's extraterritorial bases significantly complicated both the political and military dimensions of French counterinsurgency efforts. Two aspects are brought into particular relief. First, French efforts to combat the FLN's external sanctuaries were moulded by the techniques of colonial repression and the rationales of *guerre révolutionnaire*, the French theory of anti-subversive and counterinsurgency warfare. Second, within this process, the French intelligence and security services played a paramount role. Given the fiercely held conviction that the FLN's external organisation constituted the lifeblood of the Algerian rebellion, it should hardly come as a surprise that the French armed forces viewed its obliteration as a core strategic objective. According to the logic of *guerre révolutionnaire*, the destruction of the FLN's external platforms was a vital precondition for a French victory in the struggle against internal subversion, whether in Algeria or the metropole. Only by containing and domesticating the nationalists' activities could the internal forces of order suppress FLN militancy comprehensively, thus securing a *physical, military* victory in the fight for Algeria. Furthermore, the destruction of the FLN's external sanctuaries would weaken the morale and break the will of the *mujâhideen*. In so doing, it would aid French efforts to re-conquer the hearts and minds of Algerian Muslims, thus securing a *psychological* and *political* victory over the FLN.[56]

A key objective of French counterinsurgency, the destruction of external sanctuaries proved exceptionally difficult given the non-belligerent status of the host states. France's intelligence and security services played a pivotal

'Incubators', pp. 469–88; Idean Salehyan, 'No Shelter Here: Rebel Sanctuaries and International Conflict', *Journal of Politics* 70/1 (2008), pp. 54–66.

55 Byman, *Deadly*, p. 67; Salehyan, *Rebels*, p. 6.

56 The concept of *guerre révolutionnaire* will be explored in the following chapter.

part in this process since they allowed the French authorities to circumvent the norms of sovereignty and territoriality preventing the intervention by one state in the internal affairs of another.[57] Responsible on the one hand for intelligence-gathering on insurgent activities, these services, through collaborative arrangements and covert interventions, also constituted key agents in the repression of the FLN's external organisation. When one considers historian Martin Thomas's thesis about the fundamental importance that intelligence – both as an aid to policy formation (or provider of information) and as an instrument of policy implementation (or agent of state violence) – played in the maintenance and survival of colonial regimes, this development should hardly come as a surprise.[58] This book argues that French security and intelligence, in its effort to domesticate the FLN's subversive activities, ultimately achieved the opposite. To develop one of Connelly's arguments: nothing internationalised that conflict more than the attempts of the French authorities to export their methods of colonial repression and counterinsurgency.[59]

Sovereignty

The FLN's decision to use the Federal Republic as sanctuary and rear base and French efforts to combat this development were bound to impinge on West German sovereignty. In this case, sovereignty is a term broadly used to describe 'supreme and legitimate authority within a territory', the recognition of territorial statehood bestowed by members of the Westphalian international system, and a state's ability to shape and conduct its foreign relations in an independent manner. It also includes notions of just how a state should wield or project its power and authority internally and externally on the international stage.[60] Historians Nassima Bougherara, Jean-Paul Cahn and Klaus-Jürgen Müller have highlighted the extent to which the Algerian war reverberated on West German diplomacy.[61]

[57] This also explains why the CIA would later play a vital albeit doomed role in US interdiction operations against the Ho Chi Minh trail.

[58] Martin Thomas, *Empires of Intelligence. Security Services and Colonial Disorder after 1914* (Berkeley CA, 2008), pp. 1–8.

[59] Connelly, *Diplomatic Revolution*, p. 8.

[60] For a succinct introduction to the concept of sovereignty, see: Daniel Philpott, 'Sovereignty: An Introduction and Brief History', *Journal of International Affairs* 48/2 (1995), p. 357. Also: F.H. Hinsley, *Sovereignty*, 2nd edn (Cambridge, 1986), p. 17.

[61] Nassima Bougherara, *Les Rapports franco-allemands à l'épreuve de la question algérienne (1955–1963)* (Bern, 2006); Jean-Paul Cahn and Klaus-Jürgen Müller, *La République fédérale d'Allemagne et la Guerre d'Algérie (1954–1962): perception, implication et retombées diplomatiques* (Paris, 2003).

The conflict created a constant dilemma for the Adenauer government, which remained torn between its allegiance towards France (the policy of *Westbindung*) and a desire to guard German interests in the Arab world from East German encroachment (the Hallstein doctrine). Building on these studies, this book highlights how the growing Algerian presence within the Federal Republic compounded Bonn's foreign-policy dilemma. Because the FLN came to use West Germany as a refuge and base for subversive activities, and because the French authorities sought to undermine those activities using both legal and illegal means, the Algerian war came to impinge not only on West German foreign policy but increasingly also on internal law and order and hence the nation's sovereignty. The domestic authorities struggled to comprehend and contain the Franco-Algerian confrontation unfolding on their territory as the country became more directly affected by the war than any other French ally. This book describes in detail some of the internal debates instigated by this development. Contrary to received wisdom, the Adenauer government, intent on protecting the Franco-German rapprochement, did not adhere to strict neutrality in the Algerian question. Rather, it instructed officials to do what they could to support the French in their fight against Algerian nationalism. However, West German officials at times resisted the government's instructions believing they undermined not only the FRG's recently won sovereignty and territorial integrity but also its newly minted democratic order. The resultant tensions often seemed to work in the FLN's favour. Sometimes the government's view prevailed; however, it could take time for domestic officials to turn Bonn's *Diktat* on Franco-German cooperation in matters Algerian into policies that conformed to the *Rechtsstaat*, i.e. the constitution and the rule of law. At other times, the imperative of upholding German sovereignty trumped all other considerations.

The internal debates over how to respond to the FLN's implantation in West Germany also shed light on the country's efforts at moral and political rehabilitation post-World War II, a process that involved more than denazification, democratisation, and westernisation. On the international stage, rehabilitation involved an opening-up to the world and a repudiation of nationalist and imperialist patterns of thought and action.[62] As this book argues, West German responses to national liberation movements and decolonisation proved central to that process, none more so than responses to the Algerian war. After all, the Algerian

[62] See also: Hagen, 'Internationalism'.

sanctuary confronted the West German authorities with global processes usually far removed from their immediate concerns.

The same argument goes for civil-society actors, who played an important role in the process of moral and political rehabilitation on the international stage. The FLN's decision to use West Germany as a sanctuary meant that civil society, too, came to be drawn out of the insulated and introverted shell that had cocooned it since the end of World War II. As Claus Leggewie and Thomas Scheffler have shown in studies focusing on the West German Left, the Algerian war inspired the first stirrings of Third World solidarity usually associated with the protest movements of the 1960s.[63] This book goes beyond that claim, for it argues that solidarity with the FLN's cause was not the preserve of the Left. The rising presence in West Germany of Algerian refugees and militants meant that society at large became increasingly alert to events occurring beyond its provincial and Eurocentric horizon. This awareness fed into a growing willingness to support the FLN's cause, one that spanned across the political spectrum and across generational divides. The grassroots political and humanitarian activism that emerged during the Algerian war never became as cohesive as the peace and anti-nuclear movements that also witnessed their first stirrings at this time.[64] Collectively, such activism nonetheless 'confronted the prevailing limits of legitimate political participation', as Belinda Davis argues, 'and served more broadly to redefine "politics" and democratic participation', even in international affairs.[65]

In highlighting the depth and diversity of civic engagement on the FLN's behalf, this book helps revise the traditional view of the 1950s as a decade of political and emotional reserve on the part of West German society toward questions of foreign policy and national security.[66] It demonstrates the extent to which civil-society actors in the young Bonn Republic responded to, engaged with, and sought to influence international politics, in this case Algeria's independence struggle. In doing so,

63 Claus Leggewie, *Kofferträger. Das Algerienprojekt der Linken im Adenauer-Deutschland* (Berlin, 1984); Thomas Scheffler, *Die SPD und der Algerienkrieg (1954–1962)* (Berlin, 1995).

64 See, for instance: Detlef Bald, *Alternativen zur Wiederbewaffnung: Friedenskonzeptionen in Westdeutschland 1945–1955* (Essen, 2008); Markus Gunkel, *Der Kampf gegen die Remilitarisierung: Friedensbewegung in Hamburg 1950 bis 1955* (Frankfurt/Main, 2009); Forschungsstelle für Zeitgeschichte in Hamburg (ed.), *'Kampf dem Atomtod!': Die Protestbewegung 1957/58 in zeithistorischer und gegenwärtiger Perspektive* (München, 2009).

65 Belinda Davis, 'What's Left? Popular Political Participation in Postwar Europe', *American Historical Review* 113/2 (2008), p. 370.

66 It is not alone in that endeavour. See also: Detlef Bald and Wolfram Wette (eds.), *Friedensinitiativen in der Frühzeit des Kalten Krieges 1945–1955* (Essen, 2010); Holger Nehring, *Politics of Security. British and West German Protest Movements and the Early Cold War, 1945–1970* (Oxford, 2013).

these actors offset the Adenauer government's pro-French policies in the Algerian question. They also helped induce a significant re-assessment of West German foreign and security policy, one that emphasised not just traditional *Realpolitik* but also, crucially, a new 'moral grammar' of ethical and humanitarian behaviour.[67] Here, then, was a country seeking not only to reassert its sovereignty and independence but to find a new identity and role in a rapidly changing world community.

Methodology

Examining such an entangled story requires a broad approach to international history, one that embraces the roles of high and low politics, foreign and domestic policy, and that pays attention to tangible and intangible factors informing decision-making processes, whether strategic or political calculations, economic interests, public opinion or cultural preconceptions. Inspired by the transnational and transcultural perspectives and approaches central to the pursuit of 'connected' or 'entangled' history, the book also looks beyond the state to assess the roles of transnational movements (notably the FLN itself) and civil-society actors in international relations. Equally central to the book's research methodology is an understanding of insurgency and counterinsurgency warfare. Finally, the book draws on multi-archival research, particularly on a broad range of previously undisclosed files from the French and West German security and intelligence services. Used judiciously, these files serve as an indicator of the preoccupations, mentalities and knowledge that informed French and West German decision-making. They also provide crucial information on the nature, scale and reception of the FLN's activities in the Federal Republic, a subject about which we otherwise know very little given their clandestine nature, the fact that leading protagonists are deceased or untraceable, and that the files of the GPRA's Ministry for Armaments and General Logistics, which coordinated most of the FLN's subversive actions in West Germany and Europe, remain classified.[68] This book

[67] Peter Sloterdijk, *Theory of the Post-War Periods. Observations on Franco-German Relations since 1945* (Vienna, 2009), foreword by Klaus-Dieter Müller, p. 1. See also: Thomas U. Berger, *War, Guilt, and World Politics after World War II* (Cambridge, 2012), pp. 35–82; José Brunner, Norbert Frei and Constantin Goscher (eds.), *Die Praxis der Wiedergutmachung: Geschichte, Erfahrung und Wirkung in Deutschland und Israel* (Göttingen, 2009); Lily Gardner Feldman, *Germany's Foreign Policy of Reconciliation: From Enmity to Amity* (Lanham MD, 2012); Constantin Goschler, *Schuld und Schulden: Die Politik der Wiedergutmachung für NS-Verfolgte seit 1945* (Göttingen, 2005).

[68] On the Ministry's dominance in overseeing FLN activities in the FRG, see: 'Entretien avec Abdelhafid Keramane, Alger, 21.9.2000', in Bougherara, *Rapports*, pp. 209–11; Daho Djerbal,

therefore privileges the West German and French perspectives, all the more so since the author is not an Arabic speaker. To ensure the Algerian voice is nonetheless heard, the study draws on a growing number of Algerian memoirs and published sources; it takes seriously Ann Laura Stoler's advice of reading the available archives 'along the grain'.[69] Finally, a study involving such multiple perspectives, actors and themes will invariably have gaps, oversights and errors. For these, the author assumes full responsibility.

For its structural framework, the book draws on the theory of revolutionary warfare as conceived by the FLN and French military. Chapter 1 examines these understandings in greater detail and places them into a wider historical context. It traces the reasons why external sanctuaries such as the one in West Germany became so central to both Algerian and French strategy and operations. Two larger sections follow this chapter. The first focuses on the war's early years ending with the overthrow of the Fourth French Republic in May 1958. This period witnessed the FLN's initial implantation in West Germany. The second section covers the return to power of General de Gaulle and ends just before the Algerian referendum on self-determination of January 1961, which ultimately paved the way for France's disengagement from Algeria. During this phase, the FLN came to make full use of its West German sanctuary in a strategy that deliberately sought to internationalise the Algerian war. Each of these two sections contains four thematic chapters exploring different facets of the Franco-Algerian confrontation as it affected the West German state and society: the diplomatic contest; the intelligence services' struggle over the population, specifically the control of Algerian migrants and refugees; the propaganda war, or battle for "hearts and minds"; and the fight over military and non-military resources.

The thematic and chronological divisions are at times fluid and artificial; however, they provide useful frames of analysis that serve to cast important fresh light on the manner in which extraterritorial sanctuaries became contested sites between France and the FLN in a war that, as French military scholar David Galula later wrote, consisted of '20 per cent military

L'Organisation Spéciale de la Fédération de France du FLN: Histoire de la lutte armée du FLN en France (1956–1962) (Alger, 2012), pp. 367–71. On Algeria's National Archives: Abdelkrim Badjadja, 'Panorama des archives de l'Algérie moderne et contemporaine', in *Guerre d'Algérie* (eds.) Harbi and Stora, pp. 924–7, and www.archives-dgan.gov.dz/. Access to the files of the GPRA and its ministries is being liberalised, but sadly not in time to be exploited for this book.

69 Ann Laura Stoler, *Along the Archival Grain: Epistemic Anxieties and Colonial Common Sense* (Princeton NJ, 2010).

action and 80 per cent political'.[70] To use the expression of one exasperated German diplomat, West Germany did indeed become a '*Tummelplatz*' (playground) of Algerian nationalists engaging in multifarious activities.[71] French officials, both military and civilian, were bound to react to this development, and as a consequence they, too, exported aspects of their counterinsurgency campaign into West Germany – not least the resort to paramilitary operations, as demonstrated by the assassination attempt on Améziane Aït Ahcène. The story of how the FRG became a contested site between Algerian nationalists and French authorities thus adds a whole new layer to our understanding of the Algerian war, one shedding light on the role of external sanctuaries. It also helps to dispel long-held views of West Germany as disinterested in and detached from the process of decolonisation that so radically transformed the international community in the decades that followed World War II. Put simply, the Algerian sanctuary compelled the West German state and its citizens to think critically about the meanings of sovereignty and about their country's role in international society.

[70] David Galula, *Counter-Insurgency Warfare: Theory and Practice* (New York, 1964), p. 66.

[71] Entwurf eines Rundschreibens an deutsche Vertretungen in den arabischen Staaten, 15 February 1960, Politisches Archiv des Auswärtigen Amts (PA/AA), Berlin, B25/12 (italics added).

CHAPTER 1

Internationalising colonial warfare
FLN strategy and French responses

Few observers would have concluded that the thirty-odd, poorly executed and mostly bungled attacks undertaken by the FLN on 1 November 1954 marked the advent of an insurgency with global reverberations.[1] Hardly anyone had heard of the FLN, but to the small group of conspirators who launched the Algerian war, the time was ripe for armed resistance. Reforms had failed for years to address the inequities of the colonial state. In 1954, Algeria counted a Muslim population of 8,546,000 and a European population of 984,000. With Muslim birth rates 2.5 times higher than European birth rates and among the highest in the world, 52.6 per cent of the population was under the age of thirty. Neither agricultural production nor limited efforts at industrialisation could cope with the demands of this rapidly expanding population. Around 70 per cent of Algerian Muslims lived on less than 10 hectares of land, below the average required to stave off malnutrition. The most fertile soil had long been in the hands of French settlers or *colons*. Regardless of metropolitan surpluses or Algeria's predominantly Muslim culture, wine production constituted almost three-quarters of Algeria's harvest, encompassing 72 per cent of cultivable land. The consequence of this agricultural crisis, where half of the working rural population was jobless, had been a rapid rise in urbanisation. In the cities, meanwhile, rampant unemployment further pauperised the Muslim population, which had become ghettoised in squalid shanty towns. Political inequalities merely compounded these socio-economic disparities. The failure to apply the Algerian Statute of 20 September 1947 meant that Muslims continued to face political discrimination. Underrepresented in the civil administration (due, in part, to their limited access to

[1] The attacks left seven dead and a dozen wounded. Estimates of the number of militants involved range from 700 to 3,000. See: Connelly, *Diplomatic Revolution*, p. 69; Horne, *Savage War*, p. 96; John Ruedy, *Modern Algeria: The Origins and Development of a Nation* (Bloomington IN, 1992), pp. 156–7, 159; John Talbot, *The War without a Name: France in Algeria 1954–1962* (New York, 1980), pp. 38, 47–9.

education) and in the Algerian Assembly (where elections took place through two disproportionate colleges), Muslims also faced widespread vote rigging, which ensured the political dominance of the *colons*.[2]

If the domestic situation had reached an impasse in 1954, internationally, the tide was turning against the colonial powers. British troops were evacuating the Suez Canal and fighting anti-colonial insurgencies in Malaya, Kenya and soon also Cyprus. French forces suffered a humiliating defeat against the Vietminh at Dien Bien Phu and battled sedition in Morocco and Tunisia. The Geneva Accords of 20 July spelt the end of French Indochina, and Prime Minister Pierre Mendès-France's declaration at Carthage on 31 July presaged France's retreat from Tunisia and Morocco. Algerian nationalists had to act swiftly if they wanted to take advantage of this favourable climate, especially the French army's preoccupation with insurgencies elsewhere. Disgruntled with those who still sought to operate within the constitutional confines of the colonial state, a group of conspirators broke with the PPA-MTLD to set the stage for the 'violent event' that Martiniquan psychiatrist and FLN militant Frantz Fanon would deem so essential for the demolition of the colonial system.[3] The FLN's 'historical chiefs' had only one goal in mind in October 1954: to launch Algeria's war of national liberation. Matters of doctrine and the finer details of strategy remained of secondary concern.[4]

It would be wrong, however, to assume that the FLN's founders disregarded the means and methods through which to accomplish their goal. For nearly a decade, a small but determined group of PPA militants had preoccupied itself precisely with this question, galvanised into action by the 8 May 1945 massacres at Guelma, Sétif and Kheratta. Realising that Europe's liberation from fascism would not extend to them, these massacres provoked in Algerians what Hocine Aït Ahmed called an 'attitude of revolt, in the Camusian sense of the word'.[5] As one of the FLN's future

[2] Charles-Robert Ageron, *Modern Algeria. A History from 1830 to the Present* (trans.) Michael Brett (London, 1991), pp. 84–9, 105–6; Connelly, *Diplomatic Revolution*, pp. 18–21; Ruedy, *Modern Algeria*, pp. 94, 126, 152.

[3] Frantz Fanon, *The Wretched of the Earth* (trans.) Richard Philcox (New York, 2004), pp. 1, 42, 30. On the FLN's origins, see: Mohammed Harbi, *Aux origines du FLN: Le populisme révolutionnaire en Algérie* (Paris, 1975); Mohammed Harbi, *Le FLN, mirage ou réalité: des origines à la prise du pouvoir (1945–1962)*, 2nd edn (Paris, 1985), chs. 6–8; Meynier, *Histoire*, pp. 69–126.

[4] Albert Memmi, *The Colonizer and the Colonized* (trans.) Howard Greenfeld (London, 2003), p. 180. See also: Harbi, *1954*, p. 72; Abder-Rahmane Derradji, *The Algerian Guerrilla Campaign: Strategy and Tactics* (Lewiston NY, 1997), pp. 34, 108; Mohamed Boudiaf, *La préparation du 1er novembre suivi de la lettre ouverte aux algériens* (Paris, 1976), p. 44.

[5] Hocine Aït Ahmed, *Mémoires d'un Combattant. L'esprit d'indépendance 1942–1952. Document* (Paris, 1983), p. 45; Robert Merle, *Ahmed Ben Bella* (Paris, 1965), pp. 63–4; Charles-Robert Ageron, 'Mai 1945

founders, Aït Ahmed had a formative influence on the shape that revolt would take. A scion of a prominent Kabyle family, he was the first head of the *Organisation Spéciale* (OS), a paramilitary unit established in 1947 by the PPA's successor and legal front, MTLD, for the purpose of preparing an armed insurrection. Aït Ahmed's report to the MTLD's central committee of December 1948, though not an exact blueprint for Algeria's independence struggle, anticipated many of the strategies, tactics and political principles embraced by the FLN between 1954 and 1962.[6] Not only does it articulate some of the main features of the FLN's brand of anti-colonial warfare, it also expounds the reasons for which that struggle placed such an important emphasis on the international arena.

The FLN and revolutionary warfare

Inspired by colonial insurgencies from Ireland to Indochina, the Bolshevik revolution, the Chinese civil war and the global fight against fascism, Aït Ahmed argued that only a 'truly revolutionary war' in the Marxist-Maoist sense would secure an overthrow of the 'blind and brutal colonialism' in Algeria, for France would not relinquish the 'cornerstone' of her empire 'without exhausting all of the considerable assets at her disposal'.[7] Against this preponderance of French power, the strategy of revolutionary warfare held out two trumps: first, the 'moral force of a just cause' in defence 'of a crushed and humiliated humanity', which would rally the Algerian people and enable them to persevere; and second, the people's knowledge and communion with their country, which would allow the insurgents to exploit Algeria's topography and environment to their advantage.[8] After a period of preparation, a small vanguard of 'peasant soldiers' organised and trained by the OS in the techniques of modern guerrilla warfare would spearhead the resultant people's war from sanctuaries and rear bases located in Algeria's remote and inaccessible mountains. Inspired by Maoist and Vietminh tactics, Aït Ahmed argued that to operate effectively, these

en Algérie. Enjeu de mémoire et histoire', *Matériaux pour l'histoire de notre temps* 39 (1995), pp. 52–6. On the May 1945 massacres: Harbi, *1954*, p. 50; Meynier, *Histoire*, pp. 65–9. For more detail: Roger Vétillard, *Sétif, mai 1945: massacres en Algérie* (Paris, 2008); Jean-Louis Planche, *Sétif 1945: histoire d'un massacre annoncé* (Paris, 2006); Annie Rey-Goldzeiguer, *Aux origines de la guerre d'Algérie 1940–1945: de Mers-el-Kébir aux massacres du Nord-Constantinois* (Paris, 2002); Mahfoud Kaddache, *Histoire du nationalisme algérien, 1919–1951*, II (Alger, 1981), ch. 21.

6 Mohammed Harbi (ed.), *Les Archives de la révolution algérienne* (Paris, 1981), p. 15.

7 Rapport par Aït Ahmed du bureau politique du PPA au comité central élargi, December 1948, in *Archives* (ed.) Harbi, pp. 42, 22–3.

8 Ibid., p. 36.

partisans required the support of Algeria's rural masses, which in turn necessitated the creation of political-administrative cadres tasked with stimulating and sustaining the people's patriotic and revolutionary fervour. The revolution's command structure, meanwhile, was to remain decentralised so as to make effective use of the terrain.

Adopted by the PPA-MTLD in 1948, Aït Ahmed's plan was never brought to fruition, for by 1950 the French security services had dismantled the OS. As a 'laboratory' that forged both men and ideas, however, the organisation's influence on the FLN is undeniable.[9] Preoccupied by the technical problems of launching a revolutionary war against a stronger adversary, both the OS and the FLN initially favoured the development of military structures over political ones.[10] Mohamed Boudiaf, who like Aït Ahmed served in the OS and co-founded the FLN, highlighted this fixation in his description of the FLN's plan for a Maoist-style, three-phased insurgency. After an initial period dedicated to the implantation of rear bases and military structures – Aït Ahmed's vanguard of peasant *junud* (regular soldiers) and *musabbilûn* (auxiliary partisans) – the revolution would pass to a phase of generalised insecurity that implicated the masses through the creation of a counter-authority to the French colonial administration. The final stage would see the emergence of 'fortified free zones' from whence conventional troops would reconquer Algeria. Only during this third phase, Boudiaf wrote, could the movement begin to think of a 'fusion' of military and political structures with a view to preparing the stage for an independent Algerian government. Until then, armed struggle would dominate over political doctrine.[11]

Equipped with this strategy of the weak, the struggle against France's superior resources and know-how would still prove daunting. Weakness and inexperience, however, did not excuse inaction. It is 'essential that we stop conducting politics based on our means', Aït Ahmed urged in 1948: since 'only the revolution can liberate our people, "the art of the possible" must support our strategy and not disqualify it'. Algeria's dispossessed masses would provide the manpower and morale, but they could not provide the material and financial resources needed to sustain a revolutionary war. To address this problem – the insurgents' 'highest concern' – the revolution, like others before it, had to look abroad: to Algerian émigrés in metropolitan France; the wider Arab world; the Soviet bloc; and the West.[12]

[9] Harbi, *1954*, p. 72; Ibid., *FLN*, p. 53; Aït Ahmed, *Mémoires*, pp. 156–8.

[10] This propensity, Harbi argues, accentuated the FLN's authoritarian tendencies, ultimately resulting in the imposition of a military dictatorship in 1965. Harbi, *FLN*, p. 125; Ibid., *1954*, pp. 51–2, 66.

[11] Boudiaf, *Préparation*, pp. 46–7. [12] Rapport, December 1948, pp. 33–4, 40–1, 43.

Internationalising revolutionary warfare

Here, then, is the prime motive driving the internationalisation of Algeria's independence struggle, including the FLN's future presence in West Germany. To sustain their revolution, Algerians had to be guided by what Aït Ahmed called a 'strategy of openness to and expansion into the world'.[13] This strategy is echoed in the Proclamation of 1 November 1954, which outlined the FLN's two immediate and essential tasks as 'an *internal* action, both on the political level and in terms of proper [armed] action; and an *external* action with a view to making the Algerian problem a reality for the entire world'.[14] To Aït Ahmed, the international arena constituted the revolution's third and supreme trump. It was here that Algerians would secure the materiel they required and here they would inflict the greatest political and psychological damage on France, for in an age of anti-imperialism, the scrutiny of international and world opinion would ultimately undermine French colonialism.[15] This strategy would only work if Algerians avoided 'sentimental pitfalls and the blinkered attitude of dogmatism'. To exploit the ideological, geopolitical and economic contradictions and rivalries that marked the international system, Algerians had to engage in impartial analysis.[16]

With these principles in mind, Aït Ahmed identified four concentric circles from which the revolution would draw support: the Cold War world; the colonial world; the Arab-Islamic world; and the Maghreb. In the first circle, the Cold War created opportunities for aid and support, especially as the two antagonistic superpowers both claimed to oppose European colonialism. However, even in 1948 Aït Ahmed warned against leaning too closely towards the Eastern bloc, since the United States would never allow North Africa to pass under communist influence given the region's strategic importance as a base for potential military operations in Europe. Instead, Algerians ought to secure the patronage of powerful nations on *either* side of the ideological divide, a strategy that had the added benefit of driving a wedge between France and her allies. Aït Ahmed thus proposed taking full advantage not only of the bipolar world-system

[13] Ibid., pp. 33–4, 40–1, 43; Harbi, *FLN*, p. 124.

[14] Proclamation du Front de libération nationale, 31 October 1954, in *Archives* (ed.) Harbi, p. 102 (italics added).

[15] Rapport, December 1948, p. 36; Aït Ahmed, *Mémoires*, pp. 102–3. International opinion refers to the opinion of *states*, world opinion to the opinion of *people* or non-state actors, but the terms are often used interchangeably. Christopher Hill, 'World Opinion and the Empire of Circumstance', *International Affairs* 72/1 (1996), pp. 115, 117–28.

[16] Rapport, December 1948, pp. 43–5.

but also of antagonisms within the Western alliance, including European and American commercial rivalries.[17]

The revolution's genuine 'strike force', meanwhile, was located in the second circle consisting of (former) colonies, especially among the anti-colonial struggles gathering pace in Asia and Africa.[18] Well before the emergence of an Afro-Asian bloc at the UN, international tensions over Syria and Lebanon, French Indochina and the Dutch East Indies had demonstrated that diplomacy and international negotiation could contribute to the outcome of emancipatory struggles. In an era driven by the discourse of international cooperation, human rights and the Wilsonian ideal of self-determination – normative values that were enshrined in the UN's founding Charter of June 1945 as well as the 1948 Universal Declaration of Human Rights – Algerians counted on the backing of anti-colonial movements throughout the (formerly) colonised world.[19] To exploit this support, Aït Ahmed believed, Algerians had to forge ties to governments, political parties, student associations and trade unions throughout Africa and Asia.[20]

Particularly important in this regard was the Arab-Islamic world, the third concentric circle to which Aït Ahmed ascribed the roles of 'catalyst' and 'mobiliser' charged with generating wider interest in the Algerian problem. Emphasis on Islamic and pan-Arab solidarity would help to cement the revolutionaries' standing at home as well as in the wider Middle East. More importantly, it challenged French claims that Algeria was distinct from the rest of the Arab-Islamic world.[21] The creation of the League of Arab States in March 1945, seen widely as a first step towards the unification of the Arab world and its liberation from colonial subjugation, had lent vigour to these strategies. These hopes proved to be short-lived, for the League assumed a cautious stance on French North Africa. As a

[17] Ibid., pp. 40, 44. Aït Ahmed could not have foreseen this, but the revolution would equally profit from the Sino-Soviet split. See: Connelly, 'Rethinking', p. 223; Ibid., *Diplomatic Revolution*, p. 47; Odd Arne Westad, *The Global Cold War: Third World Interventions and the Making of Our Times* (Cambridge, 2007), p. 89.

[18] Rapport, December 1948, p. 43.

[19] On the influence of international and normative regimes on anti-colonial movements before, during and after World War II, see: Burke, *Decolonization*; Fabian Klose, *Menschenrechte im Schatten kolonialer Gewalt. Die Dekolonisierungskriege in Kenia und Algerien 1945–1962* (München, 2009), pp. 19–61; Erez Manela, *The Wilsonian Moment. Self-Determination and the International Origins of Anticolonial Nationalism* (Oxford, 2007); Mark Mazower, *No Enchanted Palace: the End of Empire and the Ideological Origins of the United Nations* (Princeton NJ, 2009), ch. 4.

[20] Rapport, December 1948, pp. 43–44.

[21] Ibid., p. 44. On the influence of Arab-Islamic cultural discourse on Algerian national identity, see: James McDougall, *History and the Culture of Nationalism in Algeria* (Cambridge, 2006).

representative body, however, it remained a symbolic anchor or 'leitmotiv' for Maghrebi nationalists; and by the 1950s, it became an important conduit through which they laid their claims for independence before the UN.[22] The League's headquarters at Cairo served as a point of convergence for exiled North Africans, including four of the FLN's founding fathers: Ahmed Ben Bella, a twice decorated veteran of the Italian campaign, who before going underground in the OS had briefly acted as municipal councillor in his native Oranie; Mohamed Khider, a self-educated radical who had served as MTLD deputy for Algiers since 1946; Boudiaf, another veteran of the Italian campaign; and Aït Ahmed himself. It was from Cairo that this 'external delegation' began to implement the FLN's international strategy and goals.[23]

The concentration in Cairo of Algerian, Moroccan and Tunisian nationalists helped foster the notion inspiring Aït Ahmed's final circle: that of a united Maghrebi front against French colonialism. To Aït Ahmed, the Maghreb represented one 'geometrical entity' and 'strategic whole' whose liberation could only be achieved through concerted action and a united high command.[24] This call for unity was not new, having already inspired Messali Hadj's *Étoile nord-africaine*, an early populist-nationalist movement founded in 1926. Not until the end of World War II, however, did the notion of a common front gather momentum. In 1945, the PPA signed a non-binding accord with Tunisia's *Neo-Destour* and Morocco's *Istiqlal*, in which each party pledged to coordinate their independence campaigns.[25] Three years later, the three parties created a Committee for the Liberation of the Arab Maghreb, which failed to implement a common front. Ultimately, not even a renewed accord signed in April 1954, just months before the FLN instigated its revolution, brought about the unity Aït Ahmed had desired.[26] Ben Bella later claimed he always considered the idea unrealistic, since Moroccans, Tunisians and Algerians had from the

22 Samya el-Mechat, 'L'Improbable "Nation Arabe". La Ligue des états arabes et l'indépendance du Maghreb (1945–1956)', *Vingtième Siècle* 82 (2004), pp. 57–68 here p. 68. Also: Samya el-Mechat, *Tunisie. Les chemins vers l'indépendance (1945–1956)* (Paris, 1992), pp. 11–12, 25–29, 57–78, 91–100, 163–75, 255–8; Martin Thomas, *The French North African Crisis: Colonial Breakdown and Anglo-French Relations, 1945–62* (London, 2000), pp. 24–5.

23 Aït Ahmed, *Mémoires*, pp. 103, 210, 221–3; Merle, *Ben Bella*, pp. 93–8; Harbi, *FLN*, pp. 34,54–6; Meynier, *Histoire*, pp. 73–4.

24 Rapport, December 1948, pp. 41–3.

25 Meynier, *Histoire*, p. 73.

26 Ibid., pp. 73–5, 564; Aït Ahmed, *Mémoires*, pp. 103n.1, 162–3, 189; 'Alāl al-Fāsi, *The Independence Movements in Arab North Africa* (Washington DC, 1954), pp. 285–89, 310–14; Rachid Driss, 'Le mouvement de résistance du Maghreb arabe au Caire après la Deuxième Guerre Mondiale', *Les Cahiers de Tunisie: Revue de Sciences Humaines* 117–118 (1981), pp. 295–36; El-Mechat, 'L'Improbable', pp. 59–60; Ibid., *Tunisie*, pp. 35–51, 91–100, 259–63.

start engaged in 'indubitably national' independence struggles. To Mohamed Lebjaoui, a former leader of the FLN's *Fédération de France*, the three countries, notwithstanding their many connections, each faced different hurdles in their respective liberation campaigns. As protectorates, the Moroccan sultanate and Tunisian beylical administration continued to embody at least a semblance of national sovereignty. Algeria, on the other hand, had lost both its former state structures and its traditional elites, making it much harder for the FLN to assert itself as the accepted representative of the Algerian people. In contrast to their neighbours, moreover, Algerians had to contend with a far stronger settler presence, one that conceived of itself not as a community of expatriates but as an integral part of France. Moroccan and Tunisian nationalists also promoted distinct aims and emphasised different strategies, forcing even Aït Ahmed to concede that neither *Neo-Destour* nor *Istiqlal* were as revolutionary as the PPA-MTLD, let alone the FLN. Although they, too, eventually resorted to insurgency tactics, neither party made violence the primary aspect of its independence struggle, preferring to rely on diplomacy and negotiation instead.[27]

In spite of this failure to create a common front, the Maghreb continued to represent an important source of solidarity and support. Morocco and Tunisia remained vital pillars in the FLN's independence struggle, just as Aït Ahmed had predicted, with each playing a significant part in internationalising the Algerian problem. As early as 1957, M'Hammed Yazid, one of the FLN's foremost diplomats, praised *Neo-Destour* and *Istiqlal* for their 'unconditional support' in the diplomatic arena, without which the FLN would never have secured such widespread recognition as the 'true [and rightful] expression of the Algerian resistance'. Without their help, Yazid maintained, the FLN could not have attended the Afro-Asian conference at Bandung in April 1955, which laid the groundwork for the non-aligned movement; nor would the Algerian question have been inscribed

[27] Merle, *Ben Bella*, p. 94; Mohamed Lebjaoui, *Vérités sur la Révolution algérienne* (Paris, 1970), pp. 95–6; Rapport, December 1948, p. 42; Aït Ahmed, *Mémoires*, pp. 162–3. On the international diplomacy of *Istiqlal* and *Neo-Destour*: El-Mechat, *Tunisie*, pp. 19–25, 110–19, 195–207; Azzou el-Mustafa, 'Le nationalisme Marocain et les États-Unis 1945–1956', *Guerres mondiales et conflits contemporains* 177 (1995), pp. 131–8; Kenneth J. Perkins, 'North African Propaganda and the United States, 1946–1956', *African Studies Review* 19/3 (1976), pp. 65–77; Egya N. Sangmuah, 'Sultan Mohammed Ben Youssef's American Strategy and the Diplomacy of North African Liberation, 1943–61', *Journal of Contemporary History* 27/1 (1992), pp. 129–48; Martin Thomas, 'France Accused: French North Africa before the United Nations, 1952–1962', *Contemporary European History* 10/1 (2001), pp. 91–103; Ibid., 'Defending a Lost Cause? France and the United States Vision of Imperial Rule in French North Africa, 1945–1956', *Diplomatic History* 26/2 (2002), pp. 215–47.

on the agenda of the UN General Assembly in September 1955. Both these events proved pivotal to the internationalisation of the FLN's cause.[28]

Once Tunisia and Morocco secured their independence in March and April 1956 respectively, their assistance to the FLN intensified further. Initially, many Algerian nationalists perceived the decision by *Istiqlal* and *Neo-Destour* to negotiate with Paris on the terms of self-government as a retreat from previous commitments to a united front.[29] Faced with a fait accompli and reassured of continued solidarity, the FLN quickly came to see the advantages to be garnered from these changed circumstances. As Lebjaoui noted:

> [...] the independence of Tunisia and of Morocco, even if acquired separately, could only facilitate the development of our own contest; as our struggle intensified, these two countries ended up becoming the principal bases of our political, diplomatic and military action.[30]

Algeria's neighbours thus proved most valuable to the FLN as active sponsors and hosts of extraterritorial sanctuaries. After all, as Daniel Byman notes, insurgent groups 'become far more potent if they have a sanctuary in which to organize, plan, and train'. Sanctuary, Byman continues, 'facilitates all other forms of assistance', allowing a group to 'plot, recruit, proselytize, contact supporters around the world, raise money and – perhaps most important – enjoy a respite from the enemy regime's [counterinsurgency] effort [... as well as] escape from the constant stress that characterizes life underground'.[31] Sanctuary is all the more valuable if located in a contiguous state that actively supports the insurgency's cause, providing not just shelter but logistical and material support, military training, political backing as well as economic aid.[32] Having always envisioned their actions as both internal and external, FLN leaders were clearly aware of the benefits gained from external sanctuaries. From February 1957, the height of the Battle of Algiers – the French army's campaign to expunge the FLN from the colonial capital, the movement began directing its war effort largely from safe havens beyond France's territorial control; its army established bases, training camps and weapons depots on either side of the Algerian border (as well as in Egypt and Libya). In September 1958, Tunis became the headquarters of the GPRA. From

[28] L'Action internationale du FLN, rapport par M'Hammed Yazid, July 1957, in *Archives* (ed.) Harbi, pp. 172–3. See also: Étude envoyée au C.C.E. de la prison de la Santé (April 1957), in *La Guerre et l'Après-Guerre*, Hocine Aït Ahmed (Paris, 1964), pp. 17–18.

[29] Lebjaoui, *Vérités*, p. 105. [30] Ibid., p. 106.

[31] Byman, *Deadly*, p. 65. Also: Salehyan, *Rebels*, p. 10. [32] Reider, 'External Support', p. 2.

thence, Aït Ahmed pointed out, 'the government will be both inside and outside' of Algeria: close enough to maintain contact with the fighting *mujâhideen*; yet safely out of the French authorities' reach. Extraterritoriality made it possible for the FLN's institutions to assume permanence and stability, thereby enhancing the movement's authority, legitimacy and effectiveness.[33] In harbouring the FLN's headquarters and most vital bases, Morocco and Tunisia proved invaluable allies. To Lebjaoui, their solidarity constituted one of the FLN's 'most precious trumps', for it kept the revolution alive.[34] As later chapters will show, the FLN also applied this trump in Europe, especially in West Germany, though on a different scale. Moreover, in stark contrast to Tunisia and Morocco, whose governments freely and consciously allowed the FLN to operate from their soil, authorities in Bonn never condoned this development.

The Soummam platform

External sanctuaries, however, come at a cost. While they enable much, they can reduce an insurgent group's contact with the populations it seeks to rally as well as its ability to monitor and respond to changing conditions on the ground. They can also limit an insurgent group's freedom of action. After all, even the most supportive and sympathetic host-states have their own national interests to consider and are therefore keen to preserve a non-belligerent status.[35] Extraterritorial sanctuaries thus jeopardised one of the FLN's core principles, for as Aït Ahmed insisted in 1948, Algeria's revolutionary independence struggle had to remain free from outside control:

> No subjugation to anyone, our freedom of manoeuvre must be safeguarded with firmness and tact. Our relations with other peoples, other parties and other governments must be conceived in this optic of independence.[36]

This principle was reiterated by Abane Ramdane, another FLN theoretician and the prime architect of a seminal congress of regional commanders held on 20 August 1956 in the Soummam valley of Kabylia. Convened with

[33] Étude envoyée au C.C.E., pp. 38–43. Meynier claims that Tunis was chosen because Tunisians were deemed 'effeminate' and manipulable while Moroccans were considered headstrong and warlike. *Histoire*, p. 561.

[34] Lebjaoui, *Vérités*, p. 109; Derradji, *Algerian Guerilla*, p. 199; Meynier, *Histoire*, pp. 557–69; Aleya-Sghaier, 'Tunisie', pp. 155–60.

[35] Byman, *Deadly*, p. 75; Salehyan, *Rebels*, pp. 10, 32. Also: Artens, 'Sanctuary State – Insurgency Relations'.

[36] Rapport, December 1948, p. 45.

a view to reorganising the FLN's decimated leadership and endowing the revolution with an institutionalised chain of command and politico-administrative structure, the congress elaborated a political platform to guide the FLN's future actions. On Abane's urging, this platform adopted three core tenets: the primacy of politics over the military; the principle of collective leadership; and the primacy of the interior over the exterior. The leaders assembled at Soummam staked their claim as the revolution's true guardians. They condemned the 'cult of personality' allegedly surrounding the movement's external leaders, notably Ben Bella, who had been excluded from the congress. Instead, control of the revolution's activities and organisations fell to a newly formed Committee of Coordination and Execution (CCE) consisting solely of internal leaders.[37]

Some scholars have portrayed the Soummam platform as an expression of personal rivalries and power struggles.[38] In fact, the congress echoed many of the principles articulated in Aït Ahmed's 1948 report.[39] By insisting on the primacy of politics over the military, the platform sought to integrate more effectively those MTLD 'centrists' and former opponents from the UDMA or AUMA whose parties had been dissolved into the FLN.[40] It further acknowledged that no matter how important the imperative of armed struggle, the FLN would never win its war on the military battlefield. All action, including military, had to aim to achieve 'the political isolation of France – in Algeria and in the world'.[41]

The Soummam platform thus never suggested a curtailment of external activities. Just as it called for an intensification of the insurgency within Algeria, notably through the extension of terrorist operations into urban centres, so, too, it appealed for a systematic and comprehensive expansion of the FLN's international efforts to secure moral, diplomatic and material support. To this end, the congress foresaw the creation of permanent missions at the UN and in Asian capitals such as Karachi and Djakarta, as well as mobile delegations to tour the capitals of Latin America, Africa

[37] Procès-verbal du congrès de la Soummam, 20 August 1956; lettre de Ben Bella à la direction exécutive, autumn 1956, in *Archives* (ed.) Harbi, pp. 160–8.

[38] Chikh, *Algérie en Armes*, pp. 356, 386; Horne, *Savage War*, pp. 143–6; Talbot, *War without a Name*, pp. 78; Philippe Tripier, *Autopsie de la guerre d'Algérie* (Paris, 1972), pp. 116–19.

[39] Aït Ahmed was the only 'external' to support its conclusions, though his detractors claimed he did so merely out of loyalty to fellow Kabyles like Abane and Krim Belkacem. See: Harbi, *FLN*, pp. 189–90; Meynier, *Histoire*, p. 195.

[40] Manifeste de l'Association des Oulémas, 7 January 1956; communiqué sur l'intégration des 'combattants de la libération' à l'ALN, 1 July 1956, in *Archives* (ed.) Harbi, pp. 109–12; Ibid., *FLN*, pp. 131–62; Meynier, *Histoire*, pp. 176–91.

[41] Procès-verbal du congrès, p. 166.

and Europe. FLN diplomats were to liaise not just with sympathetic governments but also with student movements, trade unions, commercial circles and humanitarian organisations across the globe. These diplomatic efforts required internal direction and control, for they had to reflect developments within Algeria.[42] Abane and his colleagues thus considered foreign policy too important to be delegated to the 'externals', whose long absence had left them out of touch with realities on the ground.

More importantly, internal direction sought to guard against outside interference. Although the Soummam platform recognised the vital importance of foreign allies and hosts, it criticised most Arab states whose 'support of the Algerian people's struggle remained limited' and 'subjected to the fluctuations of their general diplomacy', especially the 'special form of pressure' exerted on them through French economic and military aid. The ALN's commanders were frustrated with the pace and scale of the material aid they received. Nor did they entirely trust their allies. Anxious to avert French reprisals and counteract the influence of radicals such as Egypt's president, Colonel Gamal Abdel Nasser, Morocco and Tunisia still favoured a negotiated settlement in Algeria. By early 1956, even Egypt had curbed its support in an effort to secure French backing against the British-led Baghdad Pact. Nasser had persuaded the FLN's external delegates to pursue top-secret discussions with French emissaries on the terms of a provisional ceasefire and future reforms. To the FLN's internal commanders (as indeed to radicals within the French military and administration), the talks that took place in Cairo, Belgrade and Rome between April and September 1956 amounted to a 'shameful compromise', one that betrayed the revolution's very essence. In calling the 'externals' into line, the Soummam platform reaffirmed the FLN's principle of independence. Its message was clear: the FLN was 'directed neither from Cairo, nor from London, nor from Moscow, nor from Washington'; it would serve Algerian interests alone. While the FLN's internal leaders themselves would soon be forced into exile abroad, they never deviated from this line.[43]

[42] Tripier, *Autopsie*, pp. 586, 589–93, 597–600.

[43] Ibid., pp. 582, 599–600. The earlier paragraphs draw on: Connelly, *Diplomatic Revolution*, pp. 102–13; Mohamed Fathi al-Dib, *Abdel Nasser et la Révolution algérienne* (Paris, 1985), pp. 123–37; Harbi, *Le FLN*, pp. 173–97; Rédha Malek, *L'Algérie à Évian: histoire des négociations secrètes, 1956–1962* (Paris, 1995), pp. 22–8; Meynier, *Histoire*, pp. 169–76, 191–5; William B. Quandt, *Revolution and Political Leadership: Algeria, 1954–1968* (Cambridge MA; London, 1969), pp. 99–109; Chikh, *Algérie en armes*, pp. 97–102; Thomas, *French*, pp. 106–16.

French external interventions

Published in the FLN's official newspaper *El Moudjahid* on the revolution's second anniversary, the Soummam platform produced something of a paradox, for at the very moment that the FLN asserted its freedom from foreign control, the French military launched a series of external interventions aimed at stamping out the insurgency. On 22 October 1956, French intelligence orchestrated the capture of Ben Bella, Khider, Boudiaf, Aït Ahmed and information officer Mustafa Lacheraf by hijacking a DC-3 chartered by Morocco's Sultan Mohammed V to transport the five men from Casablanca to Tunis.[44] Hailed as a dazzling success, the intervention in fact did more harm than good. It neither deprived the revolution of its perceived leaders nor did it sever the FLN from its allies. Infuriated by France's disrespect of their sovereignty, the intervention merely strengthened the resolve of the governments in Rabat and Tunis to support the FLN. Enjoying only retrospective backing from Prime Minister Guy Mollet, the rogue stunt extinguished the possibility of a negotiated settlement between France and the FLN. From then on 'the guns would do the talking', as hard-liners outflanked moderates on either side of the Franco-Algerian divide.[45]

One week later, the Anglo-French-Israeli intervention at Suez proved even more counterproductive. French intelligence and policy-makers had long perceived Nasser as the foremost mastermind behind the FLN and Ben Bella as his chief puppet. An ardent supporter of pan-Arabism, Nasser made no secret of his support for Algerian nationalists.[46] By 1954, his cross-regional radio station *Voice of the Arabs*, established in 1953 to combat imperialism and promote pan-Arab unity, emitted a daily broadcast titled 'Combat in the Maghreb'. It was here that the FLN's creation was first announced.[47] Jean Vaujour, director of the Algerian *Sécurité Générale* in 1954, suspected the Egyptian army had trained many of the commandos

[44] 'North Africa: Aerial Kidnap', *Time Magazine*, 5 November 1956.

[45] Meynier, *Histoire*, p. 566. On the operation, see: Connelly, *Diplomatic Revolution*, pp. 114–15; Thomas, *French*, pp. 113–14; Irwin M. Wall, *France, the United States and the Algerian War* (Berkeley CA, 2001), pp. 50–5.

[46] Adeed Dawisha, *Arab Nationalism in the Twentieth Century* (Princeton NJ, 2003), pp. 135–59; Mohamed Heikal, *Nasser. The Cairo Documents* (London, 1972), pp. 33, 56. Nasser describes his ideas on pan-Arab unity in: *The Philosophy of the Revolution*, book I (Cairo, 1955).

[47] Charles-Robert Ageron, 'Un aspect de la guerre d'Algérie: la propagande radiophonique du FLN et des États arabes', in *La guerre d'Algérie et les Algériens 1954–1962* (ed.) Charles-Robert Ageron (Paris, 1997), pp. 245–6; Jean Vaujour, *De la révolte à la révolution. Aux premiers jours de la guerre d'Algérie* (Paris, 1985), pp. 263–4, 275.

that initiated the FLN's insurgency.[48] The security service's suspicions were not entirely unfounded. During his exile in Cairo, Ben Bella had indeed won the grace of the Egyptian *mukhabarât* (secret service), which pledged to provide money, arms and facilities to the revolution.[49] The capture on 16 October 1956 of the *Athos*, a decommissioned British minesweeper carrying Egypt's largest known arms shipment to the FLN, helped confirm these misgivings. The nationalisation of the Suez Canal Company in July thus provided an expedient pretext for the French to extirpate Egyptian meddling and eliminate Nasser altogether.[50] Like the hijacking that preceded it, this 'twenty-fifth hour intervention' to remedy the Algerian problem also backfired. It elicited near-universal condemnation of France's colonial policies and established Nasser as the undisputed leader of Arab nationalism and a key figure in the emerging non-aligned movement.[51]

French external interventions thus strengthened the bonds they intended to sever. If the debacles reveal anything, it is the extent to which the French authorities had come to obsess about the Algerian war's international dimension. From the outset, politicians, administrators, military officers and journalists blamed the insurgency on forces beyond Algeria's borders. Marshal Alphonse Juin's conviction that French Algeria was being 'assassinated' by a 'veritable international conspiracy' became a commonplace idea.[52] On 5 November 1954, Governor-General Roger Léonard announced, 'the rioters had obeyed foreign orders to the letter'.[53] The conservative daily *L'Aurore* contended that the instigators were 'armed and controlled from abroad' whereas the Catholic

[48] Vaujour, *Révolte*, pp. 99–109, 152–6, 167–8.

[49] Al-Dib's account of *mukhabarât*'s collusion with the FLN probably exaggerates the amount of aid provided.

[50] On Suez and Algeria, see: Connelly, *Diplomatic Revolution*, pp. 108–23; Horne, *Savage War*, pp. 157–64; Keith Kyle, *Suez. Britain's End of Empire in the Middle East* (London, 1991), pp. 111–12, 118, 143–6; Thomas, *French*, ch. 4; Maurice Vaïsse (ed.), *La France et l'opération de Suez de 1956* (Paris, 1997); Maurice Vaïsse, 'France and the Suez Crisis', in *Suez 1956: The Crisis and Its Consequences* (eds.) Wm. Roger Louis and Roger Owen (Oxford, 1989), pp. 131–43; Wall, *France*, ch. 2.

[51] André Beaufre, *L'Expédition de Suez* (Paris, 1967), p. 230, see also: pp. 217–18, 229–31; Heikal, *Nasser*, pp. 36–7; Maurice Vaïsse, 'Post-Suez France', in *Suez* (eds.) Louis and Owen, p. 335; Rashid Khalidi, 'Consequences of the Suez Crisis in the Arab world', in ibid., pp. 377, 380.

[52] Charles-Robert Ageron, 'Les forces internationales et la décolonisation de l'Afrique du Nord', in *Les Internationales et le problème de la guerre au XXe siècle. Actes du colloque de Rome (22–24 Novembre 1984)* (Rome: Ecole Française de Rome, 1987), p. 195; Guy Pervillé, 'Guerre étrangère et guerre civile en Algérie, 1954–1962', *Relations internationales* 14 (1978), p. 175.

[53] Cited in: Charles-Robert Ageron, 'L'Opération de Suez et la guerre d'Algérie', in *France et Suez* (ed.) Vaïsse, p. 43; Thomas, *French*, p. 210.

broadsheet *La Croix* referred to 'a plot directed from abroad'.[54] Though they were more nuanced, similar voices could also be heard from left-wing exponents of colonial devolution and reform. On 12 November 1954, Prime Minister Mendès-France declared before the National Assembly that the rebels 'had received encouragements from abroad, as well as provocations of the most extreme order'.[55] Even Claude Bourdet, a journalist well known for his anti-colonialism, commented in *France-Observateur* that one 'could not exclude the possibility that *agents provocateurs* were able to play on the exasperation of extremists in order to put a stop to any positive evolution [in Algeria] by sparking further repression'.[56]

Faced with the ignominy of Dien Bien Phu, the escalation of nationalist unrest in Morocco and Tunisia and the inflammatory rhetoric emitting from *Voice of the Arabs*, one can understand why so many French observers believed the international context had contributed to the onset of the Algerian war. After all, the FLN did draw its inspiration from global developments and did enjoy international support. Even so, no matter how jealously it guarded its independence from external control, French observers found it difficult to accept the FLN as a home-grown movement, let alone one that would come to enjoy widespread popular support. Policy-makers and military officers thus misconstrued the nature of the FLN's relationship with the foreign forces that stood accused of meddling in Algeria.

Colonial myths and conspiracy theories

What prompted this stubborn refusal to consider as real the domestic roots of the FLN's insurrection? Historians have pointed to the enduring influence of two powerful and interlocking myths: those of empire as the font of French power and prestige and of France's civilising mission.[57] Rooted in the nineteenth century, these myths experienced a revival during World War II, when both Vichy and Free France vied for the colonies' support.[58]

[54] Cited in: Harbi, *1954*, p. 26; Ageron, 'Forces internationales', p. 195.

[55] Cited in: Maria Romo, 'Le gouvernement Mendès France et le maintien de l'ordre en Algérie en novembre 1954', in *Militaires et guérilla dans la guerre d'Algérie* (eds.) Jean-Charles Jauffret and Maurice Vaïsse (Paris, 2001), p. 431.

[56] Cited in: Harbi, *1954*, p. 27 (italics added).

[57] Charles-Robert Ageron, 'La survivance d'un mythe: La puissance par l'Empire colonial (1944–1947)', in *La puissance française en question 1945–1949* (eds.) René Girault and Robert Frank (Paris, 1988), pp. 31–51; Raoul Girardet, *L'idée colonial en France de 1871 à 1962* (Paris, 1972), pp. 278–88.

[58] Martin Thomas, *The French Empire at War, 1940–1945* (Manchester, 1998); Eric Jennings, *Vichy in the Tropics. Pétain's National Revolution in Madagascar, Guadeloupe and Indochina, 1940–1944* (Stanford CA, 2001); Ruth Ginio, *French Colonialism Unmasked. The Vichy Years in French West Africa* (Lincoln NB, 2008).

The resultant profusion of eulogies exalting the empire at war's end, whether in parliament, press, cinema or even schoolbooks, ensured that the idea of *la Plus Grande France* remained ingrained in the French official and popular mind.[59] Although there was widespread agreement that the empire required fundamental political and socio-economic changes in order to become more humane, democratic and progressive, it was inconceivable that these should occur 'outside of the French bloc', as de Gaulle stated at the opening of the 1944 Brazzaville conference on colonial reform. Put simply, France's cultural identity, its global standing and, indeed, its very existence had become entwined with the continuation of colonialism. 'True France' was an imperial union, 'one and indivisible' consisting of 'one hundred million Frenchmen'.[60]

By the mid-1950s, this colonial consensus continued to attract support, particularly among an important circle of military officers who came to blame the loss of Indochina on what they perceived as the defeatism, lack of direction and general immobilism of Parisian governments.[61] To these officers, the FLN's declaration of war represented an assault on the very heart of France's imperial edifice. This view was not limited to the military: to the socialist deputy and former governor-general of Algeria, Marcel-Edmond Naegelen, the loss of Algeria would 'reduce France to the ranks of a secondary power and vassal'; to his Gaullist colleague Jacques Soustelle, it signified nothing short of 'a national disaster comparable to Sedan and June 1940'.[62] Metropolitan opinion might have been indifferent and hostile to the war in Indochina, yet in 1954, the consensus was that Algeria had to remain French.[63]

[59] The 'official mind' being understood as the self-image and aspirations of French policy-makers, administrators and military officers.

[60] Herman Lebovics, *True France: The Wars over Cultural Identity, 1900–1945* (Ithaca NY, 1991); Girardet, *Idée coloniale*, p. 286; Ageron, 'Survivance', pp. 39–41; Raymond F. Betts, *France and Decolonization 1900–1960* (Basingstoke, 1991), pp. 17, 58–61.

[61] Martin Alexander and Philip Bankwitz, 'From Politiques en Képi to Military Technocrats: de Gaulle and the Recovery of the French Army after Indochina and Algeria', in *The Aftermath of Defeat: Societies, Armed Forces, and the Challenge of Recovery* (eds.) George Andreopoulos and Harold Selesky (New Haven CT, 1994), pp. 81–6; John S. Ambler, *The French Army in Politics 1945–1962* (Columbo OH, 1966), pp. 93–117, 207–12; Raoul Girardet (ed.), *La crise militaire française, 1942–1962: Aspects sociologiques et idéologiques* (Paris, 1964), pp. 162–5; Alistair Horne, *The French Army and Politics, 1870–1970* (London, 1984), pp. 74–77; George A. Kelly, *Lost Soldiers. The French Army and Empire in Crisis, 1947–1962* (Cambridge MA, 1965), pp. 54–75.

[62] Citations from: Charles-Robert Ageron, 'L'Algérie dernière chance de la puissance française. Étude d'un mythe politique (1954–1962)', *Relations internationales* 57 (1989), pp. 113, 120–21.

[63] Charles-Robert Ageron 'L'opinion française à travers les sondages', in *Guerre d'Algérie et Français* (ed.) Rioux, pp. 25–44; John Talbott, 'French Public Opinion and the Algerian War: a Research Note', *French Historical Studies* 9/2 (1975), pp. 354–61; Christopher Harrison, 'French Attitudes to Empire and the Algerian War', *African Affairs* 326 (1983), pp. 75–95; William B. Cohen,

If the myth of power through empire shored up the idea of Algeria as France's 'last chance' at grandeur, the myth of France's '*mission civilisatrice*' also shaped attitudes and policies towards the FLN. Resting on an ambiguous fusion of Enlightenment ideas of the perfectibility of humankind, Republican notions of social emancipation and progress through the mastery of nature, and an entrenched belief in the superiority of French culture, the 'civilising mission' had lain at the heart of French imperial ideology since the mid-nineteenth century.[64] Deeply ethnocentric on the one hand and remarkably humanist on the other, the conviction that French civilisation was 'the way forward for the whole of mankind' made it difficult even for many a French anti-colonialist to fathom a nationalist uprising against France.[65] Neither were Algerians deemed capable of sustaining a nationwide insurrection nor were they believed to be interested in ending French rule given the benefits of enlightenment and modernity it supposedly brought. As Martin Evans points out, it was simply unimaginable 'that the colonies would aspire to anything else but being French'.[66]

Unable and unwilling to acknowledge the FLN as a home-grown movement, French observers and policy-makers both left and right of the political spectrum relied on conspiracy theories to explain opposition to their rule. The FLN's expansion as an organisation, the ever-increasing allegiance and support it secured from other political parties and the population at large, were rationalised as the results of terror, coercion and fanaticism. Genuine nationalist resistance seemed unthinkable, for Algeria, as was so often claimed, had never been a nation.[67] Since, as Christopher Andrew reminds us, the very idea of 'principled opposition to the universal values of French civilization was, by definition, impossible', the FLN had to be a foreign puppet whose strings were pulled by external forces out to weaken and tarnish France.[68] One decade after

'The Algerian War and the Revision of France's Overseas Mission', *French Colonial History* 4 (2003), pp. 227–39.

64 Nicolas Bancel, Pascal Blanchard and Françoise Vergès, *La République coloniale: essai sur une utopie* (Paris, 2003) and Alice L. Conklin, *A Mission to Civilize: The Republican Idea of Empire in France and West Africa, 1895–1930* (Stanford CA, 1997) bring out the civilising mission's inherent paradoxes particularly well.

65 Ageron, *Modern Algeria*, p. 27; Conklin, *Mission*, p. 17.

66 Guy Mollet's 'Third Way: National Renewal and the French Civilizing Mission in Algeria', in *French History and Civilisation. Papers from the George Rudé Seminar*, vol.2 (eds.) Vesna Drapac and André Lambelet (2009), p. 176.

67 On the origins of this myth, see: Abdelmajid Hannoum, 'The Historiographic State: How Algeria once Became French', *History and Anthropology* 19/2 (2008), pp. 91–114.

68 'France: Adjustment to Change', in *The Expansion of International Society* (eds.) Hedley Bull and Adam Watson (Oxford, 1984), p. 339.

Algeria gained its independence, the historian and former St Cyrian Philippe Tripier still wrote of an 'infiltrated Algeria' and 'general invasion of Algerian territory by the FLN', as if the movement had originated abroad.[69] Such notions remained influential because, as Connelly argues, they 'played on and perpetuated the anger and anxiety French people of all political persuasions felt about their diminished role in international affairs'. Feeding on a sense of weakness and insecurity, conspiracy theories helped explain a series of French defeats, from Sedan to Dien Bien Phu, while leaving France 'at the very center of international politics'. They also deflected responsibility for consecutive setbacks away from France, for it was easier to blame others than to acknowledge one's own fault for national misfortunes.[70] Contrary to expert anthropologists like Germaine Tillion and Pierre Bourdieu, who located the underlying causes of the war in the exploitative and racist nature of settler colonialism and its destruction of traditional social structures and values, much of the public and official French discourse would continue to portray the FLN's insurrection as an alien imposition.[71]

Foreign forces

This is not to say that French officialdom discounted the authenticity of popular discontent with the colonial situation in Algeria. The prevailing view nonetheless depicted the FLN as a fanatical minority of 'terrorists' guided from abroad that had come to exploit Algerians' legitimate grievances for foreign ends. While Egypt and other Arab states bore the brunt of these accusations, they were not the only countries accused of meddling in Algeria. The Soviet Union, too, became an immediate culprit. To give but one example: as early as 10 November 1954, Maurice Viollette, a socialist deputy and former governor of Algeria, declared before the National Assembly that although 'the signal for terrorism came from Cairo', behind the Egyptians stood 'Khrushchev and the Soviets'.[72] Europe's colonies were, of course, not spared from the Cold War. In Indochina and Malaya, communist movements had spearheaded the anti-colonial struggle, drawing inspiration, and increasingly also support from the Eastern bloc, notably Mao's China. By contrast, Moscow's

[69] *Autopsie*, pp. 70, 78. [70] Connelly, *Diplomatic Revolution*, p. 71.
[71] Tillion, *L'Algérie en 1957* (Paris, 1957); Bourdieu, *The Algerians* (trans.) Alan C.M. Ross (Boston, 1962). See also: Georges Balandier, 'La situation coloniale: approche théorique', *Cahiers internationaux de sociologie* 11 (1951), pp. 44–79.
[72] Cited in: Ageron, 'L'Opération de Suez', p. 58.

attitude remained remarkably reserved. It was not until Secretary-General Nikita Khrushchev conceded the possibility of multiple, evolutionary paths towards socialism at the Soviet Communist Party's twentieth congress in February 1956 that the Kremlin began to support non-Marxist liberation movements such as the FLN. Khrushchev's policy shift aimed at containing the rising influence not only of neutralism in the Third World but precisely also that of Communist China.[73]

As Viollette's accusation suggests, many in France perceived a much more sinister plot. Fresh out of Indochina, military officers such as Charles Lacheroy, Jacques Hogard or Lionel-Max Chassin believed that Soviet-sponsored colonial insurgencies represented Moscow's latest strategy of world domination.[74] In an age of mutually assured nuclear destruction, they argued, modern warfare would no longer be fought by conventional forces or opposing nations. Insidious and subversive in nature, it involved fifth columns, proxies and civil wars. In short, modern warfare was revolutionary warfare (*guerre révolutionnaire*) in the Marxist-Maoist sense.[75] Speaking before NATO officials in November 1957, General Jacques Allard, commander of the Algiers Army Corps, encapsulated the logic behind this new form of combat. The Soviet Union, Allard claimed,

> has concealed from many the fact that the direction of her main effort was not the East-West axis, but a vast enveloping curve passing through China, the Far East, Southeast Asia, the Middle East, Egypt, and North Africa in order to encircle Europe. [...] To wrest [Algeria] from France under the pretext of the people's right for self-determination [...] means preparing the ground – here as everywhere else – for Communist takeover and satellization. France had earlier attempted to stem Communist expansion in Indochina [...] our ultimate line of defence is Algeria.[76]

The idea that France had a 'vocation' to act as 'the guardian of the positions of the free world' or that 'the fate of France and of Europe [...]

[73] Bradley, 'Decolonization', p. 474–5, 481–2; Jerry F. Hough, *The Struggle for the Third World: Soviet Debates and American Options* (Washington, 1986), pp. 143–51, 201; Westad, *Global Cold War*, pp. 66–72.

[74] Ambler, *French Army*, ch. 11; Christopher Cradock and M.L.R. Smith, '"No Fixed Values". A Reinterpretation of the Influence of the Theory of *Guerre Révolutionnaire* and the Battle of Algiers, 1956–1957', *Journal of Cold War History* 9/4 (2007), pp. 72–6; Paul Villatoux, 'L'Institutionnalisation de l'arme psychologique pendant la guerre d'Algérie au miroir de la guerre froide', *Guerres mondiales et conflits contemporains* 4, no. 208 (2002), pp. 38–41.

[75] Galula, *Counterinsurgency*; Constantin Melnik, *The French Campaign against the FLN* (Santa Monica CA, 1967); Roger Trinquier, *Modern Warfare: A French View of Counterinsurgency* (trans.) Daniel Lee (New York, 1964).

[76] Cited in: Peter Paret, *French Revolutionary Warfare from Indochina to Algeria: The Analysis of a Political and Military Doctrine* (New York, London, 1964), p. 25.

hangs in the balance of North Africa' became a common mantra in official circles.[77] Only France's continued presence in Algeria, it was argued, would safeguard Europe's southern flank from Soviet encroachment.[78]

Such hyperbolic statements about the global Cold War were designed to garner support for *l'Algérie française*, whether at home or abroad, and were never universally believed.[79] They also contained a baffling paradox, for at the same time as the French authorities sought the backing of their foreign allies for their 'anti-communist' policies in Algeria, they accused these same allies – notably Britain and the United States, of playing a double game in the Maghreb. French misgivings were nurtured by several factors: the long history of Anglo-French colonial rivalry; the anti-colonial rhetoric of US administrations; and the memories of the Allied landing in North Africa in November 1942, which had so roused the hopes of Maghrebi nationalists for self-determination. In addition to the Arab world and Communist bloc, some voices thus also blamed '*les Anglo-Saxons*' for the Algerian quagmire. Britain, it seemed, was once again trying to undermine French imperial positions in 'a selfish and subtle game inspired by past rivalries' as one defence memorandum put it. The United States, meanwhile, stood accused of 'political inexperience', an 'anti-colonial, anti-slavery complex', as well as a desire to supplant French influence in the Maghreb.[80]

French paranoia did not stop there, however, for the Bonn Republic, too, was accused of complicity with the FLN. Ten years after the end of World War II, a 'burden of mistrust' continued to mar bilateral relations as many in France still perceived Germany as their 'hereditary enemy'.[81] In July 1954, while the National Assembly deliberated (and rejected) the plan to rearm West Germany within the framework of the European Defence Community, a French opinion poll revealed that only 29 per cent believed in the possibility of a Franco-German rapprochement.

77 Vaujour, *Révolte*, pp. 280–1; Dépêche no. 473 du Général Calliès au Premier Ministre, 4 April 1955, SHD-T, 1H/1103/D1.

78 Paret, *French Revolutionary Warfare*, pp. 26–7.

79 Martin Alexander, 'Seeking France's "Lost Soldiers": Reflections on the French military crisis in Algeria', in *Crisis and Renewal in France, 1918–1962* (eds.) Martin S. Alexander and Kenneth Mouré (New York; Oxford, 2002), pp. 242–66.

80 Plan de protection de l'Afrique du Nord contre la guerre froide par l'Inspection générale des Forces terrestres, maritimes et aériennes de l'Afrique française du Nord (INS/AFN), 4 June 1955; Dépêche no. 473, 4 April 1955, SHD-T, 1H/1103/D1.

81 Lappenküper, *Deutsch-französischen Beziehungen* 1, p. 837. On the myth of hereditary enmity: Henri Burgelin, 'Le mythe de l'ennemi héréditaire dans les relations franco-allemandes', *Documents: Revue des Questions Allemandes* (1979), pp. 76–88; Michael E. Nolan, *The Inverted Mirror. Mythologizing the Enemy in France and Germany, 1898–1914* (Oxford; New York, 2005).

A poll taken later that year fared little better: although the Mendès-France government had by then agreed to the FRG's accession to NATO and the Brussels Pact, only 9 per cent of French respondents thought positively of Germany.[82] This mentality of distrust pervaded not only public opinion but also political and diplomatic circles. Commenting on the abrogation of the Occupation Statute in May 1955, France's high commissioner in Bonn, André François-Poncet, warned of an impending 'German danger'. To this senior diplomat, the Germans remained 'the *Boches*' whose innate expansionism and nationalism had to remain checked. Past experiences and preconceptions thus continued to inform French views of their eastern neighbour.[83]

Historical analogies were equally instrumental in shaping French perceptions of German–Arab relations. Ever since the much-publicised 1898 visit of Kaiser Wilhelm II to Saladin's tomb in Damascus, German-Arab relations had a reputation of being particularly close. Legend had it in the Arab world that during his 'pilgrimage' to the Holy Land, the Kaiser had converted to Islam, earning him the title of *Hajj*.[84] In the late nineteenth and early twentieth century, this mythologised German–Arab friendship was sustained by a number of political, material and cultural factors. The works of German Orientalists, for instance, though not as bound up with the exigencies of colonial control as those of their British and French counterparts, served both academic and politico-economic ends, especially in the crumbling Ottoman Empire.[85] Influential Arab intellectuals and reformers such as Sati' al-Husri meanwhile drew on the cultural nationalism expounded by German philosophers of the Romantic era to elaborate

[82] Ziebura, *Deutsch-französischen Beziehungen*, pp. 74, 82.

[83] Cited in: Hans M. Bock, 'Zur Perzeption der frühen Bundesrepublik Deutschland in der französischen Diplomatie: Die Bonner Monatsberichte des Hochkommissars André François-Poncet 1949–1955', *Francia* 15 (1987), pp. 602, 633, 636 (italics added). Also: Hélène Miard-Delacroix, *Question nationale allemande et nationalisme. Perceptions françaises d'une problématique allemande au début des années cinquante* (Lille, 2004).

[84] Gilbert Meynier, *L'Algérie Révélée* (Paris, 1981), p. 250. See also: Jan Stefan Richter, *Die Orientreise Kaiser Wilhelm II, 1898. Eine Studie zur deutschen Aussenpolitik an der Wende zum 20. Jahrhundert* (Hamburg, 1997).

[85] Gottfried Hagen, 'German Heralds of Holy War: Orientalists and Applied Oriental Studies', *Comparative Studies of South Asia, Africa and the Middle East* 24/2 (2004), pp. 145–62; Thomas Scheffler, 'Orientalisten und Orientkenner als Väter der deutschen Politikwissenschaft?' in *Annäherung an das Fremde. XXVI. deutscher Orientalistentag* (eds.) Holger Preissler and Heidi Stein (Stuttgart, 1998), pp. 63–70; Malte Fuhrmann, *Der Traum vom deutschen Orient: zwei deutsche Kolonien im Osmanischen Reich 1851–1918* (Frankfurt/Main, 2006); Suzanne L. Marchand, *German Orientalism in the Age of Empire: Religion, Race and Scholarship* (Cambridge, 2009); Ursula Wokoeck, *German Orienatalism: The Study of the Middle East and Islam from 1800 to 1945* (Abingdon, 2009).

their notions of pan-Arabism. Others found inspiration in Germany's successful unification in 1871.[86] After the Nazi era, other professed affinities emerged. Some Arabs came to view Germany as a natural ally against the new state of Israel. Others perceived a similarity in the fact that German sovereignty remained constrained by foreign occupation, as was the case for many Arab states during the 1940s and 1950s. Germany, moreover, had never occupied the Arab lands (if one discounts the *Afrikakorps*' sojourn in Libya and Tunisia between February 1941 and May 1943). On the contrary, the country was deemed the traditional enemy of Britain and France – the two colonial powers that dominated the region.[87]

Between 1905 and 1911, European imperial rivalries had indeed extended into the Maghreb.[88] As Gilbert Meynier has shown, the two Moroccan crises helped spread the myth of '*Hajj Guillaume*' in Algeria, spurring rumours of German subversion on the one hand and hopes of liberation from colonial oppression on the other.[89] During World War I, German and Turkish propagandists used the rhetoric of *jihâd* to sow dissension among Britain and France's Muslim territories and troops.[90] This task fell to the Orient Intelligence Office, whose most prolific Muslim collaborators were the Tunisian cleric Salih as-Sarif at-Tunisi, a close associate of the Turkish War Minister Enver Pasha, and the Algerian deserter Rabah Boukabouya.[91] Muslim prisoners-of-war held in separate camps at Wünsdorf and Zossen were urged to rally to the Central Powers.[92] Subjected to poor treatment, only 1,020 Algerians out of approximately

86 Youssef M. Choueiri, *Arab Nationalism: A History* (Oxford, 2000), pp. 6–7, 116–17, 144; Dawisha, *Arab Nationalism*, pp. 52–71, 75–6, 298–9; Bassam Tibi, *Arab Nationalism: Between Islam and the Nation-State*, 3rd edn (Basingstoke, 1997), pp. 127–38.

87 For an excellent survey of German Middle Eastern policy through the First World War, see: Sean McMeekin, *The Berlin-Baghdad Express: The Ottoman Empire and Germany's Bid for World Power* (Cambridge MA, 2010). Also: Peter Hünseler, *Die außenpolitischen Beziehungen der Bundesrepublik Deutschland zu den arabischen Staaten von 1949–1980* (Frankfurt/Main, 1990), pp. 23–26; Wolfgang G. Schwanitz, 'Deutsche in Nahost 1946–1965: Sozialgeschichte nach Akten und Interviews', Habilitationsschrift, Bd.1 (Freien Universität Berlin/Princeton University, 1995), pp. 230–34.

88 Good overviews of the crises, albeit of an older vintage, are: Eugene N. Anderson, *The First Moroccan Crisis 1904–1906*, 2nd edn (Hamden CT, 1966); Geoffrey Barraclough, *From Agadir to Armageddon: Anatomy of a Crisis* (London, 1982).

89 Meynier, *L'Algérie*, pp. 249–52.

90 Hagen, 'German Heralds'; Wolfgang Schwanitz, 'Djihad "Made in Germany": Der Streit um den Heiligen Krieg, 1914–1915', *Soziale Geschichte* 18/2 (2003), pp. 7–34.

91 Peter Heine, 'Salih as-Sarif at-Tunisi, a North African Nationalist in Berlin during the First World War', *Revue de l'Occident Musulman et de la Méditerranée* 33 (1982), pp. 89–95; Meynier, *L'Algérie*, p. 510.

92 Gerhard Höpp, *Muslime an der Mark: als Kriegsgefangene und Internierte in Wünsdorf und Zossen 1914–1924* (Berlin, 1997); Margot Kahleyss, *Muslime in Brandenburg: Kriegsgefangene im 1. Weltkrieg: Ansichten und Absichten* (Berlin, 2000).

4,000 Maghrebi POWs agreed to join the Turkish ranks. The Orient Intelligence Office fared little better at inciting mass desertions: of the 173,000 Algerian soldiers who served under the French flag between 1915 and 1917, about 130 deserted.[93] Likewise, though attempts to incite sedition certainly captured people's imagination through best-selling thrillers such as John Buchan's *Greenmantle* (1916), they, too, yielded meagre results.[94] In Algeria, Muslim discontent found its expression in a popular, pro-German song – the *Ode to Hajj Guillaume*. Even so, unrest remained sporadic and localised.[95]

However meagre its outcome, German propaganda resumed during World War II. Prominent nationalists such as the Iraqi premier Rashid Ali al-Gaylani and the grand mufti of Jerusalem Amin al-Husayni collaborated closely with Nazi officials during their exile in Berlin. The *Wehrmacht* established an *Orientkorps* comprising Muslim volunteers, which included a North African company. Similarly, the Vichyite *Légion tricolore* created in July 1942 recruited heavily in Algeria, while the *Phalange africaine* did the same in Tunisia. Though under Pétainist control, both units were established to support Field-Marshal Erwin Rommel's *Afrikakorps*. Of these units, only the *Orientkorps* briefly saw active service.[96] Indeed, to avoid conflict with Vichy France and Italy, or even neutral Spain, all of which maintained strong interests in the region, Nazi authorities largely treated North Africa as a French and Italian *domaine réservé*. Although they recruited informants and spies, developed an active propaganda campaign and financially supported a number of nationalist committees, including the fanatical *Comité d'action révolutionnaire nord-africaine*, the Third Reich never went so far as to support independence or armed rebellion in the

93 Gerhard Höpp, 'Frontenwechsel: Muslimische Deserteure im Ersten und Zweiten Weltkrieg und in der Zwischenkriegszeit', in *Fremdeneinsätze. Afrikaner und Asiaten in europäischen Kriegen 1914–1945* (eds.) Gerhard Höpp and Brigitte Reinwald (Berlin, 2000), p. 131; Kahleyss, 'Muslimische Kriegsgefangene in Deutschland im Ersten Weltkrieg – Ansichten und Absichten', in ibid., p. 80; Meynier, *L'Algérie*, pp. 434, 452–4.

94 Herbert L. Müller, *Islam, Gihad ('Heiliger Krieg') und Deutsches Reich: Ein Nachspiel zur Wilhelminischen Weltpolitik im Maghreb, 1914–1918* (Frankfurt/Main, 1991); Höpp, *Muslime*; Peter Hopkirk, *On Secret Service East of Constantinople: The Plot to Bring down the British Empire* (London, 1994); Martin Kröger, 'Revolution als Programm. Ziele und Realität deutscher Orientpolitik im Ersten Weltkrieg', in *Der Erste Weltkrieg: Wirkung, Wahrnehmung, Analyse* (ed.) Wolfgang Michalka (Munich, 1994), pp. 366–91.

95 Nadya Bouzar-Kasbadji, 'La Marseillaise et ses dissonances en Algérie coloniale', *Revue du monde musulman et de la Méditerranée* 52/1 (1989), pp. 243, 249; Abdelkader Djeghloul, 'Hors-la-loi, violence rurale et pouvoir colonial en Algérie au début du XXe siècle: les frères Boutouizerat', *Revue de l'Occident musulman et de la Méditerranée* 38/1 (1984), p. 41.

96 Chantal Metzger, *L'Empire colonial français dans la stratégie du troisième Reich (1936–1945)* (Paris, 2002), pp. 467–70, 554–6; Thomas, *French Empire*, pp. 237–8.

Maghreb. To gain the indigenous populations' sympathy and collaboration, Nazi propaganda instead exploited the familiar tropes of anti-Semitism, German–Arab friendship and Germany's impending victory.[97]

This relative reserve did not prevent many French, both Pétainist and Gaullist, from suspecting North African, and especially Algerian nationalists of collusion with Nazi Germany. In 1941, Mohamed Bouras, leader of the *Scouts musulmans algériens*, paid with his life for his apparent willingness to work with the German armistice commission.[98] As Simon Kitson has shown, Vichy counter-intelligence services remained determined to pursue Nazi subversion and espionage on their territory.[99] In fact, instances of resistance far outweighed those of collaboration. Prominent nationalists such as Ferhat Abbas or Messali Hadj placed their hopes for liberation not on Nazi Germany but on the Allies. Other future leaders of the FLN, including Ben Bella, Krim Belkacem, Boudiaf and Mostefa Ben Boulaïd, participated in the liberation of Italy and France.[100] Even so, suspicions of collusion persisted. As late as May 1945, the communist newspaper *L'Humanité* blamed the Sétif uprising on Nazi *agents provocateurs*, revealing just how ingrained the French colonial mindset was.[101]

Some French circles believed that Arab ties to Nazi officials survived the Third Reich's collapse. While Germany remained occupied and demilitarised, a significant number of former Nazis did indeed find refuge in Egypt and other Middle Eastern countries, where they often served as military instructors or political and economic advisors.[102] In January 1954, French

[97] François-Georges Dreyfus, 'Les Allemagnes contre l'Algérie française', *Revue d'Allemagne et des Pays de langue allemande (RA)* 31/3–4 (1999), pp. 533–4; Roger Faligot and Rémi Kauffer, *Le Croissant et la Croix gammée. Les secrets de l'alliance entre l'Islam et le Nazisme d'Hitler à nos jours* (Paris, 1990), pp. 59–65, 99–132; Mahfoud Kaddache, 'Itinéraire d'un militant nationaliste: Ouamara Mohammed, dit "Rachid"', in *Militaires et guérilla*, pp. 503–15; Vera Henssler, 'Für die Propaganda nach dem Orient ist bei weitem die wirksamste Waffe der Rundfunk: NS-Auslandspropaganda in den Nahen Osten und Nordafrika', *Zeitschrift für Geschichtswissenschaft* 59/11 (2011), pp. 920–37; Metzger, *L'Empire*, pp. 463–5, 553, 579–83; Raffael Scheck, 'Nazi Propaganda toward French Muslim Prisoners of War', *Holocaust and Genocide Studies* 26/3 (2012), pp. 447–77. See also: Jeffrey Herf, *Nazi Propaganda in the Arab World* (New Haven CT, 2009); Gerhard Höpp et al. (eds.), *Blind für die Geschichte? Arabische Begegnungen mit dem Nationalsozialismus* (Berlin, 2004); David Motadel, *Islam and Nazi Germany's War* (Cambridge MA, 2014); Barry Rubin and Wolfgang G. Schwantiz, *Nazis, Islamists, and the Making of the Modern Middle East* (New Haven CT; London, 2014).

[98] Jacques Cantier, *L'Algérie sous le régime de Vichy* (Paris, 2002), p. 302.

[99] Simon Kitson, *The Hunt for Nazi spies: Fighting Espionage in Vichy France* (Chicago, 2008).

[100] Meynier, *Histoire*, pp. 60–1, 68; Faligot and Kauffer, *Croissant*, pp. 61–2; Kaddache, *Histoire*, pp. 565–649.

[101] Meynier, *Histoire*, pp. 65, 67; Ageron, 'Survivance', p. 43.

[102] According to Rubin and Schwanitz, over 4,000 ex-Nazis fled to the Arab world in the post-war period. See: *Nazis, Islamists*, pp. 209–10.

intelligence reported that Egyptian authorities had supposedly entrusted former *Wehrmacht* officer Franz Mertens with the task of supplying Maghrebi nationalists with armaments.[103] One year later, information surfaced whereby several Germans were helping the FLN prepare terrorist campaigns in the Oranais.[104] By August 1955, the French Foreign Ministry, or *Quai d'Orsay*, declined visas to a group of West Germans wanting to visit Morocco on the grounds that they 'might devote their attention to anti-French activities'.[105] Whether there was any truth in these and other suspicions is difficult to say, yet they highlight the continued misgivings harboured towards Germany as well as the conviction that foreign conspirators were at work in Algeria. It was therefore not surprising for the French military to maintain in June 1955 that when it came to France's problems in the Maghreb, 'Germany intrigue[d] out of nostalgia for its aspirations in the Middle East'.[106]

Internationalising *guerre révolutionnaire*

Convinced of the interconnection between the Algerian war's local, national and international dimensions yet constrained by the norms of sovereignty and territoriality that defined state power and authority, the French, as Connelly argues, had 'to think globally while acting locally' to defeat Algerian nationalism.[107] Yet as the Suez crisis or Ben Bella's hijacking attest, and as subsequent chapters will show, French governments did not confine themselves to local action: their intelligence and security services intervened globally. They did so precisely because of the importance French officials accrued to the FLN's external organisation and foreign backers. The French general staff continued to argue even after the Suez debacle that, because it was 'certain that the rebellion finds its force in the aid it receives abroad [. . .] measures must be taken to try to isolate Algeria from the rebellion's external bases of support'.[108] To secure

[103] Vaujour, *Révolte*, pp. 91–2; Faligot and Kauffer, *Croissant*, p. 185.

[104] Renseignements no. 47, Service régional des affaires militaires musulmanes (division d'Oran), 18 January 1955, SHD-T, 1H/1714/D1. These intelligence reports remain uncorroborated. Rubin and Schwanitz make similar claims, citing as evidence Boualem Sansal's award-winning novel, *Le village de l'Allemand ou le journal des frères Schiller* (Paris, 2008). See: *Nazis, Islamists*, p. 220.

[105] Note du service des visas pour la direction d'Afrique-Levant, 22 August 1955, Paris, Ministère des Affaires Etrangères (MAE), Afrique-Levant (AL)/Maroc (MAR)/26.

[106] Plan de protection, INS/AFN, 4 June 1955, SHD-T, 1H/1103/D1.

[107] *Diplomatic Revolution*, p. 106.

[108] Note d'information no.1053/INS/AFN/EM sur la situation en Afrique du Nord, 16 November 1956, SHD-T, 1H/1101/D3.

victory in the Algerian war, the French had to engage the FLN and its alleged co-conspirators in an international arena.

This strategy was rooted in the belief, shared with their adversaries, that as a revolutionary struggle, the conflict in Algeria entailed far more than military operations. French army officers defined *guerre révolutionnaire* as 'an interlocking system of actions – political, economic, psychological, military – that aims at the overthrow of the established authority in a country and its replacement by another regime'.[109] In this 'new' type of warfare, what mattered was not so much victory on the battlefield but in the battle for hearts and minds. To quote General Allard:

> In revolutionary war, pure military action [. . .] takes a back seat to psychological action, propaganda, the collecting and exploitation of political as well as operational intelligence, police measures, personal contacts with the population, social and economic programs [. . .]

All of these measures had but one goal: to isolate the FLN from the Algerian population, whose unconditional support represented 'the *sine qua non* of victory'.[110] For this purpose, Allard explained to his NATO audience, France had to carry out a 'complex program' classified 'under two categories: Destruction and Construction'.[111] Under 'Construction', Allard included economic and political reforms, social welfare and educational programmes as well as propaganda designed to win over the masses for 'the establishment of a new order' in Algeria.[112] Under 'Destruction', he included all those repressive operations designed 'to uncover, dismantle, and suppress the rebel politico-administrative framework, the nerve centre of the rebellion', as well as its machinery of war.[113] 'Construction' and 'destruction', with their inherent reliance on intelligence and policing, represented the obverse and reverse sides of what Peter Paret has called a 'policy of complete human management and control'. This policy,

109 Trinquier, *Modern warfare*, p. 6. See also: Ambler, *French Army*, chs. 6, 7, 11; Étienne de Durand, 'France', in *Understanding Counterinsurgency Warfare: Origins, Operations, Challenges* (eds.) Thomas Rid and Thomas Keaney (Abingdon and New York, 2010), pp. 11–27; Galula, *Counterinsurgency*; Girardet, *Crise militaire*, pp. 173–85; Kelly, *Lost Soldiers*, pp. 107–40; Pierre C. Pahlavi, *La guerre révolutionnaire de l'armée française en Algérie 1954–1961. Entre esprit de conquête et conquête des esprits* (Paris, 2004); Paret, *French Revolutionary Warfare*; Paul and Marie-Catherine Villatoux, *La République et son armée face au 'péril subversif': guerre et action psychologique 1945–1960* (Paris, 2005).

110 Trinquier, *Modern Warfare*, p. 8. 111 Cited in: Paret, *French Revolutionary Warfare*, p. 30.

112 Stephan Malinowski, 'Modernisierungskriege: Militärische Gewalt und koloniale Modernisierung im Algerienkrieg (1954–1962)', *Archiv für Sozialgeschichte* 48 (2008), pp. 213–48.

113 Cited in: Paret, *French Revolutionary Warfare*, pp. 30–2.

Martin Thomas reminds us, had long constituted one of the fundamental features of the colonial state.[114]

Once the FLN removed its organs of power beyond the confines of French sovereignty, engaging in this type of warfare became increasingly difficult. The exodus of Algerians from French territory – whether to Morocco and Tunisia in the Maghreb or West Germany and other neighbouring states in Europe – undermined the very system of human management and control upon which the French forces of order relied in their struggle against the FLN. As such, it constituted a direct threat to French national security and public order. French officers were acutely aware of this problem. 'As long as this considerable war potential [i.e. the FLN's bases, reserves, command structures, and support networks in non-belligerent foreign states] is not neutralised,' Colonel Roger Trinquier, one of the foremost theoreticians of *guerre révolutionnaire* maintained, 'peace, even if completely restored within our own borders, will be precarious and in continual jeopardy'. For France to win the Algerian war, it was essential not only to sever the FLN from foreign allies and external supply lines but to destroy the movement's extraterritorial sanctuaries.[115]

Achieving these goals proved complicated, for as *New York Times* journalist Michael K. Clark wrote in 1959, 'it is singularly difficult to destroy an enemy enjoying the sanctuary of an inviolable frontier'.[116] Military pursuit of the FLN across state boundaries had to be ruled out on legal and political grounds, though the rules of sovereignty did not prevent the French army from trying. As Trinquier put it, international norms and diplomatic realities were such that 'this kind of intervention would lead to reactions throughout the entire world, and certainly to an unpredictable extension of the conflict'.[117] Suez and the hijacking of the FLN's external leaders had certainly taught the French army that lesson. This put the onus on diplomatic interventions and heightened border controls, tactics that were rendered difficult by the fact that French governments refused to acknowledge they were engaged in a war for fear of legitimating the FLN. In the international arena, too, therefore, Trinquier advocated the use of unconventional means: 'Attacked on our territory with the methods of *modern warfare*, we must carry the war to the enemy with the same methods'.[118] Since military interventions on foreign territory were impossible and diplomatic ones ineffective, the French

114 Ibid., p. 59; Thomas, *Empires of Intelligence*. 115 Trinquier *Modern Warfare*, p. 97.
116 *Algeria in Turmoil: A History of the Rebellion* (New York, 1959), p. 309. See also: Salehyan, *Rebels*, pp. 20, 29; Byman, *Deadly*, pp. 67–75.
117 Trinquier, *Modern Warfare*, p. 101. 118 Ibid., p. 103.

intelligence and security services would play the leading role in this new type of warfare, both as providers of information and as covert operators. Most importantly, France had to recruit its own allies or proxies, through which to neutralise and dismantle the FLN's external sanctuaries and support networks.

These tactics allowed the French authorities to circumvent the strictures imposed by national boundaries. In April 1955, General Jean Calliès, in his capacity as inspector-general of the French armed forces in North Africa, urged Prime Minister Edgar Faure to adopt a strategy that took into account the Cold War context in the Maghreb.[119] Two months later, Calliès' staff devised a 'Plan for the protection of French North Africa against the Cold War' that reflected many of the tenets of *guerre révolutionnaire*. According to this plan, four parallel strands of unconventional warfare conducted both internally and abroad would henceforth complement all 'constructive' and 'destructive' counterinsurgency operations. First among these strands was 'psychological warfare' ('*guerre psychologique*'), which strove to win over Algerian and world opinion through extensive propaganda and other forms of psychological action. Second came the so-called war of action ('*guerre d'action*'), defined as 'a permanent secret war conducted by the special services' and which aimed to neutralise the FLN's external networks and agents. The third strand consisted of 'diplomatic warfare' ('*guerre diplomatique*') – the use of diplomatic pressure to clamp down on the FLN's international bases and isolate the movement from its foreign supporters. Finally, 'economic warfare' ('*guerre économique*') aimed to asphyxiate the FLN's funds and materiel.[120]

Calliès' 1955 plan – like Aït Ahmed's 1948 report – can be read as a blueprint for the internationalisation of French counterinsurgency warfare. Consecutive governments adopted and implemented its general recommendations. In a general directive dated 2 April 1959, for instance, Prime Minister Michel Debré reiterated that 'our embassies, our consulates, every one of our services must do everything in their power to expose and put an end to the overt and covert assistance afforded to the FLN', whatever its nature or provenance.[121] Without overlooking the internal dimension, Debré, too, focused French action on the international arena. His instructions left no doubt as to their meaning: French officials and

[119] Dépêche no. 473, 4.4.1955, SHD-T, 1H/1103/D1.

[120] Plan de protection, INS/AFN, 4.6.1955, SHD-T, 1H/1103/D1.

[121] Instruction, 2.4.1959, Archives d'Histoire Contemporaine (AHC), Paris, Fonds Michel Debré, 2DE/75*.

diplomats were to use every means – conventional and unconventional – in order to undermine the FLN's external sanctuaries and activities.

Here, then, are the prime factors explaining how and why the Bonn Republic came to be implicated in Algeria's independence struggle. On the one hand, the FLN deliberately pursued a strategy of internationalisation in order to gain the moral and material support without which its revolution could not survive. For this purpose, the movement established an increasingly elaborate external organisation, the entire purpose of which was to engage in public diplomacy, propaganda and the procurement of material supplies. More than that, the FLN relied on extraterritorial sanctuaries and bases from whence to pursue its internal struggle. On the other hand, French governments were determined to neutralise and destroy the FLN's external safe havens, which they deemed the insurgency's true motor and force. To accomplish this, the authorities resorted to methods and means that were both conventional and unconventional in nature. The case of West Germany highlights this process, for the more the FLN came to use that country as a refuge and base, the more the French authorities felt compelled to intervene. As the following chapters will show, the country soon became the target of a diverse set of counterinsurgency tactics, including the diplomatic war, the struggle over the control of the population, the battle for hearts and minds and the war of action over resources and supplies. Caught in the crossfire of what was essentially an extension of the Franco-Algerian confrontation onto their soil, the West German authorities and public had little choice but to pick a side. The country itself became a site of contestation of the Algerian war.

PART I

Creating the sanctuary
November 1954–May 1958

CHAPTER 2

West German diplomacy and the Algerian war

When the FLN launched its insurrection in November 1954, no one – not even the movement's own militants – could have guessed that West Germany would become a sanctuary and base for Algerian nationalists. After all, the Algerian war coincided with a period of unprecedented rapprochement between France and the FRG. By 1956 the Bonn and Paris governments had forged an alliance that became the driving force of European cooperation and integration. To what extent did the worsening conflict in Algeria help to shape this budding entente? Indeed, did the 'events' in Algeria affect West German diplomacy in other ways? Almost from the outset, this chapter argues, the Algerian war undercut two of the Bonn government's most vital foreign policy axioms. By destabilising the French political system, weakening NATO's defence potential and dividing the Atlantic alliance, the conflict impinged on Chancellor Konrad Adenauer's policy of *Westbindung*, or Western integration, threatening to derail its central tenet: the all-important process of reconciliation with France. That very process, meanwhile, jeopardised West German efforts to forge strong relationships with newly independent states in Asia, Africa and the Middle East, many of which sympathised with or even supported the FLN. The Algerian war thus also risked undermining the Hallstein doctrine through which Bonn's *Auswärtige Amt*, or Foreign Office, sought to isolate the GDR and uphold the Federal Republic's claim as the only legitimate German state. Filtering the Algerian question largely through a Cold War optic, policy-makers in Bonn grew ever more alarmed by the conflict's impact on West German foreign relations and national security. The government soon realised that West Germany could not avoid the Algerian war's increasingly global reverberations.

A foreign conspiracy?

At first, the FLN's liberation struggle barely registered in Bonn. Observers who paid attention depicted the uprising as the latest crisis in a chain of tribal uprisings spanning across French North Africa.[1] This indifference did not last long. By December 1954, Wilhelm Hausenstein, Bonn's *chef de mission* in Paris, presented the situation in Algeria as a 'reason for concern from a political and military perspective'. Hausenstein's alarm had been triggered by comments made by Commandant de Torquat, *chef de cabinet* to Marshal Alphonse Juin, one of France's highest military authorities. Speaking more frankly than perhaps he should have, Torquat revealed to his German interlocutor that the French army faced considerable difficulty in quelling the insurgency, whose principal theatre of operations, the Aurès mountains, remained impenetrable to armoured divisions. The rebels' numbers, moreover, appeared to be far stronger than reported in the French press; their ranks having swelled from a few hundred to roughly 20,000 within the space of just a few weeks. Thus contrary to the claims of General Paul Cherrière, the commander-in-chief of French forces in Algeria, this was no mere tribal uprising.[2]

More worrying still from Hausenstein's perspective was the fact that the French armed forces attributed the insurrection entirely to foreign intrigues. Torquat spoke of a 'communist conspiracy, whose containment represented a common concern for the West'. He claimed 'that pan-Arab circles not only supported the rebels financially and through arms smuggling, but that they also trained the rebels' cadres of agents and leaders', notably in Syria and Egypt. He then implicated the United States and Britain. In voicing their support for Western-oriented movements such as *Istiqlal* and *Neo-Destour*, Torquat claimed, the Americans 'showed very little understanding for the French position and were cherishing an illusion when it came to North Africans'. As for the British, they stood accused, in view of their 'old colonial rivalry' with France, of backing Tunisian insurgents from bases in Libya. Torquat implied that both countries now sought to extend their assistance to the FLN.[3]

What made these accusations so worrying to Hausenstein and his staff, apart from the fact that they were so widely believed, was that 'they seem[ed] to contradict every political logic'.[4] Notwithstanding the vitriolic attacks against French policies in North Africa emanating from the *Voice of*

[1] Reiner Marcowitz, '"Die Kommunisten stecken dahiner": Unionsparteien und Algerienkrieg (1954–62)', *RA* 31/3–4 (1999), p. 556; Klaus-Jürgen Müller, 'Le réalisme de la République fédérale d'Allemagne', in *Guerre d'Algérie et français* (ed.) Rioux, p. 410; Klaus-Jürgen Müller, 'Die Bundesrepublik Deutschland und der Algerienkrieg', *Vierteljahrshefte für Zeitgeschichte* 38/4 (1990), p. 611; Eckard Michels, 'Die Bundesrepublik und die Unabhängigkeit Tunesiens und Marokkos 1951–1962', *RA* 31/3–4 (1999), p. 439.

[2] Schreiben Nr.4834/54 der Vertretung Paris, 1 December 1954, PA/AA, B24/3/F2.

[3] Ibid.

[4] Ibid.

the Arabs, German diplomats in Cairo sympathised with the Egyptian government's claim that their country had far more to lose (e.g. in economic and development aid) than to gain from masterminding the Algerian rebellion.[5] Nor could German diplomats find any evidence of Soviet-bloc sponsorship of the North African rebellions. Likewise, since Prime Minister Mendès-France had already initiated the liberal reform process that both Washington and London deemed so vital for the future security of Western interests in Tunisia and Morocco, there seemed to be no reason for Britain or the United States to want to undermine France's position in North Africa.[6]

Vollrath von Maltzan, who succeeded Hausenstein as Bonn's first post-war ambassador to Paris after the abrogation of the Occupation Statute, shared his precursor's scepticism. Shortly after assuming his post in May 1955, he cautioned that 'all French claims over the role of foreign aid to the rebels should be handled with the greatest of circumspection'. To Maltzan and his staff, foreign conspiracy theories detracted attention away from the real roots of the Algerian uprising: namely, the continuing socio-economic misery of Algeria's Muslim population and the political discrimination exerted by the *colons*.[7] In such circumstances, repression alone would never extinguish the revolt. If anything, the army's heavy-handed tactic of assigning collective responsibility for terrorist acts heightened the rebels' prestige among Algerians. This, along with an elaborate propaganda campaign drawing on the dual principles of secular nationalism and holy *jihâd*, had facilitated the efforts of the FLN's internal leaders to turn their relatively localised and uncoordinated rebellions into a nation-wide insurgency: in April 1955, 'rebel actions' against the representatives and symbols of French rule averaged at an already significant 200 a month; by October, that number had risen to 900; and by March 1956, it averaged at 2,624. By then, all but the staunchest Messalists had rallied to the FLN, including the AUMA, most Muslim members of the Algerian Communist Party and even the moderate UDMA.[8] Having conceded to the nationalist aspirations of Tunisia and Morocco, Maltzan noted in December 1955 that France 'will find it more and more impossible to

[5] Schreiben Nr.3306-I, 18 November 1954, und Nr.3306-II, 24 November 1954, der Vertretung Kairo, PA/AA, B25/3.

[6] Schreiben Nr.4834/54 der Vertretung Paris, 1 December 1954, PA/AA, B24/3/F2.

[7] Schreiben Nr.3653/55 der Botschaft Paris, 3 August 1955; Schreiben Nr.4763/55 der Botschaft Paris, 3 November 1955, PA/AA, B25/3.

[8] On the rise in rebel actions: Talbot, *War without a Name*, p. 48; Tripier, *Autopsie*, p. 79. On the rallying of Algerian nationalists: Harbi, *FLN*, pp. 132–40; Meynier, *Histoire*, pp. 176–91.

pursue contrary policies that negate the existence of nationalism in Algeria'.[9]

This nationalism clashed irreconcilably with what one German diplomat called the 'sacrosanct thesis of French politics': namely, the insistence that Algeria was an integral part of France. As Torquat had explained in December 1954: 'On no account could reforms lead to a situation that called into question the "*présence française*" in North Africa [. . .] because otherwise France would cease to be a great power.'[10] To German diplomats, Torquat's comment summed up the 'unsolvable difficulties' French governments faced in Algeria. The prospect of reform remained illusory as long as French public opinion and political circles clung to the 'judicial fiction' that Algeria was an incontestable part of France. The French simply could not admit to themselves that ethnically, culturally and linguistically, Algeria was 'a part of the Arab and Muslim [. . .] Maghreb'.[11] Most unrealistic of all seemed to be the attitude of the French settlers. Renate Osiander, an attaché at the German embassy in Paris who travelled extensively throughout Algeria in December 1955, observed that few *colons* 'admitted to themselves that it was precisely the rigid clinging to traditional relations of power that [had] conjured up the present situation, and that a fundamental political reorganisation [had] become inevitable'.[12] In their reports to Bonn, German diplomats highlighted the settlers' political clout in Paris, as well as the colonial administration's tendency to ignore or sabotage metropolitan directives deemed unpopular by the *colons*.[13] Their influence and intransigence was such that successive French governments, starting with Mendès-France, pursued an awkward mixture of repression and reform in Algeria that loosely mirrored the dual precepts of *guerre révolutionnaire*.

In reality, repression quickly took precedence over reform, and the resultant policy was one of paralysis of the political process. By February 1955, German diplomats reckoned that settler obstinacy would make it impossible for Algeria's new governor-general, the anthropologist and Gaullist Jacques Soustelle, to implement his intended programme of liberal and progressive

[9] Schreiben der Botschaft Paris, 14 December 1955, PA/AA, B25/3. Also: Schreiben Nr.4148/54 der Vertretung Paris, 17 December 1954; Schreiben Nr.3653/55 der Botschaft Paris, 3 August 1955; Aufzeichnung von Attaché Renate Osiander über eine Informationsreise nach Algerien, 18 January 1956; Schreiben der Botschaft Paris, 2 March 1956; Aufzeichnung, Referat 302, 1956, PA/AA, B25/3; Schreiben Nr.2076/56 der Botschaft Paris, 25 April 1956, PA/AA, B24/308/F4.

[10] Schreiben Nr.4834/54 der Vertretung Paris, 1 December 1954, PA/AA, B24/3/F2 (italics added).

[11] Schreiben der Botschaft Paris, 14 December 1955; Schreiben Nr.4148/54 der Vertretung Paris, 17 December 1954, PA/AA, B25/3.

[12] Aufzeichnung, Informationsreise Osiander, 18 January 1956; PA/AA, B25/3.

[13] Schreiben Nr.159 der Vertretung Paris, 14 January 1955.

reforms. After the massacres perpetrated under Youssef Zighout's command at Philippeville on 20 August, Soustelle's plan for closer integration between Algeria and France was deemed a categorical failure.[14] The horrific events of that day – the insurgents' first deliberate attacks against European civilians – represented a calculated act of terrorism designed to provoke an indiscriminate and disproportionate reaction from the French. Although Zighout's unilateral offensive incurred criticism from some FLN leaders who saw it as suicidal or barbarous, it achieved its goal of dividing the colonisers from the colonised: while Zighout's offensive had left 123 dead, including 71 *colons*, French reprisals killed over 2,000 Algerians according to army estimates and up to 12,000 according to the FLN.[15]

The Philippeville massacre transformed the Algerian war. Some months earlier, Maltzan had written of French policy: 'one gets the impression that on the one hand the French government does not dare to intensify the military contest in Algeria into a kind of "total war", yet on the other hand the government cannot decide in the present circumstances to make any concessions in the form of reforms either'.[16] Mendès-France's successor, Edgar Faure, had just taken the radical decision in May to recall 8,000 reservists and extend the period of service of 100,000 draftees. Following on from his decision on 31 March to declare a state of emergency over certain regions in Algeria, this move was part of a general strategy designed to grant the military and security services a greater freedom to manoeuvre while simultaneously maintaining the legal premise that the army was not 'at war' but merely conducting 'operations for the maintenance of order' against terrorist '*hors la loi*' (outlaws). After Philippeville, the stage was set for a dramatic escalation of the conflict: not only was the FLN's struggle transformed from a 'phony rebellion' into a national revolution and people's war, but the Faure government also stepped up its efforts at military 'pacification', dispatching yet more reservists and conscripts and extending the state of emergency to all of Algeria. The determination to crush the rebels and preserve *l'Algérie française* assumed increasing priority over the search for a liberal solution to the conflict. With Soustelle's conversion to the cause of the *colons*, the prospects of reform seemed more distant than ever.[17]

14 Schreiben Nr.853 der Vertretung Paris, 25 February 1955, PA/AA, B24/3/F3; Schreiben Nr.4467 der Botschaft Paris, 28 September 1955, PA/AA, B24/4/F3.

15 Horne, *Savage War*, pp. 119–23; Meynier, *Histoire*, pp. 280–2.

16 Schreiben Nr.2557 der Botschaft Paris, 1.6.1955, PA/AA, B25/3.

17 Charles-Robert Ageron, 'L'insurrection du 20 août 1955 dans le Nord-Constantinois. De la résistance armée à la guerre du peuple', in *La guerre d'Algérie et les Algériens 1954–1962* (ed.) Charles-Robert Ageron (Paris, 1997), p. 27; Mahfoud Kaddache, 'Les tournants de la guerre de libération au niveau des masses populaires', in ibid., p. 54; Stephen Tyre, 'From Algérie française to France

This tendency to capitulate to the settlers became more pronounced still under the 'Republican Front' formed in January 1956. Distressed by the depths of *colon* hostility to the appointment of the liberal-minded General Georges Catroux to the post of resident-minister (as the post of governor-general had been rebranded), France's new Socialist premier, Guy Mollet, performed a dramatic *volte-face* after his first and only visit to Algiers on 6 February. Instead of implementing the political reforms that had constituted the election platform of the French Section of the Workers' International (SFIO), Mollet appointed his much more hawkish colleague Robert Lacoste as resident-minister and drastically escalated the counter-insurgency, further narrowing the prospects of a political solution. On 16 March, the National Assembly passed the law on 'special powers', an enabling act that strengthened the executive's hand vis-à-vis parliament and consolidated the military's power in Algeria. One month later, the government recalled yet more reservists and extended the period of military conscription.[18] To German diplomats, the 'near rebellion by the European population' in February highlighted the deadlock reached in Paris's Algerian policies. Maltzan likened Mollet's *volte-face* to an 'admission of impotence' vis-à-vis the colonial lobby.[19] The prime minister's watered-down programme of social and economic reforms did not have 'enough of a psychological effect on the Muslim population' to bring about 'a real political detente'. With Morocco and Tunisia having become independent, Maltzan also wondered 'whether a policy of categorical integration and assimilation [. . .] even remained a desirable objective for Algerians'.[20]

Global reverberations

If German diplomats voiced serious doubts over the viability of French strategy in Algeria, they were even more troubled by the Algerian war's wider ramifications. Though dismissive of foreign conspiracies, they acknowledged the conflict's international reverberations, which had begun to impinge on West German diplomatic efforts in the developing

Musulmane: Jacques Soustelle and the Myths and Realities of 'Integration', 1955–1962', *French History* 20/3 (2006), pp. 276–96.

[18] On Mollet's Algerian policies: Pascal Descamps, 'La politique algérienne du gouvernement Mollet: de la cohérence à l'enlisement', in *Guy Mollet. Un Camarade en République* (eds.) Bernard Ménager et al. (Lille, 1987), pp. 463–74; Martin Evans, *Algeria: France's Undeclared War* (Oxford, 2011), pp. 148–88; ibid., 'Mollet's Third Way', pp. 169–80.

[19] Schreiben Nr.1360/56 der Botschaft Paris, 8 February 1956, PA/AA, B25/3.

[20] Schreiben Nr.1431 der Botschaft Paris, 17 February 1956, PA/AA, B25/3; Schreiben Nr.5060/56 der Botschaft Paris, 21 December 1956, PA/AA, B24/273/F6.

world. The FLN's independence struggle resonated strongly in states that had themselves experienced forms of colonial domination. Moreover, although Germany had long lost its own colonies, the Bonn Republic could ill afford to ignore what Adenauer dismissively called 'the awakening of the coloured peoples', whose demands for political independence were transforming international politics.[21] In 1955, sixteen new nations had joined the UN, altering the make-up of that organisation. That same year, the Bandung conference gave birth to the principle of Cold War neutralism, which German Transport Minister Hans-Christoph Seebohm, in racialised terms, likened to a 'revolt of the coloured peoples against the white peoples'.[22] To many Western observers, Bandung heralded the end of the colonial era and the rise of the Afro-Asian bloc as an autonomous player in the Cold War.[23] As the first international conference to call for Algerian independence, Bandung represented an important coup and precedent for the FLN. This was followed in September 1955 by the Afro-Asian bloc's narrow success in securing the Algerian question's inscription on the agenda of the UN General Assembly.[24] Having imposed itself as the dominant nationalist force within Algeria, the FLN had also succeeded in internationalising its cause. The implications of this situation were obvious even to Adenauer, who in a cabinet meeting on 6 October referred to the FLN's triumph at the UN as a 'decisive victory of the coloured peoples', a fact he deemed 'very depressing'.[25]

The chancellor, it appears, did not share his diplomats' views on the inexorable rise of anti-colonial nationalism. Born and bred in the colonial era, Adenauer's worldview was steeped in the Christian, humanist, and

[21] Télégramme circulaire no.73 à tous postes diplomatiques, 2 October 1956, MAE, Europe (EU)/ République Fédérale d'Allemagne (RFA)/1259*.

[22] *Die Kabinettsprotokolle der Bundesregierung*, Vol. 8, *1955* (eds.) Michael Hollmann and Kai von Jena (Munich, 1997), 79. Sitzung, 20 April 1955, p. 231, n. 29. The emerging clashes between European powers and the developing world were often described in racial terms. Connelly cites one French intelligence officer who referred to Bandung as 'the beginning of the end of the supremacy of the white race'. See: Connelly, *Diplomatic Revolution*, p. 81.

[23] On Bandung's global legacy: C.J. Lee (ed.), *Making a World after Empire: The Bandung Movement and Its Political Afterlives* (Athens OH, 2010); J.C. Parker, 'Small Victory, Missed Chance: The Eisenhower Administration, the Bandung Conference, and the Turning of the Cold War', in *The Eisenhower Administration, the Third World, and the Globalization of the Cold War* (eds.) K.C. Statler and A.L. Johns (Lanham MD, 2006), pp. 153–74; Cary Fraser, 'An American Dilemma: Race and Realpolitik in the American Response to the Bandung Conference', in *Window on Freedom: Race, Civil Rights, and Foreign Affairs, 1945–1988* (ed.) B.G. Plummer (Chapel Hill NC, 2003), pp. 115–40.

[24] Thomas, 'France Accused', p. 104; Vaïsse, 'La guerre perdue?' p. 451.

[25] *Kabinettsprotokolle – 1955*, 99. Sitzung, 6 October 1955, p. 546. Also: Schreiben Nr.2983/56 (Maltzan) der Botschaft Paris, 27 July 1956, PA/AA, B25/19.

deeply racist ideologies that had underpinned Europe's imperial expansions in the nineteenth century.[26] Like many of his era he was condescending of so-called coloured peoples, as he habitually referred to non-Europeans, and firmly believed in the superiority of Western, Christian civilisation (the *christliche Abendland*). As vice-president of the German Colonial Society from 1931 to 1933, he had even advocated the return of German colonies lost at the end of World War I.[27] Adenauer thus never questioned France's right to defend its overseas possessions. He shared the French conviction that 'communist wire-pullers' stood behind the Algerian rebellion. The FLN represented another 'willing idiot of the hated Soviets', who were using the movement to gain control of a strategically and economically vital region and to penetrate Western Europe from below.[28] Doubtful of the ability of 'coloured peoples' to govern responsibly and obsessed with security, the chancellor questioned the wisdom of Algerian independence. To him, France's continued presence in the Maghreb constituted an essential bulwark against communism.[29]

However biased and amiss his views of the FLN, Adenauer also believed in the inherent interdependence of societies and states, all the more so given his country's own vulnerable position.[30] West Germany, the chancellor realised, would not stay immune to the Algerian war's global ramifications. Beyond Europe, the conflict threatened to undermine West German interests particularly in the Arab world, a region deemed vital not only geopolitically as a buffer to the communist East, but also economically as a source of oil and an export market.[31] Already marred by the 1952 restitution agreement with Israel, West German interests in the region

[26] Anneliese Poppinga, *Konrad Adenauer. Geschichtsverständnis, Weltanschauung und politische Praxis* (Stuttgart, 1975), pp. 161–70.

[27] Dirk van Laak, *Über alles in der Welt. Deutscher Imperialismus im 19. und 20. Jahrhundert* (München, 2005), p. 109.

[28] First citation: *Kabinettsprotokolle – 1955*, 95. Sitzung, 31 August 1955, p. 478; second citation: Rolf Pfeiffer, 'Ein erfolgreiches Kapitel bundesdeutscher Außenpolitik: Die Adenauer-Regierung und die Suez-Krise von 1956', *Historische Mitteilungen* 13/1 (2000), p. 226.

[29] *Die Kabinettsprotokolle der Bundesregierung*, Vol. 9 – *1956* (ed.) Ursula Hüllbüsch (Munich, 1998), 132. Sitzung, 2 May 1956, p. 328; Konrad Adenauer, *Erinnerungen 1955–1959* (Stuttgart, 1967), pp. 19, 133, 135, 398; Marcowitz, 'Unionsparteien', p. 562; Maurice Couve de Murville, *Une politique étrangère 1958–1969* (Paris, 1971), p. 36; Ulrich Lappenküper, 'Adenauer, de Gaulle und der Algerienkrieg 1958–1962', *RA* 31/3–4 (1999), p. 604; Michels, 'Bundesrepublik', p. 441; Schwarz, *Staatsmann*, pp. 238–9, 317.

[30] Poppinga, *Adenauer*, pp. 58–63.

[31] Jürgen Bellers, *Außenwirtschaftspolitik der Bundesrepublik Deutschland, 1949–1989* (Münster, 1990), pp. 105, 225; S.O. Berggötz, *Nahostpolitik in der Ära Adenauer: Möglichkeiten und Grenzen, 1949–1963* (Düsseldorf, 1998), pp. 64, 72–3, 130, 233, 236–7, 402; Gray, *Germany's Cold War*, p. 68.

faced increasingly stiff competition from the Soviet Union and GDR.[32] The visits by Heinrich Rau, East Berlin's deputy prime minister, to India and Egypt in late 1955, which resulted in the establishment of a trade mission in Cairo, marked the beginnings of an increasingly assertive East German campaign for diplomatic recognition from the non-European world. This campaign focused strongly on the Middle East, and by October 1956, it nearly registered its first major success when only the strongest of diplomatic interventions prevented Damascus from becoming the first non-communist capital to exchange consulates with East Berlin.[33] By then, Bonn's diplomats considered the Arab world 'a decisive front sector' in their personal Cold War against the so-called Eastern Zone. The *Auswärtige Amt* knew that by alienating Arab opinion, it opened a door for East Berlin and undermined the freshly formulated Hallstein doctrine.[34] To counteract this trend, Bonn instructed its ambassadors in the region to build strong and enduring Arab–German partnerships.[35]

For this strategy to succeed – especially given Bonn's policy of reconciliation with and reparations to Israel – the Adenauer government had to dissociate itself from its allies' increasingly unpopular colonial policies, particularly France's war in Algeria.[36] Whether out of political considerations, a sense of ideological obligation towards French communists, which still supported *l'Algérie française*, or distrust of the FLN's nationalist discourse, both Moscow and East Berlin had initially remained detached from the Algerian question. West German diplomats found no evidence of collusion with the FLN, commenting instead on the Soviets' 'remarkable reserve'.[37] This reserve was unlikely to last, however, for as one diplomat noted in August 1956, 'the Algerian rebellion, with its engagement of NATO [i.e. French] troops, fit well into the general concept of Soviet global strategy'. As such, the conflict presented Moscow with 'a welcome opportunity for the commencement of an alternative offensive beginning

[32] Hünseler, *Außenpolitischen Beziehungen*, pp. 63–4; Friedemann Buettner, 'Germany's Middle East Policy: The Dilemmas of a 'Policy of Even-Handedness' (*Politik der Ausgewogenheit*)', in *Germany and the Middle East. Past, Present, and Future* (ed.) Haim Goren (Jerusalem, 2003), pp. 115–16, 119–29.

[33] Gray, *Germany's Cold War*, pp. 41–9, 64–5; Hermann Wentker, *Außenpolitik in engen Grenzen: die DDR im internationalen System 1949–1989* (Munich, 2007), pp. 172–3; G.M. Winrow, *The Foreign Policy of the GDR in Africa* (Cambridge, 1990), p. 36.

[34] Protocol der Istanbuler Konferenz deutscher Botschafter im Nahen Osten, 3–7 April 1956, PA/AA, B2/94. Also: Gray, *Germany's Cold War*, pp. 5–6, 44–9, 81–6; Booz, '*Hallsteinzeit*', pp. 35–7, 78–95; End, *Zweimal*, pp. 39–41; Kilian, *Hallstein-Doktrin*, pp. 22–30.

[35] Protocol der Istanbuler Konferenz, PA/AA, B2/94; Herbert Blankenhorn, *Verständnis und Verständigung. Blätter eines politischen Tagebuchs, 1949 bis 1979* (Frankfurt/Main, 1980), p. 241.

[36] Notiz (Dr. Kassler), Referat 302, 21 December 1955; Aufzeichnung, Referat 302, 1956, PA/AA, B25/3.

[37] Aufzeichnung, Referat 302, AA, 1 August 1956, PA/AA, B25/6. Also: Müller, 'Réalisme', p. 417.

at Europe's southern flank'.[38] The *Auswärtige Amt* feared that French intransigence would ultimately drive the FLN into Soviet arms. After all, French policies were such that 'the Arabs' [sic] only choice is to fight for their independence, and this will one day bring them into another dependency'.[39]

By the time of the Suez crisis, that dependency looked set to be communist for Moscow had become increasingly vocal in its criticism of France.[40] More worrying still from the perspective of the *Auswärtige Amt*, the GDR had begun to exploit both the Algerian problem and the Franco-German rapprochement as a means through which to further its goal of gaining international legitimacy and diplomatic recognition. East German propaganda assumed an aggressive and defamatory tone that deliberately sought to associate the Bonn government with Germany's colonial and imperialist past.[41] Otto Grotewohl used the Suez crisis and Algerian war to denounce Bonn's complicity in 'the full brutality of imperialist colonial policy'. The East German premier condemned West Germany's 'imperialist alliance' with Tel Aviv and Paris.[42] In an official statement issued in April 1957, East Berlin's Foreign Ministry denounced the Adenauer government for harbouring 'neo-colonial designs' in the Arab world and accused it of being an 'active exponent of colonialism' and 'enemy of national liberation movements'. Over the following months, the Algerian war developed into an ever more prominent theme of East German propaganda depicting Bonn as the lackey of French imperialism.[43] The regime also began to furnish modest amounts of medical aid to the FLN, which it channelled through the East German Red Cross and trade union federation, the *Freie Deutsche Gewerkschaftsbund* (FDGB).

[38] Ibid. [39] Schreiben Nr.4467/55 der Botschaft Paris, 28 September 1955, PA/AA, B24/4/F1.

[40] Mohieddine Hadhri, *L'URSS et le Maghreb: De la révolution d'octobre à l'indépendance de l'Algérie, 1917–1962* (Paris, 1985), pp. 120–32, 137–49; Y.H. Zoubir, 'The United States, the Soviet Union and Decolonization of the Maghreb, 1945–62', *Middle Eastern Studies* 31/1 (1995), pp. 59, 63–6, 71–2.

[41] Luís Madureira, 'Kalashnikovs, Not Coca-Cola, Bring Self-Determination to Angola: The Two Germanys, Lusophone Africa, and the Rhetoric of Colonial Difference', in *German Colonialism* (eds.) Langbehn and Salama, p. 284.

[42] Cited in: Angelika Timm, 'The Middle East Policy of East Germany', in *Germany and the Middle East* (ed.) Goren, p. 253. Also: Jan Lorenzen, 'Die Haltung der DDR zum Suez-Krieg. Das Jahr 1956 als Zäsur in der Nahost-Politik der DDR', *Deutschland Archiv* 28/3 (1995), pp. 278–85.

[43] Erklärung des Ministeriums für Auswärtige Angelegenheiten der DDR, 10 April 1957, in *Dokumente zur Außenpolitik der Regierung der Deutschen Demokratischen Republik*, Bd. V (ed.) Institut für Zeitgeschichte (Berlin, 1958), pp. 107–10. Also: Hong, *Germany's Cold War*, pp. 148–51; Manfred Kittel, 'Wider «die Kolonialmacht der französischen Großkapitalisten und die Rüstungsmillionäre des Nordatlantikpakts»: SED und Algerienkrieg 1954–1962', *RA* 31/3–4 (1999), pp. 407–10; Fritz Taubert, *La guerre d'Algérie et la République Démocratique Allemande. Le rôle de l' « autre » Allemagne pendant les « événements » (1954 à 1962)* (Dijon, 2010), pp. 17–19.

According to French diplomats in Berlin, these donations started just after Suez in December 1956.[44] They soon accelerated and by the end of 1957 reached an estimated value of 577,000 East German marks.[45]

Dividing the Western alliance

The Soviet bloc's growing support for the FLN certainly alarmed foreign policy-makers in Bonn, yet they were even more concerned by the Algerian conflict's increasingly deleterious effect on France and the Western alliance. French politics under the Fourth Republic were already notoriously volatile, with coalition governments forming and falling at intervals of six to eight months. Early on in the war, it became apparent that Algeria would aggravate this situation; there would be five more premiers in Paris before de Gaulle's return to power in June 1958.[46] By polarising French politics, reinforcing xenophobic and nationalist sentiment, and strengthening the opponents of Western integration, the Algerian war consolidated France's reputation as 'the sick man of Europe'.[47] As early as February 1955, dissent over Algerian reforms prompted the fall of Mendès-France's government, rousing fears in Bonn over the fate of the Paris Accords signed on 23 October 1954, which, once ratified, would pave the way for an end of occupation and for West German rearmament. Although the country's sovereignty would remain qualified, and although the army – or *Bundeswehr* – would be fully integrated into NATO and the Brussels Pact, the Accords made it possible for Bonn to participate in international relations on an almost equal footing to its Western allies.[48] The accompanying declaration of La Celle-St-Cloud addressed the fate of the Saarland. It proposed a referendum on a European statute for this disputed territory, which had been tied to France in a customs union

[44] Télégramme no.290 par Bernard de Chalvron, conseillier politique au gouvernement militaire français à Berlin, 8 December 1956, MAE, AL/Algérie (ALG)/57; Dépêche no.111 par Chalvron, Berlin, 29 March 1957, MAE, AL/ALG/39.

[45] Aktennotiz für Kamerad Dr. Ludwig, Abteilung PMS, 24 December 1957, Archiv des Deutschen Roten Kreuzes (ADRK), Berlin, Akten des Roten Kreuzes der Deutschen Demokratischen Republik (DDR)/56. See also: Hong, *Cold War Germany*, pp. 143–4, 153.

[46] Vincent Wright, *The Government and Politics of France*, 3rd edn (London, 1996), p. 4.

[47] François Seydoux, *Beiderseits des Rheins. Erinnerungen eines französischen Diplomaten* (Frankfurt, 1975), p. 197.

[48] Helga Haftendorn, *Deutsche Außenpolitik zwischen Selbstbeschränkung und Selbstbehauptung* (Stuttgart, 2001), pp. 38–46; Gustav Schmidt, '"Tying" (West) Germany into the West – But to What? NATO? WEU? The European Community?' in *Western Europe and Germany. The Beginnings of European Integration 1945–1960* (ed.) Clemens Wurm (Oxford and Washington, 1995), pp. 137–74.

since 1945. The declaration's approval promised to resolve one of the most difficult problems in post-war Franco-German relations.[49] To Adenauer, the survival of the Mendès-France government was 'of the greatest significance' to the pursuit of these goals; its fall 'would render the situation for Europe and the world more difficult'.[50]

This prediction proved premature, for the Faure government that succeeded Mendès-France did ratify the Paris Accords and declaration of La Celle-St-Cloud. Even so, foreign policy-makers in Bonn became increasingly preoccupied by Algeria's impact on French political stability. To German diplomats, the *colons* lobby led by powerful politicians such as former premier René Mayer (a deputy for Constantine and Mendès-France's main rival within the Radical Party) represented not only the principal obstacle to reform within Algeria but also the decisive powerbroker in metropolitan politics.[51] Nothing proved this point more than Mollet's *volte-face* of February 1956, which convinced Maltzan that a 'further procrastination of the [political] problem [in Algeria] represented a serious danger not only for the existence of the government but also for the survival of the republican system'.[52] To Joseph Jansen, a councillor in the German embassy in Paris, the endurance of Mollet's government hung on a silk thread, 'and that silk thread is Algeria'.[53] Unable to find a workable solution to the ever-deteriorating crisis, French politics assumed the guise of what another German diplomat called 'jungle combat', where one party undermined the other through a relentless cycle of stasis and mutual recriminations.[54]

Worse still, the foreign conspiracies surrounding the FLN had generated xenophobic and anti-Western sentiments benefiting the political extremes, as witnessed by the significant gains made by both the *Parti Communiste Français* (PCF) and the reactionary Poujadist movement in the January 1956 parliamentary elections, which saw the greatest voter turnout in French post-war history (the PCF obtained 150 seats, the most of any party, while Poujade's *Union et Fraternité Française* gained 51 seats).[55] During the Suez

[49] Lappenküper, *Deutsch-französischen Beziehungen* I, p. 316.

[50] *Kabinettsprotokolle – 1955*, 68. Sitzung, 28 January 1955, pp. 113, and 69. Sitzung, 2 February 1955, p. 120.

[51] Fernschreiben Nr.51 der Vertretung Paris, 24 January 1955; Schreiben Nr. 853 der Vertretung Paris, 25 February 1955, PA/AA, B24/3/F2.

[52] Schreiben Nr.1360/56, 8 February 1956, PA/AA, B25/3.

[53] Schreiben Nr.2585/56 der Botschaft Paris, 20 June 1956, PA/AA, B24/273/F4.

[54] Schreiben Nr.4467/55 der Botschaft Paris, 28 September 1955, PA/AA, B24/4/F1. Also: Schreiben Nr.2115/56 der Botschaft Paris, 30 April 1956, PA/AA, B24/273/F3.

[55] P.M. Williams, *French Politicians and Elections 1951–1969* (Cambridge, 1970), pp. 39–63.

crisis, chauvinistic overtones rose still further. 'Never before', Maltzan wrote in November 1956, 'have the United Nations, United States, United Kingdom, Soviet Union and ultimately the entire Western world been so heavily attacked'. The ambassador feared a nationalist 'short circuit' that could undermine the entire regime.[56]

Maltzan's prediction looked set to become reality when on 8 February 1958, French forces engaged in an aerial bombardment of the Tunisian village of Sakiet-Sidi-Youssef. Justified by French generals as retaliation against cross-border skirmishes with the ALN, the raid aimed – unsuccessfully – to eliminate one of the Algerians' key external sanctuaries. A blatant violation of Tunisian sovereignty and non-belligerency, the bombardment killed sixty-eight civilians, many of them schoolchildren and women. Once again, an attempt to deny the FLN sanctuary by means of a military intervention came to spark international outrage. The Sakiet incident produced an international public relations disaster for France on a scale that surpassed even the hijacking of the FLN's external leaders and the Suez debacle. The crisis prompted an Anglo-American good offices mission to mediate between the governments in Paris and Tunis. It also exacerbated French resentment of the governments in Washington and London, especially since President Eisenhower sought to use the crisis as a means of pressuring France into a negotiated settlement of the Algerian problem.[57] French opposition to such perceived meddling prompted Bonn's Foreign Minister Heinrich von Brentano to worry that '[i]n the almost hopeless confrontation that France faces in North Africa grow the chances of a small-minded and thoroughly anti-European and nationalist school of thought in France'.[58] Some diplomats even presaged civil war. On the one hand, France faced the prospect of a reactionary national front or even military dictatorship. On the other hand, it stood on the verge of a communist-led popular front.[59] From Bonn's perspective, both scenarios portended

[56] Schreiben Nr.4469/56 der Botschaft Paris, 14 November 1956, PA/AA, B24/273/F5. Also: Schreiben Nr.1076/57 der Botschaft Paris, 11 January 1957, PA/AA, B24/310/F1.

[57] On Sakiet crisis: Geoffrey Barei, 'The Sakiet Sidi Youssef Incident of 1958 in Tunisia and the Anglo-American 'Good Offices' Mission', *Journal of North African Studies* 17/2 (2012), pp. 355–71; Connelly, *Diplomatic Revolution*, pp. 160–67; Thomas, *French*, pp. 147–52; Irwin M. Wall, 'The United States, Algeria, and the Fall of the Fourth French Republic', *Diplomatic History* 18/4 (1994), pp. 489–511; Ibid., *France*, ch. 4.

[58] Cited in: Lappenküper, 'Adenauer', pp. 605–6; Marcowitz, 'Unionsparteien', p. 556.

[59] Schreiben Nr.4467/55 der Botschaft Paris, 28 September 1955, PA/AA, B24/4/F1; Schreiben Nr.1360/56, 8 February 1956, PA/AA, B25/3; Schreiben Nr.4697/56 der Botschaft Paris, 28 November 1956, PA/AA, B24/273/F5; Schreiben Nr.1904/58 der Botschaft Paris, 11 April 1958, PA/AA, B24/275/F1.

impending doom. Either way, France would pursue neutralist and nationalist policies hostile to Adenauer's *Westpolitik*. Filtered through a Cold War logic, these worst-case scenarios would lead to West Germany's encirclement by hostile powers, incite the United States to withdraw from Europe, and thereby spell the end of NATO and of European integration. Germany itself would end up disarmed, neutralised, and reunited on Soviet terms.[60]

Of all the Algerian war's myriad repercussions, therefore, it was the strain on the Atlantic alliance that worried the Bonn government most. The conflict had already weakened NATO by drawing French forces away from Europe.[61] Whereas 693,000 French soldiers had served in Europe in 1954, only 242,000 did so in 1958. Concurrently, the number of soldiers in Algeria rose from approximately 55,000 in November 1954, to 450,000 in 1957. With the newly formed *Bundeswehr* still in its infancy, this drain of military power was acutely felt, especially as many of the transferred troops had been stationed on German soil.[62] When French troops were replaced at all, it was typically with North African garrisons. This, in turn, roused popular memories of the 1920s 'black shame', when thousands of colonial troops had occupied the Rhineland and Ruhr. As then, many Germans reacted with racist indignation to the presence of 'coloured' soldiers they deemed untrustworthy and inferior to their European counterparts.[63] In late 1955, the stationing of the 4th RTM (Moroccan infantry regiment) in rural Baden-Württemberg produced lively objections from the *Land*'s population, press, and premier.[64] Paris's decision to redeploy further

[60] Marcowitz, *Option*, pp. 13, 15–16.

[61] Ageron, 'L'insurrection', p. 29; Connelly, *Diplomatic Revolution*, pp. 64, 76; Jean-Charles Jauffret, 'L'Armée et l'Algérie en 1954', *Revue Historique des Armées* 187 (1992), p. 23.

[62] Jean Doise and Maurice Vaïsse, *Diplomatie et outil militaire, 1871–1969* (Paris, 1987), p. 454; Jacques Frémeaux, *Le Monde arabe et la sécurité de la France depuis 1958* (Paris, 1995), pp. 17, 21; Alfred Grosser, 'La France en Occident et en Algérie', in *Guerre d'Algérie et Français* (ed.) Rioux, p. 384.

[63] Initially a government campaign to generate public opposition to the occupation, the 'black shame' developed into a wider debate over the supposed threat posed by 'racially primitive' and 'sexually depraved' African soldiers, particularly to German women. Rapes, thefts, and murders allegedly perpetrated by French soldiers, whether they dated to the interwar years or the post-1945 period, were invariably blamed on 'coloured' men. See: Edgar Wolfrum, 'Das Bild der »düsteren Franzosenzeit«. Alltagsnot, Meinungsklima und Demokratisierungspolitik in der französischen Besatzungszone nach 1945', in *Vom »Erbfeind« zum »Erneuerer«. Aspekte und Motive der französischen Deutschlandpolitik nach dem Zweiten Weltkrieg* (ed.) Stefan Martens (Sigmaringen, 1993), pp. 91–2; Iris Wigger, *Die 'Schwarze Schmach am Rhein': rassistische Diskriminierung zwischen Geschlecht, Klasse, Nation und Rasse* (Münster, 2007); Christian Koller, '*Von Wilden aller Rassen niedergemetzelt': Die Diskussion um die Verwendung von Kolonialtruppen in Europa zwischen Rassismus, Kolonial – und Militärpolitik (1914–1930)* (Stuttgart, 2001), pp. 235–41.

[64] Dépêche no.34 de l'ambassadeur Louis Joxe, Bonn, 11 January 1956, SHD-T, 14S/20*.

North African regiments to West Germany in February 1956 amplified popular consternation.[65] Spurred by racial and security concerns, including an ostensible rise in crimes attributed to 'coloured' troops, even national newspapers such as *Die Welt* and *FAZ* voiced anxieties over the replacement of French combat troops by North African garrisons.[66]

These fears were exacerbated by the fact that French force reductions occurred at a time marked by rising insecurity over the fate of NATO's conventional forces. With conscription ending in 1957, Britain, too, sought to downsize its army on the Rhine. Meanwhile, the Radford Plan of 1956 and 'Overall Strategic Concept for the Defense of the North Atlantic Treaty Area' (MC 14/2) of May 1957 both advocated a nuclear first-strike strategy relying on tactical nuclear weapons to which the infant *Bundeswehr* had no access.[67] NATO's new strategy of 'massive retaliation' revived German fears of a withdrawal of American troops from Europe, a situation that might have prompted the Western allies to take up Moscow's latest plan for German reunification and demilitarisation – a scenario that remained anathema to Adenauer. When the Soviet launch of Sputnik in late 1957 triggered a race by the American military to fill the perceived missile gap with intercontinental ballistic missiles, Bonn's sense of vulnerability rose still further. The Adenauer government now distrusted even the reliability of America's nuclear umbrella. NATO's military defences thus appeared to be weakening on a number of fronts.[68]

From Adenauer's perspective, only the continued cohesion of a militarily strong Atlantic alliance could contain the Soviet menace and ensure West Germany's national security and survival. Algeria strained that cohesion. The French accused Britain and America of meddling on the one hand, but demanded Western solidarity on the other. Algeria's three northern departments were, after all, covered by the terms of the North Atlantic Treaty. Though mindful of avoiding NATO's direct interference in what to them constituted a domestic concern, French politicians insisted

[65] Dépêche no.281 de l'ambassadeur Joxe, Bonn, 29 February 1956, SHD-T, 14S/20*.

[66] Aufzeichnung, von Baudissin, 7 November 1956, PA/AA, B24/321/F1. Also: Cahn and Müller, *RFA et Guerre d'Algérie*, p. 144; Klaus-Jürgen Müller, 'La guerre d'Algérie vue par la presse ouest-allemande', *Relations internationales* 58 (1989), p. 182.

[67] Michael H. Creswell and Dieter H. Kollmer, 'Power, Preference, or Ideas? Explaining West Germany's Armaments Strategy, 1955–1972', *Journal of Cold War Studies* 15/4 (2013), pp. 77–9.

[68] On these anxieties: Werner L. Abelshauser, 'The Causes and Consequences of the 1956 West German Rearmament Crisis', in *NATO: The Founding of the Atlantic Alliance and the Integration of Europe* (eds.) Francis H. Heller and John R. Gillingham (Basingstoke, 1992), pp. 311–34; Adenauer, *Erinnerungen*, pp. 197–214, 222–8; Trachtenberg, *Constructed Peace*, pp. 232–3; Schwarz, *Staatsmann*, pp. 290–6.

that Algeria was 'part of a great world struggle against Communism' (Soustelle) and that the Cold War's newest defence line ran not along the Elbe but along the axis Paris-Algiers-Brazzaville (Mitterrand).[69] While France's allies agreed on the importance of keeping Algeria within the Western sphere, they increasingly disagreed with Parisian governments on the strategy through which to accomplish that goal. Though the Atlantic Council never openly objected to the withdrawal of French troops from NATO command, it grew sceptical of the argument that France defended strategic interests in Algeria. Most NATO members dismissed the argument that the Algerian rebellion represented a pan-Arab and Soviet plot. If anything, they argued that French practices and policies in Algeria did more to facilitate the spread of communism than the FLN. By supporting these practices, NATO would undermine the West's image in much of the developing world, making it easier for the Soviet bloc to pose as the champion of anti-colonialism.[70]

France's allies thus faced a growing dilemma over Algeria, especially Britain and the United States.[71] On the one hand, neither power could afford to alienate France, which remained a vital pillar in NATO and the European community. On the other hand, neither power wanted to estrange the nascent Third World, especially as Britain faced its own colonial crises in Africa and Asia. After the Suez debacle, Whitehall increasingly viewed colonial retrenchment and self-government as the best method for maintaining British power and influence.[72] As for the Eisenhower administration, it had long regarded the colonial empires as ideological and political liabilities for the Western alliance.[73] When it came

[69] Télégramme circulaire du MAE aux postes OTAN, 28 March 1956, MAE, AL/ALG/15; Jacques Soustelle, 'France Looks at her Alliances', *Foreign Affairs* 35 (1956), p. 116; Connelly, *Diplomatic Revolution*, p. 84; Samya El Mechat, 'Les Etats-Unis, l'Algérie et l'équilibre stratégique 1954–1962', in *Guerre d'Algérie au miroir des décolonisations françaises* (ed.) Charles-Robert Ageron (Paris, 2000), p. 343; Grosser, 'France', p. 385; Pierre Mélandri, 'La France et le «double jeu» des États-Unis', in *Guerre d'Algérie et français* (ed.) Rioux, p. 431.

[70] Grosser, 'France', p. 385; Bruno Bagnato, 'Une solidarité ambiguë: l'OTAN, la France et la guerre d'Algérie (1954–1958)', *Revue d'histoire diplomatique* 115/4 (2001), pp. 329–50.

[71] Schreiben Nr.2641/55 der Botschaft Paris, 8 June 1955, PA/AA, B24/3/F1; Aufzeichnung, Referat 211 (Verteidigung and Abrüstung), 30 July 1956, PA/AA, B14/64.

[72] On British decolonisation: John Darwin, *The Empire Project: The Rise and Fall of the British World System* (Cambridge, 2009); Ronald Hyam, *Britain's Declining Empire: the Road to Decolonisation, 1918–1968* (Cambridge, 2007); Sarah Stockwell, *The British Empire: Themes and Perspectives* (Malden MA, 2008); Wm. R. Louis and R. Robinson, 'The Imperialism of Decolonization', *Journal of Imperial and Commonwealth History* 22 (1994), pp. 462–511.

[73] On US attitudes to decolonisation: Matthew Connelly, 'Taking Off the Cold War Lens: Visions of North-South Conflict during the Algerian War for Independence', *American Historical Review* 105/3 (2000), pp. 739–69; Frank A. Ninkovich, *The United States and Imperialism* (Malden MA, 2001),

to Algeria, both powers championed a liberal solution. To contain the spread of neutralism and communism, Washington and London courted the pro-Western governments of Morocco and Tunisia but generally avoided direct interventions in the Algerian question, much to the FLN's disappointment. This 'middle-of-the-road' approach in turn reinforced French suspicions that Britain and the United States sought to undermine France's influence in the Maghreb.[74]

Non-engagement?

With tensions so high and varied, the Bonn government had to tread carefully in its handling of the Algerian war's reverberations. Discussions on how best to proceed began on the conflict's first anniversary. In a widely circulated memorandum dated 4 November 1955, Paul Frank, then a councillor at the German embassy in Paris, proposed binding the Algerian question to the Franco-German rapprochement. For decades, Frank maintained, Franco-German relations had been 'the object of a sentimental pipe-dream or a series of fatal misunderstandings'. Now, geopolitical realities had created a situation in which 'the political coalescence of both countries resulted from considerations of *Realpolitik*'. Algeria had contributed to these changed circumstances. By driving France into international isolation, Frank believed that Paris had no choice but to turn to Bonn for diplomatic support. To cement this rapprochement, the Adenauer government had to avoid everything 'that would rekindle the hostile sentiments of French public opinion towards Germany, which have only just begun to fade', and instead help alleviate France's problems. Frank recommended creating a 'community of interests' in North Africa. He believed that 'any *Schadenfreude* vis-à-vis France's difficulties in [the Maghreb] was out of place, for in the long-run this could only undermine

pp. 200–46; David Ryan and Victor Pungong (eds.), *The United States and Decolonization: Power and Freedom* (Basingstoke, 2000); Westad, *Global Cold War*, chs. 1, 4.

[74] On Anglo-American policies towards the Algerian war: Miloud Barkaoui, 'Managing the Colonial Status Quo: Eisenhower's Cold War and the Algerian War of Independence', *Journal of North African Studies* 17/1 (2012), pp. 125–41; Connelly, *Diplomatic Revolution*, pp. 119–70; Wall, *France*, pp. 9–133; Ibid., 'United States', pp. 489–511; Christopher Goldsmith, 'The British Embassy in Paris and the Algerian War: An Uncomfortable Partner?' *Journal of Strategic Studies* (JSS) 25/2 (2002), pp. 159–71; Martin Thomas, 'The Dilemmas of an Ally of France: Britain's Policy towards the Algerian Rebellion, 1954–62', *Journal of Imperial and Commonwealth History* 23/1 (1995), pp. 129–54; Ibid., *French*, pp. 130–57; Egya N. Sangmuah, 'Eisenhower and Containment in North Africa, 1956–1960', *Middle East Journal* 44 (1990), pp. 76–91.

France's position in the Mediterranean and consequently Western Europe's overall potential'. He concluded:

> If, for ideological and domestic reasons, the United States only supports France hesitantly; if England thinks that France should follow its lead on the abandonment of colonial positions; and if Russia believes it can use the Arab League to extend its reach into the Mediterranean; then this is reason enough for the Federal Republic and Western Europe to show understanding for the French policy of maintaining its positions in the European sphere of influence.

This did not imply that one should support France's 'obsolete and narrow-minded colonialism'. Rather, Frank urged the Bonn government to 'shield France propagandistically' until the Paris authorities realised that 'both countries can accomplish together what the French will not be able to manage on their own' in North Africa: namely, a gradual disengagement that ensured the region remained firmly tied to the West.[75]

Frank's recommendations divided opinions in Bonn. As Cahn and Müller have shown, officials were keen to advance Franco-German relations and ensure that France remained an integral member of the Western alliance. Overt support for Paris would, however, jeopardise West Germany's standing in the Third World. Considering, moreover, the depths of anti-French sentiments among the local populations, officials doubted the viability of bilateral or European collaboration in the Maghreb.[76] By November 1955, the Bonn government had already withdrawn from a number of joint economic projects, including the planned construction of an aeronautical plant at Agadir, after German industrialists and Arab diplomats questioned their political wisdom.[77] Resistance to such projects had also grown in France. Although plans for Franco-German economic cooperation, notably in the exploitation of Moroccan and Tunisian mineral resources, had formed an important part of the 1954 declaration of La Celle-St-Cloud, the rapidly changing situation in

[75] Schreiben Nr. 4728/55 von Paul Frank, Paris, 4 November 1955, PA/AA, B24/13/F3.

[76] Cahn and Müller, *RFA et guerre d'Algérie*, pp. 34–6; Müller, 'Réalisme', pp. 413–16; Müller, 'Bundesrepublik', pp. 617–18.

[77] Aufzeichnung Nr.4088, 27 November 1954; Fernschreiben Nr.1370, 6 April 1955; Unterredung, 30 April 1955, in *Die Bundesrepublik Deutschland und Frankreich: Dokumente 1949–1963* (BDFD), Vol. 2, *Wirtschaft* (ed.) Andreas Wilkens (Munich, 1997), pp. 391–95, 448–56, 1074; Sabah Bouhsini, *Die Rolle Nordafrikas (Marokko, Algerien, Tunesien) in den deutsch-französischen Beziehungen von 1950–1962* (Aachen, 2000), pp. 146–59; Sylvie Lefèvre, 'Associer l'Allemagne au développement économique de l'Afrique: un leitmotiv français avant la décolonisation (1950–1956)', *RA* 31/3–4 (1999), p. 477; Andreas Wilkens, 'Vom Rhein bis zum Kongo. Französisch-deutsche Wirtschaftsprojekte und Politik in Afrika 1950–1959', *RA* 31/3–4 (1999), pp. 487, 491–2.

the protectorates meant that the *Quai d'Orsay* now opposed collective initiatives in the Maghreb. Its Directorate for Economic and Financial Affairs maintained, 'it was not by enlarging these problems to discussions of the Europe of Six that one will facilitate a solution, quite the contrary'.[78] The deteriorating situation in North Africa also contributed to the *Quai d'Orsay*'s initial resistance to the European Common Market, an idea first proposed at the Messina conference of June 1955. To French diplomats, a sovereign, economically powerful Federal Republic had everything to gain from a '*relance européenne*', while France would forfeit its independence and European leadership.[79]

Contrary to Frank therefore, most German diplomats felt that any collective European or German attempts to help solve the Algerian predicament, however well intended, would result in charges of malevolent interference. After all, rumours of German meddling and subversion in North Africa, as discussed in the previous chapter, had never really gone away. They were rekindled in February 1956, when French newspaper *Combat* accused 'numerous German agents' of disseminating anti-French propaganda in Algeria.[80] To Maltzan, the accusations were symptomatic of France's discomfort over the revival of German economic and military power after the abrogation of the Occupation Statute.[81] West Germany thus had to avoid giving the impression that it was trying to acquire French economic and political positions in North Africa.[82]

This left the Adenauer government in a quandary over how best to placate French opinion in the Algerian question without being criticised by the FLN's Third World allies. One way to manage the dilemma was through what Müller and Cahn have called '*Spagatpolitik*' (policy of the splits) that sought to satisfy both sides in the Algerian war. Since the two poles of the split invariably cancelled one another out, the *Spagatpolitik* essentially amounted to a policy of non-engagement.[83] 'In questions concerning French policies in North Africa', the *Auswärtige Amt* instructed its diplomats in December 1955,

[78] Cited in: Ghislain Sayer, 'Le Quai d'Orsay et la construction de la Petite Europe: l'avènement de la Communauté économique européenne (1955–1957)', *Relations internationales* 101 (2000), p. 93.

[79] Sayer, 'Quai d'Orsay', pp. 91, 93, 98; Michael Sutton, *France and the Construction of Europe, 1944–2007. The Geopolitical Imperative* (New York, 2007), pp. 117–21.

[80] Claude Delmas, 'La discussion sur la canalisation de la Moselle. La propagande allemande en Algérie', *Combat*, 21 February 1956; 'Gibt es in Algerien deutsche Agenten? Französische Presse gibt Hinweise auf Beweismaterial', *Frankfurter Rundschau*, 22 February 1956.

[81] *Kabinettsprotokolle – 1956*, Sondersitzung, 12 April 1956, p. 301.

[82] Michels, 'Bundesrepublik', pp. 442, 444–5; Wilkens, 'Vom Rhein', p. 487.

[83] Müller and Cahn, *RFA et guerre d'Algérie*, pp. 31–36; Müller, 'Réalisme', pp. 409–28; Ibid., 'Bundesrepublik', pp. 609–41.

> the federal government principally maintains the greatest reserve, and out of consideration to relations with the Arab states it has become impossible for [Bonn] to express its opinion in any way, or even to allow for the presumption of a standpoint [. . .] through the attitude of its official representatives abroad.[84]

By the following year, the *Amt* declared that, although it welcomed 'every [. . .] initiative through which the North African problem can be solved in such a way as to satisfy Western European interests', the Bonn government would remain uninvolved.[85]

The policy of non-engagement stood in stark contrast to Frank's earlier recommendations and should have presented a straightforward balancing act for German diplomacy. In practice, it became an acrobatic feat. From the time of its inception in late 1955, non-engagement proved more of a façade than an observed policy. Though professing its neutrality rhetorically, the Bonn government in fact came to side with France in the Algerian question. Frank's arguments, it seems, had won the day. By supporting France's Algerian policies, the Adenauer government sought to bolster the fragile Fourth Republic and advance the goals of *Westbindung*, which the chancellor deemed more important than relations to the Third World. This policy was already achieving results. Thus, France's growing preoccupation with Algeria helped detract attention from the disputed fate of the Saarland, rendered acute once again when the state's population unexpectedly rejected Paris's plan for a European statute. French reactions to the outcome of the 23 October 1955 referendum only remained subdued because, by then, Algeria had come to surpass the Saarland as the country's most pressing political and security concern. From Bonn's perspective, this presented a favourable atmosphere for a speedy and final solution to the Saar question.[86] In sanctioning the Saarland's phased integration with West Germany, the resultant Treaty of Luxemburg of 27 October 1956 eliminated a major obstacle to Franco-German reconciliation. On 1 January 1957, the territory was politically united with the FRG, though it remained bound to France economically until July 1959.[87]

[84] Vermerk, Referat 302 (Dr Kassler), 21 December 1955, PA/AA, B25/3; also: Michels, 'Bundesrepublik', p. 443.

[85] Aufzeichnung Nr.3654/56, Referat 302, 1956, PA/AA, B25/3.

[86] Schreiben Nr.4728/55 der Botschaft Paris, 4 November 1955, PA/AA, B24/13/F3.

[87] Jean-Paul Cahn, *Le Second Retour: le rattachement de la Sarre à l'Allemagne, 1955–1957* (Bern, 1985); B.W. Long, 'The Saar Dispute in Franco-German Relations and European Integration: French Diplomacy, Cultural Policies and the Construction of European Identity in the Saar, 1944–1957', PhD Dissertation (Indiana University, 2007), pp. 278–333; Lappenküper, *Deutsch-französische Beziehungen* I, pp. 1076–1138.

If, as both Adenauer and Mollet maintained, the solution of the Saar dispute created a new basis for a Franco-German entente, then the Suez crisis cemented that processes still further.[88] Washington's hostility to the Anglo-French-Israeli collusion and the rapid reversal of London's attitude towards the military expedition had left France feeling isolated and betrayed. Fears of American unilateralism and isolationism reinforced convictions in Paris and Bonn of the need not just for greater Franco-German cooperation but also for a stronger Europe.[89] On 6 November 1956 as the crisis reached its peak, and against the advice of the *Auswärtige Amt*, which, sensitive of world opinion, had counselled reserve, Adenauer travelled to Paris to set a 'sign of unison' that would herald a period of unprecedented Franco-German partnership and pave the way for the disputed '*relance européenne*'.[90]

To Louis Armand, a close aid to Jean Monnet, one of the chief architects of European unity, Nasser had become 'the federator of Europe'.[91] The Suez crisis convinced the chancellor of the need to rethink Bonn's objections to the association of Europe's – especially France's – overseas territories to the Common Market and to the creation of a common overseas investment fund. Proposed at the Venice conference of foreign ministers in May 1956, the French, after initial hesitations, had made these demands the *conditio sine qua non* of their participation in the Common Market. This had sparked controversy in Bonn. Some cabinet members, especially Ludwig Erhard, the influential economics minister and architect of the *Wirtschaftswunder*, were sceptical of the proposals' economic benefits and feared they might implicate Bonn in France's colonial quagmire. Others, including Adenauer and Brentano, were more sympathetic, especially after the Suez debacle. They shared the view being propagated by the French whereby Europe could only regain an independent voice in world politics if it retained and strengthened its influence over Africa.[92] As Mollet

88 Lappenküper, *Deutsch-französische Beziehungen* I, pp. 1135–8.

89 Schreiben Nr.4961/56 der Botschaft Paris (Maltzan), 14 December 1956, PA/AA, B24/273/F5.

90 Klaus-Jürgen Müller, 'Suez 1956: Die Bundesrepublik zwischen London, Paris und Washington', in *Grossbritannien und Deutschland. Gesellschaftliche, kulturelle und politische Beziehungen im 19. und 20. Jahrhundert* (eds.) Frank Otto and Thilo Schulz (Rheinfelden, 1999), p. 195. Also: Pfeiffer, 'Erfolgreiches Kapitel', pp. 213–32.

91 Peo Hansen and Stefan Jonsson, 'Bringing Africa as a "Dowry to Europe"', *Interventions* 13/3 (2011), p. 457; Mathieu Segers, *Deutschlands Ringen mit der* Relance*: Die Europapolitik der BRD während der Beratungen und Verhandlungen über die Römischen Verträge* (Bern, 2008), pp. 13–24.

92 On the evolution of the Eurafrican idea: Marie-Thérèse Bitsch and Gérard Bossuat (eds.), *L'Europe Unie et l'Afrique. De l'idée d'Eurafrique à la convention de Lomé I* (Bruxelles, 2005); Yves Montarsolo, *L'Eurafrique contrepoint de l'idée d'Europe. Le cas français de la fin de la deuxième guerre mondiale aux négociations des Traités de Rome* (Aix-en-Provence, 2010); Thomas Moser, *Europäische Integration,*

put it in February 1957, only *Eurafrica* would save Western Europe from insignificance:

> Cooperation with Africa is the most beautiful chance that Europe has ever had. Once this matter by the foundation of the Common Market is settled on the economic level, this union of two continents will further develop in the fields of politics and strategy and will possibly form an important factor in the global balance of power.[93]

In accepting the Eurafrican idea, France's allies secured the fate of the historic treaties establishing the Common Market and Euratom, which were signed in Rome on 25 March 1957. To achieve this important foreign policy goal, Adenauer was ultimately willing to make a 'substantial sacrifice'.[94] He agreed to contribute $200 million to a newly invested European (overseas) Development Fund (EDF), which was endowed with $581.25 million for an initial five-year period. More importantly, the chancellor convinced his allies to accept Mollet's final and most controversial demand: the incorporation into the Common Market not only of France's overseas dominions but also of Algeria.[95]

Europe, then, was to become a partner in what historian Stephan Malinowski has called France's 'modernization war' in Algeria, just as Mollet claimed it would bring 'progress, happiness and democracy to Africa'.[96] Although Algeria was excluded from the EDF, which only applied to overseas territories, the Common Market was seen as vital to Algerian development. To General Jacques Massu, commander of the elite 10th Parachute Division and chief architect of French operations during the Battle of Algiers, Eurafrica provided an essential framework for *guerre révolutionnaire*, for only by drawing on the widest possible range of resources could France carry out the vast programme of socio-economic and political reforms required to win over the hearts and minds of the

Dekolonisation, Eurafrika: eine historische Analyse über Entstehungsbedingungen der Eurafrikanischen Gemeinschaft von der Weltwirtschaftskrise bis zum Jaundé-Vertrag, 1929–1963 (Baden-Baden, 2000).

93 Cited in: Louis Sicking, 'A Colonial Echo: France and the Colonial Dimension of the European Economic Community', *French Colonial History* 5 (2004), p. 212.

94 Lappenküper, *Deutsch-französische Beziehungen* I, p. 1045.

95 Sicking, 'Colonial Echo', pp. 207–28; Béatrice Dedinger, 'L'Allemagne, l'association des pays et territoires d'outre-mer français et la politique communautaire de développement', *RA* 31/3–4 (1999), pp. 497–502; Lefèvre, 'Associer', pp. 363–80; Guido Thiemeyer, 'West German Perceptions of Africa and the Association of the Overseas Territories with the Common Market 1956–1957', in *L'Europe Unie et l'Afrique*, pp. 269–86. Also: Muriam Haleh Davis, 'Producing Eurafrica: Development, Agriculture and Race in Algeria, 1958–1965', PhD Dissertation (New York University, 2015).

96 Hansen and Jonsson, 'Dowry', p. 445. Malinowski, 'Modernisierungskriege', pp. 213–48.

Algerian population.[97] As French Foreign Minister Christian Pineau declared before the UN General Assembly's Political Committee in February 1957, 'participation in Eurafrica would mean for Algeria comfort, riches – in other words, the true condition of independence'. That independence, so the argument went, could only be achieved as part of France and Western Europe.[98]

From Bonn's perspective, the Rome treaties represented a momentous step in achieving Adenauer's aims of equality and cooperation within the Western alliance. Yet the *Auswärtige Amt* remained ill at ease with Algeria's inclusion in the Common Market, which it feared would elicit further accusations on the part of the GDR or the Third World of West German collusion in France's colonial war. With allegations of French torture practices beginning to abound, particularly in the context of the Battle of Algiers, such accusations became a growing concern. At any rate, the Paris embassy considered the Common Market 'a chimera' as long as the Algerian war continued to consume all of France's energy and resources.[99] Until its resolution, the Bonn government had little choice but to build the Franco-German entente through 'persistent, patient cooperation'.[100] Most importantly, German diplomats understood that 'France will presently always measure [Germany's] readiness for a genuine cooperation in proportion to the understanding that the Federal Republic showed for France's Algerian question'.[101] In his inaugural speech as ambassador to Bonn in October 1956, Maurice Couve de Murville had stated that as long as the Adenauer government supported France in its 'overseas' troubles, French governments would also defend Bonn's standpoint on reunification and rearmament.[102] By linking France's 'overseas' (i.e. Algerian) troubles to the all-important German question, the *Quai d'Orsay* had created an effective instrument through which to pressurise the *Auswärtige Amt*. After all, as long as Germany was divided, its freedom of action remained constricted. As Karl Carstens, head of the *Amt*'s Western department, reminded ambassadors in the Middle East in April 1956, if the Bonn government wanted to implement its *Westpolitik*, German diplomats would have to avoid all controversies with Europe's 'problem child'.[103] Although they believed

[97] Schreiben Nr.1330/57 der Botschaft Paris, 1 February 1957; PA/AA, B24/274/F1.
[98] Cited in: Hansen and Jonsson, 'Dowry', p. 459.
[99] Schreiben Nr.2974 der Botschaft Paris, 5 July 1957, PA/AA, B24/263/F2.
[100] Schreiben Nr.1800/57 der Botschaft Paris, 18 March 1957, PA/AA, B24/310/F2.
[101] Aufzeichnung Nr.3654/56, Referat 302, 1956, PA/AA, B25/3.
[102] Notiz, Protokoll an Referat 302, 10 October 1956, PA/AA, B24/292/F1.
[103] Vortrag Karl Carstens, Istanbul Konferenz deutscher Botschafter, 3–7 March 1956, PA/AA, B2/94.

that 'France's efforts in North Africa were doomed to failure' and although these efforts continued to incur global condemnation, policy-makers in Bonn felt they had little choice but to support Paris in the Algerian question.[104]

Acquiescence to Algeria's incorporation into the Common Market represented just one out of several measures through which the Adenauer government sought to demonstrate this support. German diplomats also backed the *Quai d'Orsay* at the UN. Though an observer-state with no vote of its own, the FRG interceded with a number of UN member-states so as to prevent the passing of Afro-Asian resolutions calling for Algerian independence. These interventions occurred with utmost discretion not only to avoid accusations of West German collusion but also to prevent undermining France's own argument at the UN, which rested on the premise that the Algeria problem remained an internal affair. Bonn's secret demarches predominantly targeted the UN's twenty-two Latin American members, who tended to vacillate in their attitudes between sympathy for anti-colonialism and a cultural affinity for France.[105] Judging by the available evidence, Brentano first ordered these interventions on 6 February 1957 ahead of a General Assembly debate that was expected to be particularly acrimonious coming just after Suez as well as General Massu's ruthless clampdown in Algiers on an FLN-organised general strike. Brentano instructed his representatives in Latin America to underline how Moscow alone would benefit from an internationalisation of the Algerian problem.[106] The *Quai d'Orsay* 'very deeply appreciated' Bonn's mediation and requested another round of covert intercessions later that year.[107] Latin American moderation did indeed ensure that the December 1957 UN resolution on Algeria was significantly toned down.[108] Bonn's role in securing this outcome remains less clear.

104 *Kabinettsprotokolle, 1956*, Sondersitzung, 12 March 1956, p. 301. Also: Schreiben Nr.5060/56 der Botschaft Paris (Maltzan), 21 December 1956, PA/AA, B24/273/F6.

105 René Girault, 'La France en accusation à l'ONU, ou les pouvoirs d'une organisation internationale', *Relations Internationales* 76 (1993), p. 415.

106 Schreiben Nr.537/57 der Botschaft Buenos Aires, 12 February 1957, PA/AA, B25/19; Fernschreiben Nr.78 der Dienststelle des Ständigen Beobachters bei den Vereinten Nationen (VN), New York, 20 February 1957, PA/AA, B25/7.

107 Télégramme no.1584 de Jean Jurgensen, chef du service d'Europe centrale, à l'ambassade de France à Bonn, 7 February 1957, MAE, EU/RFA/1272. Also: Schreiben Nr.1588/57 der Botschaft Paris (Maltzan), 20 February 1957; Fernschreiben Nr.658 der Botschaft Paris (Maltzan), 23 August 1957, PA/AA, B25/19; Schreiben Nr.1417/57 der Botschaft Santiago, 3 September 1957, PA/AA, B24/274/F2.

108 Meynier, *Histoire*, p. 588.

Within NATO, too, the Adenauer government became France's staunchest defender.[109] State Secretary Walter Hallstein represented a shrinking minority when he urged the NATO Council in March 1956 that 'we – all partners of the Atlantic community – must help' in subduing the Algerian rebellion, if only by offering France moral support.[110] The Bonn government then practised what it preached by supporting the Paris authorities in their drawn-out dispute over Anglo-American arms deliveries to Tunis during the autumn of 1957.[111] Frustrated by the growing Algerian presence in Tunisia, where the FLN had recently established its headquarters, the French government had suspended arms shipments to Tunis, convinced that these benefited the ALN. French intransigence had prompted President Habib Bourguiba to request arms from France's NATO allies instead, especially from Washington and London. As leverage, he threatened to turn to Cairo or Moscow if his demands were not met. The Paris government, meanwhile, worked hard to convince its allies to desist from meeting Tunis's requests.[112] Adenauer defended the French argument that Western arms deliveries were likely to benefit the ALN given the Tunisian regime's open support of the Algerians. The chancellor rejected a Tunisian request for West German arms and vowed to prevent future weapons exports to North Africa.[113] Desperate to mend the growing rift within NATO, Adenauer tried to convince the influential American journalists Cyrus Sulzberger and Joseph Alsop of the strategic importance of Algeria in the war against communism. In December 1957, he promised French Premier Félix Gaillard to intervene personally in Washington and London, though he did so to little avail.[114]

By late 1957, therefore, West German policy had decisively turned away from the principle of non-engagement in the Algerian question. In an

109 Cahn and Müller, *RFA et guerre d'Algérie*, p. 34; Ziebura, *Deutsch-französischen Beziehungen*, p. 91.

110 Vortrag vor dem NATO Defence College, Berlin, 24 March 1956, PA/AA, B1/62.

111 Note par Henri Langlais, chef de la Mission de liaison pour les affaires algériennes (MLA), à Robert Lacoste, ministre-résident de l'Algérie, 18 December 1957, MAE, EU/RFA/1272.

112 Connelly, *Diplomatic Revolution*, pp. 144–54; Thomas, *French*, pp. 147–52; Wall, *France*, pp. 68, 70, 91–6.

113 Télégramme no.2271 par M. Couve de Murville à M. Pineau, 5 September 1957, *Documents Diplomatiques Français* (*DDF*), 1957, Vol.II/159, pp. 336–38; Wall, *France*, p. 92.

114 Informationsgespräche mit Cyrus Sulzberger, 6 August 1957 und mit Joseph Alsop, 13 August 1957, in *Adenauer. Teegespräche, 1955–1958* (eds.) Rudolf Morsey and Hans-Peter Schwarz (Berlin, 1986), pp. 212, 225–6; 'Unterredung zwischen Bundeskanzler Adenauer und Präsident des Ministerrates Gaillard vom 15 December 1957', in BDFD, Bd.1 (eds.) Horst Möller and Klaus Hildebrand (Munich, 1997), pp. 561–4; Kommentar von Paul Frank (Referat 302) auf Schreiben des Generalkonsulats Algiers (Hendus), 7 January 1958, PA/AA, B25/4; Adenauer, *Erinnerungen*, pp. 339–42, 401–3.

ironic twist of fate, the conflict that so roused French xenophobia and conspiracy theories had helped turn West Germany – the 'hereditary enemy' – into France's only true friend.[115] As Bonn's embassy in Paris noted, even the influential daily *Le Monde* had dropped its habitual criticism of the FRG for more appreciative tones, declaring on 3 December 1957 that Franco-German relations were no longer marred by disagreements.[116] Some months earlier, Couve de Murville reported from Bonn:

> It is clear the federal government, and in particular the *Auswärtige Amt*, very deeply desires to avoid all that can harm the harmony in Franco-German relations [. . .] we can count on the cooperation of our interlocutors.[117]

The ambassador was not mistaken. Though it did so circuitously so as to shield the government from accusations that it helped finance France's war in Algeria, Bonn agreed in January 1958 to finance 80 per cent of a European Payments Union (EPU) loan for $250 million to France, whose budgetary situation had become ruinous partly because of the Algerian conflict.[118] When the Sakiet crisis and Anglo-American "good offices" mission once again threatened the unity of the Atlantic alliance, Brentano urged the Bonn government to 'face the French with absolute openness by avoiding everything that amounts to support for France's opponents'.[119] The *Quai d'Orsay* observed that Adenauer, in particular, 'manifested a total comprehension for our current position', having even 'engaged to make his opinion known publicly during the discussion of the problem at the NATO council's session in Copenhagen next May'.[120]

The fall of Gaillard's government on 15 April 1958 prevented the chancellor from delivering on this promise. Even so, by the time the settlers' revolt broke out in Algiers on 13 May 1958, the Adenauer government could no longer claim to be a neutral bystander in the Algerian war. Instead, it had become France's closest ally and friend, offering diplomatic, moral, even financial support. Bonn's policy of support in the Algerian question

115 Ziebura, *Deutsch-französischen Beziehungen*, pp. 90–1.

116 Aufzeichnung des Presse- und Informationsamts der Bundesregierung, 4 December 1957, PA/AA, B24/279/F2.

117 Dépêche no.1107 par M. Couve de Murville à M. Pineau, 1 July 1957, DDF, 1957, Vol.II/6, p. 16.

118 *Die Kabinettsprotokolle der Bundesregierung.* Vol.10 – *1957* (eds.) Ulrich Enders und Josef Henke (Munich, 2000), 5. Sitzung, 27 November 1957, pp. 429–30; Connelly, *Diplomatic Revolution*, pp. 155–58; Cahn and Müller, *RFA et guerre d'Algérie*, p. 124.

119 Cited in: Lappenküper, 'Adenauer', p. 606. Also: Marcowitz, 'Unionsparteien', p. 556; Michels, 'Bundesrepublik', p. 444.

120 Télégramme circulaire du *Quai d'Orsay* aux postes OTAN, 2 April 1958, MAE, EU/RFA/1259*.

significantly contributed to the Franco-German rapprochement, for it helped build trust in Paris.[121] This policy came at a cost, however, for it strained relations to the Arab world, creating diplomatic opportunities for the GDR. Algeria, then, remained a 'cancerous sore', as Jansen put it, whose 'danger of contagion' grew with every day.[122] Nothing demonstrated that danger more than the Sakiet crisis. Not only did that crisis precipitate the fall of the Gaillard government, it also triggered the collapse of the entire Fourth Republic. More importantly, the Sakiet crisis highlighted the dangers of hosting insurgents. By offering sanctuary to the FLN and ALN, the Tunisian government had set itself on a perilous and ultimately deadly path of confrontation with France.[123] What made the Sakiet crisis so alarming was the fact that the Bonn government was itself no longer immune to this form of contagion. For by 1958, West Germany, too, was well on its way to becoming an extraterritorial sanctuary for the FLN.

121 On the importance of trust to Franco-German reconciliation, see: Philipp Brugger, Andreas Hasenclever and Lukas Kasten, 'Theorizing the Impact of Trust on Post-Agreement Negotiations: The Case of Franco-German Security Relations', *International Negotiation* 18 (2013), pp. 441–69. Many thanks to Jan Ruzicka for pointing out this title.

122 Schreiben Nr.1077/57 der Botschaft Paris (Jansen), 11 January 1957, PA/AA, B24/310/F1.

123 Aufzeichnung, Referat 302, 10 March 1958, PA/AA, B24/311/F1.

CHAPTER 3

The FLN's implantation in West Germany

Considering the Adenauer government's tenacious pursuit of a Franco-German entente, the Bonn Republic should have made an unlikely and unattractive refuge for the FLN.[1] And yet the period between November 1954 and May 1958 witnessed a steady influx of Algerians into West Germany, producing something of a paradox. On the one hand, the country emerged as France's only true ally in the Algerian war, and on the other it became the chief sanctuary of the FLN's *Fédération en France* that would spearhead the insurgency's second armed front. What prompted this development? And more importantly, how did authorities in Paris and Bonn respond to the emergence of an Algerian sanctuary on federal territory? This chapter highlights the extent to which the exodus of Algerians from the metropole challenged French counterinsurgency efforts. Mindful of the threat this development posed to national security, French authorities sought to restrict Algerians' movements to prevent the FLN from establishing bases and sanctuaries beyond their reach. From the perspective of the West German security services, meanwhile, the Algerians did not present an immediate threat. Their response to the FLN's presence was conditioned less by the diplomatic imperative of Franco-German reconciliation than by the domestic imperative of upholding the sovereign *Rechtsstaat*. As this chapter will show, these twin imperatives were far from compatible, producing some paradoxical results.

[1] Some sections of this chapter draw on material first published in: Mathilde von Bülow, 'Franco-German Intelligence Cooperation and the Internationalization of Algeria's War of Independence (1954–62)', *Intelligence and National Security* 28/3 (2013), pp. 397–419 (www.tandfonline.com/doi/abs/10.1080/02684527.2013.789638); Ibid., 'Exposing the "Paradoxical Citizenship": French Authorities' Responses to the Algerian Presence in Federal Germany during the Algerian War, 1954–1962', in *The French Colonial Mind. Vol. 2: Violence, Military Encounters, and Colonialism* (ed.) Martin Thomas (Lincoln NB, 2011), pp. 304–33; Ibid., 'Hôtes importuns. Des Algériens en République fédérale pendant la guerre d'Algérie', in *Migrations et identités. L'exemple de l'Allemagne aux XIXe et XXe siècles* (eds.) Jean-Paul Cahn and Bernard Poloni (Villeneuve d'Ascq, 2009), pp. 119–29.

First warnings

The first indication of an Algerian presence in West Germany came in early June 1956, when former French premier Antoine Pinay approached Bonn's minister for atomic questions, Franz-Josef Strauss, with a most unusual request. Agents of the FLN, Pinay confidentially informed Adenauer's closest political ally, had been secretly meeting with Egyptian emissaries in West Germany. Such gatherings had previously occurred in Switzerland, Pinay explained, which had long been the preferred rendezvous for Arab nationalists.[2] Recently, however, the Swiss authorities had cracked down on these meetings. French intelligence, it transpired, had even manoeuvred Swiss prosecutor-general René Dubois into authorising illicit wire taps in the Egyptian embassy in Bern, from where the FLN's external delegates supposedly coordinated much of their activity.[3] Dubois' clampdown, it appeared, persuaded the FLN to transfer some of its subversive activities to West Germany. To counter this dangerous development, Pinay proposed to Strauss the creation of an informal and transnational 'Catholic front' against the FLN. The proposition echoed French propaganda, which depicted the Algerian war as a civilisational struggle between the 'Christian West' (or *christliche Abendland*) on the one hand and Islam or communism on the other.[4] As leader of the Christian Social Union (CSU), whose power base was in staunchly Catholic Bavaria, Strauss would have been amenable to such arguments. So would Adenauer as head of the Christian Democratic Union (CDU), whose condescension for 'coloured peoples' was noted earlier.[5] In concrete terms, Pinay proposed establishing a top-secret liaison between West Germany's *Bundesamt für*

[2] Montreux was one of the FLN's five initial external bases, along with Cairo, Tanger, Nador and Madrid. See: Meynier, *Histoire*, p. 551, n. 6.

[3] Damien Carron, *La Suisse et la guerre d'indépendance algérienne (1954–1962)* (Lausanne, 2013), pp. 19, 119–30, 152–97; Charles-Henri Favrod, 'La Suisse des négociations secrètes', in *Guerre d'Algérie et français* (ed.) Rioux, pp. 397–8; Marc Perrenoud, 'La Suisse et les accords d'Évian: la politique de la Confédération à la fin de la guerre d'Algérie', *Politorbis. Revue trimestrielle de la politique étrangère* 31/2 (2002), pp. 12–14.

[4] Connelly, 'Rethinking', pp. 221–45; Ibid., 'Taking off', pp. 739–69.

[5] On the pervasiveness of ideas about the 'Christian West' and their juxtaposition with the communist or Eastern-Oriental 'Other' in post-war West Germany, see: Eric D. Weitz, 'The Ever-Present Other. Communism in the Making of West Germany', in *The Miracle Years. A Cultural History of West Germany, 1949–1968* (ed.) Hanna Schissler (Princeton NJ, 2001), pp. 219–32; Axel Schildt and Arnold Sywottek, '"Reconstruction" and "Modernization": West German Social History during the 1950s', in *West Germany under Construction: Politics, Society, and Culture in the Adenauer Era* (ed.) Robert G. Moeller (Ann Arbor MI, 1997), p. 437; Axel Schildt, *Zwischen Abendland und Amerika. Studien zur westlichen Ideenlandschaft der 50er Jahre* (München, 1999). On the transnational history of the idea: Johannes Großmann, *Die Internationale der Konservativen. Transnationale Elitenzirkel und private Außenpolitik in Westeuropa seit 1945* (München, 2014).

Verfassungsschutz (BfV), or domestic intelligence service, and France's national police, or *Sûreté Nationale*, one dedicated exclusively to Algerian affairs.[6]

Signs of FLN agitation in West Germany had indeed begun to multiply in 1956, with intelligence even warning of an attack on French diplomatic personnel on Bastille Day.[7] Though it proved false, this intelligence undoubtedly prompted another confidential demarche around the same time as Pinay's – that of Colonel Duchène, who represented the French security and intelligence services in Bonn, with BfV President Hubert Schrübbers.[8] Playing on Adenauer's policy of *Westbindung* and the ingrained anti-communism of most West German officials, Duchène depicted the FLN as a Soviet puppet. He stressed how the French press had become suspicious of Algerian–German collusion, but reassured Schrübbers that these rumours were 'obviously spread by communist sources'. The East, Duchène maintained, 'was trying to implicate the Federal Republic in the internal difficulties of France so as to upset Franco-German relations'. Like Pinay, Duchène requested the implementation of strict but discreet controls of North Africans in West Germany, of which the French security and intelligence services attached to the headquarters of the French armed forces at Baden-Baden were to be kept informed.[9]

Considering Adenauer's supportive stance in the Algerian question, one would have expected the West German domestic security services to defer to these requests. In the Federal Interior Ministry, however, constitutional considerations outweighed diplomatic ones. 'We stand before the general question', asked Walter Bargatzky, who headed the ministry's public security department, 'whether it is reconcilable with the Federal Republic's liberal democratic order, when a violent overthrow abroad [i.e. Algeria] is secretly prepared on or supported from [German] territory'. To Bargatzky, the answer was no: tolerating subversive activity not only risked diminishing Bonn's diplomatic manoeuvring room, but it also

[6] Schreiben, Strauss an Staatssekretär Hans Ritter von Lex, Bundesministerium des Innern (BMI), 4 July 1956, Bundesarchiv (BA/K), Koblenz, B106/15600.

[7] Fernschreiben, BMI an Innenminister (–Senatoren) der Bundesländer, 13 July 1956, PA/AA, B24/292/F1.

[8] The available archives do not specify for which service Duchène (sometimes spelled Duchèsne) worked or when he arrived in Bonn. They suggest he acted on behalf of the military and domestic intelligence services. See: Aufzeichnung Nr. 462/56 für Abteilungsleiter öffentliche Sicherheit (VI), BMI, 18 July 1956, BA/K, B106/15600; Vermerk, Besprechung mit Duchène, 30 April 1959, BA/K, B106/15779.

[9] Aufzeichnung Nr. 462/56/BMI, 18 July 1956, BA/K, B106/156000.

violated the constitution, or Basic Law.[10] The ministry's legal department took a more nuanced view. It argued that FLN activities on federal territory were only unconstitutional if they disturbed the peaceful coexistence of nations by fomenting world revolution or if they undermined the Bonn Republic's own democratic order. Algerian nationalists, the legal experts argued, did neither.[11] Like many in the *Auswärtige Amt*, they mistrusted the French depiction of the Algerian insurgency as a communist conspiracy. Even so, Bargatzky advised the Federal Border Guard to look into ways of keeping the BfV and its external counterpart, the *Bundesnachrichtendienst* (BND), informed of the movements of North Africans. The French authorities, however, were to be informed only when these movements appeared particularly suspicious.[12]

In the summer of 1956, then, the Interior Ministry rejected the idea of a Franco-German front against the FLN and did little to hinder the movements of Algerians. While the fight against Algerian subversion was a matter of national security for France, it hardly interested the fledgling West German intelligence and security services, whose conception of national security focused on combating communist or neo-Nazi intrigues. Compared to those of Soviet-bloc agents, the machinations of a few anti-colonial nationalists must have appeared innocuous to West German spy-hunters.[13] As shall be seen, the Bonn government's apparent unwillingness to restrict Algerian movements was often interpreted by French officials both as sympathy towards the FLN and as a deliberate snub to France. Suspicions of intentional obstructionism proved to be unjustified. If anything, they reflected French conspiracy theories. After a decade of occupation, the Interior Ministry was simply keen to reassert its sovereign control over domestic affairs. This factor, more than any other, determined the authorities' reaction to Pinay and Duchène's demarches. Officials neither ruled out close Franco-German cooperation, nor could they given Adenauer's Francophile policies. Their actions in the Algerian question were guided by a desire to protect and uphold the country's newly won sovereignty.

[10] Notiz, Bargatzky an stellvertretenden Leiter VI/A/BMI, 19 July 1956, BA/K, B106/15600.

[11] Notiz, stellvertretender Leiter I/A (Verfassungsfragen) an stellvertretenden Leiter VI/A/BMI, 30 July 1956, BA/K, B106/15600; *Die Verfassung von Berlin und das Grundgesetz für die Bundesrepublik Deutschland* (GG), Landsezentrale für politische Bildungsarbeit (Berlin, 1991 edn), Art. 26, Para. 1, p. 43.

[12] Notiz, Bargatzky, 19 July 1956; Notiz, Abteilung VI/A/3/BMI, 12 August 1956, BA/K, B106/15600.

[13] On the formation and early priorities of the BfV, see: Wolfgang Buschfort, *Geheime Hüter der Verfassung: von der Düsseldorfer Informationsstelle zum ersten Verfassungsschutz der Bundesregierung (1947–1961)* (Paderborn, 2004).

The metropolitan front

To understand both French and German reactions to the FLN's activities on federal territory, it is essential to grasp why so many Algerians began to appear in West Germany from 1956. More than anything, this development stemmed from the Algerian war's impact on Algerian migrants in the metropole.[14] During the 1920s, these workers had constituted the crucible of Algerian populist nationalism.[15] Counting between 250,000 and 350,000, by the mid-1950s they had developed into a vital reservoir of financial and political support for the PPA-MTLD. After November 1954, both FLN and MNA competed for control over this sizeable community.[16]

Initially, France's Algerian community remained a Messalist stronghold; the FLN boasted a mere 200 militants.[17] To break this monopoly, the movement had 'to convince the Algerian people of its existence, then [...] give it confidence in its capacities, and finally [...] create structures through which those capacities could overcome French power and within which the people could begin to express its nationhood'.[18] In early 1955, Mohamed Boudiaf ordered the creation of the *Fédération du FLN en France* whose mission was fourfold: first, the elimination of Messalists or their integration into the *Fédération* as sympathisers, adherents, or

[14] See: Linda Amiri, *La Bataille de France: La guerre d'Algérie en Métropole* (Paris, 2004); House and MacMaster, *Paris*, part I; Neil MacMaster, *Colonial Migrants and Racism: Algerians in France, 1900–1962* (Basingstoke, 1997), ch. 11; Benjamin Stora, *Ils venaient d'Algérie. L'immigration algérienne en France (1912–1992)* (Paris, 1992), part II; Marc Bernardot, 'Une politique de logement: la SONACOTRA (1956–1992)', thèse de doctorat (Université Paris 1-Panthéon-Sorbonne, 1997); Ibid., 'Être interné au Larzac. La politique d'assignation à résidence surveillée pendant la guerre d'Algérie (1958–1962', *Politix* 69 (2005), pp. 39–62; Emmanuel Blanchard, *La police parisienne et les Algériens (1944–1962)* (Paris, 2011); Ibid., 'Contrôler, enfermer, éloigner. La répression policière et administrative des Algériens de metropole (1946–1962)', in *La France en guerre 1954–1962. Expériences métropolitaines de la guerre d'indépendance algérienne* (eds.) Raphaëlle Branche and Sylvie Thénault (Paris, 2008), pp. 318–31; Ibid., 'Police judiciaire et pratiques d'exception pendant la guerre d'Algérie', *Vingtième Siècle* 90 (2006), pp. 61–72; Peggy Derder, *L'immigration algérienne et les pouvoirs publics dans le département de la Seine 1954–1962* (Paris, 2003); Monique Hervo, *Chroniques du bidonville: Nanterre en guerre d'Algérie 1959–1962* (Paris, 2001); Amelia H. Lyons, 'The Civilizing Mission in the Metropole: Algerian Immigrants in France and the Politics of Adaptation during Decolonization', *Geschichte und Gesellschaft* 32 (2006), pp. 489–516; Jacques Simon, *L'immigration algérienne en France des origines à l'indépendance* (Paris, 2000), part IV; Special Issue, *Matériaux pour l'histoire de notre temps* 92 (2008) on 'L'internement en France pendant la guerre d'indépendance algérienne'.

[15] See: Rabah Aissaoui, '"Nous voulons déchirer le bâillon et briser nos chaines": Racism, Colonialism and Universalism in the Discourse of Algerian Nationalists in France between the Wars', *French History* 17/2 (2003), pp. 186–209; Kaddache, *Histoire* vol. I.

[16] See note 14 and: Mohammed Harbi, *Une Vie debout: Mémoires politiques 1945–1962*, vol. I (Paris, 2001), chs. 4–7; Ibid., *FLN*, pp. 143–58; Ali Haroun, *La Septième Wilaya: La Guerre du FLN en France 1954–1962* (Paris, 1986), chs. 1, 15, 18.

[17] Djerbal, *L'OS*, p. 37. [18] Ruedy, *Modern Algeria*, pp. 156–7.

militants; second, the imposition of a 'revolutionary tax' on the Algerian community to help finance the war effort; third, the organisation of clandestine 'shock groups' to enforce discipline and collect this tax; and fourth, the sensitisation of French public opinion and formation of European support networks. For this purpose, the FLN divided France, together with Belgium and the Saarland, which at the time remained tied to France in a customs union and also boasted sizeable Algerian communities, into political and administrative districts mirroring those created in Algeria. The *Fédération* further established commissions to tackle specific issues such as press and information, hygiene, justice and the welfare of detainees. In late 1956, it created an underground army, the *Organisation Spéciale*, charged with organising the insurgency's second front. By forming alternative institutions that sought to govern a section of French civil society and claiming the right to exert legitimate violence, the *Fédération* aspired to create a state within the state. It constituted an essential appendix to the FLN.[19]

The *Fédération*'s implantation did not go unchallenged by the MNA. By 1956, the contest between the two movements had evolved into what Algerian novelist Kateb Yacine called 'a war within a war, a sinister fratricide' that would claim 4,000 Algerian lives and leave another 10,000 wounded.[20] According to Gilbert Meynier and Ali Haroun, a member of the *Fédération*'s executive, assassinations became so commonplace that the woodlands of north-eastern France and the Saarland resembled 'cemeteries of cadres' while the French and German police regularly retrieved suitcases containing dismembered bodies out of the Rhine.[21] The French press spoke of 'North African terrorism' that soon surpassed the realm of intercommunal violence, for by late 1956 the *Fédération* began to target symbols of French colonial repression: police constables and collaborators, including Algerian politicians and auxiliary police forces.[22] Through a combined

[19] See: Linda Amiri, 'La Fédération de France du Front de Libération Nationale: 1954–1962. Organisation politico-administrative', thèse de doctorat (Institut d'Études Politiques de Paris, 2013); Djerbal, *L'OS*; Meynier, *Histoire*, pp. 531–44; Haroun, *Septième wilaya*, chs. 1–3; Harbi, *Vie debout*, ch. 6.

[20] Cited in: Benjamin Stora, 'La gauche et les minorités anticoloniales françaises devant les divisions du nationalisme algérien (1954–1958)', in *Guerre d'Algérie et français* (ed.) Rioux, p. 63. See also: MacMaster, *Colonial Migrants*, p. 195; Stora, *Ils venaient*, pp. 206–9; Rabah Aissaoui, 'Fratricidal War: The Conflict between the Mouvement national algérien (MNA) and the Front de libération nationale (FLN) in France during the Algerian War (1954–1962)', *British Journal of Middle Eastern Studies* 39/2 (2012), pp. 227–40.

[21] Haroun, *Septième wilaya*, p. 259; Meynier, *Histoire*, pp. 538–9.

[22] Djerbal, *L'OS*, p. 43; Roger Faligot and Pascal Krop, *DST. Police Secrète* (Paris, 1999), pp. 190–2; Raymond Muelle, *7 ans de guerre en France. Quand le FLN frappait en métropole* (Monaco, 1994), pp. 74, 87–8, 94.

strategy of ruthless liquidations and forceful propaganda, the FLN strengthened its support among the Algerian community. By late 1957, its militants numbered over 15,000. The French police's Directorate of Territorial Surveillance, or *Direction de la Surveillance du Territoire* (DST), believed the movement had effectively marginalised the MNA, though it never managed to destroy its rival completely.[23]

Algerian workers in France also came under increasing pressure from the police and security services, which waged their own battle against the FLN and MNA. Recent works by scholars such as Emmanuel Blanchard, Linda Amiri, Jim House and Neil MacMaster have highlighted the ruthless and unrelenting nature of the police's crackdown on the Algerian community in the metropole during the Algerian war. Legally French citizens since the end of World War II, in practice, Algerians on either side of the Mediterranean remained subjected to racism, segregation and discrimination.[24] After the outbreak of the FLN's insurgency, the metropolitan security services reintroduced methods of colonial policing and repression that had largely been abolished in 1944.[25] A decree dated 22 October 1955 established a national identity card in an ostensible move to standardise administrative procedures that had previously been the preserve of departmental prefectures. Subsequent rulings made possession of the new ID card a prerequisite for passport applications, and hence foreign travel. To enable still greater control and surveillance, the authorities in March 1956 reintroduced a restrictive permit system for travel between Algeria and France.[26]

Obligatory for all French citizens, these regulations infringed on Algerians' rights in an indirect manner: they enabled the authorities to monitor the movements of Algerians and to conduct a close census of this

[23] Faligot and Krop, *DST*, p. 172; Muelle, *7 ans*, pp. 70, 88.

[24] See: John Barzman, 'Citoyens, sujets, immigrés: quelques aspects de la législation française en Algérie et à l'égard des personnes originaires d'Algérie', *Cahiers de Sociologie économique et culturelle/ Ethnopsychologie* 21 (1994), pp. 111–27; Laure Blévis, 'Droit colonial algérien de la citoyenneté: conciliation illusoire entre des principes républicains et une logique d'occupation coloniale (1865–1947)', in *Guerre d'Algérie* (ed.) Ageron (Paris, 2000), pp. 87–103; Alexis Spire, 'Semblables et pourtant différents. La citoyenneté paradoxale des 'Français Musulmans d'Algérie' en Métropole', *Genèses* 53 (2003), pp. 48–68.

[25] See: Emmanuel Blanchard, 'La dissolution des Brigades nord-africaines de la Préfecture de police: la fin d'une police d'exception pour les Algériens de Paris (1944–1953)?' *Bulletin de l'Institut Historique du Temps Présent* 83 (2004) www.ihtp.cnrs.fr/spip.php%3Farticle329&lang=fr.html (accessed 22 September 2010).

[26] Pierre Piazza, *Histoire de la Carte Nationale d'Identité* (Paris, 2004), pp. 289–99; Spire, 'Semblables', pp. 58–60; MacMaster, *Colonial Migrants*, ch. 8; Clifford Rosenberg, *Policing Paris: The Origins of Modern Immigration Control between the Wars* (Ithaca NY, 2006), ch. 5.

expanding community.[27] They were followed by the law of 26 July 1957, which introduced the first blatantly discriminatory measures by extending into France some of the 'special powers' that had previously only applied to Algeria. Apart from increased powers of arrest, the security services could now deploy arbitrary identity checks, raids and curfews against Algerians. These measures were supplemented in August 1957 by the creation of a national database of card-index files dedicated to 'dangerous individuals living in the metropole' and maintained by the police's general intelligence directorate, or *Renseignements Généraux* (RG). Similar in nature to the *Carnet-B*, a pre-World War I index system established to keep anti-militarists and peace activists under surveillance, which was also used during the interwar years to monitor anarchists and other extremists,[28] the *Fichier Z* allowed the metropolitan security and intelligence services to 'fight more effectively against subversive activities', including terrorism, and to 'follow the displacements of liaison agents, the members of commando groups, arms traffickers, etc.' A September 1957 directive specified that in compiling *Fichier Z*, security and intelligence officers were to pay particular attention to members of the FLN, that is, those 'nationalist agents whose elimination was deemed a priority' and 'who would already be incarcerated if the legal dispositions permitted it'.[29]

The exceptional and discriminatory legislation introduced between 1955 and 1957 reveals the general thrust of French counterinsurgency efforts in the metropole. At bottom, it sought to facilitate the identification and surveillance of Algerians in view of isolating and eliminating nationalist dissent. As in Algeria, the new discretionary measures served one fundamental purpose: the collection and collation of intelligence. Within the context of *guerre révolutionnaire*, accurate and actionable intelligence constituted the very bedrock upon which all other operations against the FLN were built.[30] Without it, the French security services would have struggled to dismantle the *Fédération de France*'s hierarchy of political and military

[27] Unless specified otherwise, the following paragraphs are based on Amiri, Blanchard, Bernardot, House and MacMaster referenced in note 14.

[28] Donald N. Baker, 'The Surveillance of Subversion in Interwar France: The Carnet B in the Seine, 1922–1940', *French Historical Studies* 10/3 (1978) pp. 486–516; Michael B. Miller, *Shanghai on the Metro: Spies, Intrigue, and the French between the Wars* (Berkeley CA, 1994); Rosenberg, *Policing Paris*.

[29] Cited in: Hélène Chaubin and Laurent Chevrel, 'Identifier les nationalistes algériens: les fichiers Z', in *France en guerre* (eds.) Branche and Thénault, pp. 332–3. Also: Bernard Deschamps, *Le Fichier Z, Essai d'histoire du FLN algérien dans le Gard (1954–1962)* (Pantin, 2004).

[30] Raphaëlle Branche, *La torture et l'armée pendant la guerre d'Algérie 1954–1962* (Paris, 2001), pp. 51–6, 176–211; Paret, *French Revolutionary Warfare*, chs. 4–5.

cadres or to strangulate the insurgents' resources and supplies, particularly their arms and ammunitions. With this in mind, in August 1955 the authorities had also established an inter-departmental committee (the *Service de coordination des informations nord-africaines*) that brought together representatives of the domestic police and intelligence agencies, SDECE, various social and administrative agencies, the justice ministry, and the military, and that ensured the effective dissemination and exploitation of all intelligence related to the Algerian war in France.[31]

The metropolitan authorities thus established a system of intelligence collection and anti-subversive action that strongly resembled procedures in place in Algeria. By 1958, the DST committed 70 per cent of its resources to the fight against Algerian nationalists.[32] Only after the appointment of former Vichy collaborator Maurice Papon as prefect of the Paris police in March 1958, however, did the adoption of colonial methods of policing and intelligence reach a climax in the metropole. Papon had ample experience as a colonial administrator in North Africa, having served in Constantine as inspector-general of the civil service from 1956 to 1958. In that capacity, he had enthusiastically embraced and implemented the principles of *guerre révolutionnaire*. A firm believer in the strategy of isolating the FLN by separating it from the masses, Papon constantly pushed for the full and open adoption of special powers in France, too, particularly after the outbreak on 25 August 1958 of the FLN's second front.[33]

If Papon's arrival in Paris epitomised the 'Algerianization' or 'militarization' of the metropolitan security services, as House and MacMaster argue, then it also engendered some of the same consequences.[34] Just as the army's ever more brutal and indiscriminate counterinsurgency in Algeria prompted several hundred thousand Algerians to seek refuge in neighbouring Morocco and Tunisia, so, too, the escalation of nationalist agitation and intensification of police repression in the imperial metropole motivated several thousand Algerians to seek refuge in states neighbouring France.[35] Likewise, just as the FLN came to command its war effort largely

[31] Amit Prakash, 'Empire on the Seine: Surveillance, Citizenship, and North African Migrants in Paris (1925–1975)', PhD Dissertation (Columbia University, 2010), p. 123.

[32] Philippe Bernert, *Roger Wybot et la bataille pour la DST* (Paris, 1975), p. 451; Faligot et Krop, *DST*, p. 164; Jean-Émile Vié, *Mémoires d'un directeur des renseignements généraux* (Paris, 1988), pp. 139–40.

[33] House and MacMaster, *Paris*, pp. 48–87; Maurice Papon, *Les Chevaux du pouvoir* (Paris, 1988), p. 90; Conférence par Papon sur la guerre subversive, Cercle Militaire, Constantine, 19 January 1957, Service des archives et du musée de la Préfecture de Police de Paris (SAMPP/P), Ha68*.

[34] House and MacMaster, *Paris*, pp. 27–8.

[35] Linda Amiri, 'Les espaces de voisinage dans les conflits de décolonisation: le cas de la Suisse pendant la guerre d'indépendance algérienne', *Matériaux pour l'Histoire de Notre Temps* 97/98

from extraterritorial sanctuaries in Tunisia and Morocco, so, too, the *Fédération de France*'s collective leaders sought refuge abroad. Beginning in April 1958, they directed metropolitan operations from clandestine hideouts in and around Cologne.[36]

Inter-communal strife and police repression thus prompted many Algerians to leave France for countries such as Belgium, Switzerland and especially West Germany.[37] There were particular factors that made the Bonn Republic a popular destination. For instance, some Algerians left France to evade the war and its consequences altogether, especially the payment of revolutionary dues, which was difficult in Belgium and the Saarland given their incorporation into the *Fédération de France*. Others sought to profit from West Germany's economic boom. Geographic proximity, too, played a role. After all, apart from Paris and Marseille, the principal areas of Algerian migration were the industrial centres in and around Lyon, Lille, Metz, Strasbourg and Belfort, all situated in northern and eastern regions, close to the German and Belgian frontiers.[38] An extreme permeability marked these border regions, particularly in the woodlands of the Saarland and of the Ardennes, and many Algerians used this 'green border' to enter West Germany illegally.[39] The special status of the Saarland only facilitated these movements. Over 500 Algerians worked in the mines and heavy industry in the French protectorate, who stayed on in their positions even after the Saarland's political integration into the FRG in January 1957. The state's continued economic union with France made the Saarland a useful transit point for Algerians seeking to enter West Germany.[40] The Franco-German agreement of 8 December 1956 also made it easier for Algerians to use regular border-crossings. The agreement eliminated the requirement for French and West German nationals to carry passports and obtain visas when crossing the common frontier. Henceforth, all that was needed was a valid ID card, which the French had made compulsory by the October 1955 decree. These more elastic

(2010), pp. 50–7. Approximately 80,000 Algerians sought refuge in Morocco during the war, and up to 230,000 in Tunisia: Meynier, *Histoire Intérieure*, p. 559.

36 Omar Boudaoud, *Du PPA au FLN. Mémoires d'un combattant* (Alger, 2007), pp. 162–8; Harbi, *Vie debout*, p. 222.

37 Faligot and Krop, *DST*, p. 187; Instructions de l'ambassade de France, Bonn, aux consuls en RFA, 21 January 1958, MAE, MLA/2.

38 Marcel Streng, '"Abrechnung unter Nordafrikanern?" Algerische Migranten im Alltag der französischen Gesellschaft während des Algerienkriegs (1954–1962)', *Werkstattgeschichte* 35 (2003), p. 65.

39 Cahn and Müller, *RFA et Guerre d'Algérie*, pp. 196–8.

40 Vermerk, Referat IB3/BMI, 2 October 1958, BA/K, B106/5350; Stora, *Ils venaient*, p. 147.

regulations were particularly fortuitous for Algerians, since the authorities in Algeria rarely approved their passport applications. The French state's official insistence on treating Algerians as French citizens thus helped the latter evade the very surveillance system built to contain the Algerian war.[41]

Containment

These contradictions – and the cross-border traffic of Algerians they enabled – significantly complicated the counterinsurgency efforts of the metropolitan security services, which struggled to monitor the movement of Algerians between France, Belgium and West Germany. From their perspective, wanted 'terrorists' could escape French justice only to continue their subversive activities from abroad. To Director Jean-Émile Vié of the RG, the FLN had to be prevented from creating extraterritorial sanctuaries bordering the metropole.[42] In September 1957, he instructed the border police to intensify its inspections of so-called French Muslims from Algeria. Vié exhorted the police to exercise these controls 'with judgement, avoiding vexatious measures, notably with regards to known Muslim personalities, and with a maximum of discretion in order to prevent potentially unfavourable commentaries by foreign witnesses'.[43] With France facing growing international condemnation over its Algerian policies, Vié was sensitive to the negative image that discriminatory border controls could convey, especially if they occurred in the heart of Europe. After all, his instructions contravened both the letter and the spirit of the law according to which Algerians were French citizen.

Apart from representing a potential security threat, the growing Algerian presence in West Germany also created a social and political headache for French consular officials. The liberalisation of Franco-German border traffic had made it easier for Algerians to travel, like all French citizens, however, they still required a valid passport and visa in order to gain authorisation for long-term residency, work or study in West Germany.[44] Unable to obtain employment or find housing, those who arrived in the industrial centres of

[41] Instructions aux consuls en RFA, 21 January 1958, MAE, MLA/2; dépêche no. 658 de l'ambassade de France, Bonn, 8 April 1958, EU/RFA/1272; Notiz an Breull, IB3/BMI, für die am 18–19 July 1960 stattfindende deutsch-französische Besprechung, undated, BA/K, B106/5350. Also: Spire, 'Semblables', pp. 58–9.

[42] Vié, *Mémoires*, p. 137.

[43] Instruction no. 4085/SN.RG.RAF du Directeur des RG, 12 September 1957, SAMPP/P, Ha/66*.

[44] Dépêche no. 1245 de l'ambassade à Bonn, 29 July 1957, MAE, MLA/2. Also: Heike Knortz, *Diplomatische Tauschgeschäfte: 'Gastarbeiter' in der westdeutschen Diplomatie und Beschäftigungspolitik 1953–1973* (Köln, 2008), p. 26.

the Ruhr soon found themselves in dire straits. As French diplomats reported, some managed to secure occasional work on the black market, but many depended on the aid of organisations such as the West German Red Cross (DRK) or Workers' Welfare Organisation (AWO) to survive. Some turned to the French consulates, requesting passports, financial assistance and even train tickets back to France. French diplomats feared these destitute Algerians could fall prey to the FLN.[45]

By late 1957, the embassy in Bonn petitioned the *Quai d'Orsay* for increased resources to help deal with the growing number of desperate Algerians seeking consular aid in West Germany. Whether from the humanitarian perspective of assisting citizens in need or the national-security perspective of containing anti-colonial subversion, embassy officials argued that the existing consular regulations for dealing with Algerians had become woefully inadequate. They particularly complained about the government's slow processing of passport applications. In the interim, applicants were issued with consular attestations, which they used to obtain temporary visas and residence permits from the West German police. These attestations, however, did not necessarily secure the applicants employment. In Cologne, for instance, the authorities only granted work permits to Algerians possessing a valid passport. Elsewhere, they were more lenient. More problematic still, consular attestations, being valid indefinitely, allowed Algerians to extend their sojourn even when their passport applications were rejected.[46] After all, consular officials never communicated this rejection to the West German police, which consequently had no way of knowing whether visas and residence permits should remain valid or be revoked. In the meantime, the French authorities lost all oversight, let alone control, over this migrant and itinerant population.[47]

The German authorities, too, had become increasingly concerned by the arrival of Algerians on federal territory. As early as October 1955, Labour Minister Anton Storch had warned the cabinet against the recruitment of Algerians.[48] Earlier that year, the authorities had granted seasonal work permits to thirty-odd passport-wielding Algerians, recruited directly in Algeria by a Hanoverian quarry to fill a temporary labour gap.[49] In August

45 Dépêche no. 1245 de Bonn, 29 July 1957; Dépêche no. 184 de Jean Jurgensen, chef du service d'Europe central, à l'ambassadeur à Bonn, 28 December 1957, MAE, MLA/2.

46 Dépêche no. 658 de l'ambassadeur à Bonn, 8 April 1958, MAE, EU/RFA/1272.

47 Instructions de l'ambassade aux consuls en RFA, 21 January 1958, MAE, MLA/2.

48 *Kabinettsprotokolle – 1955*, 100. Sitzung, 15 October 1955, pp. 584–5.

49 Vermerk, Referat Iib/4, Bundesministerium für Arbeit und Sozialordnung (hereafter BMA), August 1955, BA/K, B149/1514.

1955, a prominent trade union newspaper published an article accusing the quarry owner of paying the Algerians sub-standard salaries, housing them in derelict lodgings, forcing them to work off their travel costs and even abusing them physically.[50] Incited by what the Federal Employment and Welfare Office called 'communist propaganda', some of the Algerians went on strike demanding improved working conditions and benefits.[51] The affair soon gained the attention of the regional press and even the national parliament, or *Bundestag*.[52] By 1956, federal authorities intervened by ordering local employment offices to stop issuing work permits to Algerians. Having only just secured agreement on the recruitment of Italian 'guest workers' to make up for the growing labour shortage brought on by the country's rapid economic growth, they feared the negative publicity arising from the case of the Algerian quarry workers could provoke a general rejection of foreign workers by German employers. Officials further argued that the strike action by the Algerian quarry workers, rather than reflecting a justified protest against discrimination, demonstrated 'their different, and for Germans generally foreign mentality'. Deemed easily excitable and 'prone to temper tantrums', Algerians were typecast as a threat to public order.[53]

Racial prejudice thus factored strongly in the decision to reject Algerian workers in 1956. The Federal Labour Ministry was perfectly aware that its position contravened existing legislation since Algerians should have been treated as French citizens.[54] Yet the ministry enjoyed the backing of the *Auswärtige Amt*, which also objected to the recruitment of Algerian workers, though for different reasons. As one diplomat noted,

> the presence of numerous Algerians in the Federal Republic [. . .] and the related possibility of anti-French demonstrations [. . .] could force German

[50] 'Fahrgeld wird abgearbeitet. Ein Unternehmer plant menschliche Transaktionen mit Algerien', *Welt der Arbeit*, 12 August 1955; 'Ins Gesicht geschlagen. Ein grausames Spiel mit algerischen "Studenten" als Arbeiter', *Welt der Arbeit*, 30 September 1955.

[51] Schreiben, Präsident der Bundesanstalt für Arbeitsvermittlung und Arbeitslosenversicherung an den Bundesminister für Arbeit, 24 September 1955, BA/K, B149/1514.

[52] 'Kein Essen für streikende Algerier', *Rheinische Post* (Düsseldorf), 24 September 1955; 'Söhne Allahs streiken im Harz', *Goslarsche Zeitung*, 24 September 1955; Notiz, Abt.I an Abt.II, BMA, bezüglich Punkt I Tagesordnung des Bundestages, 116. Sitzung, 5 December 1955, BA/K, B149/1514.

[53] Schnellbrief, Bundesanstalt für Arbeitsvermittlung und Arbeitsversicherung an BMI, 7 July 1956. On 'guest labour' recruitment: Ulrich Herbert, *Geschichte der Ausländerpolitik in Deutschland. Saisonarbeiter, Zwangsarbeiter, Gastarbeiter, Flüchtlinge* (Bonn, 2003 edn), pp. 202–16; Ibid. and Karin Hunn, 'Guest Workers and Policy on Guest Workers in the Federal Republic. From the Beginnings of Recruitment in 1955 until its Halt in 1973', in *Miracle Years*, pp. 187–218; Knortz, *Tauschgeschäfte*, pp. 67–92; Johannes-Dieter Steinert, *Migration und Politik: Westdeutschland – Europa – Übersee, 1945–1961* (Osnabrück, 1995), pp. 209–38.

[54] Schreiben, Bundesanstalt für Arbeitsvermittlung und Arbeitslosenversicherung an BMA, 4 July 1956; Schreiben, BMA an BMI, 7 August 1956, BA/K, B149/22411.

> authorities to express a certain partisanship in the North African confrontation. This would be incompatible with the strict neutrality practiced by the federal government in all questions relating to North Africa.[55]

In other words, the *Auswärtige Amt* opposed the recruitment of Algerian workers for fear of undermining the policy of non-engagement in the Algerian question. In fact, the decision to rebuff Algerian work permits facilitated French counterinsurgency efforts for it obstructed the Algerians' ability to establish a legitimate sanctuary on German soil. When the consulate in Lyon asked for instructions in October 1956 on how to respond to the increasing number of queries from Algerians seeking employment in West Germany, it was basically told to lie by informing the latter that no jobs were available. Applications submitted to the consulate were to be sent to the Central Employment Exchange in Frankfurt, which was explicitly instructed to treat them 'in a dilatory manner' and to reject them 'after a fairly long time'.[56]

Much to the chagrin of the German and French authorities, even this blatantly discriminatory fudging of policy failed to deter Algerians from migrating to the FRG, reinforcing suspicions of subversion. Between 1956 and 1958, the French army observed a steady increase in the level of FLN activity in West Germany. The *deuxième bureau* of French forces stationed in Germany warned of fraternisation between Algerian nationalists and North African soldiers; in March 1956, it held 'secret propaganda' responsible for the low morale, 'even hostility', to be found among soldiers of the 13th RTA (Algerian Infantry Regiment). This propaganda, the army suspected, aimed to induce desertions. After all, the FLN had established a successful exfiltration/infiltration network that operated between the Bonn Republic and France to facilitate the recruitment of militants, including deserters and draft-dodgers.[57] By early 1958 intelligence suggested that this evasion and desertion network had expanded to such an extent that the Tunisian embassy in Bonn, which was thought to be its operational headquarter, struggled to support the number of Algerians seeking to join the ALN in the Maghreb.[58]

[55] Vermerk, Referat 302 (Mohrmann) an Referat 5, AA, 28 August 1956, PA/AA, B25/7; Schreiben, Botschaft Paris an AA, 1 February 1957, BA/K, B149/22411.

[56] Schreiben Nr. 433/56, BMI an BMA, 15 September 1956; Erlass, AA an Konsulat Lyon, 17 October 1956, BA/K, B149/22411.

[57] Synthèse de renseignements no. 6060, État-major des Forces Armées, deuxième bureau (EMA/2), 28 March 1956, SHD-T, 1R/352/D2*. Also: Lebjaoui, *Vérités*, p. 77.

[58] Rapport confidentiel, 24 December 1957, de la direction des affaires d'Algérie, ministère de l'intérieur, au MAE, 2 January 1958, MAE, MLA/2; Notice no. 6279/SDECE, 14 April 1958, SHD-T, 10R/578*.

By then, French diplomats in Bonn had come to believe that nearly all of the increasingly numerous Algerian 'refugees' arriving in West Germany were in fact members of the FLN.[59] In January 1958, they officially sounded the alarm. Eschewing the private and secretive demarches of the past, Ambassador Couve de Murville intervened directly in the *Auswärtige Amt* demanding tighter controls at border-crossings. He insisted the Federal Border Guard bar entry to all those Algerians arriving at checkpoints without a penny to their name.[60] The embassy's delegate in Saarbrücken, Tanguy de Courson, held similar discussions with Saarland authorities. Just as Vié had ordered French border guards to be discreet in their surveillance of Algerians, so, too, the plenipotentiary remained 'at pains to avoid any special handling of North Africans [i.e. Algerians]' on the part of German officials. He reminded officials that such handling 'could be construed by the latter as discrimination compared to other French nationals'.[61] The *Quai d'Orsay*, meanwhile, revised its consular regulations so as to exert greater control over Algerians already in West Germany. Attestations for passport applicants would henceforth only be valid for ten days, allowing the military security service of the French Forces headquartered at Baden-Baden to run background checks on the applicants. If these checks proved satisfactory, consular officials would extend their attestations for five to six weeks, giving the authorities in Algiers time to process the passport applications. If the checks threw up doubts, the ten-day attestations would not be renewed, making it impossible for rejected applicants to obtain or extend West German residence or work permits.[62]

Political asylum

Though far more stringent, and again highly discriminatory in their treatment of supposed French citizens, these regulations proved too little too late. By the time of their implementation, the influx of Algerians into the FRG had become a matter of public concern. In January 1958, Bonn's *Rheinischer Merkur* commented on the connection between the FLN's

[59] Dépêche no. 408 de l'ambassade de France à Bonn, 27 February 1958, MAE, EU/RFA/1272.

[60] Dépêche no. 3 de la MLA à la DGGA, 7 January 1958; Dépêche no. 2 de Jurgensen à l'ambassade de France à Bonn, 9 January 1958, MAE, MLA/2; Dépêche no. 658 de l'ambassadeur à Bonn, 8 April 1958, MAE, EU/RFA/1272.

[61] Schreiben der Dienststelle der Bundesregierung in Saarbrücken an BMI, 7 March 1958, BA/K, B106/5349.

[62] Instructions de l'ambassade aux consuls en RFA, 21 January 1958, MAE, MLA/2; Dépêche no. 27 du service d'Europe centrale à la direction des affaires algériennes, ministère de l'intérieure, 4 February 1958, MAE, EU/RFA/1272.

insurgency and the 'Algerian invasion' of West Germany. Other papers soon drew parallels between Algerian refugees in the FRG and those in Tunisia and Morocco, whose plight was spotlighted by the French bombing of Sakiet-Sidi-Youssef.[63] At the height of that crisis, the *FAZ* became the first major national newspaper to question the West German authorities' treatment of Algerians. In an article published on 25 February, the paper drew attention to the manifold administrative hurdles and socio-economic hardships this community faced. Though their numbers were still small – only a few hundred Algerians were deemed to have fled mainly to the Ruhr region as well as Cologne, Frankfurt, Hamburg and Bonn – the *FAZ* anticipated that ever more Algerians would seek refuge in West Germany, exacerbating an already fraught situation. The reason for this was obvious: namely, the repression and persecution of Algerians in France. Evoking the 1951 Geneva Convention on Refugees, the 1950 European Convention on Human Rights, as well as principles enshrined in §16.2 of the Basic Law, the *FAZ* demanded that Algerian refugees formally be granted political asylum in the Federal Republic.[64]

These demands caused uproar. Several French and German journalists demanded interviews with the Federal Interior Ministry and French embassy in Bonn. National and regional papers such as *Die Welt* and *Westdeutsche Allgemeine Zeitung* echoed the *FAZ*'s call for Algerians to be granted asylum.[65] The sudden publicity that accrued to the legal status of Algerians seriously alarmed Jean Jurgensen, head of the *Quai d'Orsay*'s Central European directorate. 'The Federal Republic of Germany is the first country in which the problem of the right of asylum for members of the FLN has been posed before public opinion', he noted in March 1958, concluding that 'the solution to this problem, and our [the French government's] reactions to it, will in some measure determine the attitude of other European countries [towards this question]'.[66] By conceding the right of political

[63] 'Algerier ausgewiesen', *Der Mittag* (Düsseldorf), 5 December 1957; 'Algerische Invasion? Die Ausstrahlung des französisch-algerischen Konfliktes auf die Bundesrepublik', *Rheinischer Merkur*, 31 January 1958.

[64] 'Algerier flüchten in die Bundesrepublik', *FAZ*, 25 February 1958; Dépêche no. 408 de l'ambassade de France à Bonn, 27 February 1958, MAE, EU/RFA/1272.

[65] Télégramme no. 472 de l'ambassade de France à Bonn, 26 February 1958, MAE, EU/RFA/1272. Also: 'Algerier suchen in der Bundesrepublik Zuflucht. Bonn ist beunruhigt – Asyl muss gewährt werden', *Neue Rhein Zeitung*, 1 March 1958; 'Wie steht es mit dem Asylrecht? Algerier suchen Zuflucht in der Bundesrepublik', *Die Welt*, 21 March 1958; 'Vom Regen in die Traufe des Asyls', *Aachener Nachrichten*, 7 June 1958; 'Algerier bittet um Asyl', *Westdeutsche Allgemeine* (Essen) 26 June 1958; 'Politisches Asylrecht lückenhaft', *Westdeutsche Allgemeine*, 28 June 1958.

[66] Dépêche no. 52 du service d'Europe centrale à l'ambassade de France à Bonn, 21 March 1958, MAE, EU/RFA/1272.

asylum to Algerians, the German authorities would set a dangerous precedent, one that had to be prevented at all costs. After all, the act of granting asylum constituted an implicit recognition by a foreign government, not only of the oppressive and discriminatory nature of France's treatment of Algerians, but also of the FLN as a legitimate political movement pursuing a just cause, and of Algeria itself as a culturally and politically distinct nation.

The implications of this move were certainly not lost on the authorities in Bonn either. Fearful of a backlash from French opinion and diplomacy, the *Auswärtige Amt* and Interior Ministry issued a pre-emptive press statement designed to diffuse the 'dangerous controversy' unleashed by the *FAZ* and preclude any Franco-German misunderstandings.[67] Released on 28 February 1958, the statement read:

1. Anyone who credibly maintains to be politically persecuted in his/her country cannot be refused the right to asylum [. . .] and cannot be returned, deported, or extradited by German authorities.
2. However, the question, whether someone is politically persecuted and entitled to asylum must be examined [. . .] by the competent German administrative and judicial authorities. Should the investigation conclude that there are no grounds for a political persecution, then the foreigner must reckon with deportation and extradition. Should the investigation conclude that the foreigner does suffer political persecution, then he/she will be shielded from deportation and extradition for the duration of that persecution.
   It follows from this that *criminal elements* do not benefit from the protection accorded by the dispositions of the Basic Law.[68]

The authorities in Bonn thus couched their response to the question of asylum in legalistic terms that, while upholding their constitutional and international obligations, avoided explicit references to the Algerian question. Officially, the statement once again echoed the policy of non-engagement. Particularly significant, however, was its final sentence. Without denying the right to asylum *per se*, it tacitly endorsed the French view of the FLN as a criminal and terrorist organisation.[69] Thus although its full meaning remained veiled and deliberately vague, the

[67] Télégramme no. 472 de l'ambassade de France à Bonn, 26 February 1958, MAE, EU/RFA/1272. Also: Aufzeichnung, Referat 302 (Alexander Böker), 26 February 1958; Schreiben Nr. 134/58, BMI an AA, 26 February 1958, PA/AA, B25/4.

[68] Informationsfunk der Bundesregierung, Meldung Nr. 58, 28 February 1958, PA/AA, B25/4 (underlined in original, italics added).

[69] Télégramme no. 472 de l'ambassade de France à Bonn, 26 February 1958, MAE, EU/RFA/1272.

statement in fact demonstrated the Bonn government's support of France in the Algerian war.

To secure the authorities' backing, the *Quai d'Orsay* increased its pressure on Bonn. The federal government's attitude towards Algerian refugees became a yardstick for Franco-German reconciliation. French diplomats reminded federal authorities of the fact that France was itself a signatory of the European Convention on Human Rights and Geneva Convention on Refugees. As French citizens, so the argument went, Algerians did not require asylum, for they were members of a civilised and democratic nation, one that had practically invented the rights of man. France's harsh line towards certain Algerians, the argument continued, had nothing to do with politics and everything to do with the fact that this minority comprised dangerous criminals and terrorists who ought to be extradited back to France. French diplomats informed Bonn 'that a refusal to defer to a demand of extradition [. . .] would hardly be compatible with the present spirit of Franco-German relations' and 'that we would consider the granting of political asylum to an Algerian refugee even less amicable and very detrimental to our interests'. Such steps, Jurgensen argued, 'would have serious psychological repercussions in France, where public opinion [. . .] is sensitized to events concerning the Algerian war on the one hand and to incidents arising in the sphere of Franco-German relations on the other'.[70]

French diplomacy, however, was not alone in seeking to sway the manner in which West German authorities handled the asylum question. On 24 March 1958, a secret meeting occurred in Bonn's prestigious Press Club between three unidentified agents of the FLN and two senior officials from the Federal Ministry for Refugees and Displaced Persons. According to the official record, this was the first – and for a long time the only – semi-formal meeting to have occurred between representatives of the Bonn government and the FLN. Neither the *Auswärtige Amt* nor the Interior Ministry had been informed. The Algerians opened their discussions with Drs Wolfrum and Maurach by painting an exaggerated picture of the refugee situation. Up to 1,500 Algerians now lived in West Germany, they claimed, of which only 400 to 500 were 'real refugees'. The rest

[70] Dépêche no. 52 de Jurgensen à l'ambassade de France à Bonn, 21 March 1958, MAE, EU/RFA/1272. Also: Télégramme no. 472 de l'ambassade de France à Bonn, 26 February 1958; Dépêche no. 408 de l'ambassade de France à Bonn, 27 February 1958; Note de la direction des affaires administratives et sociales, MAE, au service d'Europe centrale, 18 March 1958, MAE, EU/RFA/1272; Aufzeichnung, Referat 302, 26 February 1958; Schreiben Nr. 134, BMI an AA, 26 February 1958; Informationsfunk der Bundesregierung Nr. 58, 28 February 1958, PA/AA, B25/4.

were an itinerant lot consisting of FLN militants whose temporary sojourn served specific tasks and who mostly carried Tunisian, Moroccan or Egyptian passports; deserters and draft-dodgers en route to the Maghreb; workers possessing legitimate French papers; and a small number of students enrolled at universities. Practically all of these Algerians were single, young men.[71]

According to Wolfrum, the Algerians evidently hoped that their intercession would persuade federal authorities to recognise all of these Algerians as political refugees. Wolfrum and Maurach rejected this request, but they did not dismiss it altogether. Emphasising the imperative of Franco-German reconciliation, Wolfrum argued that Bonn's refusal to acknowledge Algerians as official refugees stemmed not from a lack of sympathy but from political and diplomatic realities. He indicated that the authorities would be willing to tolerate the presence of Algerians and even grant them a form of informal asylum provided they refrained strictly from engaging in subversive activities. Wolfrum's memorandum on the meeting suggests that the FLN representatives were satisfied by this proposal. They apparently conceded to the stipulation of refraining from political subversion and even promised to maintain order among the Algerian community themselves.[72]

This tacit accord went entirely against the grain of the government's press release of February 1958. Wolfrum justified his assurances to the FLN by claiming that it was not in Bonn's interest to allow the development of an Algerian underground organisation on federal territory, which would merely radicalise nationalist sentiments, especially among those genuine refugees who were not yet committed to the FLN. By granting them informal asylum, Wolfrum continued, the authorities would be much better placed to control Algerians, stifle their subversive activities and prevent them from using federal territory as an extraterritorial base against France. Wolfrum insisted that his reassurances to the FLN were in both France's best interests and those of Franco-German relations. He felt that 'everything is still possible to become master of the situation as quietly as possible while remaining true to German laws and to political obligations vis-à-vis France'. To work out the finer details of his plan, Wolfrum had even invited his Algerian interlocutors to another meeting scheduled on 15 April 1958.[73]

It would appear that this second encounter never took place, for on 15 April the Gaillard government fell, setting into motion the chain of events

[71] Aufzeichnung, Dr. Wolfrum, Bundesministerium für Flüchtlinge und Vertriebene, 24 March 1958, PA/AA, B1/59.
[72] Ibid. [73] Ibid.

that resulted in the Fourth Republic's demise. It is impossible to say who backed out of the meeting and why. On the one hand, the FLN's agents may have changed their minds about the desirability of close collaboration with the West German authorities. By April 1958 the leaders of the *Fédération de France* had designated the Bonn Republic as the sanctuary and base from where they intended to pursue their metropolitan activities, and for this they required freedom to manoeuvre. Wolfrum's proposal of granting Algerians informal asylum in return for a strict renunciation of political and subversive activities was therefore hardly in the FLN's interests. The entire rationale of establishing an external sanctuary was, after all, to facilitate the continuation of the struggle against France. On the other hand, Wolfrum's initiative would also have met with strong disapproval from the *Auswärtige Amt*. Officially, the Bonn government was bound by a policy of strict neutrality in the Algerian war. Unofficially, as has been seen, it lent its support to France. German diplomats were in fact mortified when they heard of Wolfrum's proposal to grant Algerians informal asylum later that year, a move they felt would have seriously undermined Franco-German relations.[74] To reinforce the argument that Algerians were *not* to be treated as refugees, the Ministry for Refugees and Displaced Persons was henceforth excluded from further discussions of the issue.

For the moment, then, the political and socio-economic problems deriving from the development of an Algerian sanctuary remained unresolved. The controversy over the question of political asylum nonetheless reveals that not everyone in West Germany shared the Adenauer government's pro-French attitude to the Algerian war. The Ministry for Refugees and Displaced Persons advocated a flexible and nuanced approach to the Algerian question, one that tacitly accepted the Algerians as refugees. German newspapers, meanwhile, called for Algerians to be formally granted political asylum. Regardless of their political tendencies, these newspapers had developed highly critical views of France's Algerian policies. Some even sympathised openly with the FLN. Indeed, the very presence in West Germany of a growing number of Algerians had helped to bring the Franco-Algerian conflict closer to home. As will be shown in the next chapter, this helped to generate interest among the West German public for the anti-colonial struggles being waged in Algeria and elsewhere in the Third World.

[74] Schreiben des Bundesministers für Flüchtlinge Theodor Oberländer an Außenminister Brentano, 28 October 1958; Notiz, Referat 712 (Flüchtlinge und Rückführung), 8 November 1958; Aufzeichnung, Karl Carstens, Abt. West/II, 15 November 1958, PA/AA, B1/59.

CHAPTER 4

Algeria and West German opinion

The 1950s are often depicted in historiography as a decade marked by parochialism, insularity and political apathy in West Germany.[1] After the traumas generated by mass political participation during the Third Reich, civil society retreated into work and the home, paying little attention to politics or international affairs.[2] To historian Wolfram Hanrieder, this view of the 1950s is a myth. Precisely because of their own recent past, he argued, most Germans possessed a sharp 'sense of the significance of international politics for the routines of daily life'. With their country occupied, divided, and at the frontline of the European Cold War, Germans perceived foreign policy as 'an all-embracing existential experience'.[3] In a similar vein, historian Eckart Conze argues that the quest for security became the defining feature of West Germany, permeating every aspect of life and society and remaining at the heart of debates about the country's reintegration into international society.[4] By the late 1950s, these debates had led to the emergence of small but articulate protest movements opposing rearmament (*Ohne Mich*) and nuclear weapons (*Kampf dem Atomtod*). West German civil-society actors thus did take an interest in matters of foreign and security policy, though their political engagement tended to centre on issues closer to home.[5]

[1] Unlike some studies of post-war German history that demarcate the 1950s as the period from 1949 to 1957 and then refer to the period from 1957 to 1974 as the 'long 1960s', this study takes the conventional approach of referring to the 1950s as the decade ending in 1959.

[2] For examples of this view over time: Anselm Doering-Manteuffel, *Die Bundesrepublik in der Ära Adenauer: Außenpolitik und innere Entwicklung, 1949–1963* (Darmstadt, 1983), pp. 212–13; Jürgen Osterhammel and Niels P. Petersson, *Geschichte der Globalisierung. Dimensionen, Prozesse, Epochen*, 4th edn (München, 2007), p. 100; Axel Schildt, *Moderne Zeiten. Freizeit, Massenmedien und 'Zeitgeist' in der Bundesrepublik der 50er Jahre* (Hamburg, 1995), pp. 314–15.

[3] Wolfram F. Hanrieder, 'The Foreign Policy of the Federal Republic of Germany, 1949–1989', *German Studies Review* XII/2 (1989), pp. 312, 314; ibid., *Deutschland*, pp. xiv–xv.

[4] Eckart Conze, *Die Suche nach Sicherheit. Eine Geschichte der Bundesrepublik Deutschland von 1945 bis in die Gegenwart* (Munich, 2009).

[5] Michael Geyer, 'Cold War Angst: The Case of West-German Opposition to Rearmament and Nuclear Weapons', in *Miracle Years*, pp. 376–408; Nehring, *Politics;* Nick Thomas, *Protest Movements in 1960s West Germany. A Social History of Dissent and Democracy* (Oxford, 2003), pp. 31–45.

The Third World, meanwhile, did not become a focal point of civic engagement or protest in West Germany until the late 1960s, influenced especially by events in Vietnam. Only then did a younger generation of civil-society actors associated with the New Left and extra-parliamentary opposition become engaged in debates about imperialism and neo-imperialism.[6] Some scholars have nonetheless argued that a small minority of mostly left-wing activists had begun to take an interest in decolonisation in the late 1950s already. Of all the colonial conflicts that marked that decade, they single out Algeria's independence struggle as the one that laid the foundations of the West German Third World movement.[7] What remains less clear is just how and why these actors became aware of the Algerian war? What role did the FLN and French authorities play in this process? And was it really only a small group of left-wing activists that took an interest in that conflict? Answering these questions is the main purpose of this chapter. It argues that the FLN's use of West Germany as sanctuary and base contributed to a rising public consciousness about the Algerian war. Contrary to received wisdom, the chapter argues that it was not just the radical Left that came to advocate Algeria's independence but a much broader cross-section of society. West German newspapers of different political persuasions took a keen interest in the FLN's insurgency; other actors would soon follow. The development of an Algerian sanctuary in the FRG contributed to this situation, for it brought the realities of the anti-colonial struggle closer to home. Precisely because the country became as sanctuary, moreover, both the FLN and the French government came to vie for German popular support.

Publishing and propaganda

As discussed in the previous chapter, many of the Algerians that had begun to reach the Bonn Republic were economic migrants or refugees seeking

[6] For two recent, excellent examples, see: Martin Klimke, *The Other Alliance: Student Protest in West Germany and the United States in the Global Sixties* (Princeton NJ, 2009); Quinn Slobodian, *Foreign Front: Third World Politics in Sixties West Germany* (Durham NC, 2012).

[7] Werner Balsen and Karl Rössel, *Hoch die internationale Solidarität: zur Geschichte der Dritte-Welt-Bewegung in der Bundesrepublik* (Köln, 1986), pp. 44, 50; Hong, *Cold War Germany*, pp. 140–3; Claus Leggewie, 'Kofferträger: Das Algerien-Projekt in den 50er und 60er Jahren und die Ursprünge des "Internationalismus" in der Bundesrepublik,' *Politische Vierteljahresschrift* 25/1 (1984), p. 171; Claudia Olejniczak, *Die Dritte-Welt-Bewegung in Deutschland: konzeptionelle und organisatorische Strukturmerkmale einer neuen sozialen Bewegung* (Wiesbaden, 1999), p. 82; Dorothee Weitbrecht, *Aufbruch in die Dritte Welt. Der Internationalismus der Studentenbewegung von 1968 in der Bundesrepublik Deutschland* (Göttingen, 2012), pp. 68–9.

respite from police repression and inter-communal rivalries in France. Others arrived with a purpose. As Pinay and Duchène had informed Strauss and Schrübbers in 1956, and as FLN representatives told Wolfrum and Maurach in 1958, many were militant nationalists charged with specific tasks. Of these, one of the first and most essential was the forging of links to individuals and organisations in West Germany that could further the FLN's cause. These links were required for three vital reasons: first, to ensure the security and stability of the sanctuary and base the FLN sought to build in West Germany; second, to expand and optimise the European support networks that proved so vital to the *Fédération en France*, especially once the organisation's leaders were themselves forced into exile; and finally, to advance the goal of winning over world opinion to the FLN's liberation struggle. Reconfirmed as a core tenet of policy at the Soummam congress of 1956, the FLN pursued its psychological battle over public opinion not just in Algeria and France but also in the international arena. The moral and material support secured in this manner would sustain and strengthen the revolution while weakening and isolating France. To implement this goal, the FLN developed sophisticated machinery dedicated to propaganda and public relations. After all, one first had to win the battle for hearts and minds before one could turn sympathy into active support.

Initially, the FLN's external propaganda campaigns were not directed at a German audience. As discussed in Chapter 1, the movement's earliest efforts focused on the Arab-Islamic world, which was deemed an important source of moral, material and diplomatic assistance. The FLN also sought to gain support and recognition from the UN as one of the principal arbiters of international relations. Considering its role as leader of the Western world and a key ally of France, the United States, too, became an important target of the FLN's psychological war. Finally, FLN propagandists sought to influence public opinion in France and thereby also French policy-making.[8]

If FLN propaganda initially ignored German opinion, the Bonn Republic did come to serve as one of their operational bases. This made it possible for Algerian nationalists to circumvent an increasingly restrictive censorship regime in France. The control of information constituted an integral component of French counterinsurgency strategy through which the authorities sought to bolster morale, prevent sedition and tighten military security.[9] The FLN eluded the French censors by printing much

[8] Connelly, *Diplomatic Revolution*, pp. 96–7; Meynier, *Histoire*, p. 549; Thomas, 'Defending', p. 242.

[9] Philip Dine, 'French Culture and the Algerian War: Mobilizing Icons', *Journal of European Studies* 28/1 (1998), p. 54; Raymond Kuhn, *The Media in France* (London, 1995), pp. 57–8; Martin Harrison,

of its promotional material abroad and then smuggling it back into France. West Germany became one of the locations serving this purpose. On 26 October 1956, French officials confiscated a package at Paris's *Gare de l'Est* that had been posted in Hamburg by one Mohamed El Garbi containing 100 copies of the FLN newspaper *Résistance Algérienne*. Earlier that year the DST had put an end to a similar smuggling operation out of Belgium run by members of the Trotskyite Fourth International, which constituted the first leftist movement actively to support the FLN.[10] On 11 November, French customs officials at Villard in Upper-Savoy seized an even larger package containing 5,000 copies of *Résistance Algérienne*, 300 copies of the FLN's official organ *El Moudjahid*, and several thousand propaganda stickers, all wrapped in West German newspapers. The Algerian who attempted to smuggle this material into France confessed to having collected his cargo from a printer close to Hamburg.[11]

With evidence mounting of the FLN's use of West German printers, French diplomats notified the authorities in Bonn, where the domestic intelligence services launched an investigation.[12] In February 1957, the BfV reported that the Hamburg-based printer Erich Balaszus had indeed printed leaflets for a Tunis-based businessman and journalist named El Gharbi and his 'Tunisian Bureau for Economic and Cultural Exchanges with Germany'. The printed material included a brochure entitled *Le Combattant*, but Balaszus denied having printed copies of *Résistance Algérienne*, *El Moudjahid*, or stickers promoting the FLN.[13] *Le Combattant*, of course, was the French subtitle for *El Moudjahid*, a fact that eluded the BfV's investigators (possibly due to a lack of command of French and Arabic), but not the French authorities, which immediately pressed for further investigations.[14] The BfV must have uncovered more substantial evidence against the FLN, for in June 1957 Hamburg's prosecutor-general ordered a nation-wide seizure of printed materials associated with Algerian nationalists on the grounds that they broke copyright law. In subsequent months, police in Hamburg, Frankfurt

'Government and Press in France during the Algerian War', *American Political Science Review* 58/2 (1964), pp. 273–85.

10 Hervé Hamon and Patrick Rotman, *Les Porteurs de Valises: la résistance française à la guerre d'Algérie* (Paris, 1979), p. 57. Also: Sylvain Pattieu, *Les Camarades des Frères. Trotskistes et libertaires dans la guerre d'Algérie* (Paris, 2002).

11 Dépêche no. 2715 de l'ambassadeur Étienne Dennery, Berne, 16 November 1956, MAE, MLA/2; Schreiben, Dr. von Kempis, BMI, an BfV, 28 December 1956, BA/K, B106/15600.

12 Ibid. 13 Schreiben, BfV an BMI, 14 February 1957, BA/K, B106/15600.

14 Erlaß zu Ermittlungen, BMI (Dr Fröhlich) an BfV, 15 February 1957; Schreiben, BfV an BMI, 28 March 1957; Schreiben, AA (Böker) an BMI, 12 July 1957, BA/K, B106/15600.

and Munich confiscated up to 2,500 brochures, some even written in German.[15]

The confiscation of printed propaganda represents an early instance of Franco-German collaboration in the fight against Algerian nationalists. Far from tolerating the FLN on their territory, West German authorities were quick to crack down on subversive activities. Though their measures aimed to protect the sovereign *Rechtsstaat*, they had the added benefit of promoting Franco-German reconciliation. And yet the prosecutor-general's clampdown failed to achieve its foremost goal, for the FLN's propagandistic activities in West Germany continued to expand. In February 1957, as the Battle of Algiers raged and the UN held a particularly acrimonious debate on the Algerian question, several members of the *Bundestag* and Chamber of Industry and Trade, including Adenauer, received two anonymously sent brochures entitled 'France's Hungary: Algeria' and 'Call of the Algerian People!'[16] Detailing Algeria's history of colonial oppression and comparing Massu's crackdown in Algiers to the Red Army's brutal repression of the 1956 Budapest uprising, both brochures were detailed, well crafted and written in impeccable German. They consisted of reprints of articles that had previously appeared in *Schweizerische Republikanische Blätter*. Since the latter was a conservative Swiss weekly published by a 'serious, politically neutral company', the BfV on this occasion saw no further reason to investigate.[17] French intelligence clearly thought otherwise. According to SDECE, the FLN had charged one of its key agents in Switzerland – Ahmed Bayoud – with the distribution of 10,000 pamphlets among West German and European political and business elites. To the French intelligence service, the two brochures represented the beginning of a much broader public-relations campaign.[18] A close associate of future GPRA President Ferhat Abbas, Bayoud was thought by SDECE to possess close contacts in West Germany dating back to World War II and his time in the German-Arab Legion. He reportedly spoke excellent German. Bayoud was also a member of the American-founded Muslim aid organisation *Jam'iyyat ul Islâm*, which at the time constituted one of the FLN's largest foreign financial

[15] 'Doch in Hamburg gedruckt', *Hamburger Abendblatt*, 13 June 1957; 'Les activités du FLN en Allemagne', *Agence France Presse* (AFP), 14 June 1957; Dépêche no. 1107 de l'ambassadeur Couve de Murville, Bonn, annexe 2, 1 July 1957, MAE, MLA/2; Schreiben, BfV an BMI, 24 January 1958, BA/K, B106/15600.

[16] Schreiben Nr. 428, AA an BMI, 4 February 1957, PA/AA, B25/7; Schreiben, AA an BMI, 7 February 1957; Brief des Bundestagsabgeordneten Dr. Georg Graf Henckel an Bundesinnenminister Dr. Gerhard Schröder, 22 February 1957, BA/K, B106/15600.

[17] Schreiben Nr. 1558/57, BfV an BMI, 2 December 1957, BA/K, B106/15600.

[18] Note d'information no. 72/2304/SDECE, 6 February 1957, MAE, AL/ALG/19.

backers.[19] Although this intelligence might have aided the BfV's investigations, French authorities never passed it on, perhaps out of distrust. The BfV thus never managed to explain who had posted the two brochures, or how many had been disseminated.[20]

Notwithstanding the authorities' attempted crackdown, the FLN pursued its public-relations activities in West Germany with relative impunity. By 1957, the movement had even begun to change its *modus operandi*. As shall be seen, the Bonn Republic was no longer just a base for producing and disseminating propaganda but became a target in and of itself. Algerian propagandists expertly drew on themes and references they knew would strike a German nerve while also resonating beyond the FRG. To conduct their increasingly diversified public-relations campaign, the FLN cleverly relied on the German media, Arab diplomats, and other civilian actors. Signalling this change in tactics was a press conference held in Bonn on 26 September 1957 by two of the FLN's top propagandists. Organised by the Moroccan and Iraqi embassies and advertised as a private event for a select group of twenty-odd journalists and numerous Arab diplomats, Ahmed Francis and Abderrahman Kiouane spoke of France's 'war of extermination' that destroyed entire villages whose inhabitants were rounded into concentration camps. They deplored the fact that 'the civilised [i.e. Western] world' unanimously condemned Soviet barbarism in Hungary but failed to speak up against French atrocities in Algeria and demanded to know whether blood 'changes colour depending on whether it flows in Budapest or in Algiers?'[21] Couve de Murville assured the *Quai d'Orsay* that the Bonn authorities had nothing to do with the event, having refused to meet Francis and Kiouane. 'The German government's attitude on this occasion was perfectly correct', the ambassador avowed, for Bonn had no authority to ban private gatherings, especially when authorities had no prior knowledge of their occurrence. Fortunately, he concluded, the conference had found only a minor echo in the press.[22]

[19] According to Meynier, *Jam'iyyat* funding dwindled considerably from 1957. This was, first, because Indonesia, the largest net donor, became preoccupied by domestic emergencies, notably the military uprising in Sumatra, and second, because Bayoud and his American collaborator, Ahmed Kamal, were arrested by Swiss police and their organisation's bank accounts frozen after the exposure of an illicit trade deal in explosives. See: Meynier, *Histoire*, pp. 580, 585.

[20] Schreiben, BfV an BMI (Dr. Toyka), 13 May 1957; Schreiben, BfV an BMI, 2 December 1957, BA/K, B106/15600; Schreiben, BMI an AA, 11 December 1957, PA/AA, B25/7.

[21] Text der Pressekonferenz abgehalten durch die Nationale Algerische Befreiungsfront im Hotel Königshof, undated Archiv der sozialen Demokratie (AdsD), Bonn, Nachlaß (NL)/Werner Plum/29; Abderrahmane Kiouane, *Les Débuts d'une Diplomatie de Guerre (1956–1962). Journal d'un Délégué à l'Extérieur* (Alger, 2000), p. 34.

[22] Dépêche no. 1709 de l'ambassadeur Couve de Murville, Bonn, 25 October 1957, MAE, EU/RFA/1272.

These reassurances only temporarily satisfied Michel Debré, the Gaullist senator and staunch supporter of *l'Algérie française*, who denounced the conference for its 'quasi-official character'.[23] On 8 January 1958, the airing of a television documentary on Algeria by the West German Public Broadcasting Corporation (ARD) produced another complaint by Debré, who took it as proof that 'German policy aims to draw closer to the leaders of the rebellion'.[24] As before, French diplomats found the senator's allegation unfounded, especially since the West German media operated independently from governmental controls. Jurgensen assured the senator that 'the attitude of the federal government was guided by the anxiety not to accord the rebels any support and to ignore their pretensions'. Moreover, the documentary depicted the French view of the Algerian conflict, its creator having filmed it with the authorities' express support.[25]

Debré was not the first to react sensitively to indications of success on the part of FLN propaganda in the FRG. High Commissioner François-Poncet had complained about West German opinion and its attitude toward Algeria as early as 1955. France's emergence as one of the post-war victors had indeed left a bitter aftertaste for many Germans, who referred to the Occupation as the '*düstere Franzosenzeit*' (dismal French time). Apart from Moscow, many Germans continued to view France as the greatest obstacle to West German rearmament and to the country's sovereignty and equality within the Western alliance.[26] An opinion poll conducted by Frankfurt University's Institute for Social Research found that whereas 48 per cent of those questioned thought Franco-German relations were 'not very good' in December 1953, 60.5 per cent thought as much in July 1954 after the French National Assembly had scuppered plans for the European Defence Community.[27] Likewise, a poll by the Allensbach Institute of Public Opinion found that while 55 per cent

[23] Dépêche no. 161 de Jean Jurgensen à l'ambassadeur Couve de Murville, Bonn, 17 October 1957, MAE, EU/RFA/1267.

[24] Dépêche no. 20 de la direction des affaires politiques à l'ambassadeur à Bonn, 31 January 1958; MAE, EU/RFA/1267.

[25] Note no. 14 de Jurgensen pour le Secrétariat Général, 26 February 1958, MAE, EU/RFA/1267.

[26] Wolfrum, 'Bild', pp. 87–113; Rainer Hudemann, 'Französische Besatzungsmacht und deutsche Bevölkerung nach zwei Weltkriegen', in *Politischer Wandel, organisierte Gewalt und nationale Sicherheit. Beiträge zur neueren Geschichte Deutschlands und Frankreichs. Festschrift für Klaus-Jürgen Müller* (eds.) Ernst Willi Hansen, Gerhard Schreiber, and Bernd Wegner (Munich, 1995), pp. 427–45.

[27] 'Image de la France. Un sondage de l'opinion publique allemande (RFA, Berlin non-compris), hiver 1953/54', Institut für Sozialforschung, Johann-Wolfgang-Goethe Universität, Frankfurt-am-Main, July 1954, MAE, EU/RFA/385.

believed the FRG should cooperate with France in March 1953, only 46 per cent felt as much in September 1954.[28] West German criticism of France became so virulent in 1954 that François-Poncet feared 'the Franco-German antagonism would again become one of the underlying facts of the international situation'.[29] Clearly, 'a large fraction of the German population' still felt a 'distrust, if not hostility' towards France.[30]

One year later, François-Poncet continued to deplore the 'systematic malevolence' and 'veritable Francophobia' of West German public opinion.[31] By then, he believed, these sentiments found their strongest expression in media portrayals of the Algerian problem, which to him contained a discernible undercurrent of *Schadenfreude*. The press depicted the entire process of decolonisation as 'a shattering [*éclatante*] revenge on those powers, which in 1918 dispossessed [the Germans] of their colonial empire'. With their inherent penchant for expansionism and greatness, so the ambassador believed, West Germans were only waiting to take France's place in the Maghreb.[32] François-Poncet considered the press's attitude towards the Algerian problem intolerable, and he bitterly complained about it to Adenauer.[33] Distrustful of the political maturity of German opinion and keen to assuage the French, the chancellor shared the ambassador's concerns.[34] During a cabinet meeting on 6 October 1955, he deplored the press's 'malicious' coverage of France's Algerian troubles. Adenauer lamented the media's lack of '*Fingerspitzengefühl*' (sensitivity), which so elicited François-Poncet's wrath and imperilled Franco-German reconciliation.[35]

Gestapo-style methods

François-Poncet's fears of German expansionism and revanchism were greatly exaggerated, yet he was right in one sense, for in contrast to Adenauer and the *Auswärtige Amt*, the West German press had begun openly to criticise France's Algerian policies. The more extreme French repression became, the more disapproving the press's tone became.

[28] Elisabeth Noelle and Erich Peter Neumann (eds.), *Jahrbuch der öffentlichen Meinung 1947–1955*, Institut für Demoskopie (Allensbach, 1956), p. 331.

[29] Cited in: Bock, 'Perzeption', p. 634.

[30] Dépêche no. 1909/EU de François-Poncet, Bonn, 25 August 1954, MAE, EU/RFA/386.

[31] Télégramme no. 3443 de l'ambassadeur François-Poncet, Bonn, 2 September 1955, MAE, EU/RFA/390; Dépêche no. 720 de François-Poncet, 20 July 1955, MAE, AL/MAR/26.

[32] Cited in: Klaus-Jürgen Müller, 'Bundesrepublik', p. 614,n. 18.

[33] Télégramme no. 3443 de François-Poncet, Bonn, 2 September 1955, MAE, EU/RFA/390.

[34] Schwarz, *Staatsmann*, pp. 145–7.

[35] *Kabinettsprotokolle – 1955*, 99. Sitzung, 6 October 1955, p. 546.

Moreover, the more the press chastised the French, the more interested it became in the FLN, which had not only imposed itself as the dominant nationalist force within Algeria but which also enjoyed the international backing of the Afro-Asian bloc and, increasingly, the socialist world. These factors had helped sensitise both French and world opinion to the Algerian war and West German opinion proved no different. Criticism of French policies became increasingly vocal, leading Parisian governments into a deepening isolation.

In France, this criticism centred on the brutality of French counter-insurgency methods, especially the army and security services' systematic practice of torture. Early civic initiatives like the 'Committee of Intellectuals against the Continuation of the War in North Africa' generated little public interest. Later ones would, especially those prompted by the supposed suicides in custody of FLN militants Larbi Ben M'Hidi and Ali Boumendjel, the disappearance of communist mathematician and FLN supporter Maurice Audin, and the torture of Audin's colleague Henri Alleg during the Battle of Algiers.[36] French army officers justified the use of torture as an effective and essential, albeit regrettable, method of intelligence collection and psychological warfare in the campaign against FLN terrorism. At the same time, they claimed that torture was never applied systematically, saying it was only employed by a few, misguided individuals.[37] Few in the French establishment actively opposed these arguments: General Jacques de Bollardière became the first and only officer to request a transfer out of Algeria in March 1957; Algiers police prefect Paul Teitgen also resigned from his post in October 1957; and *L'Express* founder Jean-Jacques Servan-Schreiber condemned the practice in his published account of service as a reservist in Algeria.[38]

Reprobation of and resistance to torture thus largely fell to French journalists and public intellectuals. As early as 1955, the militant leftist Claude Bourdet and Catholic conservative François Mauriac had launched

[36] Henri Alleg, *La Question* (Paris, 1957); Klose, *Menschenrechte*, pp. 232–7; James D. Le Sueur, *Uncivil War: Intellectuals and Identity Politics during the Decolonization of Algeria* (Philadelphia PA, 2001), pp. 197–205; Pierre Vidal-Naquet, *L'Affaire Audin 1957–1978* (Paris, 1989).

[37] Paul Aussaresses, *Services Spéciaux, Algérie 1955–1957: mon témoignage sur la torture* (Paris, 2001); Branche, *Torture*; Marnia Lazreg, *Torture and the Twilight of Empire: From Algiers to Baghdad* (Princeton NJ, 2008); Pierre Vidal-Naquet, *Torture: Cancer of Democracy. France and Algeria 1954–62*, (trans.) Barry Richard (Harmondsworth, 1963).

[38] Jacques Pâris de Bollardière, *Bataille d'Alger; Bataille de l'homme* (Paris, 1972); 'Lettre de démission par Teitgen, 24 mars 1957', in *La Guerre d'Algérie. Dossier et témoignages* (eds.) Patrick Eveno and Jean Planchais (Paris, 1989), p. 144; Jean-Jacques Servan-Schreiber, *Lieutenant en Algérie* (Paris, 1957).

a press campaign to protest the use of Gestapo-style methods in Algeria.[39] These analogies to the Third Reich would have hit a sore nerve in a post-war France intent on 'forgetting' its collaborationist past.[40] They echoed arguments propagated by Aimé Césaire in *Discourse on Colonialism* (first published in French in 1950) and Hannah Arendt in *The Origins of Totalitarianism* (1951), which both drew parallels and perceived connections between the racist brutality of European colonialism in Africa and Asia and the genocidal violence of National Socialism.[41] The Nazi regime would become a prominent point of comparison for French critics of the counterinsurgency in Algeria regardless of their ideological background or political views. Like Bourdet and Mauriac, many anti-torture campaigners were veterans of the French Resistance and had themselves been victims of Nazi brutality. Though not all advocated Algerian independence, they deplored the fact that the French army and security services resorted to practices reminiscent of the Gestapo, practices that challenged the very values of justice, freedom, dignity, democracy and equality for which they had fought.[42] In December 1955, even *Sûreté* director Jean Mairey lamented, 'it is intolerable for me to think that, by their behaviour, French police officers can remind one of the Gestapo [. . .] I shudder when I hear French soldiers compared to the S.S. brutes of the Wehrmacht'. By August 1957, he, too, had resigned from his post.[43]

Precisely because it hit a nerve, the FLN, too, used the memory of the world war to advance its international propaganda campaign. The movement's propagandists regularly accused the French authorities of applying 'German methods' in Algeria.[44] One brochure published in 1957 indicted the French for perpetrating crimes worse than those of the Third Reich, because 'German Nazism was candid, while French

[39] Bourdet first lamented these practices in 1951: Claude Bourdet, 'Y a-t-il une Gestapo en Algérie?' *France-Observateur*, 6 December 1951; Ibid., 'Votre Gestapo d'Algérie', *France-Observateur*, 13 January 1955; François Mauriac, 'La Question', *L'Express*, 15 January 1955.

[40] Henry Rousso, *Le syndrome de Vichy: de 1944 à nos jours* (Paris, 1987).

[41] These arguments have spawned a lively debate among historians over the continuities between German colonialism and the Holocaust. For overviews of this debate, see: Langbehn and Salama, 'Introduction', in *German Colonialism*, pp. ix–xxxi; Gerwarth and Malinowski, 'Arendt's Ghosts', pp. 279–300; Pascal Grosse, 'What has German Colonialism to do with National Socialism? A Conceptual Framework', in *Germany's Colonial Past*, pp. 115–34.

[42] Henri Marrou, 'France, ma patrie', *Le Monde*, 5 April 1956; Hubert Beuve-Méry, 'Sommes-nous les Vaincus de Hitler?' *Le Monde*, 13 May 1957; or generally: Martin Evans, *The Memory of Resistance. French Opposition to the Algerian War (1954–1962)* (Oxford; New York, 1997), pp. 31–72; Ibid., *Algeria*, pp. 210–14.

[43] Cited in: Vidal-Naquet, *Torture*, p. 38.

[44] FLN delegation to the UN, New York, 'The Forgotten War Continues in Algeria', *Free Algeria* II/10 (20 March 1957).

colonialism covers its crimes in a robe of morality'.[45] Leaflets and posters confiscated by the army in Algeria frequently compared French imperialism with fascism. One hand-drawn flyer depicting the 1940 invasion of France cautioned the French 'not to do unto others that which they did not want done to themselves'; another equated the *Paras* (paratroopers) to the SS.[46] FLN propaganda also played on the 'hereditary enmity' between France and Germany. Thus in one tract the movement warned: 'France weakens herself considerably by maintaining an army of over one million men. Germany grows stronger because she has no military expenses. Do you know what will happen if this continues?'[47] Other tracts, clearly directed at Germans serving in the Foreign Legion, bore messages such as: 'We do not understand why you, German, give your blood and your life for the enemy of Germany that is also our enemy'.[48]

Just one decade after World War II, such analogies struck a raw nerve in France and the Bonn Republic. Addressing the SFIO in April 1957, Mollet condemned these Nazi comparisons as 'a scandal'. 'Hitler gave orders that advocated these barbaric methods', the former premier argued, 'while Lacoste and I have always given orders in a sense that is completely contrary'.[49] The West German press, meanwhile, deplored the way some French newspapers, in a defensive reflex, blamed the army's excesses on the large number of Germans serving in the Foreign Legion: it was they, rather than French soldiers, who applied the torture methods they had learned in the SS.[50] These attempts to pass the blame on to the innately cruel '*Boches*' hardly fostered a spirit of rapprochement.[51] As for the FLN, its propaganda not only condemned French efforts to deflect responsibility for the excesses of war, but even defended the Germans serving in the Legion. In October 1957, the propaganda section attached to the ALN's 5th *wilâya* (military region) in Western Algeria ordered the distribution of tracts

45 'Les Assassins en Uniforme', *Éditions Résistance Algérienne*, 1957.

46 The leaflets can be found in SHD-T, 1H2588/D1.

47 Cited in: Daniel Lefeuvre, 'Les réactions algériennes à la propagande économique pendant la guerre d'Algérie', in *Guerre d'Algérie et Algériens* (ed.) Ageron, p. 240.

48 Cited in: Charles-Robert Ageron, 'La "guerre psychologique" de l'Armée de libération nationale algérienne', in *Guerre d'Algérie et Algériens* (ed.) Ageron, p. 207.

49 'Discours par Guy Mollet devant la fédération socialiste, 14 avril 1957', in *La Raison d'Etat* (ed.) Pierre Vidal-Naquet (Paris, 1962), p. 111.

50 It was a common misconception that most Germans in the Legion were former SS and Gestapo agents: Eckard Michels, *Deutsche in der Fremdenlegion 1870–1965. Mythen und Realitäten*, 5th edn (Paderborn, 2006), pp. 150–9.

51 'Verantwortung Deutschlands im Algerienkreig?' *Frankfurter Rundschau*, 10 May 1957; 'Die Deutschen sind an allem schuld', *Hannoversche Presse*, 27 August 1957; W. Dobritz, 'Algerien auch ein deutsches Problem', *Klarer Kurs* 5/10 (1957), pp. 16–17.

with messages such as, 'French leaders send foreign soldiers to their death [...] and spare their own children'.[52] *El Moudjahid* published articles depicting foreign – and especially German – legionnaires as victims of French oppression: just like the Algerian people, these young men had been enslaved by the French under false pretences and were now being forced to do the latter's dirty work.[53]

The French Foreign Legion

From its inception in 1831, a strong sense of mystique had shrouded the French Foreign Legion. The polyglot force made up of foreign volunteers was celebrated as an unrelenting and unforgiving elite force held together by draconian discipline and a unique *esprit de corps*. Due to its policy of anonymity, the Legion had also gained a reputation for attracting not just adventurers, romantics and runaways, but also criminals and thugs. Intimately linked to the history of colonial Algeria, where it was founded and headquartered at Sidi-Bel-Abbès, the Legion was at the forefront not only of France's colonial conquests but also of its late colonial conflicts in Indochina, Madagascar and Morocco. More importantly, its highly professional and mobile regiments spearheaded many of the counterinsurgency operations during the Algerian war.[54] From an Algerian perspective, it must have represented a potent instrument and symbol of colonial domination and brutality.

As the earlier examples indicate, however, FLN propaganda often depicted the Legion in a different light. This was hardly coincidental, for the image of the legionnaire as a hapless victim proved extremely effective in highlighting the unjust and repressive nature of French rule in Algeria, especially in countries such as West Germany, where the Legion had long been deemed a scourge. In the years prior to World War I, societies such as the 'German Protection League against the Foreign Legion' or the 'Association to Combat the Enslavement of Germans in the Foreign Legion' carried out intense propaganda campaigns to dissuade young men from enlisting. Following World War II, anti-Legion hysteria ran across the political spectrum. In the Federal Republic, youth organisations such as the *Jungsozialisten*, or *Jusos* (Young Socialists), and the Federal

[52] Publication de la section de propagande et d'éditions du commandement supérieur de la wilaya d'Oran, FLN/ALN, 12 October 1957, SHD-T, 1H/1715/D1.

[53] Examples include: 'Le véritable visage de la Légion Étrangère', *El Moudjahid* 26 (4 July 1958), p. 8; 'L'enfer de la "Légion"', *El Moudjahid* 79 (15 April 1961), pp. 11–12.

[54] Douglas Porch, *The French Foreign Legion: A Complete History* (London, 1993).

Youth Association worked together with welfare organisations like the Catholic *Caritasverband*, the Protestant relief agency *Evangelisches Hilfswerk* and the DRK to orchestrate nation-wide campaigns that sought to prevent Germans from enlisting and help those seeking to leave the Legion. Rumours of kidnappings and other dubious recruitment tactics abounded during the occupation period, especially in the tabloid and local press.[55] The *Bundeskriminalamt* (BKA), or Federal Criminal Police Office, continued to monitor the recruitment and return of legionnaires even after the abrogation of the Occupation Statute.[56]

Such protective measures were deemed necessary because Germans, and German speakers, constituted by far the strongest national group in the Legion. Of the 350,000-odd legionnaires who served between 1870 and 1962, around 100,000 were German. Of the 100,000 new recruits that joined during the wars in Indochina and Algeria, nearly 50 per cent were German. In 1953/54, Germans constituted a record 55 per cent of the Legion, dropping to 35 per cent during the Algerian war. Roughly one-third of the 50,000-odd Germans that served in Indochina and Algeria were under twenty-one and hence legal minors; a fair number were even under the minimum age of eighteen required for service in the armed forces.[57]

By linking its own cause of national liberation from colonial oppression with the German quest to "liberate" their youths from the Foreign Legion, the FLN disposed of a ready-made hook through which to bait West German public opinion. In October 1956, its National Council for the Algerian Revolution (CNRA) approved the creation of a 'Repatriation Service for Deserted Legionnaires' (*Service de rapatriement des légionnaires déserteurs*), which fell under the auspices of Abdelhafid Boussouf, the influential leader of Algeria's 5th *wilâya*. Boussouf operated largely from extraterritorial sanctuaries in Morocco, and it was in Tétouan, the former capital of Spanish Morocco, that he established the new *Service*.

As its head, Boussouf deliberately chose Winfried Müller, a German who went by the name of Si Mustapha.[58] One of the few Europeans to join

[55] Michels, *Deutsche*; Heinrich Nieder, 'Die französische Fremdenlegion – Légion Étrangère und die Auswirkungen ihrer Anziehungskraft auf Deutsche. Eine sozialwissenschaftliche Studie', PhD Dissertation (Universität Nürnberg-Erlangen, 1962); 'Verber Conundrum', pp. 84–105.

[56] Erörterung über die Fremdenlegion, Referat Z-B-3/BMI, 18 November 1955, BA/K, B106/20285.

[57] Jean-Paul Cahn, 'La République fédérale d'Allemagne et la question de la présence d'allemands dans la Légion étrangère française dans le contexte de la guerre d'Algérie (1954–1962)', *Guerres mondiales et conflits contemporains* 186 (1997), p. 96; Michels, *Deutsche*, pp. 180, 196–7, 274, 331–3.

[58] Meynier, *Histoire*, p. 484; 'Interview mit Si Mustapha', *Der Spiegel*, 2 September 1959; Klaus Polkehn, 'Die Mission des Si Mustapha – ein Deutscher kämpft für Algerien', *Comparativ* 16/2 (2006), p. 34–5.

the FLN, Winfried Müller's life remains enigmatic. Of his own admission, he was born in Wiesbaden in 1926 to a communist and part-Jewish family and spent most of World War II in concentration camps and Moscow, where he joined the National Committee for a Free Germany. Müller returned to Germany in 1945 with the communist Ulbricht Group, but was soon denounced as a Trotskyist and expelled from the Soviet Occupation Zone. His accounts are vague on what he did next. French military records indicate that Müller attempted to join the Legion in 1951 only to be rejected on the basis of his communist past.[59] By 1955, he had moved to France, where, through fellow Trotskyists, he came into contact with the FLN. Like others of the Fourth International, Müller allegedly acted as a courier for the FLN until imminent arrest precipitated his departure to Morocco. It was there in 1956 that he converted to Islam, joined the FLN, and decided 'to become an Algerian, and stay an Algerian'.[60]

Si Mustapha's mission as head of the FLN's Repatriation Service was threefold: first, to incite legionnaires to desert through a targeted propaganda campaign within Algeria, thereby weakening morale as well as the French war effort; second, to arrange for their repatriation; and third, to ensure international media coverage of said repatriations so as to score publicity points. Since German constituted the Foreign Legion's *lingua franca*, the Algerians relied on Si Mustapha's linguistic abilities to implement these goals. Charged by the FLN to target his activities on Germans and German-speaking regions, Si Mustapha recruited the aspiring journalists Hans-Peter Rullmann and Hans Karl Lindemann, based in Hamburg and West Berlin, to help publicise the Service's activities. In December 1956, these three men had formed the short-lived North-African Club, which aimed, so Couve de Murville believed, 'to weaken, through [...] propaganda, the will to fight of Germans in the Foreign Legion, and expose the ostensible atrocities committed by the French against the Algerians'. Dubbed 'Operation *Heimat*', the club produced pamphlets about the Repatriation Service and posted these to German and other European journalists as well as the families of legionnaires.[61] By late 1957, the Club

[59] Michels, *Deutsche*, p. 279.

[60] Polkehn, 'Mission', pp. 30–4; Leggewie, *Kofferträger*, pp. 89–91; Erika Fehse, 'Si Mustapha Müller – kurze Zeit des Ruhms', TV documentary (WDR, 1992); Cahn, 'Présence', p. 116; Meynier, *Histoire*, p. 484; Aufzeichnung, BfV an BMI, 21 August 1957, BA/K, B106/15600; Note de renseignements no. 25201, Service de Sécurité de la Défense Nationale et des Armées (SSDNA), 5 December 1958, SHD-T, 10T/522/D3*.

[61] Dépêche no. 908 de l'ambassadeur Couve de Murville, Bonn, 27 May 1957, MAE, MLA/2. Also: Schreiben der Botschaft Paris, 5 December 1956, PA/AA, B25/7; 'Rettung aus der Hölle Algeriens', *Der Mittag*, 11 May 1957; 'Le "Club nord-africain", section allemande du FLN organise la

had created three glossy information booklets for distribution in West Germany and other German-speaking countries: 'The Algerian People and its Revolution'; 'The True Face of the Algerian Revolution'; and 'The Revolution of the People and for the People'.[62] Together with other FLN propagandists, Si Mustapha fostered contacts to German journalists, including the foreign-affairs editors of the widely read *Süddeutsche Zeitung* (based in Munich) and *Die Welt*, the influential magazine *Der Spiegel*, and East Berlin's *Wochenpost*.[63] He extended countless invitations for journalists and photographers to visit the Repatriation Service, interview deserters, and follow the activities of the ALN. Popular tabloids such as the *Münchner Illustrierte* were particularly attracted by such invitations, though German diplomats tried to discourage them from accepting. In January 1958, for instance, the *Auswärtige Amt* asked the tabloid's editor-in-chief to call off a planned report from Tétouan for the sake of Franco-German relations.[64]

Although much of the publicity around the Repatriation Service belonged 'in the domain of fantasy', as one French official cautioned in March 1958, its impact was profound.[65] Just five months after the Service's creation, the Legion's inspector-general, Colonel Paul Lennuyeux, complained of abnormally high desertion rates particularly among two regiments stationed in Morocco. Lennuyeux blamed this development in part on the FLN's skilfully contrived propaganda campaigns. Comparing Si Mustapha's Repatriation Service to the Vietminh's *Dich Van*, which had organised desertions during the Indochina war, he concluded, 'this time we are facing a truly large-scale operation, efficiently organized and managed by the FLN, and supported by Moroccan elements'.[66] Although the FLN's claim of 4,000 repatriations was greatly exaggerated, the Service had

propagande, le trafic d'armes et la désertion des légionnaires', *Le Figaro*, 18 June 1957; 'Les révélations sensationnelles de nos envoyés spéciaux sur les agissements du FLN en Allemagne', *Jours de France*, 20 July 1957.

62 *Das algerische Volk und seine Revolution* (ed.) Résistance Algérienne, undated, SHD-T, 1H/1715/D1; Dépêche no. 1855 de l'ambassadeur Couve de Murville, Bonn, 21 November 1957, MAE, EU/RFA/1272; Hans Karl Lindemann (ed. and trans.), *Das wahre Gesicht der algerischen Revolution*, undated, BA/K, B106/15600; Winfried Müller (ed. and trans.), *Die Revolution von dem Volk und für das Volk*, El Moudjahid, undated; Dépêches nos. 407 et 1 du conseiller politique au gouvernement militaire à Berlin, 17 December 1957 and 1 January1958, MAE, MLA/2.

63 Dépêche no. 651 du consul-général Robert de Nerciat, Munich, 16 July 1957; dépêche no. 387 du conseiller politique de Chalvron, Berlin, 2 December 1957, MAE, EU/RFA/1272; Leggewie, *Kofferträger* p. 17; Polkehn, 'Mission', p. 30.

64 Schreiben, Generalkonsul Obermaier, Casablanca, 8 January 1958; Vermerk, Referat 302, 14 January 1958, PA/AA, B25/74.

65 Télégramme no. 1903 de la DGGA au Quai d'Orsay, 12 March 1958, MAE, MLA/2.

66 Cited in: Michels, *Deutsche*, p. 279.

managed not only to incite desertions, but also to sensitise West German opinion to the Algerian war.[67]

The French riposte

These successes did not go unnoticed in France, where they nourished enduring suspicions of German subversive intentions in Algeria. In June 1957, Bonn's ambassador in Paris drew attention to a significant rise in the number of newspaper-articles accusing Germans of conspiring against France and assisting the FLN. Many of the articles revolved around the machinations of the North-African Club; others made blanket generalisations. Maltzan was alarmed by the manner in which the resultant accusations spanned the political spectrum, for they were not confined to conservative or reactionary newspapers such as *l'Aurore*, *Carrefour* or *Fraternité Française* (a Poujadist paper), but could also be found in moderate and left-wing papers such as *Le Monde*, *Paris-Soir*, *Combat* and *Tribune des Nations*.[68] Even prominent politicians voiced their concern, as illustrated by Senator Debré's interventions in the case of the FLN press conference and ARD documentary. In August 1957, socialist deputy Marcel-Edmond Naegelen blamed the supposed presence of numerous Arab agitators in West Germany for poisoning Franco-German relations. Writing in the *Dépêche du Midi*, he complained that the government of Radical leader Maurice Bourgès-Maunoury did too little to counter the FLN's international public-relations efforts, especially in Western Europe.[69]

Naegelen's reproach was unwarranted, for the authorities in Algiers and Paris were steadily intensifying their counter-propaganda. In April 1957, Resident-Minister Lacoste had alerted the government to the 'indisputable' need for a new and global information campaign.[70] In the battle for hearts and minds, the French, like the FLN, had initially concentrated much of their attention on the United States, whose attitude both sides deemed pivotal to winning over international opinion, particularly at the UN. Thus while Massu's elite 10th Parachute Division had battled the FLN for control of Algiers, another French 'battalion' of secretaries, interpreters, *colons* and Francophile Algerians engaged in what Connelly

[67] Dépêche no. 908 de l'ambassadeur Couve de Murville, Bonn, 27 May 1957, MAE, MLA/2.

[68] Bericht Nr. 2806/57 der Botschaft Paris, 21 June 1957, PA/AA, B24/310/F4.

[69] Bericht Nr. 1739 des Generalkonsulats Marseille, 20 August 1957, PA/AA, B24/278/F1.

[70] Dépêche par Robert Lacoste pour René Coty et Guy Mollet, 30 April 1957, Archives Nationales (AN), Paris, 4AG/45.

called an all-out public-relations offensive in the 'battle of New York'.[71] Eager to downplay the army's destructive counterinsurgency operations and especially its excesses, which painted the French in such a negative light, the public-relations offensive focused on France's constructive counterinsurgency efforts, especially the implementation of sweeping social and economic reforms. Through brochures, newspaper articles, public lectures, radio broadcasts and film footage the authorities sought to draw attention to France's positive achievements in Algeria, whether in the realm of social work, health care, education, industrial development, or agricultural modernisation. Their propaganda dwelled on the harmonious co-existence of two ethnically and culturally diverse communities, negating the very existence of a war. Drawing on familiar colonial tropes, Pierre Baraduc, director of information and press at the *Quai d'Orsay*, aimed to depict France as a 'civilized nation' that was 'at the forefront of progress and bringing democracy and prosperity to backward populations'. He sought to highlight how France, together with Algeria, 'is striving forward into a new era epitomized by Euratom, the Common European Market, Eurafrica'. The fates of Algeria, France and Europe thus remained inherently intertwined in French propaganda.[72]

After the intense Battle of Algiers/Battle of New York, the French government's public-relations offensive rapidly expanded beyond the United States. In West Germany, too, French diplomats monitored the press with increased intensity, focusing on national and local newspapers.[73] By April 1957, the Algiers government had printed and distributed 20,000 German translations of the information booklet 'Algeria: here 9,500,000 French citizens live side by side'; 30,000 of 'Essential notions on Algeria'; and 4,000 of 'Industrial Algeria', and was preparing to print more.[74] Together with the *Quai d'Orsay*, the authorities in Algiers also began to organise information tours for carefully selected groups of so-called unbiased observers. Through a 'policy of open windows', these tours for foreign diplomats, politicians, businessmen and journalists aimed to promote a 'dispassionate and objective appraisal' of the Algerian situation, one that demonstrated the difficulties France faced, and the progress that had

[71] Connelly, *Diplomatic Revolution*, pp. 133–4, 127, 119; Vaïsse, 'Guerre perdue?' p. 454.

[72] Cited in: Connelly, *Diplomatic Revolution*, pp. 140, 138.

[73] This can be observed by the '*bordereaux d'envoi*' (cover sheets) listing newspaper clippings on Algeria dispatched by French diplomats and consular officials in the FRG found in MAE, EU/RFA/1272 and MLA/2.

[74] Dépêche par Robert Lacoste, Alger, 30 April 1957, AN, 4AG/45.

already been made in the implementation of reforms.[75] In May 1957, Mr Gramss from the Düsseldorf daily *Der Mittag* became the first German to participate on such a tour, and others soon followed.[76]

Apart from emphasising France's 'war of modernisation' in Algeria, French efforts to influence German and Western European opinion also brandished the communist card and played on racial sentiments. In combating the FLN, so the argument went, France engaged in a defence of 'Western civilization' against 'Red imperialism' and 'Islamic fanaticism'.[77] These themes, Connelly argues, resonated with the image of the 'Christian West' (*christliche Abendland*) as a bulwark against the depraved and despotic East that was so popular among Christian and conservative circles in Western Europe during the 1950s.[78] To underscore their opponents' supposed fanaticism and depravity, French propaganda concentrated on the FLN's severe and brutal treatment of those it deemed traitors (especially Muslim auxiliaries, or *harkis*, who fought alongside the French and other Francophile Algerians) or rivals (Algerians who supported the MNA). Such chastisements generally aimed to terrorise the Algerian population into compliance. Though never formally condoned by the FLN's leaders, they did at times reach sickening proportions. One such example occurred in late May 1957 in the remote Kabylian village of Mélouza, where ALN *mujâhideen* killed over 300 men in retaliation for the region's continued allegiance to the MNA. A few days later, a similar, though smaller massacre occurred in the village of Wagram in north-western Algeria.[79] The French authorities used these incidents to demonise the FLN and direct attention away from the French forces' own brutal excesses. In a radio message, President René Coty appealed 'to all civilised peoples' asking them to reject 'this horrible terrorism, which tramples on all the laws of God and man in contempt of the universal conscience'.[80] In a glossy brochure titled 'World opinion judges the savage "liberators" of Mélouza and Wagram', the Algiers government turned the tables on the FLN, now accusing the latter of Nazism.[81] France's strict censorship regime normally sought to deny foreign (and French)

[75] Lettre circulaire par Xavier de Montjoye, consul de France à Kiel, 5 August 1957, MAE, EU/RFA/1272. Also: Connelly, *Diplomatic Revolution*, p. 138.

[76] Schreiben, Generalkonsulat Algier, 16 May 1957, PA/AA, B25/7.

[77] Ibid.

[78] Connelly, *Diplomatic Revolution*, p. 134. Refer also to Chapter 3.

[79] Martha Crenshaw Hutchinson, *Revolutionary Terrorism: The FLN in Algeria, 1954–1962* (Stanford CA, 1978), pp. 44–9.

[80] 'President Coty's Message to the World on the Algerian Massacre of May 31, 1957', *French Affairs* 47/3 (3 June 1957), MAE, AL/ALG/24.

[81] LeSueur, *Uncivil War*, p. 176.

journalists access to scenes of fighting in Algeria. This time, the authorities positively encouraged reporters from agencies and newspapers around the world, including *Die Welt* and the West German Press Agency (DPA), to witness and document the atrocities for themselves.[82] The *Quai d'Orsay*, too, enjoined its representatives 'to make the best use' of the massacre, 'according to the state of opinion in the country of [their] residence on the Algerian question' and invited foreign diplomats to visit Mélouza.[83] At first, the German embassy in Paris hesitated, anxious to uphold the public appearance of neutrality. It eventually relented, dispatching a junior secretary, Hermann Munz.[84]

For a moment, Mélouza threatened to turn world opinion against the FLN, which denied all responsibility for the massacre and called on the UN to investigate both sides' conduct in the war.[85] However, the French forces' unrelenting application of mass repression and collective punishment quickly reversed this trend. By November 1957, Ambassador Couve de Murville concluded that the latest information tour organised for a group of West German journalists had failed entirely to produce the positive press coverage the French authorities so desired – and this although French diplomats had hand-picked the participants. The editor-in-chief of Essen's *Neue Rhein Zeitung*, for instance, was 'not tender' in his assessment of French policies in Algeria. He remained unconvinced by the French argument that Algeria essentially constituted a 'European task' and urged the Bonn government not to support France's new programme of reforms.[86] The Hamburg-based *Bild* tabloid took an equally critical view, arguing that Algeria's social and economic plight merely highlighted the contradictions inherent in the French claim that Algeria was part of France. In a radio broadcast for the *Westdeutsche Rundfunk*, another tour participant concluded pessimistically that France's modernisation efforts hardly changed the fact that the Algerian conflict remained insoluble. The conservative *Frankfurter Neue Presse* and *Stuttgarter Nachrichten*, and the liberal weekly *Die Zeit* were more sympathetic in their portrayals. Although these papers, too, concluded that France's programme of reforms

82 Fernschreiben Nr. 451, Botschaft Paris, 11 June 1957, PA/AA, B25/6.

83 Télégramme circulaire no. 49 de la Direction générale des affaires culturelles et techniques, 11 June 1957; Télégramme circulaire no. 2360 du cabinet du ministre, 7 June 1957, MAE, AL/ALG/24.

84 Vermerk, Referat 302 (Böker), 12 June 1957, PA/AA, B25/6.

85 Connelly, *Diplomatic Revolution*, p. 132; Thomas, *French*, p. 86.

86 Télégramme no. 2789 de l'ambassadeur Couve de Murville, Bonn, 20 November 1957, MAE, MLA/2.

failed to address the war's political roots, they at least praised French efforts as commendable.[87]

All of these responses were unsurprising to Couve de Murville, who noted how anti-colonialist in tone a large section of the West German press had become. Social-democratic and leftist newspapers such as the *Neue Rhein Zeitung*, in particular, 'lent an indulgent ear to Arab propaganda, especially that of the FLN'. As another example of this empathy, the ambassador cited the *Hamburger Echo*, which in November 1957 advertised a public screening of a film about Algeria in the local offices of the Social Democratic Party (SPD) that would include commentary by FLN militants.[88] One month later, Councillor Bernard de Chalvron in Berlin drew attention to the close contact between *Die Welt*'s chief editor Hans Zehrer and FLN propagandist Abderrahman Kiouane. The latter had supposedly persuaded Zehrer to publish a translation of Servan-Schreiber's highly critical eyewitness account to French repression and brutality, *Lieutenant en Algérie*, as well as an appeal for humanitarian aid for the Algerian victims of said aggression.[89] In highlighting cases of colonial oppression, valiant resistance, or the *liberation* of young Germans from the Foreign Legion, FLN propaganda drew on emotional and moral themes. Though it inflated the Algerians' achievements and strength, such propaganda made a deeper impression on West German journalists (and on the public) than factual stories about French administrative, industrial, or agricultural reforms. In other words, FLN propaganda was easier to sell. More importantly, FLN propaganda made it possible for West German journalists and the public to take a moral high ground vis-à-vis France. Although one should not generalise, some Germans must have secretly felt relieved, perhaps even satisfied, by the fact that they were able to draw attention to the injustice and inhumanity perpetrated by others in the name of European civilisation. The French government's information tours did little to redress this trend. By negating the existence of war and blatantly attempting to influence how foreign journalists reported the unfolding events, they made the French line appear biased and untrustworthy. In March 1958, Baraduc acknowledged that censorship had 'made the worst impression abroad' for it belied the free and democratic system the French supposedly sought to create in Algeria.[90]

[87] Télégramme no. 2816 de l'ambassadeur Couve de Murville, Bonn, 23 November 1957, MAE, MLA/2.

[88] Télégramme no. 2789, 20 November 1957, MAE, MLA/2.

[89] Dépêche no. 387 du conseiller politique à Berlin, 2 December 1957, MAE, MLA/2; 'Humanität', *Die Welt*, 29 November 1957.

[90] Cited in: Connelly, *Diplomatic Revolution*, pp. 132–3, 135.

Stirrings of civic engagement

By then, the West German press seemed universally critical of France's Algerian policies, with the Sakiet crisis of February 1958 once more proving a watershed. The crisis revealed the extent to which Algeria was perceived as 'the Achilles heel of the West', with French military action not only straining the NATO alliance but also threatening to discredit France's allies, especially in the eyes of the Arab world.[91] To Councillor François Leduc of the French embassy in Bonn, the 'unanimous condemnation' of the aerial bombardment that could be found in all the major newspapers, irrespective of their political orientation, was indicative of 'the latent hostility of public opinion toward our Algerian policies'. Even papers usually sympathetic to France and close to the CDU/CSU such as the *Bonner Rundschau* or *Münchner Merkur* openly questioned France's chances of success in Algeria.[92] Consul Maurice Ardiet in Hanover thought the entire press of Lower-Saxony conducted a 'violent campaign' against French policies in North Africa.[93] The fiercest criticism, however, came from the West German Left. For the first time, social-democratic newspapers themselves raised the spectre of Nazism. The *Frankfurter Rundschau* and *Neue Rhein Zeitung* likened the Sakiet bombing to the SS's destruction of the French village of Oradour-sur-Glane in June 1944 and chastised the Bonn government for supporting France's Algerian policies. The socialist youth organisation, *Die Falken*, drew parallels to the Luftwaffe's bombing of Coventry in 1940. Willi Eichler, a prominent member of the SPD's executive, compared Sakiet to the Nazi massacre of the Czech village of Lidice in 1942. The SPD's central organ *Vorwärts*, meanwhile, spoke of an 'act of barbarism' and, preferring a more recent parallel, warned of a 'Tunisian Budapest'. [94] Coming from Germans not long after World War II, these comparisons infuriated French diplomats. Ardiet in particular spoke of an 'excess in violence' that highlighted the depths of 'German bad taste'.[95]

Whether in bad taste or not, the moral judgements of German social-democrats exposed a deep concern over the evolution of events in North Africa. They are also representative of an earnest and growing advocacy among different sections of West German civil society for a new, human rights-based

[91] Müller, 'La guerre vue par la presse', pp. 182, 179–80.

[92] Télégramme no. 340 de l'ambassade de France, Bonn, 10 February 1958; Dépêche no. 150 du consul-général de Nerciat, Munich, 11 February 1958, MAE, EU/RFA/1272.

[93] Dépêche no. 53 du consul Ardiet, Hanovre, 17 February 1958, EU/RFA/1272.

[94] Scheffler, *SPD*, p. 49.

[95] Dépêche no. 46 du consul Ardiet, Hanovre, 11 February 1958, MAE, EU/RFA/1258.

foreign policy. Among the numerous German critiques of French policy in Algeria, one increasingly found appeals to civic engagement or foreign government intervention. The press's call for the Bonn authorities to accord Algerians in the FRG political asylum, discussed in Chapter 3, epitomised this new tone, yet one could also find other, less dramatic examples. West German university students, for instance, had begun to remonstrate the French authorities' harassment and persecution of Algerian students. Spurred into action by the Leiden-based Coordinating Secretariat of National Unions of Students (COSEC), the *Verband deutscher Studentenschaften* (VdS), an umbrella association representing all West German student unions, wrote to the French interior and foreign ministers protesting the dissolution on 29 January 1958 of its Algerian counterpart, the *Union générale des étudiants musulmans algériens* (UGEMA), and the arrest of its secretary-general Mohammed Khemisti, one month before.[96] The French Interior Ministry refused to engage with the German students' protests, demanding instead an intervention in Bonn to rein in the 'inimical and insolent' VdS. The *Quai d'Orsay*, meanwhile, responded defensively, lecturing the German association that UGEMA had become 'a cover for [the] subversive activities' of the FLN, an organisation 'that, contrary to what you might have heard, does not inconvenience itself with moral considerations or democratic principles'.[97] Such attempts to justify French repression and tarnish Algerian nationalists hardly convinced the West German student association, some of whose members had also rallied around the cause of the female student Djamila Bouhired. Captured in April 1957 while transporting correspondence between Saadi Yacef and Ali la Pointe, the chief architects of the FLN's campaign of urban terrorism during the Battle of Algiers, Bouhired's subjection to torture and subsequent death sentence sparked international protests, including public demonstrations organised by students in Göttingen and Hanover.[98]

'[F]or now', Ambassador Couve de Murville reported, such marches constituted only 'isolated protests that cannot be considered part of a systematic and orchestrated campaign'.[99] Yet he was clearly concerned this might not remain the case. After all, signs of agitation continued to mount.

[96] COSEC Circular Nr. 18, 11 December 1957; Protestbrief, Hans Grigoleit, VdS Vize-Präsident, an die französische Botschaft, Bonn, Außenminister Pineau und Innenminister Bourgès-Maunoury, 30 January 1958; COSEC Circulars Nr. 31 and 34, 7 February and 7 March 1958, BA/K, B166/1414.

[97] Dépêche no. 43 de la Direction générale des affaires politiques à l'ambassadeur de France à Bonn, 14 March 1958; Lettre de la Direction générale des Affaires politiques à Hans Grigoleit, 27 February 1958, MAE, EU/RFA/1272.

[98] Dépêche no. 44 du consul Ardiet, Hanovre, 10 February 1958; Dépêche no. 80 d'Ardiet, 7 March 1958, MAE, EU/RFA/1272.

[99] Dépêche no. 482 de l'ambassadeur Couve de Murville, 12 March 1958, MAE, EU/RFA/1272.

Already a pillar of the anti-Legion campaign, the SPD's *Jungsozialisten* supported calls by the Socialist International to aid the growing number of Algerian refugees in North Africa.[100] In a press release dated 20 April 1958, the *Jusos* called on the SPD executive to take up contact with the FLN and condemn French repression in Algeria, which 'not only infringed against the right to self-determination of nations and human rights but also constituted a betrayal of the principles of democratic socialism'.[101] Until then, the SPD had abstained from commenting on Algeria out of deference to the SFIO, one of its closest allies.[102] This changed after Sakiet. The party's branch offices in Bonn and Hamburg joined the *Jusos* in denouncing French policies in Algeria.[103] Walter Menzel and Karl Mommer, leaders of the SPD's *Bundestag* faction, called on the Adenauer government to condemn the incident. Concerned by the recently agreed EPU loan to France, party chairman Erich Ollenhauer demanded assurances that Bonn's financial aid would not benefit the French war effort in Algeria.[104] Meanwhile, the *Bundestag* deputy Peter Blachstein, one of the few party members to have met FLN propagandists during their press conference in Hamburg, came to the aid of the *Croissant Rouge Algérien* (CRA), or Algerian Red Crescent, a relief organisation formed by the FLN in January 1957 to challenge the French stranglehold on humanitarian aid and solicit moral and material aid from the international community.[105] Highlighting the substantial humanitarian assistance already being provided by the East German Red Cross in North Africa,

100 Michels, *Deutsche*, pp. 238–41; Karlheinz Schonauer, 'Geschichte und Politik der Jungsozialisten und der SPD 1946–1973. Der Wandel der SPD-Jugendorganisation von der braven Parteijugend zur innerparteilichen Opposition', PhD Dissertation (Freie Universität zu Berlin, 1980), pp. 119–21.

101 'Jungsozialisten verurteilen französische Algerienpolitik', Presseinformation, 20 April 1958, AdsD, NL/Plum/29; Scheffler, *SPD*, p. 53.

102 Jean-Paul Cahn, *Le parti social-démocrate et la fin de la Quatrième République française (1954–1958)* (Bern, 1996), pp. 155–59, 391–466; Cahn and Müller, *RFA et guerre d'Algérie*, pp. 36–44; Scheffler, *SPD*, pp. 25, 28, 40–44. On the SPD's ties to the SFIO: Talbot Imlay, '"The Policy of Social Democracy is Self-consciously Internationalist": The German Social Democratic Party's Internationalism after 1945', *Journal of Modern History* 86/1 (2014), pp. 81–123, esp. 92–5.

103 Kreisdelegiertenversammlung, SPD, Hamburg, 21 February 1958, AdsD, NL/Peter Blachstein/32; Pressemitteilung, Ortsverein Bonn, SPD, 14 March 1958, AdsD, NL/Plum/29.

104 *Verhandlungen des Deutschen Bundestages. Stenographische Berichte* (VdDBT/StB), 3. Wahlperiode 1957–1961 (Bonn), 16. Sitzung, 12 March 1958, pp. 731–2; *Verhandlungen des Deutschen Bundestages. Anlagen zu den Stenographischen Berichten. Drucksachen* (VdDBT/D) 3. Wahlperiode 1957–1961 (Bonn), Drucksache 275: Kleine Anfrage der SPD Fraktion betr. finanzielle Leistungen der BRD an Frankreich, 12 March 1958; Drucksache 309: Der Bundesminister für Verteidigung Nr. 578 I/58: Antwort auf die kleine Anfrage der Fraktion der SPD betr. finanzielle Leistungen der BRD an Frankreich, 27 March 1958.

105 Hong, *Cold War Germany*, p. 136; Jennifer Johnson Onyedum, '"Humanize the Conflict": Algerian Health Care Organizations and Propaganda Campaigns', *International Journal of Middle East Studies* 44/4 (2012), p. 719.

Blachstein contacted its West German equivalent, the DRK, urging it, too, to respond to the CRA's calls for aid.[106] In fact, the DRK had recently wired 100,000DM to the International Committee of the Red Cross (ICRC) as a contribution toward the latter's relief work in North Africa. Given Germany's own 'great debt of gratitude' for the humanitarian assistance received during the post-war period, DRK President Heinrich Weitz felt obliged to respond to the ICRC's appeals with at least this 'relatively modest aid'.[107]

By the time of the Fourth Republic's demise, therefore, West German opinion across the political spectrum not only criticised the French counterinsurgency in Algeria, but it had also started to oppose it, urging the Bonn government to do the same. French propaganda had sought to draw attention to the constructive, modernising and civilising role that France purported to play in Algeria. This image of a benevolent and nurturing France clashed invariably with the brutal and indiscriminate measures deployed against the Algerian people, which trampled on individual liberties and human rights as well as on international norms and laws. Nothing highlighted this inherent contradiction between the constructive and destructive sides to *guerre révolutionnaire* more than the plight of Algerian refugees, whether those in North Africa caught up in the Sakiet crisis, or those in the FRG whose status remained in dispute. As more and more civil-society actors called for the provision of humanitarian aid to these victims of war, it became clear that French efforts to influence West German opinion had failed in their desired effect.

Conversely, through their adept exploitation of themes that tapped into West German cultural and political sensitivities – whether the country's Nazi past, the post-war Occupation and historical enmity with France, the French Foreign Legion, or the Cold War competition with the GDR – Algerian propagandists had managed to gain sympathy not just from a significant cross-section of the West German press but also from a growing circle of civil associations. Though hardly systematic or widespread, some of this sympathy had begun to turn into humanitarian and political support. At this point, calls for civic engagement came largely

106 Lettre par Omar Boukli-Hacène, président du CRA, au président de la Croix-Rouge Allemande, 2 February 1957, PA/AA, B25/9; Werner Ludwig, 'Deutsche Demokratische Republik hilft Algerien', *Neues Deutschland*, 26 February 1958; Schreiben des Vertreters des algerischen Roten Halbmonds an Blachstein, undated; Brief, DRK an Blachstein, 8 March 1958, AdsD, NL/Blachstein/32.

107 Schreiben, Dr. Weitz, an Bundesaussenminister Brentano, 24 February 1958 and 4 March 1958, ADRK, DRK (FRG)/5173/I.

from the Left and from younger generations that embraced a new, human rights-based foreign policy. As the next chapter will show, however, another, altogether less idealistic group of civil-society actors had also begun to support the FLN: namely, West German arms dealers. The battle for hearts and minds, after all, constituted only one dimension of Algeria's independence struggle. Of equal, if not greater, significance than the psychological war was the armed struggle itself, for which the FLN required a steady supply of arms, munitions and other vital materiel. As shall be seen, West Germany would play an important part in the movement's procurement efforts. In effect, the country became an armoury of the FLN.

CHAPTER 5

FLN contraband in West Germany

In the early 1960s, Bernt Engelmann travelled to Tunisia to visit an ALN base on the Algerian frontier.[1] After twelve uncomfortable hours spent in the back of a lorry, the *Spiegel* reporter discovered, upon arrival at the base, that the crates on which he had sat were filled with anti-personnel mines. Like him, these mines had begun their clandestine journey in Western Europe. Engelmann found an army equipped with Italian Beretta pistols, American and British infantry rifles and howitzers, as well as German Mauser carbines, mortars, bazookas and anti-aircraft guns. The soldiers' sheath knives and cookware, too, were of German – *Wehrmacht* – vintage. Asked by Engelmann what he thought of the men who secretly sold these supplies to the ALN, Abdelhafid Boussouf – by then promoted to the powerful post of Minister for Armaments and General Relations in the GPRA – supposedly replied:

> You know [. . .] arms dealers are indispensible for a revolution. They serve the progress of humanity in their own way. What would have happened to the declaration of independence of the United States of America [. . .] if General Washington had not known the addresses of a few capable gun-runners? [. . .] [A]rms dealers are businessmen like any others. They take risks and want to make money, and they strive to balance their risks against their earnings. Some are honest merchants, others fraudsters – exactly as in other lines of business! And they are not half as swashbuckling and romantic as one generally imagines.[2]

What Boussouf neglected to tell Engelmann was that many of the dealers sustaining the Algerian revolution with arms were in fact German. By 1960, the Bonn Republic had become a central hub in the FLN's efforts to

[1] Some sections of this chapter incorporate material first published in: Mathilde von Bülow, 'Myth or Reality? The Red Hand and French Covert Action in Federal Germany during the Algerian War, 1956–61', *Intelligence and National Security* 22/6 (2007), pp. 787–820.

[2] Bernt Engelmann, *Meine Freunde, die Waffenhändler. Kleine Kriege – große Geschäfte* (Bergisch Gladbach, 1964), pp. 6–8.

procure war materiel. How could a country that at the time of the Algerian war's inception did not even possess its own army let alone a significant armaments industry come to play such a pivotal role in FLN supply networks? What impact did this development have on French counterinsurgency efforts, and how did the authorities react to the FLN's procurement activities in West Germany? The Federal Republic, this chapter argues, was always more than an extraterritorial refuge for FLN militants. Just as the country became an important conduit for the clandestine movement of recruits, so, too, it developed into a vital logistical base from where the FLN secretly procured the means to sustain its insurgencies in Algeria and France. As shall be seen, these clandestine machinations transformed the FRG into a prime target – and the Bonn government into a key ally – in one of the most important and understudied facets of the French counterinsurgency: the army's campaign to asphyxiate the FLN's military and non-military supplies.

Arming the revolution

Conceived as a people's struggle against colonialism, FLN strategy emphasised armed action as the ultimate path to national liberation. If recruiting the manpower to sustain the insurgency proved easy, the task of furnishing the *mujâhideen* with the equipment and supplies required to sustain a long war was far more challenging. The militants who launched the revolution in November 1954 had disposed over 400-odd firearms, hardly enough to transform a small insurrection into a people's war.[3] For this, the FLN required a steady supply of light and portable firearms and explosives that could easily be concealed both in an urban environment and in the Algerian *bled* (hinterland). To prepare for pitched battles, the ALN required heavier arms, including machine guns, bazookas and mortars. The revolution's success depended also on recourse to a range of non-military provisions, including vehicles, tents, field beds, blankets, combat rations, field-kitchen equipment, combat fatigues and boots, wire-cutters, saws, shears, knives and other tools, binoculars, compasses, pocket lights, chirurgical tools and pharmaceuticals. Radio transmitters and receivers were needed to enable communication and coordination between command posts within Algeria and across the Maghreb. From the start, therefore, the procurement of arms, munitions and non-military supplies represented one of the FLN's principal and most pressing concerns.

[3] Harbi, *1954*, p. 69.

As Mohammed Harbi argues, it became 'an obsession that would accentuate [the] militancy' of the movement's leaders.[4]

The FLN initially procured many of its supplies internally. Non-military goods were bought through inconspicuous middlemen; arms and munitions were obtained through raids on French military and police depots or seizures from captured or killed French soldiers.[5] These sources proved inconstant and insufficient, however, especially in a context of tightening economic and security controls. It fell to the FLN's external delegates, especially Ahmed Ben Bella and Mohamed Khider in Cairo, and Mohamed Boudiaf in Tétouan assisted by Larbi Ben M'hidi in the Oranais, to organise supplies from abroad.[6] As Mohamed Lebjaoui remembers it, 'the revolution's first militants for a long time remained isolated individuals who had to impose themselves painstakingly against indifference and scepticism to assemble the derisory means that would enable them to start the fight'.[7] Success also depended on funds, which were in short supply. The FLN's foreign delegates initially relied on donations from foreign allies. Morocco and Tunisia provided material and logistical support, especially after they obtained their independence.[8] Egypt also proved an increasingly important source of aid, its *mukhabarât* arranging training and logistical support for Algerian *junud* as well as a steady supply of arms. Other member-states of the Arab League, too, came to provide financial and logistical support.[9]

The early stages of the war were nonetheless marked by improvisation, a lack of coordination and a severe shortage of modern weaponry. The arms procured by the FLN's external delegates were mostly of a pre-1945 vintage – leftovers from the desert campaigns of World War II. Many were damaged or derelict, and because their makes and calibres were so diverse – Mauser, Beretta, Enfield, Sten and Statti constituting the most commonly used rifles – the procurement and allocation of suitable ammunition soon became a logistical nightmare. As the revolution grew in force during 1956 and 1957, the ALN turned its attention to standardising and

[4] Ibid., p. 24. Also: Alf Andrew Heggoy, *Insurgency and Counterinsurgency in Algeria* (Bloomington IN, 1972), p. 89; Meynier, *Histoire*, p. 308; Tripier, *Autopsie*, p. 167.

[5] Bulletin d'information no. 417/INS/AFN, 30 April 1956, SHD-T, 1H/1101/D3; Dépêche no. 1668 de Général Henri Lorillot, commandant en chef des forces françaises en Algérie (CCFFA) au résident général à Algers, 22 February 1956, 1H/1536Bis/D1. Also: Martin Thomas, 'Policing Algeria's Borders, 1956–1960: Arms Supplies, Frontier Defences and the Sakiet Affair', *War & Society* 13/1 (1995), p. 88.

[6] Harbi, *FLN*, pp. 124, 174; Meynier, *Histoire*, p. 308.

[7] Lebjaoui, *Vérités*, p. 124.

[8] Étude no. 1546, 10ème Région Militaire (Algérie), Etat-Major, Deuxième Bureau (10.RM/EM/2), 16 July 1955, SHD-T, 1H2594/D6; Lebjaoui, *Vérités*, pp. 125–38.

[9] Harbi, *FLN*, p. 174; Merle, *Ben Bella*, pp. 98–102; Meynier, *Histoire*, p. 308; al-Dib, *Nasser*, parts 1–3.

modernising its armaments. After the hijacking and capture of the FLN's initial external delegates in October 1956, the acquisition of military and non-military materiel and organisation of supply networks was delegated to Omar Ouamrane, who was put in charge of a newly created Office for Armaments and General Provisions (the *Direction de l'armement et du ravitaillement général*).[10] By then, the revolutionary tax imposed on Algerian migrants in France had begun to boost the FLN's finances.[11] Donned with a new infrastructure and mounting financial resources and aided by its Arab allies, Ouamrane's operatives turned to the international arms trade to acquire supplies. Their activities soon focused on the FRG.

West Germany and the international arms trade

The suggestion that Algerian militants purchased arms and munitions in West Germany initially met with disbelief among French officers stationed in the country. Colonel Duchène, who represented the intelligence services, and his colleague General Pierre Le Hingrat, the military attaché in Bonn, both dismissed the idea as absurd when the first rumours surfaced in July 1956. The country had been thoroughly demilitarised and disarmed after 1945, they argued. True enough, the Korean War had provoked a rethink on West German rearmament, and by 1951 the Allies had approved a resumption of the manufacture of light weaponry, yet the Allied Military Security Office oversaw the production, sale, import, export, transport and transit of all material of military significance. The manufacture and sale of conventional armaments did not resume in earnest until after May 1955. Even then, it expanded so slowly that the newly established *Bundeswehr* initially had to be equipped from allied stocks.[12]

On the surface, therefore, West Germany appeared an unlikely player in the FLN's procurement efforts, and yet the country became a 'happy hunting ground' for international arms traffickers.[13] Several factors explain the paradoxical situation that arose after the repeal of the Occupation Statute. For one, although §26.2 of the Basic Law stipulated a strict control

[10] Meynier, *Histoire*, p. 308. [11] Ibid., pp. 471–4; Haroun, *7ème Wilaya*, pp. 307–24.

[12] Schreiben Nr. 462/56 an Abteilungsleiter VI/BMI, 18 July 1956, BA/K, B106/156000; Dépêche no. 924 du Général Le Hingrat, 13 August 1956, SHD-T, 14S/20*. Also: Oliver Haller, 'German Industry, The Cold War, and the Bundeswehr', and Dieter H. Kollmer, 'Reasons of State: A Military and Foreign Trade Necessity. The International Mix of Armaments in the Build-up Phase of the Bundeswehr 1953–1958', both in *Rearming Germany* (ed.) J. S. Corum (Leiden, 2011), pp. 145–75 and 177–201; D.C. Large, *Germans to the Front: West German Rearmament in the Adenauer Era* (Chapel Hill NC, 1996).

[13] Horne, *Savage War*, p. 262.

of the production, purchase, sale, export and import, transit, storage and usage of all armaments and war-related materials, the legal framework to govern these issues – the so-called *Kriegswaffenkontrollgesetz* (law on the control of weapons of war) and *Außenwirtschaftsgesetz* (law on foreign trade) – had yet to be drafted. In the interim, the Federal Ministry for Economic Affairs regulated the arms trade by means of a temporary decree (the *vorläufige Kriegswaffen-Genehmigungsverfahren*) stipulating that the purchase and sale of armaments had to be authorised by federal authorities in both economic and political-diplomatic terms.[14]

The temporary procedures in place for obtaining said authorisations, however, contained a number of omissions and loopholes that positively encouraged illegal arms trafficking. For one, the decree only covered armaments formally classified as *Kriegswaffen* (weapons of war) and excluded so-called *Relativwaffen*, that is, such light, portable and relatively cheap arms used primarily for hunting, recreation and sport. Precisely these *Relativwaffen*, however, were ideally suited for insurgency warfare. In September 1956 the newly appointed commander-in-chief of French forces in Germany, General Pierre-Élie Jacquot, informed Adenauer that the *mujâhideen*'s principal weapon remained the hunting rifle.[15] This posed a problem, for in contrast to *Kriegswaffen*, the sale and export of which was strictly controlled by the federal government, the trade in *Relativwaffen* merely required a commercial licence obtainable from local or provincial authorities. Officials could only prohibit the export or transit of *Relativwaffen* if evidence emerged that these were intended for military use. Proving this was easier said than done, however, for the end-use certificates – required by international law for all armaments transactions and obtainable only by government authorities or internationally recognised intermediaries – never identified the Algerian insurgents as the final recipients of these arms.[16] The distinction between *Relativwaffen* and *Kriegswaffen* was itself not always readily discernible and could easily be fudged; controls were complicated further by false cargo declarations.[17]

Some West German arms dealers fully exploited the ambiguities of this provisional legal framework, establishing for themselves a lucrative trade.

[14] *Bundesanzeiger* (Bonn), Nrs. 92 and 115, 13 May and 18 June 1955; Vermerk Nr. 3372/56, Bundesministerium für Wirtschaft (BMWi), 5 May 1956, BA/K, B106/15600. Also: Cahn and Müller, *RFA et Guerre d'Algérie*, pp. 311–312, 330; Scheffler, *SPD*, p. 107, n. 274–76.

[15] Aufzeichnung, Staatssekretär Hilger van Scherpenberg, 2 October 1956, PA/AA, B14/64; Harbi, *FLN*, p. 176.

[16] Djerbal, *L'OS*, p. 112.

[17] Vermerk, Abteilungsleiter VI/BMI (Bargatzky), 10 September 1957; Schreiben Nr. 79/56, Polizeibehörde der Freien und Hansestadt Hamburg an BMI, 2 October 1956, BA/K, B106/15600.

Undiscerning in their choice of business partners, these entrepreneurs were able to work the system in such ways as to make their transactions appear legitimate. With the production of arms in West Germany still in its infancy, they mostly acted as middlemen in the transit trade of arms. Much of their business rested on the acquisition and resale of the vast quantity of arms stocks left over in Europe from World War II. As a result of their activities, the ports of Hamburg and Bremen became important thoroughfares for armaments shipments, and West German shipping companies knowingly or unknowingly became complicit in what was, at best, a semi-legal trade in arms.[18]

The FLN, too, took full advantage of this situation. With the active help of the Arab governments supporting its cause, the movement was able to cloak its external purchasing missions in a veneer of respectability and legality. More experienced and better connected, these Arab allies introduced the Algerians to German arms merchants, many of whom operated out of the Middle East. The FLN was thus able to draw on the contacts of former officers of the *Wehrmacht* or SS, thousands of whom now worked as military and technical advisers to various Arab regimes, whether in Egypt, Iraq, Syria or Libya, often with the knowledge and backing of the United States.[19] Meanwhile Egyptian, Libyan, Tunisian and Moroccan diplomats and state officials acted as middlemen for the Algerians, or they issued diplomatic passports and other identification papers to the FLN's own agents. This allowed the latter not only to travel freely and operate under the cover of diplomatic immunity but also to obfuscate the aforementioned end-use certificates.

As early as January 1955, Director Vaujour of the *Sécurité Générale* in Algeria had warned that agents 'operating from and protected by [. . .] Egyptian embassies, were charged in Brussels, Geneva, Rome, and Tripoli with the acquisition of arms [. . .] with the [. . .] financial support of the Arab states'.[20] That early in the war, however, the *deuxième bureau* found no evidence to confirm the existence of FLN contraband networks in Western Europe or the Arab world.[21] The secretive world of arms smuggling remained impenetrable

18 Engelmann, *Freunde*.

19 Rubin and Schwanitz, *Nazis, Islamists*, pp. 209–32. Also: Reinhard Gehlen, *Der Dienst. Erinnerungen 1942–1971* (Mainz-Wiesbaden, 1971), p. 271; Timothy Naftali, 'Reinhard Gehlen and the United States', in *U.S. intelligence and the Nazis* (eds.) Richard Breitman et al. (Cambridge, 2005), pp. 404–5; Schwanitz, 'Deutsche in Nahost', pp. 205–16.

20 Vaujour, *Révolte*, pp. 88, 376.

21 Étude no. 1546/10.RM/EM/2, 16 July 1955, SHD-T, 1H2594/D6; Bulletin d'information no. 417/INS/AFN, centre de renseignements avancé d'Afrique du Nord, 30 April 1956, 1H/1101/D3; Note no. 1668 du Général Lorillot au Résident-Général, 22 February 1956, 1H/1536bis/D1.

to French intelligence. This changed in June 1956, when Ambassador Étienne Dennery in Bern and SDECE drew attention to the activities of Ahmed Bayoud and his Turkish-American collaborator Ahmed Kamal of the Tripoli (Libya) branch of *Jam'iyyat ul Islâm*. As mentioned earlier, Bayoud and Kamal operated mainly out of Switzerland. They undertook frequent missions to the Netherlands, Belgium and Italy, but especially to Hamburg and Frankfurt/Main in West Germany, ostensibly for the purpose of negotiating arms deals.[22] As if to corroborate that claim, French authorities in June 1956 intercepted their first shipment of arms bound for North Africa from the FRG.[23] Two months later, Libyan authorities impounded 150,000 rounds of 9mm ammunition, 160 8mm calibre Mauser rifles and 60 signal pistols with 4,000 rounds aboard the *Gertrud*, a German vessel that had sailed from Hamburg, after French intelligence had linked the consignment to Bayoud.[24] In France, these episodes helped fuel the rumours already circulating in the press of German aid to the FLN. In July, *Paris-Presse*, a paper well connected to government circles, even implicated the notorious SS-man Otto Skorzeny whose network of Nazi contacts purportedly spanned the Middle East.[25]

Countering contraband

Though many were unfounded, such rumours worried Ambassador Maltzan, who in June had urged the government to 'prevent the Algerian insurgents at all costs from engaging in any type of activity within the Federal Republic'.[26] Of all of the FLN's real and imagined machinations in their West German sanctuary, the growth of the illegal arms trade on the FLN's behalf caused the most alarm in Paris and Algiers. The asphyxiation of the insurgents' supplies constituted one of the French army's top priorities. In April 1955, the inspector-general of French forces in North

[22] Télégramme no. 109 de l'ambassadeur Dennery, Berne, 21 June 1956; Dépêche no. 1607 de l'ambassadeur Dennery, Berne, 10 July 1956; Dépêche no. 1728 de l'ambassadeur Dennery, Berne, 3 August 1956, MAE, AL/ALG/49; Notice d'information no. 295/2304/SDECE, 5 June 1956, SHD-T, 1R/352/D9*; Notice de documentation no. 5536/232/SDECE, 8 December 1956, SHD-T, 10T/525/D1*; Meynier, *Histoire*, p. 580; Carron, *Suisse*, pp. 223–4. On Kamal and the *Jam'iyyat ul Islâm*, see also: Ian Johnson, *A Mosque in Munich: Nazis, the CIA, and the Rise of the Muslim Brotherhood* (Boston and New York, 2010), pp. 139–54.

[23] Dépêche no. 924 de l'attaché militaire à Bonn, 13 August 1956, SHD-T, 14S/20*.

[24] Télégramme no. 2526 du Quai d'Orsay à l'ambassade de France, Bonn, 7 September 1956, MAE, AL/ALG/39; Fiche sur l'appui par la Libye aux rebelles d'Afrique du Nord, 26 October 1956, SHD-T, 1R/351/D9*.

[25] 'En Algérie, la France doit se défendre aussi contre ses amis', *Paris-Presse L'intransigeant*, 11 July 1956. On Skorzeny, see: Rubin and Schwanitz, *Nazis, Islamists*, p. 211.

[26] Schreiben Nr. 2806 der Botschaft Paris, 21 June 1956, PA/AA, B24/310/F4; also: Schreiben Nr. 2557 der Botschaft, Paris, 1 June 1955, PA/AA, B25/3.

Africa General Calliès had identified the destruction of 'the aid provided to the rebels [. . .] no matter its source' as the key to the preservation of *l'Algérie française*.[27] Likewise, Defence Minister General Pierre Kœnig reminded the commander-in-chief of French forces in Algeria, General Henri Lorillot, in December 1955:

> The supply of arms, ammunition and radio material constitutes a principal concern for the rebels, for whom the problem of manpower practically does not exist. [. . .] Our continued presence or eviction from North Africa will largely depend on the failure or success of their efforts. That is why the repression of this traffic presently constitutes a major preoccupation of the government and command.[28]

The campaign against contraband thus constituted a vital facet of France's counterinsurgency against the FLN.[29] In the context of *guerre révolutionnaire*, these operations held a twofold significance, as a *deuxième bureau* memorandum from February 1956 pointed out. First, by severing the ALN from its material reinforcements, they weakened the insurgents physically, thus forcing them to surrender. Second, and more importantly, the asphyxiation of the FLN's foreign supplies robbed the insurgents of one of their most potent symbols of power and support, thus also delivering a psychological blow.[30] Such arguments enjoyed widespread support among French military and civilian authorities, which remained convinced that the fastest way to quench the FLN's insurgency was to strike at the movement's foreign aid and external sanctuaries.[31] Even after the Suez debacle, the North African Joint Command continued to argue that to fulfil their ultimate objective, 'the psychological conquest of the population', French forces first had to destroy 'the military potential of the rebellion'. Accomplishing this 'intermediary objective', however, hinged on 'factors escaping the field of action of the authorities responsible for Algeria's pacification'.[32]

27 Note no. 7/INS/AFN/EM, 4 April 1955, 1H/1103/D1.

28 Mémorandum no. 6315 du ministre de la défense au Général Lorillot, 15 December 1955, SHD-T, 1H/1536Bis/D1.

29 Erwan Bergot, *Commandos de Choc 'Algérie'. Le dossier rouge. Services secrets contre FLN* (Paris, 1990 edn), pp. 33–6; Constantin Melnik, *Mille jours à Matignon: de Gaulle, l'Algérie, les services spéciaux* (Paris, 1988), pp. 38, 112, 139.

30 Rapport au sujet du trafic d'armes entre la Libye, la Tunisie et l'Algérie, EMA/2, 2 February 1956, SHD-T, 1R/247/D1*.

31 Connelly, *Diplomatic Revolution*, p. 71; Douglas Porch, *The French Secret Services: From the Dreyfus Affair to the Gulf War* (Basingstoke, 1996), pp. 365–6; Stephen Tyre, 'The Gaullists, the French Army and Algeria before 1958: Common Cause or Marriage of Convenience?' *JSS* 25/2 (2002), p. 105.

32 Note d'information no. 1053/INS/AFN/EM, 16 November 1956, SHD-T, 1H/1101/D3.

To combat these factors – that is, the FLN's external sanctuaries and supplies – French military and civilian authorities resorted to the various strands of *guerre révolutionnaire* outlined in Calliès' aforementioned 'Plan for the protection of French North Africa against the Cold War' of June 1955.[33] By engaging in *guerre diplomatique*, for instance, French diplomats and political leaders were to dissuade foreign governments from supporting the FLN. The framework of *guerre économique*, meanwhile, covered a whole panoply of measures, including a crackdown on FLN fundraising activities, the tightening of regulations governing the import and sale of military or dual-use supplies, the reinforcing of customs controls and an intensification of maritime and aerial surveillance along Algeria's borders.[34] In 1957, Defence Minister André Morice further ordered the construction of the eponymous 'Morice line', a heavily defended barrier along the Algerian–Tunisian border. By November 1959, this barrier consisted of roughly 1,300 kilometres of electrified fencing fortified by extensive radar surveillance systems and some 1.2 million anti-personnel mines. At the peak of the 'battle of the frontiers' in early 1958, it was patrolled by over 80,000 French troops. Combined with a similar barrier along the Algerian–Moroccan frontier (the 'Pedron line'), the Morice line was pivotal to the French strategy of defeating the FLN militarily since it physically severed the internal insurgents from reinforcements and supplies.[35]

As a physical barrier, the Morice line effectively stemmed the flow of men, arms and provisions into Algeria; one estimate even claimed it reduced infiltration by as much as 90 per cent.[36] By contrast, the effectiveness of the authorities' other measures against contraband depended entirely on fast and ready access to 'exploitable' intelligence.[37] In January 1956, SDECE established a specialised section within its counter-intelligence department charged exclusively with the collection of

[33] Plan de protection no. 1887/INS/AFN/EM, 4 June 1955, SHD-T, 1H/1103/D1.

[34] Fiche sur le contrôle économique en Algérie, 10RM/EM/2, undated, SHD-T, 1H/1557/D1; Jacques Guillon, 'La contrabande des armes pendant la guerre d'Algérie', *Revue Historique des Armées* 200 (1995), pp. 105–18; Jean Kessler, 'La surveillance des frontières maritimes de l'Algérie 1954–1962', *Revue Historique des Armées* 187 (1992) p. 98; Maurice Faivre, 'Le renseignement dans la guerre d'Algérie', in *Militaires et guérilla dans la guerre d'Algérie* (eds.) Jean-Charles Jauffret and Maurice Vaïsse (Bruxelles, 2001), p. 293; Maurice Faivre, *Le Renseignement dans la guerre d'Algérie* (Panazol, 2006), pp. 193–8.

[35] Thomas, *French*, pp. 98, 149, 184–5.

[36] Talbot, *War without a Name*, p. 184. Also: Haas, 'Operations at the Border', pp. 33–4; Record, 'External Assistance', pp. 46–7; Staniland, 'Defeating', p. 32.

[37] Rapport du chef d'escadrons de Réals de l'EMA et du chef de bataillon Robert de l'INS/AFN, 2 February 1956, SHD-T, 1R/247/D1*.

information on the international arms trade. Its task was to identify the FLN's negotiators, intermediaries and suppliers; trace the FLN's financial transactions; and track the timing, means of transport, routes and destinations of shipments.[38] In June 1957, the *deuxième bureau*, too, made intelligence on the FLN's contraband in armaments and communications equipment its top collection priority after the FLN's external organisation. The FLN's extraterritorial sanctuaries and supply lines thus constituted a larger problem for the French High Command than the movement's internal structures and fighting strength. General Raoul Salan, who in January 1956 had replaced Lorillot as commander-in-chief in Algeria, subsequently instructed the intelligence services to intensify their monitoring of the international arms trade, including the financial institutions frequented by Arab clients, notably in Switzerland, as well as the shipping industry, with particular focus on the ports of Hamburg and Trieste.[39]

In the context of the war on contraband, however, SDECE was expected to do more than provide actionable intelligence. As General Calliès had pointed out to Prime Minister Faure in April 1955, the best way to combat the FLN's external aid was 'by means of "action" operations conducted against the enemy'.[40] Spearheading the *guerre d'action* according to Calliès' 'Plan for the protection of French North Africa against the Cold War' was 'the action branch of SDECE'. Operating on foreign soil, Colonel Morlanne's *Service Action*, working together with the *11ème Choc*, a parachute regiment subordinate to SDECE, would 'destroy the [FLN's] ringleaders [...] annihilate [their] clandestine means of communication [... and] wipe out the traffic, transit, and supply of armaments and other war materials for the benefit of the North African rebellion'.[41] According to writers Roger Faligot and Pascal Krop, such interventions, dubbed '*Hors jeu*' (off-side), were first sanctioned by a secret inter-ministerial decree in May 1955 that ordered the 'neutralisation' of the FLN's external leaders and principal suppliers.[42]

[38] Bergot, *Commandos*, pp. 33–4, 71; Roger Faligot and Pascal Krop, *La Piscine. Les services secrets français, 1944–1985* (Paris, 1985), p. 95; Claude Faure, *Aux Services de la République. Du BCRA à la DGSE* (Paris, 2004), p. 269.

[39] Ordre de recherché no. 3422/10.RM/EM/2, 24 June 1957, SHD-T, 1H/1740/D3*; Dépêche no. 5600 du Général Salan au ministre de la défense nationale, 2 October 1957, 1H/1540/D3*.

[40] Mémorandum no. 473/INS/AFN/EM du Général Calliès au premier ministre Edgar Faure, 4 April 1955, SHD-T, 1H/1103/D1.

[41] Plan de protection de l'Afrique du Nord, 4 June 1955, SHD-T, 1H/1103/D1.

[42] Faligot and Krop, *Piscine*, pp. 137–8.

The Schlüter affair

Armed with these conventional and unconventional means, the French authorities set about targeting the FLN's contraband networks. In so doing, they invariably came to focus on the country constituting the unexpected "centre" of the international arms trade: West Germany. French diplomats first sought the assistance of the *Auswärtige Amt* in September 1956 after the *Gertrud* affair had highlighted Bayoud's efforts to purchase arms in the FRG, ostensibly on behalf of the Libyan government.[43] Bayoud's supplier, so French intelligence believed, was a Hamburg-based arms dealer, Otto Schlüter, whose trade concentrated on Libya. Alerted by Colonel Duchène, federal authorities including the BfV and BND had started to investigate this dealer's dubious transactions as early as July 1956.[44] Their investigations, however, failed to connect Schlüter to the FLN. A claim by French intelligence that Schlüter had met Bayoud, Kamal and Mohamed Boudjemline (another Algerian *Jam'iyyat*-member) in Düsseldorf on 7 August 1956 to discuss the acquisition of 150 automatic rifles from the Luxemburg armaments company SOLA remained unconfirmed.[45] Hamburg's criminal police (*Kripo*) did verify that the city's Trade and Transport Authority had, indeed, approved the shipment of 150,000 rounds of 9mm ammunition recovered from the *Gertrud* as these were not classified as war materiel, and the end-use certificate had listed their recipient as a legitimate Libyan authority. The Federal Office for Trade and Industry had also approved another transaction with authorities in Tripoli involving Belgian machine guns for which Schlüter possessed an export license.[46] As weapons of war, this transaction required political approval from the Federal Economics Ministry, which Schlüter had failed to request. In the absence of clear regulations, however, the authorities felt unable to press charges against Schlüter for this transgression, especially since the end-use certificate identified the recipient as the Libyan government. To prosecute, the Bonn government would have had to ban the export of certain weapons types to the Arab world, a move the Federal Ministry for Economic Affairs opposed since it would damage German trade and standing in the Middle

[43] Télégramme no. 2842 par l'ambassade de France à Bonn, 12 September 1956, MAE, AL/ALG/39.

[44] Aufzeichnung Nr. 462/56, Abteilungsleiter VI/BMI, 18 July 1956; Schreiben für Unterabteilungsleiter VI-A/BMI, 28 July 1956; Vermerk Nr. 4261/56, Referat VI-A-3/BMI, 10 October 1956, BA/K, B106/15600.

[45] Schreiben Nr. 52823/56 von Vize-Präsident Radke, BfV, an BMI (Dr. Bitterkühn), 24 August 1956, BA/K, B106/15600.

[46] Polizeibehörde, Hamburg, an BMI (Dr. Bitterkühn), 13 September 1956, BA/K, B106/15600.

East. Instead, the ministry instructed customs officials to intensify their controls of arms exports and ensure that the proper authorities had provided consent. Notwithstanding the French protests about his illegal dealings with the FLN, the ministry refused to intervene and prohibit Schlüter's trade with the Libyan authorities.[47]

On 28 September 1956, the dispute took a sinister turn when a bomb exploded in Schlüter's offices, injuring his mother and killing one of his business associates, Wilhelm Lorenzen. The ensuing criminal enquiry gave the police access to the dealer's files. These revealed that Schlüter was involved in 'an extensive transitory trade in Mauser rifles and munitions', which he obtained from wartime stocks in Belgium and Austria and then re-sold to clients in countries as diverse as Iraq, Kuwait, Djibouti, Libya and Yemen. Though classified as *Kriegswaffen*, Schlüter avoided seeking federal export and transit approval by removing the rifles' bayonets, changing their visors and slightly reworking their shafts. In this manner, he could export them as hunting rifles (*Relativwaffen*), which merely required a commercial licence. In addition to this irregularity, the files also confirmed Schlüter's close connection to one 'Bioud' (i.e. Bayoud), whom the dealer confessed to having seen last in Düsseldorf not long before the attack on his office on 3 September.[48]

In view of these revelations, Bonn's Interior Ministry suspected international agents behind the bombing of Schlüter's premises and instructed both the BfV and BKA to investigate the affair.[49] Their enquiries concluded that Schlüter had attempted to export *Kriegswaffen* to Libya fraudulently on more than one occasion, including the aforementioned 150 SOLA machine guns. He did so by disguising these weapons as machinery and using the West German mechanical engineering firm Wagria as an intermediary. The latter represented one of the few West German companies licensed at the time to fabricate carbines and was considered reputable by General Le Hingrat.[50] A sequestered letter from Wagria indicated that Schlüter was seeking to purchase a number of mines, bazookas, automatic pistols and rifles, mortars and anti-aircraft guns for a Libyan client.[51]

[47] Vermerk Nr. 4281 II/56, Referat VI-A-3/BMI, 4 October 1956, BA/K, B106/15600.

[48] Schreiben Nr. 79/56 der Polizeibehörde Hamburg (Dr. Thiemann) an BMI, 2 October 1956, BA/K, B106/15600.

[49] Notiz an Abteilungsleiter VI/BMI, 2 October 1956; Schreiben, BfV an BMI, 4 October 1956; Notiz an Unterabteilungsleiter VI-A/BMI, 5 October 1956; Vermerk, Referat VI-A-3/BMI, 8 October 1956, BA/K, B106/15600.

[50] Dépêche no. 924, annexe I, SHD-T, 14S/20*.

[51] Brief, Schlüter an Hubert Meinke, Wagria Maschinen- und Gerätebau GmbH, Ascheberg/Holstein, 6 July 1956; Brief, Meinke an Schlüter, 2 August 1956, BA/K, B106/15600.

Evidence of Schlüter's shady business practices thus continued to mount. Yet the BKA and BfV still failed to connect Schlüter to the FLN, for the merchant's files identified 'Bioud' and his associates as representatives of the Libyan Trade Ministry. Schlüter, moreover, denied all knowledge of Bayoud's Algerian identity, though he admitted to BfV investigators that the latter 'has bitter enemies amongst the French, and [. . .] makes no secret of his hostility towards France'. He vehemently denied any misconduct in his Libyan transactions, including the *Gertrud* shipment. German authorities thus remained mystified by the bombing of Schlüter's premises, which they attributed to inter-Arab rivalries. The dealer himself suspected a man claiming to be a Tunisian businessman who had visited his premises twice enquiring about Bayoud.[52]

This man's identity could never be confirmed, but it is possible that he worked for French intelligence. In all likelihood, it was *Service Action* that had orchestrated the bombing on Schlüter's office, either as a warning to the dealer or as an attempt on his life.[53] After all, SDECE possessed reliable intelligence on Bayoud's activities for the FLN, having persuaded Swiss prosecutor-general Dubois to eavesdrop on his workplace in the Egyptian embassy in Bern.[54] By late 1956, intelligence indicated that most of the ALN's new arms now derived from 'foreign provenance'. At the time, Bayoud and his associates were deemed the FLN's principal purveyors in arms and explosives after Ben Bella and Boudiaf, operating in Tangier, Madrid, Barcelona, Brussels, but especially in West Germany. Coinciding as it did with the seizure of the Egyptian gunrunner *Athos*, the capture of Ben Bella and the FLN's other chief external delegates, as well as the Suez crisis, the attack on Schlüter was in fact symptomatic of the invasive approach to sanctuary denial then popular with the French military and part of a general escalation of the authorities' counterinsurgency efforts against the FLN's external organisation and foreign backers. The *deuxième bureau* of French forces in Algiers certainly concluded that Bayoud's activities and the bombing of Schlüter's premises were inherently connected.[55]

Not privy to this information and unable to link Schlüter to the FLN, the BfV wondered whether it should communicate its findings to Duchène.[56] Bonn's Economics Ministry shared this view, fearing that

[52] Schreiben Nr. 767/56, BfV an BMI (Dr. Bitterkühn), 20 October 1956, BA/K, B106/15600.

[53] Bergot, *Commandos*, pp. 160–1. [54] Chapter 3, p. 85.

[55] Bulletin d'information no. 1053/INS/AFN/EM/2, 16 November 1956, SHD-T, 1H/1101/D3; Notice no. 1774/SSDNFA/Algérie, 26 February 1957, 1H/1536Bis/D2*.

[56] Schreiben Nr. 767/56, 20 October 1956, BA/K, B106/15600.

Paris would use the Schlüter affair to demand greater restrictions on arms exports to the Arab world. The ministry advised that officials 'should not communicate information on German firms to foreign countries, which could then be used to implement measures contrary to German interests'.[57] After all, in the context of the Algerian war, the French authorities increasingly came to perceive all arms exports to the Arab world as likely aid to the ALN and hence a threat to French national security. To Bonn's Economics Ministry and especially its archliberal boss, Ludwig Erhard, arms exports helped boost foreign trade, the lifeblood of West Germany's booming economy. Moreover, they represented an effective means of expanding Bonn's influence in the Arab world to the detriment of the GDR.[58] In the context of the Suez crisis, which threatened to turn Arab opinion against the Western world, the ministry did not want to be seen as catering to French colonialism.[59] On this occasion, it seems, sovereign rights and national self-interest had to take precedence over Franco-German relations.

Trouble with Tunis

In 1956, officials in Bonn successfully contested French attempts to thwart West German arms exports to Arab states. By the following year, it became increasingly difficult to maintain that resistance, especially with ever more intelligence accumulating on the centrality of the FRG for the FLN's procurement networks. In January 1957, the *deuxième bureau* of French forces in Morocco reported that the ALN's western command had allegedly received a shipment of arms, munitions and grenades from West Germany.[60] That same month, Bayoud, Boudjemline and Kamal attended a trade conference in Cologne alongside Egyptian Foreign Minister Mohamed Fawzi, where they supposedly negotiated the purchase of explosives. French military security linked this intelligence to the arrest on 28 January at Geneva airport of Swiss arms dealer Marcel Léopold and two Algerian associates, who were caught smuggling 60kg of explosives from Hamburg to Tripoli.[61] Two months later, General Calliès warned of

[57] Vermerk Nr. 4294/56, Referat VI-A-3/BMI, 31 October 1956, BA/K, B106/15600.

[58] Berggötz, *Nahostpolitik*, pp. 130, 228, 233, 237; Hünseler, *Außenpolitischen Beziehungen*, pp. 28–9.

[59] Gray, *Germany's Cold War*, p. 68; Berggötz, *Nahostpolitik*, pp. 64, 72–3.

[60] Renseignements, Commandant-supérieur interarmées des troupes françaises au Maroc, EM/2, 14 January 1957, SHD-T, 1H/1536Bis/D2*.

[61] Notice no. 1774/SSDNFA/Algérie, 26 February 1957; Notice no. 2205/SSDNFA/Algérie, 9 March 1957, SHD-T, 1H/1536Bis/D2*; Carron, *Suisse*, pp. 224–8.

an impending 'massive delivery of armaments of Scandinavian and West German origin' to the FLN.[62] Meanwhile in Paris, the DST seized documents from the FLN's *Fédération de France*, which indicated that Egyptian intermediaries intended to purchase a substantial consignment of arms in these very countries. The consignment, which purportedly included 300 machine guns, 4,000 Mauser rifles, 200 mortars with accompanying shells, 200 bazookas and their shells, 20,000 grenades and over 8 million diverse rounds of ammunition, was to be shipped to North Africa under Moroccan licences.[63] Also in March, the BfV tried to substantiate reports whereby FLN agent Ahmed Mahsas was on an arms prospecting mission in Cologne and Bonn. After Ben Bella's capture, Mahsas had temporarily assumed responsibility for unifying the ALN's eastern command and standardising its equipment.[64]

The accumulating intelligence reinforced the French authorities' determination to asphyxiate the FLN's external supplies. After all, the movement's clandestine activities in West Germany were perceived as having a direct bearing on French counterinsurgency operations in Algeria. They consequently prompted vigorous diplomatic demarches in Bonn.[65] Meanwhile, *Service Action* intensified its campaign against Schlüter, who on 3 June 1957 became the target of a car bombing. The arms dealer once again survived the assassination attempt, which this time killed his mother and severely maimed his young daughter.[66] Because of its public nature and female victims, the attack made for sensationalist news. For the first time, rumours of Schlüter's Algerian connection received greater credence as the press speculated about French involvement in the attack.[67] On 8 June, the *Mannheimer Morgen* announced that the perpetrators' trail led to France: Schlüter had received warnings to stop his 'putrid trade', one of which came in the shape of a small coffin similar to ones allegedly used by the French resistance against Nazi collaborators during

[62] Bulletin de renseignements no. 260/INS/AFN/EM/2, 13 March 1957, SHD-T, 1R/351/D8*.

[63] Dépêche no. 5067 de la DST au chef de l'EMA/2, 22 March 1957, SHD-T, 1H/1536Bis/D2*.

[64] Schreiben, AA (Referat 302) an BMI, BMWi, Bundesministerium für Verteidigung (BMVg), 7 March 1957, PA/AA, B14/64; Schreiben, BfV an BMI, 3 April 1957, BA/K, B106/15600; Meynier, *Histoire*, pp. 308, 476.

[65] Dépêche no. 137 du Quai d'Orsay au ministère de la défense nationale, 15 March 1957, SHD-T, 1R/264/D5*; Dépêche no. 864 du Général Le Hingrat, Bonn, 29 June 1957, SHD-T, 14S/20*.

[66] Bergot, *Commandos*, p. 161; Antoine Méléro, *La Main rouge. L'armée secrète de la République* (Monaco, 1997), p. 203.

[67] Dépêche no. 335 du Consul-Général Olivier de Sayve, Hambrug, 21 June 1957, MAE, MLA/2; 'Bombenattentat auf Hamburger Waffenhändler', *Die Welt*, 4 June 1957; 'Fahndungen im Attentat Schlüter gegen Unbekannt bisher erfolgslos', *Ruhr Nachrichten* (Dortmund), 5 June 1957.

World War II.[68] Hamburg's Senate appointed a commission to investigate the affair and a young Helmut Schmidt, the future Social-democratic chancellor in whose parliamentary constituency the bombing had occurred, demanded an official pledge from Economics Minister Erhard that 'the federal government will do everything to undermine the illegal trade in arms'.[69]

Authorities in Paris insisted on similar guarantees. On 26 August 1957, shortly after ordering the Morice line's construction, the defence minister sought an outright pledge that Bonn would ban the export of all portable arms to Morocco and Tunisia.[70] Morice's demand came in response to concerns raised by General Salan in Algiers. The commander-in-chief had alerted the Paris authorities to the alarming improvement in the ALN's logistical and command infrastructure in Morocco and Tunisia, which manifested itself through increasingly daring cross-border raids, especially along the Algerian–Tunisian frontier.[71] Everything suggested that Rabat and Tunis now rivalled Cairo as the FLN's chief intermediaries in the acquisition of military supplies. In June, for instance, the Office of National Security of Tangier had supposedly received armaments worth 78,000 DM from Schlüter, which the *deuxième bureau* believed were for the ALN.[72] Similarly in August, French military security reported the delivery of a consignment of West German and Belgian munitions to the Tunisian National Guard, though 'some of these arms may in fact be for the FLN'.[73] French signals intelligence, the *Service technique de recherche* (STR), further intercepted radio messages revealing that the FLN had recently received four tonnes of communications equipment from the well-known West German company Telefunken.[74] French forces operating in the Oranais later recovered a directive from the ALN's newly created Transmissions Service highlighting the importance that the insurgents attached to such materiel: 'an absolute necessity' for any modern army, communications represented the revolution's 'central nervous system'.

[68] 'Die Spur führt nach Frankreich. Jetzt befasst sich Interpol mit dem Anschlag auf Schlüter', *Mannheimer Morgen*, 8 June 1957; Bundeskriminalblatt Nr. 740, 18 June 1957, BA/K, B106/15600.

[69] 'Erhards Erklärung zum Fall Schlüter', *Stuttgarter Nachrichten*, 13 June 1957; 'SPD fordert parlamentarische Untersuchung im Fall Schlüter', *FAZ*, 14 June 1957; 'Der Fall des Waffenhändlers Schlüter vor dem Hamburger Parlament', *Neue Rhein Zeitung*, 12 June 1957.

[70] Dépêche no. 1806 du ministre de la défense au ministre des affaires étrangères, 26 August 1956, SHD-T, 1R/351/D1*.

[71] Dépêche du Général Salan au ministre de la défense nationale, 4 August 1957, SHD-T, 1H/1775/D1.

[72] Bulletin de renseignements no. 3581/10.RM/EM/2, 29 July 1957, SHD-T, 1H/1536Bis/D2*; Notice no. 4876/SDECE, 7 November 1957, SHD-T, 10T/531*.

[73] Fiche no. 8212/SSDNFA, section navale, pour le chef, EMA/2, 26 August 1957, SHD-T, 1R/247/D6.

[74] Renseignement no. 1830/STR/E/TS, 5 June 1957, SHD-T, 1H/1552/D1.

The procurement of radio transmitters and receivers thus constituted a top priority for the Algerians, and Telefunken appeared to be their preferred brand.[75] On 6 September 1957, the *Quai d'Orsay* formally informed the Adenauer government that 'the growth of the illegal arms trade on the FLN's behalf [...] caused serious concern'.[76] Authorities in Paris and Algiers no longer contented themselves with the pledge that Bonn would only authorise arms exports to the Arab world 'if there is certainty that the material will not reach Algerian rebels'.[77] This certainty must have struck French officials as elusive given the FLN's many state-sanctioned supporters in the region.

Adding urgency to the French demarche was the fact that it coincided with the aforementioned crisis within NATO over Anglo-American arms deliveries to Tunisia. As tensions mounted within the Western alliance, German diplomats were keen to reassure the *Quai d'Orsay* that Bonn was intent on preventing FLN contraband and would reject Tunisian or Moroccan requests for arms, even if this contravened Erhard's principle of free trade. After all, the Adenauer government sought to avoid conflict with France over Algeria so as to protect and promote Franco-German cooperation, including planned projects in the realm of European defence. Spurred into action by the Radford Plan, the two countries in January 1957 had signed the protocol of Colomb-Béchar on closer collaboration in the domain of armaments production and military planning.[78] This unprecedented accord was followed ten months later by a Franco-German-Italian agreement calling for joint research and development in the realm of conventional and nuclear arms. Considering that Bonn had renounced nuclear, biological and chemical weapons in the Paris Accords, these developments proved momentous. They paved the way for what Mollet in May 1957 had called 'an integrated European nuclear force' that would grant West Germany a voice in the deployment of atomic arms and reduce Western Europe's dependency on America's nuclear umbrella.[79]

The Adenauer government was not about to jeopardise this achievement by approving arms shipments to Tunis or Rabat.[80] If anything, the NATO

[75] Instructions particulières no. 3, ALN, Transmissions, 29 August 1957, SHD-T, 1H/1690/D1; Note de renseignements no. 2210/PSN/ALGER, 24 July 1957; Renseignement no. 2937 de l'Office de liaison Algérie-Maroc-Tunisie, 11 October 1957, 1H/1552/D1.

[76] *Aide mémoire* de l'ambassade de France, Bonn, 6 September 1957, PA/AA, B25/7.

[77] Dépêche no. 864 du Général Le Hingrat, Bonn, 29 June 1957, SHD-T, 14S/20*.

[78] Creswell and Kollmer, 'Power', pp. 78–81.

[79] Cited in: Lappenküper, *Deutsch-französischen Beziehungen I*, pp. 1175, 1194.

[80] Colette Barbier, 'Les négociations franco-germano-italiennes en vue de l'établissement d'une coopération militaire nucléaire au cours des années 1956–1958', *Revue d'Histoire Diplomatique* 1/2

crisis over the Anglo-American arms delivery had made the *Auswärtige Amt* aware of the 'far-reaching significance' of the question of arms controls, which it deemed 'politically explosive to the highest degree'. Having previously shown little interest in the matter, German diplomats now insisted on being consulted in the processing of export and transit applications, which could not remain the *domaine réservé* of Bonn's Economics Ministry. The *Amt* urged the latter to tighten up its provisional regulations on the export of arms to so-called special regions, especially North Africa.[81]

The Adenauer government's promise to prohibit arms exports to North Africa for the duration of the Algerian conflict may have reassured the *Quai d'Orsay*, yet it raised objections from the Interior and Economics Ministries in Bonn. Both argued that an injunction on sales in military materiel remained legally impossible and economically undesirable. Federal authorities could ban the export of *Kriegswaffen* to North Africa, but to proscribe *Relativwaffen* and dual-use technology, they first had to be able to prove that these were intended for use in military conflagrations, i.e. the Algerian war. As the Schlüter case had shown, securing this evidence proved difficult.[82] While agreeing on the need to combat contraband, both ministries further opposed a blanket ban on the grounds that it would damage German economic and political interests in the Arab world.[83] A blanket ban was, however, precisely what the French Defence Ministry expected from Bonn. To achieve this end, French Foreign Minister Christian Pineau urged the military and the intelligence services to furnish the West German authorities with the necessary evidence of Arab collusion with the Algerian insurgents.[84]

German–Algerian complicity?

These efforts notwithstanding, the ALN's stocks and supplies continued to expand in the final months of 1957, especially in its cross-border sanctuaries

(1990), pp. 81–113; Gérard Bossuat, 'Les armements dans les relations franco-allemandes (1945–1963): les nationalismes à l'épreuve des temps nouveaux', RA 25/4 (1993), pp. 606–11; Eckart Conze, 'La coopération franco-germano-italienne dans le domaine nucléaire dans les années 1957–1958: un point de vue allemand'? *Revue d'Histoire Diplomatique* 1/2 (1990), pp. 115–32; Soutou, *L'Alliance incertaine*, pp. 66–7, 71–95.

81 Aufzeichnung, Dr. von Keller (Referat 404, Handelsabkommen), 13 August 1957, PA/AA, B25/7.

82 Vermerk Nr. 863/57 für Abteilungsleiter VI/BMI, 10 September 1957, BA/K, B106/15600.

83 Vermerk, Dr. Gieseler, BMI, 20 September 1957; Vermerk Nr. 936, Dr. Pioch, BMI, 11 October 1957, BA/K, B106/15600.

84 Dépêche no. 125 du ministre des affaires étrangères au ministre de la défense nationale, 10 September 1957, SHD-T, 1R/351/D1*.

in the Maghreb. The authorities in Algiers grew increasingly frustrated by their inability to undermine this traffic. In December, General Salan again complained that only Tunisian and Moroccan aid and sanctuary had allowed the ALN 'to conserve a certain military potential despite the heavy losses' inflicted by the French forces over the past year. Tunisia, in particular, had become a 'veritable "armaments shop"' for the Algerians as well as a 'depot where weapons and other supplies converged from both Western countries and the Middle East'. Since the Morice line could not guarantee an 'absolute hermeticity [sic]', Salan argued that this traffic had to be stopped. In the eyes of the Algiers authorities, NATO countries in particular had to do more to help their beleaguered ally, who was, after all, fighting communism on their behalf.[85]

After the perceived betrayal of *les Anglo-Saxons*, who in November 1957 agreed to deliver arms to Tunis so as to keep Bourguiba tied to the West, Algiers' irritation focused primarily on West Germany from where so many of the FLN's supplies seemed to come. While it was difficult for the authorities to change the behaviour of France's senior partners in NATO, or that of North African countries hosting the FLN, they were determined to influence their junior ally, the FRG. By the end of the year, SDECE had confirmed the delivery of at least one hundred Telefunken radio transmitters and receivers to the FLN, prompting an angry complaint from Resident-Minister Lacoste.[86] Another case of dual-use technology that fell through the cracks of Bonn's provisional export-regulations, German diplomats were at a loss about how to respond. They had already enforced a ban on the export of *Kriegswaffen* to North Africa as well as a revision of the existing control mechanisms whereby the Economics Ministry henceforth had to consult the *Auswärtige Amt* in all other transactions involving *Kriegswaffen*.[87] Yet they had failed to enforce a similar ban on *Relativwaffen* and dual-use technology. Even the *Quai* defended the Bonn government on this occasion, reassuring Lacoste that 'Chancellor Adenauer himself has adopted an attitude that in no uncertain terms favours France in the Algerian question and has given clear instructions to all ministerial departments so that these will assist us in an effective manner'.[88] These assurances failed to dislodge the French military's

[85] Dépêche no. 7420 du Général Salan au ministre de la défense nationale, 23 December 1957, SHD-T, 1H/1536Bis/D2*.

[86] Renseignements no. 4614/SDECE, 21 October 1957; Renseignements no. 4814/SDECE, 4 November 1957; Renseignements no. 5221/SDECE, 4 December 1957, SHD-T, 1H/1552/D1.

[87] *Bundesanzeiger*, Nr. 233, 4 December 1957.

[88] Note no. 276 de la MLA pour le ministre de l'Algérie, 18 December 1957; Télégramme no. 3008 de l'ambassade de France, Bonn, 12 December 1957, MAE, EU/RFA/1272.

suspicions of German-Algerian collusion, and by January 1958 Defence Minister Jacques Chaban-Delmas urged the *Quai* to maintain its pressure on Bonn, 'not only so that the Algerian rebellion would cease to be supplied with radio material but also because [such pressure] could facilitate the exposure of one of the rebels' supply networks, an effort which has hitherto almost always proved impossible'.[89]

By the New Year, the French military's frustrations with FLN contraband had spilled over into the press, which reproached West Germany of complicity with the North African nationalists. Several French newspapers reprinted accusations first raised on 10 January 1958 by Hamburg's *Bild* tabloid in an article detailing Schlüter's nefarious business in *Kriegswaffen*, including the sale of 400 sub-machine guns, 400 Mauser rifles, 340 automatic pistols and 400,000 rounds of ammunition to the Tunisian National Guard and to Tangier's National Security Office. Some, including the semi-official *Agence France Presse* (AFP), linked these transactions to the army's recent recovery in the course of skirmishes along the Algerian–Tunisian frontier of brand-new machine guns of Mauser design (MG42s and MG34s).[90] West German diplomats found the AFP report particularly damning, for it reproached the Bonn government of having sanctioned arms sales to the ALN. The *Auswärtige Amt* felt compelled to issue an immediate press release refuting this claim in which it also pointed out that Germany had ceased production of MG34s in 1942 while the manufacture of MG42s had only resumed in October 1957. The recuperated machine guns thus could not have come from the FRG. By contrast, both models were currently under production in Czechoslovakia and Yugoslavia.[91] West German diplomacy thus sought to redirect the public's attention to the FLN's growing connections to the Communist bloc. To convince the French press of Bonn's loyalty in the Algerian question, the embassy in Paris was instructed to impress upon AFP that 'the federal government did its utmost to undermine arms trafficking with North Africa' and that the discovery of World War II-era German-model weapons in Algeria hardly meant that these originated in West Germany. 'In the interest of the

[89] Dépêche no. 18 de Chaban-Delmas pour le ministre des affaires étrangères, 8 January 1958, MAE, Amérique (AM)/États-Unis de l'Amérique (EUA)/363.

[90] 'Bild kann es beweisen: Schlüter handelte doch mit Kriegswaffen', *Bild*, 10 January 1958; 'Un journal allemand: l'armurier Otto Schlüter a livré des armes en Afrique du Nord', *Le Figaro*, 11 January 1958; Fernschreiben Nr. 3 des Generalkonsulats Algier, 13 January 1958, PA/AA, B63/129; Vermerk, Referat 302 (Frank), 14 January 1958; Fernschreiben Nr. 40 der Botschaft Bonn, 15 January 1958, B12/936.

[91] 'Keine Waffen für Algerien aus der Bundesrepublik', *FAZ*, 15 January 1958; télégramme de l'ambassadeur de France à Bonn, 15 January 1958, SHD-T, 1R/352/D10*.

Franco-German rapprochement', the *Amt*'s directive read, 'one should refrain from spreading sensationalist reports that deviated from the facts, strained Franco-German relations, and only made the suppression of arms trafficking more difficult'.[92] The French authorities appeared to be reassured; even the Algiers government promised henceforth to inform the West German consul-general, Heinrich Hendus, of future confiscations of "German" arms in the interest of Franco-German cooperation.[93]

This entente lasted until the French navy's interception of the Yugoslav cargo vessel *Slovenija* on 18 January, which aggravated matters further. The vessel carried the largest arms consignment confiscated by the French since the start of the Algerian war, including 200 MG34s, 4,000 Mauser rifles and 1,000 sub-machine guns.[94] Much of the evidence suggested that the confiscated arms originated behind the Iron Curtain. As French technical experts now reminded the Algiers government, just because the seized weapons were German models did not mean they originated in West Germany; indeed, France had itself furnished wartime stocks of these same arms to Belgrade under the Tripartite Agreement of 1951.[95] The Czech state-run armaments company *Omnipol*, moreover, manufactured a range of German wartime models for sale against hard currency, even reproducing the swastika as a badge of authenticity and quality. *Omnipol* reportedly sold large quantities of arms to various Arab clients, especially in Egypt and Syria.[96] Indeed, a detailed intelligence survey titled 'Foreign interferences in the foreign rebellion' concluded, 'the year 1957 saw a decline in the activity of private traffickers, and simultaneously a considerable increase in the aid contributed by governments, amongst which Egypt and Syria occupy the first rank, followed by Russia and the [Soviet] satellites'.[97] Notwithstanding the evidence, French military and intelligence believed that the FLN continued to engage in business with 'numerous traffickers' in West Germany; Ouamrane himself was thought to have only recently purchased 'German weapons valued at 10 million [French] Francs' with Egyptian and Syrian help.[98] The French press, too, continued its tirade against Algerian–German complicity in the trafficking of arms.[99]

92 Drahterlass an Paris, 17 January 1958, PA/AA, B12/936.

93 Schreiben des Generalkonsuls Hendus, Algier, 18 January 1958, PA/AA, B63/129.

94 Guillon, 'Contrebande', p. 112; Kessler, 'Surveillance', p. 101.

95 État récapitulatif des armes saisies sur le '*Slovenija*', SSDNFA, February/March 1958, SHD-T, 1H/1542.

96 Bergot, *Commandos*, pp. 93–4; Guillon, 'Contrebande', p. 109.

97 Rapport sur les ingérences étrangères dans la rébellion algérienne, 21 January 1958, SHD-T, 1H/1753/D1.

98 Ibid. 99 Fernschreiben Nr. 5 des Generalkonsultas Algier, 21 January 1958, PA/AA, B12/936.

These allegations of German collusion with the FLN were symptomatic of France's growing malaise over the Algerian war. Even before the Sakiet crisis would exacerbate its problems, the Gaillard government had faced growing international condemnation and isolation over its pursuit of the Algerian war and domestic political tensions, too, were on the rise. The French army faced an increasingly sophisticated adversary in the ALN and was fighting pitched battles along the Algerian–Tunisian frontier. Whether in the military, press or political arena, many voices continued to blame France's inability to come to terms with the insurgency on foreign forces and on the FLN's external sanctuaries. On 21 January 1958, Joint Chief-of-Staff General Paul Ely reminded Defence Minister Chaban-Delmas of the continued need to combat these external forces, particularly in the realm of arms trafficking:

> With the actions of the FLN being directly contingent on the volume of its material means, the fight against the subversive forces' permanent current of military supplies remains indispensable and must be conducted parallel to our political and operational activities.[100]

It was precisely this kind of thinking that would precipitate the Sakiet crisis. By then, the Gaillard government knew it could count on the Adenauer government's support in combating contraband. Even so, public criticism of Bonn had reached feverish pitches in France, so much so that Foreign Minister Pineau felt compelled to intervene before the National Assembly to stifle further charges of German–Algerian collusion. On 22 January, he reminded French deputies that 'the organization of international smuggling [...] has become such that it is difficult to determine the origin of all the weapons reaching Algeria', and assured them that 'the Government of the Federal Republic has initiated a judicial investigation into this kind of traffic which it intends to halt'.[101] By the time of the Sakiet crisis, the Bonn government had included sub-machine guns and automatic revolvers under the ban on exports to North Africa; only non- and semi-automatic revolvers remained exempt from political-diplomatic approval.[102]

The Algerian war and the imperative of Franco-German reconciliation thus had had a direct bearing on West German legislation regulating the

[100] Dépêche no. 9072/EMGA du Général Ely au ministre de la défense nationale, 21 January 1958, SHD-T, 1R/247/D3*.

[101] Christian Pineau, 'France's position on the main international questions', 22 January 1958, Speeches and Press Conferences Nr. 104 released by the French embassy to the UN, New York, January 1958, MAE, AL/ALG/15.

[102] Vermerk, Referat VI-B-4/BMI, 28 March 1958, BA/K, B106/15600; Schreiben, Referat 413/AA an BMWi, 26 February 1958, PA/AA, B63/124; *Bundesanzeiger* Nr. 40, 27 February 1958.

trade in armaments. The Federal Economics Ministry had lost its bid to retain sole control over the export of *Kriegswaffen* in the name of free trade. Federal authorities investigated each suspected case of FLN contraband the French brought to their attention. Even vague rumours were scrutinised, for example an unsubstantiated report from April 1958 that a Frankfurt-based scrap-metals dealer may have acquired 2,800 tonnes of ammunition from an American military base on the FLN's behalf.[103] Although the number of "German" arms recovered in Algeria rose constantly, General Le Hingrat found no reason to fault Bonn. In April 1958, the attaché reassured the French Defence Ministry:

> [o]wing to the controls that were organised after the war by the Allies and the surveillance exercised by federal authorities, owing also to the current state of the armaments industry in this country, the [FRG] is perhaps one of the least well-placed countries to furnish German arms to the rebels in Algeria.[104]

In a similar vein, Ambassador Couve de Murville praised Bonn's cooperativeness, arguing that in many ways – especially when it came to the transit trade in arms – West German regulations were more stringent than French ones.[105]

The Adenauer government thus constituted an important collaborator in the French campaign against FLN contraband. Yet Bonn's loyalty and cooperation surpassed the fight against arms trafficking. As the past chapters have shown, the Chancellor gave his full support to the French counter-insurgency in Algeria and tried in vain to persuade his NATO allies to do the same. Though initially opposed to the very idea of a Eurafrican community, the FRG became the largest net contributor to the EDF, thereby binding the Bonn government to France's modernisation plans in sub-Saharan Africa (and soon also in Algeria). The Adenauer government was also the largest contributor to the EPU loan that rescued France from insolvency, itself largely caused by the Algerian war. Even as international and domestic opinion turned against France's brutal conflict in Algeria, West German diplomacy abetted the *Quai d'Orsay*'s efforts to influence voting at the UN. Though unable to prevent the emergence of an external sanctuary in West Germany, federal authorities refused to recognise Algerians as political

[103] Aufzeichnung, Alexander Böker, Referat 302, 14 April 1958; Schreiben, BMWi an AA, 28 May 1958; Schreiben, Dr. Gieseler, BMI, an AA, 10 July 1958, PA/AA, B63/124; Schreiben, BfV an BMI, 13 June 1958, BA/K, B106/15600.

[104] Dépêche no. 71 du Général Le Hingrat, Bonn, 22 April 1958, SHD-T, 1R/352/D10*.

[105] Dépêche no. 763 de l'ambassade de France, Bonn, 25 April 1958, MAE, EU/RFA/1280.

refugees and helped pre-empt the setting of a dangerous precedent that would have conferred upon the FLN the international legitimacy and political recognition it craved. West German authorities sought to prevent Algerian nationalists from engaging in subversive activities on federal territory, whether the printing and distribution of subversive tracts or the acquisition of military and non-military supplies.

The Adenauer government's quiet assistance in the Algerian question served three interconnected goals: to improve Franco-German relations; strengthen and stabilise the Western alliance; and enable West Germany to emerge as an equal and sovereign partner within that alliance. To secure these goals, all elements of his *Westpolitik*, the chancellor was willing to support the fragile and fractured Fourth Republic morally, diplomatically and financially. He was even prepared to sacrifice Bonn's reputation in the Third World as well as some of his government's independent room to manoeuvre. As illustrated by Ambassador Couve de Murville's repeated defence of the Bonn government whenever the Algerian question arose in Paris, and even Foreign Minister Pineau's strong exculpation of the German authorities before the French National Assembly, Adenauer's policy of unobtrusively supporting the French war effort had worked. By deferring to France in the Algerian question, the chancellor had helped build trust between the authorities in Paris and Bonn. This trust, in turn, had helped the federal government secure some of its key foreign-policy goals. It had even enabled closer Franco-German cooperation in the realms of defence and nuclear technology, a development that would have been unimaginable just a few years earlier. By April 1958, Franco-German relations were closer than they had ever been. And yet, the fall of the Gaillard government over the Sakiet crisis and the Algerian question was about to call all of the chancellor's remarkable achievements into doubt.

PART II

Contesting sanctuary and sovereignty

June 1958–December 1960

CHAPTER 6

The diplomatic war

The fall of the Gaillard government in a vote of no confidence on 15 April 1958 exposed the depths of French frustration with the FLN's ability to pursue its fight from the safety of extraterritorial sanctuaries. The French military and security service's invasive attempts at sanctuary denial had failed to eradicate the movement's external organisation. Like the hijacking of Ben Bella and his associates or the Suez intervention that had preceded it, the air strike against Sakiet-Sidi-Youssef of 8 February had backfired on the authorities, provoking international outrage at France's illegal and immoral pursuit of the Algerian war. The Eisenhower administration's attempt to link the resultant Anglo-American good-offices mission between Paris and Tunis with a political solution to Algeria's problems – one that took into account the Algerians' desire for 'self-government and self-determination' – produced an outpour of anti-American sentiments in France. Gaillard's apparent weakness in the face of this pressure proved his undoing.[1] The ensuing contest between liberals willing to pursue a negotiated settlement and hardliners determined to forestall the humiliation of a 'diplomatic Dien Bien Phu' climaxed on 13 May 1958, when a memorial service in Algiers for three French prisoners killed by the FLN in retaliation for the execution of three insurgents turned into a riotous demonstration against the investiture as prime minister of the Christian-democrat and colonial liberal Pierre Pflimlin.[2] In a violent reaction against perceived foreign meddling, a mob ransacked the American Cultural Centre before descending upon the Government-General. The military's top commanders in Algiers broke ranks with the government, joining *colons* (or *pieds-noirs*) rebels in creating a Committee of Public Safety. Two days later, the Committee's leader, Salan, demanded

[1] Connelly, *Diplomatic Revolution*, p. 166; Mélandri, 'La France et le "double jeu"', pp. 439–40.
[2] Benjamin Stora, *Algeria, 1830–2000: A Short History* (trans.) Jane Mary Todd (Ithaca NY, 2001), p. 70.

the return to power of General Charles de Gaulle, if need be by means of a coup d'état.[3]

The May crisis profoundly altered political realities in France and marked a watershed for the Algerian war and indeed for Franco-German relations. At the time, the Adenauer government thought it faced its worst security nightmare: the rise to power of reactionary and xenophobic French forces determined to pursue a policy of national grandeur. How, then, did Bonn react to the unfolding developments, and what impact did the return of de Gaulle have on Franco-German relations? In what manner did the new political realities also affect the *guerre diplomatique* between France and the FLN, and what impact did this contest have on West German foreign policy? Whatever dilemmas Bonn's diplomacy had previously faced over the Algerian war, the May crisis intensified them. In a context of heightened Cold War tensions over Berlin and quickening decolonisation, the *Auswärtige Amt* struggled to reconcile the conflicting aims of *Westbindung* with those of the Hallstein doctrine, for both France and the FLN instrumentalised the German question to their respective diplomatic ends. The resultant contest to influence West German foreign policy was unequivocally won by France. As this and the following chapters will show, far from remaining non-engaged in the Algerian question, the Adenauer government intensified its covert and overt support to the French counterinsurgency. The imperative of Franco-German reconciliation trumped even Bonn's quest for sovereign equality.

Deciphering de Gaulle

Neither the events of May 1958 nor their xenophobic, anti-American undertones came as a surprise to the Bonn government, which had long anticipated a political crisis with dire consequences for the Fourth Republic's stability and survival.[4] Though most French vitriol was directed against the United States and Britain, Adenauer maintained great reserve throughout the crisis so as not to exacerbate the situation.[5] Karl Carstens,

[3] Bernard Droz and Evelyne Lever, *Histoire de la guerre d'Algérie 1954–1962* (Paris, 1982), pp. 168–80; Horne, *Savage War*, pp. 273–98; Wall, *France*, pp. 104–56; Ibid., 'Fall of the Fourth Republic', pp. 489–511; Michel Winock, *L'Agonie de la IVe République: 13 mai 1958* (Paris, 2006).

[4] Blankenhorn, *Verständnis*, p. 294.

[5] *Der Auswärtige Ausschuß des Deutschen Bundestages: Sitzungsprotokolle,* Bd. 13/III – *1957–1961* (eds.) Joachim Wintzer, Josef Boyer and Wolfgang Dierker (Düsseldorf, 2003), 9. Sitzung, 14 May 1958, CD; *Die Kabinettsprotokolle der Bundesregierung.* Vol. 11 – *1958* (eds.) Ulrich Enders and Christoph Schawe (Munich, 2002), Sondersitzung, 28 May 1958, p. 260; Marcowitz, *Option*, pp. 11, 15.

who headed the *Auswärtige Amt*'s Western department, warned that 'any advice no matter how well intended would be perceived as meddling'.[6] Foreign Minister Heinrich von Brentano hoped France's democratic reflexes would prevail to thwart a military coup or the emergence of a popular front, scenarios that threatened to spell the end of Franco-German reconciliation, destabilise the Western alliance and imperil West German national security.[7]

Nothing, however, worried the government more than the return of de Gaulle.[8] This development came as a severe shock, especially since rumours of its possibility, though persistent, had always been discarded as unfounded by West German diplomats.[9] While the governments in London and Washington soon came to view the General as 'a preferable alternative to Fourth Republic instability', the Bonn government struggled to accept the new reality.[10] Adenauer's anxiety was so great that he instructed his close confidante and Bonn's ambassador to NATO, Herbert Blankenhorn, to persuade the wobbling Pflimlin government of the need for a strong anti-Gaullist front.[11] Blankenhorn gloomily confided in his journal that de Gaulle's return would spell 'the end of the Western European alliance'.[12]

Why did the General generate such apprehension in Bonn? One reason, historian Hans-Peter Schwarz argues, is that de Gaulle personified a brand of nationalism and unilateralism that many Germans had come to reject either by conviction or by necessity after the experience of the Third Reich.[13] The Adenauer government also lacked personal experience of de Gaulle, who had kept aloof from political life during his self-imposed retirement. German knowledge of the General was derived from his time as leader of the Free French during World War II, as president of the

[6] Aufzeichnung, Carstens, 19 May 1958, PA/AA, B24/311/F3.

[7] Drahterlass, Brentano, 19 May 1958, PA/AA, B24/311/F3; Lappenküper, *Deutsch-französischen Beziehungen II*, p. 1204.

[8] Cahn and Müller, *RFA et Guerre d'Algérie*, pp. 159–84; Lappenküper, 'Adenauer', p. 606; Marcowitz, *Option*, pp. 11–19.

[9] Schreiben Nr. 4824/I-II der Botschaft Paris, 5 December 1956, PA/AA, B24/273/F5; Schreiben Nr. 1143 der Botschaft Paris, 16 January 1957, PA/AA, B24/274/F1; Schreiben Nr. 1643 der Botschaft Paris, 3 March 1958, PA/AA, B24/272/F1.

[10] Thomas, *French*, p. 181; Connelly, *Diplomatic Revolution*, p. 169; Wall, *France*, pp. 134, 143–56; ibid., 'United States', pp. 505–11.

[11] Botschafter Blankenhorn an Bundeskanzler Adenauer und Bundesminister des Auswärtigen von Brentano, Telegramm, 23 May 1958, in BDFD 1, pp. 580–1; Cahn and Müller, *RFA et Guerre d'Algérie*, pp. 168–9; Lappenküper, 'Adenauer', p. 606; Marcowitz, 'Unionsparteien ', p. 558.

[12] Cited in: Birgit Ramscheid, *Herbert Blankenhorn (1904–1991): Adenauers außenpoliticher Berater* (Düsseldorf, 2006), p. 334.

[13] Schwarz, *Gründerjahre*, pp. 450–4.

provisional French government between 1944 and 1946 and as leader of the right-wing *Rassemblement du Peuple Français* from 1947 to 1953. Throughout this period, he had advocated Germany's dismemberment and demilitarisation; his relationship with the FRG's other occupants and allies, Britain and America, had been tense; and the Gaullists had opposed European integration, objected to West German rearmament and criticised NATO's integrated command structure.[14] To make matters worse, in 1944, de Gaulle had not only accepted communists into his government, but he had also forged a security pact with Stalin. This 'tendency to unilateral negotiations with [the] Soviets' struck Brentano as 'particularly dangerous'.[15] The federal government feared that a Gaullist France would again collaborate with Moscow, especially on the all-important German question. By provoking the May revolt, the Algerian war had come to jeopardise the central tenets of West German foreign and security policy. The General's return to power threatened not only to reverse West Germany's twelve-year progression towards sovereignty and equality but also to undermine the very foundations of Adenauer's *Westpolitik*.[16] No wonder Blankenhorn felt the crisis presaged 'the end of the European order as envisaged by Adenauer', provoking 'feelings of sheer panic' in Bonn.[17]

Events subsequently eased these fears, for de Gaulle refused to participate in Operation *Resurrection*, the French army's anticipated invasion of France. Instead, the democratic process prevailed. On 1 June, the General was invested by parliament, albeit with far-reaching powers to restore order in Algeria and draft a new constitution. The inclusion of "good Europeans" such as Mollet, Pflimlin and Pinay strengthened the provisional government's democratic and pro-Western credentials. The nomination of Maurice Couve de Murville as foreign minister further placated Adenauer and Brentano, for the erstwhile ambassador had been a staunch defender of the Bonn government, especially in matters

[14] Conze, *Herausforderung*, pp. 63–71; Maurice Vaïsse, *La Grandeur. Politique étrangère du Général de Gaulle 1958–1969* (Paris, 1995), pp. 30–4; Peter Schunck, 'De Gaulle und seine deutsche Nachbarn bis zur Begegnung mit Adenauer,' in *De Gaulle, Deutschland* (eds.) Loth and Picht, pp. 21–43; Wilfried Loth, 'De Gaulle und die europäische Einigung', in ibid., pp. 45–60; Knut Linsel, *Charles de Gaulle und Deutschland 1914–1969* (Sigmaringen, 1998), chs. 1–5.

[15] Drahterlass, Brentano, 19 May 1958, PA/AA, B24/311/F3.

[16] Cahn and Müller, *RFA et Guerre d'Algérie*, pp. 167–8; Conze, *Herausforderung*, p. 72; Lappenküper, *Deutsch-französischen Beziehungen II*, p. 1209; Paul Noack, 'Er kam und ging als Fremder. Charles de Gaulle in der westdeutschen Einschätzung zwischen 1958 und 1970', in *De Gaulle, Deutschland* (eds.) Loth and Picht, pp. 83–88.

[17] First quote: Ramscheid, *Blankenhorn*, p. 334; second quote: Lappenküper, 'Adenauer', p. 606.

Algerian.[18] Yet uncertainty persisted over de Gaulle's intentions. The General's declaration on 13 June that France belonged to the Western world 'without confining herself to it' struck German diplomats as ambiguous. What would become of Franco-German relations? Would de Gaulle accept West Germany as an equal partner or would he try to assert his dominance over the European edifice? Would he back the Adenauer government in the German question or would he seek accommodation with Moscow?[19] These anxieties were heightened by the inclusion of Michel Debré in de Gaulle's cabinet. A fervent nationalist, the former senator had never disguised his distrust of Germany, including in Algerian matters, nor his distaste for European integration.[20]

Only the historic first meeting between Adenauer and de Gaulle at Colombey-les-deux-Églises on 14 September 1958 began to dissipate some of the chancellor's many anxieties and reservations. Described as an 'historic miracle', the encounter marked the first and only time the General invited a foreign statesman to his private residence.[21] Colombey sparked what historian Jean Lacouture called 'an immediate and reciprocal stroke of seduction' between the two statesmen, one that would culminate in the Franco-German Friendship Treaty of January 1963 and transform the 'axis Paris-Bonn' into the driving motor of Europe.[22] De Gaulle, however, never considered this axis a relationship between equals. When it came to France's 'grandeur and glory', Alexander Böker of the *Auswärtige Amt* cautioned, he was likely to bypass the Adenauer government.[23] The General had already repudiated the Franco-German-Italian agreement on nuclear cooperation, declaring a Germany armed with atomic weapons one of the 'last casus belli to exist in this world'.[24] He also sought closer

18 Lappenküper, *Deutsch-französischen Beziehungen II*, p. 1210; Drahterlass Nr. 750 an Botschaft, Washington, 16 June 1958, PA/AA, B24/285/F2.

19 Schreiben Nr. 2796 von Botschaftsrat Jansen, Paris, 20 June 1958, PA/AA, B24/285/F2; Cahn and Müller, *RFA et Guerre d'Algérie*, p. 178.

20 Patrick Samuel, *Michel Debré. L'Architecte du Général* (Suresnes, 1999), pp. 86–94; Robert Frank, 'Michel Debré et l'Europe', in *Michel Debré. Premier Ministre, 1959–1962* (eds.) Serge Berstein, Pierre Milza and Jean-François Sirinelli (Paris, 2005), pp. 297–314.

21 Lappenküper, *Deutsch-französischen Beziehungen II*, p. 1230.

22 Jean Lacouture, *De Gaulle. Le souverain, 1959–1970* (Paris, 1986), p. 293. Also: Adenauer, *Erinnerungen*, pp. 424–36; Jacques Bariéty, 'De Gaulle, Adenauer et la genèse du traité franco-allemand', *RA* 22/4 (1990), pp. 540–3; ibid., 'La perception de la puissance française par le chancelier K. Adenauer de 1958 à 1963,' *Relations internationales* 58 (1989), pp. 221–2; Charles de Gaulle, *Mémoires d'espoir. Le renouveau 1958–1962* (Paris, 1970), pp. 188–94; Jean Lacouture, *De Gaulle. Le politique* (Paris, 1985), ch. 28; Schwarz, *Staatsmann*, pp. 439–57; Seydoux, *Beiderseits*, pp. 202–8; Vaïsse, *Grandeur*, pp. 226, 228–35.

23 Aufzeichnung, Alexander Böker, AA, 30 May 1958, PA/AA, B24/285/F2.

24 Cited in: Lappenküper, *Deutsch-französischen Beziehungen* I, p. 1197.

cooperation with Britain and the United States. Just days after Colombey, on 17 September, de Gaulle submitted to London and Washington his notorious memorandum on the creation of a tripartite directorate within NATO that excluded Bonn's voice altogether.[25] Gaullist France thus seemed set to become a highly capricious partner to Bonn. Doubts lingered over the steadfastness of France's solidarity with the West, especially once London and Washington rejected de Gaulle's NATO reforms.

These concerns became particularly acute on 27 November 1958, when Nikita Khrushchev issued an ultimatum on Berlin. In an effort to stabilise the economically faltering East German regime and force through a two-state solution to the German question, the Soviet premier demanded the complete removal of Western troops from Berlin, which should henceforth become a demilitarised 'free city'. Failure to comply would result in the Soviet Union signing a separate peace with the GDR. The ensuing crisis had a debilitating effect on the Adenauer government and came to dominate its foreign and security policy. Once again, the country became an object of international diplomacy, revealing the Bonn government's continued weakness and dependence on its Western allies.[26] Adenauer sought to prevent the latter from both recognising the East German regime and conceding to the formation of a unified, demilitarised German state. To push through these two aims, the chancellor increasingly turned to de Gaulle.[27]

French solidarity over Berlin would remain wavering, however, as long as the Algerian war endured. To Carstens, French support in the Berlin crisis depended entirely on de Gaulle's ability to solve the Algerian problem and to satisfy the supporters of *l'Algérie française*. Bonn's only choice was to back the General in order to forestall an even worse political alternative.[28] As the 'acid test [*Prüfstein*]' of the new regime, the Algerian problem thus remained 'of great significance' to the Adenauer government.[29] Many in

[25] Vaisse, *Grandeur*, pp. 114–23; Ibid., 'Aux origines du mémorandum de septembre 1958', *Relations Internationales* 58 (1989), pp. 253–68; Conze, *Herausforderung*, pp. 77–9.

[26] According to conventional explanations, Khrushchev sought a way to stabilise the GDR domestically and force its diplomatic recognition. The alternative view expounded by Marc Trachtenberg argues that Moscow attempted to prevent the arming of Western European armies, including the *Bundeswehr*, with American nuclear weapons. See Hope M. Harrison, *Driving the Soviets up the Wall: Soviet-East German Relations, 1953–1961* (Princeton NJ, 2003), ch. 3; Steininger, *Mauerbau*; Trachtenberg, *Constructed Peace*, chs. 7–9; Gerhart Wettig, *Chruschtschows Berlin-Krise 1958 bis 1963: Drohpolitik und Mauerbau* (München, 2006).

[27] Koopmann, *Schwierige Bündnis*, pp. 53–4; Marcowitz, *Option*, p. 150.

[28] Drahterlass Nr. 750 an Botschaft Washington, 16 June 1958, PA/AA, B24/285/F2.

[29] Aufzeichnung, Böker, 30 May 1958, PA/AA, B24/285/F2; Blankenhorn, *Verständnis*, p. 396. Also: *Auswärtige Ausschuß: Sitzungsprotokolle 13/*III, 10.Sitzung, 12 June 1958; Dépêche no. 1492 de l'ambassadeur Seydoux, Bonn, 28 August 1958, MAE, EU/RFA/1260*.

Bonn questioned de Gaulle's ability to harness the reactionary forces unleashed by the Algerian conflict, particularly among the French army. The government hoped for a prompt and lasting settlement, one that strengthened France rather than lead it – and all of Western Europe – down the path of political chaos.[30]

Faced by these circumstances, Adenauer and his diplomats kept close watch over the Algerian 'tragedy' and tried to decipher de Gaulle's plans.[31] Ever since his opening speech at the 1944 Brazzaville conference of colonial administrators, the General had a reputation as a colonial liberal, though he never advocated decolonisation.[32] A grand master of equivocation and dissimulation, de Gaulle deliberately avoided statements that could be interpreted as policy or personal opinion, leaving everyone guessing as to his intentions.[33] His notorious words – 'I have understood you!' – before an ecstatic crowd during his first visit to Algiers on 4 June 1958, only confounded this situation.[34] One Austrian journalist informed German diplomats in Paris in early May 1958 that de Gaulle had told him France had to prepare Algeria for independence. This suggested that the General favoured a policy of devolution along the lines of a Franco-Algerian federation.[35] Others argued that de Gaulle deemed overseas possessions vital for the restoration of French grandeur, which spoke for a hard line.[36] The inclusion of Debré and Soustelle in his first cabinet strengthened this view, as both ardently supported *l'Algérie française*.[37] These apparent contradictions worried German diplomats. Writing from Paris, Councillor Joseph Jansen considered the scenes of fraternisation between Algerians and *colons* in the days leading up to de Gaulle's return a 'Fata Morgana' that ignored the global trend towards national liberation. Jansen realised that de Gaulle's ambivalence was deliberate, representing 'the essence of an attempted mystification that is intended to facilitate his return to power'.

30 Dépêche no. 1289 de l'ambassade de France à Bonn, 17 July 1958, MAE, EU/RFA/1259*; Blankenhorn, *Verständnis*, pp. 298–9, 311–16; Cahn and Müller, *RFA et Guerre d'Algérie*, pp. 178–9, 183–4.

31 Seydoux, *Beiderseits*, p. 212.

32 Droz and Lever, *Histoire*, p. 184; Connelly, *Diplomatic Revolution*, p. 177; Vaïsse, *Grandeur*, p. 92; Betts, *France and Decolonisation*, pp. 58–61; Tony Smith, 'A Comparative Study of French and British Decolonization', *Comparative Studies in Society and History* 20/1 (1978), pp. 73–4.

33 On de Gaulle's theory of leadership: P.G. Cerny, *The Politics of Grandeur. Ideological Aspects of de Gaulle's Foreign Policy* (Cambridge, 1980), pp. 56–73.

34 Michèle Cointet, *De Gaulle et l'Algérie française, 1958–1962* (Villeneuve-d'Ascq, 1995), pp. 20–1.

35 Fernschreiben Nr. 2255 der Botschaft Paris, 9 May 1958, PA/AA, B24/275/F2.

36 Schreiben Nr. 2397 der Botschaft Paris, 21 May 1958, PA/AA, B24/272/F1.

37 Samuel, *Debré*, pp. 127–35; Chantal Morelle, 'Debré et l'Algérie. Quelle Algérie française?' in *Debré* (eds.) Berstein, Milza and Sirinelli, pp. 449–69.

The General 'had to swim in the "tide of ambiguity"' so as to generate support from reactionaries and liberals alike.[38]

De Gaulle's initial decisions, which combined liberal reforms with uncompromising repression, suggested a proclivity for *l'Algérie française*. The 28 September referendum on the Fifth Republic's constitution for the first time saw Algerians and Europeans vote in a single electoral chamber, as equals. De Gaulle declared its successful outcome a sign of the Algerian people's willingness 'to participate [. . .] in the grand political, economic, social, cultural project through which we intend to transform Algeria in order to deliver its inhabitants from fear and misery and assure each woman and man their liberty and dignity'.[39] If the referendum initiated the most sweeping political reforms French Algeria had ever undergone, de Gaulle's 3 October speech in Constantine instigated its largest ever programme of socio-economic modernisation. With the Constantine Plan, France committed to building homes for one million inhabitants and schools for 1.5 million children. Over the next five years, de Gaulle promised to create 400,000 new jobs and declared that 'Muslim Frenchmen from Algeria' should staff one-tenth of the civil administration. In addition to large-scale industrialisation, including the exploitation of Saharan oil and gas, the plan foresaw a redistribution of 250,000 hectares of land and committed 350 million francs to developing agriculture, forestry and hydraulics. In short, the General's intention was for 'the whole of Algeria [to take] part in all that modern civilisation can and must provide to mankind in welfare and dignity'. For this, he called upon the FLN to surrender its arms in a "peace of the brave".[40]

With these well-publicised constructive measures, so essential to the pursuit of *guerre révolutionnaire*, the Gaullist regime sought to convince Algerians and the world that Algeria's future lay with France. However, the counterinsurgency's destructive facet, too, received new impetus. Salan's temporary investment in June 1958 with both military and civilian authority in Algeria seemed to sanction the commander's hard-hitting repression and cement the military's role in shaping Algerian policies.[41] One month after the Fifth Republic's formal inception on 9 January 1959, Salan's

[38] Schreiben Nr. 2397, 21 May 1958, PA/AA, B24/272/F1.

[39] 'Allocution radiodiffusée et télévisée prononcée à l'Hôtel Matignon, 26 September 1958', in *Discours et Messages: avec le Renouveau, mai 1958-juillet 1962*, Charles de Gaulle (Paris, 1970), p. 46.

[40] 'Discours prononcé à Constantine, 3 Oct. 1958', in *Discours*, de Gaulle, pp. 48–50. Also: Cointet, *De Gaulle*, pp. 25–6; Muriam Haleh Davis, 'Restaging Mise en Valeur: "Postwar Imperialism" and the Plan de Constantine', *Review of Middle East Studies* 44/2 (2010), pp. 176–7.

[41] Doise and Vaïsse, *Diplomatie*, p. 461.

replacement as commander of French forces in Algeria, Air Force General Maurice Challe, initiated a sweeping new military offensive relying on helicopter-borne commando forces and mobile units of *harkis* to eliminate 'rebel' cadres in the *bled.* A military defeat of the FLN, which had rejected de Gaulle's "peace of the brave", thus continued to represent a vital precondition for a re-conquest of the Algerian population by constructive means.[42] As one study prepared by Prime Minister Debré's military cabinet argued:

> This war [. . .] is conducted as much, if not more, by opening roads and construction sites, building clinics, sending ever more children to school, controlling populations and [. . .] tracking the rebels' politico-administrative organisation as by destroying [. . .] their quasi-regular 'katibas' . . .[43]

Diplomatically, too, the new regime initiated a relentless pursuit of the FLN. As the new inter-ministerial committee on Algerian affairs concluded on 20 February 1959, since the 'Algerian war [constituted] a true revolutionary war [. . .] in the framework of international subversion', global initiatives had to complement internal politico-military action.[44] On 10 March, Prime Minister Debré, who became the chief executor and coordinator of the President's Algerian policies, instructed French diplomats to oppose the FLN's international activities and 'to preoccupy themselves, all other matters aside, with that which should and could be done to impede the financial, technical, military, or political aid that the rebellion sought abroad, including from our neighbours and allies'.[45] Four days later, he convened a meeting with Foreign Minister Couve de Murville and France's ambassadors in Western Europe to discuss the government's 'grand lines of diplomatic action'. Debré defined these as to:

(a) make our position known clearly and everywhere. We will never leave Algeria. The FLN cannot beat us. Aiding it will prolong an absurd and sterile struggle. We desire a ceasefire, but we reject all political negotiations with the rebellion [. . .]

[42] Evans, *Algeria*, pp. 245–50; Horne, *Savage*, pp. 330–40.
[43] Fiche, cabinet militaire du premier ministre, undated (1959), AHC, 2DE75/D1*.
[44] Compte-rendu de la réunion du comité interministériel, 20 February 1959, SAMPP/P, Ha/24*.
[45] Directives confidentielles d'information et d'action, 10 March 1959, MAE, Secrétariat d'État aux Affaires Algériennes (SEAA)/3. While Debré was the executive organ, de Gaulle remained in charge of Algerian policies though he did not make Algeria his *domaine réservé* until February 1960: 'Lettre du général de Gaulle à Debré, 8 février 1960', in *Lettres, Notes et Carnets* 8, Charles de Gaulle (Paris, 1985), p. 329; Maurice Vaïsse, 'Michel Debré et la Défense ou la voie étroite d'un Premier ministre', *Revue Historique des Armées* 236 (2004), pp. 49, 53–4.

(b) intervene to stop all material aid to the rebellion [. . .]
(c) work on political attitudes [. . .]
(d) influence political opinion wherever it is ill-disposed toward us [. . .][46]

These grand lines highlight the importance the new government continued to attach to the war's external dimensions, yet as Connelly argues, only France held the right to internationalise the conflict, and then only in view of domesticating it.[47] Through forceful diplomatic action, Debré aimed to isolate and asphyxiate the insurgents so as to make them 'realise that our friends are more and more on our side' and that surrender remained their only option. To succeed, this policy required the full backing of France's allies. 'Every indulgence or complaisance towards those who declare themselves at war with France', the premier contended, 'is incompatible with the spirit that should animate countries wishing amicable relations with France'. Admonishing the ambassadors to show 'the same energy and fighting spirit' as those engaged on the domestic front, Debré insisted that he would not tolerate breaches of European or Atlantic solidarity. 'Let it be known everywhere', he instructed, 'that the French people will judge foreign nations that claim to be its friends and allies on their attitudes toward the Algerian problem'.[48]

Blackmail in grand style?

Considering the presence on federal territory of numerous Algerian refugees and militants, the mounting evidence of FLN propaganda and arms trafficking, and the West German public's vocal criticism of French policies in Algeria, Debré's demands unsettled the Bonn government though they did not come as a surprise. Alexander Böker, head of the French desk in the *Auswärtige Amt*, predicted in May 1958 that de Gaulle would solicit 'declaration[s] of solidarity regarding North Africa' from France's allies.[49] Böker's views were mild compared to those of his colleague Paul Frank, who believed French calls for cooperation in the Algerian question were bound to increase. After all, had not the General's closest political associates – Debré and Soustelle – been some of the most

[46] Compte-rendu de la réunion sur l'Algérie, Hôtel Matignon, 14 March 1959, AHC, 2DE75/D1*.
[47] Connelly, *Diplomatic Revolution*, pp. 196–201.
[48] Compte-rendu, 14 March 1959; instruction du ministre des affaires étrangères, 2 April 1959, AHC, 2DE75/D1*.
[49] Aufzeichnung, 30 May 1958, PA/AA, B24/285/F2.

persistent and vocal critics of Bonn's supposedly nefarious 'meddling' in North Africa?[50] Once in power, Frank maintained, the Gaullists would pursue a 'policy of blackmail in grand style'. In exchange for France's continued cooperation in NATO and Europe, they would demand the West's moral and financial backing in the Algerian war.[51]

True to Frank's predictions, the exequatur of France's new ambassador to Bonn, François Clausonne de Seydoux, who took up post on 1 August 1958, contained an explicit link between the Algerian problem and the German question. Whereas Couve de Murville's investiture speech had loosely hinted at the parallel in October 1956, Seydoux's *agrément* articulated an explicit *quid pro quo*: 'when a problem particularly torments the one or the other', the document read, 'that is the case for you concerning territorial reunification, and for us concerning Africa – we know that each one can count on the comprehension and assistance of the other'.[52] The reference to Africa fooled no one. The *Quai d'Orsay* essentially likened France's non-recognition of the GDR to Bonn's support against the FLN. Blankenhorn considered the offensive passage 'a threat' imperilling both Adenauer's *Westpolitik* and West German interests beyond Europe.[53]

Eager to disentangle the two issues, the response drafted for Federal President Theodor Heuss contained carefully nuanced language. It extended to France Bonn's full comprehension in the Algerian problem, but remained silent on the question of assistance. The speech emphasised how the government and German people 'gratefully appreciate the fact that French governments have emphatically supported the [West] German position in [the German] question'. It noted that Bonn and the German public 'take a lively interest in all the problems and dangers that France faced in Africa' (i.e. Algeria) and concluded by appealing to the 'political genius' and 'great liberal traditions' of the French people to solve its problems there, but to do so alone.[54] This careful wording, the *Auswärtige Amt* hoped, would defuse a 'dangerous form of argumentation' that was becoming increasingly popular among French officials.[55]

As East–West tensions mounted in November 1958, fears again arose that France would make its support in the Berlin crisis contingent on

[50] Question écrite no. 26 posée par Debré, Sénateur, 25 October 1957; Note no. 79 pour le bureau législatif, 29 November 1957; Note no. 24 pour le bureau législatif, 28 April 1958, MAE, EU/RFA/1267.

[51] Aufzeichnung, Frank, Referat 302/204, 27 May 1958, PA/AA, B24/285/F1.

[52] Agrément, Seydoux, undated, PA/AA, B24/292/F3. [53] Linsel, *De Gaulle*, p. 151.

[54] Entwurf, Erwiderungsansprache des Herrn Bundespräsidenten, undated, PA/AA, B24/292/F3.

[55] Lappenküper, *Deutsch-französischen Beziehungen II*, pp. 1236–7.

Bonn's assistance in the Algerian conflict. Averting this scenario required stronger defences than Heuss's speech. To Herbert Müller-Roschach, deputy director of the *Amt*'s Western department, the parallel between Algeria and Berlin was fundamentally flawed. The German question, he argued, was about the reunification of two ethnically, linguistically, culturally and historically related and adjacent territories traditionally considered one nation, where one part remained under a hostile occupation that threatened the security of the other part and of Western Europe as a whole. In contrast, Müller-Roschach argued, refuting the historical myth of *l'Algérie française*, Algeria was neither ethnically nor culturally a part of France. As a co-signatory, along with Britain, the United States and West Germany, of the May 1952 General Treaty on the abrogation of the Occupation Statute, which had taken effect in May 1955, French governments furthermore had a legal obligation vis-à-vis the question of German reunification. Although covered by the Atlantic treaty, no such obligation existed for Bonn or any other NATO ally with regards to Algeria, which the French consistently treated as an internal affair.[56]

Müller-Roschach thus built a case for denying the French assistance in the Algerian question. He pushed on by proposing that Bonn should confront the Paris authorities in a 'frank conversation', asking:

1. Is the Algerian question really an existential matter [. . .] or is the war not rather a threat to the vital interests [also] of France's allies?
2. Will Western solidarity with France's war not end up driving Tunisia and Morocco into the Soviet bloc?
3. Does the continuation of this war not endanger France's positions in Africa?
4. Will France not have to decide one day whether it is a European nation, whose interests lie with [the West], or whether it is an Afro-European hybrid that will degenerate through an internal struggle between its African and European factions and rob Europe of the chance to become the true ally of independent African unions?

These questions revealed Bonn's continuing concern with the Algerian war's impact not just on European and Atlantic unity but also on Western influence and standing in the emerging Third World. Reversing the parallel between Algeria and reunification, Müller-Roschach concluded that Paris had to be made to realise how more was at stake than French glory and grandeur:

[56] Aufzeichnung, Herbert Müller-Roschach, 20 November 1958 in BDFD 1, pp. 711–12; Aufzeichnung, Müller-Roschach, für Paul Frank, 22 November 1958, PA/AA, B24/312/F4.

> Last not least one must point out that [West] Germany, too, stood before the moral decision whether to give priority to reunification, thus jeopardising the unity of the West, or to solidarity with the West, thus endangering reunification. Germany has managed to take the painful decision for the West. France cannot be spared from this fundamental choice in the Algerian question.[57]

Müller-Roschach's deliberations ignited a conceptual debate among foreign-policy makers over how to handle Algeria with the French. In a highly controversial memorandum submitted to Brentano and Adenauer on 30 December 1958, Paul Frank endorsed Müller-Roschach's views. Having championed a joint and liberal solution to the Algerian question in November 1955, Frank once again came out in favour of 'frank, open, and if need be unbending' dialogue. Citing Frederick the Great's dictum, 'to be France's ally is to be its slave', Frank vehemently opposed attempts to coerce loyalty in the Algerian question, which would only heighten Bonn's 'one-sided dependence' on France. To him, Algeria had become an 'abscess of fixation' threatening the security and credibility of all of Western Europe. Even 'passive support' of France's Algerian policies endangered 'the free world's higher goal of security and peace'. If the French wanted German solidarity and assistance in the Algerian question, Frank insisted, then it was not only 'their duty to discuss this most dangerous of European/African problems with us' as equal partners but also to pursue 'a good policy that served the interests of the entire West'. These arguments sought to buttress Bonn's independence and parity vis-à-vis the Gaullist regime. They reflected what historian Christian Hacke calls the 'primacy of intertwined interests' in German foreign policy.[58] To Frank, *l'Algérie française* had become untenable, and the sooner that territory became independent, the better for France and the Western alliance. He had lost faith even in de Gaulle's ability to solve the Algerian quandary unilaterally: its solution had to be internationalised; and Bonn should encourage France to accept that fact.[59]

Needless to say, not everyone in Bonn agreed with this bold and controversial conclusion. Adenauer found Frank's memorandum 'impossible'

[57] Aufzeichnung, Müller-Roschach, 22 November 1958, PA/AA, B24/312/F4. Also: Cahn and Müller, *RFA et Guerre d'Algérie*, pp. 230–1.

[58] Christian Hacke, 'Nationales Interesse als Handlungsmaxime für die Außenpolitik Deutschlands', in *Deutschlands neue Außenpolitik: Interessen und Strategien* (eds.) Karl Kaiser and Joachim Krause (Oldenbourg, 1996), p. 7.

[59] Ministerialdirektor Carstens an Bundesminister von Brentano, Aufzeichnung, 30 December 1958, in BDFD 1, pp. 717–23; Paul Frank, *Entschlüsselte Botschaft. Ein Diplomat macht Inventur* (Stuttgart, 1981), pp. 39–45. Also: Cahn and Müller, *RFA et Guerre d'Algérie*, pp. 231–3; Lappenküper, *Deutsch-französischen Beziehungen II*, pp. 1257–8.

and 'outrageous'. Blankenhorn, who had replaced Maltzan as ambassador to France, was equally dismayed. He vehemently counselled against broaching the Algerian problem in Paris, something he deemed all the more important given the rightward shift in French politics after the November 1958 parliamentary and presidential elections.[60] To Blankenhorn, any talk of Algerian abandonment would aggravate the 'inner reserves' that Debré, in particular, harboured against Germany.[61] He was not mistaken. In February 1959, the premier personally cautioned the ambassador 'that the solidarity of the accord between France and Germany was linked to a community of views that must, for the moment, manifest itself principally in Algeria'.[62] By the same token, Debré's cabinet director warned Frank the 'Federal Republic must choose between its sympathy for an independent Algeria and its friendship for France!'[63]

In these circumstances, there would be no internationalisation of the Algerian problem let alone dialogue between heads of state. Nor would there be much of what Cahn and Müller have called 'a policy of equidistance', marked, as Bougherara also maintains, by an extreme reserve and neutrality in the Algerian question.[64] Instead, as historian Maurice Vaïsse argues, 'Adenauer displayed an unfailing support for the General's policies in Algeria' and instructed his diplomats to do the same.[65] Apart from standard well wishes, Adenauer never initiated discussions of the Algerian question with French interlocutors, least of all de Gaulle. Having already appointed his closest diplomatic councillor to the post of ambassador in Paris, he ensured that Franco-German relations remained under his close and personal control.[66]

Adenauer's utmost priority was to protect the Franco-German rapprochement, which in the context of the Berlin crisis remained central to the success of his policy of *Westbindung*. The chancellor could ill afford to alienate the French government. He already feared that Britain or the United States might capitulate to Soviet demands on Berlin, or reach an agreement over his head. British Prime Minister Harold Macmillan's 'voyage of discovery' to Moscow in February 1959 merely exacerbated

[60] Frank, *Botschaft*, pp. 43–5. [61] Ramscheid, *Blankenhorn*, p. 336.
[62] Note a.s. de l'entretien du Premier Ministre et de M. Blankenhorn, 17 February 1959, MAE, EU/RFA/1261*.
[63] Frank, *Botschaft*, pp. 43–4.
[64] Cahn and Müller, *RFA et Guerre d'Algérie*, pp. 252–3; Bougherara, *Rapports*, pp. 81–2.
[65] Vaïsse, *Grandeur*, p. 230.
[66] On Adenauer's control of foreign policy: Gordon A. Craig, 'Konrad Adenauer and his Diplomats', in *The Diplomats 1939–1979* (eds.) Gordon A. Craig and Francis L. Loewenheim (Princeton NJ, 1994), pp. 201–27.

Adenauer's *Angst*.[67] He was relieved to find a staunch ally in de Gaulle, who refused to compromise over Berlin.[68] French policies, however, remained unpredictable. In his press conference of 25 March, for instance, de Gaulle sanctioned the Oder-Neisse line demarcating the East German–Polish border, a line the Adenauer government refused to recognise as Germany's eastern frontier.[69] Earlier that month, the withdrawal of France's Mediterranean fleet from NATO had again raised alarm over France's continued solidarity with the Atlantic alliance.[70] So did de Gaulle's reiteration in November 1959 of France's determination to become an independent nuclear power. The General's concomitant insistence that Bonn renounce all ambitions to gain access to military nuclear capabilities seemed to confirm that he did not perceive the Paris–Bonn axis as a partnership between equals.[71] This view of the Adenauer government as a junior and subservient partner that would toe the French line was reinforced further by de Gaulle's consistent refusal to broach the Algerian question with West German officials or ministers, even though, as Vaïsse points out, he discussed Algeria 'with almost all of his foreign interlocutors'.[72]

In the prevailing conditions of insecurity and uncertainty, Adenauer felt it best to give in to the French demand for a *quid pro quo*: he would support de Gaulle in the Algerian problem so that the latter would back Bonn in the German question. This *Diktat* became all the more pressing after the death in May 1959 of the fervently anti-communist US State Secretary John Foster Dulles, who had been one of the chancellor's closest allies and friends, and the failure three months later of the four-power Geneva conference on Berlin. As Eckart Conze argues, Adenauer's support of de Gaulle aimed to shore up NATO unity at a crucial point in the crisis over Berlin.[73] In contrast to Müller-Roschach and Frank's advice, even the

67 Kitty Newman, *Macmillan, Khrushchev and the Berlin Crisis: 1958–1960* (London, 2007), pp. 63–82; Steininger, *Mauerbau*, pp. 69–82; Richard D. Williamson, *First Steps toward Détente: American Diplomacy in the Berlin Crisis, 1958–1963* (Lanham MD, 2012), pp. 15–38.

68 De Gaulle's intransigence apparently had to do with power-political considerations and distaste for appeasement. The General was convinced in the righteousness of the Western position in Berlin and believed that Khrushchev was bluffing when he threatened the use of force. He preferred the status quo to the possibility of a unified Germany: Cyril Buffet, 'De Gaulle et Berlin. Une certaine idée de l'Allemagne,' *RA* 22/4 (1990), pp. 525–38; Linsel, *De Gaulle*, pp. 164–96; Vaïsse, *Grandeur*, pp. 263–83; Soutou, *L'Alliance incertaine*, pp. 123–202.

69 Conférence de presse tenue au palais d'Elysée, 25 March 1959, in *Discours*, de Gaulle, pp. 82–7.

70 Ramscheid, *Blankenhorn*, p. 336.

71 Allocution prononcée à l'École Militaire, 3 November 1959, in *Discours*, de Gaulle, pp. 125–9; Soutou, *L'Alliance incertaine*, pp. 136–9.

72 Vaïsse, *Grandeur*, p. 73.

73 Conze, *Herausforderung*, pp. 17, 82 n.69; Lappenküper, 'Adenauer', pp. 609–11; Schwarz, *Staatsmann*, p. 464.

Auswärtige Amt had concluded in April 1959 that 'every attempt to influence France [in the Algerian question], no matter how well meant, would end in failure and could even produce a negative reaction'.[74]

Thus although its assessments of the Algerian war remained as pessimistic as ever, German diplomacy continued to support the French war effort.[75] Far from upholding a policy of equidistance and non-engagement, Bonn's diplomats persisted in their efforts to persuade the Western allies of the need to back de Gaulle on Algeria. The chancellor had already tried to shore up NATO support for France prior to the UN's Algerian debate in December 1958.[76] At the time, a strongly worded Afro-Asian resolution on the 'right of the Algerian people to independence' and 'negotiations between the two parties' was only narrowly thwarted by one vote, revealing just how unpopular French Algeria had become in the international community. Many of France's key allies, including the United States, had switched from supporting France to abstaining from the vote, which the FLN interpreted as an incontestable triumph for its cause.[77] To prevent a similar or worse scenario in December 1959, Adenauer redoubled his efforts to secure allies for the UN debate. In Reykjavík and other Nordic capitals, where pro-Algerian sympathies were particularly strong, German diplomats began as early as August 1959 to remind the foreign ministries of the need for solidarity vis-à-vis the communist bloc.[78] Similar demarches occurred in London and The Hague.[79] Adenauer's state secretary, Hans Globke, informed the Greek ambassador in Bonn that the chancellor 'desired to aid France inconspicuously in the matter with different countries to which he entertained particularly good relations'.[80] In contrast to his diplomats, however, Adenauer was hardly discreet in his interventions. After a meeting of NATO representatives in Italy in August 1959, the Belgian envoy informed his French counterpart, Pierre Leusse, who had been absent, how 'the chancellor had turned into the most ardent advocate for

[74] Aufzeichnung, Dr. Sarrazin, Referat 204/205, 27 March 1959, PA/AA, B25/9.

[75] Schreiben Nr. 3505 von Botschaftsrat Kutscher, Paris, 17 July 1959, PA/AA, B24/291/F4; Schreiben Nr. 3919 von Botschaftsrat Jansen, Paris, 20 August 1959, PA/AA, B24/313/F3; Blankenhorn, *Verständnis*, p. 344; Cahn and Müller, *RFA et Guerre d'Algérie*, pp. 250–1.

[76] Schreiben des Beobachters bei den VN, New York, 16 December 1958, PA/AA, B25/12.

[77] Connelly, *Diplomatic Revolution*, p. 198; Thomas, 'France Accused', pp. 110–11.

[78] Télégramme no. 2199 de l'ambassadeur Seydoux, Bonn, 4 August 1959, MAE, EU/RFA/1273; Schreiben Nrs. 423 and 436 von Botschafter Hirschfeld, Reykjavík, 3 September and 10 September 1959, PA/AA, B24/313/F3.

[79] Aufzeichnung, Frank, Referat 204, 22 September 1959, PA/AA, B24/313/F4; Dépêche no. 707 de l'ambassadeur de Beauverger, La Haye, 5 August 1959, DDF, 1959, Vol. II, Nr. 54, p. 145.

[80] Cited in: Cahn and Müller, *RFA et Guerre d'Algérie*, p. 235; Aufzeichnung, StS van Scherpenberg, 4 August 1959, PA/AA, B2/78/F1.

France [. . .] especially when speaking of Algeria'. Adenauer 'had energetically defended the fact that the members of the Atlantic alliance should support the French viewpoint before the UN'. The Belgian diplomat concluded that he had 'rarely seen as steadfast a Gaullist' as Adenauer.[81]

The French authorities welcomed Adenauer's advocacy, especially his intervention with Eisenhower on 26 August 1959 ahead of the president's state visit to Paris, and his repeated attempts to convince other American personalities of the Cold War imperatives driving French policy in Algeria.[82] Franco-American relations had deteriorated steadily over Washington's decision to abstain from UN votes on the Algerian question. Considering, as Couve de Murville maintained, that the United States 'guided the opinion of a large part of the world and held considerable influence at the UN', this move had delivered a serious blow to France's diplomatic war against the FLN.[83] The *Quai d'Orsay* thus expressed its 'thankful recognition' to German diplomats in Paris 'for the fact that German policy [. . .] has substantially helped to generate greater comprehension among the Western allies for de Gaulle's difficult position in the Algerian question'.[84] For once, even de Gaulle acknowledged his gratitude, informing Adenauer how American attitudes in the Algerian question posed 'a risk to the Atlantic alliance', one he hoped 'had now passed'.[85]

Veiled though it was, the General's praise was revealing, for he generally eschewed any mention of the *guerre diplomatique* and rejected the UN's authority in the Algerian question. In contrast to previous governments, he instructed French representatives in New York to abstain from discussions of Algeria, 'even in the corridors'.[86] Considering the importance accruing to UN debates as a measure of moral and political support for the FLN, the General nevertheless called for 'preparatory' action to influence voting.[87] To avoid any semblance of official sanction of the UN's competency in the

[81] Télégramme no. 235 de l'ambassadeur Leusse, 1 September 1959, MAE, AL/ALG/15.

[82] Dépêche no. 2266 de l'ambassadeur Seydoux, Bonn, 15 August 1959; Dépêche no. 2383 de l'ambassadeur Seydoux, Bonn, 28 August 1959, MAE, MLA/4; Aufzeichnung, Frank, Referat 204, 12 August 1959, PA/AA, B24/287/F2; Günter Buchstab (ed.), *Adenauer: 'Um den Frieden zu gewinnen.' Die Protokolle des CDU-Bundesvorstandes 1957–1961* (Düsseldorf, 1994), Nr. 9, pp. 387, 390–1; Charles G. Cogan, 'France, the United States and the Invisible Algerian Outcome', *JSS* 25/2 (2002), p. 140; Schwarz, *Staatsmann*, pp. 464–5; Cahn and Müller, *RFA et Guerre d'Algérie*, pp. 248–9; Conze, *Herausforderung*, pp. 113–15.

[83] Compte-rendu de la réunion sur l'Algérie, Hôtel Matignon, 14 March 1959, AHC, 2DE75/D1*.

[84] Schreiben von Botschaftsrat Jansen, Paris, an Dr. Bach, Bundeskanzleramt, 17 September 1959, BA/K, B136/3624/2/F6.

[85] Lettre du Général de Gaulle au Chancelier Adenauer, 7 September 1959, AHC, 2DE65*.

[86] Note par le Général de Gaulle pour le premier ministre et le ministre des affaires étrangères, 4 December 1959, 2DE75/D1*.

[87] Lettre circulaire du MAE aux postes diplomatiques, December 1959, AHC, 2DE75/D1*.

matter or of open engagement with the FLN, this action was conducted largely through private, transnational channels linking Christian-conservative elites and organisations in what Johannes Großmann has called a 'Christian Cominform'.[88] A covert campaign that took the form of propaganda, bribery and blackmail, its chief coordinators were the prominent French lawyer and SDECE collaborator, Jean Violet, and Catholic priest Yves-Marc Dubois.[89] Bonn's diplomats played an active, albeit secret part in Violet's campaign. Prior to Eisenhower's visit with Adenauer, the chancellor and his state secretary had received a personal visit from their 'known friend' Violet who requested that German embassies distribute a brochure on the Algerian problem prepared by the Swiss, hence 'neutral', Catholic International Press Agency.[90] Former premiers Mollet and Pinay and General Allard, recently appointed to the post of commander-in-chief of French forces in Germany, undertook similarly discreet demarches.[91] Likewise, in late September 1959, a 'friend' from the Élysée palace signalled that an 'intervention in La Paz [. . .] would [also] be very useful'.[92] Bonn's diplomats clearly obliged, for that same month Counsellor Jansen from the embassy in Paris reported with satisfaction how 'a personality very close to de Gaulle told him that Bonn had demonstrated what cooperation means' and that 'the French press had been amply and emphatically orientated in this sense'.[93]

Adenauer's policy of backing the French authorities in their diplomatic war against the FLN helped considerably to consolidate the axis Paris–Bonn, for it continued to build French trust. This policy came at a cost, however, for it threatened to sully the Federal Republic's international reputation. De Gaulle's recognition on 16 September 1959 of Algeria's right to self-determination consequently came as a great relief to West German diplomacy.[94] Finally, the *Auswärtige Amt* could defend what Frank had

[88] Johannes Großmann, 'Vom "christilichen Kominform" zur "geistigen Nato". Das Internationale Comité zur Verteidigung der Christlichen Kultur als transnationale antikommunistische Propagandaagentur', *Jahrbuch für Historische Kommunismusforschung* (2011), pp. 139–54.

[89] Faligot and Krop, *Piscine*, pp. 194–6; Melnik, *Mille jours*, pp. 122, 272; Philippe Thyraud de Vosjoli, *Lamia. L'anti-barbouze* (Montreal and Brussels, 1972), pp. 306–7. On Violet broadly: Großmann, *Internationale*, pp. 437–96.

[90] Schreiben, Botschaftsrat Jansen, Paris, an Dr. Bach, Bundeskanzleramt, 17 September 1959, BA/K, B136/3624/2/F6.

[91] They are alluded to in: *Protokolle 1957–1961*, Nr. 12, 29 January 1960, p. 581.

[92] Brief von Botschaftsrat Jansen, Paris, an StS Globke, 25 September 1959, BA/K, B136/3624/2/F6.

[93] Fernschreiben von Botschaftsrat Jansen, Paris, an Dr. Bach, Bundeskanzleramt, 7 September 1959, BA/K, B136/3624/2/F6. Also: 'Adenauer: L'autorité de de Gaulle est vitale pour l'Europe. L'Algérie est la clé de la Méditerranée', *La Croix*, 26 June 1959.

[94] Allocution radiodiffusée et televisée prononcée au Palais de l'Élysée, 16 September 1959, *Discours*, de Gaulle, pp. 117–23. More broadly: Benjamin Stora, *Le Mystère de Gaulle. Son choix pour l'Algérie* (Paris, 2009).

called a 'good policy' that served Western interests. As Carstens informed Ambassador Seydoux, Bonn's pro-French attitude in the Algerian question was now much more defensible, especially vis-à-vis the Afro-Asian bloc.[95] Adenauer and Brentano spoke of de Gaulle's initiative 'in the warmest terms and with unreserved satisfaction'. Both confided to Seydoux that their confidence in the General had now been vindicated.[96] The policy of self-determination, which offered Algerians a choice of secession, 'complete francization' or federation, promised significantly to improve the climate of world opinion towards France. For the first time, a French government was willing to countenance the idea of Algerian independence. In presenting a democratic solution that conformed to the principles of the UN Charter and provided a clear timetable of implementation, the General had outmanoeuvred those calling for the Algerian problem's internationalisation.[97] German observers realised that many hurdles remained, especially the uncompromising attitudes of the French military and *colons*. The FLN, too, rejected de Gaulle's terms for a ceasefire, elections and multi-party negotiations.[98] Despite these hurdles, the 16 September speech represented the first glimmer of hope for a negotiated end to the Algerian war. In an apologetic statement – since it was 'not habitual to take position on the [internal] affairs concerning a neighbour state' – the Adenauer government publicly praised de Gaulle, whose initiative facilitated an improvement in Franco-American and hence NATO relations and laid 'the foundations for conciliation in Algeria'.[99]

How distant this conciliation remained would soon become apparent. Even after de Gaulle's apparent change of course, German diplomats in Paris and Algiers warned constantly against expressing too much optimism in France's Algerian policies. After all, notwithstanding the operational successes of the Challe offensive, the military proved unable to subdue the ALN, which according to Bonn's consul-general in Algiers demonstrated

[95] Télégramme no. 3036 de l'ambassadeur Seydoux, Bonn, 26 October 1959, MAE, MLA/4.

[96] Télégramme no. 2573 de l'ambassadeur Seydoux, Bonn, 18 September 1959, MAE, MLA/4. Also: Schreiben des Ständigen Vertreters im Nordatlantikrat an Brentano, 18 September 1959, PA/AA, B1/56; Télégramme no. 2616 de l'ambassadeur Seydoux, Bonn, 23 September 1959, MAE, EU/RFA/1262*.

[97] Cointet, *De Gaulle*, p. 56; Evans, *Algeria*, pp. 261–5.

[98] Aufzeichnungen, Frank, Referat 204, 22 September and 2 October 1959, PA/AA, B24/314/F2–3; Télégrammes nos. 2621, 2686 et 2703 de l'ambassadeur Seydoux, Bonn, 23 September, 29 September, and 30 September 1959, MAE, MLA/4. Also: Blankenhorn, *Verständnis*, pp. 352–3; Cahn and Müller, *RFA et guerre d'Algérie*, pp. 250–1.

[99] Télégramme no. 2587 de l'ambassadeur Seydoux, Bonn, 18 September 1959, MAE, MLA/4.

a 'surprising capacity to regenerate its cadres'.[100] Diplomatically, too, the FLN grew continuously in stature, especially in the context of 1960 – the 'year of Africa', which saw seventeen former colonies join the UN, all of which backed the Algerian cause. Bonn's furtive interventions had themselves failed to prevent several Latin American states from supporting the FLN at the UN. The Eastern bloc, too, had significantly extended its solidarity and aid to the Algerians, especially Communist China, which had intensified its competition with the Soviet Union.[101] To Blankenhorn, Algeria seemed to be on the verge of turning into another Cold War proxy conflict.[102]

Mostly though, the ambassador feared for French political stability. The 'week of the barricades' of January 1960 reminded Bonn just how volatile de Gaulle's position, and Algeria's future, remained. Bizarrely, the rebellion's impetus had come from an interview by the former paratrooper turned correspondent for Munich's *Süddeutsche Zeitung*, Hans-Ulrich Kempski, with General Massu, "victor" of the Battle of Algiers. Published on 18 January, the interview received worldwide attention, for in it Massu openly challenged the president's political authority. He 'questioned the army's obedience to de Gaulle's next directive and condemned the policy defined on 16 September [1959], going so far as to query the president's succession'.[103] Massu's subsequent recall sparked an uprising by reactionary settlers in Algiers on 24 January. The weeklong standoff revived fears of a civil war, especially since large sections of the army sympathised with the rebellious *colons*.[104]

Dismayed by the prospect of losing his staunchest ally, Adenauer immediately redoubled his defence of de Gaulle.[105] At a CDU conference on 29 January, he publicly chastised France's critics, especially the Americans, for what he deemed their over-simplified analysis of the Algerian war as a mere colonial problem.[106] The French authorities sought to capitalise on the chancellor's stance. Days after his speech, Violet let it be known via Defence Minister Strauss that 'official circles' in Paris had

[100] Schreiben, Generalkonsul Nostitz, Algiers, 17 January 1960, PA/AA, B25/2. Also: Schreiben, Generalkonsul Nostitz, Algiers, 7 March 1960, PA/AA, B24/374/F1; Schreiben Nr. 3505 der Botschaft Paris, 17 July 1959; Aufzeichnung, von Plehwe, 16 September 1959, PA/AA, B24/291/F4.

[101] Connelly, *Diplomatic Revolution*, pp. 195, 199; Kyle Haddad-Fonda, 'An Illusory Alliance: Revolutionary Legitimacy and Sino-Algerian Relations, 1958–1962', *Journal of North African Studies* 19/3 (2014), pp. 338–57.

[102] Blankenhorn, *Verständnis*, p. 396.

[103] Télégramme no. 175 de l'ambassadeur Seydoux, Bonn, 20 January 1960, DDF, 1960, Vol. I, Nr.25, pp. 54–5.

[104] Evans, *Algeria*, pp. 270–6; Horne, *Savage*, pp. 349–72.

[105] Lappenküper, 'Adenauer', pp. 610–12.

[106] *Protokolle 1957–1961*, Nr. 12, p. 580; Télégrammes nos. 387, 414, et 426 de l'ambassade de France, Bonn, 30 January, 1 February and 2 February 1960, MAE, MLA/5.

greatly appreciated Adenauer's 'warm words of support'. In the interest of 'intensifying Franco-German cooperation even further', they hoped the chancellor would again impress upon Eisenhower how dangerous an American abstention from UN debates on Algeria was for European security.[107] The Bonn government thus remained an important ally in the Fifth Republic's concealed efforts to sway international opinion and influence voting at the UN.

Exploiting German anxieties over French political stability, the Paris authorities also succeeded in forcing through contentious plans to tap the EDF for investments in Algeria. In an *aide mémoire* dated 24 November 1959, the Debré government had unilaterally withdrawn Mollet's pledge in 1957 to exclude Algeria from the EDF. At the time, the European Commission under Walter Hallstein had refused to recognise this decision. On 8 February 1960, Debré ordered French diplomats to redouble their efforts to overturn this opposition. Remarking on Adenauer's 'excellent words' of support during the Barricades crisis, the premier felt the moment had come 'to obtain a solution'.[108] The chancellor, however, faced stiff resistance from the *Auswärtige Amt* and Federal Ministry for Economic Affairs. Both feared that concessions on the EDF would expose West Germany to criticism from the Arab and Third World of buttressing French colonialism.[109] On 21 June, Debré noted how Bonn kept using 'one bad pretext after another to dally around' in the matter. He instructed Couve de Murville to remind Bonn how France, '[m]ore than any European nation, followed a loyal policy with regard to Germany', alluding to Paris's policy of *quid pro quo*.[110] By 5 July the premier threatened to withhold France's annual EDF contribution if Bonn and the European Commission did not change their tune.[111] In a context of heightened insecurity over Berlin, especially after the failure of the Four Power summit of May 1960, these warnings had the desired effect. At the Rambouillet meeting with de Gaulle on 29 July, Adenauer formally conceded to Paris's demands regarding the EDF.[112] Even then, the *Auswärtige Amt* requested 'that this decision not be made

[107] Schreiben von Strauss an Adenauer, 5 February 1960, BA/K, B136/3624/2/F7.

[108] Note par Debré à l'attention de M. Amanrich, 8 February 1960, AHC, 2DE/12*.

[109] Entwurf, Referat 205 AA, 24 November 1959, PA/AA, B25/67; *Die Kabinettsprotokolle der Bundesregierung*, Bd.13 – *1960* (eds.) Ralf Behrendt and Christoph Seemann (Munich, 2003), 115. Sitzung, 20 July 1960, p. 280; Lappenküper, *Deutsch-französischen Beziehungen II*, pp. 1348, 1350; Cahn and Müller, *RFA et Guerre d'Algérie*, p. 289.

[110] Lettre par Debré à Couve de Murville, 21 June 1960, AHC, 2DE/21*.

[111] Lettre par Debré à Couve de Murville, 5 July 1960, AHC, 2DE/21*.

[112] Deuxième tête-à-tête entre de Gaulle et Adenauer, Rambouillet, 29 July 1960, AN, 5AG1/160*.

public'.[113] The chancellor's policy of support for France's Algerian policies thus presented a growing cause for concern in Bonn.

West German diplomats had reason to worry, for Adenauer's concessions in the Algerian question did not go unnoticed. By siding too closely and too openly with France, the chancellor not only alienated his other Western allies, but he also damaged West German relations with the Third World. The FLN itself had issued a propaganda brochure condemning the Common Market as a neo-colonialist vehicle permitting France to maintain its dominance over newly independent countries.[114] The West German media and political opposition, too, had begun to accuse the chancellor of acting like Paris's vassal, sworn to allegiance through a myth-inspired '*Nibelungentreue*' (feudal loyalty).[115] No wonder that German diplomats pleaded for utmost discretion in the Franco-German *quid pro quo*. The *Auswärtige Amt* had repeatedly appealed for understanding over its reluctance to support French Algerian policies publicly.[116] Adenauer's staunch backing of de Gaulle helped cement the Paris–Bonn axis, but it hampered West German foreign policy in almost every other domain.[117]

Balance and blackmail?

Nowhere was this felt more acutely than in Bonn's relations with 'the so-called Bandung world', those regions of Asia, Africa and the Middle East where neutralism and anti-colonialism were on the rise and support for the FLN grew stronger with every colony to gain independence.[118] By 1960, Algeria's liberation struggle had become an international *cause célèbre* and

[113] Télégramme no. 3003 de l'ambassadeur Seydoux, Bonn, 22 July 1960, AHC, 2DE/70*.

[114] Fédération de France du FLN, 'L'Afrique se libère', mid-1960, SHD-T, 1H/1715/D1.

[115] Aufzeichnung Carstens an Brentano, 7 May 1960, PA/AA, B24/352/F2; 'Eine Axis Paris-Bonn?' *Industrie-Kurier*, 19 February 1959; 'Die Verlobung von Paris ', *Die Welt*, 9 March 1959; 'Unsere Freundschaften,' *Hamburger Abendblatt*, 14 March 1959; Müller, 'Presse ouest-allemande', p. 183. On the etymology of *Nibelungentreue*: www.germany.info/Vertretung/usa/en/__pr/GIC/TWIG__WoW/2014/08-Nibelungentreue.html (accessed 12 August 2014).

[116] Dépêche no. 1833 de l'ambassadeur Seydoux, Bonn, 9 November 1958, MAE, EU/RFA/1241; Dépêches nos. 306 et 1557 de l'ambassade de France, Bonn, 12 February and 21 August 1959, EU/RFA/1273; Télégramme no. 2105 de l'ambassadeur Seydoux, Bonn, 21 July 1959, MLA/3; Note du service d'Europe centrale, 27 November 1959, EU/RFA/1262*.

[117] The chancellor's policies also created a rift within the CDU/CSU-coalition between Gaullists and Atlanticists, who favoured closer ties to Britain and the United States: Conze, *Herausforderung*, pp. 22–4; Tim Geiger, *Atlantiker gegen Gaullisten: außenpolitischer Konflikt und innerparteilicher Machtkampf in der CDU/CSU 1958–1969* (Munich, 2008), chs. 1–3; Klaus Hildebrand, '"Atlantiker" versus "Gaullisten". Zur Außenpolitik der Bundesrepublik Deutschland während der sechziger Jahre', *RA* 23/4 (1990), pp. 583–92.

[118] Aufzeichnung, Referat 302, undated (1958), PA/AA, B24/312/F1.

prime symbol of Third World unity.[119] The FLN had not been idle since the May 1958 crisis. De Gaulle's return to power represented a dangerous and disheartening setback for the movement, one that required a strong riposte to counteract the General's charismatic appeal to the Algerian masses. After months of internal deliberations, the FLN launched a two-pronged offensive designed to lift morale and inject renewed dynamism into Algeria's independence struggle.[120]

In the first instance, the *Fédération de France* instigated its long-awaited second front to 'carry the war to France'. In contrast to Algeria, FLN terrorism in the metropole avoided French civilians, exclusively targeting strategic installations and symbols of French repression, including petroleum reservoirs, military depots, police stations, and prominent supporters of *l'Algérie française* such as Soustelle.[121] Launched on 25 August 1958, the FLN likened its second front to a 'virus that weakens colonialist France' and was 'capable of contaminating the West'.[122] By extending the armed struggle to the metropole and forcing France to concentrate some of its military resources at home, the FLN hoped to alleviate the pressure on its combatants in Algeria. By compelling the authorities to clamp down on Algerian migrants, the offensive would further rally this community to the FLN's cause. By confronting the metropolitan population, it would help convince public opinion of the necessity for Algerian independence. Finally, by re-focusing international attention on the FLN, the initiative would demonstrate to all that the FLN remained a force with which even de Gaulle would have to reckon.[123]

To underscore this final point, part two of the FLN's riposte saw the creation on 19 September of the GPRA, a government-in-exile presided over by the well-known veteran of liberal nationalism, Ferhat Abbas. Based first in Cairo, then Tunis, the GPRA's creation signalled an astute shift in FLN strategy, one outlined by Aït Ahmed from his prison cell in April 1957.[124] Henceforth, politics, diplomacy and propaganda would supersede guns and bombs as the movement's weapons of choice. Whereas the Soummam congress had stressed the internal struggle, the external dimension would now take precedence. Created on the eve of the

119 Westad, *Global Cold War*, p. 105.
120 Connelly, *Diplomatic Revolution*, pp. 180–5; Meynier, *Histoire*, p. 352.
121 Lebjaoui, *Vérités*, p. 77.
122 Bulletin d'information de la Fédération de France sur la nouvelle forme de lutte inaugurée le 25 August 1958, ses effets, September/October 1958, in *Archives* (ed.) Harbi, no. 50, pp. 228–9.
123 Boudaoud, *Du PPA au FLN*, pp. 169–72; Djerbal, *L'OS*, pp. 59–65, 226–8; Haroun, *Septième wilaya*, ch. 5.
124 Étude envoyée au C.C.E. de la prison de la Santé (April 1957), in *Guerre*, Aït Ahmed, pp. 9–57.

referendum on the new French constitution, the GPRA announced the existence of an alternative political authority when it came to Algeria. Internally and externally, the move sought to enhance the FLN's legitimacy and credibility. The GPRA claimed to incarnate the Algerian nation state, albeit one 'turned inside out' and lacking territorial sovereignty. By proclaiming its own independence rather than waiting for France to grant it, the FLN also declared itself the sole valid interlocutor for a negotiated settlement to the Algerian question.[125]

The GPRA's primary aim was to internationalise the independence struggle by means of what FLN diplomat Abderrahmane Kiouane called a '*diplomatie de guerre*', or wartime diplomacy. According to one CCE-directive from June 1958, internationalisation alone could 'weaken the enemy positions in the diplomatic sphere and hasten [. . .] victory' in the armed struggle.[126] However vital, wartime diplomacy never sought to replace the internal insurgency. As Ferhat Abbas explained to Chinese Premier Zhou Enlai in October 1960, 'the diplomatic struggle aims to complete the armed struggle', which remained essential to the attainment of national independence.[127] Strongly influenced by Aït Ahmed's strategic reflections, the GPRA subscribed to the ideology of neutralism, declaring itself indifferent to the international system's bipolarity. Its '*diplomatie de guerre*' represented a force-multiplier and equaliser vis-à-vis France's economic, military and political might. Echoing Aït Ahmed's advice from a decade earlier, Omar Ouamrane, the FLN's chief of armaments and procurement, had urged the FLN in July 1958 to exploit not only East–West divisions but also those that existed within each bloc. A 'policy of balance and blackmail', he believed, would enhance the GPRA's political clout and enable it to gain a maximum of material, financial and moral support.[128]

With its twin pillars of *Westbindung* and Hallstein doctrine, West German diplomacy turned out to be particularly vulnerable to the GPRA's diplomatic offensive. The FLN's strategy of 'balance and blackmail' sought to modify Bonn's policy of supporting *l'Algérie française* to one of backing Algerian independence. As early as March 1958, the

[125] Connelly, *Diplomatic Revolution*, pp. 195–6, 180–5. Also: Memoranda by Abbas, Bentobbal, Boussouf, Krim, and Ouamrane, in: *Archives* (ed.) Harbi, nos. 40–47, pp. 183–224; Harbi, *FLN*, pp. 218–23; Meynier, *Histoire*, pp. 210–13, 352–3.

[126] Connelly, *Diplomatic Revolution*, p. 182; Kiouane, *Débuts*.

[127] Kiouane, *Débuts*, p. iii; Derradji, *Algerian Guerrilla*, pp. 138–9, 153.

[128] Rapport au CCE par le Colonel Omar Ouamrane, responsable de la direction de l'armement et du ravitaillement général, 8 July 1958, in *Archives* (ed.) Harbi, no. 41, pp. 189–93. Also: Connelly, *Diplomatic Revolution*, pp. 183–4.

movement had addressed a sternly worded letter to Adenauer, in which it accused the Bonn government of abetting 'the colonisers' genocidal actions'. In underwriting the EPU loan that kept France financially afloat and supposedly demonstrating a 'stupefying passivity' towards the recruitment of legionnaires, West German diplomacy had 'assumed an aggressive and hostile character against the Algerian people'. The letter expressed the FLN's 'hope that West Germany would contribute by other means to re-establishing world peace, especially in martyrial Algeria'.[129] Such appeals to the federal government's democratic and humanitarian instincts were increasingly balanced by threats of turning to Bonn's Eastern rival. Thus at the same time as Ahmed Francis, in his new capacity as finance minister, visited the West German embassy in Cairo in September 1958 in view of swaying Bonn's attitude towards the GPRA, Ferhat Abbas telegrammed East Berlin requesting diplomatic recognition from the GDR.[130]

West German diplomats had reason for concern. Within ten days of its creation, thirteen states, mainly Arab and stalwarts of the 'Bandung-world' such as the People's Republic of China, North Vietnam and Indonesia, had recognised the GPRA. By October 1958, the FLN entertained diplomatic or quasi-diplomatic delegations in over twenty countries, including one in Bonn, where a clandestine mission had first been established in late 1957.[131] Federal authorities found themselves under growing pressure to state their position vis-à-vis the GPRA and its mission in Bonn. The ambassadors of Morocco, Tunisia, and the newly created United Arab Republic (UAR), as well as the Sudanese envoy all tried to rally the *Auswärtige Amt* to the FLN's cause.[132] Conversely, Couve de Murville on 20 September directed France's allies to condemn the FLN's would-be government as illegal and to ban its pseudo-diplomatic representatives from their territory. Even a *de facto* recognition of the GPRA was deemed an 'unfriendly act'. In a move reminiscent of the Hallstein doctrine, Paris threatened to sever relations with states refusing to comply.[133] True to Adenauer's policy of *quid pro quo*, Brentano reassured Ambassador Seydoux that Bonn would

[129] Brief, FLN Tétouan, an Adenauer, 17 March 1958, MAE, MLA/2.

[130] Télégramme no. 2097 de l'ambassadeur Seydoux, Bonn, 24 September 1958, MAE, MLA/2; Dépêche de Krim Belkacem au ministre des affaires étrangères de la RDA, 26 March 1960, in *Archives* (ed.) Harbi, no. 104, pp. 496–7; Taubert, *L'«autre» Allemagne*, p. 43.

[131] Bougherara, *Rapports*, p. 206.

[132] Aktenvermerk, Protokoll, 10 October 1958, PA/AA, B25/10; Aufzeichnung, Referat 708, 11 September 1958, B25/14.

[133] Of the thirteen states that recognised the GPRA, only Morocco and Tunisia maintained diplomatic relations with France given their strategic importance: Connelly, *Diplomatic Revolution*, pp. 194–5.

not recognise the GPRA and categorically rejected the presence in the FRG of 'official' representatives of this 'pseudo-government'.[134]

Faced with 'blackmail' on two fronts, West German diplomacy struggled to reconcile the conflicting diplomatic pressures exerted by the Algerian war. Recent events in the Middle East merely heightened Bonn's anxieties. The UAR's formation in February 1958 had extended Nasser's anti-Western influence over Syria. On 14 July, socialist-nationalist forces under General Abdel Karim Qassem had overthrown the pro-Western Hashemite monarchy in Baghdad. The Iraqi revolution, in turn, had prompted Anglo-American interventions in pro-Western Jordan and Lebanon.[135] As Western positions succumbed to Arab nationalism, the spectre of communism began to rise, and with it the fear of Soviet and East German inroads in the Middle East.[136] In line with Soviet policy, the GDR had itself switched from a tactic of moral support to Arab nationalists to one of material assistance. In 1958, the regime in East Berlin made an initial offer of two long-term loans to facilitate Nasser's industrialisation plans, paving the way for Otto Grotewohl's landmark voyage to Cairo, Baghdad and New Delhi in January 1959. In Egypt, the premier's visit engendered an agreement to open the regime's first consulate-general in the non-communist world, marking a significant step in East Berlin's quest for recognition.[137] East German diplomacy would continue to focus on Egypt and the UAR, whose leading role in the Arab and Third World, it was hoped, would produce a 'domino effect' to end the regime's international isolation.[138]

In a parallel move, the GDR also redoubled its efforts to woo the FLN. After all, the Socialist Unity Party shared an important common objective with the GPRA: both sought international acceptance of their right to rule

[134] Télégramme circulaire no. 114 par M. Couve de Murville aux représentants diplomatiques de France à l'étranger, 20 September 1958, DDF, 1958, Vol. II, Nr. 177, pp. 396–7; Télégramme no.2088 de l'ambassadeur Seydoux, Bonn, 23 September 1958, MAE, MLA/2.

[135] Nigel Ashton, *Eisenhower, Macmillan and the Problem of Nasser: Anglo-American Relations and Arab Nationalism, 1955–1959* (Basingstoke, 1996); Stephen Blackwell, *British Military Intervention and the Struggle for Jordan: King Hussein, Nasser and the Middle East Crisis, 1955–1958* (New York, 2009); H.W. Brands, *The Specter of Neutralism. The United States and the Emergence of the Third World, 1947–1960* (New York, 1989), ch. 7; Zachary Karabell, *Architects of Intervention: The United States, the Third World, and the Cold War, 1946–1962* (Baton Rouge LA, 1999), chs. 7–8; Wm. Roger Louis, *Ends of British Imperialism: The Scramble for Empire, Suez, and Decolonization* (London, 2006), chs. 29–30.

[136] Yevgeny Primakov, *Russia and the Arabs. Behind the Scenes in the Middle East from the Cold War to the Present* (trans.) Paul Gould (New York, 2009), p. 3.

[137] Schwanitz, 'Deutsche in Nahost', Vol. 1, pp. 395–413; Winrow, *Foreign Policy*, p. 54.

[138] Klaus Storkmann, *Geheime Solidarität. Militärbeziehungen und Militärhilfen der DDR in die 'Dritte Welt'* (Berlin, 2010), pp. 184–5.

over independent and sovereign states.[139] In October 1958, the East Berlin government responded to Ferhat Abbas's call for unilateral recognition by demanding an exchange of plenipotentiaries. The GPRA rejected this request, mindful of its need to protect the FLN's external sanctuary in West Germany. Failing unilateral recognition, the Algerians opted for an inferior form of accreditation, one that would allow the FLN to garner moral and material aid from the GDR whilst simultaneously circumventing Bonn's Hallstein doctrine. On 13 November, Ferhat Abbas countered the East German demand for reciprocal recognition by suggesting an exchange of trade missions instead. The GPRA, Abbas explained to Richard Gypter, East Berlin's envoy in Cairo, could not agree to full diplomatic recognition of the GDR, for such a move risked reprisals against Algerians based in West Germany. As historian Fritz Taubert has shown, the GPRA's unexpected refusal to recognise the East German regime clearly frustrated the authorities. Gyptner, who behaved like an ambassador though he was not accredited as one, responded by denigrating the Algerians' lack of diplomatic etiquette and treating them as amateurs. Trade Minister Heinrich Rau also rejected the proposed exchange of trade missions. From an ideological vantage point, Rau could hardly comprehend why the Algerians were interested in sustaining their sanctuary in neo-imperial West Germany. In January 1959, the regime thus opted not to recognise the GPRA 'for the time being' and to limit relations to non-governmental exchanges between trade unions, student associations or humanitarian societies.[140]

Meanwhile, the East German authorities intensified the material and moral assistance they had begun to extend to the FLN after the Suez crisis. Barely a month after the GPRA's formation, Algerian diplomat Mohammed Hadj Yala el-Charbi visited East Berlin to discuss humanitarian assistance, including studentships and apprenticeships, to Algerian refugees. In November 1958, CRA delegate Boumediène Bensmaïne held similar discussions with Werner Ludwig, head of the East German Red Cross.[141] French intelligence soon observed a marked rise in the quantity of East German aid arriving in North Africa, especially in pharmaceuticals and foodstuffs. Moreover, the regime had agreed in October 1957 to open its hospitals to injured *mujâhideen*, especially those requiring prosthetics.[142] A first group of thirteen wounded soldiers arrived in the GDR on 22 January 1959. At the

[139] Kilian, *Hallstein-Doktrin*, pp. 31–4, 359. [140] Taubert, *L'«autre» Allemagne*, pp. 45–50.
[141] Ibid., pp. 46, 21–2.
[142] Bericht, Empfang der Gäste des Algerischen Roten Halbmondes, 12 October 1957, ADRK, DDR/56.

time, East German radio announced that a total of 400 hospital beds would be made available for war invalids, though by late 1960 the number of Algerians being treated in East German hospitals did not appear to surpass seventy.[143] Though they remain unsubstantiated, reports also circulated that the regime had agreed to train Algerians as saboteurs and radio operators.[144]

The GDR's readiness to aid the FLN arose from a mixture of ideological and realist impulses. As Ludwig informed Bensmaïne during the latter's visit to Dresden in October 1957, the East German Red Cross 'genuinely' wanted to aid the Algerian struggle against 'French imperialists'.[145] This socialist, internationalist and humanitarian impulse to combat imperialism compelled the regime to support the FLN even after the latter had rebuffed East Berlin's request for reciprocal recognition. Yet as Taubert argues, the continued provision of aid also served a 'Machiavellian' end. Although it had not secured East Berlin's recognition in the short term, a policy of aid stood to improve the regime's chances of eventually achieving that important goal.[146]

Thus by the end of 1959, solidarity with Third World national liberation movements had become a central tenet of East German foreign policy. From a realist perspective, however, the GDR knew it could not recognise the GPRA before the rest of the Warsaw bloc.[147] As a junior partner to the Soviet Union, Walter Ulbricht's regime took its cues from Moscow in matters of foreign and security policy. The Soviet Union initially demonstrated considerable restraint in its treatment of the GPRA, neither extending recognition nor military aid.[148] Moscow's reserve had a variety of reasons, including commitments to the PCF. Mostly though, Soviet leaders were mindful of their relations with the new regime in France.[149] So, too, were East German leaders, who had only recently negotiated a trade agreement with France.[150] As Bonn's ambassador to Moscow Hans Kroll analysed the

143 Synthèse de renseignements no. 17566/SDECE, 26 March 1959, MAE, AL/ALG/22. Also: Hong, *Cold War Germany*, p. 145.

144 Note no. 4647/SSDNFA/Berlin, 10 May 1958, SHD-T, 1H/1721/D1; Fernschreiben Nr. 93 der Botschaft, Paris, 31 January 1959, PA/AA, B1/56.

145 Aktennotiz, Abteilung Auslandsverbindungen und Suchdienst, 15 October 1957, ADRK, DDR/56.

146 Fritz Taubert, 'Ideologie oder Macchiavellismus? Die Algerienpolitik der DDR', in *Trauma Algerienkrieg* (eds.) Kohser-Spohn and Renken, pp. 245–61.

147 Taubert, *L'«autre» Allemagne*, p. 44.

148 Ingrid Muth, *Die DDR-Außenpolitik 1949–1972. Inhalte, Strukturen, Mechanismen* (Berlin, 2000), pp. 24, 27; Winrow, *Foreign Policy*, p. 55; Connelly, *Diplomatic Revolution*, pp. 195, 226.

149 Hadhri, L'URSS et le Maghreb, pp. 120–32, 137–67; Meynier, *Histoire*, pp. 607–8; Yahia H. Zoubir, 'U.S. and Soviet Policies towards France's Struggle with Anticolonial Nationalism in North Africa', *Canadian Journal of History* 30 (1995), pp. 439–66.

150 Ulrich Pfeil, *Die 'anderen' deutsch-französischen Beziehungen: die DDR und Frankreich, 1949–1990* (Weimar, 2004), p. 92.

situation in June 1958, the Kremlin wanted to avoid alienating de Gaulle, who remained 'the man who concluded the 1944 friendship treaty with the Soviet Union, who included [PCF leader] Maurice Thorez in his [post-war] government, and who envisaged the dismemberment of Germany'.[151] After Khrushchev's Berlin ultimatum, Moscow seemed to hope that its restraint vis-à-vis the GPRA would loosen France's bonds to Bonn and the West.[152]

Soviet diplomatic restraint did not, however, prevent the East German authorities from escalating their propaganda against the Adenauer government, which they continued to accuse of abetting France's war in Algeria. This policy of denouncing West German interests in the non-European world as imperialist and (neo-)colonialist aimed not only to enhance the regime's international standing and stature but also, as Luís Madureira argues, 'to erase any lingering traces of [the GDR's own] Nazi as well as colonial past'.[153] From August 1959, West German diplomats in the Middle East and Africa observed a steady rise in communist propaganda denouncing the Federal Republic for collusion with French colonialism.[154] That month, East Berlin sent a memorandum to the participants of the Monrovia conference of African foreign ministers condemning Bonn as France's 'satellite'.[155] In October 1959, the Iraqi press reproduced newspaper articles first published by the East German *Allgemeine Deutsche Nachrichtendienst* and Soviet *Isvestiya* accusing the FRG of supplying not only the 'cannon-fodder' for France's colonialist war in Algeria (legionnaires) but the 'cannons' themselves (through economic aid). 'Such news reports', the German ambassador in Baghdad warned, 'are without a doubt much more harmful to the Federal Republic's reputation in [Iraq and the Third World] than articles over supposed [German] revanchism or militarism [in Europe]', especially since Algeria represented such a vital issue in the Middle East and Africa.[156]

The *Auswärtige Amt* urgently sought to counteract East Berlin's disinformation campaign. Paul Frank, who now headed both the French and

151 Schreiben Nr. 2120 von Botschafter Kroll, Moskau, 12 June 1958, PA/AA, B24/311/F4.

152 Evguenia Obitchkina, 'La politique gaullienne vue de Moscou: les illusions perdues', in *De Gaulle et l'Algérie, 1943–1969* (ed.) Maurice Vaïsse (Paris, 2012), pp. 111, 114.

153 Madureira, 'Kalashnikovs, not Coca Cola', pp. 283–4.

154 Schreiben der Gesandtschaft Tripoli, 28 August 1959, PA/AA, B25/9; Schreiben Nr. 438 der Botschaft Jeddah, 23 September 1959; Schreiben Nr. 503 der Botschaft Jeddah, 26 October 1959; Schreiben Nr. 1022 der Botschaft Beirut, 9 November 1959, B24/314/F2–3.

155 Schreiben der Botschaft Monrovia, 9 September 1959, PA/AA, B25/15.

156 Schreiben Nr. 347 der Botschaft Bagdad, 21 October 1959, PA/AA, B25/9. Also: Kum'a Ndumbe, *Was will Bonn in Afrika? Zur Afrikapolitik der Bundesrepublik Deutschland* (Pfaffenweiler, 1992), pp. 66–7.

Maghreb departments, had long argued that Adenauer's policy of *quid pro quo* damaged West Germany's reputation in the Arab world. 'The Algerian question', he contended, 'cannot be dissociated from the pan-Arab desire for unity' and independence since 'Algeria is part of the Arab world'. Bonn's futile support of France's 'hopeless' determination to cling to Algeria merely 'destroyed what was left of [Western] Europe's power' in the world.[157] By July 1959, Frank's line-manager Carstens, too, lamented the way in which Adenauer's policy of support for *l'Algérie française* encumbered the development of economic and diplomatic partnerships in Africa, the Middle East and the Maghreb. Since siding with the FLN remained unrealistic, Carstens believed, Bonn would only be able to activate its foreign policy in those regions if it remained strictly neutral in the Algerian question. Carstens considered active engagement a vital requisite to maintain the 'immense capital of confidence' West Germany enjoyed in the Arab world, defend its growing economic interests in Africa and Asia and keep these regions firmly tied to the West. A pro-active policy that sidestepped the Algerian issue represented nothing short of a 'national imperative'. As the representative of 'the whole of Germany', he concluded, the Bonn government had to distinguish itself from East Berlin 'through a distinct, independent, and constructive policy'.[158] Because of the need for good relations with France, however, it was almost impossible to imagine that West Germany would adopt a policy of neutrality over Algeria, which meant that the *Amt*'s conundrum remained unsolved.

After the Monrovia conference of August 1959, Frank once again drafted a memorandum drawing attention to the 'baiting' and 'defamation' through which 'the so-called GDR' sought to isolate Bonn and encourage its own diplomatic recognition. In his typically contrarian fashion, Frank believed it should be made clear to African (and other non-European) leaders 'that the federal government possessed total freedom in its African [and non-European] policies' and that the '[West] German people has no sympathy for any kind of colonial system'. Whether consciously or unconsciously, Frank's reasoning now mirrored that of the East German regime in that he advocated a policy of disassociating the FRG from the Nazi and colonial past. He even went one step further: Germany, he argued, was now itself a colonised country, one where 'Soviet imperialism denies the right of self-determination to 17 million Germans on

[157] Frank, *Botschaft*, p. 44.
[158] Ministerialdirektor im Auswärtigen Amt Carstens an Staatssekretär van Scherpenberg, Aufzeichnung, 17 July 1959, in BDFD 1, pp. 732–35.

German soil'. Soviet imperialism, he continued, represents 'the only support pillar of the 'GDR'-regime, which itself constitutes a sort of colonial system'.[159] In essence, Frank suggested garnering sympathy from the Third World by drawing a direct parallel between the colonial struggle for national liberation and Germany's own quest for reunification.

By mid-1959, therefore, West German diplomacy made a renewed effort to distance itself from French Algerian policies and assert its neutrality in the Algerian question so as to isolate the GDR and retain the sympathies of the Afro-Asian world, where political decolonisation had reached breakneck pace. The 'dynamic public relations counteroffensive' that ensued represented West Germany 'as the true champion of "self-determination"'. As William Gray has argued, Bonn's counteroffensive largely achieved its goal, for none of the African countries that gained their independence by 1960 recognised the GDR, not even socialist Guinea.[160] When it came to Algeria, however, Frank's analogy between the colonial and German struggles for liberation and independence had created a political and moral conundrum. Given the French government's own linkage of the Algerian and German questions, could the analogy really extend to the FLN? And yet, as Cahn and Müller have pointed out, how could the Adenauer government claim self-determination for Germans and Africans on the one hand and deny this same right to Algerians on the other?[161] German diplomats clearly faced a dilemma, for their support of decolonisation had to exclude Algeria, where Bonn remained bound to the policy of *quid pro quo* by its alliance with France.

It was for this reason, too, that de Gaulle's pronouncement in favour of self-determination came as such a relief to the *Auswärtige Amt.* At last, German diplomats could vindicate Bonn's pro-French attitudes in the Algerian question. In October 1959, ahead of the Addis Ababa conference of German ambassadors in Africa and the first visit by Guinean President Ahmed Sékou Touré to Bonn, Frank crafted a defence that would henceforth guide West German diplomacy vis-à-vis the Third World. In a memorandum dated 2 October, he pointed out how Bonn 'will not uncritically support every Algerian policy' pursued by France and hoped to 'make it easier for the French government to find a sensible solution' to the conflict. This statement was blatantly untrue, for notwithstanding Frank's personal quest to engage in a constructive debate on the Algerian problem, the Adenauer government had never dared to critique France and always extended its full support. No matter

159 Aufzeichnung, Frank, undated, PA/AA, B24/312/F6.

160 Gray, *Germany's Cold War*, p. 87.

161 Cahn and Müller, *RFA et Guerre d'Algérie*, p. 253.

how much strain Algeria exerted on German–Arab relations, in particular, Frank himself admitted that 'France comes first' in Bonn's foreign policy priorities.[162] In a second memorandum aimed at elucidating West German policy to its Third World critics, he therefore explained how the German question and the government's multiple and multilateral treaty obligations 'required us to treat our [French] ally with consideration and understanding and obliged us to refrain from everything that could amount to a stab in France's back'. In essence, the Bonn government remained subordinate to the authorities in Paris, on whose support it continued to depend. Ultimately, Frank continued, this Franco-German alliance was also in Africa's interest: 'without it there could be no orderly and economically powerful Europe', which 'remained a precondition for the development of Arab-African countries'. Forcing Bonn to take sides in the Algerian question was a 'wrong alternative', Frank concluded; the government's only possible 'duty was to mediate between the warring factions in order to preserve possibilities for future collaboration'.[163] West German diplomats would stick to this defence for the remainder of the Algerian war. They presumably realised that Bonn would never assume a mediating role between France and the FLN since external arbitration contravened de Gaulle's strategy of domesticating the conflict. Besides, an attempt at mediation would have jeopardised Franco-German cooperation, especially in the German question.

The FLN, however, presumably would not have cared for Bonn's mediation either. After all, in stark contrast to the *diplomatie de guerre* it pursued elsewhere, the GPRA never pushed for recognition from the Adenauer government, and this although FLN militants Améziane Aït Ahcène and Abdelhafid Keramane operated a 'clandestine, parallel embassy' in Bonn.[164] Nor did the FLN force the issue in East Berlin. In March 1960, Mohammed Harbi, in his function as under-secretary for relations with the socialist bloc, had to remind the new foreign minister, Krim Belkacem, that the GPRA never responded to East Berlin's repeated request in March 1959 for an exchange of plenipotentiaries. Harbi considered this 'lack of courtesy' unacceptable in light of the aid the East German regime extended to the revolution, which he deemed a 'fundamental criterion for the choice of alliances'. This aid and the existence in East Germany of a growing Algerian colony necessitated 'a normalisation of our relations with the GDR'.[165] Krim

162 Aufzeichnung, Referat 204/205, 2 October 1959, PA/AA, B25/12.

163 Aufzeichnung, Referat 204/205, 26 October 1959, PA/AA, B24/271/F1.

164 'Entretien avec Keramane', in Bougherara, *Rapports*, p. 209.

165 Note à l'intention de M. le ministre et du cabinet, 26 mars 1960, in *Archives* (ed.) Harbi, no. 103, pp. 495–6.

Belkacem, however, refused to contemplate recognition. Instead, he repeated the GPRA's request for an exchange of trade missions as a means of protecting the FLN's 'growing economic, social and cultural interests' in the GDR and 'tighten[ing] the bonds of friendship' between Algerians and East Germans.[166] The Algerians rejected East Berlin's overtures even after Khrushchev changed tactic in August 1960 in response to the FLN's growing closeness to communist China, extending Moscow's *de facto* recognition to the GPRA.[167]

Only the importance that accrued to West Germany – not as an ally or instrument in the FLN's *diplomatie de guerre*, but as an external sanctuary and operational base in the movement's wider war effort – can explain the GRPA's continued refusal to support Moscow's and East Berlin's two-state solution to the German problem. As deputy secretary-general of the FLN's Foreign Ministry, Mabrouk Belhocine, explained to the East German ambassador to Moscow in May 1960, West Germany constituted an expedient and essential refuge for Algerians 'who had to temporarily disappear from France'. The GPRA could not risk jeopardising this sanctuary, hence 'one had to understand why the Algerian government did not pronounce itself in the German question'.[168] One month later while visiting East Berlin, Belhocine expressed himself in similar terms. As a 'buffer zone', West Germany 'enabled the passage and exfiltration of Algerian workers from France', he informed the deputy foreign minister, Sepp Schwab, and this explained why the GPRA could not recognise the GDR.[169] Si Mustapha, who visited East Berlin in July 1960, further clarified that the FLN had 'to stay in Bonn' to ensure the procurement of arms, which was 'organised via Federal Germany'.[170]

In short, the West German sanctuary proved so important that the GPRA was willing to forsake what it craved most to protect it: diplomatic recognition. A shrewd and rational decision, the FLN's refusal to recognise East Berlin reflected its policy of 'balance and blackmail' as well as its wider strategic priorities. To protect its war effort and advance its strategic and operational aims, the movement was willing to accept a minor defeat in the diplomatic war. After all, its external sanctuary in the FRG had not only become the operational headquarters of the *Fédération de France*, but it had

166 Lettre de Krim Belkacem au ministre des affaires étrangères de la RDA, 26 mars 1960, in *Archives* (ed.) Harbi, no. 104, p. 497.

167 Hartmut Elsenhans, *Frankreichs Algerienkrieg. Entkolonialisierungsversuch einer kapitalistischen Metropole. Zum Zusammenbruch der Kolonialreiche* (Munich, 1974), p. 72.

168 Cited in: Taubert, *L'«autre» Allemagne*, p. 54.

169 Cited in: Ibid., p. 59.

170 Cited in: Ibid., p. 64.

also developed into a vital base for FLN propagandists and procurement officers. The chapters that follow will examine this sanctuary in greater depth. They explore the role the sanctuary played in different facets of the Algerian and French war efforts, and the impact this had on West Germany's complicated relationship with both France and the Third World.

CHAPTER 7

The intelligence war

On 25 July 1958, an extraordinary, top-secret meeting occurred just outside of Cologne at a *Falken*-owned conference centre, though not a single member of the socialist youth organisation was present, nor any other German.[1] The assembled delegates were all leaders of the *Fédération de France* who had sought sanctuary in West Germany in April 1958. They were assembled now to finalise preparations for the launch of the FLN's long-awaited second front.[2] The onset of this offensive exactly one month later marked a watershed in the Franco-Algerian confrontation in the metropole, one that rapidly accentuated West Germany's importance as an extraterritorial sanctuary. How did the French and German authorities respond to the mounting Algerian presence on federal territory? In what manner did the authorities seek to contain or combat the presence of Algerians in the FRG? This chapter illustrates how French officials, in their efforts to domesticate the Algerian war and crush the FLN, attempted to export to West Germany some of the core tenets of *guerre révolutionnaire*, notably their colonial 'policy of complete human management and control'.[3] Encumbered though they were by resistance on the part of German domestic authorities and by the inherent contradictions of French counterinsurgency strategy, these efforts ultimately resulted in close, even unprecedented, cooperation between the French and German security and intelligence services. As the FLN's sanctuary expanded, the Adenauer government's *Diktat* of supporting the French war effort transformed the West German police and security services into proxies in France's counterinsurgency. The country itself now became a contested site in the Algerian war.

[1] Certain sections of this chapter draw on material first published in: Bülow, 'Franco-German Intelligence Cooperation', pp. 397–419; Ibid., 'Exposing the "Paradoxical Citizenship"', pp. 304–33; Ibid., 'Hôtes importuns', pp. 119–29.

[2] Djerbal, *L'OS*, pp. 221–8; Harbi, *Vie debout*, p. 239; Haroun, *Septième Wilaya*, pp. 90–1.

[3] Paret, *French Revolutionary Warfare*, p. 59.

An 'Algerian psychosis'

If the appointment in March 1958 of Maurice Papon as police prefect in Paris had signalled the 'militarisation' of policing in the metropole, the outbreak of the FLN's second front radicalised this process still further. With the new wave of terrorism, the search for accurate and actionable intelligence again constituted 'the sinews of war'.[4] Though unwilling to go as far as they had in Algeria in effacing civic rights and judicial controls, the de Gaulle government agreed to extend discretionary measures such as curfews or spot searches to help obtain this intelligence. An ordinance dated 8 October empowered the metropolitan security forces to detain Algerians for two weeks without charges, providing ample time for interrogations. As in Algeria, the authorities approved the creation of mass holding and identification camps, such as the *Centres d'assignation à résidence surveillée* (CARS) of Vadenay, Saint-Maurice l'Ardoise, Thol, le Larzac, or the *Centre d'identification de Vincennes* (CIV). By 1962, over 15,000 Algerians had endured periods of 'house arrest' in the CARS without ever standing trial. The number of those who passed through the CIV was significantly higher still: over 67,000 Algerians in 1960 alone, of whom 3,889 were subsequently incarcerated. In the aftermath of the deadly repression on 17 October 1961 by the Paris police of a peaceful, mass demonstration organised by the *Fédération de France* – the single-most public act of police brutality against Algerians to have occurred in the metropole – the arrests numbered some 11,518 individuals.[5] By then, the practice of 'repatriating' undesired Algerians – whether FLN militants, unemployed workers or petty criminals – back into the hands of the civil and military authorities in Algeria had also established itself as an effective means of intimidation and control.[6]

With the creation in August 1958 of the *Service de coordination des affaires algériennes* (Coordinating Unit for Algerian Affairs), Papon established an umbrella organisation that integrated a range of agencies as he strove to centralise and coordinate intelligence with social action and repressive operations so as better to implement some of the core principles of *guerre révolutionnaire*. Under the unit's auspices, Papon oversaw the creation of two specialised police corps modelled closely on, and recruited heavily from, the counterinsurgency machinery in Algeria. On the constructive side was the *Service d'assistance technique aux Français musulmans d'Algérie*

[4] Branche, *Torture*, p. 51.
[5] Amiri, *Bataille*, p. 88; Blanchard, 'Police judiciaire', p. 71; House and MacMaster, *Paris*, pp. 76, 127.
[6] House and MacMaster, *Paris*, pp. 76–7; Stora, *Ils venaient*, pp. 292–4.

(Technical Assistance to French Muslims from Algeria), nominally charged with the provision of social welfare and administrative services designed to integrate Algerian workers into metropolitan society. The unit's role also extended to destructive practices, including surveillance, intelligence collection and psychological action that aimed to undermine the FLN in the metropolitan battle for hearts and minds. The unit's work closely resembled that of the French army's *Sections administratives spécialisées/urbaines* in Algeria. Likewise, an auxiliary police force established in 1959 as a quasi-military brigade of "native" police, closely resembled the *harkis* forces deployed by French forces in Algeria. With its ruthless interrogation techniques, which included torture, the auxiliary police became the violent face of metropolitan police repression.[7] Thus militarised and 'Algerianised', the 'Papon system' replicated many of the brutal and discriminatory forms of repression, social control and intelligence collection employed in Algeria. Inspired by the strategy of *guerre révolutionnaire*, the system resembled what House and MacMaster describe as 'a "totalizing" project that sought to obtain absolute knowledge of the Algerian immigrants, a mastery over every individual through an ineluctable net of bureaucratic controls, lures, intimidation, hotel inspections, *fiches*, and intelligence operations'.[8]

Papon's unrelenting crackdown, which reverberated beyond the French capital to affect Algerians throughout the metropole, produced a rapid and significant surge in the number of Algerians seeking refuge in neighbouring states. If Belgium and Switzerland, as partly francophone countries with an established Algerian migrant community (in the case of Belgium) and long-term record of harbouring Arab dissidents (in that of Switzerland), had constituted the first of the FLN's external European sanctuaries, the clampdown by the French, Swiss and Belgian security services beginning in 1956 soon turned West Germany into the more significant.[9] In early 1958, official estimates for the number of Algerians in West Germany were in the hundreds; by September, they were several thousand.[10] On 2 October, the interior minister of the Saarland reported that approximately 3,000 Algerians had arrived in the *Bundesland*, though only

[7] Amiri, *Bataille*, pp. 115–22; Blanchard, *Police Parisienne*, pp. 313–58; House and MacMaster, *Paris*, pp. 83–7.

[8] House and MacMaster, *Paris*, p. 69.

[9] Djerbal, *L'OS*, p. 50; Dominique Masset, *Une Affaire Intérieure Française? La Belgique et la guerre d'Algérie (1954–1956)* (Louvain-la-Neuve, 1988), pp. 37, 147, 151; Carron, *Suisse*, pp. 152–96.

[10] Dépêche no. 148 du Quai d'Orsay au ministère de l'intérieur, 29 September 1958, MAE, EU/RFA/1272; Schreiben, Referat IB3/BMI, an Passkontrolldirektion Koblenz, Landesministerien des Innern (hereafter LMI), und AA, 30 September 1958, BA/K, B106/15779.

about 300 had registered with the police.[11] By March 1959, police authorities in Baden-Württemberg, Berlin, Lower Saxony, North Rhine-Westphalia, Rhineland-Palatinate and the Saarland had registered 1,350 Algerians.[12] Two years later, 2,992 had registered with the police, a substantial number for a country reluctant to accept 'non-European' migrants.[13] The total number was believed to be much higher than these statistics suggested. By October 1959, the *Auswärtige Amt* had collected estimates of up to 8,000 Algerians scattered across West Germany.[14] By contrast, Belgian authorities registered 1,834 Algerians in 1959, though unofficial numbers rarely surpassed 4,000, while estimates for Switzerland averaged between 500 and 800.[15]

Bonn's inability to compile more reliable statistics had several reasons. For one, the police authorities responsible for registering foreign residents fell under the auspices of the *Bundesländer*, and information regarding the movements of Algerians was rarely communicated from one *Land* to another. The police services transmitted such details to the *Ausländerzentralregister* (Central Registry for Foreigners), which collated information on foreigners residing in West Germany. At a time before the widespread use of electronic surveillance and identification technologies, however, the reporting process suffered from delays and procedural inconsistencies.[16] The process was further encumbered by the fact that the category, 'Algerian', did not exist in international law. The authorities were meant to register Algerians as French nationals.[17] And since, as Alexis Spire points out, French identity cards no longer bore 'any specific mention capable of differentiating [Algerians] from other French citizens',

[11] Vermerk, Referat IB3/BMI, 2 October 1958, BA/K, B106/5350.

[12] Télégramme no. 503 de l'Ambassade de France, Bonn, 11 March 1959, MAE, EU/RFA/1273.

[13] Brief, BMI an UN High Commission for Refugees (hereafter UNHCR)/Germany, 5 January 1961, BA/K, B106/5352. In 1960, foreign (i.e. Italian) "guest workers" numbered 279,000 in West Germany, or 1.3% of all gainfully employed. The first non-European 'guest workers' were Turks, who only started to arrive in late 1961. See: Herbert and Hunn, "Guest Workers", pp. 196, 193. Also: Karen Schönwälder, 'Why Germany's Guestworkers Were Largely Europeans: The Selective Principles of Post-war Labour Recruitment', *Ethnic and Racial Studies* 27/2 (2004), pp. 248–65.

[14] Schreiben AA an BMI und BMA, 6 October 1959; Schreiben BMI an AA, 26 November 1959, PA/AA, B25/11.

[15] Jean L. Doneux and Hugues Le Paige, *Le Front du Nord. Des Belges dans la guerre d'Algérie (1954–1962)* (Bruxelles, 1992), p. 35; Stora, *Ils venaient*, p. 148; Perrenoud, 'Suisse', p. 4.

[16] Niederschrift, Besprechung im BMI mit Vertretern der LMI, 10 October 1958, BA/K, B106/15779; Schreiben, BMI an AA, 13 November 1958, PA/AA, B25/4; Schreiben, BMI an AA, 26 November 1959, B25/11. For an overview of French difficulties in this domain: Neil MacMaster, 'Identifying "Terrorists" in Paris. A Police Experiment with IBM Machines during the Algerian War', *French Politics, Culture & Society* 28/3 (2010), pp. 23–45.

[17] Aufzeichnung, Referat IB3, BMI, 21 October 1958, BA/K, B106/15779.

except perhaps their names and places of birth, the authorities struggled to monitor them as a distinct group of foreigners.[18]

To complicate matters further, the Algerian presence in West Germany was itself in a state of constant flux. As noted in Chapter 3, the country had become a central collection and transit point for recruits intending to join the ALN. These recruits generally stayed for short durations, awaiting transfer to the Maghreb. Even Algerians who stayed for longer periods, whether as economic migrants or militants charged with specific tasks, frequently changed residence and employer, making it difficult for police and employment agencies to keep track of numbers and whereabouts.[19] The maintenance of accurate statistics was further complicated by the fact that most Algerians entered the country illegally. Even those who crossed at border checkpoints with legitimate French ID cards or passports rarely registered with the police; many were able to find lodging and employment by bypassing the authorities.[20] Militants preferred the anonymity conferred by this illegal existence, for it not only safeguarded their freedom of movement and action but it also protected them from the German and French police.[21] In sum, the authorities were dealing with an extremely mobile population that in the colonial context of surveillance and repression had become highly adept at clandestinity and evasion. Nationalists were further able to exploit the weaknesses of the state's identification system by adopting fake ID cards and pseudonyms.[22]

In the end, it did not take statistics for the West German and French authorities and press to realise the FRG had become an important sanctuary for the FLN. Foreshadowing the outbreak of the second front, the magazine *Politik und Wirtschaft* had accused the FLN as early as 20 August 1958 of using West Germany as a refuge and base for new offensives.[23] After 25 August, French newspapers were quick to seize on these allegations, and the Paris police confirmed the existence of close ties between FLN cells in north-eastern France and Algerians in West Germany.[24] By the autumn,

[18] Spire, 'Semblables', p. 57.

[19] Schreiben, Präsident Bundesanstalt für Arbeitsvermittlung an AA, 5 January 1960, PA/AA, B25/11.

[20] Ibid.; 'Viertausend Algerier', *FAZ*, 29 March 1962; Interview with former ALN fighter, anon., Cambridge UK, 10 January 2002.

[21] Schreiben, BMI an AA, 26 November 1959, PA/AA, B25/11.

[22] MacMaster, 'Identifying', pp. 28, 39; Ibid., *Colonial Migrants*, p. 12.

[23] 'Die Umtriebe des FLN in der Bundesrepublik Deutschland', *Politik und Wirtschaft* 65 (20 August 1958).

[24] 'Les chefs FLN de France ont leur quartier général en Allemagne', *Paris-Journal*, 26 August 1958; Télégramme no.3000 du Quai d'Orsay à l'ambassade de France, Bonn, 28 August 1958, MAE, EU/RFA/1272; Fernschreiben Nr. 769 von Botschafter, Paris, 26 August 1958; Aufzeichnung, Frank, Referat 204/205, 28 August 1958, PA/AA, B24/280/F1.

even foreign newspapers commented on the mounting traffic along the 'green frontier' of the Ardennes.[25] In a cover article for the Bernese newspaper *Bund*, Swiss journalist Hans Ziegler remarked how West Germany seemed 'destined to become the European centre of Algerian nationalism'.[26] The *FAZ* reported that a veritable 'Algerian psychosis' had gripped some of the communities along the Franco-German border, where locals feared an 'invasion of Algerians from France'.[27] French authorities held similar views. To the *Quai d'Orsay*, it 'seem[ed] that the FLN presently endeavour[ed] to turn West Germany into its principal base in Europe'. The movement's ever-growing range of subversive activities from German soil included arms trafficking, propaganda and even incitement to desertion of French-Muslim troops.[28] To Papon, the city of Düsseldorf, in particular, had become 'one of the nerve centres of [FLN] terrorism throughout Western Europe'.[29] In a similar vein, SDECE concluded in October 1958 that the 'FLN considers West Germany a pivotal hub for its activities throughout Europe'.[30]

Communities along the Rhine were therefore hardly the only sufferers of an 'Algerian psychosis' in autumn 1958. The growing Algerian presence in West Germany posed a significant threat to French national security and public order, for the exodus of Algerians from France strengthened the hand of the FLN while at the same time eroding the effectiveness of French counterinsurgency measures, whether 'constructive' or 'destructive'. After all, Algerians who fled France could no longer be exposed to the social and psychological action through which the Interior Ministry sought to contain and counteract the spread of nationalism among the Algerian community in France; nor could they be subjected to the security services' severe measures of surveillance, repression and control. Furthermore, the FLN's external platforms severely impeded the collection of reliable intelligence, which threatened to undo the very system of 'human management and control' upon which the military and security services relied in their

[25] 'Die algerischen Nationalisten organisieren sich in West Deutschland. Bis jetzt 2,000 Flüchtlinge auf dem Bundesgebiet', *St. Galler Tagblatt*, 23 September 1958; 'Die algerischen Nationalisten organisieren sich in Bonn: Bundesregierung in einer peinlichen Situation', *Luxemburger Wort*, 24 September 1958.

[26] Cited in: Dépêche no. 4079 de l'ambassadeur Etienne Dennery, Berne, 13 October 1958, SHD-T, 1H/1164/D1*.

[27] 'Algerier in Lörrach: die "Badische Zeitung" in Freiburg untersuchte die Gerüchte über eine angebliche Invasion von Algeriern aus Frankreich über den Rhein', *FAZ*, 6 October 1958.

[28] Note, Service d'Europe centrale, 6 September 1958, MAE, EU/RFA/1272.

[29] Papon, *Chevaux*, p. 186.

[30] Notice d'information no. 11383/SDECE, 20 October 1958, 10T/525*.

struggle against the FLN. In November 1958, Director-General Jean Verdier of the *Sûreté Nationale* admitted to officials in Bonn that 'the total liquidation of terrorist activities in the metropole would be much more advanced today if the rebels did not possess safe havens situated on foreign territories that bordered France', particularly, he argued, in West Germany.[31] Verdier's reasoning mirrored that of officials in Algeria, whose near-obsessive efforts to eradicate the FLN's external bases and support networks had already produced the Suez and Sakiet crises. Prevented by de Gaulle's policy of 'domestication' from repeating such aggressive and detrimental interventions, especially in the heart of Europe, the security services had to find alternative methods of ensuring, as RG-Director Vié phrased it, 'that terrorists would no longer find refuge in sanctuaries that were beyond the reach of the [French] police'.[32] To Papon, the security services faced the threefold task of dismantling the FLN's external sanctuaries, neutralising foreign-based subversion and preventing the FLN from reconstituting its extraterritorial bases and safe havens.[33]

Paradoxical citizens

Achieving these objectives proved difficult, for the French security and intelligence services did not always know the identities of militants. Nor did they always know when, where, how frequently, or by what means, militant nationalists departed for an external sanctuary, let alone whether they did so legally or illegally, directly or indirectly. French authorities could not even be sure the militants in question possessed legitimate French ID cards, or whether they used counterfeit ones, or passports furnished by one of the Arab governments allied to the FLN. This uncertainty left only one avenue open in the struggle to prevent the formation of external sanctuaries: French authorities would have to stem the exodus of Algerians altogether, regardless of whether they were militants (including those of the MNA), refugees seeking to escape intercommunal feuding, or economic migrants with no interest in the politics of Algerian nationalism.

Since French governments never went so far as to declare a full-blown state of emergency in the metropole, this task, too, proved impossible. Unlike their counterparts in Algeria, the metropolitan security services

[31] Compte-rendu de la conférence entre représentants français et allemands au sujet de l'activité des rebelles algériens en RFA, 18 November 1958, MAE, MLA/2.

[32] Vié, *Mémoires*, p. 137. [33] Papon, *Chevaux*, p. 186.

were unable to fortify and seal off France's territorial borders. Nor could they impose a wholesale travel ban on Algerians in France. By contradicting official rhetoric and legislation stipulating that Algerians were French citizens – an argument reinforced by the September 1958 referendum on the new constitution – such measures would have severely undermined the very argument the authorities were fighting for: namely, that Algeria was an integral part of France. These limitations frustrated many top-ranking members of the metropolitan police and intelligence apparatus, who felt constrained in their abilities to carry out their duties. Vié complained in his memoirs that Algerian 'terrorists' were 'easily able to cross the border' and 'implant' their cadres in neighbouring countries precisely because the borders were 'insufficiently monitored' and the government refused to enact 'an appropriate legislation'.[34] Papon and his staff were equally exasperated by the freedom of circulation that Algerians enjoyed by virtue of their French citizenship, particularly among Common Market countries. One memorandum drafted by Papon's cabinet after the outbreak of the second front declared it to be 'inconceivable that in times of war an enemy can cross the border just like all inoffensive individuals'. Demanding an extension to the mainland of the same special powers he had enjoyed as prefect in Constantine, Papon argued that he would 'fight the separation that exists in the struggle against the rebellion between Algeria and France and abolish the ridiculous principle that says that everyone makes do with his Algerians'. He concluded, 'in times of war, as is the case now', one simply could not 'uphold the ridiculous taboo of civil liberties' for Algerians.[35]

Needless to say, the de Gaulle government refused to grant Papon's request. Whether on account of the mounting hostility of domestic and international opinion to French colonialism or because of its own republican rhetoric and persistent refusal to admit that France engaged in a war in Algeria, authorities in Paris simply could not break with the legal and political fiction that Algerians were French, at least not openly. Doing so would have legitimised the FLN, thereby undermining the entire premise of France's counterinsurgency. When it came to combating the FLN's external sanctuaries, the metropolitan authorities thus had little choice but to solicit the tacit cooperation of their neighbours, especially West Germany.[36]

[34] Vié, *Mémoires*, p. 137. Also: Circulaire ministérielle no. 580 pour les préfets métropolitains, 17 October 1958, SAMPP/P, Ha66*.

[35] Quelques suggestions sur la lutte à mener contre le FLN en France, undated, SAMPP/P, Ha68*. Also: House and MacMaster, *Paris*, pp. 30–1, 68–9, 101–6.

[36] Vié, *Mémoires*, pp. 137–8.

Initially, Paris hoped to obtain this support through diplomatic channels. Having averted their recognition as political refugees, the treatment of Algerian migrants and illegal aliens had become a matter of frequent exchanges between French and German diplomats.[37] The new wave of migration following the FLN's second front merely added to the urgency of these debates. By October 1958, the situation had become pressing enough from the French perspective to warrant an intervention by Ambassador Seydoux with Foreign Minister Brentano. Seydoux's demarche exposed the constraints the authorities faced by Paris's negation of the state of war. The ambassador reminded Brentano that 'it is essential to avoid all discrimination between French citizens of Algerian or metropolitan origin'. Yet he also remarked that 'it would be desirable [. . .] for the cooperation between French and German security services to be intensified, especially with regard to the search for the authors of criminal acts', and asked that 'no particular privileges (for example, the right of asylum) be accorded to Algerians who found themselves in an irregular situation in Germany'.[38] Even while insisting that *de jure* Algerians were French citizens, Seydoux thus reminded his perplexed German counterparts that *de facto* they were not.[39] The absurdity of this situation was not lost on French diplomats. As early as July 1958, Jean Jurgensen had sought to convince Bonn that controls and restrictions on Algerians 'are not at all motivated by racial discrimination or by political preoccupations, but will prevent the entry of a drifting population that is dangerous to public order'.[40]

Jurgensen's instructions highlight the contradictions and distortions that typified what Alexis Spire has called Algerians' 'paradoxical citizenship'.[41] Characterised by a stark divergence between legal categories and democratic principles stipulating that Algerians were '*Français*' and administrative practices and colonial mind-sets that continued to qualify them by the descriptor '*Musulmans d'Algérie*', the 'paradoxical citizenship' exposed French officialdom's discriminatory attitudes and policies toward Algerians. After all, in the same sentence in which Jurgensen denied that French policies were racially or politically motivated, this senior diplomat

[37] Dépêche no. 902 de l'ambassade de France, Bonn, 20 May 1958, MAE, EU/RFA/1272; Schreiben Nr. 386, BMI an AA, 15 August 1958, PA/AA, B25/10.

[38] Télégramme no. 2299 de l'ambassade de France, Bonn, 15 October 1958, MAE, EU/RFA/1272.

[39] Aufzeichnung, Referat 204/AA, 16 September 1958, PA/AA, B25/4; Vermerk, Referat 204/AA, 23 October 1958, B25/14; Aufzeichnung, Abteilungsleiter West/AA, 24 October 1958, B25/10.

[40] Dépêche no. 103 de Jurgensen à l'ambassade de France, Bonn, 12 July 1958, MAE, EU/RFA/1272.

[41] Spire, 'Semblables', pp. 48–68; Ibid., *Étrangers à la carte: L'administration de l'immigration en France (1945–1975)* (Paris, 2005), p. 195.

managed to depict Algerians – and not just those deemed subversive nationalists – as essentially rootless and ruthless, iniquitous and terrorist, untrustworthy and hence undeserving of the same rights and liberties as French citizens 'of European descent'.

Paris's conflicting demands merely added to the confusion among West German authorities over how to handle the Algerian influx. Faced with a growing number of migrants claiming to have fled police persecution, authorities in the Saarland and in Stuttgart had begun to issue so-called *Fremdenpässe* (passports for foreigners) to Algerians, a practice usually reserved for political refugees. The French embassy immediately delivered two sternly worded *aides mémoires* reminding the *Auswärtige Amt* of Bonn's pledge not to treat Algerians as asylum-seekers. The provision of *Fremdenpässe*, the embassy claimed, constituted an unfriendly act that 'contradicted the spirit of Franco-German collaboration and risked to elicit the gravest repercussions from French opinion'.[42] French diplomats further insisted on the absolute need to reject passports or IDs issued by the GPRA, reminding the Bonn authorities that France did not recognise East German identification papers either.[43] The *Auswärtige Amt* was clearly susceptible to such pressures from Paris, especially after Adenauer's historic visit to Colombey-les-deux-Églises. Yet Arab representatives, too, had begun to lobby the Bonn authorities. While the UAR's ambassador mediated with State Secretary Hilger van Scherpenberg, Moroccan Ambassador Abdelkebir El Fassi intervened directly with the chancellor complaining of Bonn's unfair treatment of Algerians.[44] Even Améziane Aït Ahcène, the GPRA's newly arrived representative in Bonn, petitioned Brentano for greater lenience towards Algerian refugees, hinting that intolerance would prompt the GPRA to turn to East Berlin instead.[45]

The Algerian presence on federal territory thus significantly magnified the conflicting pressures the Adenauer government faced in the Algerian war. Diplomatic priorities would determine Bonn's response. 'Given that the Federal Republic attaches the greatest importance to the maintenance of good relations with France [. . .] and desires to avoid all conflict with the

[42] Note, Service d'Europe centrale, 6 September 1958, MAE, EU/RFA/1272; *Aides mémoires* de l'ambassade de France, Bonn, 16 September and 23 October 1958, PA/AA, B25/4.

[43] Aufzeichnung, Referat 205/AA, 13 October 1958; Schreiben, Botschaftsrat Jacques Schricke, Paris, 15 October 1958; Aufzeichnung, Abteilung 5/AA, undated; Aufzeichnung, Referat 205/AA, 3 November 1958, PA/AA, B25/4.

[44] Aufzeichnung, van Scherpenberg, 13 November 1958, PA/AA, B25/9; *Kabinettsprotokolle –1958*, 39. Sitzung, 22 October 1958, p. 366.

[45] Télégramme no. 2108 de l'ambassadeur Seydoux, Bonn, 24 September 1958, MAE, MLA/2; Note no. 11456/SDECE, 30 September 1958, SHD-T, 10T/528/D2*.

government of General de Gaulle', the Dutch *Maasbode* predicted in late September 1958, 'it is certain that Bonn will not follow a policy of open aid on behalf of the Algerians installed on its territory'.[46] This prognostication proved accurate, though some German diplomats still reacted with exasperation to what they considered a no-win situation. Ambassador Maltzan, for instance, not only considered the metropolitan anti-terror campaign detrimental to French democratic and international prestige, but also called it 'a *demonstratio ad oculos* [manifest demonstration] of the infeasibility of the call for integration and a total repudiation of the thesis of the "*communauté nationale franco-musulmane*"'.[47] Alexander Böker, meanwhile, confessed to Jean Bouchaud of the French embassy that, 'while we do not doubt in any way that Algerians, legally speaking, are French citizens, the entire world realised that, de facto, they are not French'.[48]

Faced with opposing pressures, federal authorities on 6 and 10 October 1958 convened two inter-ministerial conferences – one at national level, the other gathering representatives of the *Bundesländer* – to determine how best to handle the rising influx of Algerians. The new regulations devised at these conferences did not seek to prevent Algerians from entering federal territory; given the legal realities, German officials felt this task should fall to the French.[49] Rather, they sought to contain and control the movements and actions of Algerians once in the FRG. To preclude formal applications for asylum, Bonn's Interior Ministry decided to issue temporary residence and work permits – so-called tolerance papers – to Algerians without French passports. In a reversal of previous policy, the ministry instructed the Federal Employment Office to find these individuals work, which – so one hoped – would keep them out of trouble with the law and beyond the FLN's reach. In exchange for temporary residence and work permits, Algerians not only had to commit themselves to regular check-ins with the police, they also had to promise to refrain from political activities. A refusal to comply with either stipulation risked expulsion. The Bonn authorities thus aimed to prevent Algerians from engaging in subversive activities deemed a threat not only to law and order, whether in Germany and France, but also, more broadly, to the Franco-German rapprochement. The new regulations upheld the legal

[46] The article, dated 26 September 1958, is cited in: Dépêche no. 804 de l'ambassade de France, La Haye, 1 October 1958, MAE, MLA/2.

[47] Schreiben Nr. 3891 der Botschaft Paris, 19 September 1958, PA/AA, B24/275/F2 (emphasis added).

[48] Vermerk, Referat 205/AA, 16 September 1958, PA/AA, B25/4.

[49] Vermerk, Referat IB3/BMI, 30 September 1958, BA/K, B106/5350.

precept that Algerians were French while simultaneously evading the politically explosive question of asylum.[50] Karl Carstens hoped they would deter Algerians, especially nationalists, from seeking refuge in West Germany. In a memorandum dated 24 October, he insisted, 'all measures must be avoided that could evoke another influx of Algerians into [the FRG] and that could somehow be interpreted by the French government as support for the Algerian rebellion'.[51]

Exporting *guerre révolutionnaire*

Carstens was right to sound the alarm, for Bonn's new regulations hardly satisfied the French security and intelligence services. For one, they did nothing to prevent Algerians from entering West Germany. For another, they did not subject Algerians on federal territory to sustained police surveillance. In the context of the FLN's second front, which the intelligence and security services knew was being coordinated from external sanctuaries beyond their control, the liaison arrangements put in place by Colonel Duchène with the security services in Bonn and those established by his counterparts in Brussels and Bern appeared inadequate for mastering the situation. Beginning in Brussels in October 1958, the French intelligence and security services thus intervened directly in view of soliciting greater cooperation in the surveillance of France's borders and in the fight against 'communist subversive warfare'. [52]

It was in this context that on 18 November, two of France's most senior intelligence directors, Verdier and Vié, convened a personal meeting in Bonn with senior representatives of the *Auswärtige Amt* and Federal Ministry of the Interior. Their aim was to explain to the German authorities the full extent and dangerous consequences of the FLN's 'terrorist activities in France and their prolongation into federal territory'. By establishing a close working relationship with their German counterparts, Verdier and Vié, hoped 'to prevent the terrorists from organizing themselves and from executing terrorist attacks against France'. To emphasise the importance the French authorities attached to this matter, Verdier insisted that he was acting

[50] Vermerk, Referat 502, Ressortbesprechung im BMI vom 6 October 1958, 8 October 1958, PA/AA, B25/10; Niederschrift, Besprechung mit Vertretern der LMI über ausländerpolizeiliche Fragen im Sammellager für Ausländer, Nürnberg, 10 October 1958; Schreiben, Nr.13514, BMI an LMIs, 13 November 1958, BA/K, B106/15779.

[51] Aufzeichnung, Carstens, 24 October 1958, PA/AA, B25/10.

[52] Vié, *Mémoires*, p. 137; Bougherara, *Rapports*, pp. 156–7. On Switzerland, see: Carron, *Suisse*, pp. 264–5.

on the express wishes of General de Gaulle. This was an astute move, for the Adenauer government was desperate to improve Franco-German relations. Verdier implied that intelligence cooperation constituted an essential component of the *quid pro quo* underpinning Parisian conceptions of the rapprochement.[53]

In the struggle to prevent the transnational displacements of FLN militants (the MNA was only ever mentioned as an afterthought), Verdier and Vié made four fundamental requests of the German authorities. First, they insisted on the institutionalisation of Franco-German intelligence cooperation in all matters Algerian, henceforth labelled 'Operation A'. Duchène would continue to represent the metropolitan security and intelligence services in Bonn. This central mechanism of exchange was to be complemented at the local level by the institution of direct channels of communication between adjacent French and German border checkpoints. In creating a system that allowed for a seamless exchange of information at multiple levels, the French security services strove to secure their second goal: namely, the prevention of both legal and illegal border crossings by FLN agents along the Franco-German frontier. To work towards this objective, Verdier and Vié agreed to share with their German counterparts intelligence from the RG's *Fichier Z*. This new readiness to share with the German authorities such sensitive and classified information indicates just how vital the issue of extraterritorial sanctuaries had become for the French security services. The intelligence thus provided, they hoped, would facilitate the identification and arrest of 'criminal outlaws' and 'terrorists' by German border guards. In exchange for this intelligence, Verdier and Vié thirdly hoped to obtain from the German authorities the identities and locations of all Algerians already based in West Germany. Finally, Verdier and Vié insisted on absolute secrecy regarding Franco-German intelligence cooperation. The conference attendees implicitly agreed that in view of the motives that underpinned these exchanges, the involvement of Interpol, whose members included states that supported the FLN, would merely provoke a harmful political backlash against both Paris and Bonn. French authorities were naturally keen to avoid such criticism, which, by highlighting the political nature of their counterinsurgency, would merely have benefited the FLN's bid for international legitimacy. The Bonn authorities, for their part, were keen to

[53] The following paragraph draws on: Niederschrift über die vertrauliche Aussprache mit Vertretern des französischen Innenministeriums über das Algerier-Problem, 18 November 1958, BA/K, B106/5350; Compte-Rendu, 18 November 1958, MAE, MLA/2.

avoid being seen as sponsors of French colonialism, which would have damaged relations with the Third World.

The high-level meeting of 18 November 1958, like those that occurred in Brussels and Bern, was of foremost importance. For the first time, foreign authorities were formally albeit surreptitiously implicated in France's counterinsurgency, contradicting the argument that Algeria remained a domestic problem. In essence, the Swiss, Belgian, and now West German security services had become third parties, or proxies, through which the French sought to influence the strategic outcome of the Algerian war.[54] In this respect, the meetings set a precedent. Verdier and Vié had secured from the German security and intelligence services the pledge to support French efforts to contain the transnational movements of Algerians and to combat FLN activities. The German police consequently became a vital auxiliary in France's counterinsurgency. Almost immediately, the RG began communicating to Bonn's Interior Ministry records from its *Fichier Z*. Much to the dismay of the German authorities, these records were not limited to a few individual cases of known and wanted nationalists. Instead, the first batch transmitted amounted to 13,000 entries – over four times the total number of Algerians thought to have fled to West Germany at that time.[55] To complicate matters, the entry cards transmitted excluded the accompanying dossiers. Hence, the German authorities could learn from these cards whether an Algerian was deemed by the RG to be 'very dangerous', 'dangerous', or 'in need of surveillance', but not why.[56]

This situation produced some frustration among the German security services, which lacked the personnel and technical resources (and in some cases, as shall be seen, even the motivation) to search for and identify every Algerian listed on the provided cards. Passport control constituted only 5 per cent of the Federal Border Guard's circa 17,000-strong service, whose paramilitary units were in any case stationed exclusively along the country's eastern frontier. Algerian nationalists hardly represented a priority for the security services, whose attention remained fixated on countering communist subversion emanating from the East.[57] In February 1959, Bonn's

[54] Andrew Mumford, *Proxy Warfare* (Cambridge, 2013), p. 1.

[55] Vermerk, Abteilungsleiter VI/BMI, 4 December 1958; Vermerk, Referat VIA-3/BMI, 16 December 1958, BA/K, B106/15779.

[56] Vermerk, Ressortbesprechung mit Staatssekretär, BMI, 2 February 1959, BA/K, B106/5350.

[57] Paulinus Dickopf, 'Die Stellung des BKA im Rahmen der internationalen Verbrechensbekämfung', in *40 Jahre Bundeskriminalamt* (ed.) Hans-Ludwig Zachert (Stuttgart, 1991), pp. 38–48; Heiner Busch et al., *Die Polizei in der Bundesrepublik* (Frankfurt/M, 1985), pp. 79–80; Falco Werkentin, *Die Restauration der deutschen Polizei. Innere Rüstung von 1945 bis zur Notstandsgesetzgebung* (Frankfurt/M, 1984), pp. 94, 146, 148.

Interior Ministry instructed the security services to focus on those cases deemed 'very dangerous' by French intelligence. After five months of investigations, the BKA and BfV had identified only a handful of individuals from the *Fichier Z,* all of whom appeared entirely inoffensive to the German security services. This was a problem, for in the absence of evidence of criminal and subversive behaviour, the authorities were unable to arrest or expel these Algerians. From a legal perspective, therefore, the shared records remained an ineffective instrument of control. After all, those Algerians who did engage in subversive activities tended to possess Moroccan, Tunisian or Egyptian passports rather than French IDs; some, like Améziane Aït Ahcène, even enjoyed diplomatic immunity.[58] Even so, the RG continued to pass on entry cards only from its *Fichier Z* dossiers. By July 1960, the number of entries communicated to the German authorities had risen to over 24,000.[59]

The French security services were equally keen to build on the formal ties established during the November 1958 conference. In May 1959, the RG invited a team of high-ranking German officials to Paris to discuss further practical measures in the joint struggle against the FLN.[60] At this meeting, Vié made five new demands of the German security services. First, he insisted that federal border guards refuse entry not just to all Algerians who failed to provide valid French IDs but also to all those lacking a 'legitimate' reason for leaving France. Henceforth, only those possessing official invitations, such as a contract of employment or university scholarship, were to be allowed across the border. The numbers of such officially sanctioned migrants were, of course, very small. In January 1960, only about one-third of the 3,000-odd Algerians registered by the police were in full-time employment, and it is doubtful that many of these individuals had managed to secure work prior even to moving to West Germany.[61] The Association of Student Unions (VdS), meanwhile, estimated in May 1960 that fewer than thirty Algerian students had gained scholarships at German universities.[62] Vié's stringent new criteria would have therefore barred the vast majority of Algerians from entering West Germany.

58 Vermerk, Referat VIA-3/BMI, 2 February 1959; BMI an Passkontrolldirektion, 20 March 1959, Vermerk, Referat VIA-3/BMI, 4 May 1959, BA/K, B106/15779; BMI an AA, 16 July 1959, PA/AA, B25/12; BMI an AA, 9 September 1959, BA/K, B106/5351.

59 Meldekopf, SG-Bonn, 1 July 1960, BA/K, B106/15783.

60 Vermerk, Unterabteilungsleiter VIA/BMI, 26 May 1959, BA/K, B106/15778.

61 Schreiben, Präsident, Bundesanstalt für Arbeitsvermittlung an BMA, 5 January 1960, PA/AA, B25/11.

62 'Die Lage der algerischen Studenten: Aus dem Arbeitsmaterial des Verbandes deutscher Studentenschaften', *Freies Algerien* 3/5 (May 1960), Dokumentarbeilage.

As his second demand vis-à-vis the German authorities in May 1959, Vié insisted that all Algerians already in the FRG who were identified from the entry cards passed on by the RG were to be delivered into French custody, even if they had obtained residence or work permits. He justified this stipulation on the grounds that the French government had recently imposed a travel ban on individuals listed in the *Fichier Z*. Third, the RG director wanted all Algerians facing expulsion from West Germany on account of illegal residence or criminal activity, but who could not be identified through the *Fichier Z*, to be handed over to the French police, even when these individuals objected on the grounds of political persecution or fear for their personal safety. Vié essentially called for the blanket extradition or expulsion of Algerians, a request that openly contravened West German laws, which stipulated that foreign nationals claiming persecution in their home country must either be granted asylum, at least until their claims could be verified, or else be deported to a third state.[63] Fourth, the director demanded the implementation of strict measures of surveillance and control targeting 'fake' Tunisians, Moroccans and Egyptians. French intelligence would supply the suspects' names. Finally, Vié expected the German security and intelligence services to share with Duchène the names, whereabouts, movements and activities of all known or suspected Algerians residing in or passing through federal territory.[64]

These new demands were far more stringent and invasive than those made in November 1958. At that time, Verdier and Vié had still taken pains to uphold the legal precept that Algerians were French. 'Of the 300,000 Algerians in metropolitan France', they had maintained, 'only a small minority could be considered to be terrorists'. It was their duty to protect all French nationals, 'including the overwhelming majority of decent Algerians' from these criminal elements. Verdier, in particular, had emphasised that 'it was not the intention of the French government to induce the German authorities to control and monitor all Algerians on federal territory', but rather to draw attention 'to a small minority of Algerians who abused German hospitality for their terrorist actions against France'.[65] The more the French authorities intensified their efforts to contain and suppress Algerian nationalism, the more difficult it became to distinguish

[63] Gregor Haas, *Die Auslieferung in Frankreich und Deutschland* (Berlin, 2000), pp. 66, 138–9; Ulrich Häde, 'Die Auslieferung – Rechtsinstitut zwischen Völkerrecht und Grundrechten', *Der Staat* 36/1 (1997), pp. 1–26.

[64] *Aide mémoire*, Vié au BMI, May 1959, BA/K, B106/15783; Vermerk, Unterabteilungsleiter VIA/BMI, 26 May 1959; Note, Vié à Duchène, 30 November 1959, B106/15778.

[65] Niederschrift, 18 November 1958, BA/K, B106/5350.

between this alleged minority of fanatical criminals and majority of faithful French citizens. Rather than targeting specific members of the FLN or MNA, Vié's new demands affected every Algerian seeking refuge in West Germany, irrespective of his or her situation, motives, or views.

For the French authorities, the May 1959 meeting sought to deepen their cooperation with the German security and intelligence services so as to dismantle and neutralise the FLN's most important European sanctuary. To accomplish this goal, the metropolitan security services aimed to extend to the FRG the apparatus of repression and surveillance that underpinned their counterinsurgency and *guerre révolutionnaire*. Fixated on maintaining 'total' control over the Algerian population in order to weed out and destroy the subversive elements that destabilised the Franco-Algerian *communauté*, this apparatus targeted, and ultimately criminalised, all Algerians, regardless of where they lived. With these goals in mind, the French security services also insisted on an intensification of bilateral collaboration at the local level. At least two further conferences were convened in July and November 1960, again under conditions of strict secrecy. Rather than focusing on questions of policy and strategy, these meetings sought primarily to iron out technical difficulties in the working relationship between French and German border checkpoints, particularly regarding the coordination of surveillance along the 'green frontier'.[66]

A '*Fédération FLN d'Allemagne*'?

In spite of the framework of cooperation established between 1958 and 1960, the French security services never felt their German counterparts were sufficiently committed to the containment of Algerian subversion. As Vié remembered, he and his associates were always well received in Bonn (or Brussels and Bern), yet the collaborative arrangements established were never effective in crushing the FLN.[67] Not only did the Algerian presence in West Germany rise constantly, the FLN's implantation also seemed to continue in an unimpeded fashion. By late 1958, leading cadres of the *Fédération de France* were firmly entrenched in West Germany.[68] Learning from his predecessors' mistakes that it was

[66] Vermerk, Referat VIA-3/BMI, bezüglich der deutsch-französischen Besprechung in Bad Dürkheim, 21 July 1960, BA/K, B106/5350, Niederschrift der deutsch-französischen Sitzung, 18 November 1960, BA/K, B106/63320.

[67] Vié, *Mémoires*, pp. 137–8.

[68] They would be joined progressively by members of the *Organisation Spéciale*. See: Djerbal, *L'OS*, pp. 367–75.

'imperative for the Federation's survival and the continuity of its action to place its directing board out of reach of French repression', the Federation's chairman Omar Boudaoud decided that even in Germany, all five committee members should remain apart. Saïd Bouaziz, who headed the OS, consequently moved to Duisburg; Kaddour Ladlani, head of the politico-administrative organisation, and Abdelkrim Souissi, responsible for finance and unions, to Essen; Ali Haroun, head of information and communication, to Mülheim-Ruhr; while Boudaoud was based in Düsseldorf.[69] In Haroun's words, the aim was to exit 'without leaving France'. Based in the densely populated North Rhine-Westphalia, the committee was ideally placed to direct and control its activities in France, the Saarland and Belgium. Assisted by the Federation's European support networks, the committee members took turns travelling secretly to France for meetings with the heads of the *wilâya(s)* or local militants, who could just as easily cross into West Germany. This system worked seamlessly, for none of the committee members were ever caught.[70] In early 1959, the Federation also opened a 'school' for militants in offices belonging to the *Falken* in Hagen. Directed by Zine-el-Abidine Moundji and run entirely by the FLN, the school trained and indoctrinated new recruits, many of whom had never received a formal education.[71]

Meanwhile, Abdelhafid Keramane set about to organise an FLN bureau in Bonn. A former teacher, who had become one of the chief animators of the UGEMA in France, Keramane first arrived in Bonn in late 1957, having been asked by Boudaoud on behalf of the FLN's Coordinating and Executive Committee to establish an operational base in West Germany. He arrived under the alias Malek Dakhlaoui. Since Keramane did not speak German, Mouloud Kacem Naït Belkacem, a PhD candidate in philosophy at Bonn University who, in addition to the FLN, also represented the Arab League, became his interpreter and assistant. Améziane Aït Ahcène, a lawyer with close ties to GPRA Vice President and Defence Minister Krim Belkacem, joined the two in mid-1958. To SDECE, Aït Ahcène was one of the FLN's most promising and uncompromising young leaders.[72] Until the attempt on his life in Bad Godesberg in November 1958, Aït Ahcène assumed the lead of the FLN's 'official'

[69] Boudaoud, *Mémoires*, pp. 163–6.

[70] 'Entretiens avec Omar Boudaoud, Ali Haroun et Kaddour Ladlani, Alger, 19.9.2000', in Bougherara, *Rapports*, pp. 220–1.

[71] Boudaoud, *Mémoires*, pp. 119–21. Also: Notice no. 32071/SDECE, 15 June 1960, SHD-T, 10T521/D2*; and interrogation transcripts, January and February 1961, SAMPP/P, H1B/16*/18*/19*.

[72] Notice no. 12357/SDECE, 28 October 1958, SHD-T, 10T/528/D2*.

delegation in Bonn, while Keramane became his deputy. They would be joined by a growing number of co-workers. In an important act of solidarity, Tunisia's first ambassador to Bonn, Mondher Ben Ammar, brother-in-law of President Bourguiba, allowed the Algerians to use his embassy as their primary operational base and listed them as embassy staff. Morocco's ambassador, El Fassi, followed suit. Thus although the GPRA had not been recognised by the Adenauer government, its delegates enjoyed the privileges of extraterritoriality. While officially in Bonn to open a 'parallel, clandestine embassy', the delegation's real task according to Keramane focused on three crucial domains: recruitment; political mobilisation, broadly defined; and procurement. Of these domains, the procurement of war materiel appears to have taken on prime importance, for although formally subordinated to the GPRA's Foreign Ministry, Keramane claims to have worked primarily for the Ministries of the Armed Forces, of Armaments and Provisions (*Ministère de l'armement et des ravitaillements généraux*), and of General Relations and Communications (*Ministère de liaisons générales et de communications*).[73]

When it came to recruitment, as Chapter 3 revealed, the FLN bureau first became a hub for Algerians wishing to join the liberation struggle in late 1957, with recruits arriving mostly from France via Belgium or the Saarland.[74] Here, the recollections of Boudaoud, Haroun and Keramane corroborate the observations of French intelligence. In essence, the Bonn bureau's role was to arrange for the new recruits' lodging and sustenance while their enlistment was being processed by the GPRA and ALN in the Maghreb. The recruits were accommodated in so-called FLN-hotels, small, cheap, family-run establishments in and around Bonn rented out entirely by the bureau in Bonn. Over the course of a month, the recruits received from the bureau a daily allowance of 3 to 5DM while arrangements were made for new identification papers and deployments. Depending on their qualifications, some were outfitted with Moroccan, Tunisian, or Egyptian passes for travel back to the Maghreb, where they entered the ranks of the GPRA or ALN; others stayed in Western Europe, while a small number departed for the socialist bloc, including the GDR.[75]

[73] 'Entretiens avec Keramane', in Bougherara, *Rapports*, pp. 206–10; Boudaoud, *Mémoires*, p. 119; Meynier, *Histoire*, p. 597.

[74] Bougherara, *Rapports*, pp. 207–8, 218, 220. Interview by author with a former recruit, anon., Cambridge, 10 January 2002.

[75] Synthèse mensuelle no. 842/CCFFA/2, 2 May 1960, SHD-T, 10T/550*; Notice no. 29311/SDECE, 26 March 1960; Notice no. 29648/SDECE, 5 April 1960; Notice no. 30587/SDECE, 3 May 1960; Notice no.2878 par la gendarmerie, Baden-Oos, 25 August 1960; Notice no. 35808/SDECE, 1 October 1960; Notice no. 36016/SDECE, 6 October 1960, SHD-T, 10T528/D2*.

In terms of the numbers involved, Keramane later recalled that 'hundreds of Algerians escaped from France every day; they flocked to the Tunisian embassy [in Bonn] to obtain ID papers and social assistance'.[76] This estimate is surely exaggerated, yet as intelligence reports reveal, the numbers were not insubstantial. According to the BKA, the Tunisian embassy in Bonn issued at least 418 flight tickets worth 168,000DM between June 1958 and September 1959. In March 1961, SDECE appraised the rhythm of departures from Bonn to the Maghreb at 50–60 recruits per week.[77]

In addition to these arrangements, the FLN bureau also expanded its influence over the growing number of Algerian migrants based in the FRG, seeking both to recruit and to mobilise them politically. As in France, the movement aimed to harness the Algerians arriving in West Germany to the war effort, whether directly as militants charged with specific tasks or indirectly through the payment of the revolutionary tax. According to Boudaoud, militants were dispatched to all the main towns, and 'within the space of three months we had organised and controlled all Algerians' in West Germany.[78] By May 1960, the *deuxième bureau* of French forces in Germany referred to the existence of a '*Fédération FLN d'Allemagne*' that imposed a monthly levy on Algerian workers, a sum supposedly raised from 20 to 30DM in August 1960.[79] In March 1961, SDECE estimated that this "*Fédération*" contributed around 25,000 to 30,000DM to the GPRA's coffers each month, suggesting that between 1,250 and 1,500 Algerians in the FRG (excluding the Saarland) paid the revolutionary tax.[80]

Organisationally, the so-called *Fédération d'Allemagne* loosely mirrored the FLN's French Federation, albeit on a much smaller scale. French military intelligence in Germany noted how, 'contrary to the situation in France, the [*Fédération d'Allemagne*] did not have a well-defined hierarchy and its contours remained imprecise'.[81] In a survey produced in June 1961, the *deuxième bureau* divided the "Federation" into three *wilâya(s)*: a northern zone, comprising Hamburg and Bremen, was thought to contain two sectors and roughly 177 militants responsible for discipline, recruitment, liaison or tax collection; a southern zone, covering Stuttgart, Frankfurt, Mannheim, Karlsruhe, Freiburg, Nuremberg, Munich, Lörrach and Stockach, included

[76] Bougherara, *Rapports*, p. 207.

[77] Fritz Keller, *Gelebter Internationalismus. Österreichs Linke und der algerische Widerstand (1958–1963)* (Wien, 2010), p. 203, n. 4; Notice no. 42468/SDECE, 17 March 1961, SHD-T, 1H/1753/D2*.

[78] Bougherara, *Rapports*, pp. 217–18.

[79] Synthèse mensuelle no. 842/CCFFA/2, 2 May 1960; Synthèse mensuelle no. 1749/CCFFA/2, 20 September 1960, SHD-T, 10T/550*.

[80] Notice no. 42131/SDECE, 9 March 1961, SHD-T, 1H/1753/D2*.

[81] Synthèse mensuelle no. 842/CCFFA/2, 2 May 1960, SHD-T, 10T/550*.

three sectors, 95 cells and 531 militants; while a western zone, spanning Bonn, Koblenz, Düsseldorf, Dortmund and Essen, encompassed five sectors, 106 cells and 573 militants.[82] Though nominally controlled by the FLN bureau in Bonn, the "*Fédération d'Allemagne*" was believed to operate as a close adjunct and partner to Boudaoud's Federation, for which it supposedly ran safe houses and clandestine networks that helped ferry militants, money and arms in and out of France.[83] Meanwhile the Saarland, due to its strategic significance as a link between West Germany, Belgium and France, remained under the auspices of the *Fédération de France*. French intelligence believed the *Land* comprised three sectors: Saarbrücken; Burbach, Völklingen and Sarrelouis; and Neunkirchen.[84]

Thus even as Verdier and Vié attempted to export the metropolitan police services' counterinsurgency across the Rhine, the FLN expanded its influence and politico-administrative organisation throughout federal territory, entrenching its sanctuary in the process. The movement achieved this by adhering strictly to the rules of clandestine organisations: secrecy; concealment; anonymity; and watertight compartmentalisation. These principles permeated all levels of the FLN's politico-organisational structures in West Germany. As Boudaoud observed, even within the "school" for militants in Hagen, students knew nothing about the identity of their instructors, who in turn knew little about their charges.[85] Ladlani, meanwhile, recalled that he counselled against leaving written traces of meetings, let alone photos of militants. For reasons of security, militants were to commit as little as possible to paper.[86] The FLN entrenched its sanctuary by maintaining a low profile and ensuring firm discipline among its cadres so as not to attract the authorities' attention. After all, only by behaving inconspicuously could the FLN protect its operations and presence in West Germany.[87] Together with its adjunct trade union federation, the *Union générale des travailleurs algériens* (UGTA), and student association UGEMA, the FLN admonished Algerians in the FRG to demonstrate 'absolute respect for [German] institutions and laws' and 'to comport themselves in a dignified and correct manner during their sojourn' by refraining from illicit and openly political activities.[88] Correspondence intercepted by the *Sicherungsgruppe* Bonn, the

[82] Synthèse mensuelle no. 2188/CCFFA/2, 15 June 1961, SHD-T, 10T/550*.
[83] Synthèse mensuelle no. 842/CCFFA/2, 2 May 1960, SHD-T, 10T/550*.
[84] Notice no. 5274/SSDNA, 3 March 1960, SHD-T, 10T/528/D2*. Also: Meynier, *Histoire*, p. 536.
[85] Boudaoud, *Mémoires*, p. 121. [86] 'Entretiens', in Bougherara, *Rapports*, p. 222.
[87] Djerbal, *L'OS*, p. 368.
[88] First citation: Extrait d'un Bulletin de liaison et d'information, UGTA, destiné aux travailleurs algériens en RFA, November 1959, SHD-T, 10T/528/D2*; second citation: Instructions, UGEMA, aux étudiants algériens, undated, 10T/521/D1*.

BKA's security service, between Keramane and his adjunct in Nuremberg, Saïd Allag, in 1960 highlighted the former's effort to maintain order among the Algerian community.[89]

If maintaining a low profile helped secure the FLN's bases and safe havens in the FRG, it also helped garner respect and support among West German society, thereby heightening the FLN's international prestige. According to Boudaoud, discipline and restraint would demonstrate to the German public that Algerians were not all 'thieves, louts and mobsters' as portrayed by the French authorities. Aware of just how anxious most Germans were about their country's security, Boudaoud claims to have ordered that 'no [public] assaults' should occur on German territory of 'anyone who undermined the FLN'. Instead, the FLN rented villas in the environs of Cologne to serve as safe houses where, away from the public's gaze, 'recalcitrants' were 'summoned' for punishment and reform.[90] One suspected militant interrogated by the security services in Stuttgart in March 1960 reiterated how Algerians had received strict orders to refrain from public fights or score settling.[91] It would appear, however, that Boudaoud was less diligent in applying these rules than Keramane. Beginning in September 1958 and throughout 1959, French consul-general Tanguy de Courson reported on a steady rise in the number and pace of brutal altercations and assassinations among Algerians in the Saarland as the FLN engaged in an open war with the MNA over influence and control.[92] The abuse became so persistent and worrisome, Keramane recalled, that GPRA-President Abbas had to reign the *Fédération de France* back in.[93]

A 'tacit accord of tolerance and neutrality'?

The Algerian war thus presented not just a foreign-policy dilemma for the Adenauer government, it increasingly also affected domestic stability.

[89] Vermerk, SG-Bonn, 12 September 1960, BA/K, B131/214. Also: 'Entretiens, Keramane', in Bougherara, *Rapports*, p. 212.

[90] 'Entretiens', in Bougherara, *Rapports*, pp. 217–18.

[91] Vernehmungsniederschrift von Mohammed Salah Boualleg durch Landeskriminalamt (hereafter LKA) Baden-Württemberg, 24 March 1960, BA/K, B131/214.

[92] Télégramme no. 112 du consul-général Courson, Saarbrücken, 22 September 1958; Dépêche no. 308 de Courson, 14 October 1958; Télégramme no. 15 de Courson, 20 January 1959, MAE, MLA/2; Télégramme no. 133 de Courson, 13 October 1958, EU/RFA/1272; Dépêches nos. 88 et 160 de Courson, 13 March and 16 May 1959, EU/RFA/1273; Note de l'ambassade de France, Bonn, April 1959, PA/AA, B25/10; Télégramme no. 10 de Courson, 7 September 1959, MAE, MLA/4.

[93] 'Entretiens', in Bougherara, *Rapports*, p. 212.

The seeming ease with which the FLN continued to go about its business in the FRG irritated the French security and intelligence services no end. An SDECE report from October 1959 indicated that West Germany now counted more known militants than any other country outside of the Arab world, bar France.[94] The French security services repeatedly voiced their frustration over what they perceived to be a deplorable leniency on the part of the West German authorities towards Algerians. They showed no understanding for the legal and political constraints that prevented Bonn from implementing Paris's ever more indiscriminate demands, such as those arising from the 'paradoxical citizenship' of Algerians, or from Bonn's non-belligerency in a war that had never been declared.[95] German border guards remained reluctant to bar Algerians with valid French IDs from entering the country since this would have contravened the Franco-German convention of 1956. Bonn continued to argue that the onus for preventing Algerians from leaving France had to rest on the French.[96] Instead, West German authorities concentrated on tightening the regulations for Algerians already in the country, especially the vast bulk of those claiming refugee status. Prior even to Verdier and Vié's visit in November 1958, the Federal Ministry of the Interior had instructed the *Länder* to replace all 'tolerance papers' with politically neutral-sounding 'blue cards', which had to be renewed every three months. To obtain these cards, and hence residence and work permits, Algerians had to sign a written oath to refrain from political activities.[97]

To the head of French military security in Germany, this system was far too tolerant, making it 'immediately' apparent 'that the attitude of German authorities vis-à-vis French North African citizens [. . .] was [. . .] remarkably liberal'.[98] One SDECE report even professed that Adenauer was the only German who truly supported France's counterinsurgency aims.[99] Only the French ambassador in Bonn seemed to believe the 'blue-card system' could render the control of Algerians more effective.[100] His opinion appears to

94 Rapport no. 23754/SDECE, 13 October 1959, SAMPP/P, Ha/24*.

95 Vermerk, Unterabteilungsleiter VIB/BMI, 20 August 1959; Vermerk, Dr. Reuter, BMI, 28 October 1959, BA/K, B106/15783; Fiche no. 2220–4/SSDNA/Allemagne, 28 October 1959, MAE, MLA/4; Fiche, SSDNA/Berlin, October 1959, SHAT, 10T/528/D2*; Synthèse no. 750/SSDNA/Allemagne, 4 June 1960; Synthèses nos. 1327 et 2339/CCFFA/2, 16 July 1960 and 15 September 1961, SHD-T, 10T/550*.

96 BMI an AA, 16 July 1959, PA/AA, B25/12; BMI an AA, 9 September 1959, BA/K, B106/5351.

97 Rundschreiben Nr. 13514, BMI an LMI, 13 November 1958, PA/AA, B25/10.

98 Notice no. 3035/SSDNA/Allemagne, 31 December 1958, SHD-T, 10T/528/D2*.

99 Notice no. 11836/SDECE, 14 October 1958, SHD-T, 10T/262*.

100 Télégramme no. 3027 de l'ambassadeur Seydoux, Bonn, 28 November 1958, MAE, MLA/2.

have been ignored, for the metropolitan security services continued to push for greater controls and restrictions. Relenting to French pressure in November 1959, Bonn's Interior Ministry issued instructions introducing even tighter – and more discriminatory – surveillance measures, including the taking of fingerprints and headshots of all registered Algerians so as to facilitate the identification of militants listed in the *Fichier Z*.[101] French officials welcomed these measures. When the Bonn authorities contemplated the reintroduction of entry visas for Algerians, however, French officials objected. This move, they argued, 'would have established an inappropriate discrimination between *Français de la Métropole* and *Français d'Algérie*'.[102] In the context of the 'paradoxical citizenship', it seems, inequity could only be taken so far.

Regardless of their efforts to master a complicated situation, the French security services continued to perceive the German authorities as indulgent and uncooperative. These views were fed by intelligence depicting the Bonn government as playing a diplomatic double-game in the Algerian question. In one SDECE report from November 1958 – a purported translation of a memorandum detailing a meeting between deputy State Secretary Karl Knappstein of the *Auswärtige Amt* and State Secretary Hans Ritter von Lex of the Federal Interior Ministry, one reads how the former complained:

> [. . .] it is not easy for the *Bund* to take severe measures [against Algerians] because [Bonn] does not want to give the impression to international opinion that it is ready, on account of general political considerations, to assail the legal principle of asylum. Moreover, Germany must look further than the present moment: one must safeguard the future. In these conditions it is preferable to compromise 'with those people' [Algerians] in order to avoid that they 'throw themselves into the arms of the East or into those of Nasser'. [He] would not be surprised if, in a year or two, Ferhat Abbas demanded the *agrément* of an ambassador in Bonn.[103]

Regardless of whether this conversation ever actually occurred, the *Auswärtige Amt* did indeed worry about the impact of Franco-German collaboration in the Algerian question on international – especially Arab and Third World – opinion. In October 1958, Soviet news agency *TASS*

101 Rundschreiben Nr. 13514B, BMI an LMI, 5 November 1959, PA/AA, B25/10; Rundschreiben Nr. 6570, BMI an LMI, 25 November 1959, B25/11; Schnellbrief, BMI an LMI, 22December 1959, BA/K, B106/15779.

102 Note pour la MLA, 31 August 1959, MAE, MLA/4. Also: Zuschrift, Referat 204 an 502, 16 July 1959; Vermerk, Referat 204/AA, 20 July 1959, PA/AA, B25/12.

103 Notice no. 13430/SDECE, 28 November 1958, SHAT, 1H/1162/D3*.

had reported the conclusion of a secret France–German accord on the control and surveillance of Algerian refugees. This report was reproduced in leftist newspapers such as Italy's influential *Il Tempo* and Egyptian daily *Al-Shaab*, prompting an immediate refutation from the *Amt*. Though the item hardly made front-page news, German diplomats in Rome, Cairo and other Arab capitals were instructed to inform their interlocutors that since the Algerian war was a French domestic affair, allegations of Franco-German intelligence collusion were 'entirely fabricated'.[104] At the time, this was a legitimate response, for Verdier and Vié had yet to visit Bonn to agree on the terms of 'Operation A'. Even in December, however, when the East German regime, through its consulate in Damascus, issued a press communiqué offering political asylum to all those 'deported' from West Germany as part of Bonn's 'unjust' treatment of Algerians, the *Amt* declared the allegations of Franco-German collusion 'freely invented'.[105]

Anxious to maintain at least a semblance of neutrality in the Algerian war, and bound by law to refuse the extradition of individuals facing the death penalty or sought for political crimes, as was the case here, the German authorities were only able to go so far in their assistance to France. As early as July 1958, the Federal Justice Ministry had rejected French requests for legal assistance and extradition based on persistent 'rumours of maltreatment [of Algerians] by the French police'.[106] To forestall applications for asylum – something even the French government hoped to avoid – the authorities felt it best to tolerate Algerians on federal territory provided they abided by the rules set out by Bonn's Interior Ministry from November 1958: namely, refraining from subversive or open political activities. Those Algerians who flouted the rules and faced expulsion were to be sent to a third country – preferably in the Maghreb – unless the courts could be absolutely satisfied that the individuals would not face political persecution in France. Though hardly ideal, these guidelines avoided the thorny question of formal asylum and placated Arab opinion while at the same time respecting the German *Rechtsstaat* and ensuring some measure of control over the Algerians arriving in West Germany.[107] Thus although the Bonn government agreed to abet the

104 Drahterlass Nr. 1318, AA, 22 October 1958, PA//AA, B25/10.

105 Schreiben Nr. 757, Generalkonsulat Damascus, 15 December 1958; Chi-Brief an Generalkonsulat Damascus, 24 January 1959, PA/AA, B25/14.

106 Vermerk, Besprechung im Bundesministerium für Justiz, 4 July 1958; Aufzeichnung, Besprechung im BMI, 21 October 1958; Niederschrift, Punkt 4, BKA Tagung, 23 November 1959, BA/K, B106/15779; Also: Haas, *Auslieferung*, pp. 243–4, 270–6.

107 Aufzeichnung, Besprechung im BMI, 21 October 1958, BA/K, B106/158779; Niederschrift, Besprechung mit LMI, 10 October 1958; Rundschreiben, BMI an LMI, 13 November 1958, PA/

French counterinsurgency, domestic authorities continuously strove also to protect the Republic's sovereign legal and democratic order.

To the French security and intelligence services, this insistence on upholding the *Rechtsstaat* smacked of lenience. They were particularly frustrated by the authorities' apparent unwillingness to prevent the FLN bureau from recruiting draft dodgers and deserters.[108] The Allied Troop Convention of 23 October 1954, French military security argued, obliged West German officials to assist in matters of desertion. The Convention's fourth article stipulated signatories should collaborate to ensure troop security; its seventh article stated that, 'German authorities can arrest a member of the allied forces in view of handing him back to allied authorities'.[109] In October 1958, the head of military security of the French forces in Germany accused the authorities of negligence in these duties:

> It seems that there is little to expect from German collaborators in this domain. The authorities prefer to ignore the nationalists' activities. [...] Everything is happening as if a tacit accord of tolerance and neutrality existed, by the terms of which the nationalists engaged themselves not to undertake any [armed] actions directed against the French forces [...] In exchange for this attitude, German authorities would abstain from all measures of repression of anti-French activities or such contrary to diplomatic customs.[110]

Even when the authorities did intervene, French security officers remained dissatisfied. This was the case on 30 June 1959, for instance, when the police searched hotels Hessler and Jagdfeld in Bonn in view of uncovering an alleged kidnapping ring targeting Algerian soldiers. The pre-dawn raid occurred after Mohand Mesbah, an Algerian private from the 13th RT (Landau/Palatinate), accused the FLN of abduction. Eighteen Algerians were found to live in the hotels, but only one – Mesbah's supposed gaoler – was arrested. Since all of the Algerians had their papers in order and none appeared to be held against their will, the police had to let the latter go for lack of evidence of malfeasance. In fact, German officers suspected that Mesbah had concocted the allegations. They considered it far more likely that Merbah had planned to desert from his post to join the FLN, only to

AA, B25/10; Aufzeichnung für StS, BMI, 20 January 1960, BA/K, B106/5352; Dolmetscherprotokoll, Besuch arabischer Botschafter bei Bundesminister von Merkatz und StS van Scherpenberg, 16 March 1960, PA/AA, B2/86.

108 Notice no. 2140/SSDNA/Allemagne, 8 October 1958, SHD-T, 1R/333/D1*.

109 Notice no. 20888/SSDNA/Allemagne, 6 November 1958, 1R/333/D1*.

110 Notice no. 19346/SSDNA/Allemagne, 14 October 1958, SHD-T, 1R/214/D5*.

change his mind, perhaps after an argument. The episode prompted an angry outburst from the head of French military security, who accused the German police of 'push[ing] too far its concern for legality' and having 'a conception of its metier that is decidedly too narrow!'[111] This criticism reflected the continued misgivings some French officials harboured towards Germans. More importantly, it reflected the deep frustration felt by many of the proponents of *guerre révolutionnaire* with the democratic and legal constraints that inhibited their struggle against the FLN, whether in Algeria, the metropole, or abroad. To destroy a 'totalitarian' enemy, they argued, one had to resort to totalitarian tactics. As Colonel Lacheroy so famously wrote: 'One does not fight a revolutionary war with the Napoleonic Code'.[112]

The French security services were equally irritated by what they perceived as the 'inertia and bad faith' of some of the *Bundesländer*, who stood accused of showing 'the greatest mansuetude' towards FLN militants, deliberately ignoring the latter's manifold subversive activities.[113] Due to the federal nature of the West German polity, police practices often varied considerably from one *Land* to another. Frontline policing remained under regional control and was therefore subject to regional and local political constellations.[114] To Ambassador Seydoux, these divergences, and the supposed permissiveness towards Algerians that ensued, were exacerbated by the ambiguities inherent in the instructions issued by the Federal Ministry of the Interior, especially those regarding the 'political activities' deemed illegal for Algerians. Pushed by Seydoux in December 1958 to describe 'political activity', the director of the ministry's department for foreign nationals replied it was 'a concept escaping all legal definition' but that included activities 'having an organised and systematic character (formation of political groups, propaganda campaigns, etc...)' and those 'that touched in any way on terrorism (arms trafficking, instruction in sabotage, etc...)'. The authorities 'could not prohibit Algerians from maintaining contacts with German political organisations or even from expressing their opinion publicly as long as they did not act as agents of

[111] Dépêche no. 4308 du chef du service de Sûreté aux Armées, Allemange, au chef du SSDNA/Allemagne, 2 July 1959, SHD-T, 10T/528/D2*. Also: Dépêche no. 87 du Colonel Dudézèrt, Chef d'État-Major du 2ème Corps d'Armée, Coblence, au Commandant-en-chef, Allemagne, 2 July 1959, 10T/528/D2*; Wochenbericht, SG-Bonn, 7 August 1959, BA/K, B131/197.

[112] Cited in: Ambler, *French Army*, pp. 173, 170–1.

[113] Synthèses mensuelles no.1327/CCFFA/2, 16 July 1960, no. 2026/CCFFA/2, 17 January 1961, no. 2111/CCFFA/2, 21 March 1961, SHD-T, 10T/550*.

[114] Alexander Clarkson, *Fragmented Fatherlands: Immigration and Cold War Conflict in the Federal Republic of Germany, 1945–1980* (New York, 2013), pp. 7–8.

a systematic propaganda campaign', because the Basic Law guaranteed their freedom of expression and of association. This definition of political activity, Seydoux concluded, gave regional and local authorities a considerable 'margin of interpretation'. Moreover their attitude towards Algerians was often guided more by their political orientation than by Bonn's directives.[115] Thus in October 1958, when the Saarland's Interior Ministry and police were led by Julius von Lautz, a member of Adenauer's CDU, Consul-General de Courson observed with satisfaction how the state government 'and especially the police' comported themselves in a manner 'very favourable to our interests'. By May 1959, de Courson's tone had changed considerably. Ever since SPD politician Kurt Conrad had taken over from Lautz, he noted, the police were 'forced to act with much greater circumspection' since the 'socialist' Conrad 'took care not to harm Algerian nationalists'.[116] One year on, French military security complained that local authorities in Bonn, Cologne, Frankfurt and Hamburg, 'to name but the most important centres', all tolerated Algerians 'so long as they did not constitute a direct menace to public order'. From the perspective of the French security services, officials in these cities all construed 'political activity' in decidedly liberal terms.[117]

In contrast to local and provincial authorities, the Bonn government generally received praise from the French authorities. 'Loyal to the chancellor's course of action – of rapprochement with France – [federal authorities] strive to oppose FLN activities as much as possible', the French military attaché remarked in March 1959.[118] In one domain, however, even Adenauer's government came under heavy attack: namely, in regard to the presence of the FLN bureau in Bonn. The Gaullist regime could hardly tolerate an Algerian 'embassy' in the capital of its closest European ally. Again and again, French diplomats urged the *Auswärtige Amt* to reject the presence of representatives of a putative government the FRG did not recognise. They also pointed out the irregularity and unlawfulness of the Tunisian embassy's behaviour in sheltering the FLN's agents.[119] From the

[115] Dépêche no. 1997 de l'ambassadeur Seydoux, Bonn, 9 December 1958, MAE, EU/RFA/1272.

[116] Dépêche no. 308 de Courson, Saarbrücken, 14 October 1958, MAE, MLA/2; Dépêche no. 160 de Courson, 16 May 1959, EU/RFA/1273.

[117] Notice no. 750/SSDNA/Allemagne, 4 June 1960, SHD-T, 10T/550*.

[118] Fiche, March 1959, SHD-T, 14S/20*.

[119] Fernschreiben Nr. 859 von Botschaftsrat Jansen, Paris, 1 October 1958, PA/AA, B25/9; Vermerk, Böker, 16 September 1958; Aufzeichnung, Böker, 13 October 1958; Vermerk, Vocano, 29 September 1958; Vermerk, Böker, 23 October 1958, PA/AA, B25/10; Télégramme no. 2101 de l'ambassadeur Seydoux, Bonn, 24 September 1958; MAE, MLA/2; Télégramme no. 2167 de l'ambassadeur Seydoux, Bonn, 30 September 1958; Télégramme no. 2299 de l'ambassadeur, Bonn, 15 October 1958, MAE, EU/RFA/

perspective both of diplomatic conventions and Franco-German relations, Bonn had every reason to shut the bureau down. As early as September 1958, the *Amt*'s legal department opined that a failure to act would be perceived as a 'politically motivated endorsement' of the bureau's existence and tacit recognition of the GPRA.[120]

Even so, it would prove near impossible for the authorities to remove the Algerians from the Tunisian embassy. When German diplomats confronted Ambassador Ben Ammar and his Egyptian and Moroccan counterparts on the matter on 10 October 1958, a united wall of resistance met them. Though the Tunisian ambassador promised to rein the Algerians in when it came to 'illegal political activity', he refused to eject them from his embassy.[121] All three ambassadors repeatedly argued that they felt morally and politically bound to protect their Algerian allies; their governments recognised the GPRA and actively supported the FLN's independence struggle even if Bonn did not; their countries were themselves vital extra-territorial sanctuaries in the Algerian war.[122]

The attempted assassination on 5 November of Améziane Aït Ahcène merely heightened the ambassadors' resolve to assist the FLN. In a statement issued the following day, Aït Ahcène's deputy, Abdelhafid Keramane, vehemently condemned the French authorities: 'The colonialist agents aided by the powerful French secret services, are conducting an operation as cunning as it is criminal, aimed at portraying everywhere the Algerian as the cause of trouble in the country where he has taken refuge, so that the governments of those countries will deny him the right to stay.' Occurring as it did on the steps of the Tunisian embassy in Bonn, the assault, he continued, represented an attempt by the French 'to implicate the FLN [. . .] in affairs of blood and violence in order to discredit and isolate it diplomatically', prompt the expulsion of Algerians from their external sanctuaries, and intimidate Tunisian and Arab diplomats, whose aid to the FLN was believed to be responsible for the continuation of the war.[123] Keramane's argument received the full backing of his Tunisian protectors. In Bonn, the Tunisian chargé d'affaires Mongi Sahli underlined

1272; *Aide mémoire* de l'ambassadeur Seydoux, 14 October 1958; Vermerk, Böker, 23 October 1958, PA/AA, B25/14.

120 Referat 500 an Referat 204/5, 24 September 1958, PA/AA, B25/10.

121 Aktenvermerk, von Braun, 10 October 1958, PA/AA, B25/10; Télégramme no. 2291 de l'ambassadeur Seydoux, Bonn, 14 October 1958, SHD-T, 1H/1164/D1*.

122 Télégramme no. 3539 de l'ambassadeur Seydoux, Bonn, 1 December 1959, MAE, MLA/5; Schreiben Nr. 442 der Botschaft Bagdad, 19 December 1959, PA/AA, B15/12; Vermerk, van Scherpenberg, 15 March 1960, PA/AA, B2/75; Dolmetscherprotokoll, 16 March 1960, PA/AA, B2/86.

123 Déclaration de la délégation extérieure du FLN à Bonn, 6 November 1958, MAE, MLA/2.

how the attack's precision revealed its orchestration by a foreign power: namely, France.[124] In Tunis, the director of national security, Driss Guiga, and Secretary General Sahbani of the Foreign Ministry uttered similar suspicions to Bonn's ambassador, Werner Gregor.[125] Even the West German press implicated the French intelligence services, relating the attack to the aforementioned Schlüter affair: the assault highlighted the ruthless nature of France's war effort against the FLN and betrayed a blatant disregard for German sovereignty. As Seydoux reported, papers and magazines such as *Bild, Die Welt, Der Stern*, or *Der Spiegel*, all critical of France's war in Algeria, prominently featured the Arab accusations.[126]

The Bonn government, meanwhile, espoused the French explanation whereby Aït Ahcène represented a victim of inter-communal feuding. After all, the police's chief suspect, Ali Ben Madani, under whose name the getaway car had been rented, was a purported member of the MNA.[127] Ambassador Seydoux and Military Attaché General Meyer both believed the incident would strengthen Bonn's hand in the fight against Algerian nationalism.[128] The police did indeed intensify its surveillance of the FLN bureau, and at the *Auswärtige Amt*, deputy State Secretary Herbert Dittmann warned Moroccan Ambassador El Fassi that Bonn 'could in no way tolerate it, if terrorist Algerian organisations now also became active on federal territory'.[129] The *Auswärtige Amt* instructed its ambassadors in Tunis, Rabat and Cairo to reiterate to the FLN's allies the inadmissibility of Algerian political activity in West Germany.[130]

Contrary to French expectations, the assault on Aït Ahcène still did not result in the FLN's expulsion from its sanctuary in the Tunisian embassy. Instead, it produced a closing of ranks among Arab diplomats in Bonn.

124 Vermerk, Müller-Roschach, 10 November 1958; Vermerk, Hasslacher, 10 November 1958, PA/AA, B25/10.

125 Fernschreiben Nr. 172 von Botschafter Gregor, Tunis, 11 November 1958, PA/AA, B25/10.

126 Télégramme no. 2662 de l'ambassadeur Seydoux, 7 November 1958; Dépêche no. 1923 de l'ambassadeur Seydoux, Bonn, 26 November 1958, MAE, MLA/2.

127 Vermerk, Carstens, 6 November 1958, PA/AA, B25/10; Télégramme no. 2662 de l'ambassadeur Seydoux, Bonn, 7 November 1958, MAE, MLA/2. Bergot claims that Ali Madani was a pseudonym for *Service Action* operative Gabriel Bardin. Both Debré's counsellor for intelligence matters, Constantin Melnik, and former SDECE agent Philippe Thyraud de Vosjoli claim de Gaulle's right-hand man in intelligence matters, Jacques Foccart, had ordered the assassination: Bergot, *Commandos*, pp. 163–7; Constantin Melnik, *La mort était leur mission. Le service Action pendant la guerre d'Algérie* (Paris, 1996), p. 110; Vosjoli, *Lamia*, pp. 339–41.

128 Télégramme no. 2628 de l'ambassadeur Seydoux, Bonn, 6 November 1958, MAE, MLA/2; Dépêche no. 185 de l'attaché militaire, Bonn, 6 November 1958, SHD-T, 14S/20*.

129 Vermerk, Dittmann, 7 November 1958, PA/AA, B25/10.

130 Manuskript, Pressekonferenz der Bundesregierung, 7 November 1958; Drahterlass an Botschafter Tunis, Rabat, Kairo, 14 November 1958, PA/AA, B25/10.

On 21 March 1959, following instructions from Prime Minister Debré, Seydoux protested against the bureau's continued presence to Adenauer himself.[131] This prompted State Secretary van Scherpenberg once again to summon the Tunisian ambassador and object to the bureau's 'political' activities. Ben Ammar insisted that Keramane and his colleagues engaged purely in humanitarian work aiding Algerian refugees.[132] Without concrete evidence to the contrary, federal authorities were wary of proceeding against the unwanted agents for fear they might request formal asylum. Nor was the *Amt* willing to alienate the entire Arab diplomatic corps in Bonn by insisting on the Algerians' ejection.[133] '[D]espite general reservations', the *Amt* agreed to tolerate the bureau provided it stuck to 'social support services' which had demonstrably 'contributed to the maintenance of calm and order among the mass of Algerians' in West Germany.[134]

Notwithstanding repeated French interventions and threats of 'disagreeable repercussions', the FLN bureau remained 'a thorn that, in the interests of Franco-German relations, required extraction'.[135] Since Seydoux's intercessions and those of the French security services had failed to dislodge the Algerians from their diplomatic sanctuary within the sanctuary, the French premier decided to intercede personally. In a letter dated 23 November 1959, Debré informed Adenauer of his intention to raise the problem of FLN activities in West Germany at the chancellor's visit to Paris the following month. Aware 'that M. François Seydoux has already discussed this problem with you and that the German authorities tried to prevent such activities from developing', the premier felt it necessary to call the chancellor's attention to the fact that 'certain individuals have not refrained from using federal territory as a base for the replenishment of arms and the intimidation of their coreligionists and of the French forces of order'. While he understood that 'it is certainly difficult to uncover these activities, which often took place via intermediaries or under diplomatic cover', he felt sure 'the German government would want [them] to stop'. Their cessation was, after all, in the interest and 'spirit of friendly cooperation between our two countries'.[136] True to his word, Debré did indeed raise the Tunisian embassy's role in

[131] Télégramme no. 807 de l'ambassadeur Seydoux, 21 March 1959, MAE, EU/RFA/1273.

[132] Vermerk, Sarrazin, 24 March 1959, PA/AA, B25/10; Télégramme no. 969 de l'ambassadeur Seydoux, Bonn, 1 April 1959, MAE, EU/RFA/1273.

[133] Vermerk, Protokoll, 7 April 1959; Aufzeichnung an Protokoll, 21 April 1959; Vermerk, Protokoll, 24 April 1959; Aufzeichnung, Abt.5/AA, 14 May 1959, PA/AA, B25/9.

[134] Schreiben, AA an BMA, 11 January 1960, PA/AA, B25/10.

[135] First citation: Télégramme no. 2036 de l'ambassadeur Seydoux, 15 July 1959, MAE, MLA/3; second: Télégramme no. 2469 de l'ambassadeur Seydoux, 5 September 1959, EU/RFA/1273.

[136] Lettre du Premier Ministre Debré au Chancelier Adenauer, 23 November 1959, AHC, 2DE/65*.

supporting the FLN bureau in Bonn during plenary discussions at the Élysée palace on 2 December 1959, noting how he 'hoped that measures could be taken to [. . .] remedy this state of affairs'.[137]

Criminalising the FLN

Debré's intervention embarrassed the Adenauer government deeply, for it highlighted a failure to deliver on the Franco-German *quid pro quo*. When Seydoux again raised the matter with Brentano on 9 December 1959, the foreign minister appeared 'visibly upset' and resigned, 'as if admitting he could no longer escape our pressure'.[138] Five days later, Adenauer took it upon himself to inform the ambassador 'very confidentially', how 'a "*Razzia*" against FLN agents was taking place that very day throughout federal territory, and especially in the Saarland' on the orders of Federal Prosecutor-General Max Güde.[139] Standard procedure in Nazi-ruled territories outside of Germany during World War II, the *Razzia* was essentially a large-scale, coordinated and unannounced police raid.[140] The operation involved the roundup, questioning and possible detention before the onset of any legal arrest of every individual found to be in a targeted (often public) space at a designated time. Though an authoritarian police practice that contravened the inviolability of person and domicile, the *Razzia* remained a common tool of law enforcement during the Occupation as a way of coping with the rampant spread of the black market, and the perceived threat of a 'foreign crime wave' by the millions of displaced persons and refugees that found themselves in post-war West Germany.[141] It remained an instrument of policing even after the abrogation of the Occupation Statute.

The execution of a countrywide, secret *Razzia* on the order of the nation's chief prosecutor indicated that a shift in federal policy and perception was afoot when it came to Algerians based in the FRG. By January 1960, the *Auswärtige Amt* urged Bonn's Interior Ministry to crack down harder on Algerian migration and subversion, for 'the disadvantages of the [FLN's]

137 Compte-Rendu de la Réunion plénière franco-allemande tenue au Palais de l'Elysée, 2 December 1959, AN, 5AG1/160*.

138 Télégramme no. 3651 de l'ambassadeur Seydoux, 9 December 1959, MAE, MLA/5.

139 Télégramme no. 3739 de l'ambassadeur Seydoux, 14 December 1959, MAE, MLA/5.

140 The German use of the term should not be confused with the '*razzias*' executed by the French army during the conquest of Algeria: Thomas Rid, 'Razzia: a Turning Point in Modern Strategy', *Terrorism and Political Violence* 21 (2009), pp. 617–35.

141 Jose R. Canoy, *The Discreet Charm of the Police State: The Landpolizei and the Transformation of Bavaria, 1945–1965* (Leiden, 2007), pp. 103–9; Clarkson, *Fragmented Fatherlands*, p. 27.

activities were beginning to outweigh the advantages'.[142] From the *Amt*'s perspective, the rapid spread and rise in FLN activity on federal territory not only impinged on West German foreign relations, but it also menaced domestic law and order. The emergence of the so-called *Fédération d'Allemagne* as a parallel authority, one that carved out its own territorial districts, sought control over the Algerian community, and claimed to wield responsibility for its conduct and security, threatened to create a clandestine state within the state. The BKA suspected the FLN of establishing 'quasi-military command structures' among the Algerian community in West Germany.[143] By collecting its own taxes from Algerian workers – often under the threat or use of coercion, by administering its own justice, and by issuing its own laws, the "*Fédération d'Allemagne*" eroded the *Rechtsstaat*, undermined German sovereignty, and compromised national security. There were reasons aplenty, therefore, for seeking to oust the FLN from federal territory.

Indeed, the West German security services did not respond lightly to immigrant activists willing to use violence to achieve their goals. As one recent study argues, by the late 1950s, police and intelligence agencies deployed complex methods through which to monitor foreign criminals and dissident political groups. Like the *Razzia*, these procedures were informed by authoritarian and xenophobic impulses acquired during the Nazi era, which was hardly surprising given the continuity of personnel found in the West German police and security services.[144] For political reasons, however, heavy-handed tactics proved difficult to deploy against the FLN. Faced by the paradoxical imperative that Algerians were and were not to be treated as French, by constitutional constraints that guaranteed asylum from political persecution, and by a united front of Arab diplomats who protected the Algerians, the only way for federal authorities to proceed against the FLN was by outlawing the movement altogether. Thus in contrast to those proponents of *guerre révolutionnaire* who sought to undermine jurisprudence, the Bonn government would fight Algerian nationalists through the legal code. Federal authorities aimed to dismantle

[142] Schreiben AA an BMA, 11 January 1960, PA/AA, B25/10.

[143] Cited in: Keller, *Gelebter*, p. 204.

[144] Clarkson, *Fragmented Fatherlands*, pp. 54–5. See also: Imanuel Baumann et al. (eds.), *Schatten der Vergangenheit: Das BKA und seine Gründungsgeneration in der frühen Bundesrepublik* (Cologne, 2011); Constantin Goschler and Michael Wala, *'Keine neue Gestapo': Das Bundesamt für Verfassungsschutz und die NS-Vergangenheit* (Hamburg, 2015); Patrick Wagner, *Hitlers Kriminalisten: die deutsche Kriminalpolizei und der Nationalsozialismus zwischen 1920 und 1960* (Munich, 2002); Dieter Schenk, *Auf dem rechten Auge blind: die braunen Wurzeln des BKA* (Cologne, 2001).

the "*Fédération d'Allemagne*" and expel the Bonn bureau by holding its members accountable to the law. To achieve this goal, they first had to criminalise the FLN. It was in this context that Max Güde ordered the secret *Razzia* to which Adenauer had referred in December 1959. In its wake, Max Güde initiated a nation-wide inquest against the FLN. The movement stood accused of conspiracy and subversion (*Geheimbündelei*) and of forming a criminal, or terrorist organisation, thereby contravening §128 and §129 of the West German criminal code.[145]

To build a successful case, Güde required watertight and legally admissible evidence against the FLN. Acquiring this evidence took time; it involved collaboration between disparate law enforcement agencies that were not always inclined to prioritise the policing of such a small and seemingly insignificant group of foreign migrants, whether for budgetary or political reasons. The arrest of FLN tax collectors in Singen (Baden-Württemberg) in February 1960 provided the authorities the opening they required to start building their case. The arrest exposed the organisation of the FLN's 'southern *wilâya*' in West Germany, especially its leader, Saïd Allag.[146] In sweeps conducted during April 1960, police in Hamburg, Munich, Nuremberg, Darmstadt, Frankfurt, Mannheim, Heidelberg, Wiesbaden and Stuttgart arrested 150 suspected militants, confiscating over 20kg of propaganda material.[147] To assist the nation-wide crackdown, the *Sicherungsgruppe* Bonn established its own centralised database on Algerian affairs.[148] By November 1960, this '*Meldekopf*' contained reports on 708 felonies committed by Algerians since December 1959. Of these, however, only thirty could be connected directly to the FLN, twenty-three alone to the forcible collection of taxes. The BKA estimated the number of offences far higher since the *Meldekopf* excluded activities directed against the French forces stationed in Germany and since not all *Länder* had implemented the crackdown in equal measure.[149] Belonging to the FLN

[145] Schreiben Nr. 1310, LKA Baden-Württemberg an BKA, 22 February 1960, BA/K, B131/214.

[146] Wochenbericht, SG-Bonn, 5 February 1960, BA/K, B131/198; Schreiben Nr. 1310 LKA Baden-Württemberg an BKA, 22 February 1960; Vernehmungsniederschrift von Boualleg, LKA Baden-Württemberg, 24 March 1960, BA/K, B131/214; Wochenbericht, SG-Bonn, 2 September 1960; Wochenbericht, SG-Bonn, 7 October 1960, BA/K, B131/199.

[147] Aufzeichnung, BKA, 7 June 1960, BA/K, B131/214; Wochenbericht, SG-Bonn, 2 September 1960, BA/K, B131/199; Notice no. 29980/SDECE, 14 April 1960, SHD-T, 10T/528/D2*; Synthèse mensuelle no. 977/CCFFA/2, 18 May 1960, SHD-T, 10T/550*.

[148] Wochenbericht, SG-Bonn, 13 May 1960, BA/K, B131/198; Schreiben, BKA an BMI, 22 May 1960, BA/K, B106/15783.

[149] Wochenbericht, SG-Bonn, 13 May 1960, BA/K, B131/198; Zusammenstellung, SG-Bonn, 3 November 1960; Schreiben, SG-Bonn an Staatsanwalt Berard, Bundesgerichtshof, 24 November 1960, BA/K, B131/214.

was itself not yet punishable, after all, nor could it always be proved. Hence unlike in France, the police could only arrest Algerians if and when they had committed a crime. In October 1960, Güde ordered investigations against fifty new suspects in Baden-Württemberg, Rhineland-Palatinate and the Saarland.[150] The following month, acting on intelligence received from French military security in Landau, police in Rhineland-Palatinate searched the premises of another sixty suspects across thirteen cities.[151] According to the *deuxième bureau*, these measures produced a temporary decline in subversive activities across West Germany.[152] Like its French counterpart, however, the "*Fédération d'Allemagne*" appears to have found ways to reconstitute its networks.[153]

Though progress in the inquest proved uneven and slow, it placated French officials, at least temporarily, and it demonstrated the Adenauer government's continued loyalty vis-à-vis Paris. Through recourse to the law, the authorities had found a way to reconcile their desire to protect the sovereign *Rechtsstaat* and democratic order with Adenauer's *Diktat* of abetting the French counterinsurgency. In December 1960, the *deuxième bureau* observed how Güde's crackdown 'proceeded from a desire – often noted – by federal authorities to take severe measures against the [. . .] Algerian rebellion in Germany and to offer [. . .] support to French military authorities'.[154] The authorities still lacked evidence, however, linking crimes committed by Algerians to the FLN bureau in Bonn. If anything, the evidence collected seemed to exonerate the movement's leaders in the FRG, especially Keramane, who cautioned his subordinates to refrain from overt political activities and to behave in accordance with the law.[155] Not even the communist card would stick. In September 1958, the BND had painted Aït Ahcène as a 'convinced communist' and argued that socialist tendencies dominated within the FLN. However, by March 1960, the BfV had ceased its enquiries into the FLN bureau on the grounds that its 'connections to communism [. . .] did not appear significant'.[156] The domestic intelligence service, in other words, did not consider the

150 Wochenbericht, SG-Bonn, 3 November 1960, BA/K, B131/199.
151 Synthèse mensuelle no. 2273/CCFFA/2, 16 December 1960, SHD-T, 10T/550*.
152 Ibid.; Synthèse mensuelle no. 1327/CCFFA/2, 16 July 1960; Synthèse mensuelle no. 2026/CCFFA/2, 17 January 1961, SHD-T, 10T/550*.
153 Synthèse mensuelle no. 9039/CCFFA/2, 14 February 1961; Synthèse mensuelle no. 2111/CCFFA/2, 21 March 1961, SHD-T, 10T/550*; Notice no. 39566/SDECE, 9 January 1961; Notice no. 42131/SDECE, 9 March 1961, SHD-T, 1H/1753/D2*.
154 Synthèse mensuelle no. 2273/CCFFA/2, 16 December 1960, SHD-T, 10T/550*.
155 Vermerk, SG-Bonn, 12 September 1960, BA/K, B131/214.
156 Unterabteilungsleiter VIA an StSI, BMI, 24 March 1960, BA/K, B106/15779.

Algerians a threat to national security. The BKA, too, had concluded in September 1959 that Algerians 'as followers of Islam possessed a mentality that clashed with communist ideology'.[157] This conclusion was supported by the *Sicherungsgruppe* Bonn, which observed in September 1960 'that MALEK [Keramane] tried to prevent Algerians living in the FRG from sliding into communist waters'.[158] With the communist card discarded, the authorities were left with only one alternative to indict the FLN bureau: they would have to concentrate on its efforts at political mobilisation and its arms trafficking, activities deemed illegal under the regulations set out by Bonn's Interior Ministry. As the following chapters will show, here, too, the authorities ran into difficulties. After all, the FLN's representatives had long devised strategies to elude official sanctions by creating coalitions that placed the onus of political action on Germans themselves.

[157] Cited in: Keller, *Gelebter*, p. 132, n. 55.
[158] Vermerk, SG-Bonn, 12 September 1960, BA/K, B131/214.

CHAPTER 8

The propaganda war

In April 1959, an officer of the *deuxième bureau* attached to the French forces in West Germany presented an overview of FLN activities in that country to his superiors. While 'the authorities are mostly well-inclined toward us', the officer began his presentation, referring to the collaborative arrangements between the French and German security services, 'we have observed just the opposite' among the public. Whether they were social-democrats, trade unionists, radical leftists and 'crypto-communists' (the Communist Party having been constitutionally banned since 1956), all espousing an anti-colonial agenda, or right-wing reactionaries out to harm France, 'numerous groups offered their support to the FLN'. For now, their 'initiatives are still scattered' – even 'a little anarchic'. Concluding his presentation, the officer observed how 'the FLN [had] made very good use of the advantages offered by the FRG: a sanctuary, a link to rebel forces [in North Africa and the metropole], and a not insignificant fraction of public opinion sympathetic to its propaganda'.[1] These conclusions raise a number of questions. For one, what prompted such widespread, albeit uncoordinated civic engagement on the FLN's behalf? Moreover, how did this engagement affect the Franco-Algerian propaganda war, and how did the authorities react to it? This chapter argues that the mobilisation of civil-society actors constituted an important strategic aim for the FLN in West Germany. In contrast to Morocco or Tunisia, whose governments actively championed its cause and tolerated its extraterritorial sanctuaries, the FLN operated in an essentially hostile environment in the FRG. Banned by the authorities from engaging overtly in political activities, the movement's representatives came to rely on Germans (as well as their Arab allies) to do their bidding for them. Just as the French security and intelligence services used their German counterparts as auxiliaries to combat the FLN's external sanctuary, so the FLN

[1] Présentation sur les activités FLN en Allemagne, CCFFA/2, April 1959, SHD-T, 10T/528/D2*.

recruited German proxies to further its political and strategic aims. Winning hearts and minds thus assumed an ever more important dimension in West Germany, for at stake was the endurance of a vital external safe haven and base. With public opinion already poised against the French counterinsurgency, the FLN managed to recruit a broad range of willing helpers. In doing so, the movement helped to shape the humanitarian and developmental policies of a diverse range of German civil-society actors who had begun to take an interest in the decolonising world. These actors consciously went on to develop an independent foreign policy vision that was distinct from official Bonn policy.

Battling for hearts and minds

By the time the FLN opened its metropolitan front, conditions were already ripe for the FLN to intensify its efforts to recruit German proxies and allies. 'Ever since the return to power of General de Gaulle', François Leduc had noted in July 1958, 'politics in the metropole and in Algeria remain a major preoccupation in the [West German] news'. The doubtful tone of reporting worried the chargé d'affaires of the French embassy in Bonn. Newspapers across the political spectrum cautioned the Adenauer government 'not to compromise itself in an affair that evoked colonialism', convinced that Third World nationalism constituted 'a central phenomenon of the twentieth century'. De Gaulle's proposed reforms failed to moderate the censorious tone with which the press reported developments in Algeria. In August, Ambassador Seydoux, too, complained how most West German journalists greeted de Gaulle's reforms with 'scepticism nuanced by anxiety'. Though he deemed the left-wing press by far the most vitriolic in its criticism of 'French oppression' in Algeria, he concluded that 'no one believes in the chances of success of a policy of integration'.[2] Concomitantly, French officials registered a marked rise in interest in the FLN. On 19 June, Hamburg's *Die Welt* had published a first interview with Lamine Debaghine, the soon-to-be foreign minister of the GPRA. On 23 September, the *Bonner Rundschau*, a paper usually close to the government, printed an interview with the GPRA's Defence Minister Krim Belkacem and Armaments Minister Mahmoud Chérif. *Die Welt*, meanwhile, reported on a meeting with Communications Minister

[2] Dépêche no. 1289 de Leduc, Bonn, 17 July 1958, MAE, EU/RFA/1259*; Dépêche no. 1492 de Seydoux, Bonn, 28 August 1958, MAE, EU/RFA/1260*. Also: Xavier de Glowczewski, 'La guerre d'Algérie au miroir de la presse allemande (1958–1962)', *RA* 31/3–4 (1999), pp. 545–6; Scheffler, *SPD*, pp. 57–8; Marcowitz, 'Unionsparteien', p. 560.

Abdelhafid Boussouf. These articles were followed on 11 October and 3 November by interviews with GPRA-President Abbas published in *Die Welt* and West Berlin's *Der Tag*.[3]

Ambassador Seydoux blamed SPD sponsorship for the FLN's rising media profile. The party, he noted in September 1958, 'has not ceased to display hostility toward us when it comes to the Algerian crisis'.[4] Ever since the Sakiet crisis, a small but determined group representing the party's left and youth wings had indeed coalesced into a loose-knit 'Algeria lobby' that sought to establish contact with the FLN, determined to show solidarity through deeds as well as words and to enact a parallel, human rights-based foreign policy. Steeped in the belief that allegiance to socialist ideals should precede loyalty to socialist parties, these social-democrats increasingly condemned the SFIO for its handling of the Algerian question.[5] One of the FLN's first and most persistent 'lobbyists' was Peter Blachstein. A conviction politician par excellence, the *Bundestag* deputy from Hamburg had first joined the SPD in 1929, aged eighteen. Arrested by the Nazis in 1933, he had spent the years 1935 to 1947 in exile. During this period, he had fought in the Spanish Civil War and continued to resist German fascism.[6] Another Hamburg deputy belonging to the 'Algeria lobby', Hellmut Kalbitzer, had joined the International Socialist League in 1929, entering the SPD after World War II. Kalbitzer became one of the party's key experts on the developing world. His pro-Algerian engagement declined in 1960, when he became vice-president of the European Parliament.[7] Far more radical in his activism was Georg Jungclas, secretary since 1946 of the Trotskyite Fourth International's West German section and member of the International's executive. Jungclas also worked for the SPD youth organisation, the *Jusos*. As discussed in Chapter 4, the organisation's members constituted some of the earliest supporters of the FLN's cause.[8] Deeply influenced by Jungclas, though of a younger generation, was Hans-Jürgen Wischnewski, a former official in the Industrial Union of Metalworkers

[3] Bulletin d'information diplomatique no. 10, 20 June 1958, MAE, MLA/0; Télégrammes nos. 2087 et 2103 de l'ambassadeur Seydoux, Bonn, 23 September and 24 September 1958, AL/ALG/25; Télégramme no. 2584 de Seydoux, Bonn, 3 November 1958, AL/ALG/22; Schreiben Nr. 4328, Botschaftsrat Jansen, Paris, 20 October 1958, PA/AA, B24/278/F2.

[4] Télégramme no. 1931 de Seydoux, Bonn, 4 September 1958, MAE, EU/RFA/1272.

[5] Talbot Imlay, 'International Socialism and Decolonization during the 1950s: Competing Rights and the Postcolonial Order', *American Historical Review* 118/4 (2013), pp. 1122–4.

[6] www.fes.de/archiv/adsd_neu/inhalt/nachlass/nachlass_b/blachstein-pe.htm (21 October 2013).

[7] Hellmut Kalbitzer, *Widerstehen oder Mitmachen. Eigensinnige Ansichten und sehr persönliche Erinnerungen* (Hamburg, 1987).

[8] Leggewie, *Kofferträger*, pp. 104–23.

(IGM) who first entered the *Bundestag* as deputy for Cologne in 1957. Between 1959 and 1961, Wischnewski was national chairman of the *Jusos*.[9] His colleague, Jockel Fuchs, had been a deputy in the provincial parliament for Rhineland-Palatinate since 1955. Fuchs had participated in the Asian-European Youth Conference in November 1956. From 1958, he promoted his anticolonial views as editor-in-chief of the Mainz newspaper, *Freiheit*.[10]

As committed internationalists steeped in a long-standing tradition of resistance against imperialism and totalitarianism, these 'lobbyists' helped push the SPD's executive to pronounce itself against the French war in Algeria and against all forms of colonialism. The party's solidarity with the SFIO, they claimed, threatened to undermine the entire non-communist socialist movement in the growing Third World.[11] The FLN first established contact to the SPD's "Algeria lobby" in spring 1958 through the mediation of French members of the Socialist International who secretly supported the FLN in France. According to Omar Boudaoud, Ali Haroun and Abdelhafid Keramane, this introduction proved indispensable to the *Fédération de France*, whose leaders had only just arrived in Cologne and desperately required local allies to secure their bases and develop their operations. The introduction proved equally vital for the embryonic FLN bureau in Bonn, which was charged with the task of political mobilisation, broadly defined.[12] Since the proviso to refrain from political activities in West Germany severely constrained the FLN's manoeuvring room, the FLN required German allies to act as mobilisers on their behalf. With their connections to youth associations, trade unions and other organisations affiliated to the SPD and to German society and politics, the Algeria lobbyists became the vehicle through which the FLN began to recruit further allies and volunteers.

To advance this aim, the lobbyists invited an FLN delegation to attend the SPD's biennial congress, which convened in Stuttgart from 18 to 23 May 1958. The delegation was sizeable, consisting of external representatives Ahmed Boumendjel, Abdelhafid Keramane and Mouloud Kacem Naït Belkacem, UGTA official Ahmed Mostefaoui, and *Fédération de France* members Aziz Benmiloud, Belkacem Benyahia, Hadj Cherchalli, Mohammed Harbi and Ali Haroun.[13] In hosting the Algerians, West

[9] Hans-Jürgen Wischnewski, *Mit Leidenschaft und Augenmaß. In Mogadischu und anderswo. Politische Memoiren* (Munich, 1989).

[10] Jockel Fuchs, *Mainzer Jahre – schöne Jahre. Erinnerungen 1945–1987* (Mainz, 1993).

[11] Imlay, 'International Socialism', pp. 1123–4; Scheffler, *SPD*, pp. 49–52.

[12] Boudaoud, *Mémoires*, p. 166; 'Entretiens avec Keramane, Boudaoud, Haroun et Ladlani', in Bougherara, *Rapports*, pp. 206–8, 221–2.

[13] Haroun, *Septième wilaya*, p. 134.

Germany's second-largest political party appeared to recognise the FLN as a political movement. Their attendance of the congress was all the more symbolic as it coincided with the May crisis in France and juxtaposed the presence of an SFIO delegation, precipitating the latter's angry departure from the congress. Not all in the SPD, however, supported the FLN's presence. Anxious to demonstrate his solidarity with the SFIO amidst the political crisis unfolding in France, party boss Erich Ollenhauer had tried to prevent the Algerians' participation. When this failed, he refused to grant the Algerians the right to speak, hoping thus to contain French anger.[14] Ollenhauer then endeavoured to dilute his party's criticism of France. In his opening speech, he lamented the Algerian tragedy, which had not only produced 'a barely repairable breach in the trust of the peoples of Africa and Asia towards the [. . .] West', but which now also threatened French democracy. Ollenhauer emphasised that Germans had no right 'to criticise or condemn' the French given their own dishonourable history. In a break with the past, however, he appealed to France and the SFIO to find a speedy settlement to the Algerian conflict, one that was 'in the spirit of self-determination and self-administration for the Algerian people'.[15] By tabling his own resolution, one that condemned the violence committed by *all* belligerents, Ollenhauer had hoped to preserve a measure of neutrality in the Algerian question. In this he failed, for the 'Algeria lobby' succeeded in having the chairman's reference to FLN terrorism omitted from the resolution's final draft.[16]

Though it hardly galvanised the entire party into action, the Stuttgart congress raised the rank-and-file's awareness of the Algerian problem. More importantly, the congress offered the FLN an entrée into West German political circles. It helped the movement's representatives establish a broad network of contacts and lay the groundwork for an expanded and multifaceted public-relations campaign, one that for security reasons was often fronted by Germans rather than Algerians. This campaign was formally launched on 2 September 1958, when the FLN bureau in Bonn, joined by its new *chef de mission* Améziane Aït Ahcène, held its first press conference in Hamburg. Though never sanctioned by the SPD executive, the event assumed a quasi-official character since it took place in the party's Hamburg headquarters (the *Kurt Schumacher Haus*). Organised by Kalbitzer to counteract the dominant French

[14] Cahn and Müller, *RFA et Guerre d'Algérie*, pp. 219–20.

[15] Cited in: Scheffler, *SPD*, p. 54. Also: Cahn, *Parti social-démocrate*, pp. 461–63.

[16] Scheffler, *SPD*, pp. 54–6. Also: Télégramme no.1203 de Couve de Murville, Bonn, 20 May 1958, MAE, MLA/2.

narrative, the conference drew attention to the Bonn government's indirect complicity in the Algerian war through its close political and economic alliance with France.[17] Aït Ahcène used the conference to announce the imminent creation of the GPRA and denounce the impending French referendum on political reforms in Algeria. He declared it a duty of world opinion 'and especially German public opinion [...] to condemn this electoral tragi-comedy and to intervene to render it null and void'.[18] Considering that only four journalists attended according to French Consul General Olivier de Sayve, the conference found a surprising echo in the press.[19] The fact that an SPD deputy had hosted it provoked a violent complaint from Ambassador Seydoux, who fumed that his 'embassy had already tried repeatedly to make the leading personalities of that party understand the consequences of such an attitude for the good relations between our two countries'. The ambassador urged the *Quai d'Orsay* to impress upon the SFIO the suggestion of using the latter's impending congress at Issy-les-Moulineaux so that 'the most qualified Frenchmen will insist once more that the SPD modify its attitude' in the Algerian question.[20]

Seydoux's irritation rose still further when on 19 September 1958 – the day of the GPRA's formation – the SPD's Parliamentary-Press-Service announced the arrival in Tunis of a small delegation of *Jusos* led by Wischnewski and Fuchs. Officially, the delegation's two-week visit served 'to discuss closer cooperation with Tunisian, Algerian, and Moroccan politicians, trade unionists, and youth representatives'.[21] In reality, Aït Ahcène and Keramane had arranged the entire visit, and the FLN together with the UGTA would host the delegates for the duration of their stay, which comprised a tour of Algerian refugee camps, including one in Sakiet; an inspection of ALN bases, including one purportedly within Algeria itself; and an encounter with seven German deserters from the Foreign Legion. Wishnewski and Fuchs also attended

[17] Schreiben Kalbitzer an SPD Vorstand, 2 September 1958, AdsD, NL/Blachstein/32.

[18] Traduction d'une conférence de presse tenue par the FLN à Hambourg, 2 September 1958; Dépêche no. 372 du consul-général de Sayve, Hamburg, 4 September 1958, MAE, EU/RFA/1272.

[19] 'Algerier: Kampf gegen Frankreich wird schärfer', *Die Welt*, 3 September 1958; 'Algerier suchen deutsche Verbündete. Das Propaganda der "Liberationsfront" in der Bundesrepublik', *Tagesspiegel* (West Berlin), 10 September 1958; 'Algerische Flüchtlinge in der BRD', *FAZ*, 16 September 1958; 'Die algerischen Nationalisten organisieren sich in West Deutschland', *St. Galler Tagblatt* 23 September 1958; 'Une délégation du 'gouvernment Algérien en exil' se trouve actuellement à Bonn', *AFP*, 27 September 1958.

[20] Télégramme no. 1931 de Seydoux, Bonn, 4 September 1958, MAE, EU/RFA/1272.

[21] 'Jungsozialisten in Nordafrika', *Parlamentarisch-Politischer Pressedienst* (SPD), 19 September 1958; Télégramme no. 2073 de Seydoux, Bonn, 20 September 1958, MAE, MLA/2.

a meeting with two of the GPRA's most senior ministers, Krim Belkacem and Mahmoud Chérif, who impressed upon the former the FLN's disappointment in the Adenauer government, which 'had gone further than any other western government' in its hostile response to the GPRA. This produced a paradoxical situation. Although Wischnewski and Fuchs declared their support for the FLN's cause and criticised Bonn's attitude in the Algerian question, both men felt compelled to defend the Adenauer government. They explained how occupation, division and the danger of Soviet aggression had led to the FRG's inescapable dependence on the Western allies and they urged the GPRA not to recognise the illegitimate GDR.[22] In a press statement delivered upon the delegation's departure from Tunis, Fuchs reminded the Algerians that 'one had to distinguish between the attitude of the federal government', which was bound to France by treaty obligations, 'and that of [West German] public opinion', which felt 'great sympathy' for Algeria's struggle for freedom. According to Bonn's ambassador to Tunis, Werner Gregor, the Algerians had found it impressive 'that the federal government's uncompromising attitude [toward the GDR] was shared even by members of the opposition'.[23] Wischnewski had assured Gregor that the GPRA would not recognise the 'so-called GDR'. Though hardly in the spirit of Franco-German cooperation, the ambassador felt certain that the visit had done a great service to German–Arab relations.[24] Civic engagement, in other words, could go a long way to compensate for the negative repercussions of Adenauer's *quid pro quo* with France.

Returning from Tunis, Wischnewski and Fuchs embarked on a broad publicity campaign, one that drew on some of the familiar tropes of FLN propaganda: the movement's effort to 'liberate' legionnaires; the discipline of the *mujâhideen*, who donned modern, Western arms and American uniforms; the plight of Algerian refugees, many of them innocent children and women; the French forces' Gestapo methods; and the Algerians' lack of sympathy for the GDR. As Thomas Scheffler has shown, Wischnewski's account of the voyage resonated in newspapers large and small across West Germany. Virulently anti-colonialist and anti-communist, Wischnewski considered the French war effort 'irresponsible and inexcusable' in the context of Cold War and decolonisation. His report to the SPD ended with an energetic call: 'Help the Algerian people in its

[22] Jockel Fuchs, 'Wetterleuchten über Algerien', *SPD-Pressedienst*, 15 October 1958, AdsD, NL/Plum/29.

[23] Fernschreiben Nr. 140, Botschafter Gregor, Tunis, 25 September 1958, PA/AA, B25/14.

[24] Schreiben von Botschafter Greger, Tunis, 3 October 1958, PA/AA, B25/22.

fight for national independence and freedom!'[25] Fuchs's report, too, interwove anti-colonial and humanitarian arguments with anti-communist ones. In his description of the international relief efforts he witnessed at Tunisian refugee camps, Fuchs lamented the fact that the DRK supposedly had not responded to the ICRC's calls for aid while 'the Soviet-zone's Red Cross virtually outdid itself with deliveries of medication and ambulances'. Fuchs saw West German aid to the Algerians as a Cold War imperative to avoid being outperformed by the GDR, yet he also called for humanitarian engagement to be free of political motives. 'Those who want freedom for their German brothers beyond the zonal border', he wrote, '[. . .] must also have the courage to afford the Algerian people the same rights'.[26]

To underscore this point, Wischnewski took his support one step further, founding the 'Working-circle for the Friends of Algeria' (*Arbeitskreis der Freunde Algeriens*). Similarly to the Belgian 'Committee for Peace in Algeria' (*Comité pour la Paix en Algérie*), which had been established in April 1958, and to the Dutch 'Action, Information Algeria' committee (*Actie Informatie Algerije*) created in 1959, the *Arbeitskreis* became a pillar of support for the FLN's international propaganda war.[27] Though only a small group that drew its members mostly from leftist-progressivist circles, especially the *Jusos* and the Socialist German Student Union (*Sozialistische deutsche Studentenbund*, or SDS), the circle aimed to expose the injustice of French rule in Algeria and rally opinion to the FLN. Like its Belgian and Dutch counterparts, it liaised closely with members of the FLN as well as the movement's French support groups. Unlike its Belgian and Dutch counterparts, the circle published a regular newsletter, *Freies Algerien*, the first issue of which appeared in September 1958. With a run of 5,000 copies financed initially by the *Fédération de France*, the newsletter contained translations of articles from *El Moudjahid* as well as statements and resolutions made by, or on behalf of, the GPRA that were furnished by Ali Haroun or the FLN bureau in Bonn.[28] The *Arbeitskreis* justified its activity by reminding readers of Germany's own recent history of human rights abuses, which made it 'a duty' for present generations 'to speak out against such violent methods', no matter where they were

[25] Wischnewski, 'Wir besuchten das algerische Volk', *Metall* 21 (1958); Scheffler, *SPD*, p. 61.

[26] Fuchs, 'Wetterleuchten'. As noted in Chapter 4, the DRK had in fact responded to the ICRC's call for aid in late 1957, but had done so quietly.

[27] Doneux and Le Paige, *Front du Nord*, pp. 98–116; Masset, *Affaire Intérieure*, pp. 84–5, 133–53; Niek Pas, *Aan de wieg van het nieuwe Nederland. Nederland en de Algerijnse oorlog, 1954–1962* (Amsterdam, 2008), pp. 90–110.

[28] Haroun, *Septième wilaya*, pp. 135–6.

applied.[29] Moral considerations had to determine West Germany's relations with the wider world. The working-circle aimed 'to help inform the German public about the true story behind the 'dirty war' in Algeria. Since it was every German's 'duty to humanity to extend aid and solidarity to a people suffering from war and repression', the *Arbeitskreis* urged readers to prove their sympathies to the Algerian people by subscribing to their newspaper.[30]

Freies Algerien essentially constituted the FLN's official voice in the German-speaking world. In format and content it closely resembled the Belgian bulletin *Algérie Libre*, Danish *Algier frit* and English-language *Free Algeria* published by the FLN delegation in New York, or its British version edited by Labour MP John Baird.[31] Though subscription numbers remain unknown, the *Arbeitskreis* was able to sustain its newsletter until April 1962, publishing twenty-three issues that combined materials supplied by the FLN with contributions appealing to a specifically German, or German-speaking, audience. These articles discussed the repatriation of legionnaires, the difficulties encountered by Algerian workers, students and refugees in West Germany and European as well as international acts of solidarity in support of Algerian independence. Each issue of *Freies Algerien* had a circulation of 3,000 to 6,000 copies, which was not insubstantial. While some copies went to individual subscribers and journalists, many were sent to political organisations, trade unions, student associations and trade associations. The newspaper's target audience was not just based in the FRG but also in Austria and Switzerland.[32]

Needless to say, *Freies Algerien* and the 'Working-circle for the Friends of Algeria' drew fierce criticism from French officials, who made it their mission to shut the publication and others like it down. The Paris government continued to accuse not just Wischnewski but the entire SPD of pursuing a pro-Algerian agenda.[33] And yet the party's leaders remained keen to avoid perceptions of partiality in the Algerian war. While solidarity with the SFIO went some way to explain this, internal party reforms played

[29] 'Vorwort', *Freies Algerien* 1/1 (1958), p. 1.

[30] 'Was will das "Freie Algerien"? Warum Arbeitskreis der "Freunde Algeriens"?' *Freies Algerien* 1/4 (1958), p. 7.

[31] Wall, *France*, pp. 80–1; Masset, *Affaire Intérieure*, pp. 142–3; Doneux and Le Paige, *Front du Nord*, p. 147; Keller, *Gelebter*, pp. 220–5; J.J. Plant, 'John Baird: A British MP Who Supported the Algerian Revolution', *Revolutionary History* 10/4 (2012), pp. 197–202.

[32] Leggewie, *Kofferträger*, pp. 173–4; Keller, *Gelebter*, pp. 91–2. Also: Notice d'information no. 13923/SDECE, 12 December 1958, SHD-T, 10R/578*; Synthèse mensuelle no. 750/SSDNA, 4 June 1960; Synthèse mensuelle no. 2026/CCFFA/2, 17 January 1961, SHD-T, 10T/550*.

[33] Instructions aux postes diplomatiques, 2 April 1959, AHC, 2DE/75*.

an equally important role. Intent on averting a repeat of its catastrophic 1957 electoral defeat, the SPD executive had begun to tone down the party's Marxist and progressive rhetoric hoping thus to appeal to a broader voter spectrum. This process culminated in the 1959 Godesberg programme, which formally transformed the SPD from a workers' party advocating capitalism's overthrow into a social-democratic party working within the capitalist framework.[34] One corollary of this policy shift was that the SPD also moved closer to the governing CDU/CSU on key foreign policy issues. By the time of Khrushchev's Berlin ultimatum in November 1958, some party leaders, including West Berlin's influential mayor Willy Brandt, had begun to call for a 'common foreign and German policy' uniting government and opposition. With party vice-chairman Herbert Wehner's famed speech before the *Bundestag* on 30 June 1960, the SPD formally endorsed all aspects of Adenauer's *Westpolitik*.[35]

Thus like the Bonn government, the leaders of the SPD regarded Franco-German reconciliation as being of far greater political significance than support for Algerian independence. Together with French and German diplomats, they pushed Wischnewski into severing his open ties to the *Arbeitskreis* and to the FLN.[36] This pressure intensified considerably after 26 November 1958, when, in the midst of de Gaulle's first visit to Bad Kreuznach for talks with Adenauer and in that very town, Georg Jungclas together with two young associates distributed copies of *Freies Algerien* from Wischnewski's Volkswagen Beetle, which they had draped in an Algerian flag. Days before the summit, Henri Langlais, head of the *Quai d'Orsay*'s liaison service with the French government in Algeria, had ordered renewed demarches with both the *Auswärtige Amt* and the SPD 'in order to motivate Wischnewski to withdraw his open aid to the enemies of France, which damaged current efforts to promote close Franco-German collaboration'.[37] Although he never personally participated in the protest action, Wischnewski's notoriety had grown to such an extent that Adenauer himself lamented the stunt as 'about the worst thing that Social-Democracy could do to harm Germany'.[38] By 1959, Wischnewski

[34] Kurt Klotzbach, *Der Weg zur Staatspartei: Programmatik, praktische Politik und Organisation der deutschen Sozialdemokratie 1945–1965* (Bonn, 1996), pp. 401–94.
[35] Marcowitz, *Option*, pp. 86–7; Scheffler, *SPD*, pp. 63–5. [36] Scheffer, *SPD*, pp. 61–5.
[37] Dépêche no. 162 de Langlais au Général Salan, 21 November 1958, MAE, MLA/2.
[38] Buchstab (ed.), *Protokolle*, Nr. 7, p. 272. Also: Wochenbericht, SG-Bonn, 28 November 1958, BA/K, B131/195; Télégramme no. 3030 de Seydoux, Bonn, 28 November 1958, MAE, EU/RFA/1272; 'Ein "Zwischenfall" ', *Kölnische Rundschau*, 27 November 1958; Leggewie, *Kofferträger*, pp. 111–13.

had relented to the pressures he faced, resigning the editorship of *Freies Algerien*, a position subsequently passed on to less prominent party members: Cologne's *Jusos* chairman Willi Glomb and municipal councillor Wilhelm Pertz. Wischnewski did not, however, sever his ties to the FLN. He kept up his engagement on the movement's behalf, but did so discreetly and in a private capacity.

As a party, the SPD thus sought to downplay its support for the FLN, refusing to host FLN delegations at any of its subsequent congresses. The "Algeria lobby", however, together with the party's more radical youth organisations, continued their pro-Algerian activities, though on an individual basis and in circuitous ways. On numerous occasions between 1958 and 1960, Blachstein, Kalbitzer and Wischnewski, along with others from the SPD's parliamentary faction, pressed the Adenauer government on the issue of German minors serving in the Foreign Legion or on the protection and repatriation of legionnaires, especially deserters.[39] This was another example of how the issue of Germans serving in the Legion tapped into widely shared anxieties about the FRG's security and stability. These anxieties found their expression in nostalgia for a romanticised *Heimat* (homeland) and chart-topping hits such as Freddy Quinn's 1958 song, *Der Weg nach Haus ist schwer – für einen Legionär* (the path home is difficult – for a legionnaire).[40]

As a topic that continued to elicit cross-party rancour, the French Foreign Legion and its recruitment of minors continued to represent an effective yet indirect vehicle through which to attack the French war effort in Algeria. It remained a preferred vehicle for pro-Algerian propaganda. Paris's intransigence over the recruitment of minors helped paint the French as villains and contrasted negatively with the FLN's efforts to "liberate" German legionnaires. The ALN's Repatriation Service consequently attracted ever more media coverage. In October 1958, *Die Welt* correspondent Gert von Paczensky published a series of articles on Legion

[39] Mündliche Anfrage Nr. 252 des Abgeordneten Mommer, 7 February 1958; kleine Anfrage Nr. 291 der SPD betreffend Zeitungsberichte über Hinrichtung von Deutschen in der Fremdenlegion, 19 March 1958; Antwort Nr. 320 des BMAusw., 2 April 1958; Antrag Nr. 288 der SPD betreffend Junge Deutsche in der Frendenlegion, 19 March 1958; mündliche Anfrage Nr. 854 des Abgeordneten Bauer, 12 February 1959; mündliche Anfrage Nr. 1265 der Abgeordneten Wischnewski und Blachstein, 8 October 1959; Antrag Nr. 1463 der SPD betreffend Junge Deutsche in der Fremdenlegion, 8 December 1959 Anfrage Nr. 2077 des Abgeordneten Kalbitzer, 23 September 1960, in VdDBT/D, 3. Wahlperiode. Also: 16. Sitzung, 12 March 1958; 28. Sitzung, 8 May 1958; 60. Sitzung, 30 January 1959; 64. Sitzung, 25 February 1959; 81. Sitzung, 14 October 1959; 124. Sitzung, 28 September 1960, in VdDBT/StB, 3. Wahlperiode.

[40] Axel Schildt and Detlef Siegfried, *Deutsche Kulturgeschichte: die Bundesrepublik – 1945 bis zur Gegenwart* (Bonn, 2009), pp. 98–120; Leggewie, *Kofferträger*, pp. 83, 92.

deserters, praising the FLN for its humanitarian efforts, and claiming that over 3,000 legionnaires had been repatriated via Tétouan and another 2,000 via Tunis. Seydoux saw 'nothing surprising' in these articles, especially as *Die Welt* stylised itself as 'the champion of anti-colonialism'.[41] The ambassador's nonchalance would soon end, however. Intelligence obtained in March 1959 suggested that the FLN planned a public exhibition as well as radio broadcasts on its Repatriation Service in West Berlin. Seydoux immediately informed the *Auswärtige Amt* in order to prevent this unfriendly and "political" act. The *Amt*'s State Secretary Hilger van Scherpenberg subsequently wrote to West Berlin's Senate underscoring Bonn's disapproval of the FLN's planned exhibit. He further contacted the broadcasters *Rias* and *Radio Freies Berlin* 'to dissuade them from backing the creation of programmes' on the Repatriation Service. In another expression of the government's policy of supporting the French counter-insurgency, Scherpenberg went so far as to ask West German radio and television broadcasters to refrain voluntarily from airing programmes on Algeria, as these could damage West Germany's foreign relations, especially with France.[42] The French authorities remained wary, however, and when the Aachen-based photo-journalist Karl Breyer departed for Morocco in May 1959 to create a documentary on the ALN and its Repatriation Service, Prime Minister Debré again ordered the Bonn embassy 'to obtain assurances from the German authorities that they will take measures to ensure that Brayer's [sic] radio report and film will not be broadcast by media stations or cinemas in the Federal Republic'.[43]

By then, the return of repatriated legionnaires had itself become a media event. Like the public release of French POWs in North Africa, the staged arrival in the FRG of Legion deserters strove to paint the FLN in a positive, humanitarian light.[44] Thus on 31 March 1959, a group of seven German deserters landed at Frankfurt/Main airport amid a large journalistic presence. Their arrival was stylised as an 'Easter present' from the FLN to the German people. Likewise, the press widely reported the arrival on 7 August 1959 of five German 'prisoners of war' who had been 'liberated' by the FLN.[45] Interest also rose in the man who orchestrated these

[41] Dépêche no. 1705 de Seydoux, Bonn, 16 October 1958, MAE, MLA/2.

[42] Dépêche no. 591 de Seydoux, Bonn, 25 March 1959, MAE, EU/RFA/1273.

[43] Télégramme no. 2494 de Jacques Roux, sous-directeur du département d'affaires politiques, à Bonn, 13 May 1959, MAE, MLA/3.

[44] Klose, *Menschenrechte*, pp. 157–8; Onyedum, '"Humanize"', p. 721.

[45] Dépêche no. 668 de Seydoux, Bonn, 4 April 1959, MAE, MLA/3; Dépêche no. 1480 de l'ambassade à Bonn, 10 August 1959, MLA/4.

repatriations. In March 1959, French officials had still disparaged Si Mustapha for impressing journalists with the 'rare elegance' of his German when he claimed before a private meeting arranged by the social-democratic *Saarbrücker Allgemeine Zeitung* that the FLN had helped liberate 6,000 legionnaires, including 4,000 Germans.[46] Six months later, their derision had dissipated. At the time, Si Mustapha toured West Germany on a publicity campaign that resonated deeply in public discourse, climaxing on 14 September in a 'genuine press conference' in Aachen.[47] French military security estimated that well over fifty German newspapers had covered the tour.[48] The prominent political weekly *Der Spiegel* published a long interview with Si Mustapha, who now declared that the ALN had helped 2,814 deserters return home, including 1,952 Germans, most of them minors. Si Mustapha claimed to have established 'a veritable network of agents within the Legion', and that deserters only had to exclaim they were 'Alemani' to find refuge with Algerians.[49]

Although Si Mustapha's statistics were clearly inconsistent and exaggerated, there was no denying that the Foreign Legion constituted what Seydoux called 'a favourite and efficient propaganda theme for the FLN', one that 'found a large echo among German opinion given its susceptibility in that domain'.[50] The French military, too, deemed the Legion an effective weapon in the FLN's psychological war, so much so its *deuxième bureau* believed in December 1960 that Si Mustapha had been nominated for a *Bundesverdienstkreuz*, the highest award for services rendered to the Bonn Republic.[51] Though this proved untrue, French anxiety was not unfounded. The press's interest in the topic had prompted the *Jusos* to resurrect their anti-Legion campaigns in late 1959. Under Wischnewski's leadership, the organisation promoted the ALN's Repatriation Service, extolling its accomplishments in various social-democratic publications.[52] Both the West German Association of Conscientious Objectors and the youth wing of the Friends of Nature International (*Naturfreundejugend*) actively supported the *Jusos*. Under their secretary, Klaus Vack, a committed pacifist and anti-nuclear weapons

[46] Dépêche no. 74 de Tanguy de Courson, Saarbrücken, 5 March 1959, MAE, EU/RFA/1273.

[47] Notice no. 4656 de l'Institut d'Études Européennes de Strasbourg, 17 September 1959; Dépêche no. 135 du consul-général Duflos, Düsseldorf, 17 September 1958, MAE, MLA/4.

[48] Notice no. 18511/SSDNA/Berlin, 30 September 1959, SHD-T, 10T/528/D2*

[49] Si Mustapha, 'Wer desertiert muss "Alemani" rufen – Die Flucht aus der Fremdenlegion', *Der Spiegel* 36 (2 September 1959), pp. 55–9.

[50] Télégramme no. 2451 de Seydoux, Bonn, 3 September 1959, MAE, MLA/4.

[51] Synthèse mensuelle no. 2273/CCFFA/2, 16 December 1960, SHD-T, 10T/550*.

[52] Michels, *Deutsche*, pp. 309–19; Wischnewski, *Leidenschaft*, p. 109.

activist who stood in direct contact with Si Mustapha, members of the *Naturfreundejugend* distributed flyers denouncing France's war in Algeria and became active in a letter-writing campaign promoting the Repatriation Service and encouraging legionnaires in Algeria to desert.[53] By then, Si Mustapha had solicited the assistance also of *Bundestag*-deputy Blachstein in distributing pro-Algerian publications.[54] Starting in July 1960, Si Mustapha produced a monthly German-language information bulletin, the *Mitteilungen des Rückführungsdienstes*, which he sent to Austrian, Swiss and German journalists such as Werner Plum, a leading expert on North African affairs. With headlines such as 'German minor tortured to death', 'German losses in the Algerian war' or 'French crimes against three legionnaires', the bulletin effectively reinforced the connection between Algeria's struggle against the injustice of colonialism and the "liberation" of German legionnaires.[55]

The Legion, however, only constituted one flank in the FLN's battle for German hearts and minds. Profiting from contacts established during the SPD's Stuttgart congress in May 1958, Keramane and his German-speaking assistant Kacem partook in ever more regular speaking engagements across West Germany and beyond.[56] Their audiences varied considerably but frequently consisted of leftist-progressivist youth associations with strong anti-colonial and anti-militarist proclivities. Between June and December 1958, Karamane and Kacem reportedly spoke before audiences of up to 250 in Bonn, Stuttgart, Heidelberg, Mannheim and Hamburg, mostly on invitation from local branches of the *Jusos*, SDS or Trade Union Youth (*Gewerkschaftsjugend*). French intelligence painstakingly traced these 'information evenings', which eluded the authorities' efforts to suppress Algerian political activism.[57] Organised by Germans as private or academic events, Kacem – a doctoral candidate – and Keramane – a former teacher – were able to circumvent the embargo on 'political activity'. Federal

[53] Leggewie, *Kofferträger*, pp. 88, 99–100; Balsen and Rössel, *Hoch*, pp. 75–8; Klaus Vack, 'Der eigene Weg 1958-1965', in *Das andere Deutschland nach 1945 – als Pazifist, Sozialist und radikaler Demokrat in der Bundesrepublik Deutschland – Klaus Vack* (eds.) Wolf-Dieter Narr et al. (Köln, 2005), pp. 59–62.

[54] Schreiben Si Mustapha an Blachstein, 8 July 1959, AdsD, NL/Blachstein/32; Schreiben Si Mustapha an Blachstein, 16 June and 2 September 1960, NL/Blachstein/33.

[55] *Mitteilungen des Rückführungsdienstes* Nr. 3 (September 1960); Nr. 4 (25 October 1960); Nr. 6 (15 December 1960), AdsD, NL/Plum/26.

[56] Keller, *Gelebter*, p. 102

[57] Dépêche no. 1124 du chargé d'affaires, Bonn, 26 June 1958, MAE, EU/RFA/1272; Dépêche no. 374 du chargé d'affaires in Stuttgart, 4 July 1958, MLA/2; Notices nos. 4451/CCFFA/Sûreté et 4591/CCFFA/Sûreté, 22 July and 28 July 1958, SHD-T, 10T/528/D2*; 'Film über die algerische Befreiungsarmee von Hamburger Studenten präsentiert', ADN, 16 December 1958.

authorities sought to prevent these engagements by exerting pressure on the authorities under whose auspices they occurred. On occasion, these interventions succeeded. Thus in May 1959, French and German diplomats prevented a lecture by Kacem at Düsseldorf University by intervening with North Rhine-Westphalia's Cultural Ministry. Six months later, they persuaded the *Land*'s interior minister to ban Kacem from speaking in Bielefeld before the youth wing of the liberal Free Democratic Party, an erstwhile coalition partner of Adenauer's CDU/CSU.[58]

As French diplomatic pressure magnified and federal prosecutor Güde launched his nation-wide inquest into FLN activities in December 1959, the Bonn authorities warned Keramane and Kacem to refrain from their 'academic' and 'private' appearances or face expulsion.[59] The chance came on 15 June 1960. After an engagement in Copenhagen, federal border guards denied Kacem re-entry into West Germany for an appearance before Hamburg's branch of the Women's Peace Movement. Although he possessed both a Moroccan passport and a valid student visa, the authorities argued that Kacem, who openly professed being an FLN militant, had too often flouted the ban on "political activities".[60] In a personal appeal to Foreign Minister Brentano, Kacem accused the Bonn authorities of stifling his academic development and contravening his constitutional right to freedom of opinion and expression.[61] It took repeated interventions by Wischnewski to persuade the authorities to lift the ban. With the French government about to initiate a first round of negotiations with the FLN at Melun, the deputy argued that Bonn could ill afford to treat the movement's delegates as outlaws.[62] Wischnewski warned Brentano of the 'incalculable' diplomatic damage that would arise if the GPRA moved its delegation from Bonn to East Berlin, 'since the FLN's political influence in all Arab and African countries is well-known'.[63] Wischnewski's Cold War reasoning helped change the *Amt*'s mind. In September 1960, the authorities permitted Kacem to resume his

58 Note de l'ambassade de France à Bonn à l'AA, 28 April 1959; Vermerk, Referat 502 an Referat 204, 26 May 1959, PA/AA, B25/9; Fernschreiben Nr. 134, BMI an LMI Nordrhein-Westfalen, 1 December 1959, B25/10; Télégramme no. 3723 de Seydoux, Bonn, 12 December 1959, MAE, MLA/5.

59 Télégramme no. 3723 de Seydoux, 12 December 1959, MAE, MLA/5.

60 Aufzeichnungen, Referat 204/205, 14 June 1960, and van Scherpenberg, 15 June 1960, PA/AA, B12/932.

61 Schreiben BMI an AA, 22 June 1960; Vermerk, Peter Limbourg, 23 June 1960, PA/AA, B12/932; Schreiben Kacem an Brentano, 8 July 1960, B25/11.

62 Aufzeichnung, van Scherpenberg, 23 June 1960; Vermerk, Limbourg, 23 June 1960; Schreiben Wischnewski an Brentano, undated, PA/AA, B12/932.

63 Telex, Wischnewski an Brentano, 6 July 1960, PA/AA, B25/11.

studies in Bonn, though under strict orders to refrain from speaking engagements.[64]

Though his case proved troublesome, Kacem was neither the first nor the most prominent Algerian propagandist to face bans and expulsions in the FRG. In May 1959, Blachstein had invited the GPRA's Information Minister Ahmed Boumendjel to speak before Hamburg University and the *Neue Gesellschaft*, an SPD-backed organisation for political education. To score a 'large echo' in the press, Blachstein had timed Boumendjel's visit to coincide with the upcoming congress of the Socialist International, which was set to convene in Hamburg on 14 July – Bastille Day – and whose participants included SFIO leaders Guy Mollet, Jules Moch and Christian Pineau.[65] Learning of the deputy's plans on 11 July, French diplomats immediately protested, prompting the *Auswärtige Amt* to refer the matter to Hamburg's Senate, which in turn pressured Hamburg University's rector into prohibiting Boumenjdel's scheduled appearance. To Debré's 'great annoyance', the Senate had less success with Hellmut Kalbitzer's *Neue Gesellschaft*. According to his diplomatic councillor, Gérard Amanrich, the French premier could not understand how Boumendjel had even been allowed to enter West Germany. As a senior member of the GPRA, he would have featured prominently in the *Fichier Z* cards shared with the West German security and border services.[66] Under intense pressure, Hamburg's social-democratic Minister-President Max Bauer was ultimately forced to intervene. On 16 July 1959, he ordered Boumendjel's expulsion and banned him from entering the FRG.[67]

This move boosted FLN publicity far more than Boumendjel's speech at the *Neue Gesellschaft* ever would have.[68] The left-wing press criticised Bauer's decision as undemocratic, arguing that such treatment did not befit someone who was internationally recognised as one of the GPRA's top ministers. The *Frankfurter Rundschau* accused the Bonn government of '*Polizeistaatlichkeit*' (resorting to police-state methods).[69] Writing in

64 Wischnewski, *Leidenschaft*, pp. 114–15.

65 Schreiben Blachstein an Boumendjel, 26 May 1959, AdsD, NL/Blachstein/32.

66 Fernschreiben Nr. 552, Botschaft Paris, 13 July 1959, PA/AA, B24/287/F2.

67 Télégramme no. 1999 de Seydoux, Bonn, 11 July 1959; Télégramme no. 3322 du secrétaire-général Louis Joxe à Seydoux, 13 July 1959; Télégrammes nos. 2013 and 2016 de Seydoux, Bonn, 14 July 1959; Télégramme no. 2040 de Seydoux, Bonn, 15 July 1959; Télégramme no. 2064 de Seydoux, Bonn, 17 July 1959, MAE, MLA/3.

68 Vermerk, Referat 204/205, 18 August 1959, PA/AA, B25/4.

69 '. . . und Monsieur Bumendschel [sic] sprach doch. Hamburgs Senat liess zwei Bundesministerien abblitzen und schützte die Redefreiheit', *Frankfurter Rundschau*, 24 July 1959; 'Der Fall des Herrn Bumendschel [sic]', *Hamburger Echo*, 25 July 1959.

Vorwärts, Kalbitzer called the expulsion an 'act of compliance'. He accused the French government of living 'under the false pretence that the governments of the *Bund* and *Länder* are the political guardians [*Vormünder*] of the German people', and that the French, in turn, considered themselves Bonn's guardian, 'who can decide what German citizens are allowed to know about French colonial policies and what not'.[70] In an open letter published on 11 September 1959 by *Bild*, *Hamburger Echo* and *Hamburger Morgenpost*, Kalbitzer further attacked the Federal Interior Minister Gerhard Schröder for unlawfully ordering the surveillance of *Neue Gesellschaft*, where Algerian 'refugees' held fortnightly meetings.[71] Just weeks before, *Der Spiegel* had published an interview with Ferhat Abbas in which the GPRA president spoke of the 'disgrace' of Bonn's support for the French government's 'mass murder' of Algerians, warning of its 'danger for the future relations between Germany and a free Algeria'.[72] To the *deuxième bureau*, the interview constituted 'a new summit in the virulence of FLN propaganda in West Germany'.[73] That summit was in fact reached two months later, when *Der Spiegel* featured Abbas on its cover as the Algerian revolution's '*bon papa*'.[74]

The open and frequent publicity accorded to the FLN worried French authorities, especially as it was no longer confined to print. In January 1959, Debré and Couve de Murville jointly convened Bonn's ambassador Blankenhorn to protest the primetime airing of a fifteen-minute interview with Abbas by ARD.[75] Though televisions were not yet widely owned, the authorities appreciated their power as a communications and propaganda tool.[76] Unlike the French authorities, however, the Bonn government wielded little control over media contents even when it came to public

[70] Hellmut Kalbitzer, 'Der unerwünschte Gast aus Algerien. Ein Versuch zur politischen Bevormundung der Bundesbürger', *Vorwärts*, 24 July 1959.

[71] Dépêche no. 336 du vice-consul Daniel Couderc, Hamburg, 11 September 1959, MAE, EU/RFA/1273.

[72] 'Hört auf, den Massenmord zu unterstützen. Ein SPIEGEL-Gespräch mit dem Ministerpräsidenten der algerischen Exilregierung, Ferhat Abbas', *Der Spiegel* 34 (19 August 1959), p. 37.

[73] Notice no. 6276/État-major général de la Défense Nationale (EMGDN)/2, 20 August 1959, SHD-T, 10T/528/D2*.

[74] 'Ferhat Abbas – Le bon papa', *Der Spiegel* 44 (28 October 1959), pp. 55–70.

[75] Fernschreiben Nr. 70, Blankenhorn, Paris, 26 January 1959, PA/AA, B25/9; Note, 29 January 1959, AHC, 2DE/70*.

[76] Andreas Fickers, 'Radio und Fernsehen als nationale Sozialisierungsinstanzen? Der Rundfunk im Rahmen der westdeutschen und französischen Wiederaufbaumodernisierung der 1950er Jahre', in *Wandel und Integration. Deutsch-französische Annäherung der fünfziger Jahre* (eds.) Hélène Miard-Delacroix and Rainer Hudemann (Munich, 2005), p. 297; Axel Schildt, 'Der Beginn des Fernsehzeitalters: ein neues Massenmedium setzt sich durch', in *Modernisierung im Wiederaufbau. Die westdeutsche Gesellschaft der 50er Jahre* (eds.) Axel Schildt and Arnold Sywottek (Bonn, 1993), pp. 477–92.

broadcasters, since freedom of expression was constitutionally guaranteed. According to Felix von Eckardt, head of the Federal Press Office (*Bundespresseamt*), the government could not prevent future transmissions on the FLN even if it tried.[77] All the authorities could do was ask television and radio directors to refrain voluntarily from broadcasts that strained Franco-German relations and Western solidarity, as Scherpenberg would do. The media corporations responded to this subtle form of pressure by defending their programme choices and pointing to their statutory duty to inform the public in a fair and balanced manner.[78] As it happened, although the broadcast irritated the authorities in France, German diplomats consoled themselves with the fact that it appeared to impact favourably on Arab opinion. Coinciding with Grotewohl's voyage to Cairo and a personal invitation by Walter Ulbricht, the secretary general of the Socialist Unity Party, for Abbas to visit East Berlin, the ARD's interview with the latter had at least helped to counterpoise the GDR's efforts to gain recognition in the Middle East.[79]

If public broadcasters proved difficult to handle, the Bonn government faced similar difficulties in controlling the activities of the various civil associations that had begun to champion the Algerian cause. These organisations, too, enjoyed constitutional guarantees of the rights to associate and express opinions freely. One such association was the SDS. Politically far more radical and openly anti-imperial in outlook than its patron, the SPD (with whom relations had become increasingly strained), the Algerian question had developed into the socialist student union's principal cause beyond Europe.[80] In this, it collaborated closely with the Arab Student Union in (West) Germany (ASVD), which by 1960 supposedly represented some 7,000 students.[81] Beginning in 1958 and alongside members of the *Falken, Jusos* and *Naturfreundejugend*, SDS and ASVD adherents in Cologne, Bonn, Kassel and Stuttgart organised regular demonstrations and wreath-layings in protest against the Algerian war. For impact, these

77 Vermerk, Karl Carstens, 28 January 1958, PA/AA, B25/9.

78 Brief Carstens an Fernsehdirektor Clemens Münster (*Bayerischer Rundfunk*, Munich), Programmdirektor Arnold (*Norddeutscher Rundfunk*, Hamburg), und Intendant Friedrich Bischoff (*Süd-West-Funk*, Baden-Baden), 28 January 1959; Brief, Intendant Walter Hilpert, *Nord- und Westdeutscher Rundfunkverband*, an Carstens, 31 January 1959, PA/AA, B25/9.

79 Fernschreiben Nr. 93, Blankenhorn, Paris, 31 January 1959, PA/AA, B1/56; Schreiben, Botschaft Kairo, 9 February 1959, B25/9.

80 Balsen and Rössel, *Hoch*, p. 86; Tilman Fichter and Siegward Lönnendonker, *Kleine Geschichte des SDS: der Sozialistische Deutsche Studentenbund von Helmut Schmidt bis Rudi Dutschke*, 4th edn (Essen, 2007), p. 82.

81 Schreiben, LfV Bayern, an Bayerische Staatskanzlei, 1 July 1960, PA/AA, B25/2.

events were organised to coincide with important political anniversaries: international workers' day (1 May); human rights day (10 December); and of course the anniversary of the Algerian war itself (1 November).[82] The presence of Arab and other foreign students, whose visas required them to refrain from activities inimical to official interests, often permitted the authorities to disrupt these events. Thus on 1 November 1959, police in Cologne arrested *Falken* member Heinz Peiffer for causing public disorder when he spoke before a small crowd that had gathered at the French Institute to commemorate the Algerian war's fifth anniversary. One week later, the police prevented a march by 100-odd Arab and German students in Bonn on similar grounds.[83] The following month, SDS and ASVD members in Göttingen, Braunschweig, Hamburg, Kiel, Bonn and Frankfurt organised an "Algeria week" with silent marches, public presentations and fundraisers. Interventions by French and German authorities again disrupted many of the students' plans. In Bonn, city officials banned the planned parade on the grounds that it endangered public security; all other activities had to be confined to university premises. French Consul General Jean Fernand-Laurent's protests in Hamburg prompted the university to prohibit the ASVD from using its facilities for overtly political demonstrations. In Braunschweig, too, officials forbade 'anti-French' protests on university premises.[84]

Although they attracted only small crowds that never surpassed a few hundred individuals, the authorities clearly considered these acts of solidarity damaging to Franco-German relations. Hence their anxiety to prevent further demonstrations. The authorities' heavy-handed tactics, however, merely encouraged the students to intensify their civic engagement in support of the FLN. The state-imposed bans and clampdowns were taken as evidence of the undemocratic and discriminatory treatment inflicted upon Algerians, whether in Algeria and France or now in West Germany. Seen as symptomatic of the evils of colonialism, the students remained undeterred by such measures. As the *deuxième bureau* reported in 1960, SDS members in Tübingen, Frankfurt, Freiburg, Kiel, Munich and Saarbrücken organised renewed demonstrations and wreath-layings to mark the war's sixth anniversary.[85]

[82] Leggewie, *Kofferträger*, pp. 110–11, 113–14.

[83] Télégramme no. 3185 de Seydoux, Bonn, 9 November 1959, MAE, AL/ALG/39.

[84] Dépêche no. 342 du consul Maurice Ardiet, Hanover, 5 December 1959; Dépêche no. 348 d'Ardiet, 10 December 1959; Dépêche no. 491 du consul-général Jean Fernand-Laurent, Hamburg, 18 December 1959; Dépêche no. 359 d'Ardiet, 22 December 1959; Dépêche no. 2308 de Seydoux, Bonn, 28 December 1959, MAE, EU/RFA/1273.

[85] Dépêche no. 195, Sûreté aux Armées, 5ème Brigade Blindée, 9 December 1960, SHD-T, 14S/20*; Synthèse mensuelle no. 2273/CCFFA/2, 16 December 1960; Synthèse mensuelle no. 2026/CCFFA/2, 17 January 1961, 10T/550*.

By then, French officials were at a loss as to how they could influence West German public opinion in a manner conducive of their Algerian policies. The *deuxième bureau* of French forces in Germany complained bitterly about the attacks on France found in tabloids, glossy magazines and local and regional papers. At the end of the day, the majority of Germans remained indifferent or ignorant of the Algerian war: only 52 per cent of respondents in an Allensbach Institute survey had followed the May 1958 crisis; only 38 per cent correctly identified the rebels behind the 1960 "week of the barricades" as French not Muslim; and only 44 per cent of students, according to another survey, actively discussed the Algerian war. Yet this was not how it appeared to the French security and intelligence services.[86] The FLN, it seemed, was clearly winning the battle for West German hearts and minds.

French officials, of course, had not remained idle in the Franco-Algerian propaganda war. After all, the persistent disapprobation with which the European press reported events in Algeria negatively affected not only public opinion but also the attitudes of European governments upon whose cooperation the French authorities relied to dismantle the FLN's external sanctuaries. France's allies, the *Quai d'Orsay* feared, might again try to pressgang Paris into negotiations with the FLN.[87] Returning from a tour of European cities, Lieutenant Jean-Yves Alquier of the general secretariat for Algerian affairs urged the Paris government in late 1958 to intensify its international propaganda.[88] To Alquier, 'the vast majority of foreigners are still either incapable of understanding the [Algerian] problem, or hostile by "jealousy" or prejudice'. A former officer in the *Sections administratives spécialisées* who fully embraced the principles of *guerre révolutionnaire*, Alquier recommended an activation of French psychological action abroad. To isolate the FLN effectively, especially now that it had created a government-in-exile, France had to win over not just the masses in Algeria but world opinion at large. This could only be achieved through a dynamic propaganda campaign that included the invitation of foreign personalities to Algeria, lecture tours abroad by both French and Muslim 'Ambassadors of Algeria', and rigorous action by French diplomats, whom Alquier accused of idleness in the Franco-Algerian propaganda war. French psychological action, Alquier concluded, had to

86 Synthèse mensuelle no. 2273/CCFFA/2, 16 December 1960, SHD-T, 10T/550*; Elisabeth Noelle and Erich Peter Neumann (eds.), *Jahrbuch der öffentlichen Meinung 1958–1964* (Allensbach-am-Bodensee, 1965), pp. 563–4; Weitbrecht, *Aufbruch*, p. 49.
87 Dépêche, Langlais, MLA, à Paul Delouvrier, DGGA, 29 December 1958, MAE, MLA/2.
88 Pas, *Nederland*, pp. 56–9.

'convince the world of the justness of our cause, of the liberalism of our policies, of the communist danger in Algeria, of the interest for all of the West of the Saharan oil, etc.'[89]

Due to the size and significance of the Algerian presence east of the Rhine, the FRG became an important target of French psychological action. The aim was to isolate the FLN both physically and morally from West German society and opinion. By the eve of the conflict's fourth anniversary on 30 October 1958, the French General Staff had grown so alarmed by the West German press's interest in the FLN that it, too, urged the *Quai d'Orsay* to intensify its public-relations campaigns. French diplomats were to explore possible actions in order 'to inform the [. . .] West German public of the ways in which the French treat the Algerian question', for example by organising more frequent information tours for journalists in Algeria.[90] Two weeks later the commander-in-chief of French forces and temporary head of the civil administration in Algeria, General Salan, repeated this request. Salan further asked the French embassy in Bonn to find a publisher for Alquier's book, *Nous avons pacifiés Tasalt* (Robert Laffont, 1957), which he deemed 'liable to present the French army in a more objective light that certain other publications'.[91] He was referring to works condemning French military and colonial practices in Algeria, such as Alleg's *La Question*, Servan-Schreiber's *Lieutenant en Algérie* and the novels of Algerian writers Kateb Yacine, Mohammed Dib and Mouloud Feraoun, which had already been translated into German.[92]

The *deuxième bureau*, too, urged greater psychological action in West Germany. In March 1959, it lamented the 'complete incomprehension of almost the totality of German public opinion with regards to the Algerian problem, even in those circles that are well-disposed towards us'. The bureau blamed this situation on 'the total lack of serious French information on the Algerian problem', which meant that German curiosity

[89] Note, 10.RM/EMI/5, action à l'étranger concernant l'Algérie, J.-Y. Alquier, 1958, SHD-T, 1H/2592/D1.

[90] Lettre no. 192/EMDN/PSY du vice-amiral Cabanier au Quai d'Orsay, 30 October 1958, MAE, MLA/2.

[91] Lettre no.1863 du Général Salan au Quai d'Orsay, 13 November 1958, MAE, MLA/2.

[92] These works had by then all been translated into German: Alleg, *Die Folter* (trans.) Hede von Ullmann (Wien, München, Basel, 1958); Servan-Schreiber, *Lieutenant in Algerien* (trans.) Lutz Meunier (Hamburg, 1957); Yacine, *Nedschma* (trans.) W.M. Guggenheimer (Frankfurt/M, 1958); Dib, *Algerische Trilogie* (trans.) Herbert Bräuning and Karl Heinrich (Berlin/East, 1956 and 1957); Feraoun, *Die Heimkehr des Amer-u-Kaci* (trans.) Hermann Schreiber; *Der Sohn des Armen; Die Wege hügelan* (trans.) Grete Steinböck (Würzburg and Wien, 1956–1958).

was being satisfied by the FLN. Like Alquier, the *deuxième bureau* advocated measures such as tours of Algeria and conferences to clarify and promote French policy. The bureau once again drew a direct parallel between the Algerian problem, the German problem and the Berlin crisis when it suggested foregrounding arguments such as: 'The defence by the Free World of 1.5 million French citizens of European extraction [in Algeria] was equally worthy as the safeguarding of 2.5 million West Berliners.' The bureau criticised French officials for doing too little to dispel the negative preconceptions propagated by the FLN, which meant that 'Germans often [had] the impression that France hides its difficulties in Algeria like a "shameful affliction"'. Contrary to the FLN, French officials in the FRG avoided discussing the counterinsurgency, which they treated as an internal affair, and while French Institutes carried ample material on metropolitan cultural and economic matters, 'their role in the diffusion of information on Algeria appeared non-existent'.[93]

This situation had to change. In November 1958, Henri Langlais proposed organising a new round of information tours for German journalists and politicians. At the same time, he warned the General Staff of the difficulties in wooing German opinion:

> Whatever the amplitude of our action, we should not disguise the fact that we find ourselves in [West] Germany in the presence of social-democratic elements that have entirely espoused the rebels' cause, either by conviction or for political ends, and that it will be very difficult, if not impossible, to convince them of greater comprehension towards our problems.[94]

Langlais nevertheless considered it sensible to include social-democrats in French initiatives, which struck him as a viable means 'to oppose successfully the hostile actions [...] of the extremists' from the SPD's 'Algeria lobby'.[95] A two-week tour in October 1958 by Hermann Finckh, a CDU deputy in Baden-Württemberg, had already produced 'very positive' results.[96] French diplomats were equally pleased by the 'very honourable' outcome of a tour organised for mainly conservative journalists in December 1958. Hans Becker of the *Frankfurter Neue Presse*, for instance, had demonstrated 'commendable objectivity' when he argued that France's presence in Algeria prevented North Africa from turning

93 Note no. 66/EMGDN/2, 9 March 1959, MAE, MLA/3.
94 Note no. 92 de Langlais au Général Fourquet, EMA, 15 November 1958, MAE, MLA/2.
95 Dépêche no. 162 de Langlais à Salan, 21 November 1958, MAE, MLA/2.
96 Dépêche de Langlais au délégué-général Delouvrier, 29 December 1958, MAE, MLA/2. See also: Reisebericht, Hermann Finckh, undated, PA/AA, B25/12.

communist. Dieter Kiehl of the *Münchner Merkur* had lauded the French army as 'the most popular occupation force ever to have existed', which was a double-edged compliment considering its implication that France remained an alien force in Algeria.[97]

In March 1959, French officials built on these advances by organising an extensive tour for twelve *Bundestag* members led by Waldemar Kraft (CDU) and comprising of five further CDU/CSU deputies, four members of the SPD, including Blachstein, and one deputy each from the Free Democrats and German Party.[98] Blachstein's inclusion raised concerns among French administrators in Algiers, who objected to his contacts to the FLN bureau in Bonn. Convoked by Seydoux before the group's departure, the ambassador asked the deputy to refrain from press statements during his trip, warning him that 'those who are not with us are against us'.[99] Such threats did not impress Blachstein. Of the participating delegates, he and his colleague Willi Birkelbach remained intractable in their views, with Seydoux bemoaning that they had 'learned nothing'.[100] In a wilful act of defiance, Blachstein had even ended his French-financed tour with a GPRA-sponsored visit to Algerian refugee camps and ALN bases in Tunisia. Apart from meeting his ailing friend Aït Ahcène, who had returned to Tunis after the attempt on his life, the deputy held meetings with Krim Belkacem and the GPRA's chief diplomat in New York, M'Hammed Yazid.[101] Once home, Blachstein publicly accused Bonn and Washington of financially and militarily abetting France's criminal war against the Algerian people and called on Germans to support the FLN.[102] As for Blachstein's conservative colleagues, Seydoux concluded that the voyage had 'fortified their opinions' that French influence in Algeria remained indispensable, politically as well as economically. The tour had also 'developed their reflex of solidarity with France'. The CDU/CSU deputies had been particularly pleased by the opportunity to speak to German legionnaires, a deft and deliberate move on the part of the tour organisers, who realised that the Legion represented the one issue that could undermine even the conservatives' support for *l'Algérie française*.[103]

97 Dépêche no. 65 de Seydoux, Bonn, 13 January 1959; Dépêche no. 175 de Seydoux, 23 January 1959; Dépêche no. 360 de Seydoux, 19 February 1959, MAE, MLA/2.

98 Schreiben AA an Botschaft Paris, 27 February 1959, PA/AA, B25/12.

99 Télégramme no. 529 de Seydoux, Bonn, 26 February 1959, MAE, MLA/2.

100 Dépêche no. 588 de Seydoux, 25 March 1959, MAE, EU/RFA/1273.

101 Brief Blachstein an Krim Belkacem, 5 May 1959, AdsD, NL/Blachstein/32.

102 Dépêches nos. 886 et 983 de Seydoux, 27 April and 20 May 1959, MAE, EU/RFA/1273.

103 Dépêche no. 588 de Seydoux, 25 March 1959, MAE, EU/RFA/1273.

The tour organised for West German deputies constituted only one part of a vigorous new propaganda offensive, which continued to represent an important pillar of France's global counterinsurgency against the FLN. In a two-pronged attack, diplomats – especially in countries allied to France – were instructed to insist with 'firmness' on the banning of all propaganda 'slandering France', whether by the FLN or its 'accomplices', while concurrently dispelling the public's 'ignorance' of French policy in Algeria. The aim, as one directive by Foreign Minister Couve de Murville emphasised, was to 'bring about the FLN's isolation [. . .] to sow confusion among the rebellion's political leaders, to make them feel, contrary to what one might have believed in the past, that the Western world trusted France in her determination and effort to find a democratic and just solution [to the Algerian problem]'. To achieve this aim, French diplomats were exhorted in April 1959 to 'persuade world opinion that our cause is just and conforms to France's democratic and generous tradition'.[104]

Secure in their knowledge of Bonn's cooperation, the *Quai d'Orsay* still found it easier to proceed against the FLN's propaganda efforts or those of its German or Arab allies than to convince public opinion of the righteousness of France's own policies in Algeria. An information tour organised for members of the German-Atlantic Society to conflict zones in Algeria in September 1959 may have turned *Bundestag* Vice-President Richard Jäger (CSU) into an outspoken proponent of France's war effort. Yet as Military Attaché Alain Le Ray lamented (who until recently had commanded campaigns in Algeria), this still did not improve the average German's understanding of the Algerian problem.[105] French officials stepped up their public-relations campaign by organising speaking engagements and film screenings of their own.[106] In October 1959, Marshal Alphonse Juin addressed the Franco-German Association in Ludwigsburg; three months later, Seydoux appeared before the Workinggroup of Franco-German Societies.[107] To reach local audiences, French authorities also began to target communal politicians. In June 1959, the Association of Mayors of Algeria invited thirty-six European city-heads on

104 Instructions aux postes diplomatiques, 2 April 1959, AHC, 2DE/75*.

105 Dépêche no. 974 du consul-général de Nerciat, Munich, 24 November 1959, MAE, EU/RFA/1273; Reisebericht, 12 October 1959, PA/AA, B25/12; Dépêche no. 1264 de l'attaché militaire Le Ray, Bonn, 24 September 1959, SHD-T, 14S/20*.

106 Dépêche no. 1668 du SEAA à la MLA, 8 April 1959, MAE, MLA/3.

107 Schreiben, Prof. Hils, Staatliche Akademie der Bildenden Künste, an Verteidigungsminister Strauss, 16 October 1959, PA/AA, B1/56; François Seydoux de Clausonne, 'Das Algerienproblem', *Mitteilungen für die Deutsch-Französischen Gesellschaften* 7 (January 1960), PA/AA, B1/56.

an information tour, including twelve German mayors.[108] Their reactions were deemed so favourable that authorities in Algeria organised two further tours in February and October 1960, this time exclusively for German mayors.[109]

By and large, however, the French propaganda offensive achieved only marginal success in the FRG. In August 1959, the German press lambasted Debré's speech at l'île Bouchard in which the premier had demanded Western solidarity and support in the Algerian question.[110] Returning from his summit meeting with de Gaulle in December 1959, Adenauer continued to deplore the German press's attitude towards France, which he claimed jeopardised the Franco-German rapprochement.[111] In February 1960, a French diplomat told Paul Frank that French opinion considered the chancellor the sole supporter of Franco-German reconciliation while 'the vast majority of Germans was hostile towards France'. This hostility, the diplomat warned, could drastically alter Paris's attitude in the Berlin crisis. With German journalists increasingly accusing Adenauer of '*Nibelungentreue*' vis-à-vis de Gaulle, Frank conceded that Bonn's policies towards France 'lacked the necessary public support', especially when it came to Algeria.[112]

Humanitarian aid

In contrast to the Adenauer government, then, West German public opinion overwhelmingly rejected the notion of *l'Algérie française*. As seen in Chapter 4, disapproval of the French counterinsurgency ran so deeply among certain sections of civil society that some individuals and groups had begun to support the FLN beyond the realm of propaganda. After the May crisis of 1958, this trend merely accelerated. The Franco-Algerian battle for hearts and minds yielded in victory for the FLN, whose aim was always to mobilise moral as well as material and financial support. The movement succeeded in turning sympathy into solidarity, words into actions. The feat was all the more important as it helped safeguard

108 'Dr. Roser berichtet über seine Reise nach Algerien', *Stuttgarter Nachrichten*, 8 July 1959; Dépêche no. 443 du vice-consul René Eschemann, Düsseldorf, 31 July 1959, MAE, MLA/3.

109 Télégramme no. 2 du consul-général Philippe Kœnig, Sarrebruck, 3 March 1960; Télégramme no. 920 de Seydoux, 4 March 1960, MAE, MLA/5; Schreiben, Generalkonsul Nostitz, Algiers, 17 November 1960, PA/AA, B25/2.

110 Télégrammes nos. 2235 et 2298 de Leduc, Bonn, 19 August and 21 August 1959, MAE, AL/ALG/39.

111 Reinhard Schiffers (ed.), *Die CDU/CSU-Fraktion im Deutschen Bundestag. Sitzungsprotokolle 1957–1961* (Düsseldorf 2004), 170. Sitzung, 8 December 1959.

112 Vermerk, Referat 204/205 (Frank), 8 February 1960, PA/AA, B24/352/F2.

the Algerians' sanctuary in the FRG. While Werner Balsen and Karl Rössel argued that pro-Algerian civic engagement constituted West Germany's 'first internationalist solidarity movement after the war', Leggewie considered it the 'primordial, first stratum of the 60s protest movements' that helped 'de-provincialize' the Bonn Republic. Christoph Kalter, too, stresses the continuities between the FLN's German allies and the 'transnational avant-garde and revolutionary New Left' of the 1960s.[113] Leftist-progressivist groups did indeed play a leading role in organising pro-Algerian solidarity campaigns, especially those of the younger generation, yet they were not the sole font of West German civic engagement during the Algerian war. When it came to humanitarian action, those helping the FLN spanned political divides. United by an internationalist and humanitarian outlook that stressed the importance of compassion and benevolence as the driving forces of West German foreign policy, a diverse group of social actors came to champion aid to Algerians. These actors drew on the motto that the Bonn Republic was itself a nation composed of wartime refugees, one that after the defeat of Nazism and during the Occupation had benefited against all odds from others' generosity, in particular from Marshall aid. With their country returning to prosperity and international legitimacy, the time had come for West Germans to help others. One way to do so was by relieving the plight of Algerian civilians, especially the 200,000 to 300,000 refugees based in Tunisia and Morocco.

French complaints over the humanitarian aid efforts of German civil-society actors were frequent, unrelenting, and generally in vain. More often than not, the authorities lacked the legal and political means to prevent German citizens from engaging in international humanitarian relief efforts, though this did not prevent the Bonn government from seeking to influence their behaviour. On advice of the *Auswärtige Amt*, the DRK, for instance, never responded to the Algerian Red Crescent's first appeal for aid in February 1957. Considering its overt links to the FLN, German diplomats doubted the CRA's political neutrality.[114] The ICRC had not recognised the CRA as a national Red Crescent society, though it did send large-scale relief supplies to the refugee camps in Morocco and Tunisia as well as resettlement centres in Algeria.[115] The DRK contributed to these efforts, though its early donations remained small. In addition to the grant

[113] Balsen and Rössel, *Hoch*, p. 14; Leggewie, *Kofferträger*, p. 10; Leggewie, 'Kofferträger', p. 169; Christoph Kalter, 'Das Eigene im Fremden: Der Algerienkrieg und die Anfänge der Neuen Linken in der Bundesrepublik', *Zeitschrift für Geschichtswissenschaft* 55/2 (2007), p. 145.

[114] Lettre du président du CRA au président de la Croix Rouge Allemande, 2 February 1957; Schreiben, AA an DRK, 2 March 1957, PA/AA, B25/9.

[115] Klose, *Menschenrechte*, pp. 156, 165.

of 100,000DM in late 1957, the society in March 1958 had sent one delegate to help coordinate ICRC efforts in Morocco. The DRK had also lent one lorry to the Moroccan Red Crescent to facilitate the delivery of supplies.[116] Reliant on financial subsidies from the federal authorities for its international activities,[117] the DRK could not significantly augment its contributions to the ICRC's work in North Africa until attitudes in Bonn began to shift on the matter of humanitarian aid. From Tunis, Werner Gregor noted in November 1958 how regrettable it was that the DRK could not do more for Algerian refugees. The ambassador believed that lack of humanitarian engagement on the part of the DRK fuelled communist (especially East German) propaganda and weakened the Bonn Republic's reputation in the Arab world.[118]

Gregor was right to be concerned, for humanitarian aid had indeed become highly politicised in the context of the Algerian war. The FLN deliberately used the CRA and its relief work to broaden the movement's international appeal by fostering a humanitarian image of the FLN.[119] French authorities, meanwhile, rejected even the ICRC's efforts on behalf of Algerian refugees, who, as French citizens, remained their sole responsibility. They argued that humanitarian donations benefited the ALN rather than Algerian refugees. To complicate matters further, both the United States and the Soviet bloc used humanitarian aid to win over allies in the Third World.[120] So did the GDR, which continued to deliver aid shipments to North Africa through the intermediary of its Red Cross society and Free Trade Union Federation (FDGB). Far from being entirely altruistic, East Berlin deliberately deployed health care and humanitarianism to advance its national interest of diplomatic recognition.[121] According to the regime's official mouthpiece, *Neues Deutschland*, 562,000 eastmarks in medicines, surgical equipment, blankets and other supplies had been sent to Algerian refugee camps in February 1958. CRA statistics indicate that these donations were followed up by four additional shipments in June and July, which goes some way to corroborate SDECE

116 DRK Jahresbericht (Bonn, 1958), p.12, ADRK.
117 Schreiben, DRK Präsident Weitz an Bundesaussenminister Brentano, 24 February 1958, ADRK, DRK/5173/F1.
118 Schreiben, Botschaft Tunis an AA, 18 November 1958, PA/AA, B25/14.
119 Onyedum, 'Humanize', pp. 714, 719, 721. 120 Connelly, *Diplomatic Revolution*, p. 140.
121 Young-sun Hong, '"The Benefits of Health Must Spread Among All": International Solidarity, Health and Race in the East German Encounter with the Third World', in *Socialist Modern: East German Everyday Culture and Politics* (eds.) Katherine Pence and Paul Betts (Ann Arbor MI, 2008), pp. 183–210; Ibid., *Cold War Germany*.

estimates that East German contributions amounted to roughly 800,000 east-marks in 1958.[122]

Thus when the CRA repeated its request for West German aid in December 1958, the *Auswärtige Amt*'s reticence had markedly declined. By January 1959, the *Amt* encouraged the DRK to augment its contributions to the ICRC's North African relief efforts, and contributed 10,000DM from its own aid budget while insisting this donation remain anonymous so as not to upset the French government.[123] Upon returning from their visit to refugee camps in Tunisia and Morocco in early 1959, Kalbitzer and Blachstein, too, urged the DRK to intensify its relief efforts.[124] In the context of the UN's World Refugee Year of 1959–1960, these appeals fell on much more receptive ears. On 3 June 1959, DRK President Heinrich Weitz urged Foreign Minister Brentano to donate at least another 100,000DM in federal assistance. In his appeal, Weitz echoed Blachstein's claim that Algerians were increasingly critical of the fact 'that countries like Sweden, Egypt and especially the so-called GDR have continuously provided extraordinary levels of aid while the West German Red Cross's help has remained relatively low'. Even ICRC officials had admitted to Blachstein how 'the aid provided by the DRK by no means compared to donations from the GDR and that one had expected more from the Federal Republic given its "economic miracle"'.[125]

With the rhythm of East German deliveries remaining unchanged – between January and March 1959 the regime had sent 50,000kg in material aid – the *Amt* was inclined to support Weitz's request for financial assistance, hoping that this way, 'Arab states would be pacified [over] our supposed [...] support to France in the Algerian war'. Humanitarian aid, Wilfried Sarrazin of the *Amt* argued, 'would wrest a significant propaganda instrument from the Soviet zone'.[126] Channelling it through the DRK, meanwhile, would 'guarantee [the aid's] neutral and purely humanitarian character'.[127] If Sarrazin thought this would prevent the French from objecting, he was wrong. In August, Henri Langlais demanded the *Amt*

[122] Liste des dons par la Croix Rouge de la RDA, 18 October 1958, AdsD, NL/Plum/25; Notice d'information no. 17566/SDECE, 26 March 1959, MAE, AL/ALG/22.

[123] Lettre par Mostafa Benbahmed, vice-président du CRA, à Heinrich Weitz, président de la DRK, 7 December 1958; Vermerk, Referat 204/205 (Frank), 14 January 1959, PA/AA, B25/9.

[124] Peter Blachstein, 'Kennt Europa noch Solidarität?' *SPD-Pressedienst* 13 April 1959; Brief Kalbitzer an DRK, 6 March 1959, AdsD, NL/Blachstein/32.

[125] Schreiben, Weitz an Brentano, 3 June 1959, AdsD, NL/Blachstein/32.

[126] Vermerk, Sarrazin, Referat 205, an Referat 712, 10 June 1959, PA/AA, B25/12; Liste des dons, par pays, depuis janvier 1959, CRA, 23 March 1959, AdsD, NL/Plum/25.

[127] Vermerk, Sarrazin, Referat 205, 13 June 1959, PA/AA, B25/9.

refrain from financial contributions to the ICRC via the DRK on the grounds that Paris planned to shoulder the full cost of the ICRC's relief work in North Africa.[128] The *Quai d'Orsay* further alleged that the lorry lent by the DRK to the Moroccan Red Crescent in fact served to transport arms to an ALN base at Oujda, a charge that was proved false only after a lengthy international investigation.[129] With even humanitarian aid rousing French misgivings, Brentano remained hesitant to release the requested 100,000DM. This prompted Blachstein to appeal to the foreign minister in November 1959 to renew financial support for the DRK.[130]

In spite of accusations of neglecting its duty of humanitarianism and growing unease over East Berlin's relief efforts, solidarity with France prevented the Bonn government from extending assistance to Algerian refugees. Where official aid remained dormant, however, non-governmental organisations and civil society stepped in to fill the gap. Even the DRK had turned to private donors to assist the relief efforts being spearheaded by the ICRC and League of Red Cross Societies. By September 1959, it had raised 115,000DM worth in aid for refugees in Morocco.[131] It was the churches, however, that ultimately led the way in the provision of humanitarian aid. During World Refugee Year, they organised fundraising events in virtually every parish, including in the GDR. Over the Easter holiday in 1959, the Catholic Church's freshly inaugurated *Misereor* programme against world hunger raised a staggering 35 million DM. The Protestant Church, meanwhile, launched an analogous programme, 'Bread for the World', which raised its first 19 million DM over the 1959 Christmas holidays, including over 4.7 million DM in the GDR.[132] At a time when church attendance was high, the fundraising efforts by the Catholic and Protestant churches became a hugely successful and fixed feature of West German humanitarian and development aid in the Third World.[133] Generalist and global in reach, the annual fundraisers organised through *Misereor* and 'Bread for the World' never singled out individual benefactors. The funds collected went to

[128] Vermerk, Frank, Referat 205, 11 August 1959, PA/AA, B25/9.

[129] Note de l'ambassade de France à Bonn, 10 July 1959; Schreiben Nr. 296 der Botschaft Rabat, 28 August 1959; Brief, DRK an AA, 9 September 1959; Brief, DRK an AA, 14 October 1959; Brief, ICRC an DRK 12 October 1959, PA/AA, B25/71.

[130] Brief Blachstein an Brentano, 21 November 1959, AdsD, NL/Blachstein/32.

[131] 'Kreuzfahrt durch die Wüste. Deutscher Delegierter unterstützt Hilfsaktion für algerische Flüchtlinge in Marokko', *Deutsches Rotes Kreuz* 9 (September 1959), p. 5.

[132] Karl Osner, *Kirchen und Entwicklungshilfe. Ziele, Leistungen und Arbeitsweise kirchlicher Organisationen in Deutschland* (Kevelaer, 1965), p. 34.

[133] Bastian Hein, *Die Westdeutschen und die Dritte Welt. Entwicklungspolitik und Entwicklungsdienste zwischen Reform und Revolte 1959–1974* (München, 2006), pp. 60–1.

numerous causes and campaigns, including Algerian refugees. Thus in late 1959, *Misereor* set aside an initial 30,000DM to pay for the room and board of fifty Algerian orphans in Tunisia. To the Catholic Church, the initiative represented a test case. More importantly, it was an opportunity for German Christians to demonstrate solidarity not only with the episcopacy in France and North Africa, many of whose members opposed the French war effort in Algeria, but also with a Muslim people.[134] The Protestant Church thought similarly. By February 1960, 'Bread for the World' donations had raised approximately 200,000DM for foodstuffs, textiles and other supplies for Algerian refugees; six months later, the programme had collected another 500,000DM to go towards meals and blankets specifically for Algerian children.[135] The *Auswärtige Amt* encouraged such non-governmental engagement, commenting in April 1960 that it 'welcomed every [private] donation' so long as it was channelled through the ICRC or UN High Commission for Refugees (UNHCR) whilst indicating West Germany as donor country.[136]

By then, West German civil-society actors had inaugurated a number of campaigns geared specifically towards Algerian refugees. Again under the auspices of World Refugee Year, the Red Cross Youth in April 1959 had launched a year-long, nation-wide fundraiser to raise funds for the purchase of condensed milk for Algerian children. This "Milk Bottle campaign" was backed by the Federal Youth Council, whose chairman, the social-democrat Heinz Westphal, was a strong advocate of Third World engagement.[137] The action found a 'surprising echo' even by the DRK's expectations. By December 1959, the campaign had raised over 90,000DM, mostly through pennies donated by schoolchildren. Total donations eventually amounted to 175,000DM.[138] In a letter to Blachstein in August 1960, whose personal interventions had produced a sextupling of contributions in Hamburg since December 1959, Youth Secretary Fehr explained the donations had enabled the DRK to send 216,000 cans of condensed milk to Tunisia and Morocco, corresponding to

[134] Heime für algerische Flüchtlingskinder in Tunesien und Marokko, undated (1959), Archiv des Deutschen Caritasverbandes e.V. (ADCV), Freiburg, Zentralarchiv (ZA)/116 + 187 I/Fasz.01.

[135] Liste der Algerien-Nothilfe, I. Afrika, Algerien, undated, Archiv des Evangelischen Werks für Diakonie und Entwicklung (AEWDE), Berlin, Brot für die Welt (BfdW)/P315.

[136] Vermerk, Referat 205 an Referat 410, 6 April 1960, PA/AA, B25/68.

[137] 'Algerische Jugend bittet um Hilfe', *Bonner Rundschau*, 26 June 1959; Heinz Westphal, *Jugend braucht Demokratie. Demokratie braucht Jugend. Mein jugend-politisches Engagement 1945–1974* (Rostock, 1994), pp. 124, 128.

[138] DRK Jahresbericht (Bonn, 1959), p. 76; DRK Jahresbericht (Bonn, 1960), p. 54, ADRK.

648,000 rations, with another 30,000 to 40,000 cans on the way. Owing to its private fundraising efforts, the DRK had also been able to donate a further 30,000DM to the ICRC to support that organisation's relief work in the Maghreb.[139]

While the Red Cross Youth's 'Milk Bottle' campaign targeted school children, university students instigated a fundraising campaign to help support the beleaguered UGEMA. The socialist SDS is often credited with being the only West German student association to take an interest in decolonisation during the 1950s.[140] In fact, it was the politically neutral VdS that took the lead in organising this campaign following the April 1958 Special International Conference of National Unions of Students, which had been organised in London to condemn UGEMA's forced dissolution. The VdS conducted its aid effort under the auspices of COSEC, which coordinated an international campaign to help Algerian students. In June 1958, COSEC appealed to its national members 'to make available either office equipment to enable UGEMA to resume its normal activities' or, where possible, 'to provide either medical supplies, food or other items [. . .] for transfer to UGEMA and distribution to Algerian students' in the Maghreb.[141] Endorsing this initiative at its 10th annual congress, the VdS contacted UGEMA on 3 July 1958 requesting advice on how best to help.[142] The Algerian union responded by inviting VdS chairman Lenhard Holschuh to attend the first congress of North African student associations, which convened in Tunis from 20 to 23 August. Returning from Tunisia, where he had toured refugee camps, Holschuh urged the VdS to assist the Algerians, appalled by the 'indifference with which the [West] German authorities [have] treated this issue'. He was motivated by more than humanitarian concern, having observed first-hand the heavy presence in Tunis of the Prague-based International Union of Students. Holschuh feared UGEMA might gravitate towards the communist camp if unions in the West did not do more to help.[143]

Roused into action by a mixture of international solidarity, social conscience and Cold War competition, the VdS appealed for donations not only from its member unions, comprising around 200,000 students, but

[139] Brief, Fehr, Jugendrotkreuz, an Blachstein, 16 December 1959, AdsD, NL/Blachstein/32; Brief, Fehr an Blachstein, 16 August 1960, NL/Blachstein/33.

[140] Weitbrecht, *Aufbruch*, p. 15.

[141] COSEC circular no. 49/265/2, 16 June 1958; COSEC circulars no. 41/265/1 and 42/265/1, 13 May 1958, BA/K, B166/1414.

[142] Brief Holschuh an UGEMA, Tunis, 3 July 1959, BA/K, B166/1414; 'Hilfe für algerische Studenten. Deutsche Kommilitonen wollen dem Sog aus dem Osten begegnen', *Die Welt* 18 August 1958.

[143] Reisebericht, Holschuh, undated, BA/K, B166/1414.

also from a range of West German businesses. The results achieved were meagre compared to those of the churches or Red Cross Youth. Over the coming months, the association received contributions ranging from 40 cutlery sets, 61kg of milk powder and an undisclosed quantity of vitamin pills, to stationery, office supplies and financial donations.[144] By April 1959, the VdS had raised just over 5,000DM in material donations, at which point the association decided to concentrate its efforts primarily on fundraising.[145] The West German section of the World University Service fared only marginally better. By April 1960, it had raised 11,876DM in funds and material aid for Algerian refugees.[146] Meanwhile, a small group of students and *Jusos* volunteered for a COSEC-backed project that united students from fifty-four nations to assist in the rebuilding of the school destroyed by the Sakiet air strike.[147] The students' participation prompted a French complaint with the *Auswärtige Amt* in June 1959. Since the VdS received government subsidies, French diplomats argued, federal authorities should exert greater control over the association's activities, which were inimical to France. The VdS rejected this accusation, pointing out that it coordinated its initiatives not just with COSEC but also with the National Union of French Students, which itself strove to help Algerian students. Alluding to the Cold War competition over the Third World, the VdS defended the students' right to participate in voluntary humanitarian relief work as a legitimate and respectable expression of international solidarity. Considering Germany's recent past, the association argued, the FRG's presence in the world had to be a force for good.[148]

144 Notiz, VdS, 19 January1959; Dankschreiben Holschuh an Deutsche AG für Nestle Erzeugnisse, 11 December 1958; Schreiben Holschuh an Bayern AG, 18 November 1958; Dankschreiben Holschuh an Leitz Briefordnerfabrik und Firma Soennecken, 16 September and 8 September 1958; Schreiben Holschuh an Firma Beiersdorf & Co und Firma Gerlach, 24 September and 25 December 1958; Schreiben Holschuh an Axel Springer & Sohn, 23 December 1958; Allgemeiner Studentenausschuss Darmstadt an Holschuh, 10 December 1958; Dankschreiben Hoffmann an Studentenschaften Köln und Göttingen, 16 September and 26 September 1958; Schreiben Allgemeiner Studentenausschuss Berlin an Holschuh, 8 September 1958, BA/K, B166/1414.

145 Vermerk, Referat 604 an Referat 204, 16 March 1959, PA/AA, B25/12; Aktennotiz, Hoffmann, 8 May 1959, BA/K, B166/1414.

146 Working Paper D/8, 9th International Student Conference, Klosters, Switzerland, 21–30 August 1960, BA/K, B166/1418.

147 COSEC, 'The Sakiet Work Camp – a story of international student solidarity', Supplement, *Information Bulletin*, October 1959, www.gaudeamus.com/SAKIET/SAKIET.BROCHURE.pdf (accessed 12 November 2013).

148 Vermerk, Sarrazin, Referat 204/205, 18 June 1959; Schreiben AA an VdS, 23 June 1959; Schreiben VdS an AA, 6 July 1959; Aufzeichnung, Referat 204/205, 20 July 1959, PA/AA, B25/39.

These same arguments also underpinned the humanitarian relief efforts of West German workers' organisations, many of which considered socialist internationalism an integral part of their identity. Under the instigation of Werner Thönnessen, personal assistant to union boss Otto Brenner (and PhD candidate under Theodor Adorno), the IGM organised a first collection on behalf of Algerian refugees in the spring of 1959, raising 10,000DM. The Metalworkers' Union used these funds to purchase a Volkswagen van, food staples and blankets, which it donated to the Algerian trade union federation UGTA in Tunis. Later that year, the Trade Union of Public Transport Workers gave 10,000DM towards the Red Cross Youth's 'Milk Bottle' campaign.[149] The Workers' Welfare Association (*Arbeiterwohlfahrt*, AWO), too, organised charitable collections. In July 1959, it donated twenty large boxes of clothing and soap to UGTA.[150] The association further supported a project headed by UGTA to build a children's home and training centre in La Marsa, Tunisia, named after the Algerian federation's first Secretary General Aïssat Idir, whose mysterious death in July 1959 after years of incarceration in the notorious French military camp of Birtraria had sparked international condemnation among trade union circles.[151] By March 1960, the *Arbeiterwohlfahrt* had set aside 20,000DM towards the project and hoped to raise more funds still.[152]

Mostly though, West German workers' organisations focused on assisting Algerian refugees and labourers in West Germany rather than those based in the Maghreb. After all, the Algerians arriving in German cities from late 1958 were in dire need of social assistance. Many spent their first days or weeks living on the streets and avoiding the authorities. Their first point of contact with German welfare services was often the *Arbeiterwohlfahrt*, which provided them with temporary shelter and daily meals.[153] Local AWO branches, however, often lacked the resources to help all of the arriving refugees. To contain a growing social problem and alleviate the Algerians' plight, some city officials, social workers and activists came together on an ad

149 Schreiben, Thönnessen an Blachstein, 5 June 1959; Brief, Fehr, Jugendrotkreuz, an Blachstein, 16 December 1959, AdsD, NL/Blachstein/32.

150 Schreiben, Arbeiterwohlfahrt an UGTA Tunis, 31 July 1959, AdsD, NL/Blachstein/32.

151 Mathilde von Bülow, 'Irving Brown and ICFTU Labor Diplomacy during Algeria's Struggle for Independence (1954–1962)', in *American Labor's Global Ambassadors: The International History of the AFL-CIO during the Cold War* (eds.) Geert van Goethem and Robert A. Waters Jr. (Basingstoke, 2013), pp. 225–6.

152 Schreiben, Arbeiterwohlfahrt an Blachstein, 23 March 1960, AdsD, NL/Blachstein/33; Scheffler, *SPD*, p. 67.

153 Fritz Henker, 'Algerische Arbeiter in der Bundesrepublik', *Zeitschrift für Kulturaustausch* 20/2 (1970), p. 234

hoc basis to form so-called *Hilfskomitees*, or relief committees. The earliest and largest of these committees operated in Stuttgart under the direction of Fritz Henker, Fritz Lamm, Louis Pilz and Kurt Schwab, local functionaries in the West German Confederation of Trade Unions (*Deutscher Gewerkschaftsbund*, DGB).[154] Another committee, founded in Frankfurt/Main in January 1959, operated under Thönnessen. Blachstein, meanwhile, played an instrumental role in the creation of a *Hilfskomitee* in Hamburg, although DGB functionary Manfred Elsner handled its day-to-day business.[155] By late 1960, *Hilfskomitees* for Algerian refugees had formed in Hanover, Dortmund, Essen, Cologne, Mannheim/Heidelberg, Karlsruhe, Ludwigsburg, Esslingen, Singen, Nuremberg and Ulm – key centres of Algerian migration. Apart from trade unionists, committee members included not only officials from other local branches of workers' or leftist associations, such as the *Arbeiterwohlfahrt, Naturfreunde*, or SPD, but also members of the much larger Christian welfare providers, such as the Protestant Church's *Innere Mission* and the Catholic *Caritasverband*.[156] The archbishop of Freiburg, Hermann Schäufele, admonished German Catholics to 'integrate the Algerians coming to Germany in a brotherly manner, assist them in their adaptation to German conditions [. . .] and bring them into contact with Catholic organisations and parishes so that they will not isolate themselves, but rather use their time in Europe for their personal, cultural and professional development'.[157]

Based entirely on private initiatives and personal contacts, the *Hilfskomitees* provided emergency funds and helped organise shelter and employment for Algerian refugees. They acted as intermediaries with the authorities to help secure residence and work permits (the 'tolerance papers' and 'blue cards' discussed in the previous chapter), and even provided legal council to those who ran into trouble with the law. In this respect, the committees resembled the *Comité pour la paix en Algérie*, which had fulfilled a similar function in Belgium since April 1958.[158] Unlike the

[154] Leggewie, *Kofferträger*, pp. 170–8.

[155] Bericht, Thönnessen, über die Tätigkeit des Frankfurter Hilfskomitees für algerische Flüchtlinge im Jahre 1959; Bericht, Elsner, über die Lage der Algerier in Hamburg, 1959, AdsD, NL/Blachstein/33.

[156] Henker, 'Arbeiter', p. 234; 'Entretiens avec Keramane', in Bougherara, *Rapports*, p. 210; Haroun, *Septième wilaya*, pp. 135–6; 'Verwirklichte Solidarität: Aus der Arbeit eines Hilfskomitees für algerische Flüchtlinge in der Bundesrepublik', *Freies Algerien* 4/1–2 (1961), p. 8.

[157] Die Kirche und die algerischen Flüchtlinge in Deutschland, 14 December 1960, ADCV, Auslandsabteilung (AA)/187 I + 195(65)/Fasz.07.

[158] Masset, *Affaire intérieure*, pp. 151–2.

Belgian committee, however, the *Hilfskomitees* limited their field of action exclusively to social welfare. They maintained low profiles, avoiding political statements. Only one exception proved the rule: namely, the 'Committee for a Free Algeria' founded on 24 September 1960 in Saarbrücken by Friedrich Regitz, deputy head of the Saarland SPD, and Oskar Detemple, secretary general of the Saarland DGB. In contrast to other *Hilfskomitees*, the Saarbrücken committee conceived of its remit in political terms, hence its name.[159] French opposition was swift and vehement, with complaints launched simultaneously with the Saarland's Minister-President Franz-Josef Röder (CDU) and Interior Minister Kurt Conrad (SPD), the *Auswärtige Amt* and SPD executive.[160] Due to the French authorities' allegations that the committee sponsored FLN terrorism, it even came under scrutiny from Prosecutor-General Güde.[161] Pressured by his party and by the authorities, Regitz soon promised to limit activities to the realm of social welfare.[162] The committee thus never became the hotbed of political activism it set out to be.

Although all of the *Hilfskomitees* thus ultimately restricted their activity to the realm of social welfare, they did cooperate closely with the FLN's representatives in West Germany. Since few Algerians spoke German and many Germans equally spoke no French, let alone Arabic or Kabyle, the committees sought out the FLN's assistance to facilitate communication with the arriving refugees. According to Thönnessen, they also relied upon the FLN's representatives to ensure that Algerians requesting support from the committees were neither delinquent nor 'political suspect'. This demonstrates the extent to which Germans had come to perceive the FLN – not the French (or the MNA) – as the legitimate representative of the Algerian people. To facilitate this process, the FLN bureau in Bonn appointed representatives to act as local community leaders of the Algerians and liaise with the *Hilfskomitees* on their behalf. From the committees' perspective, the FLN representatives were meant to care for the welfare of the Algerian refugees and help maintain law and order.[163]

159 'Gründung eines Komitees für ein Freies Algerien im Saarland', *DPA*, 27 September 1960.

160 Télégramme du consulat à Sarrebruck, 27 September 1960; Dépêche no.929 du consul Kœnig Sarrebruck, à l'ambassade de France à Bonn, 29 September 1960; Télégramme no.4316 de Seydoux, 6 October 1960, MAE, MLA/6; Note de l'ambassade de France à Bonn, 29 September 1960, PA/AA, B25/13.

161 Brief, BMI an AA, 12 October 1960, PA/AA, B25/13.

162 'Komitee für ein Freies Algerien erklärt sich gegen den Terrorismus', *DPA*, 4 October 1960; Dépêche no.3038 du consul Kœnig, 5 October 1960, MAE, MLA/6; Schreiben, Bundesministerium für Bund-Länder Beziehungen an AA, 2 February 1961, PA/AA, B25/13.

163 Bericht, Thönnessen, AdsD, NL/Blachstein/33.

Their role, in other words, was conceived in strictly apolitical terms. In fact, these local representatives proved vital for the creation of the '*Fédération d'Allemagne*' for they helped the FLN establish a firm hold over Algerian workers and refugees arriving in West Germany. Those deemed worthy of assistance by the FLN's representatives were thus co-opted into the movement's politico-administrative organisation.

Whether inadvertently or not, the *Hilfskomitees* facilitated the consolidation of the FLN's sanctuary in the FRG. Through the committees, militants gained access to localities for fortnightly or monthly meetings with the Algerians under their charge, such as those mentioned above that occurred in Hamburg's *Neue Gesellschaft*. According to Elsner, these meetings ostensibly served to discuss problems the Algerians faced in their daily lives, which FLN delegates would consequently relay to the *Hilfskomitees*.[164] Free from German supervision, however, the Algerians undoubtedly also deliberated questions pertaining to the FLN and its independence struggle. The meetings certainly roused the suspicions of the intelligence and security services.[165] Surveillance became such a problem at Hamburg's *Neue Gesellschaft*, for instance, that by January 1960 it was decided to congregate in the offices of the local DGB branch instead.[166] Later that year, police executed a search of the DGB's premises in Stuttgart as part of the nation-wide inquest launched by Prosecutor-General Güde. The police confiscated a number of FLN newsletters as well as other propaganda material about Algeria's independence struggle.[167]

To deflect accusations of political activism and subversion, the FLN by then had replaced its local representatives with UGTA delegates and encouraged Algerian workers in West Germany to join its affiliated union.[168] Adherence to UGTA made it possible for the FLN to maintain its hold over the Algerians while at the same time protecting the movement's cadres from the authorities. A member of the Brussels-based International Confederation of Free Trade Unions (ICFTU) since its

164 Bericht, Manfred Elsner, über die Lage der Algerier in Hamburg, 1960, AdsD, NL/Blachstein/33.

165 Synthèse mensuelle no.1498/CCFFA/2, 10 August 1960; Synthèse mensuelle no.1749/CCFFA/2, 20 September 1960, SHD-T, 10T/550*; Notice d'information no.24869/SSDNA, 10 October 1960, 10T/528/D2*.

166 Bericht, Elsner, über Algerienfragen, January 1960, AdsD, NL/Blachstein/33.

167 Schreiben, Ludwig Rosenberg, stellvertretender Vorsitzender DGB, an Vorsitzende der Gewerkschaften/Industriegewerkschaften/DGB-Landesbezirge, 17 November 1960, AdsD, 5/DGAJ/209.

168 Aktenvermerk, Klaus Wedel (Abt. Ausland), über Gespräch mit Mostefaoui, 4 August 1959, AdsD, 5/DGAZ/297.

foundation in 1957, the UGTA was an internationally recognised trade union federation and an ally of the DGB. Thus while the authorities attempted to criminalise the FLN, they tolerated the UGTA.

Although rank-and-file members of the DGB were often key animators of local *Hilfskomitees*, the confederation's directors initially regarded the UGTA with some reserve. After all, the union's founding members came from the French communist trade union confederation (*Confédération générale du travail*). Its new, young cadres, meanwhile, were 'parachuted' into the organisation by the FLN.[169] DGB leaders thus doubted their commitment to free and democratic trade unionism. The UGTA's unabashed acceptance of aid from affiliates of the communist World Federation of Trade Unions raised these misgivings further. West German union leaders particularly resented the UGTA's close ties to the FDGB, which played a leading role in coordinating East German aid for Algerians. Unlike local cadres, union leaders were therefore slow to assist their beleaguered associate.

In the context of the global Cold War, this inactivity on the part of the DGB's executive came to trouble even German diplomats. Alerted by its ambassador in Tunis to the close ties between the UGTA and FDGB, the *Auswärtige Amt* complained in February 1959 that the 'DGB had not yet used the weight of its six million members to immunise [North African trade unions] against relations with Eastern trade unions through positive contributions' in the domain of labour internationalism. The *Amt* suggested the DGB take as its 'role model' the American Federation of Labor-Congress of Industrial Organizations, whose close relationship to North African and sub-Saharan labour organisations had helped further American official interests.[170] Though the DGB would 'need to be considerate of French sensitivities' in its dealings with the UGTA, Paul Frank believed that the confederation 'could achieve positive results' in securing West German interests in North Africa in a way the Bonn government could not.[171] Blachstein shared this belief. In June 1959, he urged DGB President Willi Richter to invite UGTA delegates to the confederation's upcoming fifth congress. Unlike Frank, however, the deputy felt consideration for French sensitivities was 'futile and politically obtuse'. In his opinion, Germans 'should not be complicit in a development that caused North African trade unions to drift towards the East's forced labour unions

169 Meynier, *Histoire*, p. 524.

170 Aufzeichnung, Referat 205, 12 February 1959; Schreiben von Botschafter Gregor, Tunis, 27 January 1959, PA/AA, B25/4. On the AFL-CIO, see: Bülow, 'Brown', pp. 217–36.

171 Aufzeichnung, Frank, Referat 205, 20 February 1959, PA/AA, B25/4.

against their own will'.[172] The ICFTU's Secretary General Jacobus Oldenbroek offered similar advice. 'Despite and then again precisely because of certain reservations vis-à-vis the "young people" that had succeeded the arrested older, experienced trade unionists (their voyages to communist-ruled states, acceptance of Soviet-zonal financial and material assistance)', Oldenbroek supported the idea of inviting UGTA delegates to the DGB's congress.[173]

Faced with these pressures, DGB leaders struck up what became a close relationship to UGTA's chief delegate, Ahmed Mostefaoui, who had arrived in Düsseldorf in May 1959.[174] At the DGB's congress in Stuttgart from 7 to 12 September, Mostefaoui appealed to the assembled delegates to support the work of the *Hilfskomitees*, whose efforts proved vital in enabling Algerian workers to escape discrimination and repression in France, a motion the congress accepted.[175] Even so, Algerians continued to face considerable hurdles in their day-to-day existence in the FRG. As numerous reports by Mostefaoui, Thönnessen and Henker make clear, many Algerians struggled to secure residence and work permits. Local authorities for the most part continued to insist on their possession of a French passport even though the regulations introduced by Bonn's Interior Ministry in November 1958 had rendered this requirement obsolete. Local authorities evidently applied some discretion in their application of federal regulations. In many cases, the police threatened the Algerians with expulsion if they failed to procure valid IDs from French consular authorities.[176] To Blachstein, this practice was both 'morally and politically unacceptable'. In a letter addressed both to Hesse's Minister-President Georg Zinn (SPD) and to the mayor of Frankfurt/Main Werner Bockelmann (SPD) in February 1960, Blachstein protested that one 'could impossibly demand of refugees to get themselves legitimated by their persecutors'.[177] Some months earlier, the deputy had urged Walter Menzel, chair of the SPD's *Bundestag* faction, to raise the issue of political asylum in parliament. Out of deference to France, the SPD's leaders

[172] Schreiben, Blachstein an Richter, 8 June 1959, AdsD, 5/DGAJ/209.

[173] Notiz für Kollegen Willi Richter, 4 August 1959, AdsD, 5/DGAJ/209.

[174] Haroun, *Septième wilaya*, p. 136.

[175] Vertreter, UGTA, an Delegierten des 5. Ordentlichen Bundeskongresses des DGB, September 1959, AdsD, 5/DGAJ/209; Scheffler, *SPD*, pp. 68–9.

[176] Schreiben, Henker an Wischnewski, 22 October 1959, AdsD, NL/Blachstein/32; Bericht, Thönnessen; Bericht, Elsner, January 1960, AdsD, NL/Blachstein/33; Bericht, Mostfaoui, über algerische Arbeiter in der BRD, 16 November 1960, 5/DGAJ/209; Bericht, Elsner, Algerienfragen, Mai-Sept.1960, 5/DGAZ/297.

[177] Brief, Blachstein an Zinn und Bockelmann, 4 February 1960, AdsD, NL/Blachstein/33.

continued to reign in the 'Algeria lobby'. Menzel responded that it was better to help the Algerians 'privately' than to turn their plight into a political problem.[178]

If the precariousness of their legal status represented an ongoing worry for Algerians, it was not their only problem. Even those who managed to secure residence and work permits found it difficult to integrate into West German society. Reporting to the DGB in August and November 1959, Mostefaoui highlighted some of the challenges these individuals faced: of the 2,000-odd Algerians registered by the authorities in the FRG, roughly 70 to 80 per cent were functionally illiterate; 70 per cent were unskilled labourers; and only 1 per cent skilled craftsmen. These circumstances alone made it difficult to integrate the Algerians into the highly skilled German labour market. Even those possessing a learned profession faced an intractable language barrier.[179] Elsner's reports from Hamburg alluded to other problems. On account of their poverty, for instance, Algerian workers often shared cramped, unhygienic and unheated accommodation; many lacked the funds to purchase clothing and shoes suitable for the northern German weather. So scarce were their resources that many suffered from malnutrition and other ailments, particularly tuberculosis.[180] As Harbi remembers, relying on the 'culinary art' of food banks and cafeterias proved a 'hell' of its own for his Muslim compatriots, since the staple of German cooking was pork.[181] North African labour expert Werner Plum, meanwhile, considered racism the single largest hurdle for Algerians. A decade after the end of World War II, racial prejudices continued to determine West German responses to migrant communities.[182] Plum wanted German society to show more tolerance and acceptance for the manifold difficulties that shaped Algerians' behaviour, especially the decades of colonial repression under which they had lived.[183]

To overcome these hurdles, the *Hilfskomitees* by mid-1959 had begun to supplement their social welfare activities with language classes designed to help Algerians integrate into German society and working environments.[184]

178 Brief, Blachstein an Menzel, 14 September 1959; Brief, Menzel an Blachstein, 28 September 1959, AdsD, NL/Blachstein/32.

179 Bericht, Mostefaoui, 11 November 1959, AdsD, 5/DGAJ/209; Aktennotiz, Wedel, 4 August 1959, 5/DGAZ/297.

180 Berichte, Elsner, January–February 1960, AdsD, NL/Blachstein/33.

181 Harbi, *Vie debout*, p. 232. 182 Clarkson, *Fragmented Fatherland*, p. 20.

183 Plum, Aufsatz über die algerische Einwanderung in Deutschland, undated, AdsD, NL/Plum/25; Plum, 'Algeriche Arbeiter in der Bundesrepublik', *Gewerkschaftliche Monatshefte* 11/8 (1960), pp. 469–70.

184 Bericht, Thönnessen, AdsD, NL/Blachstein/33.

The results achieved were not always positive. In Hamburg, the DGB by February 1960 had cancelled its first attempt at weekly evening class for Algerians, who due to shift work were often unable to attend. The teacher, too, had struggled, since some students only spoke Arabic or Kabyle while he only spoke French.[185] The *Hilfskomitees* persisted in their efforts, however. Mostefaoui considered language tuition so essential that he encouraged the DGB to enlist the support of local Goethe Institutes and other organisations specialising in adult education or international outreach.[186] In November 1959, he suggested supplementing language classes with lessons in German 'social norms' and the rudiments of Western trade unionism and called on the DGB also to provide vocational training. Such training, Mostefaoui argued, fell 'under the remit of the [government's] technical aid programme for underdeveloped countries'.[187]

Development aid

What had begun as a practical measure to help Algerians adjust to life in the FRG thus took on a much broader political meaning. After all, Mostefaoui demanded recognition of the Algerians as legitimate recipients of one of the federal government's earliest forms of bilateral development aid, one reserved for the newly independent states of the Third World.[188] Mostefaoui's argument rested on the premise that Algeria's independence was merely a question of time and that any assistance provided now represented an investment in the country's future. His demands were not new, for they had become commonplace in the FLN's strategy of rallying international support and underpinned much of the labour and student diplomacy pursued by the movement's auxiliaries, UGTA and UGEMA. The latter, in particular, campaigned for university placements to absorb some of the 1,800-odd students whose existence in France and Algeria had become precarious since the French ban on the UGEMA.[189] At his first and only press conference in Hamburg in September 1958, Aït Ahcène, too, had appealed for assistance in educating the future leaders of an independent Algeria. In an effort to demonstrate foresight and plan ahead, the GPRA

185 Bericht, Elsner, undated and February 1960, AdsD, NL/Blachstein/33.
186 Aktennotiz, Wedel, 4 August 1959, AdsD, 5/DGAZ/297.
187 Bericht, Mostefaoui, 16 November 1959, AdsD, 5/DGAJ/209.
188 Hein, *Entwicklungspolitik*, p. 36; Heide-Irene Schmidt, 'Pushed to the Front: The Foreign Assistance Policy of the Federal Republic of Germany, 1958–1971', *Contemporary European History* 12/4 (2003), p. 479.
189 Clement Moore and Arlie Hochschild, 'Student Unions in North African Politics', *Daedalus* 97/1 (1968), p. 27.

repeatedly called for the provision of studentships, apprenticeships and training places for Algerians who would one day have to rebuild an under-developed and war-torn country.

In West Germany, these appeals had so far achieved only meagre results. After Aït Ahcène's press conference, Kalbitzer and Blachstein had organised a campaign among Hamburg's SPD members that raised enough money for one studentship.[190] By April 1959, the two deputies had managed to secure six fully funded, four-year training placements with the Industrial Union of Construction Workers (*IG Bau-Steine-Erden*).[191] Responding to COSEC and UGEMA appeals in 1958, Holschuh, too, had attempted to secure funds for forty studentships from the *Bundesverband der deutschen Industrie* (BdI), or Federation of German Industries. If it had not been for the assassination attempt on Aït Ahcène, the VdS chairman claimed he may well have succeeded, but the BdI reneged, fearful of the fallout such aid could have on Franco-German economic relations.[192] Holschuh had also appealed to the *Auswärtige Amt*, which initially greeted the VdS's initiative.[193] However, when the French embassy warned in August 1958 that federal authorities should 'under no circumstances award scholarships to Algerian students unless these are from the contingent available to all French students', and that separate studentships for members of UGEMA 'implied [. . .] a political taking of sides', the *Amt*, too, declined its help.[194] Under no circumstances would the Bonn government sanction the use of government funds to subsidise Algerians linked to UGEMA or other FLN affiliates.

German diplomats did not, however, prevent the VdS from raising scholarships through private channels. They merely asked the association to proceed with maximum discretion and to avoid a politicisation of its efforts so as not to jeopardise the Franco-German rapprochement.[195] These instructions went also for the DGB and other non-governmental organisations helping the Algerians, especially after Verdier and Vié's secret visit to Bonn in November 1958. Both men accused Algerian students and trainees of using their German grants to pursue 'terrorist activities' against

190 Rundschreiben, Kalbitzer, an SPD Mitglieder, Hamburg, 2 September 1958; Lettre de Tewfik El-Madani, ministre des affaires culturelles du GPRA, à M. Blokchtein [sic], 5 October 1958, AdsD, NL/Blachstein/32.

191 Schreiben, Kalbitzer an Blachstein, 15 April 1959, AdsD, NL/Blachstein/32.

192 Aufzeichnung, VdS, undated, BA/K, B166/1414.

193 Vermerk, Referat 205 an Referat 604/1, 2 July 1958, PA/AA, B25/12.

194 First citation: Aufzeichnung, Referat 204, 19 August 1958, PA/AA, B25/12; second citation: Dépêche no.1456 de Seydoux, Bonn, 20 August 1958, MAE, EU/RFA/1272.

195 Aufzeichnung, Referat 204, 5 September 1958, PA/AA, B25/12.

France.[196] In a meeting in June 1959 with the DGB's Secretary for Foreign Affairs, Klaus Wedel, German diplomats encouraged the latter to intensify the confederation's support of the UGTA whilst at the same time cautioning him to limit this support strictly to trade union affairs. Under no circumstances should the DGB offer financial assistance, for instance, which, 'given the Algerian trade union's close connection with the FLN, could understandably be interpreted by France as inimical to its interests'. By contrast, the *Amt* cautiously supported the idea of trade union sponsored studentships and apprenticeships, since these constituted a practical, neutral form of development aid that would help young Algerians secure a better future for themselves and their country and would 'influence [them] in a Western sense'. The only crux was that the DGB had to 'prevent the infiltration of FLN partisans'.[197] Even in the context of development aid, therefore, policy-makers remained torn between a desire to demonstrate good faith towards Algerians and an obligation to act in solidarity with France. Adenauer's policy of *quid pro quo* precluded the release of government funds for what essentially amounted to technical development aid. Instead, the *Auswärtige Amt* encouraged private engagement in this domain, which it considered 'an act of humanitarian aid'.[198] Even then, private aid came with the strict proviso that donors and recipients refrain from political activism that could benefit the FLN.

Although some diplomats, such as Paul Frank, undoubtedly sympathised with the Algerians and felt morally obliged to help, the *Amt*'s decision to sanction the provision of privately funded technical aid rested predominantly on Cold War considerations. As Quinn Slobodian has shown, both German states had by 1958 developed an active educational strategy targeting students from the Third World. Aware that these students represented the future political and intellectual elites of their countries, educational grants aimed at convincing the recipients of the superior nature of the socialist-egalitarian or liberal-democratic models of modernity. The students' choice would not only decide the outcome of the German question one day, but 'might also determine the future of Europe', as one West German pamphlet put it in 1959.[199] With 8,522 students from developing countries enrolled in universities in the West in 1959 as opposed to 1,342 in the East, the Bonn government was clearly

[196] Niederschrift, BMI, 18 November 1958, BA/K, B106/5350.

[197] Aufzeichnung, Sarrazin, Referat 204/205, 22 June 1959, PA/AA, B25/4.

[198] Schreiben AA an Studentenschaft, Heidelberg, 26 March 1959, BA/K, B166/1414.

[199] Cited in: Quinn Slobodian, 'Bandung in Divided Germany: Managing Non-Aligned Politics in East and West, 1955–63', *Journal of Imperial and Commonwealth History* 41/4 (2013), p. 647.

the frontrunner in this campaign.[200] And yet the Algerian crisis threatened to upset this lead. Western aid to the Algerians compared poorly to the generous humanitarian assistance provided by the Sino-Soviet bloc in 1959, and West German aid paled in comparison to the GDR's. On 13 November 1958, East Berlin's Foreign Ministry had issued another press release denouncing the Bonn government for supporting France's colonial war against Algerians, especially its efforts to curtail the freedom of action of Algerian refugees. At the same time, the East German regime announced its offer of asylum, employment and education to all Algerians persecuted by the Bonn authorities.[201] The *Auswärtige Amt* sought to counter this open invitation by encouraging the provision of privately funded West German scholarships and apprenticeships. For the first time, the federal government could not and would not deploy its considerable economic and financial resources to outperform its Eastern rival.

This dilemma was evident even to those critical of Bonn's reserve vis-à-vis the Algerians in West Germany. Although individuals such as Blachstein and Thönnessen or organisations such as the VdS and DGB undeniably acted out of a sense of solidarity with the Algerians, whose colonial subjugation and humanitarian plight they genuinely deplored, not even they were immune to the Cold War logic behind the provision of educational aid. Thus in December 1959, Blachstein urged the DGB to make more paid apprenticeships available to Algerian workers. '[E]ach placement that we can create here,' the deputy reasoned, 'will relieve the overflowing refugee camps in Tunisia and Morocco and provide young people a chance at a career and a meaningful education to contribute to their country's future.' Each placement, moreover, created 'a counterbalance to schooling in Prague, Peking and Moscow'.[202] Thönnessen, too, believed the 'advance of communism in Africa can only be stopped if colonialism is ended quickly and in combination with comprehensive measures of [Western] aid'.[203] The VdS, meanwhile, lamented the fact that it had only managed to secure funds for two Algerian scholarships by the end of 1958 while East Berlin supposedly offered 150. In these circumstances, and considering the hardships of Algerian youths under French colonialism, the UGEMA was literally being 'forced to accept the offers made by the FDJ [Free German Youth] and FDGB'. To the VdS,

200 Burkhard Schade, *Das Studium im Ausland als prychologischer Prozess. Orientierungsprobleme bei Studenten aus Entwicklungsländern an deutschen Hochschulen* (Bonn, 1968), p. 25; Slobodian, 'Bandung', p. 647.
201 'Erklärung des MfAA vom 13 November 1958', in *Außenpolitik der DDR* VI, pp. 117–18.
202 Schreiben, Blachstein an Richter, 11 December 1959, AdsD, 5/DGAJ/209.
203 Bericht, Thönnessen, AdsD, NL/Blachstein/33.

this dilemma – 'for which we [West Germans] are not blameless' – created the danger that ever more Algerian students – 'who would one day play key roles in the ruling classes of their country' – would receive their education in communist countries.[204]

To counteract this danger, the VdS persisted in its efforts to raise funds for scholarships and created an Algerian solidarity fund. The association repeatedly appealed to its affiliated student unions to organise regular collections on the UGEMA's behalf. Similar requests were sent to West German industry and business.[205] Informed by the UGEMA of a continued flow of Algerians to universities in East Berlin, Leipzig and Dresden, VdS chairman Holschuh in January 1959 again solicited aid from the *Auswärtige Amt*.[206] Although official subsidies remained anathema to the *Amt*, it no longer objected to Holschuh's plans to petition the private sector for financial support. In April, deputy State Secretary Dittmann even agreed to encourage the president of the Society for Foreign Affairs to assemble a meeting of 'men of business and industry' that would constitute a suitably 'neutral framework' in which a German diplomat could rally support for the VdS's initiative.[207] It is unclear whether this meeting ever occurred, but by the end of 1960, the VdS had managed to increase the number of studentships it could offer to Algerians from two to fifty-one. The financial contributions that made this possible, however, came not from the private sector but from monthly collections and running donations among student circles.[208] These collections took time to bear fruit. In the interim, the VdS resolved at its 11th general assembly in March 1959 to host the UGEMA's next congress.[209] This demonstration of good faith went one step too far for the *Auswärtige Amt*. The French embassy warned of 'severe repercussions' in Paris should the congress proceed.[210] In light of its outspoken politics, the *Amt* consequently informed the VdS, hosting the UGEMA on federal territory 'diametrically opposed federal policies'; the congress delegates would be denied entrance into West Germany.

204 Aufzeichnung, VdS, undated, BA/K, B166/1414.

205 For instance: Aktennotiz, Hoffmann, 8 May 1959; Schreiben, Holschuh an Dr. Bergemann (Unilever-Konzern) und Dr Wagner (BdI), 17 January 1959, BA/K, B166/1414.

206 Schreiben, Holschuh and Brentano, 7 January 1959, PA/AA, B25/12.

207 Schreiben, Dittmann, an Theodor Steltzer, Deutsche Gesellschaft für Auswärtige Politik, 13 May 1959, PA/AA, B25/12; Schreiben, von Hardenberg, Büro StS, an Dr. Bergemann, Unilever-Konzern, Hamburg, 15 April 1959, BA/K, B166/1414.

208 Schreiben, Hoffmann, an Gerhard Imhof, Erlangen, 21 February 1961; Spendenaufruf, undated, BA/K, B166/1420.

209 Schreiben, Holschuh an Kassem [sic], Tunesische Botschaft, Bad Godesberg, 26 March 1959; Aktennotiz, Pangritz/Hoffmann, Besuch bei UGEMA, Lausanne, 11 June 1959, BA/K, B166/1414.

210 Télégramme no.2123 de Seydoux, 22 July 1959, MAE, EU/RFA/1273.

Faced by this ultimatum, the VdS had to relent.[211] Instead, at its March 1960 assembly, the association asked its 200,000 members to contribute 5 pfennig each so that Algerian students in the FRG would be able to participate in the UGEMA's July Tunis congress.[212]

The VdS was not alone in raising funds to support Algerian students and trainees. Blachstein, too, remained a tireless lobbyist in this regard. By June 1960, the deputy had secured eight further placements with the Industrial Union of Construction Workers, six with the Printing and Publishing Union, and two with the Food, Beverages and Catering Union.[213] The DGB, too, had increased its technical aid to the Algerians. Thus in early 1960, the confederation's executive agreed to fund an initiative by Louis Pilz of the Stuttgart *Hiflskomitee* to offer ten Algerians language tuition and basic training in trade unionism.[214] Having invited Willi Richter to Tunis in April 1960, UGTA leaders Abdelkader Maachou, Mohamed Kalache, Embarek Djilani and Safi Boudissa further impressed upon the DGB president the importance they placed on the training of future trade union cadres. They defended the UGTA's acceptance of placements in socialist countries on the grounds that ICFTU members had done so little to help in this regard.[215] Richter's visit to Tunis proved advantageous to the UGTA. The DGB subsequently agreed to subsidise a permanent UGTA bureau headed by Mostefaoui based in Cologne.[216] Moreover, the confederation agreed to organise an eighteen-month-long training programme for twenty-five Algerians selected by the UGTA.[217] By December 1960, the DGB had set aside 250,000DM specifically for this purpose, and by the New Year, the twenty-five chosen candidates had begun their preliminary language tuition at Goethe Institutes in Bad Arolsen, Hesse, and in Brilon, North-Rhine-Westphalia.[218]

211 Aufzeichnung, Frank, Referat 204/205, 22 July 1959. Also: Schreiben, Scherpenberg an Pangritz, 18 September 1959, PA/AA, B25/12.

212 Dépêche no.441 de Seydoux, 11 March 1960, MAE, EU/RFA/1218.

213 Schreiben, Blachstein, an UGTA Tunis, 27 May and 16 June 1960, AdsD, NL/Blachstein/33.

214 Schreiben, Pilz, DGB-Ortsausschuss Stuttgart, an Bernhard Tacke, DGB, 12 February 1960; Schreiben, Hauptabteilung Organisation und Werbung, an Geschäftlichen Bundesvorstand, 8 March 1960, AdsD, 5/DGAZ/297.

215 Notiz für Richter, 12 April 1960, AdsD, 5/DGAJ/207.

216 Schreiben, Wilhelm Gronau an Geschäftlichen Bundesvorstand, 15 July 1960; Auszug, Punkt 3, Protokoll der 39.Sitzung des Geschäftlichen Bundesvorstandes, 18 July 1960, AdsD, 5/DGAJ/207.

217 Auszug, Punkt 13, Protokoll der 37.Sitzung des Geschäftlichen Bundesvorstandes, 4 July 1960, AdsD, 5/DGAZ/297.

218 Auszug, Punkt 6, Protokoll Bundesausschuss-Sitzung, 7 December 1960, AdsD, 5/DGAJ/207; Vermerk, Referat 205, 21 January 1961, PA/AA, B25/13.

Within the space of under two years, West German civil-society actors had caught up considerably with East German aid measures, whose pull on Algerians had begun to decline. Indeed, the number of Algerian students, trainees and workers in the GDR was always lower than generally assumed. As Taubert argues, it never surpassed a few hundred.[219] Going on the UGEMA's propaganda, the VdS assumed in late 1958 that 150 Algerians studied at East German universities. The FDGB, meanwhile, recorded only 52. One year later, FDGB records listed 113 Algerians as attending East German universities and a further 21 enrolled in trade union education. The UGEMA, however, only recorded 83 students in the GDR in 1959.[220] By then, Algerian–East German relations had deteriorated. In September 1959, the authorities in East Berlin singled out fifteen Algerian students to Belaïd Abdesselam of the GPRA's Ministry for Cultural Affairs who, they claimed, neglected their studies and behaved in an 'insolent' and 'disgraceful' manner, especially towards East German women. UGEMA President Messaoud Aït Chaalal regretted the students' behaviour, yet he chafed even more at the authorities' refusal to allow his union to install its own officials in East Berlin to supervise the Algerians studying in the GDR.[221] That same month, moreover, the VdS took charge of its first Algerian 'refugee from the East', who claimed to have abandoned his studies at Leipzig's Karl-Marx University because of the obligation imposed on all foreign students to attend lectures on Marxism-Leninism and to participate in political manifestations. The association must have been encouraged by the student's belief that other Algerians would soon follow him to the West to avoid this type of political indoctrination.[222]

In the context of Algeria's independence struggle, it was precisely the relative freedom they enjoyed in West Germany that made that country an ultimately more attractive destination for most Algerians than the GDR. Though supervised and circumscribed, this freedom was essential to the students and trainees, who also represented the FLN or one of its auxiliaries. Indeed, the candidates selected by the UGTA or UGEMA for study or training in West Germany were often found to be unqualified; they often failed to attend their classes. This suggests ulterior motives behind

[219] Taubert, *L'«autre» Allemagne*, p. 140.

[220] Patrice G. Poutrus, 'An den Grenzen des proletarischen Internationalismus. Algerische Flüchtlinge in der DDR', *Zeitschrift für Geschichtswissenschaft* 55/2 (2007), p. 162; Taubert, *L'«autre» Allemagne*, pp. 162–3.

[221] Rapports de Belaïd Abdesselam et Messaoud Aït Chaalal, 10 September and 18 September 1959, in *Le FLN, documents et histoire: 1954–1962* (eds.) Mohammed Harbi and Gilbert Meynier (Paris, 2004), pp. 715–16.

[222] Aktennotiz, Scheib an Hoffmann, 5 September 1959, BA/K, B166/1420.

their selection and secondment.[223] In one case, an Algerian scholarship recipient apologised to Blachstein (his sponsor) for his persistent absence from Hamburg's engineering school, which he blamed on 'the claims made on his time by the FLN'.[224] Though he was fully committed to the FLN's cause, even SDS activist Reimar Lenz lamented to Blachstein that one should support Algerians for whom academic studies 'made sense' and not such 'who will start on the first day of their stay in Germany to buy guns'.[225]

Clandestine networks

Placements at a university, vocational school or trade union college thus frequently served as cover for militant nationalists – Kacem of the Bonn bureau being a prime example. Funded either fully or partly by West German organisations that also acted as the recipients' sponsors, such placements allowed the FLN to infiltrate militants, create networks and reinforce logistics and communications. In sum, they helped secure the FLN's sanctuary in West Germany. They did so, moreover, in a seemingly legitimate manner, for as members of the UGTA or UGEMA, their recipients' political and subversive activities were less likely to attract the authorities' attention.

Where some students and trainees played a part in the politico-administrative structures of the '*Fédération d'Allemagne*', others helped recruit German allies into the clandestine European networks providing vital logistical support to the *Fédération de France*. Run by a mix of left-wing intellectuals, dissident communists and progressivist Christians, these networks had become active in metropolitan France early on in the Algerian war. In a context of police surveillance and repression, the FLN relied on their assistance for safe houses, transport, communication and liaison both within France and beyond. One network animated by French journalist Jacques Vignes specialised in smuggling militants across national frontiers via an intricate system involving 'opening cars' that crossed the border at regular checkpoints, acting as scouts to warn of closures and controls, and 'load-bearing cars' transporting the Algerians to points from which the border could be crossed on foot, where they were then collected

[223] Bewertung Bennacefs und Benghenissas, Staatliche Gewerbeschule Maschinenbau, 11 June 1959; Schreiben Blachstein an Boumendjel, GPRA Informationsministerium, 6 October 1959, AdsD, NL/Blachstein/32.

[224] Schreiben, Bennacef an Blachstein, 26 June 1959, AdsD, NL/Blachstein/32.

[225] Schreiben, Lenz an Blachstein, 6 February 1960, AdsD, NL/Blachstein/34.

by the 'opening cars'. Vignes worked closely with a network established by Marxist philosopher Francis Jeanson, which smuggled the *Fédération de France*'s monthly tax collections out of France. The sums involved were substantial – over 400 million French francs a month by early 1958 – and would soon constitute 80 per cent of the FLN's overall budget.[226] Other auxiliaries contributed to an operation run by the *Organisation Spéciale* and dubbed '*Hirondelle*' (swallow). The operation sought to address the OS's constant shortage of arms and munitions jeopardising the FLN's second front and involved the smuggling of thousands of revolvers and hundreds of sub-machine guns, grenades and other explosives into France. West Germany was the vital hub in this logistical operation.[227]

In view of the illegal and risky nature of their activities, the '*passeurs de frontiers*' (border-crossers) and '*porteurs de valises*' (baggage-carriers) operated under conditions of strict secrecy and compartmentalisation. Just as the *Fédération de France* came to rely on sanctuaries beyond the metropole, the FLN's French auxiliaries began to recruit other Europeans, including West Germans, into its support networks. After all, these recruits were better placed to organise safe houses and maintain communications in the sanctuary-states than the networks' French members. One of the first Germans to offer his clandestine support was SPD-deputy Wischnewski, who together with his wife allowed FLN militants to congregate regularly in his home and to use his car for errands. At one point, Wischnewski even gave one of his Algerian friends access to his checking account, prompting bank officials to question the deputy about the sudden appearance (and disappearance) in his account of an enormous sum of 1.8 million DM.[228] Wischnewski was also responsible for establishing the Algerians' link to the socialist youth organisation, *Die Falken*, whose conference centres, as has been seen, proved vital as venues for top-secret FLN meetings and for the clandestine training of new recruits.[229] Although the rumour has never been substantiated, French intelligence even suspected the deputy of direct involvement in the preparation and coordination of terrorist offensives in France.[230]

226 Hamon and Rotman, *Porteurs*, pp. 85, 142–3; 'Entretiens avec Boudaoud, Haroun et Ladlani', in Bougherara, *Rapports*, p. 224. Also: Evans, *Memory*; Marie-Pierre Ulloa, *Francis Jeanson: A Dissident Intellectual from the French Resistance to the Algerian War* (trans.) J.M. Todd (Stanford CA, 2008); LeSueur, *Uncivil War*.

227 Haroun, *Septième wilaya*, pp. 214–15; Djerbal, *L'OS*, pp. 100, 110–15, 275.

228 Notice d'information no. 11455/SDECE, 30 September 1958, SHD-T, 10R/578*; Notice d'information no. 13650/SDECE, 5 December 1958, 10T/528/D2*; Wischnewski, *Leidenschaft*, pp. 108–9.

229 Haroun, *Septième wilaya*, p. 315.

230 Notice d'information no. 14062/SDECE, 15 December 1958, SHD-T, 10R/578*.

Members of the *Falken*, meanwhile, would also play an important role in secretly assisting *Jeune Résistance*, a militant underground network established in 1959 by French army deserter Jean-Louis Hurst. *Jeune Résistance* operated mostly out of Switzerland and West Germany and worked closely both with the FLN and the Jeanson network. In July 1960, the movement held its first clandestine congress near Darmstadt. Since conscientious objection to military service was illegal in France (but not in West Germany), *Jeune Résistance* incited French and Algerian conscripts and reservists to insubordination and desertion, offering support to those who took the leap into illegality. Operating beyond French frontiers, *Jeune Résistance* required the assistance of local allies. In Baden-Württemberg, Rhineland-Palatinate and Hesse, the network secured the aid of members not just of the *Falken* but also of the *Naturfreundejugend* and Association of Conscientious Objectors. Already a keen supporter of the FLN's anti-Foreign Legion campaign, the head of the *Naturfreundejugend*, Klaus Vack, proved particularly active in organising West German allies. Whether in West Germany, Switzerland or Belgium, *Jeune Résistance*'s supporters organised shelter for deserters and draft-dodgers with local families. Less likely to rouse the authorities' suspicion than an Algerian or French national, the network's West German supporters also distributed propaganda inciting desertion and insubordination among the North African troops stationed at French bases in Tübingen, Reutlingen, Freiburg, Landau and Konstanz. Through their help, several hundred Algerian and French deserters and draft-dodgers safely escaped the clutches of the French military police.[231]

In October 1960, Cologne's *Falken* further hosted what SDECE described as 'the most important conference held in [...] Germany since the beginning of the [Algerian] war'.[232] The conference delegates supposedly included the FLN's representatives in Western Europe, members of *Jeune Résistance*, Francis Jeanson and others from his support network. Its objective consisted of reorganising the *Fédération de France*'s support networks, whose vital activities had been severely disrupted by French police repression.

[231] According to Tramor Quemeneur, 886 French soldiers deserted during the Algerian war, 420 were classified as conscientious objectors, and 10,831 men recalled to service practised insubordination. See: 'Une guerre sans « non »? Insoumissions, refus d'obéissance et desertion de soldats français pendant la guerre d'Algérie (1954–1962)', thèse de doctorat (Université Paris VIII, 2007); Hamon and Rotman, *Porteurs*, pp. 215–22, 274–6; Haroun, *Septième wilaya*, pp. 136–7; Leggewie, *Kofferträger*, pp. 75, 85; Carron, *Suisse*, pp. 292–301; Klaus Vack, 'Die Algerien-Solidarität der Naturjugendfreunde', in *Hundert Jahre Kampf um die freie Natur. Illustrierte Geschichte der Naturfreunde* (eds.) Wulf Erdmann and Jochen Zimmer (Essen, 1991), pp. 105, 109–10.

[232] Notice d'information no. 36981/SDECE, 27 October 1960, SHD-T, 10T/528/D2*.

The conference came after a wave of arrests that began in France in February 1960 and that culminated in the trial in September 1960 of seventeen French and six Muslim members of Jeanson's network.[233] Owing to these arrests, Vignes's transportation network increasingly relied on antennae established in Frankfurt, Brussels, Geneva and Milan. The *Club Voltaire*, a socialist group founded in Frankfurt by local *Falken* chairman Heiner Halberstadt, became the backbone of the network's clandestine activities in West Germany. Starting its life as a reading circle fostering a café and counter-culture, *Club Voltaire* promoted practical socialist youth work and was already active in the West German pacifist movement (especially in the Easter marches).[234] Recruited by Vignes' confidante, Cécile Marion, the club's members sheltered deserters and militants and distributed propaganda. Some, like sociology student Walmot Falkenberg, helped smuggle militants, money, documents and even arms across European frontiers.[235]

Falkenberg was particularly useful to Vignes and the FLN, who frequently employed women as liaison agents and couriers since they were less likely to arouse the suspicion of the security services.[236] According to historian Daho Djerbal, this proved a preferred strategy for the *Fédération de France*. Militants of the *Organisation Spéciale* frequently made use of European women to smuggle much-needed arms into the metropole. A young German socialist, Gisela Goethner, is cited as one such woman, who often worked alongside her husband, Adolf. Omar Boudaoud, meanwhile, relied heavily on his German wife, a former exchange student in Paris. Inge Huscholtz, too, was recruited by her Algerian boyfriend whilst an exchange student in Paris. Huscholtz worked closely with the Algerian *mujahida* (female resister) Zina Haraigue, who was herself half German. The two women were arrested in May 1960 attempting to transport nine suitcases containing handguns and rifles through Paris.[237]

233 Ibid.; Notice d'information no. 36837/SDECE, 25 October 1960; SHD-T, 10T/528/D2*.

234 Nehring, *Politics*, p. 243.

235 Notice d'information no. 40266/SDECE, 26 January 1961; Notice d'information no. 42897/SDECE, 31 March 1961, SHD-T, 1H/1753/D2*; Leggewie, *Kofferträger*, pp. 59–80; Samuel Schirmbeck, 'Konspirativ: Wie der hessische Untergrund den algerischen Freiheitskampf unterstützte', Fernsehreportage, '*Hauptsache Kultur!*' *Hessen Fernsehen*, 23 March 2002, 21h45 (ht tp://static.hr-online.de/fs/hauptsachekultur/themen/230302thema1.html); Ute Bönnen and Gerald Endres, 'Der Algerienkrieg: Kampf an vielen Fronten', Manuskript und Dokumentarfilm, Erstausstrahlung bei ARTE, 1998 (http://home.snafu.de/endres/index.html); Djerbal, *L'OS*, p. 166.

236 Hamon and Rotman, *Porteurs*, pp. 119–20, 146–7, 153; Haroun, *Septième wilaya*, p. 110; Leggewie, *Kofferträger*, pp. 61–5.

237 Djerbal, *L'OS*, pp. 107, 114, 116–17, 143, 334–5. Also: Boudaoud, *Mémoires*, pp. 133–4; Rachid Haraigue, *Le Combat d'un Lieutenant FLN en France pendant la Guerre d'Algérie*. (Paris, 2001), pp. 122–3; 'L'Organisation Spéciale du FLN avait reçu des armes venant d'Allemagne et de Belgique', *Le Monde*, 4 June 1960.

In addition to women, the FLN relied on diplomats as couriers and facilitators, benefiting from their immunity. Although these diplomats were usually fellow Arabs, the *Fédération* managed to recruit a most unlikely agent considering the Bonn government's policy of *quid pro quo* in the Algerian question: Jakob Moneta, a member of the West German embassy in Paris. A life-long Trotskyist, militant trade unionist and close friend of "Algeria lobbyist" Georg Jungclas, Moneta had been seconded to the embassy in 1953 as social and labour attaché. He was first approached by Michel Raptis (alias Pablo), the Greek secretary of the Fourth (Trotskyite) International, about placing his Paris flat at the FLN's disposal. Moneta agreed, and his clandestine engagement on behalf of the FLN escalated from there. By 1958, he and his wife not only smuggled militants across the border into Belgium or West Germany using their diplomatic car, they also handled the transportation of tax collections, which they delivered either to Ernest Mandel, the Fourth International's secretary in Brussels, or directly into Swiss banks.[238]

As militants who saw in anti-colonialism an opportunity to advance the cause of world revolution and in the FLN the 'only active revolutionary force', Trotskyists had long constituted a key pillar of support for the FLN.[239] As experienced revolutionaries, they established what Sylvain Pattieu considers the FLN's first European support network.[240] Michel Raptis constituted the driving force in the network's expansion, which rapidly developed transnational proportions. Just how extensive and subversive the Trotskyists' activities were became evident on 10 June 1960, when police in France, the Netherlands and West Germany dismantled a forgery ring and arrested its chief animators, including Raptis and Sal Santen, the secretary of the International's Dutch section. The forgery workshop was based in the West German city of Osnabrück. It was operated by Albertus Oeldrich, a Dutch printer, and his German comrade, Helmut Schneeweiss, and financed by Ahmed Abbas, an FLN militant based in Cologne. The supposed brainchild of *Fédération* bosses Haroun and Boudaoud, the workshop primarily replicated French ID cards to make it easier for FLN militants to evade the French police and security services. Yet the German police also discovered state-of-the-art equipment for the forging of 9.6 billion old francs, which amounted to 80 million DM. Oeldrich and Schneeweiss admitted under interrogation that the

[238] 'Erinnerungen an die Algeriensolidarität. Ein Kofferträger', *Sozialistische Zeitung*, February 2005, p. 20; Harbi, *Vie Debout*, p. 228; Sylvain Pattieu, 'Le « camarade » Pablo, la IVe Internationale, et la guerre d'Algérie', *Revue Historique* 303/3 (2001), p. 702.

[239] Pas, *Nederland*, p. 145.

[240] Pattieu, 'Pablo', p. 696.

counterfeit money had been intended to subvert the French economy. Questioned by the authorities, the FLN bureau in Bonn denied all knowledge of the project. In light of the FLN's strict policy of secrecy and compartmentalisation, this was probably true.[241] While Raptis and Santen were tried in Amsterdam, Prosecutor-General Max Güde was able to build a watertight case against Oeldrich, Schneeweiss and Abbas that came to trial in early 1961.[242] Seydoux hoped the affair would finally convince the Bonn authorities 'of the criminal activity of FLN-members in [West Germany]'.[243] Indeed, Foreign Minister Brentano reportedly lamented to Wischnewski: 'The Sahara is so vast, but it has to be in Münster [sic] of all places that they have to do something like this!'[244]

Brentano's outburst was highly prescient, for under Raptis a group of Trotskyists had indeed established underground workshops in North Africa. Located close to Kenitra in north-western Morocco, these workshops became operational in 1959. Under the cover of fruit plantations and processing plants, they produced handguns and grenades for the ALN. One of the project's chief coordinators in Europe was Cologne-based Georg Jungclas, whom Keramane considered 'one of the pillars of the FLN'.[245] Jungclas oversaw the supply of funds, equipment and skilled volunteers for the Moroccan workshops. According to Leggewie, much of the machinery came from communist China while the workers were everything from Algerian, Dutch, Venezuelan, Argentinian, Greek, British and French. Jungclas also recruited a number of German machinists, including *Falke* Heinz Peiffer, who had been arrested for his pro-Algerian engagement in 1959, and Kurt Henker, the son of one of the animators of the Stuttgart *Hilfskomitee*. Although the workshops never produced a sufficient quantity and quality of arms to enhance the ALN's war effort, they were vital to the morale of the Algerian *mujâhideen* and became a useful propaganda ploy.[246]

Trotskyite engagement represented a striking and particularly radical example of international solidarity with the FLN's cause. In the battle for

[241] Télégramme no. 2384 de Seydoux, Bonn, 15 June 1960, MAE, MLA/6; Wochenbericht, SG-Bonn, 1 July 1960, BA/K, B131/198; Schreiben, Generalbundesanwalt Karlsruhe an BMJ, 21 July 1960, PA/AA, B25/11. Also: Sylvain Pattieu, *Les Camarades des Frères. Trotskistes et libertaires dans la guerre d'Algérie* (Paris, 2002), p. 179; Pas, *Nederland*, pp. 145–52.

[242] Aufzeichnung für Referat 204, 15 February 1961, PA/AA, B25/2; Télégramme no. 765 de Seydoux, Bonn, 20 February 1961, Dépêche no. 709 de Seydoux, Bonn, 19 April 1961, MAE, MLA/7.

[243] Télégramme no. 2424 de Seydoux, Bonn, 16 June 1960, MAE, MLA/6.

[244] Wischnewski, *Leidenschaft*, p. 115.

[245] 'Entretiens avec Keramane', in Bougherara, *Rapports*, p. 208.

[246] Leggewie, *Kofferträger*, pp. 55, 118–23; Pattieu, *Camarades*, pp. 174–9; Harbi, *Vie Debout*, p. 229.

hearts and minds, the movement had managed to secure propagandistic, humanitarian and developmental aid from a broad spectrum of international helpers, including a wide range of West German civil-society actors. Far from being drawn exclusively from the Left, these actors spanned the political spectrum. Though hardly a coherent or coordinated group, they constituted a force multiplier that bolstered the FLN's insurgency against France, whether morally, materially or logistically. Civil-society actors made it possible for the FLN to entrench its positions in West Germany and exploit the benefits of external sanctuary. Pursuing an alternative and private foreign policy that defended Algeria's right to independence and condemned French colonialism, the FLN's German helpers both challenged and complemented the Bonn government's policy of supporting the French counterinsurgency. Irrespective of their nationality, the Trotskyists took their assistance one step further. By seeking to subvert the French economy, their aid represented what German prosecutor Heinz Linke declared a 'frontal attack on France'.[247] By assembling handguns and grenades, Jungclas's network contributed directly to the FLN's war effort in Algeria. This was important, for even though the Challe offensive had decimated the *mujâhideen* within Algeria, armed insurrection remained a salient feature of the FLN's strategy. Defeat on the battleground constantly impelled the ALN to improve and augment its military capabilities. The armaments factories established in Morocco with Trotskyist help constituted one initiative through which the ALN sought to secure a steady supply in war materiel. Since their products were often defective, however, the ALN also looked to alternative sources. Indeed, the FLN continued to rely on the international arms trade to fuel its armed struggle in Algeria and France. As a centre in this dubious trade, the FLN's procurement efforts – and the French authorities' countermeasures – would once more concentrate on the FRG.

[247] 'Zuchthausstrafen für die Geldfälscher gefordert', *FAZ*, 21 April 1961.

CHAPTER 9

The war of action

From the moment its militants took refuge in West Germany, the FLN defied the French and German authorities seeking their expulsion.[1] Even though its room to manoeuvre was limited, the movement managed to organise Algerians arriving in the FRG into a politico-administrative framework that harnessed them to the war effort, whether as militants, adherents or sympathisers. More importantly, the FLN managed to enlist a wide range of West German civil-society actors, whose aid and support proved vital not just to the FLN's propaganda war but to the security and stability of the sanctuary itself. The previous two chapters have highlighted the extent to which FLN militants, assisted by their auxiliaries in the UGTA and UGEMA, worked indefatigably and successfully to entrench their external sanctuary and promote the cause of national liberation. They did so by hiding behind the law, exploiting the democratic order, and working through local allies, whether Arab, French or German. However, recruitment and political mobilisation only represented two of the FLN's three fundamental tasks in West Germany. To Abdelhafid Keramane, the head of the FLN bureau in Bonn, the third – the procurement of military and non-military supplies – in many ways proved most vital, for the insurgency depended on a steady source of war materiel.[2] How, then, did the governments in Paris and Bonn respond to the FLN's continued procurement efforts? The war on contraband, this chapter argues, remained a central concern for the French authorities, one pursued even more doggedly under the Fifth Republic than under its predecessor. French interventions against the FLN's supply networks became increasingly aggressive and unilateral, so much so that the FRG itself transformed into a battleground in SDECE's *guerre d'action*. A blatant violation of

[1] Certain sections in this chapter again draw on material first published in: Bülow, 'Myth or Reality?' pp. 787–820.

[2] 'Entretiens', in Bougherara, *Rapports*, pp. 206–10.

West German sovereignty, the secret services' campaign against contraband highlights once more just how unequal and volatile Franco-German relations remained during the Algerian war. It underlines further just how far the French authorities were willing to go in internationalising their counterinsurgency so as to destroy the FLN's external sanctuaries and support networks. The war of action undermined the FLN's procurement activities in West Germany. In the grand scheme of things, this did more harm than good to France's counterinsurgency campaign.

A supply base

With the onset of the second front in August 1958, the procurement of arms, munitions and other war materiel once again assumed great significance to the FLN, which now had to ensure regular provisions for its combatants on multiple fronts. A central hub in the international arms trade, West Germany had already become an important pivot in the FLN's supply chain. As seen in Chapter 5, Algerian operatives and their Arab intermediaries had established close contacts to German companies and middlemen. The ports of Hamburg and Bremen already served as important departure points for the transport or transit of goods to the FLN's bases in the Maghreb. The Saarland, meanwhile, proved an ideal base for the smuggling of arms into metropolitan France.[3] Under conditions of strict secrecy and compartmentalisation, the FLN bureau in Bonn was charged with expanding and securing the movement's supply chains in West Germany. Keramane recalled being tasked with managing the financial transactions. Meanwhile, Yaïci Abdelkader (alias Abdelkader Nouasri), Mabed Mehdi (alias Chitane or Dr Serghini) and Youssfi M'Hamed, based mainly in Frankfurt and Cologne, handled the purchasing, assisted by a number of 'moving' agents.[4] After the formation of the GPRA, the agents received their orders from Abdelhafid Boussouf's Ministry for General Relations and Communications, which controlled its own budget for the procurement of communications equipment, and Mahmoud Chérif's Ministry for Armaments and Provisions. In January 1960, these ministries were fused into one, the powerful Ministry for Armaments and General Relations (*Ministère de l'armement et des liaisons générales*, MALG) headed by Boussouf.[5]

[3] Rapport no. 6969/10R.M./EMI/2, 10 October 1958, SHD-T, 10T/531*; Notice no. 26375/SSDNA, 19 December 1958, 10T/528/D2*; Haroun, *Septième wilaya*, p. 208.

[4] 'Entretiens avec Keramane', in Bougherara, *Rapports*, pp. 209–11.

[5] Meynier, *Histoire*, pp. 475–6.

While the files of these ministries remain inaccessible,[6] French and German diplomatic and intelligence records offer frequent and surprisingly detailed descriptions of their extensive activities in West Germany. These records do not necessarily present an accurate or full account of the FLN's procurement efforts. They do, however, offer an insight into the French and German intelligence and security services' self-declared state of knowledge as well as their preoccupations and preconceptions. Moreover, they reveal a French obsession with the legal and illegal arms trade that would have dangerous repercussions. By October 1958, the *deuxième bureau* of French forces in Algeria had identified three countries as the FLN's 'principal sources in provisions'. In the East, Czechoslovakia and Yugoslavia had replaced the Arab states as the FLN's chief state-sanctioned suppliers of arms and munitions. In the West, the FRG, or rather West German arms dealers, were singled out as the FLN's third significant source of provisions.[7] Although conceding that most ALN arms – even those of German make – did not originate in the Bonn Republic, military intelligence believed West German merchants helped furnish the FLN with an array of military and non-military supplies. Their importance was such that the GPRA was thought to have established its only permanent procurement mission outside of the Arab world in West Germany, an assumption corroborated by Keramane's recollection.[8] An intelligence bulletin from March 1959 again identified the country as an operational headquarters and important transit route for FLN contraband.[9]

French intelligence compiled an impressive list of purchases purportedly made by the FLN in West Germany. In mid-1958, Libyan agents allegedly ordered fifteen lorries and all-terrain vehicles from Mercedes and Volkswagen for the FLN. By early autumn, a Hamburg establishment supposedly offered to sell the Algerians an unspecified quantity of MG42 rifles.[10] Later that year FLN operatives reportedly requisitioned 3,200 revolvers, 1,890 automatic pistols, 50,000 rounds of 9mm ammunition, 5,000 grenades, 500kg of TNT and 1,000m of lighting-cord for the *Fédération de France*.[11] In September 1959, the French naval command at

[6] This was, at least, the state of affairs when this manuscript was written.

[7] Note no. 6969/10.RM/EMI/2, 10 October 1958, SHD-T, 10T/531*; Notice d'information no. 19644/SDECE, 2 June 1959, SHD-T, 10T/530/D1*.

[8] Fiche no. 8007/10R.M./EMI/2, 4 December 1958, SHD-T, 10T/531/D3*. Also: Djerbal, *L'OS*, p. 367.

[9] Bulletin de renseignement, March 1959, SHD-T, 1H/1164/D2.

[10] Notice no. 10139/SSDNA/Alger, 24 October 1958, SHD-T, 1H/1536Bis/D2*.

[11] Notice no. 12745/SDECE, 10 November 1958, SHD-T, 10T/528/D2*.

Bizerta in Tunisia received word from a 'highly exposed' source the authorities clearly deemed reliable, who claimed that at least four separate businessmen based in Frankfurt/Main, Cologne and Munich, including one Helmuth Müller, had supplied compasses, binoculars, wire-cutters, combat fatigues, boots and tents to Nadir Benghabrit, the FLN's head of logistics and procurement in Tripoli.[12] One year later, SDECE contended that the FLN's shopping list for West Germany included: 40,000m of olive-green textiles; 20,000m of tent fabric; 22,000 combat fatigues; 5,000 belts; 10,000m of 'special' fabric; 6,000 cans of corned beef; 30,000 boxes of combat rations; 3,500 wire-cutters; 800 saws; 800 binoculars; 30 telemeters; and an undefined quantity of vehicles, field-kitchen equipment, radios, shears, razors, pocket-lights and chirurgical tools.[13] Signals intelligence indicated that Benghabrit had tried to purchase several large transport vehicles from the West German companies Borgward and Mercedes in 1960, including thirty Unimogs equipped as mobile communications platforms.[14]

To pay for these purchases, the GPRA was thought to have established several bank accounts in West Germany in addition to those it held at Swiss financial institutions.[15] In September 1958, the *deuxième bureau* reported that the *Fédération de France* supposedly transferred 15 million old francs to a Deutsche Bank account in Frankfurt/Main held in Abdelkader Nouasri's name.[16] Wireless communications intercepted by French signals intelligence in 1960, meanwhile, revealed that Keramane had opened an account with the Commerzbank in Bonn, while Benghabrit had opened one with Hamburg's Bank für Gemeinwirtschaft.[17] The GPRA appeared to dispose of substantial sums in the FRG. According to *deuxième bureau*, the government-in-exile spent over 85.5 million old francs in West Germany in April and May 1959, which still only represented a fraction of the FLN's estimated annual procurement budget of 3.3 billion old francs. Intelligence suggested that Benghabrit had purchased a further 200 million old francs worth of

[12] Aufzeichnung, Etzler, Referat 413, 29 July 1959, PA/AA, B25/12; Notice no. 1231/EM/2, Commandement Supérieur de la Base stratégique de Bizerte, 17 September 1959, SHD-T, 1H/1540/D1*; Notice no. 1150/SDECE, 16 December 1960, SHD-T, 1H/1580/D1*.

[13] Notice no. 935/SDECE, 4 October 1960, SHD-T, 1H/1580/D1*.

[14] Dossier 'E' (Écoutes), 17 July 1960; Notice no. 3236/SSDNA, 25 October 1960; Notice no. 53/SDECE, 10 January 1961, SHD-T, 1H/1580/D1*.

[15] Carron, *Suisse*, pp. 255–63.

[16] Notice no. 8007/10.RM/EMI/2, 4 December 1958, SHD-T, 10T/531/D3*.

[17] Dossier 'E', 21 July 1960, 7 September 1960, and 14 November 1960, SHD-T, 1H/1580/D1*.

materiel in the FRG and Western Europe between June 1960 and January 1961.[18]

Though reliable and regular figures are hard to come by, the estimates above help explain why the French authorities singled out West Germany for increasingly punitive interventions. After all, the suppression of contraband remained a priority for the military and security services, one that sought to prevent the Algerian insurgency from gaining in strength and effectiveness. As early as January 1958, the chief of the defence staff, General Paul Ely, had advocated a major overhaul of French strategy to achieve the 'neutralisation of [supply] networks'. Ely called for 'everything to be done to increase the efficacy of intelligence collection' and for a coordination of action 'at executive level'. He proposed a four-pronged attack against FLN contraband consisting of:

> (a) *diplomatic action*, the character of which would be adapted to each case;
> (b) *clandestine action* by our special services, which translates into direct interventions against the activities of trafficking rings;
> (c) *police action* to fight effectively against the FLN's collection of funds in France and Algeria; this action would partly drain the FLN's financial means;
> (d) specific *military action* that can only be exercised in the final stages of an arms shipment; this currently manifests itself by a surveillance of the [North African] coast, borders, and air space.[19]

Ely's recommendations were echoed one year later in the Fifth Republic's reinvigorated, multipronged counterinsurgency outlined earlier. As the head of the *deuxième bureau* Colonel Levain explained to regional commanders in December 1958, since the 'assistance to the rebellion [...] is situated at a global echelon [...] the counterinsurgency we are conducting in ALGERIA is only part of an unyielding struggle that we must conduct on a much vaster scale'.[20] While the Challe offensive aimed to isolate and neutralise the FLN within Algeria and the 'Papon system' did much the same in the metropole, the war on contraband targeted the FLN's external sanctuaries and international supply networks. The campaign required

[18] Notice no. 5850/EMGDN/2, 17 May 1960, SHD-T, 1H/1688/D1; Notice no. 4/SDECE, 2 January 1961, 1H/1580/D1*.

[19] Dépêche no. 9072/EMGA du Général Ely au ministre de la défense, 21 January1958, SHD-T, 1R/247/D3* (italics added).

[20] Exposé par Colonel Levain, chef de l'EMA/2, 29 December 1958, SHD-T, 1H/1687/D2 (capitalised in original).

a concerted effort by French authorities, whether the military, security services, civil bureaucracy or diplomacy.

Prime Minister Debré's directives of early 1959 did not elaborate on the specifics of the campaign against FLN contraband, yet they left no doubt as to the importance the de Gaulle government attached to this facet of the war. Action against the FLN's 'material aid' represented the prime pillar of France's global counterinsurgency.[21] One missive dated 2 April instructed French diplomats to intensify their efforts to uncover and protest against the 'secret assistance' provided to the insurgency and 'to raise the threat of retaliatory measures'.[22] The intelligence services, meanwhile, were instructed to improve their collection efforts, which until then had produced 'fragmentary knowledge relating only to one stage of each [contraband] affair: prospecting, negotiations, closing of a deal, payment, transport, or delivery'.[23] By August 1959, the General Staff had devised a new order of research focusing on sources and methods of acquisition and purchase, on procedures of payment, on means of transport and on storage. The General Staff considered it 'pointless to try to document and identify the multiple and highly dispersed sources of supply' emanating from the Arab and Sino-Soviet bloc, because the French government 'cannot exercise any action' against this state-sponsored aid. As such, the General Staff recommended concentrating intelligence collection on the West. It did so for two reasons. First, the FLN was believed to be coordinating most of its procurement activities from Western Europe, especially the FRG. More importantly though, only in the West might French action against contraband actually prove effective. The actions envisioned by the General Staff proved similar to Ely's recommendations from January 1958 involving diplomatic intercessions to block specific exports; military operations to intercept shipments at the point of transport; police raids to disrupt financial flows; and covert action to neutralise specific trafficking rings.[24]

Diplomatic and police action

Considering its perceived importance as an FLN supply base, West Germany remained a focal point in the Fifth Republic's reinvigorated

[21] Compte-rendu de la réunion sur l'Algérie tenue à l'Hôtel Matignon, 14 March 1959, AHC, 2DE75/D2*.

[22] Instructions aux postes diplomatiques, 2 April 1959, AHC, 2DE75/D2*.

[23] Notice no. 4351/EMGDN/2, 7 April 1959, MAE, AL/ALG/22.

[24] Projet de plan particulier de renseignements concernant le trafic d'armes, no.131/EMGDN/2, 31 August 1959, SHD-T, 10T/531/D3*.

war on contraband. To the Gaullist regime, material aid to the FLN – whether state-sanctioned or not – constituted an intolerable interference in France's domestic affairs and an inadmissible breach of French sovereignty. Having never declared war, the purchase of arms and non-military supplies by the FLN and its allies did not allow the French authorities to invoke the 'right of pursuit' or 'riposte' in international law.[25] It did, however, produce vigorous and unremitting diplomatic interventions. French diplomats in Bonn demanded restrictions to the export and transit of military and non-military goods to the Arab world. The Debré government was able to exert considerable pressure on authorities in Bonn, threatening to withdraw its solidarity in the Berlin crisis. In March 1959, Seydoux assured Debré that 'the government's attitude and notably that of the chancellor has always been very favourable' and that the 'German administration sought to help us' when it came to fighting the FLN's clandestine supply networks. 'As soon as the authorities were made aware of [a case of contraband]', the ambassador continued, they took action to investigate and imposed sanctions against those responsible.[26]

The French authorities expected a common front in the war on contraband and used the collaborative arrangements introduced by *Sûreté* director Verdier and RG director Vié to further their war aims. The ensuing joint efforts produced a number of successful interventions along the Franco-German border, where both FLN and MNA operated smuggling rings to ensure a steady supply of arms and munitions for their militants in France. As early as December 1957, the *Landeskriminalamt* of Rhineland-Palatinate had launched an investigation into how revolvers from a consignment sold by German arms dealer Hans Demmer of Ludwigshafen to the Compagnie générale de transport in Paris had ended up with MNA militants in Strasbourg. The Parisian company, it turned out, functioned as cover for MNA operative Sid Ramdane, who had also used it to purchase ammunition from a merchant in Kaiserslautern and handguns from a company in Saarbrücken.[27] Writing to Papon in August 1958, Verdier praised the German police for pursuing this case so doggedly.[28] The investigation was soon closed, however, for the police

[25] On the legal arguments, see: Fraleigh, 'Algerian Revolution', pp. 205–10.

[26] Compte-rendu de la réunion sur l'Algérie tenue à l'Hôtel Matignon, 14 March 1959, AHC, 2DE75/D2*.

[27] Schreiben LKA Rheinland-Pfalz an LMI, 13 December 1957; Vermerk, Bargatzky, BMI, 7 January 1958; Schreiben LKA Rheinland-Pfalz an LMI, 30 January 1958; Schreiben, LKA-Rheinland-Pfalz an LMI, 7 March 1958, BA/K, B106/15600.

[28] Dépêche no. 19275 de Verdier à Papon, Paris, 4 August 1958, SAMPP/P, Ha/25*.

failed to indict Demmer for illegal trafficking. It was only reopened in February 1959 when French border guards at Vogelbach (Saarland) caught the merchant *in flagrante delicto* attempting to smuggle 1,000 rounds of ammunition, 50 pistols and 1 Colt revolver into France.[29]

Demmer's indictment proved one of several victories in the war on contraband along the Franco-German border. By December 1958, police in Bavaria, Rhineland-Palatinate and North Rhine-Westphalia had dismantled a trafficking ring seeking to purchase weapons for a prison break in Paris.[30] Authorities in Baden-Württemberg, meanwhile, investigated the smuggling activities of Singen innkeeper Edmund Honold, who had been denounced by an Algerian informer. A search of Honold's property failed to uncover evidence, yet he, too, was eventually caught red-handed when he attempted to smuggle four pistols and ammunition across the border at Breisach in September 1959.[31] Enquiries were also afoot in the Saarland, which French intelligence considered the epicentre of FLN and MNA smuggling operations into the metropole.[32] In April 1959, the *Sicherungsgruppe* Bonn began to investigate the activities of a Saarland-based FLN militant, Bougherara El Hadz [sic], whom Colonel Duchène accused of having purchased 100 automatic pistols from a Karlsruhe merchant.[33] While the case led nowhere, Saarland police did arrest two other Algerians for stealing explosives in March 1960.[34] Later that year, police apprehended yet another Algerian at Saarbrücken train station whose suitcase contained five sub-machine guns, one automatic pistol and 1,256 rounds of ammunition. In January 1961, French border guards at Forbach caught two further Algerians coming from the Saarland whose luggage contained FLN propaganda tracts and arms.[35]

While police collaboration yielded some results, most contraband along the Franco-German border appears to have been discovered haphazardly through routine police or customs inspections. Arrests and prosecutions remained rare. Although supply never lived up to demand, Ali

29 Schreiben Nr. 10022–9/58, BfV an BMI, Dr. Toyka, 8 October 1958; Schreiben Nr. 10022–2a/59, BfV an BMI, Dr. Toyka, 19 February 1959, BA/K, B106/15600.

30 Wochenbericht, SG-Bonn, 5 December 1958, BA/K, B131/195.

31 Schreiben Nr. II/5/K-996/59, Polizeipräsidium Südbaden (Freiburg) an LKA Baden-Württemberg, 22 December 1959, BA/K, B131/214.

32 Synthèse no. 750/SSDNA/Allemagne, 4 June 1960; Synthèse mensuelle no. 2107/CCFFA/2, 18 November 1960, SHD-T, 10T/550*.

33 Note de l'ambassade de France à Bonn, April 1959, PA/AA, B25/10; Wochenbericht, SG-Bonn, 5 June 1959, BA/K, B131/196.

34 Wochenbericht, SG-Bonn, 1 April 1960, BA/K, B131/198.

35 Synthèse mensuelle no. 2107/CCFFA/2, 18 November 1960, SHD-T, 10T/550*; 'Waffenschmuggel an der deutsch-französischen Grenze', *Neue Zürcher Zeitung*, 23 January 1961.

Haroun and Daho Djerbal both emphasise just how successful the *Organisation Spéciale* was at smuggling arms from West Germany into France as part of Operation *Hirondelle*. By mid-1958, the OS had established a number of workshops in small-town garages in West Germany, where mechanics such as Aïssa Abdessemed installed secret arms and document caches in the vehicles used by members of the FLN's European support networks. These workshops operated in an undisturbed manner until the war's end. It would appear, therefore, that most of the arms consignments organised for the OS in fact escaped the vigilance of the French or German police.[36]

If the authorities struggled to obstruct the relatively small-scale contraband organised along the Franco-German border, they found it even harder to penetrate the transcontinental trafficking rings reaching from West Germany to the Maghreb. In May 1958, the Federal Ministry of the Interior unsuccessfully investigated claims by an informant whereby FLN logistics no longer relied on Otto Schlüter for arms supplies but on several Frankfurt-based merchants with extensive Eastern-bloc connections.[37] This new trafficking ring had supposedly supplied the FLN with an alarming array of *Kriegswaffen*: 50,000 carbines; 20,000 pistols; 20,000 machine guns; 50,000 automatic rifles; 5,000 MG42 rifles; as well as mines; mortars; and howitzers. Unable to discover even a shred of evidence of this vast trade, the authorities ultimately discarded the informant's claims.[38] The Frankfurt connection, however, would soon rear its head again.

Meanwhile, Franco-German relations were tested by another affair. On 12 December 1958, Casablanca port authorities confiscated 1,456 crates, many of which were labelled 'battlefield ammunition' although they had been declared as 'hunting ammunition'. The crates had arrived from Bremen on the *Ravensberg*, a freighter belonging to Deutsche-Levante-Linie, a Hamburg-based shipping company.[39] To SDECE, the cargo constituted a clear case of contraband, especially since its recipient, the Casablanca establishment Serghini & Benani, was a suspected FLN cover (Serghini being one of Mabed Mehdi's aliases). The French military believed that part of the confiscated freight was subsequently transferred

36 Haroun, *Septième wilaya*, pp. 209–19; Djerbal, *L'OS*, pp. 110–15; Chabane Merkal, 'Abdessemed Aïssa (dit Ali): Un homme de parole', *El Watan* (Algiers), 14 October 2009, www.djazairess.com/fr/elwatan/140131 (accessed 14 December 2013).

37 Schreiben Nr. 10033–9/58, BfV an BMI, 16 June 1958, BA/K, B106/15600.

38 Schreiben, Willy Höhner, 7 May and 14 May 1958, BA/K, B106/15600.

39 Fernschreiben Nr. 82, Botschaft Rabat, 13 December 1958; Fernschreiben Nr. 1835 an Bundesministerium der Finanzen (BMF), 16 December 1958, PA/AA, B25/74; 'Deutscher Frachter mit Munition beschlagnahmt', *Frankfurter Neue Presse*, 15 December 1958.

to an ALN base near Oujda, making the Moroccan authorities complicit in the contraband.[40] The *Ravensberg* affair prompted an investigation into how the export of battlefield munition had gone unapproved and unnoticed by West German customs officials.[41] The bullets had been sold to Serghini & Benani by Genschow & Co., a Cologne-based company that had previously been implicated in an illicit sale of revolvers to Algerians in France.[42] Arguing that this 'notorious trafficker' could only have exported the shipment with the 'complicity of the [German] administration and customs authority', the *Quai d'Orsay* in February 1959 ordered Seydoux to take the matter directly to Adenauer.[43] As ever, this tactic proved effective, for the *Auswärtige Amt* subsequently initiated criminal proceedings against Genschow.[44] Insufficient evidence of deliberate deceit meant the company was once again able 'to extract its head from the noose', as Scherpenberg lamented in October 1960. The failure to prosecute companies like Genschow & Co., the state secretary believed, rested on 'the lack of resolution of the Economics Ministry and its subordinate agencies'. Customs officials, he argued, displayed insufficient vigilance in the export of armaments, failing especially to authenticate end-use-certificates, and this, in turn, strained Franco-German relations.[45]

That strain was felt once again on 5 October 1959, when French authorities blamed yet another case of transcontinental contraband on the negligence of West German customs officials. The affair began when officials at Brussels airport confiscated 300 disassembled machine guns aboard a Sabena flight en route from Frankfurt/Main to Rabat.[46] The accompanying customs declaration innocuously listed the weapons as 'machinery', leaving little doubt as to the cargo's illicit nature. In the ensuing investigation, German customs officials established that an unidentified Frankfurt-based merchant acting on behalf of Nouasri had purchased the machine guns from the Luxemburg establishment SOLA.

40 Notice no. 23754/SDECE, 13 October 1959, SAMPP/P, Ha/24*; Notice no. 632/EMGDN/AFN, 14 April 1959, SHD-T, 1R/352/D3*.

41 Note du l'ambassade de France à Bonn, 15 December 1958; Fernschreiben Nr. 1835 an BMWi und BMF, 16 December 1958; Fernschreiben Nr. 1867 an Bundesministerium für Verkehr (BMV), 5 January 1959, PA/AA, B25/74.

42 Schreiben Nr. 159, BfV an BMI, 13 August 1957; Schreiben, BMI an LMI Nordrhein-Westfalen, 28 August 1957; Schreiben LMI Nordrhein-Westfalen an BMI, 18 October 1957; Telefonatsprotokoll, Bernhardt, BMI, und Karstens, BfV, 5 November 1957, BA/K, B106/15600.

43 Note de la MLA sur le ravitaillement de la rébellion algérienne, 9 February 1959, DDF 1959, Vol. I, Nr. 80, pp. 187–90. Also: Télégramme no. 807 de Seydoux, 21 March 1959, MAE, EU/RFA/1273.

44 Aufzeichnung, Hebich, 18 July 1961, PA/AA, B25/2.

45 Aufzeichnung, StS, 25 October 1960, PA/AA, B2/75.

46 Fernschreiben Nr. 830, Botschaft Paris, 9 October 1959, PA/AA, B25/12.

This company subsequently delivered the arms to another Frankfurt-based middleman, Otto Gandeski, who then arranged their export to Morocco. The investigation concluded that the arms had been bought for the ALN.[47] It corroborated previously unsubstantiated intelligence indicating that Nouasri and two German associates – Helmuth Müller and Otto Gandeski – had delivered at least four other shipments of innocent-sounding 'detached machinery' from Luxemburg via Frankfurt/Main to Casablanca aboard Sabena's bi-weekly flight in the preceding two months.[48]

FLN contraband thus eluded the French and German authorities by relying on falsified cargo declarations, on European or Arab middlemen, on commercial fronts, and on other forms of concealment and deception. Sometimes, however, officials simply lacked the power to intervene. Such was the case with Telefunken, whose continued export of radio transmitters and receivers to Tunisia in 1958 prompted repeated French complaints.[49] Determined to disrupt ALN communications, General Salan in June 1958 launched an all-out assault against Algerian radio networks. At the same time, French diplomats in Bonn demanded tighter controls – if not an outright cessation – of German trade in communications equipment with Tunisia.[50] Initially, these demarches had some success, for the Adenauer government in June 1958 refused to sanction the export of 200 Telefunken portable transmitters to the Tunisian army notwithstanding personal protests by President Habib Bourguiba. Angered by Bonn's intransigence, the Tunis government threatened to establish economic relations with East Berlin and to scupper three lucrative bids by West German companies to modernise Tunisia's broadcasting and telephone networks and hospitals.[51] When it transpired that French companies had also bid for these contracts and that the Debré government itself intended to supply radio transmitters as part of a new arms deal with Tunis, the *Auswärtige Amt* questioned the wisdom of upholding its opposition to Telefunken exports.[52] Once again, however, the Adenauer

[47] Schreiben Nr. 1570, BMF an BMJ, 17 February 1960, PA/AA, B25/12.

[48] Notice de renseignements, CCR/Casablanca, 9 September 1959, SHD-T, 1R/247/D9*.

[49] For greater detail on this affair, see: Mathilde von Bülow, 'The Telefunken Affair and the Internationalization of the Algerian War 1957–1959', *JSS* 28/4 (2005), pp. 703–29 (http://www.tandfonline.com/doi/abs/10.1080/01402390500336380).

[50] Directive no. 4335/EM/10/2/RIDO, 19 June 1958, SHD-T, 1H/1555/D3; Note no. 11/MLA, 21 June 1958, MAE, MLA/0.

[51] Vermerk, Referat 205, 10 June 1958, PA/AA, B25/12; Aufzeichnung, Referat 410, 21 June 1958; Vermerk, Carstens, 26 July 1958, B25/37.

[52] Télégramme no. 2540 à l'ambassade à Bonn, 4 July 1958; Télégrammes nos. 1547 et 1600 de Seydoux, 11 July and 18 July 1958, MAE, EU/RFA/1272; 'Bourguiba von Bonn enttäuscht', *Industrie-Kurier*, 30 July 1958.

government prioritised Franco-German over German–Tunisian relations. Although French objections seemed to have more to do with economic protectionism than national security, the export ban was upheld.

Bonn's opposition did not last long, however, for in August 1958, the NATO Coordinating Committee for East-West Trade Policy (COCOM) removed most of the radio equipment the company sought to export to Tunis from its embargo list of 'material of military importance'. This embargo list prohibited the export of sensitive, dual-use technologies to the Sino-Soviet bloc and socialist-leaning countries, and had served as the legal basis for Bonn's injunction against Telefunken's trade with Tunis. With the transmitters' removal from the list, the *Auswärtige Amt* had to relent in its attitude towards Telefunken.[53] Though granted under strict conditions – notably a pledge by the Tunisian authorities not to transfer equipment to the ALN – Bonn's approval of Telefunken's trade deal met with fierce opposition from military leaders in Algeria, who believed that Telefunken together with Siemens had become the FLN's chief furnishers of communications equipment. By the end of August, General Salan demanded another intervention in Bonn, 'so that West Germany [. . .] be invited to cease delivering radio material to the FLN, whether directly, or through Egyptian, Moroccan, Tunisian (or other) intermediary agencies'.[54] The head of French forces in Algeria essentially sought assurances that German communication companies would cease business in the Arab world, which made no secret of its support of the Algerians' cause. To the military, this trade had substantially improved GPRA and ALN communication networks in North Africa, rendering the insurgency far more effective. In November 1958, Salan again emphasised the importance of putting an end to contraband in radio equipment, insisting, 'the greatest attention be paid to this question'.[55]

In the absence of concrete evidence of Telefunken's or Siemens' connection to the FLN, which the French intelligence services refused to share, the Bonn government could not prohibit the export of materiel classified neither as *Kriegswaffen* under §26.2 of the Basic Law nor as 'material of military importance' under COCOM embargo lists. After all, the companies never directly traded with the FLN. In a free market economy that

[53] Télégramme no. 1803 de Seydoux, 14 August 1958, MAE, EU/RFA/1272; Aufzeichnung, Abt. 2, 25 August 1958, PA/AA, B25/37.

[54] Dépêche no. 5949/10.RM/EM/2/EG, 30 August 1958, SHD-T, 1H/1552/D2.

[55] Dépêche no. 7882/10.RM/EM/2/EG de Salan au ministre des armées, 28 November 1958, SHD-T, 1H/1552/D1.

relied heavily on foreign trade, Telefunken and Siemens were lawfully entitled to export certain communications equipment to Arab clients so long as the latter furnished end-use certificates.[56] Even when they did possess reliable intelligence of FLN involvement the authorities struggled to contain the export of dual-use equipment. Thus in October 1960 police in Stuttgart kept close watch over Benghabrit's dealings with automobile makers Daimler-Benz and Borgward, aware of his FLN connection. The *Sicherungsgruppe* Bonn, however, advised against intervention, for Benghabrit acted under diplomatic cover as an agent of the Libyan government, not the GPRA, and it would be difficult to prove otherwise. Legally, therefore, there was little the authorities could do to prevent Benghabrit from concluding contracts with the carmakers.[57] Since the Algerians either relied on their Arab allies or negotiated under assumed Arab identities and diplomatic covers, the authorities felt powerless to prevent the FLN's procurement activities in West Germany, especially when it came to innocuous-sounding materiel such as textiles, shears or binoculars. They could only try to dissuade German companies from trading with Arab clients.

The Bonn Republic's economic liberalism thus favoured the FLN. To counter this, the government would have to change the regulations governing foreign trade. Beginning in May 1958, the *Auswärtige Amt* did indeed push to increase its veto powers over German exports by insisting on the inclusion of a national-security clause in the *Außenwirtschaftsgesetz* being drafted by the Economics Ministry. This clause (§5) would give German diplomats the possibility 'to prevent the export and transit of goods [. . .] that, while not weapons, could be of similar importance in armed conflicts, for instance communications equipment, special vehicles, accessories, etc.'[58] Not coincidentally, the listed items were all being sought by the FLN. The clause aimed to thwart exports that represented 'a serious threat of the relations of [. . .] West Germany to other countries'. Once ratified, it would allow the Bonn government to block the export of goods that fell neither under COCOM embargo lists nor under the planned *Kriegswaffenkontrollgesetz*.[59] This law, too, had to assume more draconian

[56] Schreiben, Referat 413 an Referat 204, 20 October 1958, PA/AA, B25/12.

[57] Fernschreiben Nr. 1368, Polizeipräsidium Stuttgart an SG-Bonn, LKA Baden-Württemberg, *Kripos* Köln, Frankfurt/Main, 13 October 1960; Fernschreiben ZA/M-1679/60, SG-Bonn an Polizeipräsidium Stuttgart, LKA Baden-Württemberg, *Kripos* Köln, Frankfurt/Main, 13 October 1960, BA/K, B131/214.

[58] Vermerk, Etzler, Referat 413 an Referat 400, 20 May 1958, PA/AA, B63/124.

[59] Aufzeichnung, Referat 404, 21 July 1958, PA/AA, B63/124.

proportions, particularly when it came to the export of *Relativwaffen* and the transport of foreign arms by German shipping companies. Here, too, the *Amt* pressed for the inclusion of a national-security clause (§6) granting diplomats a veto over transactions that threatened relations with third nations.[60]

These attempts to restrict foreign trade, especially in non-military goods, met with considerable resistance from economic circles, who resented what they perceived as the Bonn government's acquiescence to French protectionism in the Arab world.[61] The Federal Transport Ministry opposed the *Amt*'s proposal to tighten controls of transit trade in German ports. Such measures, the ministry argued, breached the shipping industry's right to secrecy and discriminated against German ship-owners, placing them at a serious disadvantage in a highly competitive industry.[62] The Federal Economics Ministry also objected to the *Amt*'s proposals. Though it conceded the need for tougher controls on the export of *Relativwaffen*, the ministry balked at the idea of restrictions on the export of non-military products not on COCOM lists, fearing serious damage to the competitiveness and reputation of West Germany's export-orientated industry and trade. In the end it took Adenauer's personal intervention in September 1958 to impose the national-security clauses on the archliberal Economics Ministry.[63]

The French war on contraband thus had a direct bearing on the formulation of West German trade laws. Once again, foreign-policy-makers prioritised relations with France over those to other countries. The *Auswärtige Amt*'s victory was only partial, however, for the *Kriegswaffenkontrollgesetz* was not actually ratified until 22 February 1961, becoming law two months later, while the *Außenwirtschaftsgesetz* only took effect on 1 September 1961.[64] For nearly three years during which time the Algerian war continued unabated, the *Amt* thus continued to struggle to contain FLN contraband. Efforts to persuade Bonn's Economics Ministry of the need to impose temporary export bans, especially on communications equipment, failed to produce the desired effect. Having been forced to give way on the national-security clauses, Ludwig Erhard, who did not share Adenauer's 'Gaullist' proclivities, was in no mood to give in to Brentano's continued appeals.[65]

[60] Vermerk, Adt, Referat 413 an Referat 404, 20 August 1958, PA/AA, B63/124.

[61] Berggötz, *Nahostpolitik*, p. 126. [62] Vermerk, Referat 413, 14 July 1958, PA/AA, B63/124.

[63] Wochenbericht, Referat 404, 15 September 1958; Aufzeichnung, Referat 413, 26 November 1959, PA/AA, B63/124.

[64] VdDBT/StB, 3. Wahlperiode, 144. Sitzung, p. 8162; Bellers, *Außenwirtschaftspolitik*, p. 248.

[65] Schreiben, Brentano an Erhard, 14 November 1958; Schreiben, Erhard an Brentano, 20 February 1959, PA/AA, B25/12. Also: Franz Eibl, *Politik der Bewegung: Gerhard Schröder als Außenminister 1961–1966* (Munich, 2001), p. 185.

The *Amt*'s inability to restrict the export of radio transmitters and other dual-use materiel exasperated French authorities no end. SDECE contended that Erhard's ministry 'counted on France's defeat' in the Algerian war, seeking to replace French influence in the Arab world.[66] In December 1958, de Gaulle personally ordered his diplomats to caution Bonn that 'the delivery without guarantees of radio material to states that openly support the FLN's cause endangers the common policies of NATO and constitutes an act whose severity is plainly felt by French public opinion'.[67] By April 1959 and in line with Debré's tough new directives, the *Quai d'Orsay* again warned Telefunken to cease its trade in North Africa or risk economic reprisals. The Paris government threatened to cancel its contracts with Telefunken-France, the financial value of which greatly surpassed any deals the company had concluded with Arab clients.[68] Such reprisals proved useless, since Telefunken-France was no longer under German control, yet the company still came under attack in the French National Assembly. In speeches on 4 and 16 June 1959, Debré threatened to publish a blacklist of businesses supporting the FLN, warning that France 'will take retaliatory measures that will cost those dearly who do not understand the fundamental need for solidarity [...] in this fight for freedom'.[69] The prime minister refrained from naming specific companies, but *Gauche Démocratique* senator Bernard Lafay singled out Telefunken. By July, the shares of Telefunken's parent-company AEG had been banned from trading on the Paris stock exchange.[70]

In line with the principle of '*guerre économique*', French authorities took seriously their threat of retaliation against those deemed to be providing material aid to the insurgency. The Telefunken affair had revealed the limits of diplomatic interventions, which proved ineffective in the war on contraband. Bonn's inability to clamp down on the company thus helped convince the French authorities that the only way to neutralise FLN supplies effectively was through muscular and unilateral action. As Counsellor François Leduc warned the *Auswärtige Amt* in April 1959, 'France had to defend its interests [in Algeria] very vigorously'. Given the 'great sacrifices' made there, the government demanded that states 'allied to France refrain from everything that could give an advantage to the

66 Notice no. 11836/SDECE, 14 October 1958, SHD-T, 10T/262*.

67 Dépêche no. 1286/EMGDN/AP/AFN du Général de Gaulle à Murville, 13 December 1958, SHD-T, 1R/351/D1*; Dépêche no. 188 de Jurgensen à Seydoux, 22 December 1958, MAE, EU/RFA/1272.

68 Vermerk, Referat 205, 10 April 1959, PA/AA, B25/12.

69 Cited in: Carron, *Suisse*, p. 256.

70 Fernschreiben Nr. 454 und 458 der Botschaft Paris, 17 June and 18 June 1959; Drahterlass Nr. 772 an Botschaft Paris, 28 July 1959, PA/AA, B25/12.

rebels'. If political and economic pressure failed to undermine FLN contraband, Leduc continued, France had no choice but 'to resort to illegal measures' to protect its territorial integrity and national security.[71] The measures to which Leduc referred usually took the form of forced naval inspections of ships at sea or covert operations. Blatant and often shocking breaches of national sovereignty and international law, these measures demonstrated again just how far the French authorities would go in internationalising their counterinsurgency.[72]

A case of piracy?

A relatively benign method of intervention in the arsenal of military action, the French General Staff considered the time of transport the most propitious moment to intercept and neutralise illegal arms shipments.[73] Interceptions at sea consequently became 'the priority mission of French naval forces in the Mediterranean and the greatest responsibility of the [...] navy' in the Algerian war.[74] So central was this tactic to the French counterinsurgency that de Gaulle cited it as a pretext for his withdrawal of France's Mediterranean fleet from NATO's integrated command in March 1959.[75] That same month, the new commander-in-chief in Algeria ordered an intensification of intelligence collection and naval patrols. 'Experience has shown', General Challe argued, 'that since the ATHOS affair (October 1956), all arms transports for the rebellion by sea have been entrusted to regular shipping-companies [...] or negotiated by charter companies'. He instructed his subordinates, that:

> [...] it is of the greatest importance to discover the diverse contacts that FLN representatives have established to maritime circles, transport and charter companies in the principal ports of the world. This intelligence will effectively allow [us] to identify possible vessels [for interception]. It is equally important to gain information on freight agreements, particularly in London and HAMBURG [sic].[76]

Until Challe's initiative, French Maritime Surveillance (*Surmar*) had approached inspections on the high sea in a selective manner. This restraint

[71] Aufzeichnung, Unterabteilungsleiter Außenhandel, 27 May 1959, PA/AA, B25/12.
[72] Thomas, 'Policing', p. 85.
[73] Projet de plan particulier no. 131/EMGDN/2, 31 August 1959, SHD-T, 10T/531/D3*.
[74] Kessler, 'Surveillance', p. 98; Michel Debré, *Gouverner. Mémoires 1958–1962* (Paris, 1988), p. 212; Faivre, 'Renseignement', p. 293; Melnik, *Mille jours*, pp. 90–1.
[75] Vaïsse, *Grandeur*, p. 67.
[76] Notice no. 572/10.R.M./EMI/2, 18 March 1959, SHD-T, 1H/1540/D3*.

had been prompted by a lack of resources, a dearth of intelligence, and especially by legal qualms, since the policy of forced naval interceptions of foreign cargo vessels in fact violated international laws guaranteeing the freedom of the seas during peacetime (French governments never having declared war on the FLN).[77] Whereas *Surmar* only had an average of sixteen vessels at sea on a monthly basis in 1956, that number rose to thirty in 1959.[78] Under the Fourth Republic, only one West German vessel had been subjected to a forced inspection. Intercepted on 18 October 1957 en route from Alexandria – then one of the FLN's chief supply centres – the *Helga Böge* had been forced to dock at Algiers.[79] Customs authorities had found nothing untoward, prompting the vessel's Hamburg-based owner, Johann Blumenthal, to demand an apology and indemnity from the French Navy.[80] The latter presented its apology to the German embassy in Paris in November 1957 but ignored Blumenthal's request for reparations.[81] On 24 February 1958, the German embassy in Paris had presented a verbal note to the *Quai d'Orsay*, which explained that, 'while understanding the French situation in Algeria and taking account of the friendly [bilateral] relations', the legal situation was such that Bonn could not 'contest the right of [*Helga Böge*'s] proprietor to demand compensation'.[82] Considering the note's apologetic tone, German diplomats were clearly embarrassed by the affair, which clashed with Adenauer's supportive stance in the Algerian question, all the more so since it coincided with the Sakiet crisis. Obliged to defend the interests of West German citizens and businesses, on this occasion Bonn's intervention succeeded, for in October 1959 Blumenthal received an indemnity of 21,185DM.[83]

After the May crisis of 1958, the Bonn government's reticence to uphold private shipping rights intensified further. At the same time, the de Gaulle government pursued a much more rigorous approach to naval interceptions than its predecessors had, one that hit German shipping companies particularly hard. The Fifth Republic's tough new stance is explained partly by the general intensification of the counterinsurgency, and partly by a rising spate of suspected contraband cases involving German-owned

[77] Fraleigh, 'Algerian Revolution', p. 203. [78] Kessler, 'Surveillance', p. 101.
[79] Dépêche no. 2018, DGGA, cabinet militaire, à Langlais, MLA, 17 March 1959, MAE, EU/RFA/1272.
[80] Aufzeichnung, Referat 302, 21 December 1957, PA/AA, B24/349/F1.
[81] Vermerk, Frank, Referat 302 an Referat 500, 22 November 1957, PA/AA, B24/349/F1.
[82] Dépêche no. 50 de Langlais à la DGGA, 11 March 1958, MAE, EU/RFA/1272.
[83] Aufzeichnung, Rechtsabteilung, 8 December 1960, PA/AA, B24/349/F2.

vessels. In addition to the *Ravensberg* mentioned earlier, Algiers port authorities in December 1958 seized a large shipment of military cloth from a West German cargo vessel en route to Tunis, suspecting the consignment was for the ALN.[84] One month later, officials in Casablanca acting on the French authorities' behest confiscated nearly 900 tonnes of arms and munitions from the freighter *Mönkendamm*.[85] In January and February 1959, *Surmar* further intercepted the *Bonita* and *Ursula Rickmers* on suspicion of contraband.[86] And in November 1959, customs officials in Algiers confiscated 8,950kg of batteries from the *Valencia*, which they claimed were for use in the ALN's portable radio transmitters and receivers.[87]

While none of these cases prompted any serious disagreement between Paris and Bonn, the re-routing of the *Bilbao* on 4 November 1959 did. En route from Hamburg to Casablanca, the vessel was forced to dock at Cherbourg, where authorities confiscated 100 crates of hunting munitions and 73 crates containing storm lights. According to the ship's manifest, the crates were intended for the Casablanca establishment Coframa, which French intelligence suspected of being an FLN front.[88] The *Bilbao*'s owner, the Oldenburg-Portugiesische-Dampfschiffs-Reederei, and the manufacturer of the storm lights, Hermann Nier K.G., both protested their innocence and solicited the *Auswärtige Amt*'s assistance in defending their reputations and business rights. The ensuing investigation confirmed that a legitimate Moroccan establishment had ordered the storm lights and munitions, prompting Cherbourg port authorities to release the confiscated goods in December 1959. Even so, Hermann Nier K.G. demanded 96,200DM in moral and material indemnities while the shipping company demanded 298,700DM. Although the companies had been cleared, their trade had been disrupted and reputations publicly tarnished, French newspapers having accused them of collusion with the FLN.[89] The German

[84] Télégramme no. 2829 de la DGGA au Quai d'Orsay, 22 December 1958; Télégramme no. 573 de l'ambassade de France, Tunis, 3 February 1959, MAE, AL/ALG/39.

[85] Notice no. 632/EMGDN/AFN, 14 April 1959, SHD-T, 1R/352/D3*; Guillon, 'Contrebande', p. 112.

[86] Notice no. 166/EMG/2/Marine, 24 February 1961, SHD-T, 1R/352/D3*.

[87] Dépêche no. 2130 de Seydoux, Bonn, 26 November 1959, MAE, MLA/4; Dépêche de la DGGA au Quai d'Orsay, 3 December 1959, MLA/5; Fernschreiben Nr. 1000 von Botschaft Paris, 2 December 1959, PA/AA, B25/12.

[88] Notice no. 166/EMG/2/Marine, 24 February 1961, SHD-T, 1R/352/D3*.

[89] Fernschreiben, Oldenburg-Portugiesische Dampfschiffs-Reederei, Hamburg, an AA, 4 November 1959; Schreiben, Hermann Nier KG an Fachverband Stahlblechverarbeitung e.V., 16 December 1959; Schreiben, Oldenburg-Portugiesische Dampfschiffs-Reederei an BMV, 18 December 1959, PA/AA, B24/349/F1; Note Verbale, Botschaft Paris an Quai d'Orsay, 1 April 1960, MAE, EU/RFA/1274.

press, meanwhile, compared the *Bilbao* incident to an act of piracy and questioned Paris's sincerity as an ally.[90] In the *Bundestag*, the SPD echoed the press's calls for Adenauer to use the December 1959 Paris summit to defend German shipping rights.[91] The chancellor's refusal to raise the matter with either de Gaulle or Debré merely highlighted his reticence to discuss the Algerian question even when it impinged directly on West German sovereignty and economic interests. Instead, the *Auswärtige Amt* sought to depoliticise the affair by pursuing the companies' compensation claims through confidential channels.[92]

Bonn's strategy of containment worked until another high-seas inspection of a freighter belonging to the Oldenburg-Portugiesische-Dampfschiffs-Reederei again caught the press's attention. En route from Antwerp to Casablanca, the *Las Palmas* was forced on 10 September 1960 to divert to the Algerian naval base at Mers-El-Kébir. There, authorities confiscated fifteen crates containing 'agricultural material' listed in the ship's manifest as crop-dusters. *Surmar*'s intervention had been based on intelligence indicating that the FLN sought to purchase 100 flame-throwers and the napalm-like substance metavon through a West German supplier.[93] In January 1960, the cargo vessel *Melilla* had allegedly disembarked 2,718kg of metavon in Casablanca, despatched by the Karlsruhe armaments company Dimex owned by Walter Heck.[94] Five months later, Dimex supposedly delivered another 100 barrels of metavon through a Hamburg-based intermediary Schryver [sic] to Zenatia Import-Export in Rabat, a known cover for the MALG. The barrels allegedly arrived in Casablanca on 6 July 1960 aboard the *Lisboa*, having escaped *Surmar*'s net.[95] In September, a 'habitually reliable source' subsequently reported

90 'Piraterie unter Verbündeten', *SPD-Pressedienst*, 6 November 1959; Horst Möller and Klaus Hildebrand (eds.), *BDFD*, Bd.3, *Parteien, Öffentlichkeit, Kultur* (Munich, 1997), p. 592; Télégramme no. 3502 de Seydoux, 28 November 1959; Télégramme no. 759 de Chalvron, Berlin, 1 December 1959; Télégramme no. 3561 de Leduc, Bonn, 3 December 1959, MAE, EU/RFA/1262*; Dépêche no. 455 du consul-général Fernand-Laurent, Hambourg, 26 November 1959, MLA/4; Dépêche no. 468 de Fernand-Laurent, 1 December 1959, EU/RFA/1273; Dépêche no. 451 de l'attaché naval Captaine Labrousse, Bonn, à l'EMGM/2, 2 December 1959, SHD-T, 14S/20*.

91 Kleine Anfrage der SPD betreffend Rechtssicherheit, 1 December 1959, VdDBT/D, 3.Wahlperiode, Nr. 1440; Antwort des Bundesministers des Auswärtigen, 15 December 1959, Nr. 1494; VdDBT/StB, 3. Wahrperiode, 91. Sitzung, 2 December 1959, p. 4930.

92 Aufzeichnung, Büro StS, 7 January 1960, PA/AA, B2/75.

93 Fiche no. 372/EMG/2/SEC, 12 September 1960, SHD-T, 1R/352/D3*.

94 Résumé des renseignements connus, Annexe 1, EMI/2, 12 September 1960, SHD-T, 1H/1541.

95 Message de Marine, Oran, au commandant-en-chef Algérie, 22 June 1960; Message du commandant-en-chef Algérie à la Défense Nationale, 28 June 1960; Message de la Défense Nationale au commandant-en-chef Algérie, 28 June 1960; Message du commandant-en-chef, Rabat, au commandant-en-chef Algérie, 31 July 1960, SHD-T, 1H/1543/D1.

that *Las Palmas's* manifest listed twenty-five [sic] cases of crop-dusting equipment sent by Dimex, again using Schriver [sic] as intermediary, to Zenatia Import-Export. The *deuxième bureau* concluded the shipment was unlikely to contain agricultural equipment.[96]

Not privy to this intelligence, the high-sea seizure of the *Las Palmas* triggered further protests in the West German press while East Berlin's *Neues Deutschland* used the incident to ridicule Bonn's weakness vis-à-vis a 'fascistic' France.[97] In the *Bundestag*, the Free Democrats questioned the government over its proposed action. The liberal party echoed the widespread belief that Bonn should not tolerate such overt breaches of West German sovereignty and had to protect the rights and reputation of West German trade.[98] The pressure emanating from parliament and the press obliged the *Auswärtige Amt* to assume a more forceful stance in defence of ship-owners. On 3 October 1960, its speaker defended *Las Palmas's* owner, insisting the confiscated equipment was harmless.[99] The French Navy begged to differ for a technical analysis had determined with 'quasi-certitude' that the so-called crop-dusters assembled into twenty flame-throwers and 105 reservoirs.[100] Having inspected the cargo on 16 September, German consul Werner Matz confirmed that it consisted of old *Wehrmacht* materiel.[101] Even so, German officials rejected the charge of contraband, sticking to the legal precept *in dubio pro reo* (when in doubt, for the accused).[102] Only once it had been informed of the shipment's despatcher and recipient did the government concede before parliament on 7 December that *Las Palmas* had transported illicit goods, though it refused to hold the shipping company accountable for that transgression.[103]

This admission did not silence German deputies, who continued to raise a string of questions in the *Bundestag* about the illegality of France's

96 Fiche no. 372/EMG/2/SEC, 12 September 1960, SHD-T, 1R/352/D3*.

97 'Die Botschaft in Paris protestiert', *FAZ*, 15 September 1960; 'Verbündete unter sich', *Neues Deutschland* (Berlin/Ost), 16 September 1960; 'Nebelgeräte aus der Dachstube', *FAZ*, 21 October 1960; 'Las Palmas hatte keine Waffen', *Der Tagesspiegel* (Berlin/West), 1 October 1960.

98 Kleine Anfrage der FDP betreffend Aufbrindung des Frachters Las Palmas, 5 October 1960; Antwort des Bundesministers des Auswärtigen, 17 October 1960, VdDBT/D, 3. Wahlperiode, Nrs. 2102 and 2153.

99 Note de la MLA à l'EMGDN, 6 October 1960, SHD-T, 1H/1541.

100 Fiche, EMG/2/Marine, 14 September 1960, SHD-T, 1R/352/D3*; Notice, DGGA/BE, au directeur-général des finances, Algiers, 22 September 1960, SHD-T, 1H/1541.

101 Dépêche no. 497 du Vice-Amiral Querville, préfect de la 4ème région maritime, 23 September 1960, SHD-T, 1H/1541.

102 Aufzeichnung, Scherpenberg, 25 October 1960, PA/AA, B2/75.

103 134. Sitzung, 7 December 1960, VdDBT/StB, 3. Wahlperiode, p. 7617.

actions.[104] The parliamentary debate coincided with an unprecedented wave of high-seas inspections. Between 1 October 1960 and 24 February 1961, *Surmar* boarded no fewer than forty-six vessels, of which at least twelve were West German, far more than any other nationality.[105] One case generated particularly vitriolic protests. Intercepted on 4 December 1960, the *Morsum* had been on a direct course from Turkey and Greece to Bremen carrying 42,000 cases of munitions purchased by the *Bundeswehr* from the Turkish government, a NATO ally, through the intermediary of the West German company Meyersson.[106] In view of the cargo's state-sanctioned character, its confiscation prompted a sharp protest from State Secretary van Scherpenberg.[107] Outraged by another interception of a West German vessel, Hamburg's Senate temporarily banned French warships from the city's harbour, a move the *Auswärtige Amt* regretted not only for its hostility but also its futility given the fact that no warships were actually scheduled to visit the city.[108]

The French Navy, however, had no intention of ceasing its forced inspections. Unbeknownst to the Germans, its decision to intercept the *Morsum* stemmed from intelligence indicating the FLN had recently been prospecting in Turkey.[109] *Surmar* intercepted more vessels in December 1960 than at any other time during the Algerian war because intelligence strongly suggested the FLN expected a major shipment of arms. As early as May 1960, the *deuxième bureau* had warned, 'the FLN is currently proceeding with massive arms sales, principally in West Germany, where a purchasing commission has been outfitted with substantial financial means and is deploying a great deal of activity, but also in Czechoslovakia, Poland, and Hungary'.[110] French intelligence expected the arms purchased as a result of this activity to be delivered in December. Of the twenty-six vessels intercepted at sea that month, only the Yugoslav *Martin Krpan* was

[104] Mündliche Anfragen, FDP-Abgeordneten Ewald Bucher, 9 December 1960, Nr. 2301; SPD-Abgeordneten Hannsheinz Bauer, 2 December 1960, Nr. 2266; DP-Abgeordneten Herbert Schneider, 13 December 1960 und 10 March 1961, Nrs.2311 und 2593; SPD-Abgeordneten Hermann Hansing, 13 December 1960, Nr.2311, all in VdDBT/D, 3. Wahlperiode. Also: 134. Sitzung, 7 December 1960, p. 7617; 136. Sitzung, 14 December 1960, pp. 7753–5; 151. Sitzung, 15 March 1961, p. 8577, all in VdDBT/StB, 3. Wahlperiode.

[105] Notice no. 166/EMG/2/Marine, 24 February 1961, SHD-T, 1R/352/D3*. For an overview from the diplomatic perspective: Cahn and Müller, *RFA et Guerre d'Algérie*, pp. 313–32.

[106] Message de la Défense Nationale à la Marine, 8 December 1960, SHD-T, 1H/1543/D1.

[107] Drahterlass Nr. 1175 an Botschaft Paris, 6 December 1960, PA/AA, B2/75.

[108] Aufzeichnung, Presseabteilung, 20 December 1960, PA/AA, B1/57.

[109] Message no. 6471/10.R.M./EMI/2 à la Défense Nationale, 7 December 1960, SHD-T, 1H/1543/D1. On the dilemmas of Turkish policy in the Algerian question, see: Eyüp Ersoy, 'Turkish Foreign Policy Toward the Algerian War of Independence', *Turkish Studies* 13/4 (2012), pp. 683–95.

[110] Fiche, EMG/2, 20 May 1960, SHD-T, 1R/352/D3*.

found to carry 2,057 undeclared cases of munitions and explosives.[111] Although the *Morsum's* manifest proved perfectly in order, the Navy still refused to release its cargo, unconvinced the munitions would not end up in Algerian hands. French authorities in fact demanded a public statement from the Bonn government guaranteeing the cargo's intent for the *Bundeswehr*. In response to West German 'agitation on the subject of naval inspections', Prime Minister Debré even asked his cabinet 'whether one could not make an indiscretion in the press about the *Morsum*' so as to implicate the latter in sordid affairs.[112] The incident thus highlights the conspiratorial suspicions the French continued to harbour towards West Germany and the high-handed manner in which the Gaullist regime approached its German ally. Franco-German reconciliation, it would appear, still had a long way to go. Even intelligence sharing proved far more problematic than the liaison arrangements instituted by Verdier and Vié would have one believe. The *Auswärtige Amt* for its part refused to issue a public statement that could be taken as legitimising France's high-sea inspections. It did, however, convey to the French authorities a confidential copy of the *Bundeswehr's* contract with Meyersson, for only this would secure the munitions' release.[113]

Although the *Morsum* incident was resolved quietly, French high-seas inspections had placed considerable strain on Franco-German relations. In the FRG, economic circles, public opinion and parliament increasingly pressured the Adenauer government to protect the reputation of the shipping industry and uphold West German sovereign rights. In addition to accusations of piracy, allegations grew that France deliberately targeted West German vessels for high-seas inspections, leaving American, British and Soviet freighters untouched.[114] Indeed, intelligence obtained by the BKA back in March 1959 suggested that one German trafficker deliberately used British- or Russian-owned ships to transport arms so as to circumvent the French inspections.[115] This opinion came to be echoed by the West German consul-general in Casablanca Franz Obermaier, and even by a number of CDU deputies, who considered France's actions a sign of 'a very disagreeable lack of

111 Notice no. 166/EMG/2/Marine, 24 February 1961, SHD-T, 1R/352/D3*; Kessler, 'Surveillance', p. 101.

112 Note, Debré, pour Amanrich, 19 December 1960, AHC, 2DE/13.

113 Aufzeichnungen, Scherpenberg, 9 December and 12 December 1960, PA/AA, B2/75; Message no. 304/EMGDN à la Marine, 12 December 1960, SHD-T, 1H/1543/D1.

114 'Unmögliche Zustände', *General-Anzeiger* (Bonn), 21 December 1960.

115 Telex, 3–4 March 1959, BA/K, B106/15783.

respect' vis-à-vis Bonn.[116] To Seydoux, such 'absurd insinuations' were a misplaced expression of 'injured national pride'. His embassy justified *Surmar*'s interventions by pointing to Bonn's repeated failure to prevent contraband.[117] Meanwhile, the Association of German Shipowners (VdR), Federal Transport Ministry, governments of Bremen, Hamburg and Schleswig-Holstein, and parliamentary faction of the SPD, all demanded a stop to the interceptions as well as reparations for the damages incurred.[118] Formulaic protests in Paris no longer satisfied the German public even if Ambassador Blankenhorn delivered them personally, as in the case of the *Paul Rickmers* on 22 December 1960.[119]

Though frustrated by the Navy's repeated transgressions, German diplomats generally sympathised with France's war on contraband.[120] Moreover, in view of Paris's persistent demand for loyalty in the Algerian question, the *Auswärtige Amt* strenuously rejected the public's calls for Adenauer to draw attention to the illegality of high-seas inspections.[121] The Bonn government required a *modus vivendi* that would satisfy the French authorities' demand for stringent export controls while at the same time protecting the rights of German ship-owners and upholding German sovereign rights and national interests. The new State Secretary at the *Auswärtige Amt*, Karl Carstens, therefore urged parliament to hasten the ratification of the *Außenwirtschafts* and *Kriegswaffenkontrollgesetz* so as finally to enable foreign-policy-makers to impose sanctions on exports liable to harm Franco-German relations.[122] The *Amt* further proposed a system to replace *Surmar*'s inspections whereby the German authorities, including the VdR, would themselves conduct voluntary, pre-emptive controls of cargoes bound for North Africa. To be effective, these controls required the free sharing of intelligence between all parties involved.[123] German shipowners were amenable to this proposal but made their cooperation

[116] Télégramme no. 5469 de Seydoux, 13 December 1960, SHD-T, 1H/1543/D1; Schreiben Nr. 619 Generalkonsul Obermaier, Casablanca, 16 September 1960, PA/AA, B24/349/F1.

[117] Seydoux, *Beiderseits*, p. 251. Also: Bougherara, *Rapports*, p. 137.

[118] Schreiben, Brentano an Minister-Präsident Kai-Uwe von Hassel, Schleswig-Holstein, 8 December 1960; Fernschreiben Nr. 4348, BMV an AA, 9 December 1960; Fernschreiben, VdR Hamburg an AA, 9 December 1960; PA/AA, B24/349/F2; Aufzeichnung, Scherpenberg, 2 January 1961, PA/AA, B2/75.

[119] Drahterlass an Botschaft Paris, 21 December 1960, PA/AA, B24/349/F2.

[120] Aufzeichnung, Scherpenberg, 25 October 1960, PA/AA, B2/75.

[121] Briefentwurf, Adenauer an de Gaulle, 22 December 1960, PA/AA, B24/349/F3; Cahn and Müller, *RFA et Guerre d'Algérie*, p. 324.

[122] Bundestagserklärung, Carstens, 14 December 1960, VdDBT/StB, 3. Wahlperiode, 134., Sitzung, pp. 7753–4.

[123] Cahn and Müller, *RFA et Guerre d'Algérie*, pp. 325–6.

contingent on compensation for losses already incurred. Although they had previously honoured such demands, the French authorities now refused to recognise even the principle of indemnification and steadfastly defended their right to board and inspect ships at sea whenever suspicions warranted such interventions on national-security grounds.[124] The Debré government instead suggested that German officials communicate to the French Navy the manifests of all commercial vessels servicing North African ports. This proposal in turn met with fierce opposition in Bonn where it was deemed neither practical nor politically or legally acceptable.[125]

After lengthy discussions with Bonn's Economics and Transport Ministries as well as the VdR, the *Auswärtige Amt* issued a counter-proposal: federal authorities would inform the French of all freighters departing for Moroccan and Tunisian ports (though without details of ships' manifests); the VdR would temporarily and voluntarily agree to suspend the transport of war materiel to the Maghreb; and the French would supply as much intelligence on contraband as possible so that German authorities could themselves intervene whenever suspicions arose.[126] In January 1961, the VdR accepted this arrangement provided the French indemnified German shipping companies for present and future damages.[127] French diplomats, too, agreed in principle, conscious that it would prove difficult to fight the shipping companies' legal claims given that France was not formally at war. The French armed forces, however, remained obstinate. They argued that as long as Bonn could not guarantee the control of all German vessels departing for the Mediterranean, including those loaded in transit ports such as Rotterdam or Antwerp, *Surmar* would reserve the right to intervene in the name of national security.[128]

Ultimately, a gentlemen's agreement emerged based on the voluntary and confidential sharing of information between the French and German authorities and on self-regulation by the shipping companies.[129] In an effort to reduce tensions, the French General Staff had issued instructions on 21 December 1960 limiting interceptions of German vessels to cases

[124] Notiz, Weinhold, Referat 204, 30 December 1960, PA/AA, B2/75.
[125] Aufzeichnung, Unterabteilungsleiter West, 13 December 1960, PA/AA, B24/349/F2.
[126] Aufzeichnung, undated; Vermerk, Referat 204, 30 December 1960, B24/349/F3.
[127] Aufzeichnung, Weinhold, Referat 204, 2 January 1961, PA/AA, B2/75.
[128] Télégramme no.52 du directeur des affaires politiques à Seydoux, 6 January 1961, MAE, MLA/7; Cahn and Müller, *RFA et Guerre d'Algérie*, pp. 323, 331.
[129] *Der Auswärtige Ausschuß: Sitzungsprotokolle*, Bd. 13/III, 59. Sitzung, 9 February 1961.

where strong suspicions of contraband existed. In such instances, the military attaché in Bonn was to notify German authorities of *Surmar*'s intentions, and if Bonn provided the ship's manifest, the interception could possibly be suspended.[130] When the French military attaché informed the German Defence Ministry of the imminent interception of the *Paul Rickmers* on 22 December, the action was greeted by the *Auswärtige Amt* as a 'first positive step towards Franco-German cooperation in this matter' even though the two-hour notice hardly gave authorities a chance to intervene.[131] French officials subsequently informed the Bonn government of each case arousing their suspicions.[132] On 29 March 1961, for instance, the Debré government asked German authorities to prevent the delivery of eight Borgward all-terrain vehicles aboard the *Ravensberg* to Tripoli, since French intelligence suspected these of being part of a contract negotiated by FLN-agent Benghabrit. Because Borgward's contract was with the Libyan Red Crescent, and the vehicles concerned were not classified as military equipment, the authorities were unable to prevent the delivery.[133] *Surmar* therefore intercepted the *Ravensberg*, confiscating the vehicles on 24 April. Although the manoeuvre prompted renewed calls for compensation, including from the Libyan government, German diplomats on this occasion dared not protest *Surmar*'s move.[134]

Bonn's attitude towards forced interceptions thus remained highly reserved, reflecting the general deference the Adenauer government demonstrated towards France in the Algerian question. Instead of defending German sovereignty and rights, the *Auswärtige Amt* tolerated *Surmar*'s transgressions and tried to persuade German shipping companies of the need for moderation and patience in the matter of restitutions. Bonn's protests were timid and symbolic gestures intended to appease domestic and Arab opinion, not to confront the French. Although they did not question the companies' legal right to indemnification where these could prove their innocence, German diplomats considered it pointless to pursue the matter. For as long as the Algerian war continued, they argued,

130 Message no. 329/EMGDN/Algérie, 21 December 1960; Message no. 5/EMGDN/Algérie aux Marine, Quai d'Orsay, Ministère des Armées, 3 January 1961, SHD-T, 8S/258/D4*.

131 Message no. 386 de l'attaché militaire à Bonn à l'EMGDN/Algérie, 22 December 1960, SHD-T, 8S/258/D4*.

132 Cahn and Müller, *RFA et Guerre d'Algérie*, pp. 315–16, 321–3.

133 Vermerk, Referat 205, 29 March 1961; Vermerk, Referat 204, 30 March 1961; Aufzeichnung, Referat 204, 30 March 1961; Schreiben, BMV an AA, 7 April 1961, PA/AA, B24/350/F1.

134 Note verbale du Ministère des Affaires Étrangères de Libye à l'ambassade d'Allemagne, Tripoli, 15 May 1961, PA/AA, B24/350/F1.

the French government would remain intransigent and defensive.[135] Even after the Évian Accords of 18 March 1962 produced a ceasefire with the FLN, Councillor Weinhold of the French desk argued that any attempt to raise the issue of reparations before a definitive end of hostilities would merely produce 'discord'.[136] By then, the German shipping industry had become impatient. On 17 July 1962, shortly after Algeria became independent, the VdR's representative in Bonn urged State Secretary Carstens to commence negotiations with the French. Only then did the German embassy in Paris remind the *Quai d'Orsay* of the 'urgent' and 'emphatic' need to settle the reparations question.[137] Negotiations finally commenced in 1963 and in some cases settlements were not reached until 1966.[138] By then, of course, the political climate had changed considerably. Not only had the Algerian war ceased to impinge on Franco-German relations, but the Berlin crisis, too. Once the "Atlanticist" Erhard replaced the "Gaullist" Adenauer as chancellor in October 1963, the Bonn government no longer trod as carefully vis-à-vis France and was far more likely to stand up for its rights.[139]

The *Red Hand*?

If the Adenauer government responded meekly to *Surmar*'s forced inspections at sea, it proved even more reluctant to stand up to covert interventions on German territory. General Ely's 1958 call for the neutralisation of the FLN's supply networks by means of 'clandestine action' was hardly new; it reflected the '*guerre d'action*' first set out by the French army in its 'Plan for the protection of French North Africa against the Cold War' of June 1955. This strategy had found its first application in West Germany under the Fourth Republic when *Service Action* targeted Otto Schlüter in September 1956. If the explosion that killed his associate had not dissuaded the Hamburg arms dealer from his nefarious trade with North African clients, the car bomb that slayed his mother and maimed his daughter in June 1957 had. Acts of sabotage and assassination were therefore nothing new in the context of France's global counterinsurgency.

[135] Cahn and Müller, *RFA et Guerre d'Algérie*, p. 331.

[136] Vermerk, Weinhold, Referat 204 an Referat 500, 29 May 1962, PA/AA, B24/354/F2.

[137] Vermerk, StS Carstens, 17 July 1962, PA/AA, B2/75; Schreiben Nr. 3170 Botschaftsrat Knoke, Paris, 8 August 1962, PA/AA, B12/935.

[138] Cahn and Müller, *RFA et Guerre d'Algérie*, pp. 331–2.

[139] On the tensions between "Atlanticists" and "Gaullists" and their impact on foreign policy, see: Conze, *Herausforderung*, pp. 260–94; Hildebrand, 'Atlantiker', pp. 583–92.

Under the Fifth Republic, however, clandestine action against the FLN would assume entirely new proportions. The assassination attempt on Aït Ahcène of November 1958 merely represented the opening salvo of a drawn-out campaign across Western Europe, the Middle East and the Maghreb. According to Debré's security and intelligence councillor Constantin Melnik, the premier's 'ministry of action' orchestrated a relentless pursuit 'of arms traffickers in the four corners of Europe' and beyond.[140] The war of action constituted a key component of France's reinvigorated counterinsurgency, providing vital support for military and police operations in Algeria and France.[141] 'This war, we must win it', Debré wrote in his memoirs, and for that purpose he accepted even the most dubious of methods.[142]

French military and civilian authorities felt justified in resorting to muscular, clandestine interventions because, for as Melnik later noted, '[t]here are certain circumstances in which the State, representing [...] the common interest, must, if it does not want to succumb, oppose violence with violence'.[143] Although it breached international and domestic laws, the recourse to state-sanctioned sabotage and murder was rationalised as legitimate self-defence in the interest of national security. These methods received even the president's full backing, notwithstanding his oft-noted disinclination for the 'vulgar and subaltern' world of intelligence.[144] According to Melnik, de Gaulle fully tolerated and condoned the war of action, only imposing three restrictions on covert operations: that they occur in times of war and outside of France; that the targets were not French citizens; and that all operations were approved by the head of state and prime minister.[145] Though it remained undeclared, the language used in internal memoranda makes it clear that French military and civilian authorities considered themselves at war against the FLN, an enemy they did not perceive as French. Between January 1959 until April 1962, executive decisions on covert operations thus rested in the hands of three officials: Prime Minister Debré, to whom SDECE and its *Service Action* were officially subordinated; Debré's security and intelligence counsellor Melnik; and Jacques Foccart, de Gaulle's own adviser on intelligence and African affairs, who was himself a reservist in the *11ème Choc*.[146] Foccart later denied Melnik's involvement in this triumvirate, emphasising instead

[140] Melnik, *Mille jours*, pp. 59, 29. [141] Ibid., p. 33; Debré, *Gouverner*, pp. 207–13.
[142] Debré, *Gouverner*, p. 212. Also: Samuel, *Debré*, pp. 254–6. [143] Melnik, *Mille jours*, p. 80.
[144] Bergot, *Commandos*, p. 210; Faligot and Krop, *Piscine*, p. 173; Melnik, *Mille jours*, p. 58; Porch, *French Secret Services*, p. 404.
[145] Melnik, *Mille jours*, pp. 255–6. [146] Ibid., pp. 58–9, 66–7, 90, 255–6.

his own centrality in the decision-making process.[147] This claim is contradicted by Debré, however, who not only 'flattered himself for having fought effectively' to undermine arms trafficking and FLN support networks, but who also maintained in his memoirs that it was Melnik who liaised directly with the head of SDECE, General Paul Grossin, and *Service Action*, whilst Foccart – and through him de Gaulle – was merely kept informed.[148] Had de Gaulle disapproved of the war of action, he would almost certainly have intervened to put an end to it, removing key personnel such as Grossin in the process, just as he eliminated Roger Wybot, the long-time chief of the DST, after the latter's loyalty came into question in December 1958.[149]

Convinced as the French intelligence services were of West Germany's centrality to the FLN's procurement networks, it is hardly surprising that the country became a focus for covert interventions. The war of action entailed two types of operations. The first type involved acts of sabotage, codenamed *Arma* operations, which aimed to disrupt FLN supply chains and intimidate companies accused of collusion with the Algerians. By targeting suspected gunrunners, SDECE strove physically to destroy either a consignment of arms before it could reach its target or its means of transport. Thus in July 1957, frogmen scuttled two vessels – the *Bruja Rocha* and *Typhoon* – in the port of Tangier belonging to the Astramar import-export company run by German arms dealer Georg Puchert. According to MALG-operative Aïssa Abdessemed, Puchert had replaced Schlüter as one of the FLN's most important suppliers of war materiel.[150] On 1 October 1958, a detonation in the port of Hamburg subsequently scuppered the cargo vessel *Altas* belonging to the German Atlas-Levante-Linie. BKA investigators concluded the ship's hull had been sabotaged deliberately by means of an explosive device, though they were unable to prove allegations the ship had been carrying war materiel for the FLN.[151] Some time later, another freighter belonging to the Atlas-Levante-Linie

[147] Philippe Gaillard, *Foccart Parle: entretien avec Philippe Gaillard*, Vol. I (Paris, 1995), pp. 360–2.

[148] Debré, *Gouverner*, p. 212. Also: Olivier Forcade, 'Michel Debré et les fins politiques du renseignement', in *Debré* (eds.) Berstein, Milza and Sirinelli, pp. 489–502.

[149] Porch, *French Secret Services*, pp. 397–8, 421; Melnik, *Mille jours*, pp. 58–60, 212, 255–6; Faligot and Krop, *Piscine*, pp. 173–4.

[150] Aïssa Abdessemed, 'Témoignage à titre posthume', *El Watan*, 13 July 2005 (http://justesdalgerie.forumactif.org/t69-georg-puchert-mort-pour-l-algerie, accessed 24 January 2015); Bergot, *Commandos*, pp. 30–2.

[151] Dépêche no. 455 du consul-général de France à Hambourg, 23 October 1958, MAE, EU/RFA/1256; Schreiben, Generalstaatsanwalt Hamburg an den Senat Hamburg, 20 May 1959, PA/AA, B25/11; Schreiben, BKA an BMI, 20 July 1959, BA/K, B106/15783; Guillon, 'Contrebande', p. 111.

suffered a similar fate. On 15 January 1960, the *Marmara* experienced an explosion at sea shortly after departing from Bremen. Again, investigators determined that the damage had been inflicted by means of a bomb.[152] French intelligence considered the sabotage of vessels identified as gun-runners an effective tactic in the war on contraband. If Melnik can be believed, then SDECE incapacitated at least seven merchant ships in 1961 alone.[153] Melnik further claims that *Service Action* set fire to one of Telefunken's manufacturing plants in Bavaria, determined to undermine that company's business with the FLN. This allegation remains unsubstantiated, though technical experts from the *Sicherungsgruppe* Bonn did conduct investigations at the company's plant in Ulm, which had been badly damaged by a fire in early 1960.[154]

Service Action also continued to carry out a second type of operation: assassinations. According to uncorroborated statistics provided by Melnik, the service 'eliminated' some 135 arms traffickers and FLN agents in 1960 and another 103 in 1961.[155] Most of these liquidations would have occurred in North Africa and the Middle East, which remained the undisputed hubs of FLN activity throughout the war. Given its central role in FLN supply networks, however, West Germany, too, became a prime target of homicide operations. The attempts on Schlüter and Aït Ahcène were only the first in a chain of attacks on federal territory. On 3 March 1959, Georg Puchert, whom French intelligence had come to view as one of the FLN's most important contacts in the illicit arms trade, became the victim of a car bombing in Frankfurt/Main. The notorious Baltic-German had failed to heed previous warnings to sever his contacts to the Algerians.[156] Nine months later, on 31 December 1959, Puchert's Algerian business associate Nouasri lost both his hands to a parcel bomb delivered to his Frankfurt/Main hotel room.[157] In September 1960, meanwhile, the Frankfurt-based businessman Helmuth Müller, who had been implicated in a number of contraband affairs, survived two consecutive road accidents, each caused – as

152 Télégramme no. 112 de Seydoux, 16 January 1960, MAE, EU/RFA/1274; Wochenbericht, SG-Bonn, 5 February 1961, BA/K, B131/198.

153 Melnik, *Mille jours*, p. 58.

154 Melnik, *Mort*, p. 77; Philippe Bernert, *SDECE Service 7. L'extraordinaire histoire du colonel Le Roy-Finville et des clandestins* (Paris, 1980), p. 209; Wochenbericht, SG-Bonn, 14 April 1960, BA/K, B131/198; Letter from Doris Rangnick, AEG-Archiv, Frankfurt/Main, to author, 1 March 2003; Letter from Karl B. Fischer, Telefunken a.D., München, to author, 11 June 2004.

155 Melnik, *Mille jours*, pp. 58, 256; Ibid., *Mort*, p. 7.

156 Dépêche no. 12, AFP, Bonn, 4 March 1959; '"Rote Hand" legte Puchert um. Frankfurter Attentat sollte internationale Waffenhändler warnen', *Bonner Rundschau*, 7 March 1959.

157 'Der Algerier Nouasri arbeitete mit Puchert zusammen', *FAZ*, 2 January 1960.

police determined – by explosive devices that had been attached to his car.[158] Wilhelm Beißner was less fortunate. On 16 October 1960, this Munich-based arms dealer suffered serious injuries when a bomb ripped through his vehicle. He, too, traded mostly with the Middle East.[159] Meanwhile, Walter Heck, whose armaments company Dimex had been implicated in the *Las Palmas* affair, was killed in a drive-by shooting in front of his Karlsruhe home on 28 June 1961.[160] Later that year, Hamburg authorities foiled an assassination attempt on Ernst Wilhelm Springer, a former SS officer turned entrepreneur known for his Middle Eastern business contacts and support of the banned neo-Nazi Sozialistische Reichspartei. In Springer's case, too, the police discovered and removed a bomb from the underside of his car.[161]

Because of their gangster-style nature, these assassination attempts caused a sensation in the West German press, unleashing a torrent of speculation over the perpetrators involved. One thing seemed certain: the attacks taking place all had a common denominator – the Algerian war. Rumours circulated in the press that the culprits belonged to a French underground organisation composed of thugs, former parachutists, retired policemen and right-wing radicals. Some newspapers and magazines, such as the *Frankfurter Rundschau, Frankfurter Abendpost, Der Spiegel* and *Bild*, implicated renegade French intelligence officers, especially the mysterious Colonel Marcel Mercier, who had already been caught up in the espionage scandal surrounding the suicide of Swiss prosecutor-general Dubois, and who now served as SDECE's liaison to the BND.[162] Only rarely did these rumours lead to direct charges against the French intelligence services. Although some newspapers replicated allegations first voiced by *Paris-Journal* that French special services had assassinated Puchert, they never pursued this claim.[163] The shared consensus seemed to be that only Soviet-bloc or renegade agents, radicals and criminals were

[158] Wochenbericht, SG-Bonn, 7 October 1960, BA/K, B131/199.

[159] 'Die mysteriösen Bombenanschläge der Roten Hand', *Stuttgarter Zeitung*, 24 October 1960; 'Beißner-Attentat wahrscheinlich von der "Roten Hand"', *FAZ*, 26 October 1960.

[160] 'Auf der Straße angeschossen', *FAZ*, 30 June 1961; 'Karlsruher Waffenhändler gestorben', *FAZ*, 8 July 1961.

[161] 'Rote Hand, OAS – oder die Konkurrenz', *SZ*, 25 January 1962.

[162] Télégramme no. 3135 de Seydoux, 8 December 1958, MAE, MLA/2; Dépêche no. 630 de Seydoux, 26 March 1959, MLA/3.

[163] Télégramme no. 1111 de l'ambassade de France, Bonn, 14 April 1959, MAE, MLA/3; 'Mord an Waffenhändler Puchert ein Werk französischer Agenten? Enthüllungen einer Pariser Zeitung', *Die Welt*, 14 April 1959; 'Die Sprengstoffanschläge in Deutschland. Eine Pariser Zeitung beschuldigt den französischen Geheimdienst', *FAZ*, 15 April 1959; Schreiben Nr. 2302, Botschaft Paris, 17 April 1959, PA/AA, B24/280/F3.

capable of committing such reprehensible crimes, but not the representatives of a democratic government and ally.

Mostly, therefore, the press blamed the attacks on shadowy and reactionary French counter-terrorist organisations such as the *Green Crescent, White Hand* or ODAT (*Organisation de défense anti-terroriste*).[164] Parallels were drawn to assassinations elsewhere, including the deaths of the French liberal publicist Jacques Lemaigre-Dubreuil in Casablanca in June 1955, the Swiss arms dealer Marcel Léopold in Geneva in September 1957, and Ben Bella's French attorney Auguste Thuveny in Rabat in November 1958. In a confidential interview with Wolfgang Löhde of *Der Stern* and former police commissioner Alfred Martin in June 1959, the foreign-affairs editor of the conservative French paper *L'Aurore*, Alain Roy, claimed that the assassinations had been perpetrated by *Catena*, a secret society founded by French officers after World War II.[165] French journalist Pierre Péan, meanwhile, blamed the so-called *Grand O*, a semi-fascist society, also linked to the French military, which he likened to 'the new Cagoule' in reference to the Secret Committee of Revolutionary Action that had sought the overthrow of the French Popular Front during the late 1930s.[166] Whether these extremist organisations ever existed and whether they pursued the FLN's arms dealers is difficult to say, but at the time, such stories received a remarkable amount of attention and credence. *Die Welt* correspondent Paczensky reasoned that French counter-terrorists aimed to 'intimidate not only the North Africans – especially the Algerians – but also those in other countries that show sympathy for them'. Paczensky accused the Paris government of tolerating and encouraging such behaviour; yet he, too, stopped short of implicating the French authorities in the assassinations taking place.[167]

In the absence of viable explanations for the crimes being committed on German soil, conspiracy theories had clearly captured the public's imagination. One name soon came to dominate all public speculations: the *Red Hand*. By early 1959, the German press identified this secret society as the

164 'Die Spur führt nach Frankreich. Jetzt befasst sich Interpol mit dem Anschlag auf Schlüter', *Mannheimer Morgen*, 8 June 1957; Télégramme no. 2628 de Seydoux, 6 November 1958; Télégramme no. 2662 de Seydoux, 7 November 1958; Dépêche no. 1923 de Seydoux, 26 November 1958, MAE, MLA/2; Aufzeichung, StS II Dittmann, 7 November 1958, PA/AA, B25/10; Télégramme no. 630 de Seydoux, 26 March 1959, MAE, MLA/3.

165 Vermerk, SG-Bonn, zur Vernehmung des Informanten Alain Roy, 20 June 1959; Niederschrift über Besprechung mit Kriminalrat a.D. Martin, 29 June 1959, BA/K, B106/15783; Bericht, SG-Bonn, 24 June 1959, PA/AA, B25/10.

166 Pierre Péan, *Le Mystérieux Docteur Martin (1895–1969)* (Paris, 1993), pp. 399–400, 413–17.

167 'Täter, die nie gefaßt werden. Die "Rote Hand" und ihre Opfer... ', *Die Welt*, 4 April 1959.

chief suspect for the entire chain of unexplained attacks on federal territory since 1956.[168] The *Red Hand* was said to have its roots in the French settler communities of the Maghreb, specifically in the brothels, karate clubs and weight rooms of Tunis, Rabat and Casablanca. Rumour had it that during the early 1950s, European vigilance committees had tried to prevent Tunisian and Moroccan nationalists from realising their goal of self-government. Known as *la Main Rouge* in Tunisia and *la Main Noire* or ODAT in Morocco, these reactionaries were credited with the assassinations of several advocates of decolonisation, including the Tunisian trade union leader Ferhat Hached in 1952, and Lemaigre-Dubreuil in Casablanca. Following the independence of Morocco and Tunisia in March 1957, the vigilance committees supposedly turned their attention to protecting France's remaining outpost in North Africa. Coalescing into the *Red Hand*, reactionary settlers allegedly vowed to pursue the enemies of French Algeria, especially the FLN and all those who supplied its insurgency with arms.[169]

So persistent were rumours of the *Red Hand*'s machinations that the West German police and judicial authorities began to investigate their veracity. In March 1959, Frankfurt/Main's prosecutor Heinz Wolf received an anonymous telephone call from a purported member of the *Red Hand* claiming that Puchert was only the latest victim in a chain of ten attacks perpetrated by the organisation on West German soil so far. At a press conference on 16 April, Wolf announced that police wanted to interrogate three men in connection with Puchert's murder: Jean Viary, a retired French police inspector; and his accomplices Christian Durieux and Jean-Baptiste van Cottem (alias 'Pedro'). All three men, Wolf claimed, were leading members of the *Red Hand*. Wolf also implicated Mercier, though his role remained obscure.[170] The prosecutor seemed to believe that while SDECE's representative may have known about or facilitated Puchert's assassination, he had not been directly involved. Thus the authorities, too,

[168] 'Rote Hand legte Puchert um', *Bonner Rundschau*, 7 March 1959; 'Der Killer', *Der Spiegel*, 25 March 1959; 'Täter, die nie gefaßt werden', *Die Welt*, 4 April 1959; 'Die Rote Hand tötete Waffenhändler Puchert', *DPA*, 16 April 1959.

[169] Faligot and Krop, *Piscine*, p. 202; Jacques Follorou and Vincent Nouzille, *Les Parrains Corses: leur histoire, leurs réseaux, leurs protections* (Paris, 2006), pp. 191–218; René Gallisot, 'La décolonisation du Maghreb: de l'Afrique du Nord française au Maghreb en suspens', in Harbi and Stora (eds.), *Guerre d'Algérie*, pp. 49, 56; Horne, *Savage*, p. 129; Méléro, *Main rouge*, chs. I–V; Porch, *French Secret Services*, pp. 371–6, 400–1; Bernard Violet, *L'Affaire Ben Barka* (Paris, 1995), pp. 62–76.

[170] Bericht, Referat VI/A/3 BMI, 6 April 1959; Schreiben, hessischer Justizminister an BMJ, 17 April 1959, BA/K, B106/15783; Télégramme no. 1133 de Seydoux, Bonn, 16 April 1959, MAE, MLA/3.

shied away from openly accusing SDECE of complicity in attacks on arms dealers and FLN members.

Wolf's declarations had an immediate impact. As the German embassy in Paris reported, the French press mostly scorned Wolf's allegations, claiming instead that the attacks against Puchert, Aït Ahcène and others like them had been the product of rivalries among Algerians or arms dealers. Some, like *Paris-Presse*, accused Wolf of having read too many crime novels.[171] As *Paris-Journal* opined, 'the mysterious Red Hand only appears to exist in the imaginations of a group of Francophobe former Nazis'. The conservative paper *Parisien libéré* was equally sceptical, writing:

> One has to wonder that a German prosecutor has used his authority to give credence to preposterous stories and has adopted the hypotheses of the Algerian rebels. Such an attitude does not correspond to the official policy of Chancellor Adenauer. French public opinion would rather hear that the German police is observing the arms dealers closely and is striving to undermine their activities.[172]

Wolf's comments prompted French diplomats to protest to an embarrassed *Auswärtige Amt*. Unable to intervene in judiciary procedures, there was little that diplomats could do to prevent such public accusations. Ambassador Seydoux assured the *Quai d'Orsay* that they did not reflect official perceptions; Frankfurt and Hesse were ruled by Social-Democrats who were little inclined to heed Bonn's line in the Algerian problem.[173]

Already pressurised by the French, German diplomats also faced growing domestic pressures, especially once allegations surfaced of Franco-German collusion in the *Red Hand* affair, with some German papers, including the *Frankfurter Abendpost, Der Spiegel* and *FAZ*, even alluding to the federal authorities' top-secret meeting with Verdier and Vié of November 1958.[174] Barely a week after Wolf's press conference, the *Bundestag* faction of the SPD demanded to know what measures the government was taking to prevent the activities of 'secret organisations' on German territory and whether there had been any collaboration between French and German intelligence in the planning and execution of attacks on German soil.[175] Bonn's Interior Ministry flatly denied these allegations, contending that there was no evidence of secret French

171 Fernschreiben Nr. 289, Botschaft Paris, 18 April 1959, PA/AA, B24/280/F4.
172 Both citations are from: Fernschreiben Nr. 285, Botschaft Paris, 17 April 1959, PA/AA, B24/280/F4.
173 Télégramme no. 1156 de Seydoux, Bonn, 17 April 1959, MAE, MLA/3.
174 Cahn and Müller, *RFA et Guerre d'Algérie*, p. 258.
175 Kleine Anfrage der SPD betreffend ausländische Geheimdienste in der Bundesrepublik, 22 April 1959, VdDBT/D, 3. Wahlperiode, Nr. 1023.

interference in German internal affairs and that there was certainly no Franco-German collaboration in this matter.[176] The *Auswärtige Amt* echoed this response. In a joint declaration with the Interior and Justice Ministries, it proclaimed that Wolf's allegations constituted 'one of many working hypotheses' applicable only to the Puchert case for which the Frankfurt prosecutor was responsible.[177]

Though intent on playing down the scenarios circulating in the press, federal authorities, too, had grown concerned by the overspill of political violence from the Algerian war, so much so that Bonn's Interior Ministry raised the matter with the French domestic security services. In May 1959, Vié responded to these concerns by claiming that the *Red Hand* represented a propaganda ploy devised by the FLN to discredit the French. He suggested that Algerian nationalists rather than reactionary settlers had created the *Red Hand*.[178] While the RG director shifted the blame to the FLN, the *Sûreté Nationale* retorted that it was 'absurd to think' an organisation like the *Red Hand* could even exist.[179] Duchène, too, emphasised on more than one occasion that French authorities would never tolerate the supposed activities of the *Red Hand*. He implied that Paris would neither condone nor order such blatant transgressions against West German sovereignty and national security.[180] At the same time, the French security services did not discount the possibility that the attacks had been perpetrated without their knowledge by 'ultras' in defence of *l'Algérie française*.[181]

The German authorities did not quite know what to make of these contradictory hypotheses. According to the BKA, the perpetrators almost certainly belonged to a single French organisation. Comparing the attacks on Schlüter in Hamburg, Puchert in Frankfurt/Main and Thuveny in Rabat, investigators determined that all three cases shared remarkable likenesses. Apart from similar motives – all three men had strong connections to the FLN – there were striking parallels in the

[176] Antwort des Bundesinnenministers, 5 May 1959, VdDBT/D, 3. Wahlperiode, Nr. 1088.

[177] Drahterlass Nr. 159 an Botschaft Paris, 20 April 1959, PA/AA, B24/280/F4; 'Rote Hand', *FAZ*, 20 April 1959.

[178] Note du service de liaison au ministère fédéral de l'intérieure à Bonn, opération 'A', 23 May 1959, BA/K, B106/15783.

[179] Vermerk, Unterabteilungsleiter VI-A/BMI, 26 May 1959, BA/K, B106/15778.

[180] Vermerk, Vorsprache Duchène, BMI, 30 July 1959; Vermerk, Besprechung mit Duchène, Referat VI-A-3/BMI, 21 November 1959, BA/K, B106/15783.

[181] Sprechzettel für die Sitzung des Bundestagsausschusses für Inneres, Referat VI-A-3, 20 October 1959, BA/K, B106/15783.

execution of the attacks, even in the use of explosives.[182] The BKA also established similarities in the explosions that scuttled the *Atlas* and the *Al Kahira*, a freighter that sank in the port of Ostend on 13 March 1959. On both occasions, similar types of explosives and clamps had been mounted in such a manner as to inflict maximum damage. What's more, the BKA had traced this equipment to a factory in Aubagne in southern France. Investigators further believed that only a person with expert training as a frogman and access to specialised equipment would be able to execute such professional acts of sabotage. Here, too, the BKA concluded that the perpetrators belonged to a single organisation emanating from France, though its report stopped short of naming that organisation, let alone pointing the finger at the secret services.[183]

In light of these conclusions, it is hard to fathom why federal authorities did not press the French government for assistance in their criminal investigations. After all, the implications of the BKA's report were clear enough. Instead, the Bonn government remained mute, preferring to concentrate its investigations on the suppression of FLN activities and hence on facilitating the French counterinsurgency rather than exposing the perpetrators behind the attacks on German citizens and property. Puchert, for instance, had been under investigation by the *Sicherungsgruppe* Bonn ever since a 'confidential' source, probably the rival arms dealer Hans-Joachim Seidenschnur, had denounced the former in December 1958 of abetting the FLN. These investigations continued even after Puchert's death and would form an important part of Prosecutor-General Güde's federal lawsuit against the FLN.[184] The authorities' decision to concentrate on FLN contraband rather than SDECE's illicit activities was typical of Bonn's deference to the French in the Algerian question, which went so far as to tolerate blatant transgressions of German sovereignty that posed a direct threat to public security. Police in Frankfurt/Main and Hamburg continued their inquests into the attacks against Schlüter, Puchert and the *Atlas*, but they received little assistance from federal authorities.[185] By July 1959, Hamburg's prosecution

[182] Schreiben, Justizminister Hessen an BMJ, 17 April 1959, BA/K, B106/15783.

[183] Bericht, BKA an BMI, 20 July 1959, BA/K, B106/15783.

[184] Schreiben, Generalbundesanwalt Güde an BMJ, 22 April 1959; Bericht E1279/SG-Bonn, 13 May 1959, PA/AA, B25/10. On Puchert and Seidenschnur: 'Der Tod kommt mit der Post. Spiegel-Serie über Frankreichs "Rote Hand"', *Der Spiegel* 10 (2 March 1960); Bergot, *Commandos*, pp. 153–6; Leggewie, *Kofferträger*, pp. 179–87.

[185] Schreiben, Justizminister Hessen an BMJ, 28 April 1959; Schreiben, Staatsanwaltschaft Hamburg an Justizabteilung, Senat Hamburg, 20 May 1959, PA/AA, B25/11.

suspended its investigations due to insufficient evidence; other inquests fared little better.[186]

Meanwhile, the failure to bring to justice the architects behind these attacks occurring on German soil heightened public hysteria, especially given a spate of similar assaults implicating the *Red Hand* in Italy, France and Belgium. On 22 May 1959, FLN attorney Ould Aoudia had been assassinated in Paris. Just over ten days later, a bomb had destroyed a car belonging to the FLN's representative in Rome, Tayeb Boulahrouf. Detonated prematurely, the bomb had killed a young boy and severely injured at least two others. Subsequently on 5 October, Belgian border guards arrested the former Poujadist deputy Jean Berthommier together with two associates at Bléharies, having discovered an un-primed bomb in the boot of their car. The discovery unleashed speculation over their membership in the *Red Hand*.[187] Again and again, the evidence pointed to French perpetrators, raising questions as to why the Bonn authorities had not sought French legal cooperation.[188] One of the 'Algeria lobbyists', SPD deputy Kalbitzer, demanded to know from Interior Minister Schröder 'why the French assailants of the Algerian Aït Ahcène, of the arms dealers Puchert and Schlüter and of the steamer *Atlas* in the Hamburg harbour were not being prosecuted'.[189] The attempted assassination of three Algerians in front of Cologne's train station in October 1959 further fuelled this debate. While the press accused the *Red Hand*, federal authorities used the opportunity to clamp down on Algerians in the FRG, arguing that the assaults sprang from inter-communal feuding. On this occasion, they were probably right, for all three Algerians had recently defected to the FLN; the attack on them was therefore likely to have been an act of retribution by the MNA.[190]

186 Schreiben Nr. 411E Justizabteilung Senat Hamburg an AA, 16 July 1959, PA/AA, B25/10.

187 'Kinder Opfer einer Bombe', *FAZ*, 6 July 1959; 'Bombenschmuggel über die Grenze. Attentäter der "Roten Hand" in Belgien festgenommen', *Die Welt*, 6 October 1959; 'L'ex-député poujadiste Berthommier est arrêté en Belgique', *Le Monde*, 6 October 1959; 'Un procureur général allemand avait déjà parlé de la « Main rouge »', *Le Monde*, 6 October 1959; 'Auf der Spur einer Organisation französischer Terroristen', *Neue Zürcher Zeitung*, 7 October 1959.

188 'Die "Rote Hand"', *FAZ*, 18 April 1959.

189 Hellmut Kalbitzer, 'Der unerwünschte Gast aus Algerien. Ein Versuch zur politischen Bevormundung der Bundesbürger', *Vorwärts*, 24 July 1959; Mündliche Frage des Abgeordneten Kalbitzers, 11 June 1959, VdDBT/D, 3. Wahlperiode, Nr. 1159; Antwort, StS Anders, BMI, 77. Sitzung, 19 June 1959, VdDBT/StB, 3. Wahlperiode, p. 4225.

190 'Schwierige Spurensicherung beim Kölner Attentat', *FAZ*, 24 October 1959; Vermerk, Marmann, Referat 503, 26 October 1959, PA/AA, B25/10; Télégramme no. 3047 de Seydoux, 27 October 1959, MAE, MLA/4; Wochenbericht, SG-Bonn, 6 November 1959, BA/K, B131/197.

By October 1959, even the *Bundestag*'s Commission for Internal Affairs expressed alarm over the *Red Hand*, for the recent spike in assassinations constituted a clear threat to the public.[191] Criminal investigations having led nowhere, the Commission recommended vigorous diplomatic action. The *Auswärtige Amt* was to advise Paris that French counter-terrorist organisations were causing German authorities 'the greatest difficulties' and that the country 'could under no circumstances become a secondary theatre of war'. The Commission wanted Adenauer to raise the matter directly with de Gaulle at the Paris summit planned for December 1959.[192] While the Commission pressed for a forthright exchange of views in defence of West German interests, the authorities in Bonn balked at the idea of seeking French legal assistance in the prosecution of the *Red Hand*, fearing this might prompt the Paris government to demand reciprocal action over Algerians sought for political crimes in France. As the Federal Justice Ministry pointed out, the principle of political asylum and France's resort to the death penalty made it impossible for Bonn to fulfil French extradition requests, which meant that Paris would equally reject any such demands made by the German authorities.[193] Considering their failure to clamp down on the FLN's external sanctuary, the Bonn authorities found it difficult to protest against French transgressions against West German sovereignty. Given the French government's linkage of the Algerian and German questions, moreover, the Commission's recommendations struck the authorities as legally and politically ill-advised.

The West German press, meanwhile, did not share these legal and political compunctions and heavily criticised the Bonn government for its passivity in the pursuit of the *Red Hand*. As in previous instances, the tenor assumed by the press was moralistic, juxtaposing German lawfulness against French criminality. Indeed, the nefarious activities of this enigmatic organisation had reinforced the image in the press of the FLN's independence struggle as a just cause against ruthless colonial oppressors. On 28 November 1959, the *FAZ* argued:

> It has to be made clear that in a constitutional state [*Rechtsstaat*] the whole severity of the principle of order will be brought up against such misdeeds. Even in the best political alliance between two countries there can be no

[191] 'Beratung über die "Rote Hand"', *FAZ*, 22 October 1959.

[192] Aufzeichnung, 13 November 1959, PA/AA, B25/10. Also: 'Diskussion über die "Rote Hand"', *FAZ*, 13 November 1959.

[193] Aufzeichnung, 13 November 1959, PA/AA, B25/10.

> place for complicity with law-breakers. One cannot excuse oneself with the argument that the victims were just 'arms traffickers [. . .]'[194]

A few days later, the influential paper again urged the government to intervene in Paris, writing that the 'forbearance of an ally has its limits [. . .] goodwill cannot be strained forever unpunished'.[195] The *FAZ* further highlighted one of the principal obstacles in the *Red Hand*'s prosecution:

> One difficulty in putting foreign secret organisations out of business [. . .] is the fact that collaboration between our fragmented criminal police-services with the *Bundeskriminalamt* is complicated and cumbersome. Many villains escape through the net of federalism. If that is so, then the executive powers of the *Bundeskriminalamt* should be reinforced. [. . .]the Federal Republic cannot remain a playground for foreign secret services.[196]

Collaboration between local, provincial and federal authorities was indeed fraught with tensions as each sought to maintain its executive powers and approached the Algerian question with a different perspective and degree of urgency. The division of powers between *Bund* and *Länder* already impeded the surveillance and control of Algerians. Now, it affected investigations into the *Red Hand*.[197]

The *FAZ*'s exhortations appeared at a time of frenzied reporting on the topic. Rumours resurfaced of the French authorities' possible complicity in the *Red Hand*'s criminal activities. In October 1959, Cologne's *Neue Rhein Zeitung* had alleged, '[o]ne of the leaders of the [*Red Hand*] was a member of the French embassy' in Bonn, an accusation that Counsellor Leduc considered 'idiotic'.[198] Bonn's *General-Anzeiger* singled out French press-attaché Louis Hirn, leading German diplomats to advise the French embassy to pursue libel charges.[199] The greatest sensation, however, came on 27 November 1959, when the conservative British tabloid *Daily Mail* published an interview with alleged *Red Hand* killer Christian Durieux, wanted in Frankfurt/Main in connection with Puchert's assassination. Durieux's open boasts of his pursuit of FLN arms suppliers fuelled public outrage in West Germany.[200] In parliament, the SPD charged the

[194] 'Seltsame Bekenntnisse', *FAZ*, 28 November 1959.

[195] 'Griff nach der Roten Hand', *FAZ*, 2 December 1959.

[196] 'Seltsame Bekenntnisse', *FAZ*, 28 November 1959. [197] Ibid.

[198] Télégramme no. 3102 de Seydoux, 31 October 1959, MAE, MLA/4; Vermerk, Carstens, 6 November 1959, PA/AA, B24/292/F3.

[199] 'Sitzt die "Rote Hand" in der Botschaft?' *General-Anzeiger*, 26 November 1959; Aufzeichnung, Rechtsabteilung, 26 November 1959, PA/AA, B24/292/F3.

[200] 'Frankfurter Staatsanwalt prüft Bekenntnis der "Roten Hand"', *Die Welt*, 28 November 1959; 'Die "Rote Hand" bekennt sich zu den Attentaten', *FAZ*, 28 November 1959.

Adenauer government of inaction vis-à-vis the Paris authorities, which stood accused of protecting the *Red Hand* from prosecution.[201] Munich's influential *Süddeutsche Zeitung* criticised the government for its apparent refusal to help the police bring this organisation to justice.[202] Prosecutor-General Güde, other papers argued, should take charge of the inquest, which had become a matter of national security.[203] The Atlas-Levante-Linie even demanded compensation from the French government for the damages incurred to the sunken *Atlas*.[204]

By December 1959, public agitation over the *Red Hand* seriously strained relations between Paris and Bonn, and that at a particularly sensitive time in the Berlin crisis.[205] Before departing for the Paris summit, Brentano assured the *Bundestag* Commission for Foreign Affairs that judicial authorities would receive the *Auswärtige Amt*'s full backing in the pursuit of *Red Hand* assassins and promised to 'speak very frankly with the French' about this matter.[206] In fact, the foreign minister made only vague references to French transgressions during the Paris summit while promising de Gaulle and Debré that Bonn would use 'all its available resources' to suppress Algerian agitation, which it had failed thus far to do 'due to the devolution of [police] powers to the *Länder* and constitutional guarantees on the respect of individual liberties'.[207] State Secretary van Scherpenberg, too, stretched the truth considerably when he told the *Bundestag* in December 1959 that 'the federal government stood in constant contact with the French services' over the *Red Hand*. In fact, no such conversations appear to have taken place. The *Auswärtige Amt* and Interior Ministry kept remarkably mute over the breaches of sovereignty ostensibly committed by French counter-terrorists, fearful of straining the Paris–Bonn alliance over Berlin.[208] In a circular to German diplomatic missions in the Arab

[201] Mündliche Anfrage des SPD-Bundestagsabgeordneten Walter Menzel, 26 November 1959, Nr. 1430; kleine Anfrage der SPD betreffend Rechtssicherheit, 1 December 1959, Nr. 1440; Antwort des Bundesministers des Auswärtigen, 15 December 1959, Nr. 1494, VdDBT/D, 3. Wahlperiode; Behandlung, 91. Sitzung, 2 December 1959, VdDBT/StB, 3. Wahlperiode, p. 4930–1.

[202] 'Die "Rote Hand" geistert durch das Land. Deutsche Staatsanwaltschaften müssen bei der Untersuchung der Mordanschläge im dunkeln tappen', *SZ*, 3 December 1959.

[203] 'Die "Rote Hand" eine Staatsgefährdende Organisation', *FAZ*, 30 November 1959; Télégramme no.3520 de Seydoux, 30 November 1959, MAE, MLA/4.

[204] Schreiben, BMV an AA, 9 December 1959; Vermerk, Referat 503 an Referat 204, 22 December 1959, PA/AA, B25/11.

[205] Télégramme no. 3539 de Seydoux, 1 December 1959, MAE, MLA/5.

[206] *Der Auswärtige Ausschuß: Sitzungsprotokolle*, Bd. 13/III, 39. Sitzung, 4 December 1959.

[207] Compte-rendu des discussions plénaires franco-allemandes au Palais de l'Elysée, 2 December 1959, AN, 5AG1/160*.

[208] Aussage, StS van Scherpenberg, 91. Sitzung, 2 December 1959, VdDBT/StB, 3. Wahlperiode, pp. 4930–1.

world dated 15 February 1960, the *Amt* instructed its representatives to blame the assassinations and sabotage acts on inter-Algerian rivalries and to deny all French involvement.[209] The government's declarations of firmness concerning the *Red Hand* thus amounted to empty promises. Even the BKA's efforts had come to naught, especially once it transpired that Durieux' boasts to the *Daily Mail* had merely been a student hoax. Arrested by German border guards at Lörrach-Stetten in February 1960, Durieux denied his previous claims and was ultimately released for lack of proof.[210] With no more leads to go on, the government was able to extract itself from its promised demarches in Paris.[211]

With Durieux exposed as a fraud, the question remained, was there ever a *Red Hand*, or was the organisation a figment of the press's imagination? Is it possible, as Faligot and Krop have claimed, that the myth was fabricated by French counter-intelligence? Did SDECE set up Durieux's interview with the *Daily Mail*, and did French intelligence instigate a 'secret' press conference of the *Catena* at Versailles in April 1960?[212] The accessible archival records provide no evidence to prove or disprove these allegations, yet it is unlikely the organisation ever existed. According to Constantin Melnik, the *Red Hand* was 'one of the most beautiful subterfuges [*intoxications*] in the history of secret services'.[213] The *Red Hand* provided France's war of action with plausible deniability, that is the ability of a government to argue credibly that it was not responsible for – or involved in – the covert operations pursued by its secret services.[214] Even when SDECE's secret war on contraband generated very public results, the real perpetrators of the shootings and bombings targeting the FLN and its suppliers remained secret. On the one hand, French officials could quite rightly deny the existence of the *Red Hand* or *Catena*. On the other hand, these fictional organisations drew attention away from SDECE, allowing French governments to abnegate responsibility for the crimes committed in West Germany and elsewhere. Thus when reports circulated that French intelligence agents like Mercier were involved in the

209 Drahterlass an deutsche Missionen in Amman, Baghdad, Beirut, Damascus, Jeddah, Cairo, Tripoli, Tunis und Rabat, 15 February 1960, PA/AA, B25/12.

210 'Nur ein Studentenulk', *FAZ*, 7 December 1959; Bericht, SG-Bonn, 23 February 1960, BA/K, B106/15783.

211 Schreiben, AA an BMV, 3 February 1960, PA/AA, B25/11.

212 Faligot and Krop, *Piscine*, pp. 201–3; Yves Courrière, 'La chasse aux trafiquants d'armes', *Historia. Hors série* 23 (1971), p. 99.

213 Melnik, *Mort*, p. 141.

214 Gregory F. Treverton, *Covert Action. The Limits of Intervention in the Postwar World* (New York, 1987), p. 5.

Red Hand, they were easily refuted. Considering the passions roused by the Algerian war among the settler community in Algeria, which would soon produce a real counter-terrorist organisation – the Secret Army Organisation, or *Organisation de l'armée sécrète* (OAS) – the myth of the *Red Hand* provided plausible cover to discredit any rumours of official involvement in the crimes perpetrated in France's name.

The *Red Hand* thus represented a classic case of deception. Its myth was substantiated and sustained through fiction and film even after the exposure of Durieux's hoax, and without much effort on the part of French intelligence. In 1960, a first novel appeared on the subject in France. Published under the pseudonym Pierre Genève, the book's real authors allegedly worked for SDECE.[215] Two years later, a German-born American journalist, Joachim Joesten, also published an account of the *Red Hand*'s machinations.[216] Meanwhile, the German writer Gerhard Borris attempted in 1959 to create a film about the organisation entitled '*Bombengeschäfte*' ('Bomb Business'). On this occasion, German diplomats managed to block the screenplay's production on the grounds that it endangered both national security and Franco-German relations.[217] They were less successful in the case of '*Die Rote Hand*', a film by Austrian director Kurt Meisel, which was released in October 1960. Fortunately for Bonn, Meisel's film received mostly negative reviews, *Der Spiegel* calling it 'a perfect synthesis between fabrication and boredom'.[218]

The press, too, continued to follow the *Red Hand*'s purported exploits, and not just those committed in West Germany. In March 1960, the history professor Georges Laperches and teacher Pierre Le Grève became victims of letter bombs similar to the one that had maimed Nouasri in Frankfurt/Main three months earlier. Both men had been active in the Belgian *Comité pour la paix en Algérie*.[219] That same month, Bernt Engelmann, who had recently visited ALN bases in Tunisia, published a four-part series on the *Red Hand*'s terrorist machinations in *Der*

[215] Pierre Genève, *La Main Rouge* (Paris, 1960). Also: Faure, *Aux Services*, p. 274; Faligot and Krop, *Piscine*, pp. 203–4.

[216] Joachim Joesten, *The Red Hand: The Sinister Account of the Terrorist Arm of the French Right-Wing 'ultras' in Algeria and on the Continent* (London & New York, 1962).

[217] Schreiben, Referat 204/205, an BMI, 20 August 1960; Schreiben, BMI an Frank, 13 September 1960, PA/AA, B25/11.

[218] 'Die Rote Hand', *Der Spiegel* 47 (16 November 1960), p. 88.

[219] 'Die "Rote Hand" in Brüssel aktiv', *FAZ*, 28 March 1960; 'Die mysteriösen Bombenanschläge der "Roten Hand" ', *SZ*, 24 October 1960; 'Beißner-Attentat wahrscheinlich von der "Roten Hand"', *FAZ*, 26 October 1960; Doneux and Le Paige, *Front du Nord*, pp. 145–55.

Spiegel.[220] Angered by the articles' intensely anti-French tone, Seydoux suggested authorities in Paris retaliate by banning the magazine from reporting on Khrushchev's upcoming visit to Paris.[221] Such threats had ceased to have any effect, however, and the press continued to report rumours suggesting the *Red Hand* threatened the lives of German and Arab personalities or companies suspected of pro-Algerian activities and opinions. Among those supposedly targeted were the Walther arms factory in Ulm and the Oldenburg-Portugiesische-Dampfschiff-Reederei in Hamburg, the arms dealers Ernst Remer (another founding member of the Sozialistische Reichspartei) and Hans-Joachim Seidenschnur, the journalists Hans-Ulrich Kempski, Hans-Jürgen Hoffmann and Karl Breyer, and even SPD deputy Wischnewski.[222]

Under pressure from the *Bundestag* Commissions for Foreign and Internal Affairs, these rumours contributed to Güde's decision in February 1960 to open a nation-wide inquest into *Red Hand* activities.[223] The SPD's parliamentary secretary Karl Mommer demanded even stronger action from the government. With the tone of moral superiority that had become so infuriating to the French, Mommer argued that the 'treatment of humans by the French was a disgrace and [...] represented a serious burden for Franco-German relations'.[224] Güde's inquest, meanwhile, produced findings that helped extricate and exonerate the authorities in Bonn and Paris. Many of the *Red Hand*'s most recent threats, it turned out, had been fabricated by one of the organisation's purported victims, journalist Hans-Jürgen Hoffmann, who had invented them to raise his own profile.[225] Hoffmann's exposure reinforced the argument that the *Red Hand* constituted a mere figment of the press's overactive imagination. Federal authorities could point to the police's genuine efforts in attempting to track the organisation's alleged members. That these were never apprehended was not the Paris government's fault. By deflecting all

[220] 'Der Tod kommt mit der Post. Spiegel-Serie über Frankreichs "Rote Hand"', *Der Spiegel* 10 (2 March 1960); 11 (9 March 1960), 12 (16 March 1960); 13 (23 March 1960).

[221] Télégramme no. 1020 de Seydoux, 10 March 1960, MAE, MLA/5.

[222] Dépêche no. 247 de Seydoux, 10 February 1960; Dépêche no. 165 du Consul Ardiet, Hanover, 28 June 1960, MAE, EU/RFA/1274; 'Kurzmeldung zum Bonner Büro der Arabischen Liga', *FAZ*, 23 January 1960; 'Die Tätigkeit der Roten Hand', *Neue Zürcher Zeitung*, 26 February 1960; 'Kein Polizeischutz für Remer', *FAZ*, 1 June 1960; 'Todesdrohung der "Roten Hand"', *FAZ*, 17 August 1961.

[223] 'Staatsanwaltschaft zur "Roten Hand"', *FAZ*, 27 February 1960; *Der Auswärtige Ausschuß: Sitzungsprotokolle*, Bd. 13/III, 43. Sitzung, 10 March 1960; 'Akten der "Roten Hand" bei Güde', *FAZ*, 19 March 1960; Wischnewski, *Leidenschaft*, p. 120.

[224] *Der Auswärtige Ausschuß: Sitzungsprotokolle*, Bd. 13/III, 43. Sitzung, 10 March 1960.

[225] Wochenbericht, SG-Bonn, 13 May 1960, BA/K, B131/198.

responsibility onto a fictitious organisation, the *Red Hand* thus not only absolved the French state from responsibility for SDECE's transgressions, it also became a pretext for inaction in Bonn, for how could one prosecute an organisation that did not exist? In the context of Adenauer's *Diktat* in the Algerian question, federal authorities deliberately turned a blind eye to *Service Action*'s dubious activities on German soil. They wilfully ignored rumours of French secret service collusion in the organisation's exploits; and they positively 'avoided implicating the French secret services in [discussions in] the *Bundestag*'.[226] Although uncorroborated, some witnesses and commentators even claim the BND, which took its orders from the Chancellor's Office, went beyond the call of duty by transmitting intelligence on the whereabouts and dealings of German arms dealers to SDECE.[227]

Consequences

While the myth of the *Red Hand* helped extricate Bonn and Paris from public calls to bring the perpetrators of *Service Action*'s transgressions to justice, the question remains whether France's war of action eradicated the FLN's international arms supplies. The French secret services registered rather mixed results in this domain. Thus in May 1960, the *deuxième bureau* drew attention to a marked decline in intelligence on FLN procurement activities. 'If it is true that our diplomatic action and special services have neutralised the arms traffickers,' the bureau observed, 'that can explain the absence of intelligence from SDECE'. While this suggested the war of action had been effective, the bureau proved unconvinced: 'unfortunately we are certain that the traffic in war materiel [. . .] has developed considerably [. . .] and without punishment, notably in Tunisia but also in Morocco, and it continues'. Indeed, while ALN arms stocks within Algeria had declined significantly thanks to the combined effects of the Morice line and Challe offensive, the bureau observed a 'very significant augmentation' at the ALN's external bases. In Tunisia, armaments levels were thought to have risen from 10,000 'weapons of war' in February 1959 to 60,000

226 Schreiben, BMI an Bundespresseamt (BPA), 28 August 1959, BA/K, B106/15783.

227 Peter F. Müller und Michael Mueller, *Gegen Freund und Feind. Der BND: Geheime Politik und schmutzige Geschäfte* (Reinbek, 2002), pp. 304–5; Erich Schmidt-Eenboom, *Schnüffler ohne Nase. Der BND – die unheimliche Macht im Staate* (Düsseldorf, 1993), pp. 183–4; Faligot and Kauffer, *Croissant*, pp. 206–8; Faligot and Krop, *Piscine*, pp. 206–7; Bergot, *Commandos*, p. 114; Méléro, *Main Rouge*, pp. 199–200, 204, 220; Melnik, *Mille jours*, p. 122; Ibid., *Mort*, pp. 116–17; Vosjoli, *Lamia*, p. 345.

in May 1960. In Morocco over that same period, arms stocks were believed to have risen from 1,500 to 7,000. As a result, the ALN had become a potent symbol of Algeria's struggle for independence, and yet, as the *deuxième bureau* concluded, 'our intelligence service is practically mute on that traffic'.[228]

French intelligence, in other words, had been undermined by the very success of its campaign of sabotage and assassinations, for the war of action had forced the Algerians to rely on aid from the Sino-Soviet bloc. By December 1960, the *deuxième bureau* concluded:

> State organizations have replaced the arms traffickers. The [ALN's] war material comes from government stocks and the bargaining takes place with pseudo-functionaries of the GPRA at a governmental level. Furthermore, the material is transported on Eastern-bloc cargos that belong to state-owned companies; it is shipped from harbours situated behind the Iron Curtain . . . [although] for the time being, the transports are not executed by Soviet vessels but by satellite ships.[229]

In sum, the governments of Czechoslovakia, Yugoslavia and China had substituted private arms dealers as the FLN's principal purveyors, providing weapons in exchange for hard currency.[230] This shift in procurement strategy threatened to undermine the war on contraband for several reasons. First, it severely impaired the collection of intelligence, which according to the *deuxième bureau* became:

> – more rare: our agents behind the Iron Curtain being less numerous and the movements of ships in the bloc's ports not being signalled in advance by the specialised press;
> – less precise: for the same reasons;
> – more delayed: as a consequence of the difficulties in communication with possible sources and of the fact that ship movements only become known retrospectively.[231]

A dearth in actionable intelligence, in turn, affected 'the efficiency of our [. . .] maritime surveillance'. While the interception of West German cargo vessels produced few qualms, the *deuxième bureau* worried about the political consequences of high-seas inspections of Eastern-bloc vessels,

[228] Fiche, EMG/2, 20 May 1960, SHD-T, 1R/352/D3*.
[229] Note, EMG/2, 6 December 1960, SHD-T, 1R/352/D3*.
[230] Meynier, *Histoire*, pp. 612–613; Melnik, *Mort*, p. 185.
[231] Note, EMG/2, 6 December 1960, SHD-T, 1R/352/D3*. Also: Melnik, *Mille jours*, p. 112; Ibid., *Mort*, p. 13; Vosjoli, *Lamia*, p. 348.

especially as rumours had surfaced that Eastern-bloc arms shipments were protected by Soviet or Egyptian submarines.[232] The bureau consequently predicted 'a diminution of the effectiveness of repression [of contraband] and an increase in the indictments against [. . .] maritime surveillance, at least as long as there is no substantial amelioration of our intelligence'.[233] Finally, the official nature of Eastern-bloc aid eliminated the possibility of direct, covert interventions.[234] After all, it was one thing to liquidate a handful of shady arms dealers in West Germany, where the French could count on Bonn's compliance; it was quite another thing to challenge Soviet-bloc governments who were hostile to France. Militarily, therefore, the war of action proved counterproductive. By eliminating the FLN's 'merchants of death', French intelligence had undermined its own operations, generating more problems than it could solve.[235]

From a political and psychological perspective, too, the war of action did more damage than good. Here, too, French strategy had played into the FLN's hands. Although the movement's procurement efforts had long ceased to affect the military situation within Algeria, they remained vital from a political and psychological perspective. The continued flow of war materiel to the FLN's sanctuaries in Tunisia and Morocco helped boost morale among the *mujâhideen*. It became an important symbol of the FLN's vitality and determination in the face of French military superiority. Meanwhile, France's heavy-handed interventions against the FLN's supply networks had helped to generate sympathy for the movement's cause in the international battle for hearts and minds. Whether perpetrated by *Service Action* or by the *Red Hand*, acts of sabotage and assassination were considered to be in bad taste and criminal. They smacked of desperation, revealing just how untenable French Algeria had become. By transgressing the sovereignty of foreign nations and endangering the lives of innocent bystanders, the war of action also reduced the psychological effect of some of the FLN's own unlawful and immoral actions in the Algerian war, whether its terrorist campaigns in Algiers and Paris, or its merciless treatment of perceived traitors and foes.

FLN propagandists successfully exploited this situation. On the war's fifth anniversary, *El Moudjahid* ran a long article condemning the *Red*

[232] Fiches nos. 895/INS/AFN et 1125/INS/AFN, 4.7. and 9 September 1958, SHD-T, 1H/1101/D3; Aufzeichnung, Scherpenberg, 2 October 1956, PA/AA, B14/64; 'Unmögliche Zustände', *General-Anzeiger*, 21 December 1960; Melnik, *Mille jours*, p. 114.
[233] Note, EMG/2, 6 December 1960, SHD-T, 1R/352/D3*.
[234] Projet de plan no. 131/EMGDN/2, 31 August 1959, SHD-T, 10T/531/D3*.
[235] Porch, *French Secret Services*, pp. 370, 372.

Hand, which the author claimed had 'become one of the favourite weapons of French diplomacy in the European countries where Algerians reside'. While the French committed crimes and trampled on the rights of foreign nations, the FLN 'will continue to respect the neutrality of countries that granted asylum and security to Algerians persecuted by French colonialists'. By exporting France's dirty war to foreign countries, *El Moudjahid* argued, 'the Algerian reality has imposed itself each day more clearly on the German, Italian, Belgian, and Swiss people'; the 'war conducted by France against the Algerian people has become apparent to these people as fundamentally unjust and contrary to law and equity'. The *Red Hand* had given the FLN 'an ever larger audience among the [...] masses' in Western Europe, where '[c]ommittees of support have been created' and '[n]otable personalities from political, intellectual, and labour circles have spoken out in favour of Algeria's independence and [...] support the FLN in its fight against French colonialism'.[236]

The war of action, in other words, had helped the FLN consolidate its sanctuaries abroad, including in West Germany. The arguments put forth in *El Moudjahid* were echoed in the Arab world and in Western Europe.[237] In November 1959, the UGTA instructed its members not to react to attempts by the 'sorry individuals of the *Red Hand*, aided by the MNA [...] to sow trouble' for Algerians in West Germany.[238] In February 1960, the UGEMA, too, drew attention to the 'gang of killers in the service of colonialism' that sought to discredit Algerian refugees in the FRG and elsewhere.[239] West German student and labour groups, too, used the *Red Hand* as a prominent theme in their pro-Algerian propaganda, as reported by *Freies Algerien*.[240]

The use of heavy-handed tactics aimed at dismantling the FLN's external sanctuaries and supply lines backfired on the French authorities, just as it had previously during the Suez crisis and at Sakiet. Whether through naval inspections at sea, sabotage operations or assassinations, the French war on contraband had reinforced the image of France as the villain and aggressor in the Algerian war. Instead of highlighting the illegal and unethical activities of shady arms traffickers such as Puchert or Beißner

[236] 'Des tueurs à la solde des colonialistes français', *El Moudjahid*, 1 November 1959.

[237] Fernschreiben Nr. 586, Botschaft Cairo, 24 October 1959; Schreiben, Botschaft Cairo, 2 December 1959, PA/AA, B25/10; Schreiben, Botschaft Baghdad, 4 April 1960, PA/AA, B12/932.

[238] Extraits, bulletin d'information, UGTA, November 1959, SHD-T, 10T/528/D2*.

[239] Communiqué de presse, UGEMA, 12 February 1960, BA/K, B166/1462.

[240] 'Grundsätzliches zum Fall Puchert', *Freies Algerien* 1/6 (July 1959); 'Die Rote Hand', *Freies Algerien* 3/1–2 (January/February 1960); 'Die Rote Hand mordet weiter', *Freies Algerien* 3/5 (May 1960).

(most of whom remained Nazis), French tactics had transform these men into romanticised heroes, or as Seydoux put it in March 1959, a 'type of adventurous German [. . .] on the whole sympathetic, who had placed his skills and courage in the service of a good cause, in this case the fight by the Algerian insurgents for their liberty'.[241] In May 1960, even SDECE had to concede that the war of action had rendered 'the greatest of services' to the FLN.[242] By violating international laws and failing to respect the principle of territorial sovereignty, the secret war on contraband had 'helped to neutralize potential French propaganda victories in the face of FLN terrorist outrages' and had 'succeeded in making even France's allies eager to end the [Algerian] war'.[243]

Although this sentiment was widely shared among official German circles, the war of action illustrated the lengths to which the federal authorities continued to go to uphold their *quid pro quo* with France. Not even *Service Action*'s gross infringements of West German sovereignty and national security could weaken the Adenauer government's resolve to defer to France. Yet the war of action also produced mounting pressures on the Bonn government, both internal and external. These pressures led to growing calls for policy change, including a tougher, more independent posture towards France, one that defended the FRG's territorial integrity and national interests. At the time, the Bonn government was able to resist these pressures and adhere to Paris's *Diktat*. As the Algerian war entered its third and final phase, however, the policy of *quid pro quo* became an increasingly dangerous liability for the Bonn Republic. The *Auswärtige Amt*, in particular, now faced the seemingly impossible challenge of reconciling its support of the French war effort with the realisation that the counterinsurgency was doomed to fail.

241 Dépêche no. 630 de l'ambassadeur Seydoux à Bonn, 26 March 1959, MAE, MLA/3.
242 Notice no. 31389/SDECE, 24 May 1960, SHD-T, 10T/523*.
243 Porch, *French Secret Services*, p. 372.

PART III

Asserting sovereignty

January 1961–July 1962 and beyond

CHAPTER 10

From sanctuary to sovereignty

The referendum of 8 January 1961 marked a decisive turning point in the Algerian war. In the metropole, 76.25 per cent approved de Gaulle's policies. So did the majority in Algeria, notwithstanding a high rate of abstentions.[1] The overwhelming vote for self-determination signalled a clear preference on either side of the Mediterranean for the formation of an *Algérie algérienne* (an 'Algerian Algeria'), an option de Gaulle had first endorsed in a press conference on 5 September 1960.[2] By relying on the democratic process, de Gaulle had secured the public mandate he needed to prepare for France's withdrawal from Algeria. Thence started a new phase in the war, one marked by the search for a political settlement. A highly volatile period ensued, one marked by political posturing through which both the French government and GPRA sought to gain the upper hand in negotiations that opened in Évian on 20 May 1961.[3] In the context of increasingly violent resistance on the part of the newly formed OAS and growing divisions within the FLN, the negotiations proved difficult, but on 18 March 1962, the terms of a permanent ceasefire were finally agreed.[4] The Évian Accords were hailed as a triumph for compromise.[5] France conceded Algeria's territorial integrity and sovereignty and agreed to provide substantial economic assistance. The FLN's negotiators,

[1] Evans, *Algeria*, pp. 290–1.

[2] Conférence de presse tenue au Palais de l'Élysée, 5 September 1960, in *Discours*, de Gaulle, p. 241; Cointet, *De Gaulle*, p. 119.

[3] On the negotiations: Jeffrey J. Byrne, 'Négociation perpétuelle: de Gaulle et le FLN 1961–1968', in *De Gaulle* (ed.) Vaïsse, pp. 299–312; Connelly, *Diplomatic Revolution*, pp. 240–64; Evans, *Algeria*, pp. 299–312; Meynier, *Histoire*, pp. 626–34.

[4] On the OAS: Olivier Dard, *Voyage au cœur de l'OAS* (Paris, 2005); Georges Fleury, *Histoire secrète de l'O.A.S.* (Paris, 2003); Alexander Harrison, *Challenging de Gaulle: The O.A.S. and the Counterrevolution in Algeria, 1954–1962* (New York, 1989); Paul Henissart, *Wolves in the City: The Death of French Algeria* (New York, 1970). On FLN rivalries: Harbi, *FLN*, pp. 292–376; Meynier, *Histoire*, pp. 637–76.

[5] Jeffrey J. Byrne, 'Our Own Special Brand of Socialism: Algeria and the Contest of Modernities in the 1960s', *Diplomatic History* 33/3 (2009), p. 431.

meanwhile, pledged to guarantee the rights and property of the *colons*, lease key installations to the French military – including the nuclear test sites in the Sahara, and accord French firms privileged access to Algeria's oil and gas reserves. Though bitterly contested by French *ultras* and Algerian radicals alike, the Accords paved the way for Algeria's independence on 5 July.

The closing phase of Algeria's liberation struggle presented new challenges for the Adenauer government, which realised it had persistently backed the wrong side. How, then, did West German diplomacy adjust to the new realities created by the referendum? To what extent did the Adenauer government's loyalty to France endure in this final phase of the war? And how did the new Algerian state take to Bonn's erstwhile support for France? In exploring these questions, this chapter explains how the Bonn authorities ultimately managed to reconcile two seemingly incompatible foreign-policy goals. After all, the Adenauer government emerged from the Algerian war having consolidated the Franco-German rapprochement, an achievement facilitated in no small way by the chancellor's unfailing loyalty to de Gaulle and one epitomised by the historic Élysée Treaty of 22 January 1963. At the same time, Bonn also emerged from the war having secured diplomatic recognition from independent Algeria. Thus in spite of Adenauer's policy of *quid pro quo* with France, the government had managed to uphold the Hallstein doctrine. It had trumped East Berlin even though Algeria declared itself a socialist and neutralist People's Democratic Republic. Traditional interpretations would argue that in Algeria, as elsewhere in the Third World, the Bonn government secured its interests by outspending its eastern rival in the provision of development aid. This chapter argues that economic power alone was not enough to secure recognition. To understand Bonn's triumph over the GDR, one must also take account of the Federal Republic's wartime role as sanctuary as well as the extensive engagement of West German civil-society actors, who supported Algeria's liberation struggle even when Bonn did not.

Clampdown

In January 1961, the Adenauer government still adhered to the *Diktat* imposed by Paris whereby federal authorities were to do everything in their remit to support de Gaulle's Algerian policies in exchange for French backing in the German question. This made sense, for just as Algeria remained France's number one concern, the Berlin crisis continued to dominate the agenda in Bonn. Paris's stick-and-carrot approach highlighted the asymmetry that continued to characterise Franco-German relations. As Lappenküper has argued, French policy was marked by the 'mentality of an occupying power' while Adenauer remained resolved to avoid disagreements with France.[6] Although German diplomats deplored the analogy between Algeria and Berlin, they no longer counselled an independent or concerted approach to the Algerian question. After all, not even the '*entente personnelle*' between Adenauer and de Gaulle had produced a frank exchange of views.[7] When the chancellor finally broached the question with the General in February 1961 – alarmed by the amplification of Chinese and Soviet aid to the FLN – he merely expressed his hope 'that France will soon find a solution to the grave Algerian problem in order to have free hands' in its foreign relations.[8] De Gaulle did not respond to the remark. His silence spoke volumes when one considers that he discussed Algeria 'with almost all his foreign interlocutors'.[9]

In relegating the Adenauer government to the ranks of a silent and junior partner in France's counterinsurgency, the *Diktat* imposed by de Gaulle had secured a measure of success in combating the FLN's sanctuary in the FRG. In the context of the war on contraband, the *Diktat* had helped to mute Bonn's protests against heavy-handed and illegal transgressions of West German sovereignty, whether *Surmar*'s interception of cargo vessels at sea or *Service Action*'s unfettered campaign of sabotage and assassinations. Although they failed to liquidate the FLN's supply networks entirely, the interventions by *Surmar* and *Service Action* noticeably reduced the FLN's clandestine procurement activities in West Germany. So, too, did the passage in 1961 of the long-awaited *Kriegswaffen-* and *Außenwirtschaftsgesetze*, which finally made it possible for German diplomacy to veto the export of war materiel to the FLN's Arab allies. Federal authorities had also closed in on some of the FLN's other subversive activities in the FRG. The arrest of the Osnabrück forgers, whose trial opened in February 1961, had thwarted a potentially crippling strike against France's fiscal economy.[10] By the time that trial ended, Max Güde was preparing for his ultimate strike to dismantle the FLN sanctuary. On 20 April 1961, having assembled over twenty-three evidence dossiers, the federal prosecutor issued a warrant of arrest against the

[6] Lappenküper, 'Adenauer', p. 614.

[7] Lappenküper, *Deutsch-französische Beziehungen* II, p. 1343.

[8] Entretiens de Gaulle-Adenauer de Paris, 9 February 1961, *DDF* 1961, Vol. I, Nr. 59, p. 170.

[9] Vaïsse, *Grandeur*, p. 73.

[10] Aufzeichnung, Abt. 5 an Referat 204, 15 February 1961, PA/AA, B25/2; Dépêche no. 709 de Seydoux, 19 April 1961, MAE, MLA/7.

FLN bureau in Bonn. Its three permanent members, Keramane, Kacem and Abdelhamid Bouattoura (alias Alberto or Oubraham Boualem), were charged with conspiracy, subversion and spearheading a criminal and terrorist organisation in contravention of §128 and 129 of the criminal code.[11]

Although the wheels of justice had turned slowly, Güde's clampdown marked the climax of the Franco-German intelligence war to eradicate the FLN's most vital sanctuary in Western Europe. Characterised by Scheffler as anachronistic, the arrests were the logical outcome of the German authorities' legalistic approach to *guerre révolutionnaire*.[12] The *Rechtsstaat* had become Bonn's principal weapon against the FLN, one the government could justify vis-à-vis the movement's Third World allies. After all, diplomatic pressure had failed to dislodge the FLN from its extraterritorial sanctuary within the Tunisian embassy. Time and again, German diplomats had encountered a united Arab front shielding the GPRA's representatives. In March 1960, Tunisian Ambassador Ben Ammar had again refused on moral grounds to banish the FLN delegates.[13] In a collective demarche with seven other Arab ambassadors, he had protested against Bonn's hostility towards the FLN. The *Auswärtige Amt* had tried in vain to pacify the ambassadors, assuring them that Bonn's objections to the FLN bureau rested on diplomatic conventions and international law. Put simply, it was illegal to incorporate third-country agencies into embassies. Ben Ammar and his Moroccan counterpart El Fassi had again appealed to the bureau's humanitarian work, which they claimed helped preserve order among Algerian refugees in West Germany. UAR Ambassador Ibrahim Sabri had deemed its toleration an expression of German–Arab friendship.[14] The governments in Jeddah, Amman and Baghdad, too, had warned of serious repercussions if Bonn continued its 'discriminatory' attitude against the Algerians.[15]

At a time of rapid decolonisation, such warnings did not go entirely unheeded in Bonn, where diplomats had only just prevented newly independent Guinea from establishing full diplomatic relations with East Berlin.[16] The *Auswärtige Amt* had consequently relented in its persistence

[11] Wochenbericht, SB-Bonn, 7 April 1961, BA/K, B131/200; Télégramme no. 1678 de Seydoux, 21 April 1961, MAE, MLA/7.

[12] Scheffler, *SPD*, p. 70. [13] Aufzeichnung, Scherpenberg, 15 March 1960, PA/AA, B2/75.

[14] Dolmetscherprotokoll, 16 March 1960, PA/AA, B2/86.

[15] Fernschreiben, Botschaft Jeddah, 21 March 1960. Also: Fernschreiben, Botschaft Amman, 24 March 1960; Schreiben, Botschaft Baghdad, 4 April 1960, PA/AA, B12/932.

[16] Gray, *Germany's Cold War*, pp. 107–15; Amit Das Gupta, 'Ulbricht am Nil. Die deutsch-deutsche Rivalität in der Dritten Welt', in *Das doppelte Deutschland. 40 Jahre Systemkonkurrenz* (eds.) Udo Wengst and Hermann Wentker (Bonn, 2008), p. 122.

to see the FLN expelled from the Tunisian embassy. Instead, it had sought alternative solutions. As early as August 1959, Paul Frank, in his unceasing effort to reconcile both Arab and French interests in the Algerian question, had proposed replacing the FLN bureau with an independent welfare office. The idea was astute, for it would have removed the Algerians from the protection of the Arab diplomatic corps, thereby allowing the authorities to impose stricter controls on FLN activities. Moreover, given their claims that the FLN only ever engaged in humanitarian activities in West Germany, an independent office would have demonstrated goodwill towards the movement's Arab allies.[17] French diplomats, however, had objected to the idea on the grounds that the welfare of Algerians fell exclusively under French jurisdiction.[18] The *Auswärtige Amt* consequently feared that an independent FLN office 'would only lead to massive French interventions calling for its closure'.[19] The FLN, too, had rejected the idea, preferring to conduct its activities under diplomatic cover. After all, the bureau's remit far exceeded humanitarian tasks.

Indeed, only the Tunisian and Moroccan ambassadors had proved receptive to Frank's proposal, having grown weary of Bonn's repeated protests.[20] When *Gauche Démocratique* senator Bernard Lafay on 7 June 1960 accused Ben Ammar of harbouring wanted terrorists, the ambassador had urged his government to remove the FLN from his embassy. Though he decried Lafay's accusation as 'false and malicious', Ben Ammar thought the Algerians' presence had come to weigh too heavily on Tunisia's relationship to West Germany and France.[21] Ambassador El Fassi, it appears, proved equally reticent to host Keramane and his colleagues in the Moroccan embassy, especially since both the French and German governments had donated significant aid to the victims of the Agadir earthquake of 29 February 1960, which had killed over 12,000 Moroccan citizens.[22] Telegrams intercepted by French signals intelligence suggest that it took several strongly worded interventions by the GPRA, including one with

[17] Aufzeichnung, Frank, 11 August 1959, PA/AA, B25/10; Aufzeichnung, Scherpenberg, 17 March 1960; Aufzeichnung, Sarrazin, 24 March 1960; B12/932; Aufzeichnung, Scherpenberg, 21 March 1960, B2/75.

[18] Aufzeichnung, Frank, 11 August 1959, B25/10; Aufzeichnung, Frank, 18 August 1960, B25/12.

[19] Handschriftliches Kommentar, Aufzeichnung, Frank, 18 August 1959, PA/AA, B25/12.

[20] Aufzeichnung, van Scherbenberg, 15 March 1960, PA/AA, B2/75; Dolmetscherprotokoll, 16 March 1960, B2/86.

[21] Texte remise à la presse par l'ambassade de Tunisie, Bonn, 9 June 1960; Aufzeichnung, van Scherpenberg, 9 June 1960; Note verbale de l'ambassadeur Ben Ammar au Quai d'Orsay, 9 June 1960, PA/AA, B12/932.

[22] Informations-Bulletins der Bundesregierung Nrs. 43, 4 March 1960 and 46, 9 March 1960 PA/AA, B25/68.

Sultan Mohammed V himself, before Rabat consented to the Algerians' transfer to the Moroccan embassy in June 1960.[23]

Diplomatic pressure thus had finally dislodged the FLN bureau from one extraterritorial sanctuary, yet its activities had merely shifted to another. After an interlude of restraint that coincided with Kacem's temporary ban from federal territory between June and September 1960, the FLN bureau resumed its political activities. In early November 1960, it hosted a private party to mark the sixth anniversary of the independence struggle that was attended by members of the Arab, Turkish, Greek, Venezuelan and Ceylonese diplomatic corps.[24] Two months later, the FLN's chief lobbyist in Bonn, Wischnewski, organised another private function attended not only by Third World diplomats but also members of the SPD, several journalists and even a few industrialists, including representatives of the powerful construction corporation Hochtief. Coinciding with the January 1961 referendum, the function had sparked angry demarches by Seydoux with Foreign Minister Brentano and Adenauer's State Secretary Hans Globke.[25] The ambassador insisted that only Keramane and Kacem's expulsion would demonstrate 'tangible proof of [Adenauer's] comprehension and solidarity' in the Algerian question.[26] He warned the *Amt* 'that it would not be wise to let the malaise created in France by [Bonn's] attitude towards our number-one problem weigh on [Adenauer's] approaching visit to Paris'.[27] At a time of rising tensions over Berlin, Seydoux's threats spurred German diplomats back into action, though they still failed to enforce the bureau's closure. This time, the judiciary was to blame. Pending the outcome of Güde's national inquest, federal authorities had to suspend all other moves against the FLN's militants.[28]

In the interim, FLN efforts at political mobilisation became increasingly brazen. In March 1961, the head of the European and Western department in the GPRA's Foreign Ministry, Hassan Aziz (alias Hadi Ghani), visited Bonn for private meetings with a select group of politicians and businessmen. The purpose of Aziz's visit, Seydoux speculated, was 'to prepare the "future foreign relations of an independent Algeria", reassure the Germans

[23] Dossier 'E': 4 February 1960; 19 April 1960; 30 April 1960; 1 May 1960; 25 May 1960; 26 May 1960; 13 June 1960; 14 September 1960, SHD-T, 1H/1579/D3*.

[24] Télégrammes no. 4868, 7 November 1960, et no. 4884, 9 November 1960, de Seydoux, MAE, MLA/6.

[25] Télégramme no. 135 de Seydoux, 10 January 1961, MAE, MLA/7; Schreiben, LMI Nordrhein-Westfalen an BMI, 1 February 1961, PA/AA, B12/931.

[26] Télégramme no. 164 de Seydoux, 11 January 1961, MAE, MLA/7.

[27] Télégramme no. 434 de Seydoux, 27 January 1961, MAE, MLA/7.

[28] Télégramme no. 513 de Seydoux, 2 February 1961, MAE, MLA/7.

of [the FLN's] pro-Western orientation and pressurise them by brandishing the threat of recognising the [GDR] so as to obtain [. . .] promises of economic cooperation'.[29] True to the Paris government's *Diktat*, German diplomats refused to meet with the emissary. Even so, Aziz's visit marked a sea change. With the help of Wischnewski, the emissary for the first time secured introductions to members of the governing parties, including Ernst Majonica, an influential member of parliament who chaired the CDU's Commission for External Affairs and who found Aziz 'sympathetic'.[30] Majonica's willingness to meet a representative of the GPRA was indicative of a growing malaise within the CDU/CSU with Adenauer's "Gaullist" foreign policy.[31] Even the *Amt* envisioned a bolder, more balanced and autonomous policy in the Algerian question, especially now that independence was only a matter of time. In March 1961, it argued that official contacts to Algerian emissaries 'would be conceivable at the earliest when official negotiations began between the French government and the GPRA'.[32]

Güde's strike on 20 April must therefore have come as a shock to West German foreign-policy-makers who were once more preparing to challenge Adenauer's policy of *quid pro quo* in the Algerian question. Only nine days previously, de Gaulle had publicly presaged the emergence of a sovereign Algerian state.[33] In his press statement on 21 April, meanwhile, Güde charged Keramane and his co-accused of being the ringleaders of a nation-wide organisation that:

> under the name 'Front de Libération Nationale' [. . .] perpetrated acts of terror against Algerians living in the Federal Republic. The organisation has arrogated police powers for itself and imposed monetary fines and corporal punishments on its fellow countrymen. In a series of cases, Algerians who refused to join or support the organisation have been threatened, beaten and robbed.[34]

Having first encouraged the prosecutor-general in his legal fight against the FLN's politico-administrative structures, the *Auswärtige Amt* now regretted Güde's move. German diplomats were embarrassed and

[29] Télégramme no. 1272 de Seydoux, 15 March 1961, MAE, MLA/7.
[30] Ernst Majonica, *Das politische Tagebuch, 1958–1972* (eds.) Hans-Otto Kleinmann and Christopher Beckmann (Düsseldorf, 2011), p. 145.
[31] Conze, *Herausforderung*, pp. 22–4; Geiger, *Atlantiker*, chs. 1–3; Hildebrand, '"Atlantiker"', pp. 583–92.
[32] Vermerk, Referat 204, 16 March 1961, PA/AA, B12/932.
[33] Conférence de presse tenue au Palais de l'Élysée le 11 avril 1961, in *Discours*, p. 292.
[34] Schnellbrief BMJ an BMI, 21 April 1961, BA/K, B106/15780.

infuriated by the fact the prosecutor had neither consulted nor informed them of the impending arrests. For once, they fully agreed with Wischnewski, who argued the incarcerations' timing 'shortly before the Évian negotiations was extraordinarily unfortunate' and would cause 'inescapable damage' in the Arab world.[35] Majonica was even blunter; he called the arrests 'an idiotic move'.[36] The German press, meanwhile, hailed Keramane as an influential personality whose 'moderate, anti-communist' convictions would keep the GPRA anchored in the West.[37] Even Adenauer, so Seydoux believed, regretted the prosecutor's move.[38] German diplomats tried in vain to reassure the Tunisian and Moroccan embassies that the arrests were not politically motivated. The Algerians were accused of contravention against the criminal code, State Secretary van Scherpenberg argued: it was illegal for any organisation – domestic or foreign – to appropriate and exercise coercive and executive powers belonging to the sovereign West German state.[39]

Having previously sought their expulsion, the Bonn government now tried to secure the men's release. The separation between the executive, legislative and judicial branches of government, however, prevented federal authorities from intervening. Evidence seized from the accused's domiciles, which included 202,000DM in cash and a vehicle stolen from a French army base in West Germany, merely incriminated the three men further. Indeed, among the seized documentation, police found evidence of the bureau's involvement in at least one execution.[40] The Chancellor's Office suggested securing the men's release by applying §154b.3 of the criminal procedure code, which allowed a case to be abandoned if the accused were expelled from federal territory.[41] This option, Seydoux observed, struck the *Auswärtige Amt* as 'by far preferable' to 'a spectacular lawsuit'.[42] After all, a high-profile, cross-party team had assembled to ensure the Algerians' defence consisting of Wischnewski, his parliamentary colleague Gustav Heinemann, who was a lawyer by profession as well as a member of the

[35] Aufzeichnung, Referat 205, 21 April 1961, PA/AA, B25/2. [36] Majonica, *Tagebuch*, p. 150.

[37] Télégramme no. 1810 de Seydoux, 27 April 1961, MAE, MLA/2; 'Auswärtiges Amt peinlich berührt', *General-Anzeiger* 21 April 1961.

[38] Télégrammes nos. 1706, 21 March 1961, et 2016, 10 May 1961, de Seydoux, MAE, MLA/7.

[39] Aufzeichnung, Referat 5, 21 April 1961, PA/AA, B25/2.

[40] Wochenbericht, SG-Bonn, 4 May 1961, BA/K, B131/200; Vermerke, Referat 205, 26 April 1961 and 6 May 1961, PA/AA, B25/2.

[41] Aufzeichnung, StS I, 21 April 1961, PA/AA, B25/2; Notiz, Scherpenberg an Globke, 21 April 1961, B2/76.

[42] Télégramme no. 1782 de Seydoux, 25 April 1961, MAE, MLA/7; Aufzeichnung, StS I, 21 April 1961, PA/AA, B25/2.

SPD-executive and a future president of the Republic, the CDU's Majonica and a legal counsellor from the *Caritasverband*.[43] Expulsion, the *Amt* reckoned, would prevent a public trial of Bonn's pro-French policies in the Algerian war while at the same time meeting French demands and dampening Arab and Third World protests.

Contrary to expectations, international reactions to the arrests were initially muted. Keramane himself demonstrated remarkable sympathy towards his gaolers. Having failed to rein in the FLN's more insidious activities on federal territory, especially the score-settling with the rival MNA in the Saarland, he observed retrospectively how '[o]ur arrest was understandable'. Considering their justified concern for the *Rechtsstaat*, Keramane felt the authorities had 'tolerated a lot'.[44] The GPRA, too, at first responded to Güde's clampdown with reserve.[45] 'We await the results of a demarche by Tunisian [and Moroccan] diplomats in Bonn before we make further decisions', one of the government's spokespersons declared on 26 April. If the representatives were not released, however, the GPRA would 'have to think of other measures', including a transfer to East Berlin.[46] Wischnewski beseeched the *Auswärtige Amt* for once to empower its ambassadors in Tunis and Cairo to contact the GPRA to explain why an immediate, unconditional release of Keramane and his colleagues was legally and administratively impossible. The deputy had tried to appease the GPRA through private channels but feared that unofficial expressions of regret no longer sufficed to 'contain the political damage'.[47]

That damage did indeed grow. German diplomats registered daily new protests from Accra and Conakry, Beirut, Baghdad, Amman, Cairo, Tripoli and Rabat.[48] To calm the situation, Scherpenberg requested the assistance of the Arab League's Secretary General, Abdul-Khalek Hassouna, who had arrived in Bonn on 5 May, assuring the latter that federal authorities were trying to secure the speedy release and deportation

[43] Aufzeichnung, StS II, 28 April 1961; Aufzeichnung, Referat 204/5, 5 May 1961, PA/AA, B25/2; Wischnewski, *Leidenschaft*, p. 117.

[44] 'Entretiens, Keramane', in *Rapports*, p. 212.

[45] DPA-Spezial Nr. 7, 22 April 1961, PA/AA, B25/2.

[46] Fernschreiben Nr. 2789, Bundespresseamt, 26 April 1961, PA/AA, B25/2.

[47] Aufzeichnung, Sanne, Referat 205, 25 April 1961, PA/AA, B25/2.

[48] Note de l'ambassade du Maroc, 21 April 1961, PA/AA, B2/76; Aufzeichnung, Referat 205, 21 April 1961; Vermerk, Referat 205, 26 April 1961; Schreiben, Botschaft Accra, 29 April 1961; Aufzeichnung, van Scherpenberg, 30 April 1961; Fernschreiben Nr. 42, Botschaft Tripoli, 3 May 1961; Vermerk, Referat 205, 6 May 1961; Schreiben, Botschaft Amman, 10 May 1961; Fernschreiben Nr. 119, Botschaft Rabat, 11 May 1961; Schreiben, Botschaft Beirut, 12 May 1961; Fernschreiben, Nr. 145, Botschaft Baghdad, 15 May 1961; Fernschreiben Nr. 473, Botschaft Cairo, 16 May 1961, B25/2.

of Keramane and his colleagues. Scherpenberg gratefully accepted Hassouna's help 'to prevent spectacular measures and protests on the Arabs' part' while the judiciary worked towards this solution.[49] Three days later, Brentano personally urged Güde to drop his case against the Algerians.[50]

The slow wheels of justice, however, roused Hassouna's concern. At the press conference marking the end of his official visit on 15 May, the secretary-general emphasised how a 'positive solution' to the crisis was 'necessary to avoid a deterioration of German–Arab relations'.[51] Bonn's new ambassador in Tunis, Herbert Richter, complained about the absurdity of the Algerians' incarceration at a time when 'not just the eastern bloc, but Washington, London, and even Paris' had extended *de facto* recognition to the GPRA. With the Évian negotiations about to commence, an FLN spokesman had warned the ambassador of the GPRA's dwindling patience.[52] To Richter, Keramane's continued imprisonment had become so 'grotesque' and 'ridiculous' that 'even a few hundred million [DM] in development aid will not wipe away the bad impression' it left on Algeria's future leaders.[53] To the FLN, Bonn's attitude connoted animosity just when it had a particular need for international recognition to strengthen its hand in the impending negotiations.[54] On 12 May, the GPRA issued a communiqué first in Tunis, then in Cairo, calling the charges against Keramane and his collaborators, 'false', 'arbitrary and tendentious'. The communiqué made a 'direct connection' between Güde's crackdown and 'the latest military putsch in France', which on 21 April had seen Generals Raoul Salan, Maurice Challe, Edmond Jouhaud and André Zeller launch a last-ditch, ultimately failed attempt to salvage *l'Algérie française*.[55] Bonn's reactionary behaviour contrasted poorly with that of the GPRA, 'which since 1956 [. . .] has liberated thousands of German legionnaires' from French oppression. The communiqué underlined 'the gravity of [the situation], which constitutes [. . .] a manifestation of hostility toward Algeria'.[56]

49 Vermerk, Referat 205, 6 May 1961, PA/AA, B25/2.

50 Vermerk, Referat 204, 8 May 1961, PA/AA, B25/2.

51 Télégramme no. 2126 de Seydoux, 16 May 1961, PA/AA, B25/2.

52 Fernschreiben Nr. 94, Botschaft Tunis, 9 May 1961, PA/AA, B25/2.

53 Schreiben Botschaft Tunis, 12 May 1961, PA/AA, B25/2.

54 Connelly, *Diplomatic Revolution*, pp. 255–6.

55 On the putsch, see: Pierre Abramovici, *Le Putsch des Généraux* (Paris, 2011); Maurice Vaïsse, *Alger, le putsch (1961)* (Bruxelles, 1983).

56 Télégramme no. 2153 de l'ambassade de France à Tunis, 13 May 1961, MAE, MLA/7; Fernschreiben Nr. 3271, Bundespresseamt, 12 May 1961; Communiqué, GPRA, MAE, Service de l'Information, Cairo, 14 May 1961, PA/AA, B25/2.

The only authorities genuinely happy about the Algerians' imprisonment were indeed the French, who had finally achieved their desired clampdown on the FLN's most important sanctuary in Europe. 'It goes without saying', the *Quai d'Orsay* observed on 28 April, 'that we cannot but congratulate ourselves for the measures taken by the German judiciary against the FLN's principal agents in Bonn'. The *Quai* instructed Seydoux to maintain his pressure on the federal government so as to ensure an absolute dismantlement of the FLN's politico-administrative structures in West Germany.[57] That pressure was easy enough to exert since the generals' putsch had sent renewed waves of panic through Bonn, prompting Adenauer to reaffirm his full loyalty to de Gaulle.[58] French diplomats had every reason to believe the federal government would heed its warnings that the Algerians' liberation 'would be severely judged in France', where one 'counted [...] on the fact that German justice will stand firm in this affair'.[59] In a confidential telegram to Debré dated 29 April, Seydoux commented how Bonn's Interior Ministry 'naturally is ready to help us' in that regard.[60]

French consternation must therefore have been great when on 19 May, just one day ahead of the opening of the Évian negotiations, the judiciary relented to executive pressure by transmuting its charges against Keramane and Kacem on the convoluted grounds that 'one could not hold the FLN leaders in Bonn responsible for the terror acts of an organisation' – the '*Fédération d'Allemagne*' – that allegedly acted in the movement's name.[61] 'Paris would certainly take this matter very badly', Seydoux now warned the *Auswärtige Amt*.[62] Indeed, the *Quai d'Orsay* chastised the Bonn authorities for being decidedly too liberal and democratic in their treatment of Algerians, deploring 'the benevolence thus manifested toward the rebel representatives'.[63] On 24 May, Bouattoura, too, was released on bail, though in his case the charges were neither transmuted nor dropped.

As all three men secretly left the country, the *Auswärtige Amt* fell silent, clearly embarrassed by the entire affair. German diplomats hoped the deportations would assuage the French government, but Prime Minister Debré remained profoundly dissatisfied. As retaliation, he ordered French

57 Télégramme no. 1738, MLA à Bonn, 28 April 1961, MAE, MLA/7.

58 Télégramme no. 1784 de Seydoux, 25 April 1961, MAE, MLA/7; Cahn and Müller, *RFA et guerre d'Algérie*, pp. 381–7.

59 Télégramme no. 1881, MLA à Bonn, 9 May 1961, MAE, MLA/7.

60 Télégramme no. 1870 de Seydoux, 29 April 1961, AHC, 2DE/65*.

61 'Die Drei Algerier', *FAZ*, 20 May 1961.

62 Télégramme no. 2162 de Seydoux, 18 May 1961, MAE, MLA/7.

63 Télégramme no. 2028, MLA à Bonn, 19 May 1961, MAE, MLA/7; Bougherara, *Rapports*, p. 107.

newspaper *Paris-Presse* to publish 'an oriented indiscretion' tarnishing Bonn.[64] Those who opposed Adenauer's 'Gaullist' policies, meanwhile, tried to reassure the GPRA. Wischneski and Majonica quietly travelled to Switzerland, where the FLN's negotiators had set up camp. A spokesperson for the SPD assured Seydoux that Wischnewski's visit 'bore no relationship' to Keramane and Kacem's release. The deputy intended to 'contact privately a certain number of Algerian personalities, including [GPRA Foreign Minister] Krim Belkacem', to discuss 'strictly German questions' such as the repatriation of legionnaires.[65] Upon his return, Wischnewski declared, 'the relations between the Federal Republic and GPRA would no longer suffer', although he denied having apologised for the treatment to which Keramane, Kacem and Bouattoura had been subjected.[66] Majonica, meanwhile, claimed to have gone to Switzerland for meetings with Polish exiles. Unconvinced, Seydoux commented that 'it is hard for me not to see a connection between his voyage and the contacts he had already established [. . .]to an FLN envoy'. While he expected such behaviour from members of the parliamentary opposition, the ambassador felt betrayed by Majonica, who belonged to Adenauer's CDU. So long as the deputy refused to deny he had spoken to Algerians, Seydoux argued, 'we will no longer be able to entertain [. . .]the trusting relations' that had until then existed with him.[67]

Competing for recognition

French irritation thus remained palpable. For the first time, foreign-policymakers in Bonn had defied Paris's wishes in the Algerian question, having pushed Güde not only to release the three men but also to drop the case against them. German diplomats justified their defiance by pointing to Arab opposition, even going so far as to raise the question: 'Mr Malek [as Keramane was known], might he not one day be ambassador in Bonn?'[68] In the context of the Évian negotiations, the *Auswärtige Amt* did not want to jeopardise its chances of establishing relations with the nascent Algerian republic. The question of diplomatic recognition could no longer be

64 Note pour Melnik, 27 May 1961, AHC, 2DE/20*.

65 Télégramme no. 2266 de Seydoux, 24 May 1961, AHC, 2DE/65*.

66 Télégramme no. 2326 de Seydoux, 26 May 1961, MAE, MLA/7.

67 Télégramme no. 2313 de Seydoux, 25 May 1961, MAE, MLA/7. Majonica did indeed meet with Polish emissaries, but he also contacted Kacem and Keramane, who agreed the deputy should not pursue further meetings with Krim Belkacem, as this would cause 'too much commotion'. See: Majonica, *Tagebuch*, p. 156.

68 Télégramme no. 2016 de Seydoux, 10 May 1961, MAE, MLA/7.

avoided now that the war was coming to an end, especially since East German policy-makers had come to regard Algeria as 'a touchstone' for the entire Third World: if they could win over the GPRA, then other anti-colonial liberation movements and newly independent governments would follow.[69]

The German–German contest over sovereignty and recognition thus became inherently entwined with Algeria's own. In the context of the Berlin crisis, moreover, which saw thousands of citizens leave the GDR on a daily basis, the Politburo urgently sought international recognition to compensate for the regime's dwindling domestic legitimacy.[70] The Algerian problem thus figured centrally in East Berlin's efforts to break through the isolation imposed by the Hallstein doctrine. So far, these efforts had achieved only partial success.[71] By the end of 1960, the Ulbricht regime had concluded trade agreements with twenty-eight Third World countries and established a number of trade missions, including one in Tunis. Apart from the UAR, however, only socialist Guinea had agreed to the opening of a consulate. While these missions had enabled the GDR to enhance its presence outside of the Sino-Soviet bloc, they did not carry the political and symbolic weight of a full diplomatic mission. East Berlin continued to suffer setbacks in this domain. Even Guinea's President Ahmed Sékou Touré had reneged on his promise to become the first Afro-Asian leader to extend full diplomatic recognition to the GDR.[72]

The arrest of the FLN's delegates in Bonn thus came at an opportune time for the Ulbricht regime, which intensified its propaganda in the hope of avoiding another setback à la Guinea.[73] Güde's crackdown offered East Berlin further opportunity to depict the Adenauer government as France's lackey. *Neues Deutschland* published a series of articles condemning Bonn's anti-Arab prejudice and support for French colonialism. The newspaper mimicked the GPRA, denouncing federal authorities for their 'dubious role' in the generals' putsch: by abetting the French Foreign Legion in its recruitment of German soldiers, the argument went, Bonn had furnished

69 Kittel, 'SED', p. 419.

70 Ibid., p. 415; Young-Sun Hong, 'Kalter Krieg in der Ferne. Dekolonisierung, Hygienediskurse und der Kampf der DDR und der USA um die Dritte Welt', in *Umworbener Klassenfeind. Das Verhältnis der DDR zu den USA* (eds.) Uta A. Balbier and Christiane Rösch (Berlin, 2006), pp. 87–8; Ibid., *Cold War Germany*, pp. 145–6; Winrow, *Foreign Policy*, p. 42.

71 Kittel, 'SED', p. 419; Joachim Scholtyseck, *Die Außenpolitik der DDR* (München, 2010), p. 24. More generally: Alexander Troche, *Ulbricht und die Dritte Welt: Ost-Berlins 'Kampf' gegen die Bonner 'Alleinvertretunganmaßung'* (Erlangen, 1996), pp. 23–38.

72 End, *Zweimal*, p. 46; Gray, *Germany's Cold War*, pp. 121–2; Winrow, *Foreign Policy*, pp. 41, 58–9.

73 Taubert, *L' «autre» Allemagne*, pp. 208–9.

the very 'henchmen' through whom the French reactionaries had sought to perpetuate colonialist rule in Algeria.[74]

Such propaganda gained in significance on 13 August 1961, when East Berlin's security forces sealed the border to the West. A last-ditch effort to halt the GDR's relentless haemorrhage of workers and professionals, the construction of the Berlin Wall marked a new highpoint of East–West tensions. Western governments criticised the Ulbricht regime for acting in a militarist and totalitarian manner.[75] To deflect this censure and justify the construction of the 'anti-fascist protective wall', the authorities in East Berlin retaliated by highlighting the Adenauer government's role in facilitating the French counterinsurgency against the FLN. They accused the Bonn authorities of complicity even with the racist and reactionary *Red Hand* and OAS. In exposing the 'neo-colonial policies and true aims of [West] German imperialism in Africa', the regime once again sought to depict the Bonn Republic as the inheritor or Germany's colonial and fascist past. These negative depictions of the FRG were contrasted to the GDR's own positive contributions to the FLN's cause, whether humanitarian aid, medical care for injured *mûjahideen*, or asylum for refugees.[76]

These by now familiar tropes of East German propaganda were echoed in articles in *Neues Deutschland* marking the Algerian war's seventh anniversary in November 1961, which also denounced the *Sicherungsgruppe* Bonn for running a 'special commission for the pursuit of Algerian citizens' in the Federal Republic. The paper accused the director of the BND, Reinhard Gehlen, of supplying intelligence to the *Red Hand* and facilitating that organisation's campaign of assassinations and sabotage.[77] East Berlin's accusations of West German collusion and collaboration with French colonialism were repeated in radio transmissions destined for North African and Middle Eastern audiences, where they seemed to hit a nerve.[78] Reporting from Baghdad on 22 December, Ambassador Werner von Bargen sounded the alarm after the entire Iraqi press replicated a statement by the GPRA's former Minister for Cultural Affairs Ahmed Tewfiq el-Madani condemning the Adenauer government for its persecution of Algerians and solidarity with France.[79] The statement echoed many of the arguments that featured in East German propaganda, including

[74] Cited in: Kittel, 'SED', p. 413. [75] Taubert, *L'«autre» Allemagne*, p. 207.
[76] Kittel, 'SED', pp. 413–14; Hong, *Cold War Germany*, p. 151.
[77] 'Bonn arbeitet für "Rote Hand"', and 'Gehlen liefert Algerier ans Messer', *Neues Deutschland*, 18 November 1961.
[78] Radio de la RDA en arabe, 9 September 1961, MAE, SEAA/9.
[79] Fernschreiben Nr. 392, Botschaft Baghdad, 22 December 1961, PA/AA, B12/932.

accusations of Bonn's purported collusion with the OAS, whose members included former (German) legionnaires.[80] Concerned by the FLN's influence and prestige in the Middle East, Ambassador Bargen hoped to persuade the FLN's remaining cadres in West Germany to issue a collective *démenti* to el-Madani's allegations, a suggestion the *Auswärtige Amt* emphatically refused to carry out.[81]

To reinforce the image of the Federal Republic as reactionary, colonialist and anti-Algerian, the Ulbricht regime also increased its material assistance to the FLN, thus augmenting its claim of representing a paragon of anti-imperialist solidarity. In July 1961, the Free German Youth movement pledged 50,000DM aid to Algerian refugees, supplementing the East German Red Cross's ongoing relief efforts. By then, the latter had delivered over twenty-four shipments of material aid to refugees in North Africa and was about to despatch a further two worth over 173,000 marks.[82] While East German hospitals continued to treat an indeterminate number of injured *mujâhideen*, the regime in September donated furnishings and equipment for an entire hospital to the GPRA. This alarmed Bonn's consul-general in Algiers, Siegfried von Nostitz.[83] After all, in a context of growing power struggles within the FLN, mounting retributions against those deemed collaborators with the colonial state, especially the *harkis*, and increasingly vindictive scorched-earth tactics by the OAS, Algeria was in bitter need of humanitarian assistance, which the GDR continued to provide.[84] As Young-Sun Hong argues, this emphasis on medical and pharmaceutical aid reflected the regime's wider strategy of humanitarian and proletarian solidarity with the Third World whereby medicine and hygiene became symbols of socialist modernity.[85]

80 Fernschreiben Nr. 12, Botschaft Baghdad, 13 January 1961, PA/AA, B12/932; 'Westdeutsche Waffen für OAS', *Neues Deutschland*, 13 January 1962.

81 Schreiben, Botschaft Baghdad, 11 January 1962; Schreiben, AA an Botschaft Baghdad, 25 January 1962, PA/AA, B12/932.

82 Schreiben, Vizepräsident Dr. Weitbrecht, Rote Kreuz, an CRA Rabat, 22 April 1961; Schreiben, Generalsekretär Röhricht, Rote Kreuz, an das Zentralkomitee der SED, 9 August 1961, ADRK, DDR/222.

83 Taubert, *L'«autre» Allemagne*, p. 190; Siegfried von Nostitz, *Algerisches Tagebuch 1960–1962* (Düsseldorf, 1971), p. 86. Records indicate that another fifteen injured soldiers arrived in East Berlin in December 1961. There is no evidence to support the claim that up to 500 ALN wounded found treatment in the GDR. See: Hong, *Cold War Germany*, p. 151, versus: Keller, *Gelebter Internationalismus*, p. 71.

84 For analyses of this period: Shepard, *Invention*; Yann Scioldo-Zürcher, *Devenir Métropolitain. Politique d'intégration et parcours de rapatriés d'Algérie en métropole (1954–2005)* (Paris, 2010), pp. 31–158.

85 Hong, 'Kalter Krieg', pp. 77–94; Ibid., 'Benefits', pp. 183–210; and more broadly: Ibid., *Cold War Germany*.

In a context of flagging domestic legitimacy and serious economic crisis, this strategy proved unable to secure rapid returns. Increasingly desperate to break through the barriers of international isolation, the Ulbricht regime rekindled the question of exchanging diplomatic emissaries. Until then, the GPRA had refused to recognise the GDR, though its representatives had become regular visitors to East Germany to discuss matters of aid. The FDGB and East German Red Cross were in close contact with FLN ancillaries such as the UGTA and CRA.[86] In June 1961, the Ulbricht regime decided once more to table a proposal for reciprocal recognition. The recent failure of the Évian negotiations would have amplified the Algerians' need for international allies, the regime's Foreign Ministry reasoned, making them more receptive to East German overtures. On 16 June, East Berlin's consul in Cairo, Wolfgang Kiesewetter, put this proposal to Mabrouk Belhocine, secretary general of the GPRA's Foreign Ministry, repeating the offer to Foreign Minister Krim Belkacem on 10 July, just days before Franco-Algerian negotiations were set to resume at Lugrin. Kiesewetter's interlocutors both refused to consent to reciprocal recognition without further consultations.[87] Responding to Kiesewetter's proposal hardly constituted a priority for the GPRA, which remained preoccupied by more pressing concerns. After all, the failure of the Lugrin negotiations further exacerbated the tensions within the FLN. The second National Council of the Algerian Revolution (CNRA), which convened in Tripoli in August 1961, continued to divide hardliners and doves, the GPRA and the ALN. While it failed to produce a clear negotiating line, the Council did form a radical new government presided by Benyoucef Benkhedda.[88]

Policy-makers in East Berlin initially welcomed this development. Relieved that they no longer had to deal with Ferhat Abbas's 'petty bourgeois and nationalist-capitalist attitudes', they hoped Benkhedda's leftist-progressivist impulses would strengthen the GDR's hand.[89] This last assessment proved wrong, for on the matter of reciprocal diplomatic recognition, the new GPRA remained just as cagy as its predecessor. In January 1962, the new secretary general in the Algerian Foreign Ministry, Abdel Aziz Zerdani, informed an exasperated Kiesewetter that the GPRA was still looking into his request for diplomatic recognition. One month later, while Franco-Algerian negotiations resumed at Les

[86] Taubert, *L'«autre» Allemagne*, pp. 109–11. [87] Ibid., p. 224.

[88] William B. Quandt, *Revolution and Political Leadership: Algeria, 1954–1968* (Cambridge MA, 1969), pp. 141–47.

[89] Cited in: Kittel, 'SED', p. 420; Taubert, *L'«autre» Allemagne*, pp. 232–3.

Rousses, the Ulbricht regime finally abandoned its efforts.[90] The Évian Accords of 18 March 1962 would have marked a perfect opportunity for East Berlin to recognise the GPRA unilaterally, thus demonstrating goodwill and solidarity. After all, even Moscow and many of its satellites at that point extended *de jure* recognition to the GPRA. Oddly, the Ulbricht regime did not, resentful perhaps of the Algerians' refusal to recognise East Berlin.[91] Only on 4 July 1962 did Prime Minister Otto Grotewohl announce the GDR's unilateral and *de jure* recognition of the new Algerian state, one day after de Gaulle had formally pronounced Algeria an independent country, and one day before the FLN would do the same.[92] Adherence to protocol, it seems, had won the day in East Berlin.

The GDR's recognition of Algeria alarmed the Bonn government, which had yet to follow suit. As one of the first liberation movements to have fought a colonial state and won, the FLN enjoyed remarkably high prestige in the Third World and its actions were likely to set a precedent.[93] Bonn's consistent solidarity with France compared poorly with East Berlin's open policy of support for the Algerian liberation struggle. Although the FLN had remained cagy on the point of recognition, Algerian nationalists had repeatedly expressed their appreciation for East German aid. After the Évian Accords, a spokesperson in Cairo extended the GPRA's 'gratitude to the GDR and all socialist states' for the support they extended to the FLN 'from the rebellion's start'.[94] On 7 April 1962, a speaker for the GPRA's Foreign Ministry announced that Algerians were 'eager to strengthen the bonds that connect us to the East German people'.[95] Federal authorities also took note of comments made by the communist journalist and FLN collaborator Henri Alleg, whose personal account of torture had done so much to turn world opinion against the French counterinsurgency. Algeria would 'support the GDR's demand for a peace treaty' and two-state solution to the German question, Alleg maintained on 5 April 1962 while accepting an award from the Association of East German Journalists, since 'the anti-fascist part of

90 Taubert, *L'«autre» Allemagne*, pp. 224–5. 91 Elsenhans, *Frankreichs Algerienkrieg*, p. 82.

92 'DDR erkennt Algerien an', *Neues Deutschland*, 4.7.1962.

93 See: Westad, *Global Cold War*, p. 106; Jeffrey J. Byrne, 'Algiers between Bandung and Belgrade: Guerrilla Diplomacy and the Evolution of the Third World Movement, 1954–1962', in *The Middle East and the Cold War: Between Security and Development* (eds.) Matteo Gerlini and Massimiliano Trentin (Newcastle-upon-Tyne, 2012), p. 28. See also Byrne's forthcoming book, *Mecca of Revolution*.

94 BPA, Aktivität der Sowjetischen Besatzungszone (SBZ) im Ausland, March 1962, PA/AA, B12/932.

95 BPA, Aktivität der SBZ im Ausland, 10 May 1962, PA/AA, B12/932.

Germany [had] always supported us during the terrible years of war'. In a subsequent interview with *Radio Berlin International*, Alleg declared:

> I think the Algerians will never forget the friends who stood by them during their darkest days. They differentiate very clearly between the Germans of the Federal Republic, who sided with France the entire time and who supported the French colonialists by sending thousands of mercenaries, and the Germans of the Democratic Republic, who stood on their side to help fight for their independence.[96]

With signs aplenty suggesting that the FLN favoured the Ulbricht regime, the *Auswärtige Amt* sought to ensure that an independent Algeria would not recognise the GDR. To achieve this, the Bonn government had to make amends with the FLN. The question was, how? After all, Adenauer's loyalty to de Gaulle remained resolute. France's ascendancy to the ranks of the nuclear powers in March 1960 had once more exacerbated the chancellor's fears of French unilateralism in defence and foreign-policy matters and heightened the asymmetry of power between Paris and Bonn.[97] John F. Kennedy's presidential inauguration in January 1961, meanwhile, caused Adenauer, who feared the young Democrat would reach a compromise with Khrushchev over Berlin, to move even closer to France.[98] These anxieties help explain why in February 1961 the chancellor gave his support to de Gaulle's controversial Fouchet Plan for an intergovernmental European political union that, under French leadership, would act as a third force in international affairs.[99] Two months later, the attempted generals' putsch in Algiers reminded Adenauer of just how volatile France's future – and that of Europe – remained.[100] During their meeting in Bonn on 20 May 1961, the very day the Évian negotiations opened, the chancellor congratulated de Gaulle for seeing through the political crisis. Only now, for the first time, did the General speak about his Algerian plans with Adenauer, emphasising how 'he [knew] he [was] addressing himself to

[96] Ibid. [97] Lappenküper, *Deutsch-französische Beziehungen* II, pp. 1355–73, 1645.

[98] Frank Mayer, 'Adenauer and Kennedy: An Era of Distrust in German-American Relations?' *German Studies Review* 17/1 (1994), pp. 83–4. For the newest research, see: Fabian Rueger, 'Kennedy, Adenauer and the Making of the Berlin Wall, 1958–1961', PhD Dissertation (Stanford University, 2011), pp. 66–133.

[99] Jacques Bariéty, 'Les entretiens de Gaulle-Adenauer de juillet 1960 à Rambouillet: prélude au Plan Fouchet et au traité de l'Élysée', *RA* 29/2 (1997), pp. 167–76; Koopmann, *Schwieriges Bündnis*, pp. 125–83; Marcowitz, *Option*, pp. 49–108; Andrew Moravcsik, *The Choice for Europe: Social Purpose and State Power from Messina to Maastricht* (Ithaca NY, 1998), pp. 176–97; Craig Parsons, *A Certain Idea of Europe* (Ithaca NY, 2003), pp. 117–46.

[100] Fernschreiben Nr. 462, Botschafter Blankenhorn an AA, 5 May 1961, in BDFD/I, p. 770; Lappenküper, 'Adenauer', p. 612; Marcowitz, 'Unionsparteien', p. 564.

good allies' and how he hoped the war's conclusion would open new perspectives of collaboration between Europe and Africa.[101]

De Gaulle's meaning was not lost on Adenauer. The General's response had been a reward for the latter's loyalty over Algeria. Convinced that self-determination offered the only viable solution to the Algerian problem, Adenauer would not sanction any moves that jeopardised de Gaulle's position.[102] The *Auswärtige Amt*'s flirtation with greater autonomy thus proved short-lived.[103] After the expulsion of the FLN's three representatives in Bonn, the government reverted to its usual policy of restraint and support in the Algerian question. The construction of the Berlin Wall merely strengthened this policy. Considering his 'psychopathic fear' of compromise between Washington and Moscow, the chancellor relied on de Gaulle as never before.[104] Neither the federal elections of 17 September 1961, which saw the CDU/CSU lose their absolute majority, nor Brentano's subsequent replacement as foreign minister by the "Atlanticist" Gerhard Schröder had any effect on Bonn's "Gaullist" course in matters Algerian.[105] After all, in his previous capacity as interior minister, Schröder had overseen the implementation of the Franco-German intelligence war against the FLN sanctuary in the FRG.

West German policy-makers thus remained guarded vis-à-vis the movement's remaining cadres in West Germany. Although he suspended all legal action against Keramane, Kacem and Bouattoura, Güde instructed the BKA in October 1961 to continue its investigations into Algerian subversion and reserved the right to re-open his case against the FLN if new incriminating evidence came to light.[106] On the eve of the war's seventh anniversary, the BKA itself reminded the security forces of the *Länder* of their continued obligation to prevent Algerians from engaging in political activities on German soil, while the *Auswärtige Amt* requested increased protection for the French diplomatic corps. State Secretary Karl Carstens considered this continued loyalty 'urgently necessary' in view of the government's efforts to forge an axis Paris–Bonn.[107] On 1 November 1961,

[101] Entretien entre le Général de Gaulle et le Chancelier Adenauer, 20 May 1961, AN, 5AG1/160*.

[102] Lappenküper, 'Adenauer', p. 613; Marcowitz, 'Unionsparteien', pp. 564–5.

[103] Cahn and Müller, *RFA et guerre d'Algérie*, pp. 355–6, 379.

[104] Schwarz, *Epochenwechsel*, p. 127; Steininger, *Mauerbau*, p. 360. Also: Lappenküper, *Deutsch-französische Beziehungen* II, pp. 1405–15; Buffet, 'De Gaulle et Berlin', pp. 525–38; Trachtenberg, *Constructed Peace*, pp. 324–39; Koopmann, *Schwierige Bündnis*, pp. 157–66.

[105] Lappenküper, 'Adenauer', p. 611; Marcowitz, 'Unionsparteien', pp. 561–2.

[106] Wochenbericht Nr. 674, SG-Bonn, 3 November 1961, BA/K, B131/201.

[107] Referat IB3 an Referat VIB4, BMI, 26 October 1961, BA/K, B106/47459; Fernschreiben Nr. 12674, BKA an BMI und LMIs, 31 October 1961, B131/214; Télégramme no. 5080 de Seydoux, 26 October 1961, MAE, MLA/7.

Hassan Aziz, who had replaced Keramane in Bonn, issued a press release in which he urged the Adenauer government to extend economic aid and establish contact to the GPRA. These measures would no longer harm Franco-German relations, Aziz argued, since Paris itself now negotiated with the FLN. Instead, they would 'create a psychological climate of friendship' between Algeria and West Germany that could serve as 'the basis of any future economic cooperation'.[108] Although it had previously considered taking up such communication with Algerian emissaries during the phase of negotiations, the *Amt* now ignored Aziz's invitation.

With the Évian Accords drawing closer, the Adenauer government's continued embargo even on informal contacts with members of the FLN nevertheless troubled some of Bonn's diplomats. Writing from Algiers, Nostitz observed in September 1961 how the refusal to engage the GPRA caused Bonn to 'miss one chance after another' while the 'Ulbricht people moved heaven and earth to curry favour with the Algerians'.[109] Nostitz's senior colleague in Tunis, Herbert Richter, felt similarly. In early March 1962, the ambassador lamented how he was trying 'to do the reasonably possible' to counteract efforts by East Berlin's trade mission in Tunis to woo the GPRA, 'without ending up in collision with our commitments as allies to France'. Richter warned that 'under no circumstances can we come too late' in recognising the GPRA.[110] His warning had little effect, for contact with the GPRA remained anathema to the Adenauer government so long as France retained sovereign control over Algeria. The *Auswärtige Amt* refused to infringe on what was, as yet, a French sphere of influence.[111] Not even Keramane, now the GPRA's top diplomat in Tunis, could persuade the authorities otherwise. Just days before the Algerian referendum on the Évian Accord, Keramane confidentially advised Richter that 'relations between the Federal Republic and Algeria would immediately start on friendly terms' if Bonn recognised the GPRA imminently after independence.[112] His plea, too, proved in vain. The Bonn government did not follow suit when first France and then the GDR recognised the new Algerian state.[113]

Why, then, did Bonn fail to follow suit? If protocol and resentment accounted for the timing of East Berlin's recognition of the GDR, the

[108] Fernschreiben Nr. 9357, BPA, 2 November 1961, PA/AA, B12/932.
[109] Nostitz, *Tagebuch*, pp. 85–6.
[110] Schreiben, Botschaft Tunis, 9 March 1962, PA/AA, B12/932.
[111] Circulaire no. 23 aux représentants diplomatiques de la France, 18 March 1962, in *DDF* 1962, Vol. I, no. 90; Nostitz, *Tagebuch*, p. 132.
[112] Fernschreiben Nr. 107, Botschaft Tunis, 27 June 1962, PA/AA, B12/932.
[113] Aufzeichnung, Abt. 2, 2 July 1962, PA/AA, B12/932. French recognition came on 3 July 1962.

policy of *Westbindung* did so in the case of the FRG. After all, Algeria's independence coincided with a landmark moment in the Franco-German rapprochement: Adenauer's historic state visit to France, an honour usually reserved for heads of state rather than heads of government. A milestone in the process of reconciliation, the chancellor's visit was followed by de Gaulle's own first official state visit to the FRG in September 1962. Considered by Carstens as 'one of the great political occasions in the history of our country', Adenauer hoped to use both voyages to recalibrate the Franco-German relationship, expanding it into new domains, including closer military cooperation. Now that France had successfully completed the process of decolonisation, having finally extricated itself from the Algerian quagmire, the chancellor hoped to persuade the General to focus his policies on Europe. His state visit to France paved the way for the historic Élysée Treaty, designed to seal the axis Paris–Bonn indelibly.[114]

In this context, a rapid move to recognise Algeria hardly appeared opportune, especially as the political situation in Algiers remained so precarious. Divisions within the FLN had become increasingly pronounced after March 1962. Freshly released from prison and supported by Houari Boumediène, the powerful head of the ALN General Staff, Ahmed Ben Bella bitterly criticised the GPRA for having conceded too much in the 'neo-colonialist' Évian Accords. An attempt in June by the CNRA failed to bridge the gap between the quarrelling factions. By the time of Algeria's independence, the country faced an open political crisis between the GPRA and a newly formed FLN Politburo headed by Ben Bella.[115] With civil war looming, the *Auswärtige Amt* decided to postpone recognition until the crisis abated.[116] After two months of internecine violence, elections finally took place on 20 September 1962 for a National Constituent Assembly based on a single list of FLN-approved candidates purged of many of Ben Bella's opponents. On 26 September, this Assembly appointed the latter president. Only then, on 28 September, did Nostitz visit Ben Bella and his new Foreign Minister Mohammed Khemisti to request an exchange of ambassadors.[117] Such was Adenauer's reserve, however, that it took him another week before he followed the examples of the

[114] Schreiben, Carstens an Blankenhorn, 10 July 1962, PA/AA, B2/75. Also: Bariéty, 'De Gaulle, Adenauer', pp. 539–64; Conze, *Herausforderung*, pp. 242–9; Marcowitz, *Option*, pp. 70–85; Lappenküper, *Deutsch-französische Beziehungen* II, pp. 1721–32; Soutou, *L'alliance*, pp. 203–59; Vaïsse, *Grandeur*, pp. 249–58.

[115] On the crisis, see: Quandt, *Revolution*, pp. 164–74; Meynier, *Histoire*, pp. 644–71.

[116] Drahterlass Nr. 82 an Konsulat Algier, 9 August 1962, PA/AA, B12/932.

[117] Nostitz, *Tagebuch*, pp. 217–19; Fernschreiben Nr. 167, Nostitz, 29 September 1962, PA/AA, B12/932.

American, British and Italian leaders, who had sent personal telegrams congratulating Ben Bella.[118]

At this point, Adenauer's hesitation probably had less to do with loyalty to de Gaulle than apprehension over Algeria's general development. After all, the proclamation of a People's Democratic Republic did not sit well with the fiercely anti-communist chancellor. Ben Bella founded his policies on the CNRA's Tripoli Program of June 1962, which became an ideological roadmap for a radical, socialist transformation of the Algerian state, economy and society. His government declared Algerian culture to be 'national, revolutionary and scientific', albeit tempered by Islam. In its foreign policy, the new Algerian state practised the principle of neutralism and would soon emerge as a leader of the Non-Aligned Movement. At its September 1961 founding conference in Belgrade, this movement had nearly endorsed the two-state solution for Germany that the Bonn government so fiercely opposed.[119]

The Non-Aligned Movement made it clearer than ever that West Germany no longer wielded a monopoly in diplomatic legitimacy.[120] In subscribing to the movement, the Ben Bella government signalled that it did not feel bound by the Hallstein doctrine. Although he expressed a desire for close collaboration with Bonn, the president prevaricated on the future status of Algeria's relations with East Berlin.[121] Given Algeria's debt of gratitude to the GDR, Algerian officials hinted on more than one occasion that they would accept the opening of an East German trade mission at the very least.[122] Ben Bella also stalled in the accreditation of a West German ambassador. To expedite the process, Nostitz urged Foreign Minister Schröder to write a personal message to his Algerian counterpart, a step he somewhat patronisingly felt might satisfy the 'known sensitivity of Arab governments in matters of protocol and their need for prestige'.[123] Even then, the Algerians challenged Bonn's claim to exclusivity. Thus in his first speech before the UN General Assembly in October 1962, Foreign Minister Khemisti demanded a continuation of four-power negotiations to find a solution to the German question that 'took account of realities'.[124] Khemisti's

[118] Fernschreiben Nr. 170, Nostitz, 2 October 1962, PA/AA, B12/932; Telegramm Adenauer an Ben Bella, 3 October 1962, B12/933.
[119] Mahfoud Bennoune, *The Making of Contemporary Algeria, 1830–1987* (Cambridge, 1988), pp. 95–104; Byrne, 'Socialism', pp. 427–32.
[120] Gupta, 'Ulbricht', p. 125; End, *Zweimal*, p. 48.
[121] Fernschreiben Nr. 167, 29 September 1962, PA/AA, B12/932.
[122] Nostitz, *Tagebuch*, pp. 196, 199.
[123] Fernschreiben Nr. 169, Nostitz, 2 October 1962, PA/AA, B12/932.
[124] Fernschreiben Nr. 627, Gesandtschaft New York, 12 October 1962, PA/AA, B12/932.

implicit endorsement of the two-state solution alarmed Bonn, as did the presence in Algiers since August 1962 of an East German diplomatic delegation led by Günter Scharfenberg.[125] Nostitz vehemently protested against the latter's invitation to the independence celebrations planned for 1 November 1962. Echoing the Hallstein doctrine, the consul warned Ben Bella and the FLN's Secretary General Mohamed Khider that Scharfenberg's inclusion 'would virtually ensure the rupture of [Bonn's] relations' with Algeria.[126] Algiers and Bonn now both played hardball to secure their respective interests. Relenting somewhat, Algiers' Foreign Ministry assured Nostitz that only Bonn had received a formal invitation to the festivities, while the East German delegates had only been issued informal invites given the Ulbricht regime's as yet 'ambiguous' status.[127]

This *modus vivendi* hardly reassured Bonn's diplomats, whose apprehension rose further when it was announced in early November that Ben Bella would receive ambassadorial *agréments* in the order in which countries had recognised the GPRA.[128] The announcement rekindled East German hopes of finally securing their goal of recognition from Algeria. East Berlin's Foreign Ministry was therefore bitterly disappointed, when in late November 1962 the Ben Bella government decided against the initiation of diplomatic relations. After all the rhetoric in support of the two-state solution, Algeria, Mohamed Khider explained, could not recognise two German states, just as it could not accept the existence of two states in Palestine. Ultimately then, 1962 had turned into 'a year of deceptions' for the GDR.[129] In April 1963, Ben Bella did agree to the opening of an unofficial East German trade mission in Algiers. At that point, however, he had already normalised relations with the FRG.[130] Even when the Ben Bella government severed its relations with Bonn in 1965 in response to the latter's recognition of Israel, it refused to recognise the GDR. Nor did Ben Bella's successor, Boumediène, who assumed power in a coup d'état that same year. Ultimately, it would take another five years before Algeria granted East Berlin full and reciprocal diplomatic recognition in May 1970 at a time of East–West détente.[131]

[125] Fernschreiben Nr. 126, Nostitz, 26 August 1962; Schreiben, Nostitz, 9 October 1962, PA/AA, B12/807; Taubert, *L'«autre» Allemagne*, p. 243.

[126] Nostitz, *Tagebuch*, p. 222.

[127] Ibid., pp. 221–4; Fernschreiben Nr. 188, Nostitz, 22 October 1962, PA/AA, B12/932.

[128] Fernschreiben Nr. 218, Nostitz, 8 November 1962, PA/AA, B12/932.

[129] Taubert, *L'«autre» Allemagne*, pp. 229,257.

[130] Aufzeichnung, Referat 205, 8 January 1961, PA/AA, B12/807; Aufzeichnung, Referat IB4, 23 September 1963, B1/219.

[131] Taubert, *L'«autre» Allemagne*, p. 228; Winrow, *Foreign Policy*, pp. 55, 70.

Meanwhile, the Bonn authorities received the news of Algeria's decision in November 1962 not to recognise East Berlin with considerable relief. The Hallstein doctrine had proved effective, or so it appeared. On 7 January 1963, Ben Bella formally recognised Herbert Richter as Bonn's first ambassador to Algiers.[132] The choice proved astute, for Richter had built up a strong knowledge of the Maghreb while serving in Tunis. He had also been an early advocate of contacts and aid to the FLN. The fact that Ben Bella opted to receive Richter separately from other ambassadors and that their meeting found 'an exceptional echo' in the Algerian press seemed to bode well for the future of German–Algerian relations, so Richter felt.[133] The ambassador encouraged the *Auswärtige Amt* to accept Keramane as his counterpart in Bonn.[134] The former head of the FLN bureau in Bonn was characterised by the *Amt* as 'reasonable and willing to compromise'.[135] Extraordinarily gracious about his past treatment in West Germany, for which 'he felt no resentment', the *Amt* considered him a 'Germanophile' who would defend the FRG's interests in Algeria and beyond.[136] On 14 June 1963, just over two years since his ignominious arrest and expulsion, Keramane returned to Bonn and presented his *agrément* to President Heinrich Lübke. German–Algerian relations were finally normalised.[137]

Chequebook diplomacy?

West Germany emerged from the Algerian war as the clear victor in the German–German contest for recognition and legitimacy. This was a tremendous feat considering Adenauer's latent hostility towards the FLN, his fretfulness over France–German reconciliation, and the nerve-racking tensions over Berlin, three factors that had consistently pulled the federal government to side with France in the Algerian question. How, then, does one explain Algeria's choice for Bonn over East Berlin? Cahn and Müller attribute this outcome to the effective implementation of a 'policy of equidistance'. Though conscious of the fact that Paris expected the Adenauer government to be '*plus royaliste que le roi*' (more royalist than

[132] Schreiben, Botschaft Algier, 9 January 1963; Déclaration du Président Ahmed Ben Bella à l'occasion de la remise des lettres de créances par l'Ambassadeur de la RFA, 7 January 1963, PA/AA, B12/932.
[133] Schreiben, Botschaft Algier, 11 January 1963, PA/AA, B12/932.
[134] Schreiben, Botschaft Algier, 1 February 1963, PA/AA, B36/2/F3.
[135] Aufzeichnung, Abt. 2, 9 November 1962, PA/AA, B12/932.
[136] Abt. IB4 an Protokoll, 14 February 1963, PA/AA, B36/2/F3.
[137] Aufzeichnung, Protokoll, 14 June 1963, PA/AA, B36/2/F3.

the king), the *Auswärtige Amt* successfully defended West Germany's wider interests, even if this meant going against France. Through subtle manoeuvring, they argue, the Bonn government secured East Berlin's diplomatic isolation while forging the axis Paris–Bonn.[138] Bougherara argues similarly, contending that foreign-policy-makers in Bonn 'refused to follow passively a policy [they] deemed radical and leading to impasse'. In other words, they opposed French efforts to cling to Algeria.[139]

This book proposes an alternative explanation. It has argued that Bonn was highly sensitive in its handling of the French government, often to the detriment of its interests beyond Europe. It agrees with Vaïsse, who has argued that the Adenauer government practised 'unfailing support' over Algeria.[140] And it has taken that argument further by suggesting that Bonn in fact became an essential pillar and proxy of the French counterinsurgency, especially in the diplomatic arena and in the fight against the FLN's sanctuary in West Germany. This support proved vital to building trust and did far more to advance the Franco-German rapprochement than some historians have realised.

To account for Algeria's choice for Bonn, traditional interpretations would point to West Germany's economic clout. Political independence, after all, was accompanied by a drive for economic decolonisation as Third World leaders sought to modernise their countries' economies, reduce their dependence on their former colonial masters and transform entire social orders. As Arne Westad argues, it was this impulse for radical transformation that propelled the Third World into the path of the competition between Washington and Moscow to 'change the world [and] prove the universal applicability' of the ideologies that underpinned their respective models of modernity. Like other Third World governments, the Ben Bella regime turned to the Soviet model, which better reflected its preferences for a strong, centralised state, rapid industrialisation and social justice.[141] To implement their ambitious development plans, however, Third World states required foreign capital and technical knowhow, and Algeria was no different in that regard.

When it came to these needs, so the argument goes, the Bonn government simply outperformed East Berlin. After all, 'soft power' was rapidly becoming the key instrument of West Germany's mounting influence both

[138] Cahn and Müller, *RFA et guerre d'Algérie*, pp. 457, 379, 471. [139] Bougherara, *Rapports*, p. 110.
[140] Vaïsse, *Grandeur*, p. 230.
[141] Westad, *Global Cold War*, pp. 4, 90–3. For a historiographical survey: Corinna Unger, 'Histories of Development and Modernization: Findings, Reflections, Future Research', H-Soz-u-Kult 09 December 2010 (http://hsozkult.geschichte.hu-berlin.de/forum/2010–12–001).

inside and outside of Europe.[142] The country's booming economy was but one component of that power. And yet with its substantial export surpluses, as Ulrich Damm argued, West Germany's 'chequebook diplomacy' was consistently able to outbid its eastern rival in the provision of development aid, even then when a government's ideological sympathies lay with the latter.[143] Algeria, one could argue, proved no exception to this rule. The Ben Bella government had to rebuild a war-torn society. In the chaos and violence that followed the Évian Accords, the exodus of the *colons* had prompted massive capital flight and drained Algeria of its foremost professional, economic and technical classes. The scorched-earth tactics of the OAS had destroyed much of Algeria's infrastructure. The displacement of several million Algerians returning from French resettlement sites, detention centres and refugee camps had produced widespread famine and disease.[144]

Economic calculations thus undoubtedly featured strongly in Algiers' decision to recognise the Bonn government. According to SDECE, Hassan Aziz's time as FLN representative in Bonn was chiefly spent fostering ties to West German industry; the movement also sought to maintain strict discipline within its sanctuary so that Algerians would 'merit the Germans' respect through their actions and demeanour'.[145] In an interview with DPA while at the UN in October 1962, Ben Bella emphasised how 'he was very aware' that West Germany absorbed one-third of Algerian exports while trade with the GDR remained non-existent. The president expressed his hope that West German development aid and private investment would contribute to the implementation of his ambitious industrialisation plans.[146]

142 Konrad H. Jarausch and Michael Geyer, *Shattered Past: Reconstructing German Histories* (Princeton NJ, 2003), pp. 193–6. I use the term "soft power" broadly here to refer to a state's ability, both in terms of its resources and behaviour, to use appeal, attraction and non-coercive means to achieve its foreign policy goals. On the concept, see: Joseph Nye, *Soft Power: The Means to Success in World Politics* (Cambridge MA, 2004); Giulio Gallarotti, 'Soft Power: What is it, Why It's Important, and the Conditions Under Which it Can Be Effectively Used', *Journal of Political Power* 4/1 (2011), pp. 25–47; Jeffrey J. Anderson, 'Hard Interests, Soft Power, and Germany's Changing Role in Europe', in *Tamed Power: Germany in Europe* (ed.) Peter J. Katzenstein (Ithaca NY, 1997), pp. 80–107.

143 Ulrich Damm, *Versuch einer Darstellung der politischen Beziehungen der Bundesrepublik Deutschland zu den Entwicklungsländern unter besonderer Berücksichtigung der Entwicklungshilfe* (Geneva, 1965), p. 120. Also: Hein, *Entwicklungspolitik*, p. 31; End, *Zweimal*, pp. 48,125; Winrow, *Foreign Policy*, p. 42; and more broadly: Gray, *Germany's Cold War*; Gupta, 'Ulbricht'; Kilian, *Hallstein-Doktrin*.

144 Bennoune, *Making*, pp. 89–90.

145 Notice de renseignements no. 10076/SDECE, 23 March 1962. Also: Notices de renseignements nos. 12948/SDECE, 29 May 1962, 14137/SDECE, 29 June 1962, SHD-T, 10T/262*.

146 Fernschreiben Nr. 605, Gesandtschaft New York, 11 October 1962, PA/AA, B12/929. French government statistics from 1960 indicate that at 9.6 and 9.8 per cent of the respective totals, West Germany stood in second place behind France when it came to imports to and exports from

For this reason, and notwithstanding his previous ties to Benkhedda, Nostitz felt certain Ben Bella would approve Keramane's appointment as ambassador to Bonn. As Rabah Bitat, vice president of Algeria's Council of Ministers, had told the consul, Keramane's 'extensive personal connections to industrial and trade-union circles in the Federal Republic made him indispensable for that post'.[147] In early November 1962, Boumediène, the defence minister and 'strong man' of Ben Bella's cabinet, likewise noted his 'great respect' for West Germany's post-war economic recovery in a conversation with Nostitz. 'Algeria needed technical aid in all domains' to achieve a similar reconstruction, Boumediène maintained. He hoped the FRG would contribute to the equipment of the newly founded National People's Army and the construction of housing for the millions displaced by the war.[148]

To Nostitz, these supplications for aid reflected the 'latent goodwill' and 'high regard' that Germany enjoyed in Algeria, a case also made by the German defence attaché, Wilfried Hofmann, who had toured the country in December 1961.[149] Wherever he went, Hofmann reported, he had encountered a 'naïve enthusiasm' among the Muslim population for all things German, whether the carmakers Mercedes and Volkswagen, or the World War II *Afrikakorps* commander Erwin Rommel. To Hofmann's regret, this enthusiasm sometimes stemmed from a belief that Germans were 'born French-haters and anti-Semites' and that a common enmity of France and Israel made them a natural ally of Muslims and Arabs.[150]. Whatever its source, Algerians were eager to emphasise the 'genuine sympathy' they felt for Germany, as noted also by Bonn's defence attaché in Cairo. They invariably expressed their hope that the country would help implement Algeria's modernisation plans.[151]

As Dirk van Laak contends, however, this historic 'German bonus' applied to the GDR just as much as it did to the FRG.[152] In this optic, economic and technical assistance constituted both a lever and a lure

Algeria, with numbers rising rapidly. See: Rapport sur le commerce extérieur, DGGA, 1960, pp. 58, 82, 88–9, SHD/T, 1H/1106/D4.

147 Fernschreiben Nr. 187, Gesandtschaft Algier, 19 October 1962, PA/AA, B12/932.

148 Fernschreiben Nr. 216, Nostitz, 7 November 1962, PA/AA, B12/932.

149 Schreiben, Generalkonsulat Algier, 14 May 1962, PA/AA, B12/932.

150 Reisebericht, Generalkonsulat Algier, 14 February 1962, PA/AA, B12/932. Hofmann would serve as West German ambassador to Algeria from 1987–1990. He converted to Islam in 1980, assuming the name Murad.

151 Schreiben, Militärattaché Kairo, 25 May 1962; Fernschreiben Nr. 216, Nostitz, 7 November 1962, PA/AA, B12/932.

152 Dirk van Laak, *Imperiale Infrastruktur. Deutsche Planungen für eine Erschließung Afrikas 1880 bis 1960* (Paderborn, 2004), p. 361.

through which to ensure that Algeria opted for strong ties to the West. Shortly before the Évian Accords, Ambassador Richter had urged the *Auswärtige Amt* 'to start thinking about future development aid' in order to achieve this scenario.[153] His colleague Nostitz encouraged the *Amt* to plan for a Goethe-Institute in Algiers so as to cement cultural exchanges and support scholarships for study in the FRG. The sooner such measures were implemented, the consul argued, the better for thwarting East Berlin's advances. Both of these proposals remained academic, however, since 'France still trumped' in the *Amt.* So long as Algeria remained French, Nostitz observed in his diary, 'nothing can happen that Paris could take amiss'.[154] Even so, the consul kept up his efforts to stimulate German diplomacy into action. In May 1962, he reminded the *Amt* how in 1961 the European Commission had approved the provision of roughly 100 million new French Francs from the EDF for the implementation of infrastructure projects linked to the Constantine Plan. In contributing the lion's share of the EDF's budget, the Bonn government already subsidized Algeria's economic development, albeit indirectly, and would continue to do so for at least another three years. Direct investment by private West German companies, meanwhile, only amounted to 23.1 million DM, flowing primarily into the extractive industries, especially the burgeoning oil and gas sector. Nostitz urged the Bonn government to make an initial offer of development aid totalling 100 million DM as soon as Algeria became independent and to follow this up with additional public and private aid, including the provision of credits, guarantees on investments and technical assistance.[155]

As Algeria's independence approached, discussions were therefore under way on how best to deploy West German economic and cultural power in order to outperform the GDR. Within the context of rapid decolonisation, development aid had become Bonn's newest foreign-policy instrument. Western governments – especially the United States had put significant pressure on Bonn to increase the assistance it offered the newly independent states of Asia and Africa. According to the prevalent logic of the day, Western development aid, in facilitating the process of modernisation along free-market lines, would prevent the spread of socialist and revolutionary ideas in the Third World whilst allowing the West to retain access to new markets and vital natural resources.[156] The Adenauer government

153 Schreiben, Richter, 9 March 1962, PA/AA, B12/932.

154 Nostitz, *Tagebuch*, p. 132.

155 Schreiben, Nostitz, 14 May 1962, PA/AA, B12/932.

156 Schmidt, 'Pushed', pp. 474–79; Corinna R. Unger, 'Modernization à la Mode: West German and American Development Plans for the Third World', *GHI Bulletin* 40 (2007), p. 149.

had taken decisive steps to augment its provision of such aid. Created in 1961, a Federal Ministry for Economic Cooperation was tasked with overseeing the coordination and implementation of development policies. That same year the aid budget underwent a 'quantum leap' from 730 million DM in 1960 to 4,145 billion DM in 1961. By 1962, West Germany spent 1.06 per cent of its GDP on foreign aid, in fifth place behind the Netherlands, France, Belgium and Britain, all former colonial powers, but ahead of the United States.[157] By then, the Adenauer government had articulated its own approach to development aid. In contrast to Washington, which favoured sweeping, multilateral state grants, Bonn preferred to fund individual projects that involved close and direct cooperation between public and private partners. Such projects aimed to promote sustainable development and growth and foster durable bilateral trade relations.[158]

The Adenauer government also recognised the political significance of humanitarian aid. It would be no coincidence that just after Güde's ill-timed crackdown on the FLN bureau in Bonn, the *Auswärtige Amt* approached the Finance Ministry about a donation of 300,000DM towards the UNHCR's relief work in North Africa. The request, Bonn's largest donation yet, was approved in July 1961.[159] At the same time, the *Amt* had instructed its embassy in Cairo discreetly to inform the GPRA Foreign Ministry of another recent donation by the Bonn authorities, this one of 150,000DM to support the ICRC's relief work in North Africa.[160] To forestall French complaints, these state-sanctioned contributions continued to be channelled through multinational humanitarian aid organisations, a policy that remained in place even after the Évian Accords. Thus although the *Auswärtige Amt* encouraged the DRK in March 1962 to augment its assistance to Algerian refugees, it did so on the condition that all aid continued to flow through the ICRC.[161] By then, the FRG's Inter-Departmental Committee on Capital Assistance had agreed to ring-fence 5 million DM of its annual budget for Algerian food aid, something French authorities considered 'unobjectionable'.[162] In April, the

[157] Hein, *Entwicklungspolitik*, p. 41; Unger, 'Modernization', p. 149; Schmidt, 'Pushed', pp. 479–82.

[158] Hein, *Entwicklungspolitik*, pp. 30–60; Massimiliano Trentin, 'Modernization as State Building: The Two Germanies in Syria, 1963–1972', *Diplomatic History* 33/3 (2009), pp. 489–90.

[159] Fernschreiben Nr. 101, Bundesfinanzministerium an AA, 12 May 1961, PA/AA, B12/933; Brief, Brentano an Blachstein, 31 July 1961, AdsD, NL/Blachstein/34.

[160] Aufzeichnung, Referat 204, 4 May 1961, PA/AA, B12/933.

[161] Vermerk, Referat 204, 29 March 1962, PA/AA, B12/933.

[162] BMWi an Referentenausschuß für Kapitalhilfe, 19 February 1962; Ergebnisbericht, Referentenausschuß für Kapitalhilfe, 23 February 1962, BA/K, B136/2973/F9.

UNHCR, which had begun to coordinate efforts to repatriate the millions uprooted and displaced by the Algerian war, appealed urgently for 360 tonnes of sugar and 120 tonnes of soap worth approximately 1 million DM. The *Amt* sought to obtain broad approval to respond to this request, pointing out how 'every measure of help for Algerian refugees from the Federal Republic was followed attentively in the entire Arab world and was bound to have a positive echo whose political significance was not to be underestimated'.[163] Even so, it took two months before the Inter-Ministerial Committee on Development Aid approved the sugar request. The committee rejected the appeal for soap, which did not fall under the remit of food aid. With Algerian independence now looming, the *Amt* hoped to donate the sugar directly to the new Algerian authorities, bypassing the UNHCR so as to achieve 'the greatest possible political effect'.[164] For that same reason, officials were instructed to emphasise the quantity of sugar – 1,500 tonnes – rather than its market value. At 500,000DM, the donation amounted to 10 per cent of the original budget set aside for food aid, making federal authorities worry that its 'political effect might be lost'.[165]

While officials in Bonn emphasised the altruistic nature of their help, the above example illustrates just how cumbersome the inter-departmental decision-making process was. Although the humanitarian crisis escalated from day to day, it took until late August 1962 for the promised sugar to arrive in Algeria. More importantly, the example highlights just how politicised simple charitable gestures had become in the struggle between Bonn and East Berlin. Even Nostitz could not escape this Cold War logic, though his diary reflects genuine concern over the unfolding crisis. In June, the consul appealed urgently for surgeons to help staff the many hospitals left unattended by the departing *colons*. By sending doctors, Nostitz reasoned, West Germany could help prevent a 'looming catastrophe' and simultaneously 'gain goodwill'.[166] The *Amt* agreed but found it impossible to recruit civilian volunteers who spoke French (or Arabic or Berber) and were willing to take the personal risk that service in Algeria entailed at that time. These difficulties prompted diplomats to consider despatching *Bundeswehr* medics in civilian clothing, even securing the *Quai d'Orsay*'s approval. Defence Minister Strauss, however, pointed out that Bonn could not withdraw its servicemen from NATO command for use in unilateral

[163] Schreiben, AA an Bundesministerium für Ernährung, Landwirtschaft und Forsten, 9 April 1962, BA/K, B136/2973/F9.
[164] Vermerk, Referat 6, 18 June 1962, BA/K, B136/2973/F9.
[165] Vermerk (c.July 1962), BA/K, B136/2973/F9. [166] Nostitz, *Tagebuch*, p. 170.

foreign missions, even civilian ones.[167] In July, the Federal Border Guard offered to send a small team of paramedics as an interim solution, while the Inter-Departmental Committee on Technical Aid agreed to set aside 2 million DM towards medical aid for Algeria.[168] Paramedics could not replace doctors and surgeons, however, prompting Foreign Minister Schröder again to request the release of *Bundeswehr* doctors – to no avail.[169] By August, the *Amt* had recruited two civilian surgeons, a modest offering when compared to East German medical aid.[170]

Unable to mobilise doctors, West German diplomacy instead sent a fully equipped and staffed Clinomobil.[171] The Clinomobil enabled the Bonn government to achieve two goals at once: provide humanitarian aid; and impress the Algerians with West German technical prowess. Donated initially for three months, this state-of-the-art, mobile clinic made for an apolitical, practical and 'representative' offering on the occasion of Algeria's independence. In harnessing technical and scientific expertise to the improvement of health and hygiene, the Clinomobil symbolised all the benefits of West German modernity. Having been used as an independence gift in the past ('even in insignificant, for example African states'), the clinic constituted a tangible counterpart to East German aid.[172] To heighten its impact, Nostitz hoped to present the Clinomobil in the same 'ceremonious transfer' being arranged for Bonn's long-awaited sugar donation and urged the *Amt* to donate the clinic indefinitely. 'The positive publicity to be expected from such a move', he argued, would help neutralise the recent arrival of 6,500 tonnes of Soviet grain.[173]

Like its eastern counterpart, therefore, the Bonn government used medical technology to demonstrate the advantages of Western modernity and win over hearts and minds. Medical assistance, however, was not the only weapon in Bonn's soft-power arsenal. By the time the Clinomobil arrived in Algiers in late August 1962, federal authorities had turned their thoughts to the question of financial and economic assistance. In the

[167] Aufzeichnung, Abt. 2, 18 June 1962; Fernschreiben Nr. 688, Botschaft Paris, 21 June 1962; Aufzeichnung, Abt. 6, 7 July 1962, PA/AA, B12/933.

[168] Schreiben, AA an BMI, 10 July 1962; Aufzeichnung, Abt. 8, 18 July 1962, PA/AA, B12/933.

[169] Brief Schröder an Strauss, 16 July 1962, PA/AA, B12/933.

[170] Fernschreiben, Bundesgesundheitsministerium an AA, 24 August 1962, PA/AA, B12/933.

[171] Aufzeichnung, Abt. 6, 16 July 1962, PA/AA, B12/933.

[172] Referat 205 an Referat 204, 28 May 1962, PA/AA, B12/931; Unger, 'Modernisation', p. 157, n. 32.

[173] Fernschreiben Nr. 118, Nostitz, 16 August 1962, PA/AA, B12/931; Fernschreiben Nr. 122, Nostitz, 20 August 1962, BA/K, B136/2973/F9. By 1963, the donation had in fact turned into a public-relations disaster for Bonn, since the doctors chosen to work in the mobile clinic not only embezzled funds but neglected and usurped their duties. See: Hong, *Cold War Germany*, p. 159.

matter of multilateral aid, especially Algeria's future access to the EDF, the *Amt* counselled 'absolute restraint' and deference to France. Considering Algeria's regional and international standing, however, it felt 'one should not wait too long' with offers of bilateral assistance.[174] On 3 July 1962, Bonn's Economics Ministry sent a memorandum to the Inter-Departmental Committee on Capital Assistance in which it, too, emphasised the urgent need for bilateral aid and proposed reserving an initial sum of 40 to 50 million DM for this purpose. The committee endorsed this plan, settling on the higher sum of 50 million.[175] In principle, the offer of aid was contingent on agreement over specific development projects, however, the political uncertainties plaguing Algeria made it impossible to formulate clear proposals. On 28 September, the day Bonn recognised the Ben Bella government, the Inter-Ministerial Committee on Development Aid empowered Richter to communicate Bonn's offer immediately upon the presentation of his diplomatic credentials. This move was contrary to protocol. German diplomats had managed to overcome the Finance Ministry's objections to a large and open-ended commitment on the grounds that a promise of aid would counter Soviet-bloc donations and satisfy the Algerians, whose 'expectations were considerably higher' than the proposed aid.[176] Shortly after his arrival in Algiers on 21 December 1962, Richter informed the Algerian Foreign Ministry of Bonn's pledge, the specifics of which were to be decided jointly. Further public and private assistance, he assured the Algerians, would soon supplement the initial sum of 50 million DM.[177]

While the Bonn government had been slow to react to Algeria's humanitarian and economic crisis, its belated efforts did pay dividends. In October 1962, Nostitz had used personal funds to open a German school in Algiers as a first step towards the founding of a Goethe-Institute.[178] By then, the number of surgeons working in Algeria had tripled to six. Two months later, three Algerian hospitals were under West German administration. This increase finally compared positively to the medical aid supplied by the GDR, whose own shortage of surgeons meant that it preferred to train medics at home rather than second personnel to the Third World.[179] In late 1962, the *Amt* evaluated the prospects

[174] Referat 204 an Referat 200, 8 June 1962, PA/AA, B12/932; Vermerk (c.July 1962), BA/K, B136/2973/F9.
[175] Schreiben, BMWi, 3 July 1962; Protokollauszug, 7 August 1962, BA/K, B136/2973/F9.
[176] Protokollauszug, 49. Sitzung, 28 September 1962, BA/K, B136/2973/F9.
[177] Fernschreiben Nr. 267, Botschaft Algier, 26 December 1962, PA/AA, B12/932.
[178] Nostitz, *Tagebuch*, pp. 220–1. [179] Ibid., pp. 208, 243; Hong, 'Benefits', p. 188.

of Algerian–West German economic cooperation optimistically. Although the Ben Bella government adopted socialist policies in matters of state, party and economy, it accepted Bonn's offer of development aid.[180] As soon as diplomatic relations were formally established, Algerian and West German officials initiated negotiations on a number of development projects, including the construction of a petrochemical plant, a vast irrigation scheme in north-eastern Algeria, and the reconstruction of the commercial harbour at Annaba in the north-west, one of Algeria's most important industrial cities. These negotiations eventually produced the bilateral agreement on technical cooperation signed on 17 December 1964.[181] By then, the Bonn government had contributed nearly 131 million DM in development aid to Algeria, a sum that included credits, technical assistance and guarantees on investments.[182] As for the Ulbricht regime, while it provided substantial humanitarian assistance throughout the independence struggle and after (French intelligence in July 1961 estimated its total worth at roughly 3 million DM), it never matched the Bonn government's eleventh-hour offers of development aid.[183]

Cognitive dissonance?

If Bonn's largesse played an important part in Algeria's decision to recognise West rather than East Germany, it was not the only factor contributing to that outcome. Frictions between Algerians and East Germans might also explain Ben Bella's choice for Bonn, for relations between the FLN and Ulbricht regime were never as cordial as public statements implied. As mentioned in Chapter 8, tempers had first begun to flare between UGEMA and the authorities in East Berlin over the behaviour and treatment of Algerian students. Tensions also emerged between Algerian workers in the GDR, of which there were approximately 120–180, and their East German co-workers and superiors. Historians Taubert and Patrice Poutrus have shown how on the German side, complaints frequently arose over the Algerians' supposedly lax work ethic, their alleged refusal to integrate or participate in workers' demonstrations, and their apparent lewdness towards women. On the Algerian side, grievances centred on the cold,

180 Protokollauszug, 28 September 1962; Fernschreiben Nr. 204, Nostitz, 4 November 1962, BA/K, B136/2973/F9.

181 For an overview, see the files contained in BA/K, B136/2973/F9 and F10.

182 Tabelle, Entwicklungshilfe für Algerien, May 1964 [probably compiled by the Federal Ministry for Economic Cooperation], ADCV, ZA/116 + 187 I/Fasz.01.

183 Meynier, *Histoire*, p. 606; Hong, *Cold War Germany*, pp. 155-60.

cramped and damp living conditions, the pork-based diets served in workplace cafeterias, the racism to which they were frequently subjected, and the authorities' relentless attempts at ideological indoctrination.[184] As in West Germany, many of these grievances resulted from a mutual case of cultural misunderstanding and miscommunication. Unlike West Germany, where local *Hilfskomittees* had been created precisely for that purpose, there was no one to translate or mediate between the two communities in East Germany's closed and caged society.

The arrival in September 1960 of Ahmed Kroun as UGTA's permanent representative in East Berlin was intended to rectify this situation. Unfortunately, Kroun's arrival exacerbated the situation. Within eight months, the authorities demanded his departure.[185] To East German officials, Kroun's role consisted of pastoral care and ensuring that Algerian workers and trainees understood East German work standards and cultural norms. Kroun, meanwhile, believed he had exclusive authority over all Algerians in East Germany. Charged by the GPRA with maintaining order and enforcing obedience to the FLN rather than the GDR, he had identified 'recalcitrants' whose behaviour warranted 'repatriation' to North Africa for the purpose of 're-education' within the ranks of the ALN. Those affected were mostly student members of the Algerian Communist Party whose alleged refusal to toe the FLN line had prompted unanimous condemnation at UGEMA's national congress in July 1960. The East German authorities appeared to protect these 'recalcitrants', whom they considered the only politically reliable Algerians.[186]

The ensuing dialogue of the deaf was symptomatic of what Meynier refers to as the 'cognitive dissonances' and Taubert as the 'political autism' that consistently marred relations between the FLN and Ulbricht regime.[187] From East Berlin's doctrinaire and legalistic perspective, the

184 Poutrus, 'Grenzen', pp. 162–78; Taubert, *L'«autre» Allemagne*, pp. 140–59. The Algerians' experience reflects that of other foreign workers in the GDR, notably the large Vietnamese community that arrived during the 1980s. See: Dennis Kuck, 'Für den sozialistischen Aufbau ihrer Heimat?' Ausländische Vertragsarbeitskräfte in der DDR', in *Fremde und Fremd-Sein in der DDR. Zu den historischen Ursachen der Fremdenfeindlichkeit in Ostdeuschland* (eds.) Jan C. Behrends, Thomas Lindenberger and Patrice Poutrus (Berlin, 2003), pp. 271–82; Annegret Schüle, ' "Die ham se sozusagen aus dem Busch geholt": Die Wahrnehmung der Vertragsarbeitskräfte aus Schwarzafrika und Vietnam durch Deutsche im VEB Leipziger Baumwollspinnerei', in ibid., pp. 283–98; Jonathan R. Zatlin, 'Scarcity and Resentment: Economic Sources of Xenophobia in the GDR, 1971–1989', *Central European History* 40/4 (2007), pp. 683–720.

185 Taubert, *L'«autre» Allemagne*, pp. 112–18.

186 UGEMA, Motion sur les 'rappelés' de D.D.R., Tunis, July 1960, BA/K, B166/1462; Poutrus, 'Grenzen', pp. 170–2; Meynier, *Histoire*, p. 609.

187 Meynier, *Histoire*, p. 603; Taubert, *L'«autre» Allemagne*, p. 272.

FLN's attitude towards Algerian communists was undemocratic and diplomatically unacceptable. Indeed, Kroun's behaviour suggested the GPRA wanted to enjoy all the prerogatives of state recognition, including control over Algerian nationals, without reciprocating the favour.[188] Kroun and his superiors, meanwhile, justified the repatriations as a necessary measure to counteract the heavy losses inflicted by the Challe offensive, improve discipline, replenish the ALN and reinvigorate the armed struggle. In December 1960, Boumediène had personally interceded with the FLN's leading cadres in Europe to secure fresh recruits for the ALN. After all, to hardened revolutionaries, the 'easy' existence of Algerian students and workers in Europe hardly constituted commitment to the independence struggle.[189]

When East German authorities refused to release the 'recalcitrants' identified by Kroun, the FLN accused the GDR of rigidity and intransigence. After a visit in June 1960, Messaoud Aït Chaalal once more complained that East Berlin's demands for 'compensation' from the FLN after years of 'unilateral concessions' were 'discourteous' and approached 'a real *Diktat*'. To the UGEMA president, East Berlin's objections to an FLN bureau were an attempt to force the issue of diplomatic recognition.[190] The GPRA, too, saw no link between the matter of population control and the question of diplomatic recognition, insisting on its right to decide over the fates of Algerians in the GDR. In August 1961, UGTA Secretary General Embarek Djilani sent a scathing letter to the FDGB. Protesting against Kroun's recent expulsion, Djilani observed how the treatment of nearly 4,000 Algerian workers, students and refugees 'was handled much better in West Germany', where the UGTA and DGB cooperated closely. In pointing out how the UGTA maintained a central office in Düsseldorf with representatives 'in all the *[Bundes]länder*', Djilani sought to force political concessions out of East Berlin.[191] He conveniently ignored the fact that in West Germany, too, the UGTA's manoeuvring room was formally restricted to trade union affairs while the police sought to dismantle the '*Fédération d'Allemagne*'. He also ignored Güde's crackdown against the FLN's bureau in Bonn, and the fact that the bureau had owed its existence to the protection proffered by the Tunisian and Moroccan embassies, an option that did not exist in the GDR.

188 Meynier, *Histoire*, p. 608.
189 Haroun, *Septième Wilaya*, p. 79; Taubert, *L'«autre» Allemagne*, p. 177.
190 Rapport de Mission en DDR, juin 1960, in *Archives* (ed.) Harbi, pp. 497–500.
191 Cited in: Taubert, *L'«autre» Allemagne*, p. 128.

Needless to say, the Ulbricht regime responded by rejecting the GPRA's claim to authority over the Algerians in East Germany. And while the FLN undoubtedly appreciated the medical, material and technical assistance provided by the GDR, it continued to resist East German attempts at ideological indoctrination and its demands for reciprocal recognition. Unable and unwilling to understand the other's viewpoint or compromise on their respective demands, the two sides never overcame their mutual recriminations. In the run-up to independence, relations between the UGTA and FDGB waned noticeably as the Algerians reneged on previous agreements, even rejecting an offer of much-needed radiology equipment. By the time the Ben Bella government banned the Algerian Communist Party in November 1962, the Ulbricht regime realised its efforts to break out of diplomatic isolation had failed.[192]

Wilâya Germany

In contrast to East Berlin's perceived obstinacy, West German attitudes towards Algerians must have appeared positively liberal to the FLN, a fact that was not unimportant given the FRG's importance as external sanctuary. Indeed, as Wischnewski observed in September 1962, of the 196 candidates that stood for election to the Algerian Constituent Assembly, nearly 50–60 per cent had experienced the Bonn Republic first-hand during the independence struggle, if only for a short period of time.[193] These circumstances, too, will have contributed to Ben Bella's decision to recognise Bonn over East Berlin. In spite of the FRG's alliance with France, including joint efforts to undermine anti-colonial subversion, West German civil society had largely tolerated the Algerian presence in its midst. Non-state actors had even cooperated with the UGTA and UGEMA in matters concerning the welfare of Algerian workers and students. Thanks to their 'paradoxical citizenship', Algerians could move and live relatively freely in West Germany so long as they appeared to abide by residency regulations. 'If only they kept calm', Nostitz wrote in his diary, 'then our generous policy of [unofficial] asylum could turn into an asset for us'. Instead, the consul lamented, their underground conspiracies and rivalries had 'compelled our police to intervene'.[194] In January 1961, the *Quai d'Orsay* had noted how West Germany remained 'one of the European countries where FLN activity is greatest'.[195] Proximity to

[192] Taubert, *L'«autre» Allemagne*, pp. 253, 270. [193] Scheffler, *SPD*, p. 74.
[194] Nostitz, *Tagebuch*, p. 86. [195] Note, MLA, 31 January 1961, MAE, MLA/7.

France certainly contributed to West Germany's significance as an external sanctuary, yet the FLN also took advantage of the country's democratic and federal order. The necessity of protecting that sanctuary was one of the key reasons why the GPRA had persistently refused to recognise the GDR during the war. Strategically, logistically and operationally, West Germany's importance was such that the FLN dared not risk any moves that might force federal authorities to clamp down on Algerians more robustly.[196] The arrest of Keramane and his associates in April 1961 had highlighted just how volatile the sanctuary remained. While the authorities may have tolerated the Algerians' presence in the FRG, they attempted to suppress all political or subversive activities.

Güde's crackdown thus served as a reminder of the importance of secrecy, compartmentalisation and discipline not only to entrench an external sanctuary but to secure its utility towards an insurgency. This dictum remained valid right to the Algerian war's end. After all, Keramane's arrest did not spell the end of '*wilâya* Germany'.[197] According to SDECE, interim representatives rapidly assumed control over the day-to-day operations of the so-called *Fédération d'Allemagne*, while regional and local cadres remained largely unaffected by Güde's crackdown.[198] As Keramane recalled, around fifty full-time militants remained in place in April 1961 to look after the FLN's politico-administrative structures and interests.[199] By October, Hassan Aziz was running the Bonn bureau. The fact that the GPRA Foreign Ministry replaced Keramane with his superior in the European and Western department is itself a testament to the importance the FLN attached to its German sanctuary.[200] SDECE reckoned Aziz would find it easy to rekindle severed ties and create new ones.[201] The *deuxième bureau* of the French forces in Germany also detected a recrudescence in subversive activity following Aziz's arrival. After a period of relative calm, it observed, the FLN had returned to pursuing 'its "struggle", and its activity on federal territory – propaganda, collection of taxes, incitement to desertion – was not slowing down'. The military's concern was palpable, for in 1961 an unprecedented total of forty Algerians had deserted from French army bases in Baden-Württemberg and Rhineland-Palatinate.[202] By December, the Bonn bureau

[196] Meynier, *Histoire*, p. 610. [197] Leggewie, *Kofferträger*, p. 45 (italics added).

[198] Notices de renseignements nos. 46141/SDECE, 29 June 1961, 46942/SDECE, 21 July 1961, SHD-T, 1H/1753/D2*; Notice de renseignements no. 47499/SDECE, 8 August 1961, 1H/1579/D3*.

[199] 'Entretiens', in *Rapports*, Bougherara, p. 213. [200] Ibid.

[201] Notices nos. 4409/SDECE, 25 November 1961, 6646/SDECE, 30 December 1961; 9687/SDECE, 14 March 1962, SHD-T, 1H/1753/D2*.

[202] Synthèses nos. 2416/CCFFA/2, 16 October 1961; 2501/CCFFA/2, 11 November 1961, SHD-T, 10T/550*; Niederschrift, Besprechung im AA, 19 January 1962, BA/K, B106/47459.

was back to organising cocktail parties for allies and friends. According to SDECE, attendees included the usual suspects: the SPD's 'Algeria lobbyists', Wischnewski, Blachstein and Kalbitzer; DGB executive members Richter and Wedel; journalists and Third World diplomats; but also a growing number of Adenauer's political allies, including Majonica, his parliamentary colleague Gerhard Fritz, Catholic Youth leader Walter Molt and representatives of the Christian aid organisations *Caritasverband, Innere Mission* and *Pax Christi*, a peace movement established for the promotion of Franco-German reconciliation.[203] In May 1962, Aziz finally vacated the Moroccan embassy to establish the independent bureau that Paul Frank had previously advocated.[204] Two months later, Aziz was reassigned to Algeria. As SDECE observed, only then did the FLN bureau cease its operations. In August, the Tunisian government took charge of Algerian consular interests until Algiers could open its own embassy in Bonn.[205]

Meanwhile, the activities of the UGTA and UGEMA had remained virtually unaffected by Güde's ill-fated crackdown. In contrast to the GDR, both auxiliaries operated openly in West Germany thanks to their respective affiliation to the ICFTU and COSEC and close ties to the DGB and VdS. In July 1960, UGTA representative Ahmed Mostefaoui had even founded a 'Social Welfare Office for North African Workers' in Cologne. The office owed its existence to Wischnewski, who had hired the premises, and to the DGB, which paid Mostefaoui a monthly subsidy of 1,000DM. In August 1960, Omar Belouchrani took over operations, having replaced Mostefaoui as the UGTA's chief delegate in West Germany.[206] The Cologne office ostensibly functioned as a coordinating centre between the UGTA, DGB and the West German authorities. It assisted arriving Algerians in finding employment or training placements and helped them organise accommodation and language tuition. The office also coordinated and controlled the work of the UGTA's regional and local representatives in West Germany, whose task it was to work with local *Hilfskomitees*, supervise Algerian workers and collect union dues.[207] According to SDECE, Belouchrani claimed in November 1961 to have secured jobs

[203] Notice no. 6646/SDECE, 30 December1961, SHD-T, 1H/1753/D2*.

[204] Aufzeichnung, Abt. 2, 23May 1962, PA/AA, B12/932.

[205] Notices nos. 15328/SDECE, 3 August 1962, 15430/SDECE, 7 August 1962; SHD-T, 10T/262*; Schreiben Aziz (Ghani) an Blachstein, 9 July 1962, AdsD, NL/Blachstein/34; Note verbale de l'ambassade de Tunisie à Bonn, 27 August 1962, PA/AA, B12/932.

[206] Protokollauszug, 39. Sitzung des Geschäftlichen Bundesvorstandes, Punkt 3, 18 July 1960; Aktenvermerk, Abt. Vorsitzender, 22 July 1960; Lettre du président de l'UGTA, Maachou, à Richter, 23 August 1960; Bescheinigung, 13 September 1960, AdsD, 5/DGAJ/207.

[207] Plum, *Gewerkschaften im Maghreb* (Hannover, 1962), p. 71.

and union affiliation for approximately 2,100 Algerians since his arrival in Cologne. Although they paid their union dues, Belouchrani further maintained that most of these workers were active neither in a trade union capacity nor in a political one, desiring only social stability and security.[208]

Even so, French intelligence remained suspicious of the UGTA, and not just because the collected union dues were seen as buttressing the FLN's war coffers. In June 1961, Colonel Duchène asked the German security services to investigate reports whereby the Cologne office in fact functioned as a clandestine school for militants of the *Fédération de France*.[209] The following month, he claimed the office served to conceal the activities of Omar Haraigue, deemed by French intelligence to be one of the OS's top operatives.[210] German officials failed to confirm either suspicion. As late as April 1962, they considered groundless the claim that Belouchrani's office trained FLN militants and commandos and they never located Haraigue. This was unsurprising, for the latter had long departed from Europe to work for the GPRA's Ministry of Social Affairs in Morocco.[211] The German security services felt satisfied that the UGTA stuck to its trade union and social-welfare remit. In fact, the only organisation that continued to run afoul of the German authorities for its open pursuit of political activities was the UGEMA. According to the association's own records, the number of Algerians studying in West Germany had risen from 27 in mid-1960 to 84 in mid-1961, while the number in East Germany had declined from 102 to 75 – a further indication that all was not well between Algeria and the GDR.[212] French intelligence repeatedly highlighted how the students arriving in the FRG, aided by fellow German and Arab students, continued to organise pro-Algerian meetings and rallies well after Güde's crackdown on the FLN, whether in Saarbrücken, Freiburg, Heidelberg, Göttingen, Stuttgart or Bonn.[213]

Finally, Güde's crackdown never disturbed the day-to-day operations of the *Fédération de France* or of the *Organisation Spéciale*. Judging by the

208 Notice de renseignements no. 4432/SDECE, 27 November 1961, SHD-T, 1H/1753/D2*.

209 Vermerk, SG-Bonn, 15 June 1961, BA/K, B131/214.

210 Note par Duchène, 7 July 1961, BA/K, B131/214.

211 SG-Bonn an französische Botschaft, 12 April 1962; Bericht, LKA Nordrhein-Westfalen, 5 September 1961, BA/K, B131/214; BMI an Duchène, 13 September 1961, B106/15778; Haraigue, *Combat*, pp. 117, 135.

212 UGEMA, rapport sur les effectifs estudiantins, July 1960, BA/K, B166/1462; UGEMA Comité Exécutif, Effectifs des étudiants boursiers, in Notice no. 1308/A/SDECE, 27 September 1961, SHD-T, 1H/1723/D1*.

213 Synthèses nos. 2567/CCFFA/2, 18 December 1961, 2029/CCFFA/2, 13 January 1962, 10T/550*; Notice de renseignements no. 8436/SDECE, 10 February 1962, 1H/1722/D1*; SG-Bonn an BMI, 27 October 1961, BA/K, B106/15780.

available records, the German security and intelligence services never managed to uncover, let alone dismantle, the Federation's cadres on German territory. While the 'Papon system' had managed to decimate the FLN's European support networks in the metropole, they had found new recruits in neighbouring countries, including West Germany. Operations by the FLN's European support networks to infiltrate and exfiltrate militants, communications, propaganda and weapons thus continued to run smoothly. Only in late 1961 did federal border guards begin to detect some of the networks' elaborate evasive manoeuvres.[214] Their discovery helps to highlight the extent to which West Germany remained a vital safe haven and base for Algerians from the metropole even as the war drew to a close. The country's significance rose and fell with the rhythm of metropolitan police repression, which did not cease with the onset of the Évian negotiations. Papon's notorious final push to eradicate nationalist subversion from Paris in October 1961 is a case in point. The prefect's crackdown climaxed with the deadly suppression of a peaceful mass demonstration on 17 October organised by the *Fédération de France* to protest the tightening of controls limiting Algerians' freedom of movement and expression. Although its death toll remains disputed, ranging from thirty-two to two hundred, the Paris massacre, as House and MacMaster remind us, constitutes the single most public act of police brutality in post-war France. The ensuing days witnessed the arrest of over 14,000 Algerians.[215] In this context of mass repression that soon spilled beyond the capital, French intelligence observed a marked 'effluence of Algerians' into West Germany.[216] According to Fritz Henker of the DGB and Stuttgart's *Hilfskomitee*, roughly 6,000 Algerians resided in the FRG at the time of the Évian Accords.[217] The subsequent release of prisoners from metropolitan detention centres in accordance with an amnesty included in the Accords produced a further swell of new, albeit temporary, arrivals. The FLN bureau in Bonn remained an important hub for those seeking to

[214] Vermerk, Zollkommissar Rumbach, 9 November 1961; Grenzschutzdirektion Koblenz an BMI, 24 November 1961, BA/K, B106/63320.

[215] House and MacMaster, *Paris*, pp. 88–136. Also: Amiri, *Bataille de France*, pp. 123–76; Jean-Paul Brunet, *Police contre FLN. La drame d'octobre 1961* (Paris, 1999); Ibid., 'Police Violence in Paris, October 1961: Historical Sources, Methods, and Conclusions', *Historical Journal* 51/1 (2008), pp. 195–204; House and MacMaster's response, pp. 205–14; Jean-Luc Einaudi, *Octobre 1961: un massacre à Paris* (Paris, 2001); Jim House and Neil MacMaster, 'La Fédération de France du FLN et l'organisation du 17 Octobre 1961', *Vingtième Siècle* 83 (2004), pp. 145–60.

[216] Synthèses nos. 2416/CCFFA/2, 16 October 1961, 2501/CCFFA/2, 11 November 1961, SHD-T, 10T/550*.

[217] Henker, 'Algerische Arbeiter', p. 234.

return to North Africa. Only in May 1962 did French intelligence register a diminution in the activity of this transit network. By then, the *Fédération de France* was also winding down its operations, having received orders to return to Algeria.[218]

Although the French ceasefire and amnesty had reduced the need for an external sanctuary, the Algerian community in West Germany did not experience a noticeable contraction even after independence. As late as October 1962, the *deuxième bureau* of the French forces in Germany reported that while 'notorious individuals' (i.e. militants) had 'disappeared' (i.e. been recalled or transferred), most migrants appeared hesitant about returning to Algeria. The bureau speculated that Algerians were reluctant to relinquish the jobs and aid from which they benefited in West Germany, especially considering the political and economic crisis back home.[219] While this may have been the case for some, it is far more likely that the continued presence of Algerians had more to do with a lack of funds and travel documents than anxiety over Algeria's future let alone the supposed generosity of West German aid. After all, while the *Hilfskomitees* and other welfare associations tried to alleviate the migrants' plight, the West German press continued to highlight how most Algerians lived in conditions of abject poverty, emphasising the need for greater charity and 'Christian aid'.[220] Even SDECE had commented on the harshness of life '*á l'allemande*' for Algerians.[221] Since few possessed valid IDs and since the FLN bureau in Bonn had now disbanded, a voyage home had become practically impossible. The Tunisian embassy rapidly fell behind in issuing travel passes, such was the demand. By October 1962, a source deemed reliable by SDECE revealed, the embassy had to request increased resources to deal with the problem, including authorisation to issue travel passes directly in Bonn rather than going through channels in Tunis and Algiers.[222]

By then, the continued presence of Algerians also preoccupied the West German authorities. With Algeria now a sovereign state, albeit one whose administrative structures remained weak and in the process of formation, Bonn's Interior Ministry started to amend the extraordinary measures that had been used to register and control Algerians during the past four years.

[218] Synthèse no. 2210/CCFFA/2, 18 May 1962, SHD-T, 10T/550*.

[219] Synthèse no. 2388/CCFFA/2, 27 October 1962, SHD-T, 10T/550*.

[220] 'Emigranten auf Zeit', *Rheinischer Merkur*, 3 March 1961; 'Viertausend Algerier in Deutschland', *FAZ*, 29 March 1962.

[221] Notice no. 9229/SDECE, 1 March 1962, SHD-T, 1H/1722/D1*; Notice no. 15531/SDECE, 10 August 1962, 10T/262*.

[222] Notice no. 17145/SDECE, 20 October 1962, SHD-T, 10T/262*.

In September 1962, the ministry lifted its ruling whereby Algerians had to be screened through the *Fichier Z*, whose entries – by then well over 30,000 – were to be archived.[223] Two months later, the ministry modified its entry conditions as well as those for the provision of residence and work permits. Algerians wishing to enter the country would henceforth have to present a valid Algerian or French passport to do so. Those already in the country who wished to prolong their stay were required to apply for an Algerian or French passport. In the interim, the old system of 'blue cards' would continue to apply.[224]

These regulations reflected the Algerians' transitory status as France and Algeria underwent a period of legal disaggregation. In contrast to the *colons* or to Algerian Jews, whose French legal status remained uncontested, Algerian Muslims, the German embassy in Paris reported, had until 31 December 1962 to apply for the retention of their French citizenship, something they could only do in France. All Algerian Muslims who failed to apply for retention of their French citizenship would subsequently become Algerian nationals.[225] Algerians based in West Germany or elsewhere in Western Europe were consequently stuck in limbo. Those who wanted to take advantage of the ruling, in so far as they knew about it, rarely possessed the means to travel to France in order to submit their applications. The Algiers government, meanwhile, lacked the resources to issue passports for all those seeking Algerian citizenship ahead of the 31 December deadline. Countless Algerians soon found themselves with neither French nor Algerian IDs. As such, they were unable to leave West Germany and at the same time unable to stay. In February 1963, police authorities in Baden-Württemberg and Hamburg sought guidance from the federal government on how to deal with the continuing arrival of these undocumented and stateless individuals.[226] Official regulations called for their ejection, but as officials in Bonn noted, most Algerians continued to resist expulsion or extradition to France notwithstanding the government's promise to uphold the amnesties that formed part of the Évian Accords. The Algiers government, however, remained equally wary of accepting them without first checking their identities and credentials.[227]

[223] BMI an Bundesverwaltungsamt, 13 September 1962, BA/K, B106/15779; Vermerk, Referat IB3/BMI, 19 August 1962, BA/K, B106/5350.
[224] Runderlaß BMI an LMIs, 14 November 1962, BA/K, B106/15783.
[225] Schreiben, Botschaft Paris, 16 November 1962, BA/K, B106/47459. Also: Shepard, *Invention*, pp. 229–47.
[226] LMI Baden-Württemberg an BMI, 8 February 1963; Polizei Hamburg an BMI, 26 February 1963, BA/K, B106/47459.
[227] Vermerk, Referat IB3/BMI, 20 February 1963, BA/K, B106/47459.

Thus one year into Algeria's independence, West Germany's role as sanctuary had still not diminished. A solution to the presence of stateless and undocumented Algerians remained elusive. In July 1963, Councillor Benouis of the recently opened Algerian embassy estimated that up to 4,000 Algerians remained in West Germany. Whilst many had contacted the Algerian embassy to regulate their papers, whether for the purpose of leaving or extending their residence and work permits, the very fact that most of these individuals lacked even French IDs now impeded the Algerian authorities' efforts to ascertain their identities and issue passports. Benouis believed that it would take another four to five months before the backlog of passport applications had been cleared. In the interim, he asked that residence and work permits be granted and extended, a request to which the Bonn authorities obliged.[228] Ultimately, the Interior Ministry did not lift its temporary and extraordinary regulations until May 1964.[229] Only then was the status of Algerians finally normalised, and only then did the FLN's German sanctuary effectively cease to exist.

Citizen diplomacy

If the FRG's status as sanctuary played an important role in Algiers' decision to recognise Bonn over East Berlin, then the contacts that Algerian militants had forged with civil-society actors within that sanctuary proved just as vital. Civic engagement on the FLN's behalf continued to grow during the independence struggle's final phase, laying the foundation of the future German–Algerian relationship. By the time of the Évian Accords, the disparate activities of West German citizens on behalf of Algerian independence came to represent what German legal scholar Heinrich Triepel called 'private foreign policy' or American legal scholar James Marshall termed 'citizen diplomacy'. Such popular participation in international affairs occurred when private citizens or non-state organisations 'independently sought to shape the relations of their state to foreign states' in the knowledge that their actions compensated for, complemented, or counteracted official governmental policies.[230]

[228] Schnellbrief AA an BMI, 20 July 1963, BA/K, B106/47459.

[229] Runderlaß BMI an LMIs, 14 May 1964, BA/K, B106/15778.

[230] Heinrich Triepel, 'Die auswärtige Politik der Privatperson', *Zeitschrift für ausländisches öffentliches Recht und Völkerrecht* 9/1 (1939), pp. 6, 8, 16–18. James Marshall, 'Citizen Diplomacy', *American Political Science Review* 43/1 (1949), pp. 83–90 Also: Markus Heintzen, *Private Außenpolitik. Eine Typologie der grenzüberschreitenden Aktivitäten gesellschaftlicher Kräfte und ihres Verhältnisses zur staatlichen Außenpolitik* (Baden-Baden, 1988), pp. 12–22.

Algerian militants had established a web of contacts to West German civil-society actors, who provided day-to-day practical, logistical, propagandistic, moral and material support to the FLN's war effort. Though they acted in an unofficial, at times even unlawful, capacity through private channels and transnational networks, the support provided by these actors played a fundamental role in helping the FLN sustain and secure its sanctuary in West Germany. This was not overlooked in Algiers. Since the Adenauer government forbade all official contact to the FLN prior to independence and sought to restrict the movement's freedom of action within the sanctuary, the engagement with West German civil-society actors was instrumental in securing Bonn's diplomatic recognition. It expanded the FLN's manoeuvring room and kept open the channels of communication that would prove vital for the future of German–Algerian relations. Directly or indirectly, civil-society actors buttressed the FLN's insurgency in three important ways by helping, first, to win over public opinion and reinforce the movement's legitimacy; second, to procure humanitarian aid as well as war materiel; and third, to secure the future viability of the Algerian state. As such, they (if one excludes the arms traffickers) contributed to what Blachstein called the 'un-bloody war' waged internationally by a broad range of private actors to support the FLN in the very bloody war being waged in Algeria and France.[231]

In the contest for hearts and minds, voices sympathetic to the anti-colonial struggle continued to dominate West German press coverage of Algeria. Only as the Évian Accords grew nearer did Ambassador Seydoux observe 'the current of opinion appears in general to be turning [. . .] in a favourable direction' for France.[232] Approval of de Gaulle's disengagement policy did not, however, translate into favourable coverage of Bonn's pro-French attitude. Chastisement of the Adenauer government for its '*Nibelungentreue*' to France in matters Algerian remained a common theme, particularly after Güde's ill-fated clampdown on the FLN. The closer Algeria edged towards independence, the more the press expressed concern over Bonn's enduring reserve vis-à-vis the Algerians. Considering that even the French authorities had extended their *de facto* recognition to the FLN, Bonn's obstinacy seemed out of step to the press, merely benefiting the GDR.[233]

The press's critical coverage of the Algerian war and its general disapproval of colonialism helped moderate the impact of Adenauer's "Gaullist"

[231] Schreiben an Ahmed Boumendjel, February 1960, AdsD, NL/Blachstein/33.
[232] Télégramme no. 5025 de Seydoux, 23 October 1961, MAE, MLA/7.
[233] Cahn and Müller, *RFA et guerre d'Algérie*, p. 404.

foreign policy. So did the ongoing interest the West German public took in the Algerian war. Even after Güde's crackdown, the FLN continued its propaganda war in West Germany in a bid to strengthen its hand in negotiations with France. FLN militants relied on local allies to pursue and expand these efforts. The 'Working-circle for the Friends of Algeria' circulated regular issues of *Freies Algerien* until April 1962. West German publishers continued to print translations of first-hand accounts of the Franco-Algerian conflict, most of them critical of the French war effort, including a 'black book' edited by Keramane.[234] An enduring supporter of Algerian independence, Werner Plum published studies on North African history and trade unionism and even an anthology of Algerian poetry. All of these works sought to dispel the French government's claims that Algerians lacked a culture, history or national identity of their own.[235] While symbolically important, these publications hardly reached a wide readership and as such did not elicit inimical reactions from the authorities. The same could not be said of the decision by West Berlin's *Schlosspark* theatre to premier French dramatist Jean Genet's controversial *Les Paravents* (The Screens) on 19 May 1961. Set within the context of the Algerian war and explicitly political in its message, the play had been banned in France, where it would not be performed until 1966.[236] Though truncated and poorly translated, the Berlin staging led to a flurry of French diplomatic interventions. Intimidated, the theatre voluntarily ended performances one month after *Les Paravents*' premier.[237]

In addition to print culture and plays, the Algerian war had also reached the small screen. On 24 January 1961, the ARD aired a fifty-minute documentary on 'The Seven Years' War' produced by former *Welt* correspondent Paczensky, whose anti-colonial views were well known and who now hosted West Germany's first political TV talk-show, *Panorama*. To Seydoux, the film constituted 'a violent indictment of France and systematic glorification of the FLN'.[238] Such were the depths of French

[234] Hafid Keramane, *Schwarzbuch Algerien: Dokumente* (Hamburg, 1961); Jules Roy, *Schicksal Algerien* (trans.) Ulrich F. Müller (Hamburg, 1961); Robert Davezies, *Die Front* (trans.) Caesar Rymarowicz (Berlin, 1961); Pierre Leulliette, *Sankt Michael und der Drache* (trans.) Wilhelm P. Fink (Reinbek, 1962).

[235] *Algerische Dichtung der Gegenwart* (Nürnberg, 1959); *Nordafrika* (Nürnberg, 1961); *Gewerkschaften im Maghreb* (Hanover, 1962).

[236] Gene A. Plunka, *The Rites of Passage of Jean Genet: The Art and Aesthetics of Risk Taking* (Cranbury NJ, 1992), p. 241.

[237] Télégrammes du gouvernement militaire français de Berlin, nos. 669, 24 May 1961; 719, 31 May 1961; 755, 19 June 1961, MAE, MLA/7.

[238] Télégramme no. 383 de Seydoux, 25 January 1961, MAE, MLA/7.

anger over the programme, that it received mention in several French and German newspapers. Debré had Blankenhorn called in about the 'ignoble' film to remind the ambassador of Bonn's promise that 'programmes of such nature would not be permitted'.[239] Given the evolution of events, however, the *Auswärtige Amt* had lost its power to influence broadcasters over Algeria-themed content.[240] What made this situation all the more frustrating for the authorities was that television was rapidly displacing the radio as the medium through which households received their news.[241] With access to television, the FLN could begin to reach an ever-wider audience. As the war's seventh anniversary approached, the newly founded Second German Television Station (ZDF) aired what Seydoux termed another 'very disagreeable' programme about France's 'weakness and powerlessness' in Algeria.[242] On 5 November 1961, the ZDF also televised a ten-minute primetime interview with the GPRA's new president, Benkhedda. This was followed, on 10 December, by an extended ARD documentary about the ALN and its Repatriation Service for Deserted Legionnaires.[243]

The ARD's decision to commission, produce and air this documentary highlights the public's continued fixation with the French Foreign Legion, which remained the FLN's most effective propaganda theme in West Germany and other German-speaking countries. Even as the war drew to a close, Si Mustapha kept up his work for the FLN. He continued to care for deserters, organising and staging their repatriations; he also continued to produce a monthly information bulletin and organise tours of ALN bases and FLN-run refugee camps in Morocco for journalists and other interested parties. These tours sought to demonstrate the Algerians' organisational capacity, modernity, humanity and resilience. They enabled young photojournalists like Dirk Alvermann to produce some of their first work.[244] The ALN only began to wind down the Repatriation Service's activities in May 1962.[245] As Si Mustapha explained to Blachstein, by then

[239] Lettre à Couve de Murville, 27 January 1961, AHC, 2DE/21*; Note, 17 February 1959, 2DE/70*; 'L'Ambassade de France à Bonn s'élève contre une émission tendancieuse de la télévision allemande sur l'Algérie', *Le Monde*, 27 January 1961; 'Auswärtige Amt kritisiert Algerien-Fernsehsendung', *Die Welt*, 28 January 1961.

[240] Aufzeichnung, D2, 25 January 1961, PA/AA, B24/375/D4.

[241] Schildt, *Moderne Zeiten*, pp. 208, 265–8, 274.

[242] Télégramme no. 5025 de Seydoux, 23 October 1961, MAE, MLA/7.

[243] Télégramme no. 5272 de Seydoux, Bonn, 6 November 1961; Télégramme no. 5970 de Seydoux, Bonn, 13 December 1961, MAE, MLA/7.

[244] 'Zehn Tage Algerien, von Dirk Alvermann', *Freies Algerien* 4/4–5 (1961); *Algerien* (Ost-Berlin, 1960 and Göttingen, 2012).

[245] Communiqué der ALN, Tétouan, 4 May 1962, AdsD, NL/Plum/26.

the service was 'no longer of political (or military) use' to the ALN even though the demand for repatriations supposedly remained high.[246]

In addition to Blachstein and a series of journalists, Si Mustapha also maintained close contact to socialist youth organisations in the FRG. In April 1961, he hosted a delegation of *Naturfreundejugend* led by Klaus Vack, who had long been a pillar of the anti-Legion campaign and worked closely with *Jeune Résistance*. One month later, the delegation pushed through a resolution at their organisation's seventh national congress condemning the Foreign Legion for 'torture methods that barely differ from Gestapo practices' and participation in April's 'fascist putsch'. The resolution continued by declaring how the Legion 'harmed [West Germany's] reputation and tarnished [its] people with the charge of stabbing the [ALN] in the back', and this although the latter had done so much to "liberate" Germany's young men from the Legion's clutches. Working with the ALN's Repatriation Service, the *Naturfreundejugend* pledged to continue their efforts to educate the West German public about Algerian realities and lobby for the interdiction of Legion recruitment.[247]

Si Mustapha also supplied information for another youth initiative that came to attract the French authorities' attention in 1961: an itinerant exhibition organised by students belonging to West Berlin's section of the International League for Human Rights, or *Argument-Club*. Conceived largely by SDS activist Reimar Lenz as a 'significant action with political accents', the exhibit opened in a student hall on 21 February 1961.[248] Under the title, 'Why should Algeria matter to us?', the photos and documents on display 'came from French, Algerian, German and international organisations, editorial staffs, publishers, and aid organisations'.[249] French intervention denouncing the exhibit as communist propaganda was swift but ineffectual. Before long, it was displayed on university campuses in Kiel, Braunschweig, Heidelberg, Cologne, Mainz, Göttingen, Frankfurt/Main and even the Villigst home in Schwerte (a Protestant scholarship foundation).[250] The displays themselves were simplistic and crude; they rarely generated

[246] Brief Si Mustapha an Blachstein, 16 April 1961, AdsD, NL/Blachstein/34.

[247] Entschließung, Naturfreunde Bundesjugendkonferenz, 26–28 May 1961, AdsD, NL/Blachstein/34. Also: Vack, 'Algerien-Solidarität', pp. 110–14.

[248] Schreiben, Arbeiterwohlfahrt an Blachstein, 23 March 1960; Brief, Peter Hoffmann an Blachstein, 18 November 1960, AdsD, NL/Blachstein/33; Brief, Peter Hoffmann an VdS, 18 November 1960, BA/K, B166/1420.

[249] Brief, Lenz an Blachstein, 18 February 1961, AdsD, NL/Blachstein/34.

[250] Schreiben, Leiter der Protokoll- und Auslandsabteilung der Berliner Senatskanzlei an Berliner Bürgermeister, 23 February 1961; Referat 204 an Legationsrat Kunisch, 29 March 1961, PA/AA, B25/13.

publicity outside of university circles. Writing in the SPD paper *Vorwärts*, publicist Ansgar Skriver claimed the exhibit only 'appeared sensational because of the concentration of long-known but oft-ignored facts'.[251]

Lenz himself first presented the motives behind the exhibit in an article published in the *Argument-Club*'s journal in March 1960. Algeria, he wrote, represented a moral and humanitarian problem that concerned everyone but especially Germany, a country that had both experienced and perpetrated totalitarian and genocidal policies in the recent past. 'Those who remain indolent in the Algerian question', Lenz argued, 'forfeit the right to demand the release of political prisoners in the "GDR" [and] to condemn terrorist justice'. If 'we keep silent on Algeria', he continued, 'then we cannot hope to be immune against totalitarianisms of the left or right'. More than any others, therefore, it was incumbent on Germans to condemn injustice and defend democratic rights and freedoms. A failure to do so meant Germans would indeed 'carry a share of responsibility' for the French army's crimes in Algeria.[252]

That same message was echoed in a speech by the up-and-coming poet and activist, Hans Magnus Enzensberger, marking the exhibit's opening in Frankfurt/Main in June 1961. 'I want to invite you to a thing you don't want to know about, that nobody wants to know anything about [but] that concerns us all', Enzensberger began. In a gibe at the French government's propaganda efforts, he noted that the exhibit was 'no perfect product mounted by a public-relations department' but that it was better for its simplicity since it 'hid nothing', not even the FLN's crimes. Like Lenz, Enzensberger went on to draw parallels between the Algerian war and Germany's Nazi past:

> Once before we all didn't want to know anything. We didn't want to know about six million murdered Jews. Back then we said: they concealed everything from us; we couldn't do anything; the dictator was all-powerful. But we can inform ourselves, we can even help. We no longer have excuses. It's all written on two dozen cardboard panels. [. . .] Help, immediate redress: that isn't just an act of humanity but also one of self-defence; because peace and freedom are indivisible, as are torture, hunger and war. Either we end them, or they will end us.[253]

Like others before him, Enzensberger advocated a foreign policy based on humanitarian engagement and the defence of human rights. His speech

[251] 'Studenten stellen aus', *Vorwärts*, 3 March 1961.
[252] 'Der Krieg in Algerien. Unsere Mitverantwortung für Algerien', *Das Argument* 2/15 (1960), p. 162.
[253] Hans Magnus Enzensberger, 'Algerien ist überall', in Balsen and Rössel, *Hoch*, pp. 72–4.

marked a minor watershed in West German civic engagement on behalf of a Third World movement of national liberation. For the first time, a public intellectual had openly supported the cause of Algerian independence. Whereas intellectual heavyweights had long discussed Algerian events in France, German-speaking intellectuals had so far shown little interest in the conflict. In November 1960, *Argument-Club* did publish a leaflet in which a number of prominent writers, including Heinrich Böll, Erich Kästner, Max Frisch, Luise Rinser, Friedrich Dürrenmatt, Ingeborg Bachmann and Enzensberger, declared themselves in solidarity with the "Manifesto of the 121". Published on 6 September 1960 to coincide with the start of the trial of the Jeanson network, and signed by some of the most influential French intellectuals of the day, the Manifesto had called on the Debré government to recognise the legitimacy of Algeria's independence struggle and to respect the choices of conscientious objectors.[254] Although the *Argument-Club* went on to publish a statement by French novelist Françoise Sagan condemning torture as well as an open letter by Jean-Paul Sartre in defence of Jeanson, nothing became of these attempts to foster transnational, anti-colonial intellectual solidarity.[255] For the time being, West German intellectuals remained focused on matters closer to home, especially the topic of nuclear disarmament.[256]

This lack of public engagement by prominent intellectuals did not prevent a variety of civil-society actors from supporting the FLN's cause, especially when it came to the provision of humanitarian aid. The longer the conflict wore on, the more it drew attention to the plight of Algerian refugees. On the one hand, the *Hilfskomitees* continued to support Algerians arriving in West Germany. On the other hand, the humanitarian campaigns that had been initiated during World Refugee Year also endured to the Algerian war's end.[257] In 1961, the DRK contributed material goods worth 50,000DM towards international relief efforts in North Africa and seconded a nurse to work in the refugee camps in Morocco. The federal government donated 15,000DM towards these efforts, the rest having been raised through private donations. As the humanitarian crisis climaxed in May and June 1962, the DRK seconded two further

[254] 'Solidarität mit dem Manifest der 121!' *Das Argument, Flugblatt-Sonderausgabe* 1 (1960), pp. 1–2. On the Manifesto, see: Le Sueur, *Uncivil War*, pp. 232–8. On the trial: Ulloa, *Jeanson*, pp. 206–23.

[255] Françoise Sagan, 'Die Folterung der Algerierin Djamila Bouhired', *Das Argument* 2/17 (1960), pp. 1–2; Jean-Paul Sartre, 'Brief an das Gericht im Jeanson-Prozess', *Das Argument* 3/18 (1961), pp. 3–7.

[256] Weitbrecht, *Aufbruch*, p. 68; Nehring, *Politics*, p. 184.

[257] Niederschrift einer Besprechung, Lemke, Arbeitsgemeinschaft der Spitzenverbände der Freien Wohlfahrtspflege Deutschlands, 12 March 1962, ADCV, AA/187 I +195/Fasz.07/Akte 4.

delegates to help with the repatriation of Algerian refugees, while also running a nation-wide campaign that raised 393,000DM in clothing.[258] The *Arbeiterwohlfahrt*, meanwhile, persisted in its efforts to raise funds for the construction of a children's home at La Marsa. Having raised 'several 100,000 DM' by mid-1961 through 'energetic efforts', Lotte Lemke of the association's executive was bitterly disappointed when both the UGTA and CRA refused to allocate these funds to the planned home. Neither organisation would give the *Arbeiterwohlfahrt* an assurance over how the funds would be spent, let alone any co-determination in the matter. The funds were consequently withheld. Instead, the welfare association initiated a clothing drive that aimed to collect outerwear for 15,000 Algerian children.[259]

The case of the *Arbeiterwohlfahrt* indicates that relations between Algerian organisations and German non-state actors did not always run smoothly. Most German charities conceived of their contributions in purely humanitarian and social terms and were fearful that funds raised might be used to sustain the war effort. The *Arbeiterwohlfahrt*, as Lemke put it, wanted to prevent its funds from 'flowing into political channels'.[260] Like the Bonn government in its provision of development aid, the charity preferred to control the manner in which its aid was deployed. For the Algerians, however, humanitarian aid was inherently political, representing a gesture of support for the independence struggle. Control over donations and decision-making was fundamental to that fight. Politicians such as Blachstein understood the Algerians' reasoning. Regretting the *Arbeiterwohlfahrt*'s decision to pull out of the La Marsa project, he urged the association to continue its collaboration with the UGTA, for 'considering the extensive Eastern-bloc aid it received, any remittances coming from [the FRG], especially from a workers' organisation, would be of extraordinary political significance' and would help anchor an independent Algeria in the West.[261]

Another notable development during these final years of the war was the growing role played by the churches in the provision of humanitarian relief, whether at home or abroad. Writing to Blachstein in early 1960, Lemke lamented how her organisation – indeed all West German workers' associations – 'lagged behind the Churches' in providing humanitarian relief to Algerian refugees.[262] At a grassroots level within Germany,

[258] DKR Jahresbericht (Bonn, 1961), pp. 11, 58; DRK Jahresbericht (Bonn, 1962), p. 14, ADRK.
[259] Schreiben Lotte Lemke an Blachstein, 19 July 1961, AdsD, NL/Blachstein/34. [260] Ibid.
[261] Schreiben Blachstein an Lemke, 22 July 1961, AdsD, NL/Blachstein/34.
[262] Schreiben Lemke an Blachstein, 23 June 1960, AdsD, NL/Blachstein/33.

Catholic charities such as the *Caritasverband* and *Pax Christi*, as well as their Protestant equivalent, *Innere Mission*, continued to support local *Hilfskomitees*, organising shelter and providing funds as well as legal and administrative aid.[263] Due to its ecumenicism and historical support for Foreign Legion deserters, the *Caritasverband* had begun to work closely with sister branches in the Maghreb, providing social aid to Algerian refugees. It was in these camps in 1960 that the Catholic Church shot its first publicity film for the *Misereor* programme.[264] In March 1961, the episcopal committee running that programme set aside 100,000DM for relief work in Tunisia.[265] Through 'Bread for the World', the Protestant Church, too, had significantly stepped up its fund-raising activities. By June 1962, it had donated well over 1,600,000DM in emergency aid for Algeria's refugees.[266]

After the Évian Accords, Christian relief efforts focused increasingly on Algeria itself, where French organisations like *Mission de France* (Catholic) and *Cimade* (Protestant) had long supported displaced persons. As Darcie Fontaine points out, at stake for many of these largely 'progressivist' priests and social workers was not just the future of Christian–Muslim relations in Algeria but the future of global Christianity in a world radically altered by decolonisation. Under constant threat from the OAS, which accused them of treason, these Christians had continued their work towards reconciliation and social justice, smuggling aid into the besieged Casbah, even working with the FLN.[267] In this, they increasingly counted on international support, including that of *Caritas Internationalis*, the Lutheran World Federation and World Council of Churches, which each independently appealed for

[263] Joseph Scheu, 'Auf Friedensmission. Algerien-Vietnam-Biafra-Polen', in *Menschlichkeit als Spiritualität. Georg Hüssler zum 85. Geburtstag* (ed.) Deutscher Caritasverband (Freiburg, 2006), p. 150; 'Emigranten auf Zeit', *Rheinischer Merkur*, 3 March 1961; 'Viertausend Algerier in Deutschland', *FAZ*, 29 March 1962; Notices d'information nos. 27868/SDECE, 15 February 1960, 28061/SDECE, 18 February 1960, 29963/SDECE 14 April 1960, SHD/T, 10T/528/D2*; 'Entretiens avec Keramane', in Bougherara, *Rapports*, p. 210.

[264] On the organisation's aid to legionnaires, see: Michels, *Deutsche*, pp. 205, 238–41, 251, 280–3, 324; on its aid to Algerian refugees, see: Scheu, 'Friedensmission', p. 151.

[265] Bericht, Hüssler, über Projekt Sachspende für algerische Flüchtlinge, 20 March 1961, ADCV, AA/187 I + 195(65)/Fasz.06.

[266] Liste der Algerien-Nothilfe, I. Afrika, Algerien, undated, AEWDE, BfdW/P315.

[267] Darcie Fontaine, 'Treason or Charity? Christian Missions on Trial and the Decolonization of Algeria', *International Journal of Middle East Studies* 44 (2012), p. 736. See also Fontaine's PhD dissertation, 'Decolonizing Christianity: Grassroots Ecumenism in France and Algeria, 1940–1965' (Rutgers University, 2011), and André Nozière, *Algérie: les chrétiens dans la guerre* (Paris, 1979); Geoffrey Adams, *The Call of Conscience: French Protestant Responses to the Algerian War, 1954–1962* (Waterloo ON, 1998); Sybille Chapeu, *Des chrétiens dans la guerre d'Algérie: l'action de la Mission de France* (Paris, 2004).

assistance in early 1962.[268] Subsequently, the *Evangelische Hilfswerk* in November 1962 donated two fully equipped and staffed Clinomobile to the transnational Christian Committee for Service in Algeria.[269] Meanwhile, Georg Hüssler, general secretary of the *Caritasverband*, became one of the first Germans to travel to Algiers in June 1962 on orders of the Vatican-based umbrella organisation.[270] Hüssler had been invited by the Archbishop of Algiers, Léon-Étienne Duval, a champion of religious dialogue and social justice, who denounced the OAS's campaign of violence as 'an offence against God' and humanity.[271] The head of the *Caritasverband* was one of many who helped put together an international plan of action to secure material aid and spiritual help for those suffering from trauma and loss in Algeria.[272] Earlier that year, he had organised an interfaith seminar in Freiburg on 'social obligations in tomorrow's Algeria', which SDECE cynically interpreted as an effort to devise a 'mission for German Catholics after France's departure from Algeria'.[273] This was followed by a conference in Frankfurt/Main on 12 May 1962 with members of *Caritas Internationalis*.[274] While French intelligence saw yet another conspiracy, faith-based social work, as Fontaine argues, helped secure the continued presence of Christianity in the land of St Augustine. Like its Protestant counterpart, the German Catholic Church remained committed to these efforts. Ahead of the Frankfurt conference, the episcopal committee committed 1 million DM of *Misereor* funds for immediate humanitarian aid and reconstruction efforts in Algeria. Much of this aid, which would subsequently rise further, was channelled through the *Caritasverband*. It contributed to a number of schemes, including a community-development project in the villages of Tablat and Aïn-Bessem and the provision of medical aid in Biskra.[275]

[268] Rundschreiben 731/62 von Caritas Internationalis an Mitglieder, 13 April 1962; Rundschreiben, World Council of Churches, 16 March 1962, ADCV, AA/187 I + 195(65)/Fasz.06.

[269] 'Zwei fahrbare Kliniken für Algerien', Informationsdienst I (1962), AEWDE, BfdW/P235bIII.

[270] Brief Hüssler an Hadi Ghani, 13 June 1962, ADCV, ZA/116 + 187 I/Fasz.02; Nikolaus Frank, 'Weltweite Caritas', in *Menschlichkeit*, pp. 116–17.

[271] Nostitz, *Tagebuch*, pp. 172–3; Reisebericht, Hüssler, 15–25 June 1962, ADCV, ZA/116 + 187 I/Fasz.02. On Duval: Fontaine, 'Treason', p. 738; 'Algeria: Offense against God', *Time Magazine*, 9 February 1962.

[272] Michael Albus, 'Ich habe die Verantwortung gespürt. Erfahrungen mit Menschen unterwegs. Ein Interview mit Georg Hüssler', *Ost-West Europäische Perspektiven* 3 (2003), www.owep.de/artikel/361/ich-habe-verantwortung-gespuert (accessed 27 October 2014).

[273] Notice no. 9628/SDECE, 9 March 1962, SHD/T, 1H/1753/D1*; 'Viertausend Algerier in Deutschland', *FAZ*, 29 March 1962.

[274] Caritas Internationalis, Programme d'aide à l'Algérie, Compte-rendu de la réunion tenue à Francfort, 12 May 1962, ADCV, AA/187 I + 195(65)/Fasz.6.

[275] Aktennotiz, Projekt Nr. 111-0/5, verschiedene Hilfsmassnahmen für Algerien, 30 October 1963; Brief, Hüssler, an Brencklé, Caritas Algérienne, 10 March 1964; Lettre du président de Caritas

Meeting in Algiers in 1966, *Caritas Internationalis*' executive committee was positively surprised at just how active its members remained among the Muslim population.[276]

Though hardly thinking in terms of national self-interest, these Christian actors were driven by moral and humanitarian considerations, but also by thoughts about West Germany's role in international society. For the *Evangelische Hilfswerk*, just like the DRK, the aid it provided to Algerians and others was an expression of gratitude for the international help the Federal Republic had received after 1945.[277] Christians, however, were not alone in this reasoning. Conscious of the importance international aid had played in their country's own post-war recovery, the FLN's German helpers were only too aware of the trials a war-ravaged nation faced. Many considered it their duty to help others secure the foundations of a prosperous, free and just social order. If some were swayed by Cold War considerations, others wanted to make amends for Germany's past crimes. Many more were driven by a desire to provide practical assistance that would prepare the young Algerian state for the socio-economic challenges that lay ahead. In the case of the DGB, this meant expanding the programme of training for Algerian trade unionists first instituted in 1960. In September 1961, UGTA leaders Omar Belouchrani and Djillali Damerdji met with DGB representatives to plan a second such round of training for another twenty trade unionists to commence in early 1962.[278] As UGTA Secretary General Ali-Yahia Abdennour noted, the chosen participants would play an important role in driving Algeria's future economic and trade union development; they also represented 'the best artisans of Algerian-German friendship and cooperation'.[279]

Although DGB leaders did concern themselves with the future of trade unions in an independent Algeria, it still took concerted pressure from the UGTA and ICFTU to galvanise the confederation into greater activity. Reporting back from a visit to Algeria in April 1962, ICFTU Secretary General Omar Becu informed the DGB executive that Algeria needed

Algérienne à Monsignor Dossing, directeur de Misereor, 6 November 1963 ADCV, AA/187 I + 195(65)/Fasz.07/Akte 4; Bericht, Hüssler, über das Projekt Aïn-Bessem, 1 June 1964, AA/187 I + 195(65)/Fasz.04.

276 Fontaine, 'Treason', p. 734; Frank, 'Weltweite', p. 117.

277 'Aus Spenden der Aktion "Brot für die Welt"', *Hannoversche Allgemeine Zeitung*, undated newsclipping, AEWDE, BfdW/P235bIII.

278 Notiz für Richter und Tacke, 8 September 1961, AdsD, 5/DGAJ/207; Protokollauszug, 94. Geschäftsführende Bundesvorstandssitzung, 18 September 1961, 5/DGAJ/209. On ICFTU support to UGTA: Bülow, 'Brown', pp. 224–9.

279 Lettre, Ali-Yahia Abdennour à Willi Richter, 20 October 1961, AdsD, 5/DGAJ/209.

'urgent help' if it was to remain a part of the free world.[280] Until then, the ICFTU had supported the UGTA through means from its International Solidarity Fund, a multi-purpose 'freedom fund' that relied on members' contributions and assisted 'workers who fall victim to repressive measures whether emanating from totalitarian regimes, colonial regimes, or from hostile governments and employers'.[281] These means, Becu warned, no longer sufficed. To prevent Algeria from drifting from colonial into communist oppression, he issued a 'solemn appeal' for material and financial aid:

> Offices need to be opened; campaigns initiated for advertising and organising, and for that [the UGTA requires] vehicles and countless pamphlets; [it needs] to create administrative structures; render services to workers; recruit competent personnel.

Most importantly, 'the [free] Algerian trade union movement must secure itself a firm and prominent place among society, and do so as a bulwark of democracy'.[282]

To advance this goal, the ICFTU initiated a campaign whereby affiliates would promote the sale of 'solidarity stamps' celebrating Algeria's independence among their members. The DGB executive endorsed this campaign, a fact much appreciated by Abdennour, who had long pressed for 'the participation of all German labourers' in 'popularising the Algerian problem and reinforcing the links between our two working classes and our two peoples'.[283] To maximise impact and 'promote a taste for [international] solidarity' among rank-and-file, Willi Richter timed the campaign's launch not just with Algeria's formal accession to independence on 5 July 1962, but also with the ICFTU's seventh world congress, which opened in West Berlin that same day as a mark of protest against the Berlin Wall. The DGB pledged to sell three million stamps among its six million members, which would raise at least 600,000DM to support the UGTA in the task of reorganising Algeria's trade union movement and rebuilding its war-torn economy.[284] Deteriorating conditions in Algeria prompted the DGB executive to suggest an upfront transfer of the proceeds so as to alleviate the hunger crisis and

[280] Protokollauszug, 119. Geschäftsführende Bundesvorstandssitzung, 9 April 1962, AdsD, 5/DGAJ/207.

[281] ICFTU memorandum, 4 March 1957, George Meany Memorial Archives, Silver Spring MD, RG18/004, Series 2, Box 23, File 10.

[282] Rundschreiben IBFG, 9 April 1962, AdsD, 5/DGAJ/207.

[283] Lettre, Ali-Yahia Abdennour à Richter, 18 April 1962; Protokollauszug, 119. Geschäftsführende Bundesvorstandssitzung, 9 April 1962, AdsD, 5/DGAJ/207.

[284] Protokollauszug, 28. Bundesvorstandssitzung, Punkt 11, 8–10 May 1962, AdsD, 5/DGAJ/207.

offset the aid arriving from Eastern-bloc countries.[285] This combination of Cold War competition and humanitarian empathy impelled Richter twice to petition Adenauer to shore up official aid to Algeria. Predictably, the Chancellor's Office responded by arguing that such aid would jeopardise Bonn's relations with France. It did, however, welcome a bolstering of unofficial assistance.[286] To offset its own continued reserve vis-à-vis Algeria, the Bonn government now positively encouraged West German non-state actors to step up their own provisions of humanitarian and technical aid.

Meanwhile, the DGB's 'solidarity stamp' campaign produced mixed results. In some quarters, racial typecasting and suspicion of Ben Bella's socialist agenda prevailed. Members of the Printers' Union refused to 'support the civil war in Algeria', a country they deemed 'disinclined to work and communist-minded'.[287] Despite such resistance, by September 1962 the campaign had managed to raise enough funds for the purchase of fifteen Volkswagens, which Richter personally presented to UGTA in Algiers.[288] Like other West German union leaders, the DGB chairman soon grew alarmed at the widening rift between the UGTA's executive and Ben Bella's Politburo. In December, the IGM argued that 'Algeria's trade unions must be made so strong that they will be able to preserve their independence vis-à-vis the new government' and that West German workers had 'a duty' to assist their 'brethren organisation' in this task.[289] Invited to observe the UGTA's first official congress in Algiers in January 1963, West German union leaders were bitterly disappointed when it became clear, as one observer noted, that the delegates' 'spontaneous sympathies [...] lay with the East'. While Ben Bella, in his opening address, warned against the emergence of a 'workers' cult', FLN Secretary General Khider described the UGTA as the party's 'executing organ [...] tasked with popularising the Politburo's decisions among the masses'. The observer

285 Richter an Hauptverbände, 9 August 1962; Gewerkschaft Nahrung-Genuß-Gaststätten an DGB, 14 August 1962; IGM an Richter, 21 August 1962, AdsD, 5/DGAJ/207.

286 Schreiben Richter an Bundeskanzler, 12 July and 2 August 1962 BA/K, B136/6233/F3; Schreiben Globke an Aussenminister Schröder, 22 July 1962; Schreiben StS Carstens an Globke, 14 August 1962, PA/AA, B12/933; Schreiben Adenauer an Richter, 22 August 1962, AdsD, 5/ DGAJ/209.

287 Schreiben, IG Druck und Papier, Ortsgruppe Neuenburg, an DGB, 4 September 1962. Also: Schreiben, IG Druck und Papier, Ortsgruppe Metzingen, 6 September 1962, AdsD, 5/DGAJ/207.

288 Schreiben Nostitz, Generalkonsulat Algier, 19 September 1962, PA/AA, B12/933; Richter an Ali-Yahia Abdennour, UGTA, 14 September 1962; Richter an IGM Vorstand Brenner, 20 September 1962, AdsD, 5/DGAJ/209.

289 Rundschreiben Nr. 26, IGM, 6 December 1962, AdsD, 5/DGAJ/207. On the rift between the UGTA and the FLN's Politburo: Amar Mohand-Amer, 'L'Union générale des travailleurs algériens (UGTA) dans le processus de transition', in *Le Maghreb et l'indépendance de l'Algérie* (Oran, 2012), pp. 39–49; François Weiss, *Doctrine et action syndicale en Algérie* (Paris, 1970), pp. 69–92.

concluded 'that the classical concept of [free] trade unionism had no place in the Algerian revolution'.[290] One year later, the DGB would severe its ties to the UGTA.

By then, other civil-society actors had come to share the confederation's sense of trepidation and disappointment. Though they continued to assist Algerian students financially and administratively, relations between West German student associations and the UGEMA had become increasingly fraught towards the war's end. The number of Algerians studying in West Germany had jumped markedly in 1961 thanks to the GPRA's student recall from Eastern Europe, which in turn had reinvigorated West German fundraising efforts. The new arrivals stimulated the VdS to coordinate its activities both with Catholic and Protestant student organisations and with the West German branches of the World University Service and International Student Union.[291] More importantly, they enabled the Association to play the Cold War card and tap into Foreign Office funds usually reserved for 'refugees from the East'.[292] By tapping into these resources, the VdS managed to sponsor over seventy Algerian studentships by early 1962, including fourteen for 'refugee-students' from the East.[293]

Significantly, not all of the UGEMA's leaders welcomed the Association's eagerness to embrace these 'refugees'. After all, many of these Algerians had received express orders to join the ALN, not to take up studies in the West.[294] In a striking parallel to developments in East Germany, the support given to these students led to a growing disagreement between the UGEMA and VdS over who controlled Algerian stipendiaries. The dispute started as a clash between Joachim Hoffmann, head of the VdS's international section, and Mohamed Benzian, the head of the UGEMA's West German section.[295] Sent to Bonn in February 1961 to diffuse these tensions, UGEMA executive member Mohamed Baghli believed that the 'distrust and friction' between these two men stemmed from a personality clash brought on by Benzian's 'tendency to want to do

[290] Aufzeichnung, Sozialreferent Dr. Bohr, Botschaft Rabat, 23 January 1963, AdsD, 5/DGAJ/207.

[291] Schreiben, Joachim Hoffmann, an Evangelische Studentengemeinde in Deutschland, World University Service, International Studentenbund, Katholischer Akademischer Ausländerdienst, 10 January 1961, BA/K, B166/1420.

[292] Schreiben, Maaß, VdS, an Evangelische Akademie Bad Boll, 6 July 1961; Arbeitsmaterial für Lage der algerischen Studenten, 3. Auflage, February 1962, BA/K, B166/1420.

[293] Bericht über die afrikanischen Flüchtlingsstudenten aus der DDR, VdS, 22 March 1962, BA/K, B166/1420.

[294] Motion sur les 'rappelés' de D.D.R. adoptée à l'unanimité au 4ème congrès national, UGEMA, Tunis, July 1960, BA/K, B166/1462.

[295] Résolution des étudiants algériens en Allemagne fédérale, Bad Boll, 17 July 1960, BA/K, B166/1420.

everything himself so as to arrogate successes' in West Germany, while Hoffmann, 'given his extensive personal engagement on behalf of Algerian students, had a tendency to interfere in matters internal to the UGEMA'. Baghli hoped the dispute would not disrupt the otherwise 'effective and close cooperation' between UGEMA and VdS.[296]

Five months later, however, German–Algerian student relations were again marred by tensions. This time, they arose over Kamel Bouaka, a former medical student in Sofia who had approached the Catholic Academic Exchange Service (KAAD) for a grant to study in West Germany. By July 1961, the KAAD had secured government funds for Bouaka as an Eastern-bloc refugee. The Service proposed applying a similar procedure 'to open the doors to other Algerians behind the Iron Curtain'. As KAAD Secretary Hans Limbach explained, for this procedure to work, the candidates had to sever ties with the UGEMA because the 'German authorities have become quite sensitive about the disciplinary regime exercised by Algerian organisations'.[297] Though no doubt well-intended, Limbach's presumption highlighted his political naiveté and hardly met with the UGEMA's approval. On principle, President Aït Chaalal emphatically rejected the KAAD's offer to support Bouaka. Instead, he insisted on the latter's return to Bulgaria, arguing that 'it was up to the UGEMA alone to determine a student's allocation to this or that country' and demanding that others 'respect our independence and freedom of action'. Aït Chaalal reminded Limburg:

> Algerian students are not Eastern-bloc refugees but Algerian refugees who were chased from their home, Algeria, by a colonial war. Quite the contrary, they have been sent across the world, to the East as well as the West, to resume their studies thanks to an international solidarity that for us is neither bounded nor exclusive. Moreover, we reaffirm that all assistance only then assumes meaning for us insofar as it is aimed not at individuals detached from their true environment, but at members of a community that is fighting and that suffers for clear and specific goals.[298]

To achieve these goals, the FLN had established a government-in-exile as well as auxiliary organs such as the UGTA or UGEMA. Having arrogated to itself the rights and responsibilities of a sovereign nation-state, this government and its auxiliaries claimed to wield exclusive decision-making powers

[296] Aktennotiz, Lutz Erbring, VdS, 20 February 1961, BA/K, B166/1420.

[297] Schreiben Hans Limbach, KAAD, an Aït Chaalal, UGEMA, 21 July 1961, AdsD, NL/Plum/26.

[298] Lettre par Aït Chaalal, UGEMA, à Hans Limbach, KAAD, 24 July 1961, AdsD, NL/Plum/26 (underlined in original).

over Algerians. Aït Chaalal's response underlined that the UGEMA would not allow outside interference in matters pertaining to Algerian students. Nor would it tolerate others' attempts to manipulate the Algerian question for the sake of point-scoring in the competition between East and West or any other political goal. The FLN alone spoke for Algerians regardless of where they were.

By 1962, this tendency to claim absolute control over Algerians had come to alarm even some of the FLN's most idealistic and ardent supporters in West Germany. The internal power struggles that followed the Évian Accords, the efforts by Ben Bella's Politburo to stymie dissent, the purge of cadres and imposition of one-party rule – these developments proved disconcerting to all but the most radical of the FLN's German helpers. While reminiscing on his humanitarian and propagandistic engagement in support of Algerian independence, Catholic youth leader Walter Molt summed up the disappointment felt by many German students and workers:

> We had pinned our hopes on Algeria. After all, we really identified with developments there. We had read the Algerians' texts, which spoke of a new man, of a new social order. [. . .] And we discovered that it was easier to declare one's solidarity with the oppressed than with the conditions that followed the liberation.[299]

Algeria's independence struggle thus furnished important lessons to the FLN's younger and more radical allies in the FRG. Idealists to the core, many were unwilling to compromise their moral values and political principles once the war drew to an end. This was a revelation, especially given the weight of self-loathing and the lack of assurance that rightfully burdened German society after 1945. For some, disillusionment came gradually. Socialists and Trotskyists such as Klaus Vack, Helmut Wendler, Kurt Henker and Heinz Peiffer, whose clandestine activities had gone well beyond the 'poster-bearing activism' that characterised much of the pro-Algerian engagement of West German youths, initially identified with Ben Bella's policies.[300] To these young radicals, Algeria represented a harbinger of the revolution that proved so annoyingly elusive in Europe. They enthused over experiments with agricultural and industrial self-management, admiring Algeria's determination to build a socialist society with genuine grassroots democracy.[301] Their attitude resembled

[299] Cited in Balsen und Rössel, *Hoch*, pp. 90–1. [300] Schonauer, 'Jungsozialisten', p. 114.
[301] On Algerian post-war economic conditions and policies: Bennoune, *Making*, pp. 93–111.

that of the so-called *pieds-rouges*, those French and European militants who chose to stay or move to independent Algeria to help build a new social order.[302] However, the emergence of new elites and a new techno-bureaucratic regime as well as the adoption of state-planning soon shattered these hopes. To Henker and Peiffer, their 'total engagement' had had 'zero effect', having neither revolutionised society in Algeria nor achieved socio-political change at home.[303] By the time Boumediène ousted Ben Bella in 1965, even the most radical activists had experienced what Vack called an 'inner fissure' that led them to turn their backs on Algeria and the FLN. Though he received repeated invitations from his former friends, Vack never visited the country whose liberation struggle he had so ardently supported. This need to defend the moral high ground expressed by Vack and others reveals the idealism that inspired the internationalist activism of some civil-society actors in the FRG. It was also indicative of the emerging split within the West German Left that would ultimately produce the far more militant solidarity movements of the late 1960s.[304]

Not all of the FLN's German helpers were quite so idealist or militant, of course. For Wischnewski the Algerian war constituted 'an important and informative chapter' that transformed the deputy into a lifelong champion of German-Arab cooperation, a stance for which he later, as cabinet minister, earned the sobriquet 'Ben Wisch'. Notwithstanding his radical roots, Wischnewski preferred 'pragmatic, realistic policies' to revolutionary change.[305] This pragmatism, Leggewie argues, ensured that he 'became the central hub of pro-Algerian activity in the Federal Republic, a master organiser who operated swiftly, effectively combining objective returns with personal gain'.[306] By the time of Güde's crackdown on the FLN, the *enfant terrible* whose pro-Algerian proclivities had long strained Franco-German relations, jarring even with his own party's foreign-policy reorientation, had transformed into Bonn's unofficial ambassador to the GPRA. During the war's final phase, Wischnewski became indispensable to the *Auswärtige Amt* as a means of communication with the FLN that would not (further) affront the French.[307] When it came to choosing the delegates to represent the Adenauer government at

[302] Catherine Simon, *Algérie, les années pieds-rouges. Des rêves de l'indépendance au désenchantement (1962–1969)* (Paris, 2009).

[303] Cited in: Leggewie, *Kofferträger*, p. 123.

[304] Balsen and Rössel, *Hoch*, pp. 91, 86–9. Also: Kalter, 'Eigene im Fremden', pp. 142–61.

[305] Wischnewski, *Leidenschaft*, pp. 122–3. [306] Leggewie, *Kofferträger*, p. 148.

[307] Frank, *Botschaft*, pp. 172–3; Letter from Paul Frank to author, 23 May 2003; Nostitz, *Tagebuch*, p. 196. Also: Aufzeichnung, Abt. 2, 5 March 1962, PA/AA, B12/932.

celebrations marking Algeria's independence in November 1962, German diplomats insisted on including Wischnewski. Though he belonged to the opposition, the deputy's ties to the FLN's leaders made his exclusion unthinkable. Besides, as Councillor Jansen argued, he 'has always been cooperative and, as far as we know, loyal toward the *Auswärtige Amt*'.[308] As a young politician with ambitious career plans, this loyalty endured. Wischnewski pushed the Bonn government to make Algeria a focus of its development policies. By 1964, however, even he had begun to express frustration at Ben Bella's 'duplicity' given his government's refusal to sever ties to East Berlin.[309]

Wischnewski's pragmatic and statesmanlike attitude towards the FLN highlights the pervasiveness of the German–German rivalry that had become such an enduring feature of West German official and unofficial foreign policy.[310] His attitude contrasted sharply with that of his elder colleague, Blachstein, another pillar of the SPD's 'Algeria lobby'. Blachstein had used his extensive political, trade union and journalistic contacts to help create *Hilfskomitees*, garner humanitarian aid, raise funds, arrange work, college placements as well as language courses, and find shelter for Algerians, especially in his own constituency of Hamburg. Like Wischnewski, he, too, wanted to see the young, free Algerian state firmly anchored in the West. As late as August 1962, Blachstein would write to Foreign Minister Schröder pressing for generous humanitarian and development aid to help secure that goal.[311] Soon after, however, and unlike Wischnewski, he became one of the first of the FLN's German allies to turn his back on the Ben Bella regime. Blachstein's disillusionment with postwar Algeria is highlighted in his correspondence with Si Mustapha, one of the few German '*pieds-rouges*'. In August 1962, Blachstein wrote to Si Mustapha, expressing his concern about political developments in Algeria.[312] Si Mustapha responded in early September that while the country's economic problems were undeniable, the political situation was 'not as sinister as the European press made it out to be'. A supporter of Ben Bella's Politburo, which he depicted as 'a dynamic and socialist-inclined leadership group', Si Mustapha urged the deputy to visit Algeria so he could witness developments for himself.[313] The deputy declined, evidently expressing further alarm at the ALN's growing power, many members of

308 Aufzeichnung, Jansen, 19 October 1962, PA/AA, B12/931. 309 Scheffler, *SPD*, p. 77.
310 Weitz, 'Ever Present Other', pp. 219–32.
311 Brief Blachstein an Schröder, 13 August 1962, PA/AA, B1/219.
312 Brief Blachstein an Si Mustapha, 13 August 1962, AdsD, NL/Blachstein/34.
313 Brief Si Mustapha an Blachstein, 10 September 1962, AdsD, NL/Blachstein/34.

which now served in the Constituent Assembly. Once again, Si Mustapha sought to reassure. If ALN cadres had entered politics, this was because they constituted Algeria's 'best political elements [. . .] forced by circumstances to don uniform and take up arms'. Far from fostering a militaristic regime, these 'antimilitaristic' cadres represented neither 'a dominant class nor a professional army' that would oppose revolutionary change. Si Mustapha declared the multi-party system unworkable, defending the fact that the Constituent Assembly's members were chosen from a single, Politburo-approved list. Algeria, he claimed, is 'the most free and democratic African country' where 'freedom of opinion both inside and outside the party is absolute'.[314] Blachstein, however, was not persuaded. 'I would like to tell you again', the deputy emphasised in November 1962, 'that North Africa's freedom can only then be secured if there exists freedom for the press and for organisations to voice their criticism'. Blachstein conceded that such genuine democracy could be difficult in times of transition, yet it was 'precisely in such times that the government must remain open to public censure and influence'. Only then, he felt, could freedom and democracy survive.[315] In his response, Si Mustapha again sought to justify the Politburo's actions. If the FLN opposed trade unionists, for example, it did so because 'the UGTA had never really existed, its external officials had never been voted in nor approved'. The union, Si Mustapha argued, was an instrument of former GPRA Foreign Minister Krim Belkacem and other Kabyles, who, as bourgeois 'estate owners', opposed Ben Bella and the socialist policies and land reform he planned to implement.[316]

In his last known missive, dated 11 December 1962, Blachstein still refused to compromise. The news conveyed by Si Mustapha, the deputy began, had been 'valuable but unsettling'. Indeed, as someone who had spent the better part of his life resisting and fighting fascist, totalitarian and militarist regimes, whether Nazi Germany, Francoist Spain, Stalinist Russia or colonial France, Blachstein could not shake the 'great alarm' he felt over Algeria's move toward single-party rule.[317] This, clearly, was not what he wanted for the Algerian people, nor was it why he had engaged himself to help Algerians and the FLN. In Blachstein's case, moral principle and a deep commitment to social-democracy outweighed any sense of personal let alone national gain. To him, Algeria's Cold War alignment mattered little so long as the country remained on its present path of single-party rule.

[314] Brief Si Mustapha an Blachstein, 15 October 1962, AdsD, NL/Blachstein/34.
[315] Brief Blachstein an Si Mustapha, 13 November 1962, AdsD, NL/Blachstein/34.
[316] Brief Si Mustapha an Blachstein, 30 November 1962, AdsD, NL/Blachstein/34.
[317] Brief Blachstein an Si Mustapha, 11 December 1962, AdsD, NL/Blachstein/34.

As 1962 drew to a close, therefore, relations between the new Algerian nation and West Germany could hardly be called close. On the one hand, the Federal Republic had achieved a significant victory, having managed to secure independent Algeria's recognition while at the same time using the Algerian war to forge the axis Paris Bonn. On the other hand, the Ben Bella government remained politically and ideologically closer to East Berlin. With its pragmatic and realist approach to foreign policy, the Bonn government could live with that outcome. So, too, could the churches. Determined to secure a future for Christianity in Algeria, they continued to provide humanitarian and development aid to the newly independent country regardless of its political makeup. However, those in West Germany whose civic engagement on the FLN's behalf had stemmed from deeply held political and ideological convictions found it harder to come to terms with the new realities in Algiers. Whether out of idealism or self-interest, one by one Algeria's more militant supporters in the FRG turned their backs on the movement they had lionised, just as that movement increasingly turned away from them. In doing so, the FLN's erstwhile German allies grew stronger in their conviction that their country should and could become a positive force in the world.

Conclusion

Algeria's independence struggle is often hailed as a classic example of a counterinsurgency during which the French won every battle but lost the war.[1] Although tactically and operationally the French military proved highly successful, the reliance on armed force could not compensate for the lack of political vision so essential to winning over the Algerian population. The sweeping political and economic reforms introduced by de Gaulle and his predecessors, while essential elements of the constructive counterinsurgency, proved too little too late to turn the war's tide in France's favour. The brutal, inhumane and undemocratic nature of the destructive counterinsurgency undermined these reforms before they could ever bear fruit. Whether the 'militarisation' of policing or the resort to collective punishments, mass internments and torture, the destructive tactics deployed by the French military and security services on the domestic front went against the normative values for which the Republic claimed to stand. So, too, did many of the heavy-handed measures deployed on the international front, as highlighted here by the authorities' efforts to export methods of colonial policing to West Germany, and by their willing use of interceptions at sea, sabotage and assassinations to neutralise the FLN's West German supply networks. Ultimately, the preponderance of French military power undercut the rhetoric of inclusiveness and equality that underpinned the constructive counterinsurgency. The duality of the French war effort ensured that success in one domain cancelled out victory in the other.[2] With opinion both at home and abroad increasingly condemning French counterinsurgency methods, the cognitive dissonance between those fighting for

[1] James S. Corum, *Bad Strategies: How Major Powers Fail in Counterinsurgency* (Minneapolis MN, 2008); Gil Merom, *How Democracies Lose Small Wars: State, Society, and the Failures of France in Algeria, Israel in Lebanon, and the United States in Vietnam* (Cambridge, 2003).

[2] Ambler, *French Army*, p. 163.

a *French* Algeria and those demanding an *Algerian* Algeria became unbridgeable.[3]

Meanwhile, the tenacity and bravery of the FLN's militants in the face of the full ferocity of French repression had lent the insurgency a dynamic of its own. To Algerian diplomat Rédha Malek, the insurgency's strength lay 'in its rootedness among the population', though these roots were far from secure.[4] Whether in Algeria, France, or even West Germany, they sometimes had to be reinforced by coercive means. This should not detract from the fact, observed first-hand by Pierre Bourdieu, 'that the struggle was able to draw on strong popular sentiment for its vital strength and purpose, a sentiment inspired by an objective situation' – the colonial situation.[5] Those who spearheaded the French counterinsurgency, however, continued to depict the FLN as a foreign, illegitimate force with no real rootedness among the people.

Here, too, one can see signs of cognitive dissonance. To the French authorities, the movement's external activism betrayed its ultimate weakness and alien character. In actuality, it was a sign of the FLN's resilience. Popular support was not the insurgency's only source of strength. Equally important, as Malek explained, was the FLN's 'policy of openness at the international level, which gave it quite exceptional influence for a liberation movement'.[6] From the start, as has been seen, FLN strategy emphasised the importance of the principle of internationalisation. In addition to moral and material support, the movement sought to gain recognition of its belligerent status and to legitimise its cause. To achieve these ends, the FLN established a government-in-exile in Tunis to mimic French authority in Algeria and subvert the French government's claim to speak for Algerians. It created a 'veritable diplomatic apparatus' whose representatives, 'had at their disposal extensive liberty to forge relationships with the most politically influential circles: journalists, trade unionists, intellectuals, academics, political parties, youth organisations, humanitarian institutions'.[7] One could also include merchants and manufacturers, especially those in the international arms trade. Although they often lacked formal training and experience, the FLN's international agents, who included members of the UGTA, UGEMA and other auxiliary outfits, proved to be highly adept and resourceful diplomats and propagandists. The FLN's activities in

[3] Connelly, *Diplomatic Revolution*, p. 4; Martin Thomas, *Flight or Fight: Britain, France and their Roads from Empire* (Oxford, 2014), p. xii.

[4] Malek, *L'Algérie*, p. 72.

[5] Pierre Bourdieu, *The Algerians* (trans.) Alan C.M. Ross (Boston, 1962), p. 145.

[6] Malek, *L'Algérie*, p. 72. [7] Ibid., pp. 72, 74.

West – and East – Germany highlight just how skilfully the insurgents were able to tailor their political rhetoric not only to the specific national or international contexts in which they operated, but also to the distinctive interests and causes pursued by their local state and non-state allies, whose ideological, political and socio-economic agendas often diverged from their own. Algeria's 'diplomatic revolution' thus proved highly successful. The GPRA came to be treated as a *de facto* and in some cases *de jure* government by most of the Third World and Sino-Soviet bloc, and, indeed, even by parts of the West. The movement's auxiliaries, meanwhile, had firmly entrenched themselves in the international trade union, youth, peace and humanitarian movements. The moral recognition, political legitimacy and material aid thus gained helped boost morale and sustain the FLN's struggle in a way the internal insurgency could not.

Sanctuary

If the 'foreign policy of national liberation' proved vital to the insurgency, it could not secure Algeria's independence alone. To succeed, the policy of internationalisation itself rested on another, oft overlooked principle, one that played an equally important role on the domestic front: namely, freedom of manoeuvre. To achieve that freedom, this book has argued, the FLN relied on external sanctuaries. Only by taking refuge beyond the confines of the sovereign French state could the movement's militants escape the clutches of the military and security services (as indeed could thousands of Algerian refugees not engaged in the liberation struggle). Whether in the Maghreb or in Europe, bordering states such as West Germany came to serve not just as safe havens offering respite from the pressures of the war, but as vital strategic, operational and logistical bases in their own right. External sanctuaries, as has been seen, proved essential for the purposes of recruitment, mobilisation, propaganda and procurement. Even though they did not always influence the military course of the insurgency, they remained of immense political, diplomatic and psychological value.[8] As such, external sanctuaries counterbalanced the French preponderance of coercive force and reduced the asymmetry of power between coloniser and colonised. Without access to external havens, the FLN would have been hard-pressed to sustain and expand both its internal and external insurgency. To quote one study prepared by the cabinet of

8 Eqbal Ahmad, 'Revolutionary Warfare and Counterinsurgency', in *Guerrilla Strategies: An Historical Anthology from the Long March to Afghanistan* (Berkeley LA, 1982), p. 252.

Prime Minister Debré in May 1959: the 'external rebellion essentially embodies a "*base*" in the sense given to that term by the theoreticians of *guerre révolutionnaire*: at once a ground of departure, zone of logistical support, headquarters, crucible of revolutionary training, [and] contact point with exterior allies'.[9] In protecting the movement's freedom of manoeuvre, enabling its consolidation and ensuring its survival, this 'base' helped to secure the FLN's ultimate victory over France; it helped to establish Algeria's sovereignty.

The literature on the Algerian independence struggle has hitherto paid little attention to the specific role, organisation, and impact of the FLN's external sanctuaries, which as has been seen, comprised multiple operational and command centres and safe havens.[10] Although the historiography on the conflict's international dimension is extremely rich, it has taken for granted the fact that Tunisia and Morocco (and Egypt and Libya) harboured the FLN's executive organs, including the GPRA, as well as numerous ALN bases and refugee camps. Only in passing have scholars looked at how these North African sanctuaries functioned or how they affected host states and societies. Only rarely have scholars examined the extent to which these sanctuaries raised the costs and reduced the effectiveness of the French counterinsurgency. The same can be said of France's European neighbours. Although, as Gilbert Meynier has argued, Western 'Europe was more directly affected by the Algerian drama' than any other region beyond the Maghreb, studies of how the FLN's European sanctuaries impacted the French counterinsurgency, or host societies, remain scarce.[11]

Of these European countries, one, above all, came to be caught up in the war: namely, West Germany. The country accepted more refugees seeking shelter from the insurgency's dramatic reverberations in France than any other neighbouring state outside of North Africa. It became the operational base of the *Fédération de France* as well as the nerve centre of the FLN's manifold European operations. This book set out to explain just how and why a country that had no colonial interests, that had only just regained its own national sovereignty, that remained divided and dependent on France, and that was still seeking its place in international society after a decade of deserved ostracism, became so entangled in Algeria's independence struggle. In so doing, it highlighted the immense impact

9 Étude sur la situation générale en Algérie, 13 April 1959, AHC, 2DE/75/D1* (italics added).

10 Djerbal, *L'OS*, p. 105.

11 Meynier, *Histoire*, p. 598. I am, of course, going by the state of "Western" historiography, as I do not read Arabic.

that external sanctuaries can have not only on the course and outcome of insurgencies but also on the host countries themselves.

If external safe havens proved indispensable to the success of the FLN's liberation struggle, they also contributed to the failure of French strategy. After all, *guerre révolutionnaire*, like most 'classical' counterinsurgency, was rooted in a tradition of imperial and colonial 'small wars' that never had to face such thorny issues as sovereignty or legitimacy.[12] These questions, however, were at the very core of Algeria's independence struggle and indeed the entire process of decolonisation. They would hamper France's counterinsurgency in more ways than one. Whether in Europe or the Maghreb, external sanctuaries were an important part of that process. Since the principle of territorial sovereignty forbade transgressions of national boundaries, external sanctuaries thwarted efforts to destroy the FLN's politico-administrative organisation and fighting potential, all the more so, since French governments refused to acknowledge they were 'at war' with the FLN.[13] International norms and agreements, as has been seen, did not prevent the French authorities from engaging the FLN in the international arena. They, too, worked from the premise that in order to defeat the insurgents, France would have to pursue a global war effort. Convinced that the entire insurgency survived only on account of the support it received from foreign forces, the French counterinsurgency sought desperately to eradicate the FLN's external sanctuaries in Europe and the Maghreb. Using West Germany as an example, this book has highlighted the avenues through which the French authorities sought to achieve that goal. The measures deployed were diverse and elaborate involving secrecy, subterfuge and a range of actors. From the *guerre diplomatique* and *guerre psychologique* to the *guerre économique* and *guerre d'action*, and even the intelligence war, French counterinsurgency strove to neutralise and destroy the FLN's German sanctuary. To achieve their goal, the authorities resorted to both legal and illegal means.

These efforts proved unsuccessful and even counterproductive. The global war on contraband is an important case in point. In his classic study of *guerre révolutionnaire*, Peter Paret noted that armed retaliation beyond France's borders, of which the Suez debacle and bombing of Sakiet-Sidi-Youssef were only the most prominent examples, 'resulted in little military gain, while costing a great deal in diplomatic complications

[12] Alex Marshall, 'Imperial Nostalgia, the Liberal Lie, and the Perils of Postmodern Counterinsurgency', *Small Wars & Insurgencies* 21/2 (2010), pp. 235, 245.

[13] Fraleigh, 'Algerian Revolution', pp. 181.

and unfavourable public opinion'.[14] The same was true both for *Surmar*'s interceptions at sea of West German (and other) cargo vessels and for *Service Action*'s campaign of state-sanctioned sabotage and assassinations in the Federal Republic (and elsewhere). Although these operations helped weaken the FLN's reliance on West German merchants for the procurement of vital military and non-military supplies, even the French intelligence services came to consider them as a strategic failure. Instead of asphyxiating the FLN's external supplies, the insurgents merely became reliant on the Sino-Soviet bloc for aid (though the overall importance, particularly of Chinese military assistance, was probably exaggerated).[15] The ALN thus continued to accumulate modern armaments, although extensive border fortifications and surveillance prevented these from reaching the principal theatres of war in Algeria.

If the military ramifications of France's global war on contraband ultimately proved inconsequential, the same cannot be said of the campaign's impact on France's psychological war against the FLN. The Navy's interceptions of cargo vessels contravened the peacetime principle guaranteeing the freedom of the seas; SDECE's campaign of assassinations and sabotage violently transgressed against the sovereignty of foreign states. Heavy-handed, sensational and unlawful, the global war of action played right into the hands of FLN propaganda depicting France as an imperial aggressor in pursuit of an unjust cause. While the myth of the *Red Hand* served as a convenient cover for *Service Action*, it also drew the public's attention to the dirty nature of France's counterinsurgency. As such, the war of action undermined the public-relations campaigns by which French governments sought to highlight to an international audience the constructive side of their counterinsurgency (their 'modernising mission') as well as the FLN's own brutal tactics. The illegal resort to coercion and dirty tricks thus helped undo French efforts to win global hearts and minds.

These mistakes alone, however, could not account for the failure of France's psychological war in the international arena. As has been seen, the authorities also faced a highly adept adversary. In West Germany, the FLN skilfully and deliberately adapted its propaganda so as to exploit French and German sore points. Through frequent analogies to Gestapo methods and Nazi atrocities, its propagandists imbricated the Federal Republic in the Algerian war in a way that embarrassed not only the French by highlighting the inhumanity and injustice of their coercive means, but also the West Germans who were desperate to overcome (or at the very least forget)

[14] Paret, *French Revolutionary Warfare*, pp. 33–4. [15] Haddad-Fonda, 'Illusory alliance', p. 339.

their terrible past. The ALN's Repatriation Service for Deserted Legionnaires devised a highly successful propaganda campaign that consciously linked Algeria's liberation from French colonial oppression to the 'liberation' of Europe's misguided youths from the clutches of the French Foreign Legion, an institution that had long elicited public condemnation among France's neighbours, especially Germany. French officials found it increasingly difficult to parry the FLN's publicity campaigns. Whereas censorship had become an integral part of the psychological war in Algeria and the metropole, this instrument proved ineffective in the international arena. Here, attempts to stifle open debate, criticism and opposition to the French war effort usually backfired on the authorities. In West Germany, moreover, freedoms of expression and assembly were constitutionally guaranteed, hampering French efforts to undermine the active and passive support that West German civil-society actors gave to the FLN. Thus in the FRG, as elsewhere, human rights and democratic values had become an effective 'anti-colonial weapon' for FLN propagandists, one that helped the movement garner international sympathy and support.[16]

Concern for human rights and democratic principles also obstructed the intelligence war that aimed to expel the FLN – and indeed all Algerians – from West Germany and other Western European sanctuaries. The exodus of Algerians to neighbouring countries undermined the 'system of complete human management and control' through which the metropolitan security and intelligence services sought to destroy the FLN's clandestine politico-administrative structures whilst also isolating and immunising the Algerian population against the FLN's influence. Top-secret collaborative arrangements between the French security services and their foreign counterparts were meant to secure a way around the legal and political constraints imposed by this exodus. Host-country security services thus became proxies through which French officials sought to garner intelligence and exert influence over Algerian populations beyond their reach. Such arrangements were only possible with allied countries that hosted the Algerians unwillingly. Even then, however, the case of West Germany highlights how the contradictions inherent not only in the duality of France's counterinsurgency strategy but also in the 'paradoxical citizenship' of 'French Muslims' severely hamstrung the intelligence war. Considering the indiscriminate and brutal nature of the destructive counterinsurgency, even in the metropole, French authorities feared Algerians might seek

[16] Klose, *Menschenrechte*, p. 275.

political asylum in the FRG, a move that would have set a dangerous political precedent. Even as they depicted every Algerian as a potential 'rebel' and 'terrorist', officials in Paris thus continued to insist that Algerians abroad had to be treated as French citizens. The Bonn authorities consequently had little choice but to tolerate the Algerians arriving in West Germany, though they forbade them from engaging in 'political activities'.

This toleration proved vital for the FLN's militants. It helped them secure and expand the movement's covert and overt networks in the FRG, whether those of the *Fédération de France* and "*Fédération d'Allemagne*", those of the GPRA's procurement agents, or those of the UGTA and UGEMA. In attempting to arrogate for itself the powers of a sovereign state, however, the FLN came to undermine the *Rechtsstaat* and threaten domestic security. A growing threat to West German sovereignty, the authorities' tolerance only reached so far. Anxious to put an end to Algerian subversion, the federal prosecutor-general initiated a nation-wide inquest into the FLN's 'political activities', seeking to fight the insurgents through the criminal code. The court's enquiries proved lengthy and cumbersome, and when the judiciary finally struck, the timing could not have been worse. Güde's eleventh-hour crackdown on the FLN bureau in Bonn deeply embarrassed the Adenauer government. Not only did it fail to dislodge the Algerians from West Germany, but it also drew international condemnation of Bonn's collusion with France at the very moment the FLN made significant strides towards securing Algeria's independence.

Indeed, even the diplomatic war had failed to produce results against the FLN's external sanctuary in West Germany. French diplomats seeking to pressure the Bonn government into action had to contend not only with the legal and constitutional constraints outlined above but also with a united Arab front. After all, the FLN's chief militants tended to work under Arab diplomatic cover; the Tunisian and Moroccan embassies in Bonn functioned as the FLN's head office in the Federal Republic, creating an extraterritorial sanctuary within the sanctuary, one that proved difficult to combat. Even the shooting of Améziane Aït Ahcène on the steps of the Tunisian embassy had failed to remove the Algerians from the safe haven provided by their North African allies. As others before it, this brazen and criminal attack on foreign ground once again backfired on French authorities. It reinforced bonds they had hoped to sever, and it helped the FLN secure further local and international allies. On balance, then, the attempts by the French and German authorities to dislodge the FLN from West Germany merely helped to entrench that sanctuary further.

Sovereignty

France's global counterinsurgency against the FLN's external bases and supply networks thus miscarried on all accounts, and the Federal Republic was no exception. Efforts to eject the Algerians from their West German sanctuary were unsuccessful and counterproductive. This failure might have been understandable in Morocco and Tunisia, host countries that actively sponsored the FLN, but it was striking in the case of West Germany. After all, the Bonn government was firmly allied to France, and it possessed both the means and the will to clamp down on political organisations that posed a threat to the country's security, sovereignty and foreign relations. Some scholars have interpreted the Adenauer government's apparent toleration of Algerian refugees and militants as proof that West German diplomacy pursued a 'policy of equidistance' vis-à-vis both France and the Arab world in the Algerian question. Bonn's principle aim throughout the Algerian conflict, they claim, was to preserve its sovereign decision-making. Moreover, the government proved unwilling to jeopardise its reputation and interests in the Third World for a French cause it considered unwinnable. As such, Bonn's diplomats engaged in what Cahn calls 'level-headed manoeuvring' and 'hard-headed trickery', and Bougherara describes as 'a strange ballet of inventive strategies'.[17] The Franco-German rapprochement, in other words, was not sacrosanct, and Bonn did not blindly toe the French line in the Algerian question. Instead, critical reasoning and sovereign decision-making prevailed to ensure that the newly independent Algerian state would recognise Bonn over East Berlin.

Drawing on previously unused sources from the French and German security and intelligence services, this book has painted a rather more nuanced picture of West German official policy in the Algerian question. A ballet requires choreography, just as a ruse entails a calculated plan of action. This author has found no such foresight in German policy-making. Equidistance and neutrality were certainly the desired goals of West German diplomacy when it came to Algeria's liberation struggle, at least on the part of mid-ranking officials. However, they generally lacked the wherewithal to resist French pressures. While maintaining an outward appearance of non-engagement, the Bonn government usually deferred to France in the Algerian question, demonstrating little independence of thought or action. Adenauer himself unwaveringly defended the French war effort in the international arena, even against the advice of some of his

[17] Cahn, 'Bundesrepublik', in *Herausforderung* (ed.) Conze, p. 155; Bougherara, *Rapports*, p. 92.

diplomats. He instructed the domestic authorities to collaborate with French diplomats and security services in undermining FLN machinations in West Germany. The chancellor's attitude stemmed in part from his belief, rooted in a colonialist and Cold War mind-set, that Algerian independence would expand Soviet influence to North Africa, leading to Western Europe's encirclement. More importantly, it derived from his devotion to Franco-German reconciliation, an attitude merely reinforced by the return to power of de Gaulle. Even the *deuxième bureau*, which usually remained distrustful of France's neighbour, applauded Bonn's quiet cooperation in March 1961:

> While feigning disinterest in the FLN's activities in Federal Germany for legal and political reasons [i.e. Güde's national inquest], the Bonn government nonetheless exercises, through its security services, a tight control on North Africans installed or passing through German territory. Whilst ensuring the country's security, these measures have the additional advantage of being not too displeasing to the French partner.[18]

It would be wrong, however, to assume that Adenauer's policy of collaboration in the Algerian question was entirely volunteered. Ultimately, his government had little choice but to toe the French line, especially once Paris made its support in the German question contingent on Bonn's attitude towards Algeria. With the onset of the second Berlin crisis, French support in the German question became a matter of national survival for the Bonn Republic, or so Adenauer believed. Thus rather than pursuing a sovereign line in the Algerian question, the chancellor became the staunchest supporter of the French counterinsurgency. His loyalty not only made sense in the context of growing Cold War tensions over Berlin, but it also paid dividends. In building trust, promoting reconciliation, and strengthening bilateral cooperation, Adenauer's *quid pro quo* in matters Algerian ensured France's continued backing in the all-important German question, thus safeguarding West Germany's security from the East. In enabling what de Gaulle in July 1962 (the very month Algeria gained its independence) called 'the miracle of our times', the chancellor's loyalty had also cemented the axis Paris–Bonn, paving the way for the Élysée Treaty of 1963 and securing a fundamental goal of his policy of *Westbindung*.[19]

[18] Synthèse de renseignements no. 2111/CCFFA/2, 21 March 1961, SHD-T, 10T/550*.

[19] Ulrich Lappenküper, 'Diplomatische Faktoren: die deutsch-französische Annäherung im europäischen und transatlantischen Zusammenhang 1950–1958', in *Wandel und Integration. Deutsch-französische Annäherungen der fünfziger Jahre* (eds.) Hélène Miard-Delacroix and Rainer Hudemann (München, 2005), p. 69.

Considering the quiet but constant support the Adenauer government gave to the French counterinsurgency, it seems paradoxical that the FLN sanctuary survived for as long as it did. At more intermediate levels, West German diplomats always harboured reservations as to the value of trying to keep Algeria French. As has been seen, they worried deeply about the impact of their pro-French stance on West German relations to the nascent Third World, especially in the context of Bonn's Cold War rivalry with the GDR. Once Algerian independence drew near, even Adenauer perceived the dangers of his policy, as demonstrated by the Chancellery's response to Güde's crackdown on Algeria's future ambassador to Bonn. These misgivings alone, however, did not lead to greater independence in the Algerian question. If the Bonn authorities tolerated the presence of Algerian refugees and militants, this was largely due to legal and constitutional constraints: the devolution of police powers restricted Bonn's ability to interfere in matters concerning domestic law and order; the Basic Law forbade the authorities from deporting individuals facing political persecution (or the death sentence); and officials in Paris in any case insisted that Algerians had to be treated as French citizens. In spite of the imperative of Franco-German reconciliation, moreover, domestic authorities sought to protect the *Rechtsstaat* and uphold the country's internal sovereignty. Though powerless against the transgressions of the French Navy and of *Service Action*, Bonn's Interior Ministry devised a legal regime that tolerated Algerians in the Federal Republic, though its principles in fact emulated the French goal of creating a system of 'human management and control'. This independent framework was itself born out of an effort to assist the French security and intelligence services in their war against nationalist subversion.

Although their freedom was limited and controlled, the authorities' tolerance left a favourable mark on the FLN. Reminiscing on his wartime experiences, including his arrest and expulsion, Abdelhafid Keramane asserted that the FRG was the one Western European country 'that did the most for the Algerian cause, for [Algerian] refugees, for the FLN, and for [its] external delegation'.[20] To exploit fully the benefits of sanctuary, the insurgents knew they would have to walk a fine line in West Germany. For this reason, the FLN and its auxiliaries persistently called on their militants to behave unobtrusively so as not to arouse the host-country's opposition. Although gratefully accepting the substantial material and humanitarian assistance offered by the GDR, the GPRA steadfastly resisted

20 'Entretien', in *Rapports*, Bougherara, p. 214.

East Berlin's calls for reciprocal recognition for fear of a backlash from the authorities in Bonn. Although socialist and neutralist in outlook, even the Ben Bella government ultimately chose to recognise the 'collaborationist' FRG in lieu of the 'anti-imperialist' GDR. Having first endorsed the two-state solution to the German question, independent Algeria ultimately reneged. The new state abided by the Hallstein doctrine and did so even past the severing of Algerian–West German relations in 1965.

By the end of the Algerian war, therefore, the Bonn government had achieved two seemingly incompatible goals. On the one hand, it had been able to use its support in the Algerian question to build trust and cement the Franco-German rapprochement. On the other hand, it had secured success in the competition for diplomatic recognition and legitimacy with East Berlin. West Germany's importance as a wartime sanctuary had certainly contributed to this latter victory, yet so did other factors. For one, the Adenauer government could draw on the latent and historic goodwill that Germans enjoyed in the Arab world; it could also deploy West Germany's new status as an international economic powerhouse. Constrained in its manoeuvring room by the Cold War divide and the Western alliance, Bonn increasingly came to rely on these classic examples of soft power to exert its influence and define its role in the new international order that emerged through decolonisation. The Ben Bella government, too, knew it could advance its own international status as a leading power of the Third World more by recognising Bonn than East Berlin, for the GDR remained politically ostracised outside of the Sino-Soviet bloc. More importantly, the Ulbricht regime lacked the economic and financial clout to provide the kind of development aid and direct foreign investment Algiers required to see through its ambitious programme of socio-economic reforms.

If the FRG's reputation and its *Wirtschaftswunder* enabled the Bonn government to secure recognition from Algeria in spite of its consistent siding with France, there was another kind of soft power that proved even more essential: the citizen, or civic diplomacy of West German non-state actors vis-à-vis the FLN. The Algerian war helps to debunk the cliché of the 1950s as a decade marked by provincialism, insularity and society's deliberate withdrawal from politics and divestiture from international affairs. Well before the international solidarity of the anti-Vietnam War generation, a whole range of West German civil-society actors came to support the FLN in its long and bitter struggle for national liberation. These actors spanned the political and generational divide and included journalists, merchants and arms dealers, Catholic and Protestant aid organisations, trade unions and workers' welfare associations, student associations as well as pacifist movements, and a growing circle of activists and parliamentarians who were mostly, but not exclusively, from the political Left. The nature and scale of engagement on the part of these actors varied considerably, nor did they ever converge into a single, coherent social movement. Their significance has consequently been downplayed in the existing literature. Whatever their motives (and they were surely not always the same), this book has highlighted just how wide a cross-section of civil society responded to, engaged with, and sought to influence in some small measure the conflict between France and the FLN. In spite of claims to provincialism and insularity, West Germans located themselves in global contexts and took an active interest in decolonisation.[21] Both in Paris and in Bonn, policy-makers repeatedly commented on the anti-colonial views espoused in the West German press and the pro-Algerian engagement of civil-society actors, particularly the younger generations. Thanks to Algeria, Karl Carstens observed in 1959, 'the fight against so-called colonialism has become a strong component of the political world view of our youth'.[22] So long as it remained within the scope of the law and did not interfere with the superior goal of Franco-German reconciliation, West German diplomacy did not much mind this civic diplomacy. Mid-ranking diplomats, as has been seen, shared many of the ideological and political impulses that compelled West German civil-society actors to help Algerians and the FLN. Towards the end of the war, the *Auswärtige Amt* positively encouraged the less radical elements within this expanding "Algeria lobby" to augment the aid they provided the FLN, especially the West German trade unions, student associations and humanitarian organisations. In this manner, the *Amt* hoped to offset the Adenauer government's reserve towards Algeria and decolonisation.

This dual approach combining official foreign policy with unofficial civic engagement consequently became a salient feature of West German diplomacy towards the Third World.[23] Constrained by the FRG's full integration into the Atlantic alliance and dependence on the Western allies, especially in the German question, the Bonn government sometimes lacked the freedom and flexibility enjoyed by civil-society actors to engage in an independent foreign policy, whether in Europe or beyond. Civic diplomacy pursued by non-state actors had the ability to complement or even counteract the official foreign policy of the government in Bonn, an

[21] Marcia Klotz, 'Introduction', *European Studies Journal* 16/1 (1999), pp. 1–8.
[22] Aufzeichnung für Addis-Abeba Botschafterkonferenz, 2 October 1959, PA/AA, B25/12.
[23] See also: Hagen, 'Internationalism'.

option that suited the authorities' soft-power approach to international relations. Civic diplomacy, in other words, could compensate for the country's limited power and sovereignty. Thus even in the early Bonn Republic, foreign policy was not always the preserve of Adenauer and his diplomatic elite, as the case of Algeria demonstrates. Here, a division of labour between official and citizen diplomacy proved essential in securing West Germany's conflicting foreign policy goals.

Algeria's independence struggle ultimately played a pivotal role in helping the Federal Republic find ways to use its newly granted sovereignty in order to facilitate the country's rehabilitation and reintegration into the international community. The conflict helped instigate a wider debate about the nature and purpose of West German foreign policy, both in Europe and beyond, and about the Federal Republic's place in international society. This debate occurred not just among the disparate and diverse civil-society circles that espoused the FLN's cause, but it also found strong echoes in the mainstream press and even within the *Auswärtige Amt.* Although they remained wedded to Adenauer's "Gaullist" policies, some diplomats such as Paul Frank, Herbert Müller-Roschach, Herbert Richter and even Karl Carstens (who would rise to become president of the FRG) had begun to challenge the chancellor's orthodoxy. Together with the FLN's civil allies and many in the press, they called for a re-think of West Germany's place in a rapidly changing international order. Economic power and technological prowess proved salient pillars of the soft-power approach through which the Bonn Republic would secure its future role and influence in the non-European world. But so would less tangible, cultural and normative factors.

As has been seen, West Germans often presented colonialism not only as something in which they were not involved but also as something that their own country (or rather a part of it) had to endure. As 'victims' of Soviet imperialism and militarism, West Germans sought to proclaim their solidarity with Third World movements fighting for liberation from colonialism. By ignoring Germany's own brutal albeit short-lived colonial past in Africa and Asia (not to mention the country's more recent colonial enterprise in Eastern Europe), West Germans were able to take a moral high ground vis-à-vis their European allies in the crises of decolonisation that fundamentally altered the international system. This selective amnesia further helped them fight back against East German propaganda depicting the Bonn Republic as imperialist and neo-imperialist.[24] If the colonial past

[24] Friedrichsmeyer, Lennox and Zantop, 'Introduction', p. 25.

remained largely forgotten, the more recent Nazi past did not. It became a common frame of reference for critiques of French counterinsurgency methods. In the context of the Third World's struggles over normative values such as human rights, social justice, equality and freedom, many in West Germany – whether they were civil-society actors or diplomats – began to feel their country had the ability and, indeed, the responsibility to act as a voice of conscience and moral agent against tyranny and oppression. Although it infuriated their French allies, they did so precisely because of Germany's recent crimes against humanity, which rightfully burdened and shamed German society. The questions posed by the Algerian war – especially when combined with the Algerian presence in their midst – had allowed a wide range of elements in West German society to start thinking about how, and whether, their country could be a positive force in international society. For now, their musings and actions remained disparate and uncoordinated. And yet in one shape or another, they came to define West German foreign policy in increasingly anti-imperialist, anti-racist and humanitarian terms.

It is in Algeria's independence struggle, then, that we first locate the roots of the Third World movement that gained prominence during the Vietnam War. The conflict highlighted the importance of conciliation, or *Wiedergutmachung*, not just with the West or with Israel but also with the rest of the world. This policy became a defining feature of West German diplomacy during the controversial and metamorphic ministry of Willy Brandt, whose foreign policy produced a normalisation of the Bonn Republic's relations not just with the GDR and the East, but also with the Third World. Algeria's independence struggle thus had a much deeper, transformational impact on West German foreign policy than Adenauer's outwardly "Gaullist" policies would have one assume, especially if one looks beyond the traditional foreign-policy-making elite. The conflict was indeed one of the 'hottest irons' in West German diplomacy during the late 1950s and early 1960s.[25] It set in motion lasting changes both in terms of the practice and the substance of West Germany diplomacy. To defend its sovereignty, the Republic would draw ever more on soft power, civic diplomacy and normative values.

These transformations were not simply a result of the discursive and cognitive shifts that occurred in response to National Socialism. As Quinn Slobodian has shown in a recent study of German student activism during the 1960s, they also resulted from direct contact and personal experience.[26]

[25] Lappenküper, 'Adenauer', p. 604. [26] Slobodian, *Foreign Front*.

Which brings us full circle to the FLN's sanctuary: it was the Algerian presence in West Germany that created the vital link between the local, national and international spheres. Far more than the atrocities being committed in Algeria or the violence occurring in metropolitan France, it was the influx of Algerian workers, refugees and militants that directly confronted both the authorities and civil society with the realities of French colonialism. It was through direct interaction with these Algerians that West German civil-society actors came to respect and support the FLN's cause. German–Algerian relations thus came about as a result of the FLN's decision to use the Bonn Republic as an external sanctuary during its independence struggle, as well as Algeria's later need for West German technical and financial aid. These decisions were born out of expediency as well as necessity rather than affinity and principle. Once the sanctuary outlived its use and official government aid had been secured, the relationships forged between Algerians and West German civil-society actors rapidly lost their purpose and use. Indeed, many of the FLN's erstwhile allies became disillusioned with Ben Bella's one-party regime. The fragile bonds formed during the years of struggle thus did not survive Algeria's liberation from colonial rule. For the young German Republic, however, the experience of combining official with civic diplomacy gained through the FLN's use of the FRG as sanctuary not only proved formative and fundamental to maintaining the country's sovereignty, it also helped West Germans redefine their place in international society.

Glossary of foreign terms

A NOTE ON TRANSLITERATIONS: As a non-Arabic speaker, I refer only to such terms that are commonly known or used in the literature, making use of international phonetic transliterations. French transcriptions were retained for Arabic terms that have been absorbed into the French language. Except in cases where the plural form is widely used and hence familiar to non-Arabic speakers, plurals are marked by an (s) in parentheses at the end of a word. For the sake of uniformity, the personal names of Algerians, Moroccans, Tunisians and other Arab actors mentioned in this study are spelled according to the vulgar transliterations used by the colonial authorities at the time.

Agrément (French) Diplomatic approval
Algérie française (French) French Algeria
Arbeitskreis der Freunde Algeriens (German) Working-circle of the Friends of Algeria
Außenwirtschaftsgesetz (German) Law on foreign trade
Auswärtige Amt (German) Foreign Office
Bled (French, from Arabic) Hinterland
Boches (French) Pejorative slang for Germans
Bund (German) Federation or Federal government
Bundesland/Bundesländer (German) Federal State/s
Bundestag (German) Federal Parliament
Bundeswehr (German) Federal army
Caritasverband (German) Catholic charity
Chef de cabinet (French) Chief of cabinet
Chef de mission (French) Chief of mission
Christliche Abendland (German) Christian West
Colons (French) European settlers in Algeria
Deuxième Bureau (French) Military intelligence
El Moudjahid (Arabic) FLN official newspaper
Evangelisches Hilfswerk (German) Protestant relief agency
Die Falken (German) Socialist youth organisation
Fédération d'Allemagne (French) The FLN's politico-administrative organisation in West Germany
Fédération de France (French) The FLN's politico-administrative organisation in metropolitan France
Fichier Z (French) National database of card-index files on Algerians in metropolitan France
Freies Algerien (German) 'Free Algeria' – newspaper
Gestapo (German) *Geheime Staatspolizei* – Secret State Police during the Third Reich
Guerre d'action (French) War of action – covert operations
Guerre économique (French) Economic warfare

Guerre politique (French) Political warfare
Guerre psychologique (French) Psychological warfare
Guerre révolutionnaire (French) (Counter-)Revolutionary warfare
Harkis (Arabic) Term used for Muslim Algerian auxiliaries fighting in the French army
Hilfskomitee(s) (German) Relief committee(s)
Innere Mission (German) Protestant relief agency (domestic)
Jam'iyyat ul islâm (Arabic) International Islamic aid organisation
Jeune Résistance (French) Organisation for French deserters and draft dodgers
Jihâd (Arabic) Sacred struggle, or holy war
Junud (Arabic) Regular soldier
Jungsozialisten (Jusos) (German) Young Socialists, SPD
Kriegswaffen (German) Weapons of war
Kriegswaffenkontrollgesetz (German) Law on the control of weapons of war
Kripo (German) *Kriminalpolizei* – criminal police
Land/Länder (German) State/s
Meldekopf (German) Database and reporting system
Mitteilungen des Rückführungsdienstes (German) Information bulletin of the Repatriation Service for Deserted Legionnaires
mukhabarât (Arabic) secret service
Mujâhideen (Arabic) Male resisters of the FLN/ALN
Naturfreunde(jugend) (German) Friends of Nature International (Youth Section)
Neue Gesellschaft (German) New Society, SPD, Hamburg
Nibelungentreue (German) Feudal loyalty
Pax Christi (German) International Catholic charity
Pieds Noirs (French) European settlers in North Africa
Quai d'Orsay (French) French Foreign Ministry
Rechtsstaat (German) Constitutional state; rule of law
Relativwaffen (German) Weapons used for hunting and recreation
Schadenfreude (German) Malicious pleasure
Service Action (French) Covert action branch of the French foreign intelligence service (SDECE)
Sicherungsgruppe Bonn (German) Federal security and protection service
Sûreté (Nationale) (French) National police
Surmar (French) Maritime Surveillance
Ultras (French) Name given to reactionary settlers, Frenchmen and soldiers who resisted change in Algeria
Westbindung (German) Western integration (literally binding)
Westpolitik (German) Western policy
Wilâya(s) (Arabic) Military region
Wirtschaftswunder (German) Economic miracle

Bibliography

Archives

I France

Series and sub-series marked with an asterisk * were consulted *sur dérogation*, as were individual dossiers in series or sub-series marked (*).

Archives Diplomatiques, Ministère des Affaires Étrangères (MAE), Paris

AL/ALG – Département Afrique-Levant/Algérie
AL/MAR – Département Afrique-Levant/Maroc
AM/EUA – Département Amérique/États-Unis d'Amérique
EU/RFA(*) – Département Europe/République Fédérale d'Allemagne
MLA – Mission de liaison pour les affaires algériennes
SEAA* – Secrétariat d'état pour les affaires algériennes

Archives d'Histoire Contemporaine (AHC), SciencesPo, Paris

2DE* – Fonds Michel Debré

Archives Nationales (AN), Paris

4AG* – Présidence de la IVème République: Secrétariat général et cabinet
5AG1* – Présidence de la Vème République: Cabinet du Général Charles de Gaulle
F60 – Présidence du Conseil de la IVème République

Services des Archives et du Musée de la Préfecture de Police (SAMPP/P), Paris

Ha* – Archives algériennes du cabinet du préfet de la période, 1954–1962
H1B* – Service de coordination des affaires algériennes

Service Historique de la Défense – Armée de Terre (SHD-T), Vincennes

1H(*)	– Les Archives de l'Algérie: Cabinet militaire de la Délégation générale du Gouvernement en Algérie; Deuxième bureau de l'État-Major Interarmée; Troisième bureau de l'État-Major Interarmée; Cinquième bureau de l'État-Major Interarmée; Journaux des marches et opérations des secteurs et des quartiers
1R*	– Cabinet du Ministre de la Défense Nationale
10R*	– Service de Documentation Extérieure et de Contre-Espionnage (SDECE)
8S*	– Division Organisation et Logistique de l'État-Major des Armées
14S*	– Division Attachés des Forces Armées de l'État-Major des Armées
10T*	– Deuxième Bureau de l'État-Major de l'Armée « Terre »

II Germany

Archiv des Deutschen Caritasverbandes e.V., Freiburg (ADCV)

AA	– Auslandsabteilung
ZA	– Zentralarchiv

Archiv des Evangelischen Werks für Diakonie und Entwicklung, Berlin (AEWDE)

BfdW	– Brot für die Welt (Bread for the World)

Archiv der sozialen Demokratie, Bonn (AdsD)

5/DGAJ & 5/DGAZ	– Deutscher Gewerkschaftsbund (DGB): Bundesvorstand, Internationale Abteilung, Abteilung Ausland
NL/Blachstein	– Nachlass (NL)/Peter Blachstein
NL/Plum	– Nachlass (NL)/Werner Plum

Bundesarchiv, Koblenz (BA/K)

B102	– Bundesministerium für Wirtschaft (BMWi)
B106	– Bundesministerium des Innern (BMI)
B131	– Bundeskriminalamt (BKA) and Sicherungsgruppe (SG) Bonn
B136	– Bundeskanzleramt
B149	– Bundesministerium für Arbeit (BMA)
B166	– Verband deutscher Studentenschaften (VdS)

Politisches Archiv des Auswärtigen Amts (PA/AA), Berlin

B1 – Büro Aussenminister
B2 – Büro Staatssekretäre
B12 – Abteilung 7: Ost
B14 – Referat 211/301/II A 7: Verteidigung und Abrüstung
B24 – Referat 302/204/I A 3: Frankreich, Benelux, Italien
B25 – Referat 205: Nordafrika, bis 1962
B36 – Referat I B 4: Nordafrika, ab 1962
B63 – Referat 413/III A 6: Ost-West Handel

Printed sources

I *Newspapers and periodicals*

Algerian

El Moudjahid (FLN official newspaper)
El Watan
Freies Algerien (West Germany)

French

Agence France Presse (AFP)
Combat
L'Express
Le Figaro
France-Observateur
Jours de France
Le Monde
Paris-Journal
Paris-Presse

German

Aachener Nachrichten
Allgemeiner Deutscher Nachrichtendienst (ADN – East Berlin)
Das Argument
Bild (Hamburg)
Bundesanzeiger (Bonn)
Deutsche Presse Agentur (DPA)
Frankfurter Allgemeine Zeitung (FAZ)
Frankfurter Neue Presse
Frankfurter Rundschau
General-Anzeiger (Bonn)
Goslarsche Zeitung
Hamburger Abendblatt
Hamburger Echo
Hannoversche Presse
Klarer Kurs

Kölnische Rundschau
Mannheimer Morgen
Metall
Der Mittag (Düsseldorf)
Neue Rhein Zeitung (Essen)
(Neuer) Vorwärts (SPD)
Neues Deutschland (East Berlin)
Parlamentarisch-Politischer Pressedienst (SPD)
Politik und Wirtschaft
Rheinische Post (Düsseldorf)
Rheinischer Merkur (Bonn)
Ruhr Nachrichten (Dortmund)
SPD-Pressedienst
Der Spiegel (Hamburg)
Stuttgarter Nachrichten
Stuttgarter Zeitung
Süddeutsche Zeitung (SZ – Munich)
Tagesspiegel (West Berlin)
Die Welt (Hamburg)
Welt der Arbeit (DGB)
Westdeutsche Allgemeine Zeitung (Essen)

Other

COSEC Information Bulletin
Luxemburger Wort
Maasbode
Neue Zürcher Zeitung
St. Galler Tagblatt
Times Magazine

II Memoirs, diaries and personal accounts

Adenauer, Konrad. *Erinnerungen 1955–1959*. Stuttgart, 1967.
Aït Ahmed, Hocine. *La Guerre et l'Après-Guerre*. Paris, 1964.
Mémoires d'un Combattant. L'esprit d'indépendance 1942–1952. Documents. Paris, 1983.
Alleg, Henri. *La Question*. Paris, 1957.
Aussaresses, Paul. *Services Spéciaux, Algérie 1955–1957: mon témoignage sur la torture*. Paris, 2001.
Beaufre, André. *L'Expédition de Suez*. Paris, 1967.
Blankenhorn, Herbert. *Verständnis und Verständigung. Blätter eines politischen Tagebuchs, 1949 bis 1979*. Frankfurt/Main, 1980.
Bollardière, Jacques Pâris de. *Bataille d'Alger; Bataille de l'homme*. Paris, 1972.
Boudaoud, Omar. *Du PPA au FLN. Mémoires d'un combattant*. Alger, 2007.
Boudiaf, Mohamed. *La préparation du 1er novembre suivi de la lettre ouverte aux algériens*. Paris, 1976.
Debré, Michel. *Gouverner. Mémoires 1958–1962*. Paris, 1988.

al-Dib, Mohamed Fathi. *Abdel Nasser et la Révolution algérienne*. Paris, 1985.
Dickopf, Paulinus. 'Die Stellung des BKA im Rahmen der internationalen Verbrechensbekämfung'. In *40 Jahre Bundeskriminalamt*. Ed. Hans-Ludwig Zachert. Stuttgart, 1991, pp. 38–48.
al-Fāsi, 'Alāl. *The Independence Movements in Arab North Africa*. Washington DC, 1954.
Frank, Paul. *Entschlüsselte Botschaft. Ein Diplomat macht Inventur*. Stuttgart, 1981.
Fuchs, Jockel. *Mainzer Jahre – schöne Jahre. Erinnerungen 1945–1987*. Mainz, 1993.
Gaillard, Philippe. *Foccart Parle: entretien avec Philippe Gaillard*. Vol. I. Paris, 1995.
de Gaulle, Charles. *Mémoires d'espoir. Le renouveau 1958–1962*. Paris, 1970.
Haraigue, Rachid. *Le Combat d'un Lieutenant FLN en France pendant la Guerre d'Algérie*. Paris, 2001.
Harbi, Mohammed. *Une Vie debout: Mémoires politiques 1945–1962*. Vol. I. Paris, 2001.
Haroun, Ali. *La Septième Wilaya: La Guerre du FLN en France 1954–1962*. Paris, 1986.
Heikal, Mohamed. *Nasser. The Cairo Documents*. London, 1972.
Kalbitzer, Hellmut. *Widerstehen oder Mitmachen. Eigensinnige Ansichten und sehr persönliche Erinnerungen*. Hamburg, 1987.
Kiouane, Abderrahmane. *Les Débuts d'une Diplomatie de Guerre (1956–1962). Journal d'un Délégué à l'Extérieur*. Alger, 2000.
Lebjaoui, Mohamed. *Vérités sur la Révolution algérienne*. Paris, 1970.
Majonica, Ernst. *Das politische Tagebuch, 1958–1972*. Ed. Hans-Otto Kleinmann and Christopher Beckmann. Düsseldorf, 2011.
Malek, Rédha. *L'Algérie à Évian: histoire des négociations secrètes, 1956–1962*. Paris, 1995.
Méléro, Antoine. *La Main rouge. L'armée secrète de la République*. Monaco, 1997.
Melnik, Constantin. *The French Campaign against the FLN*. Santa Monica CA, 1967.
Mille jours à Matignon: de Gaulle, l'Algérie, les services spéciaux. Paris, 1988.
La mort était leur mission. Le service Action pendant la guerre d'Algérie. Paris, 1996.
Merle, Robert. *Ahmed Ben Bella*. Paris, 1965.
Couve de Murville, Maurice. *Une politique étrangère 1958–1969*. Paris, 1971.
Nostitz, Siegfried von. *Algerisches Tagebuch 1960–1962*. Düsseldorf, 1971.
Papon, Maurice. *Les Chevaux du pouvoir*. Paris, 1988.
Primakov, Yevgeny. *Russia and the Arabs. Behind the Scenes in the Middle East from the Cold War to the Present*. Trans. Paul Gould. New York, 2009.
Servan-Schreiber, Jean-Jacques. *Lieutenant en Algérie*. Paris, 1957.
Seydoux, François. *Beiderseits des Rheins. Erinnerungen eines französischen Diplomaten*. Frankfurt, 1975.
Vack, Klaus. 'Die Algerien-Solidarität der Naturjugendfreunde'. In *Hundert Jahre Kampf um die freie Natur. Illustrierte Geschichte der Naturfreunde*. Eds. Wulf Erdmann and Jochen Zimmer. Essen, 1991, pp. 104–14.
Vaujour, Jean. *De la révolte à la révolution. Aux premiers jours de la guerre d'Algérie*. Paris, 1985.

Vié, Jean-Émile. *Mémoires d'un directeur des renseignements généraux*. Paris, 1988.

Thyraud de Vosjoli, Philippe. *Lamia. L'anti-barbouze*. Montreal & Brussels, 1972.

Westphal, Heinz. *Jugend braucht Demokratie. Demokratie braucht Jugend. Mein jugend-politisches Engagement 1945–1974*. Rostock, 1994.

Wischnewski, Hans-Jürgen. *Mit Leidenschaft und Augenmaß. In Mogadischu und - anderswo. Politische Memoiren*. Munich, 1989.

III Official publications, period publications and document collections

Adenauer: 'Um den Frieden zu gewinnen'. Die Protokolle des CDU-Bundesvorstandes 1957–1961. Ed. Buchstab Günter. Düsseldorf, 1994.

Der Auswärtige Ausschuß des Deutschen Bundestages: Sitzungsprotokolle. Bd. III – *1957–1961*. Eds. Joachim Wintzer, Josef Boyer and Wolfgang Dierker. Düsseldorf, 2003.

Der Auswärtige Ausschuß des Deutschen Bundestages: Sitzungsprotokolle. Bd. IV – *1961–1965*. Eds. Wolfgang Hölscher, Joachim Wintzer and Josef Boyer. Düsseldorf, 2004.

Balandier, Georges. 'La situation coloniale: approche théorique'. *Cahiers internationaux de sociologie* 11 (1951), pp. 44–79.

Bourdieu, Pierre. *The Algerians*. Trans. C.M. Alan Ross. Boston, 1962.

Die Bundesrepublik Deutschland und Frankreich: Dokumente 1949–1963 (BDFD). Eds. Horst Möller and Klaus Hildebrand. Bd. 1. *Außenpolitik und Diplomatie*. Ed. Ulrich Lappenküper. Munich, 1997.

Die Bundesrepublik Deutschland und Frankreich: Dokumente 1949–1963 (BDFD). Eds. Horst Möller and Klaus Hildebrand. Bd. 2. *Wirtschaft*. Ed. Andreas Wilkens. Munich, 1997.

Die Bundesrepublik Deutschland und Frankreich: Dokumente 1949–1963 (BDFD). Eds. Horst Möller and Klaus Hildebrand. Bd. 3. *Parteien, Öffentlichkeit, Kultur*. Ed. Herbert Elzer. Munich, 1997.

Die CDU/CSU-Fraktion im Deutschen Bundestag. Sitzungsprotokolle 1957–1961. Ed. Reinhard Schiffers. Düsseldorf, 2004.

Documents Diplomatiques Français (DDF), 1956, Vols. I–III. Ed. Ministère des Affaires Étrangères, Commission de Publication des Documents Diplomatiques. Paris, 1988–1990.

Documents Diplomatiques Français (DDF), 1957, Vols. I–II. Ed. Ministère des Affaires Étrangères, Commission de Publication des Documents Diplomatiques. Paris, 1990–1991.

Documents Diplomatiques Français (DDF), 1958, Vols. I–II. Ed. Ministère des Affaires Étrangères, Commission de Publication des Documents Diplomatiques. Paris, 1992–1993.

Documents Diplomatiques Français (DDF), 1959, Vols. I–II. Ed. Ministère des Affaires Étrangères, Commission de Publication des Documents Diplomatiques. Paris, 1994–1995.

Documents Diplomatiques Français (DDF), 1960, Vols. I–II. Ed. Ministère des Affaires Étrangères, Commission de Publication des Documents Diplomatiques. Paris, 1996.

Documents Diplomatiques Français (DDF), 1961, Vols. I–II. Ed. Ministère des Affaires Étrangères, Commission de Publication des Documents Diplomatiques. Paris, 1997.

Documents Diplomatiques Français (DDF), 1962, Vols. I–II. Ed. Ministère des Affaires Étrangères, Commission de Publication des Documents Diplomatiques. Paris, . . .

Dokumente zur Außenpolitik der Regierung der Deutschen Demokratischen Republik. Bd. V and VI. Ed. Institut für Zeitgeschichte. Berlin/Ost, 1958 and 1959.

Eveno, Patrick and Jean Planchais. Eds. *La Guerre d'Algérie. Dossier et témoignages.* Paris, 1989.

Fanon, Frantz. *The Wretched of the Earth.* Trans. Richard Philcox. New York, 2004.

Galula, David. *Counter-Insurgency Warfare: Theory and Practice.* New York, 1964.

de Gaulle, Charles. *Discours et Messages: avec le Renouveau, mai 1958-juillet 1962.* Paris, 1970.

Lettres, Notes et Carnets. Vol. 8. Paris, 1985.

Giáp, Võ Nguyên. *The Military Art of People's War.* Trans. R. Stetler. Ann Arbor MI, 1970.

Harbi, Mohammed. Ed. *Les Archives de la révolution algérienne.* Paris, 1981.

and Gilbert Meynier. Eds. *Le FLN, documents et histoire: 1954–1962.* Paris, 2004.

Jahrbuch der öffentlichen Meinung 1947–1955. Institut für Demoskopie. Eds. Elisabeth Noelle and Erich Peter Neumann. Allensbach am Bodensee, 1956.

Jahrbuch der öffentlichen Meinung 1958–1964. Institut für Demoskopie. Eds. Elisabeth Noelle and Erich Peter Neumann. Allensbach am Bodensee, 1965.

Die Kabinettsprotokolle der Bundesregierung. Bd. 8 – 1955. Eds. Michael Hollmann and Kai von Jena. Munich, 1997.

Die Kabinettsprotokolle der Bundesregierung. Bd. 9 – *1956.* Ed. Ursula Hüllbüsch. Munich, 1998.

Die Kabinettsprotokolle der Bundesregierung. Bd. 10 – *1957.* Eds. Ulrich Enders and Josef Henke. Munich, 2000.

Die Kabinettsprotokolle der Bundesregierung. Bd. 11 – *1958.* Eds. Ulrich Enders and Christoph Schawe. Munich, 2002.

Die Kabinettsprotokolle der Bundesregierung. Bd. 13 – *1960.* Eds. Ralf Behrendt and Christoph Seemann. Munich, 2003.

Memmi, Albert. *The Colonizer and the Colonized.* Trans. Howard Greenfeld. London, 2003.

Morsey, Rudolf and Hans-Peter Schwarz. Eds. *Adenauer. Teegespräche, 1955–1958.* Berlin, 1986.

Nasser, Gamal Abdel. *The Philosophy of the Revolution*, Book I. Cairo, 1955.

Soustelle, Jacques. 'France Looks at Her Alliances'. *Foreign Affairs* 35 (1956), pp. 116–30.

Tillion, Germaine. *L'Algérie en 1957*. Paris, 1957.
Trinquier, Roger. *Modern Warfare: A French View of Counterinsurgency*. Trans. Daniel Lee. New York, 1964.
Tse-Tung, Mao. *On Guerrilla Warfare*. Trans. S.B. Griffith. New York, 1961.
Selected Military Writings. Peking, 1967.
Verhandlungen des Deutschen Bundestages. Anlagen zu den Stenographischen Berichten. Drucksachen (VdDBT/D) 3. Wahlperiode, 1957–1961. Bonn.
Verhandlungen des Deutschen Bundestages. Stenographische Berichte (VdDBT/StB) 3. Wahlperiode, 1957–1961. Bonn.
Vidal-Naquet, Pierre. *L'Affaire Audin 1957–1978*. Paris, 1989.
Ed. *La Raison d'Etat*. Paris, 1962.
Torture: Cancer of Democracy. France and Algeria 1954–62. Trans. Barry Richard. Harmondsworth, 1963.

Secondary sources

I Books and articles

Abelshauser, Werner L. 'The Causes and Consequences of the 1956 West German Rearmament Crisis'. In *NATO: The Founding of the Atlantic Alliance and the Integration of Europe*. Eds. Francis H. Heller and John R. Gillingham. Basingstoke, 1992, pp. 311–34.
Abramovici, Pierre. *Le Putsch des Généraux*. Paris, 2011.
Abu-Lughod, Ibrahim. 'Lebanon and Palestine: Some Contrasts in the Application of the Principles of National Liberation'. *Arab Studies Quarterly* 7/4 (1985), pp. 78–88.
Adams, Geoffrey. *The Call of Conscience: French Protestant Responses to the Algerian War, 1954–1962*. Waterloo ON, 1998.
Ageron, Charles-Robert. '"L'Algérie dernière chance de la puissance française". Étude d'un mythe politique (1954–1962)'. *Relations internationales* 57 (1989), pp. 113–39.
'Un aspect de la guerre d'Algérie: la propagande radiophonique du FLN et des États arabes'. In *La guerre d'Algérie et les Algériens 1954–1962*. Ed. Charles-Robert Ageron. Paris, 1997, pp. 245–59.
'Les forces internationales et la décolonisation de l'Afrique du Nord'. In *Les Internationales et le problème de la guerre au XXe siècle. Actes du colloque de Rome (22–24 nov. 1984)* Ed. École Française de Rome. Rome, 1987, pp. 195–218.
'La "guerre psychologique" de l'Armée de libération nationale algérienne'. In *La guerre d'Algérie et les Algériens 1954–1962*. Ed. Charles-Robert Ageron. Paris, 1997, pp. 201–29.
'L'insurrection du 20 août 1955 dans le Nord-Constantinois. De la résistance armée à la guerre du peuple'. In *La guerre d'Algérie et les Algériens 1954–1962*. Ed. Charles-Robert Ageron. Paris, 1997, pp. 27–50.

'Mai 1945 en Algérie. Enjeu de mémoire et histoire'. *Matériaux pour l'histoire de notre temps* 39 (1995), pp. 52–6.

Modern Algeria. A History from 1830 to the Present. Trans. Michael Brett. London, 1991.

'L'opération de Suez et la guerre d'Algérie'. In *La France et l'opération de Suez de 1956*. Ed. Maurice Vaïsse. Paris, 1997, pp. 43–60.

'L'opinion française à travers les sondages'. In *La Guerre d'Algérie et les Français.* Ed. Jean-Pierre Rioux. Paris, 1990, pp. 25–44.

'La survivance d'un mythe: La puissance par l'Empire colonial (1944–1947)'. In *La puissance française en question 1945–1949*. Ed. René Girault and Robert Frank. Paris, 1988, pp. 31–51.

Ahmad, Eqbal. 'Revolutionary Warfare and Counterinsurgency'. In *Guerrilla Strategies: An Historical Anthology from the Long March to Afghanistan*. Ed. Gérard Chaliand. Berkeley LA, 1982, pp. 241–62.

Aissaoui, Rabah. 'Fratricidal War: The Conflict between the Mouvement national algérien (MNA) and the Front de libération nationale (FLN) in France during the Algerian War (1954–1962)'. *British Journal of Middle Eastern Studies* 39/2 (2012), pp. 227–40.

'"Nous voulons déchirer le bâillon et briser nos chaines": Racism, Colonialism and Universalism in the Discourse of Algerian Nationalists in France between the Wars'. *French History* 17/2 (2003), pp. 186–209.

Albrecht, Monika. *'Europa ist nicht die Welt'. (Post) Kolonialismus in Literatur und Geschichte der westdeutschen Nachkriegszeit.* Bielefeld, 2008.

'Postcolonialism and Migration into Germany's Colonial Past'. *German Life and Letters* 65/3 (2012), pp. 363–77.

Albus, Michael. 'Ich habe die Verantwortung gespürt. Erfahrungen mit Menschen unterwegs. Ein Interviw mit Georg Hüssler'. *Ost-West Europäische Perspektiven* 3 (2003), www.owep.de/artikel/361/ich-habe-verantwortung-gespuert (accessed 27 October 2014).

Alexander, Martin. 'Seeking France's "Lost Soldiers": Reflections on the French Military Crisis in Algeria'. In *Crisis and Renewal in France, 1918–1962*. Eds. Martin S. Alexander and Kenneth Mouré. New York and Oxford, 2002, pp. 242–66.

and Philip Bankwitz. 'From Politiques en Képi to Military Technocrats: de Gaulle and the Recovery of the French Army after Indochina and Algeria'. In *The Aftermath of Defeat: Societies, Armed Forces, and the Challenge of Recovery*. Eds. George Andreopoulos and Harold Selesky. New Haven CT, 1994, pp. 79–102.

Aleya-Sghaier, Amira. 'La Tunisie: base-arrière de la révolution algérienne (1954–1962)'. *Revue d'Histoire Maghrébine* 118 (2005), pp. 155–60.

Alwan, Mohamed. *Algeria before the United Nations.* New York, 1959.

Ambler, John S. *The French Army in Politics 1945–1962*. Columbus OH, 1966.

Ames, Eric, Marcia Klotz and Lora Wildenthal. Eds. *Germany's Colonial Past.* Lincoln NE, 2005.

Amiri, Linda. *La Bataille de France: La guerre d'Algérie en Métropole*. Paris, 2004.

'Les espaces de voisinage dans les conflits de décolonisation: le cas de la Suisse pendant la guerre d'indépendance algérienne'. *Matériaux pour l'Histoire de Notre Temps* 97/98 (2010), pp. 50–7.

Anderson, Eugene N. *The First Moroccan Crisis 1904–1906*. 2nd Ed. Hamden CT, 1966.

Anderson, Jeffrey J. 'Hard Interests, Soft Power, and Germany's Changing Role in Europe'. In *Tamed Power: Germany in Europe*. Ed. Peter J. Katzenstein. Ithaca NY, 1997, pp. 80–107.

Andrew, Christopher M. 'France: Adjustment to Change'. In *The Expansion of International Society*. Ed. Hedley Bull and Adam Watson. Oxford, 1984, pp. 335–44.

Artens, Hannes. 'Sanctuary State – Insurgency Relations in Ethnic Conflicts: A New Explanatory Model'. *Oficina do CES* 392 (November 2012), pp. 1–23.

Ashton, Nigel. *Eisenhower, Macmillan and the Problem of Nasser: Anglo-American Relations and Arab Nationalism, 1955–1959*. Basingstoke, 1996.

Badjadja, Abdelkrim. 'Panorama des archives de l'Algérie moderne et contemporaine'. In *La Guerre d'Algérie 1954–2004. La fin de l'amnésie*. Eds. Mohammed Harbi and Benjamin Stora. Paris, 2004, pp. 924–7.

Bagnato, Bruno. 'Une solidarité ambiguë: l'OTAN, la France et la guerre d'Algérie (1954–1958)'. *Revue d'histoire diplomatique* 115/4 (2001), pp. 329–50.

Baker, Donald N. 'The Surveillance of Subversion in Interwar France: The Carnet B in the Seine 1922–1940'. *French Historical Studies* 10/3 (1978), pp. 486–516.

Bald, Detlef. *Alternativen zur Wiederbewaffnung: Friedenskonzeptionen in Westdeutschland 1945–1955*. Essen, 2008.

and Wolfram Wette. Eds. *Friedensinitiativen in der Frühzeit des Kalten Krieges 1945–1955*. Essen, 2010.

Balsen, Werner and Karl Rössel. *Hoch die internationale Solidarität: zur Geschichte der Dritte- Welt-Bewegung in der Bundesrepublik*. Cologne, 1986.

Bancel, Nicolas, Pascal Blanchard and Françoise Vergès. *La République coloniale: essai sur une utopie*. Paris, 2003.

Baranowski, Shelley. *Nazi Empire: German Colonialism and Imperialism from Bismarck to Hitler*. Cambridge, 2011.

Barbier, Colette. 'Les négociations franco-germano-italiennes en vue de l'établissement d'une coopération militaire nucléaire au cours des années 1956–1958'. *Revue d'Histoire Diplomatique* 1/2 (1990), pp.81–113.

Barei, Geoffrey. 'The Sakiet Sidi Youssef Incident of 1958 in Tunisia and the Anglo-American 'Good Offices' Mission'. *Journal of North African Studies* 17/2 (2012), pp. 355–71.

Bariéty, Jacques. 'Les entretiens de Gaulle-Adenauer de juillet 1960 à Rambouillet: prélude au Plan Fouchet et au traité de l'Élysée'. *Revue d'Allemagne et de Pays de langue allemande* 29/2 (1997), pp. 167–76.

'De Gaulle, Adenauer et la genèse du traité franco-allemand'. *Revue d'Allemagne et de Pays de langue allemande* 22/4 (1990), pp. 539–64.

'La perception de la puissance française par le chancelier K. Adenauer de 1958 à 1963'. *Relations internationales* 58 (1989), pp. 217–25.

Baring, Arnulf. *Außenpolitik in Adenauers Kanzlerdemokratie*. Munich, 1969.

Barkaoui, Miloud. 'Managing the Colonial Status Quo: Eisenhower's Cold War and the Algerian War of Independence'. *Journal of North African Studies* 17/1 (2012), pp. 125–41.

Barraclough, Geoffrey. *From Agadir to Armageddon: Anatomy of a Crisis*. London, 1982.

Barzman, John. 'Citoyens, sujets, immigrés: quelques aspects de la législation française en Algérie et à l'égard des personnes originaires d'Algérie'. *Cahiers de Sociologie économique et culturelle/Ethnopsychologie* 21 (1994), pp. 111–27.

Bellers, Jürgen. *Außenwirtschaftspolitik der Bundesrepublik Deutschland, 1949–1989*. Münster, 1990.

Bennoune, Mahfoud. *The Making of Contemporary Algeria, 1830–1987*. Cambridge, 1988.

Berggötz, Sven O. *Nahostpolitik in der Ära Adenauer: Möglichkeiten und Grenzen, 1949–1963*. Düsseldorf, 1998.

Berger, Thomas U. *War, Guilt, and World Politics after World War II*. Cambridge, 2012.

Bergot, Erwan. *Commandos de Choc 'Algérie'. Le dossier rouge. Services secrets contre FLN*. Paris, 1990.

Berman, Russell A.. *Enlightenment or Empire: Colonial Discourse in German Culture*. Lincoln NE, 1998.

'German Colonialism: Another *Sonderweg?*' *European Studies Journal* 16/2 (1999), pp. 25–36.

Bernardot, Marc. 'Être interné au Larzac. La politique d'assignation à résidence surveillée pendant la guerre d'Algérie (1958–1962)'. *Politix* 69 (2005), pp. 39–62.

Bernert, Philippe. *Roger Wybot et la bataille pour la DST*. Paris, 1975.

SDECE Service 7. L'extraordinaire histoire du colonel Le Roy-Finville et des clandestins. Paris, 1980.

Besson, Waldemar. *Die Außenpolitik der Bundesrepublik. Erfahrungen und Maßstäbe*. Munich, 1970.

Betts, Raymond F. *France and Decolonization 1900–1960*. Basingstoke, 1991.

Bitsch, Marie-Thérèse and Gérard Bossuat. Eds. *L'Europe Unie et l'Afrique. De l'idée d'Eurafrique à la convention de Lomé I*. Bruxelles, 2005.

Blackwell, Stephen. *British Military Intervention and the Struggle for Jordan: King Hussein, Nasser and the Middle East Crisis, 1955–1958*. New York, 2009.

Blanchard, Emmanuel 'Contrôler, enfermer, éloigner. La répression policière et administrative des Algériens de metropole (1946–1962)'. In *La France en guerre 1954–1962. Expériences métropolitaines de la guerre d'indépendance algérienne*. Ed. Raphaëlle Branche and Sylvie Thénault. Paris, 2008, pp. 318–31.

'La dissolution des Brigades nord-africaines de la Préfecture de police: la fin d'une police d'exception pour les Algériens de Paris (1944–1953)?' *Bulletin de l'Institut Historique du Temps Présent* 83 (2004) www.ihtp.cnrs.fr/spip.php%3Farticle329&lang=fr.html (accessed 22 September 2010).

'Police judiciaire et pratiques d'exception pendant la guerre d'Algérie'. *Vingtième Siècle* 90 (2006), pp. 61–72.

La police parisienne et les Algériens (1944–1962). Paris, 2011.

Bleiker, Roland. *Popular Dissent, Human Agency and Global Politics*. Cambridge, 2000.

Blévis, Laure. 'Droit colonial algérien de la citoyenneté: conciliation illusoire entre des principes républicains et une logique d'occupation coloniale (1865–1947)'. *In La Guerre d'Algérie au miroir des décolonisations françaises*. Ed. Charles-Robert Ageron. Paris, 2000, pp. 87–103.

Bock, Hans M. 'Zur Perzeption der frühen Bundesrepublik Deutschland in der französischen Diplomatie: Die Bonner Monatsberichte des Hochkommissars André François-Poncet 1949–1955'. *Francia* 15 (1987), pp. 579–658.

Booz, Rüdiger Marco. '*Hallsteinzeit*'. *Deutsche Außenpolitik 1955–1972*. Bonn, 1995.

Bossuat, Gérard. 'Les armements dans les relations franco-allemandes (1945–1963): les nationalismes à l'épreuve des temps nouveaux'. *Revue d'Allemagne et de Pays de langue allemande* 25/4 (1993), pp. 601–15.

Bougherara, Nassima. *Les Rapports franco-allemands à l'épreuve de la question algérienne (1955–1963)*. Bern, 2006.

Bouhsini, Sabah. *Die Rolle Nordafrikas (Marokko, Algerien, Tunesien) in den deutsch-französischen Beziehungen von 1950–1962*. Aachen, 2000.

Bouzar-Kasbadji, Nadya. 'La Marseillaise et ses dissonances en Algérie coloniale'. *Revue du monde musulman et de la Méditerranée* 52/1 (1989), pp. 241–50.

Bradley, Mark Philip. 'Decolonization, the Global South, and the Cold War, 1919–1962'. In *The Cambridge History of the Cold War*. Vol. I. Eds. M.P. Leffler and O.A. Westad. Cambridge, 2010, pp. 464–85.

Branche, Raphaëlle. *La guerre d'Algérie: une histoire apaisée?* Paris, 2005.

La torture et l'armée pendant la guerre d'Algérie 1954–1962. Paris, 2001.

Brands, H.W. *The Specter of Neutralism. The United States and the Emergence of the Third World, 1947–1960*. New York, 1989.

Briggs, Thomas. *Cash on Delivery: CIA Special Operations during the Secret War in Laos*. Rockville MD, 2009.

Brugger, Philipp, Andreas Hasenclever and Lukas Kasten. 'Theorizing the Impact of Trust on Post-Agreement Negotiations: the Case of Franco-German Security Relations'. *International Negotiation* 18 (2013), pp. 441–69.

Brunet, Jean-Paul. 'Police Violence in Paris, October 1961: Historical Sources, Methods, and Conclusions'. *Historical Journal* 51/1 (2008), pp. 195–204.

Police contre FLN. La drame d'octobre 1961. Paris, 1999.

Brunner, José, Norbert Frei and Constantin Goscher. Eds. *Die Praxis der Wiedergutmachung: Geschichte, Erfahrung und Wirkung in Deutschland und Israel*. Göttingen, 2009.

Bruscino Jr., Thomas A. 'Out of Bounds: Transnational Sanctuary in Irregular Warfare'. *Global War on Terrorism Occasional Paper* 17. Fort Leavenworth KA, 2006.

Bülow, Mathilde von. 'Exposing the "Paradoxical Citizenship": French Authorities' Responses to the Algerian Presence in Federal Germany during the Algerian War, 1954–1962'. In *The French Colonial Mind. Vol.2: Violence, Military Encounters, and Colonialism*. Ed. Martin Thomas. Lincoln NB, 2011, pp. 304–33.

'Franco-German Intelligence Cooperation and the Internationalization of Algeria's War of Independence (1954–62)'. *Intelligence and National Security* 28/3 (2013), pp. 397–419.

'Hôtes importuns. Des Algériens en République fédérale pendant la guerre d'Algérie'. In *Migrations et identités. L'exemple de l'Allemagne aux XIXe et XXe siècles*. Ed. Jean-Paul Cahn and Bernard Poloni. Villeneuve d'Ascq, 2009, pp. 119–29.

'Irving Brown and ICFTU Labor Diplomacy during Algeria's Struggle for Independence (1954–1962)'. In *American Labor's Global Ambassadors: The International History of the AFL-CIO during the Cold War*. Ed. Geert van Goethem and Robert A. Waters Jr. Basingstoke, 2013, pp. 217–36.

'Myth or Reality? The Red Hand and French Covert Action in Federal Germany during the Algerian War, 1956–61'. *Intelligence and National Security* 22/6 (2007), pp. 787–820.

'The Telefunken Affair and the Internationalization of the Algerian War 1957–1959'. *Journal of Strategic Studies* 28/4 (2005), pp. 703–29.

Buettner, Friedemann. 'Germany's Middle East Policy: The Dilemmas of a "Policy of Even-Handedness" *(Politik der Ausgewogenheit)*'. In *Germany and the Middle East. Past, Present, and Future*. Ed. Haim Goren. Jerusalem, 2003, pp. 115–60.

Buffet, Cyril. 'De Gaulle et Berlin. Une certaine idée de l'Allemagne'. *Revue d'Allemagne et de pays de langue allemande* 22/4 (1990), pp. 525–38.

Burgelin, Henri. 'Le mythe de l'ennemi héréditaire dans les relations franco-allemandes'. *Documents: Revue des Questions Allemandes* (1979), pp. 76–88.

Burke, Roland. *Decolonization and the Evolution of International Human Rights*. Philadelphia, 2010.

Busch, Heiner et al. *Die Polizei in der Bundesrepublik*. Frankfurt/M, 1985.

Buschfort, Wolfgang. *Geheime Hüter der Verfassung: von der Düsseldorfer Informationsstelle zum ersten Verfassungsschutz der Bundesregierung (1947–1961)*. Paderborn, 2004.

Byman, Daniel. *Deadly Connections: States that Sponsor Terrorism*. Cambridge, 2005.

Byman, Daniel, Peter Chalk, Bruce Hoffman and William Rosenau. *Trends in Outside Support for Insurgent Movements*. Santa Monica CA, 2001.

Byrne, Jeffrey J. 'Algiers between Bandung and Belgrade: Guerrilla Diplomacy and the Evolution of the Third World Movement, 1954–1962'. In *The Middle East and the Cold War: Between Security and Development*. Eds. Matteo Gerlini and Massimiliano Trentin. Newcastle-upn-Tyne, 2012, pp. 11–28.

'Négociation perpetuelle: de Gaulle et le FLN 1961–1968'. In *De Gaulle et l'Algérie, 1943–1969*. Ed. Maurice Vaïsse. Paris, 2012, pp. 299–312.

'Our Own Special Brand of Socialism: Algeria and the Contest of Modernities in the 1960s'. *Diplomatic History* 33/3 (2009), pp. 427-47.

Cahn, Jean-Paul and Klaus-Jürgen Müller. 'Die Bundesrepublik Deutschland, Frankreich und der Algerienkrieg'. In *Die Herausforderung des Globalen in der Ära Adenauer*. Ed. Eckart Conze. Bonn, 2010, pp. 147–55.

'Le parti social-démocrate allemand face à la guerre d'Algérie (1958–1962)'. *Revue d'Allemagne et des pays de langue allemande* 31/3–4 (1999), pp. 589–602.

Le parti social-démocrate et la fin de la Quatrième République française (1954–1958). Bern, 1996.

La République fédérale d'Allemagne et la Guerre d'Algérie (1954–1962): perception, implication et retombées diplomatiques. Paris, 2003.

'La République fédérale d'Allemagne et la question de la présence d'allemands dans la Légion étrangère française dans le contexte de la guerre d'Algérie (1954–1962)'. *Guerres mondiales et conflits contemporains* 186 (1997), pp. 95–120.

Le Second Retour: le rattachement de la Sarre à l'Allemagne, 1955–1957. Bern, 1985.

Campana, Aurélie and Benjamin Ducol. 'Rethinking Terrorist Safe Havens: Beyond a State-Centric Approach'. *Civil Wars* 13/4 (2011), pp. 396–413.

Cann, John P. 'Securing the Borders of Angola, 1961–1974'. *Revista Militar* 2495 (2009), www.revistamilitar.pt/artigo.php?art_id=531 (accessed 12 December 2014).

Canoy, Jose R. *The Discreet Charm of the Police State: The Landpolizei and the Transformation of Bavaria, 1945–1965*. Leiden, 2007.

Cantier, Jacques. *L'Algérie sous le régime de Vichy*. Paris, 2002.

Carron, Damien. *La Suisse et la guerre d'indépendance algérienne (1954–1962)*. Lausanne, 2013.

Celeski, Joseph D. 'Attacking Insurgent Space: Sanctuary Denial and Border Interdiction'. *Military Review* 86/6 (2006), pp. 51–7.

Cerny, P.G. *The Politics of Grandeur. Ideological Aspects of de Gaulle's Foreign Policy*. Cambridge, 1980.

Chapeu, Sybille. *Des chrétiens dans la guerre d'Algérie: l'action de la Mission de France*. Paris, 2004.

Chaubin, Hélène and Laurent Chevrel. 'Identifier les nationalistes algériens: les fichiers Z'. In *La France en guerre 1954–1962. Expériences métropolitaines de la guerre d'indépendance algérienne*. Ed. Raphaëlle Branche and Sylvie Thénault. Paris, 2008, pp. 332–39.

Checkel, Jeffrey T. Ed. *Transnational Dynamics of Civil War*. Cambridge, 2013.

Cheong, Yong Mun. *The Indonesian Revolution and the Singapore Connection, 1945–1949*. Singapore, 2004.

Chikh, Slimane. *L'Algérie en armes ou le temps des certitudes*. Paris, 1981.

Choueiri, Youssef M. *Arab Nationalism: A History*. Oxford, 2000.

Clark, Michael K. *Algeria in Turmoil: A History of the Rebellion*. New York, 1959.

Clarkson, Alexander. *Fragmented Fatherlands: Immigration and Cold War Conflict in the Federal Republic of Germany, 1945–1980*. New York, 2013.

Cogan, Charles G. 'France, the United States and the Invisible Algerian Outcome'. *Journal of Strategic Studies* 25/2 (2002), pp. 138–58.

Cohen, William B. 'The Algerian War and the Revision of France's Overseas Mission'. *French Colonial History* 4 (2003), pp. 227–39.

Cointet, Michèle. *De Gaulle et l'Algérie française, 1958–1962*. Villeneuve-d'Ascq, 1995.

Conklin, Alice L. *A Mission to Civilize: The Republican Idea of Empire in France and West Africa, 1895–1930*. Stanford CA, 1997.

Connelly, Matthew. *A Diplomatic Revolution: Algeria's Fight for Independence and the Origins of the Post-Cold War Era*. Oxford, 2002.

'Rethinking the Cold War and Decolonization: The Grant Strategy of the Algerian War of Independence'. *International Journal of Middle East Studies* 33/2 (2001), pp. 221–45.

'Taking off the Cold War Lens: Visions of North-South Conflict during the Algerian War for Independence'. *American Historical Review* 105/3 (2000), pp. 739–69.

Conrad, Sebastian. *Deutsche Kolonialgeschichte*. Munich, 2008.

Conze, Eckart. 'La coopération franco-germano-italienne dans le domaine nucléaire dans les années 1957–1958: un point de vue allemand?' *Revue d'Histoire Diplomatique* 1/2 (1990), pp. 115–32.

Die gaullistische Herausforderung. Die deutsch-französischen Beziehungen in der amerikanischen Europapolitik 1958–1963. Munich, 1995.

Die Suche nach Sicherheit. Eine Geschichte der Bundesrepublik Deutschland von 1945 bis in die Gegenwart. Munich, 2009.

Corum, James S. *Bad Strategies: How Major Powers Fail in Counterinsurgency*. Minneapolis MN, 2008.

Courrière, Yves. 'La chasse aux trafiquants d'armes'. *Historia. Hors série* 23 (1971), pp. 95–103.

Cradock, Christopher and M.L.R. Smith. '"No Fixed Values". A Reinterpretation of the Influence of the Theory of *Guerre Révolutionnaire* and the Battle of Algiers, 1956–1957'. *Journal of Cold War History* 9/4 (2007), pp. 68–105.

Craig, Gordon A. 'Konrad Adenauer and his Diplomats'. In *The Diplomats 1939–1979*. Eds. Gordon A. Craig and Francis L. Loewenheim. Princeton NJ, 1994, pp. 201–27.

Crenshaw Hutchinson, Martha. *Revolutionary Terrorism: The FLN in Algeria, 1954–1962*. Stanford CA, 1978.

Creswell, Michael H. and Dieter H. Kollmer. 'Power, Preference, or Ideas? Explaining West Germany's Armaments Strategy, 1955–1972'. *Journal of Cold War Studies* 15/4 (2013), pp. 55–103.

Damm, Ulrich. *Versuch einer Darstellung der politischen Beziehungen der Bundesrepublik Deutschland zu den Entwicklungsländern unter besonderer Berücksichtigung der Entwicklungshilfe*. Geneva, 1965.

Dard, Olivier. *Voyage au coeur de l'OAS*. Paris, 2005.

Darwin, John. *The Empire Project: The Rise and Fall of the British World System*. Cambridge, 2009.

Davis, Belinda. 'What's Left? Popular Political Participation in Postwar Europe'. *American Historical Review* 113/2 (2008), pp. 363–90.

Dawisha, Adeed. *Arab Nationalism in the Twentieth Century*. Princeton NJ, 2003.

Dedinger, Béatrice. 'L'Allemagne, l'association des pays et territoires d'outre-mer français et la politique communautaire de développement'. *Revue d'Allemagne et des Pays de langue allemande* 31/3–4 (1999), pp. 497–508.

Derder, Peggy. *L'immigration algérienne et les pouvoirs publics dans le département de la Seine 1954–1962*. Paris, 2003.

Derradji, Abder-Rahmane. *The Algerian Guerrilla Campaign: Strategy and Tactics*. Lewiston NY, 1997.

Deschamps, Bernard. *Le Fichier Z, Essai d'histoire du FLN algérien dans le Gard (1954–1962)*. Pantin, 2004.

Descamps, Pascal. 'La politique algérienne du gouvernement Mollet: de la cohérence à l'enlisement'. In *Guy Mollet. Un camarade en république*. Eds. Bernard Ménager et al. Lille, 1987, pp. 463–74.

Dickinson, Edward R. 'The German Empire: An Empire?' *History Workshop Journal* 66 (2008), pp. 129–62.

Dine, Philip. 'French Culture and the Algerian War: Mobilizing Icons'. *Journal of European Studies* 28/1 (1998), pp. 51–68.

Djeghloul, Abdelkader. 'Hors-la-loi, violence rurale et pouvoir colonial en Algérie au début du XXe siècle: les frères Boutouizerat'. *Revue de l'Occident musulman et de la Méditerranée* 38/1 (1984), pp. 37–45.

Djerbal, Daho. *L'Organisation Spéciale de la Fédération de France du FLN: Histoire de la lutte armée du FLN en France (1956–1962)*. Alger, 2012.

Doering-Manteuffel, Anselm. *Die Bundesrepublik in der Ära Adenauer: Außenpolitik und innere Entwicklung, 1949–1963*. Darmstadt, 1983.

Doise, Jean and Maurice Vaïsse. *Diplomatie et outil militaire, 1871–1969*. Paris, 1987.

Doneux, Jean L. and Hugues Le Paige. *Le Front du Nord. Des Belges dans la guerre d'Algérie (1954–1962)*. Bruxelles, 1992.

Dreyfus, François-Georges. 'Les Allemagnes contre l'Algérie française'. *Revue d'Allemagne et de Pays de langue allemande* 31/3–4 (1999), pp. 533–40.

Driss, Rachid. 'Le mouvement de résistance du Maghreb arabe au Caire après la Deuxième Guerre Mondiale'. *Les Cahiers de Tunisie: Revue de Sciences Humaines* 29/117–118 (1981), pp. 295–36.

Droz, Bernard and Evelyne Lever. *Histoire de la guerre d'Algérie 1954–1962*. Paris, 1982.

Durand, Étienne de. 'France'. In *Understanding Counterinsurgency Warfare: Origins, Operations, Challenges*. Eds. Thomas Rid and Thomas Keaney. Abingdon and New York, 2010, pp. 11–27.

Eibl, Franz. *Politik der Bewegung: Gerhard Schröder als Außenminister 1961-1966*. Munich, 2001.

Einaudi, Jean-Luc. *Octobre 1961: un massacre à Paris*. Paris, 2001.

Ellis, Stephen. *External Mission: The ANC in Exile, 1960–1990*. New York, 2013.

Elsenhans, Hartmut. *Frankreichs Algerienkrieg. Entkolonialisierungsversuch einer kapitalistischen Metropole. Zum Zusammenbruch der Kolonialreiche.* Munich, 1974.

End, Heinrich. *Zweimal deutsche Außenpolitik. Internationale Dimensionen des innerdeutschen Konflikts 1949–72.* Cologne, 1973.

Engel, Ulf and Hans-Georg Schleicher. *Die beiden deutschen Staaten in Afrika: Zwischen Konkurrenz und Koexistenz 1949–1990.* Hamburg, 1998.

Engelmann, Bernt. *Meine Freunde die Waffenhändler. Kleine Kriege, Große Geschäfte.* Bergisch Gladbach, 1964.

English, Richard. *Armed Struggle: A History of the IRA.* Basingstoke, 2004.

Ersoy, Eyüp. 'Turkish Foreign Policy Toward the Algerian War of Independence'. *Turkish Studies* 13/4 (2012), pp. 683–95.

Evans, Martin. *Algeria: France's Undeclared War.* Oxford, 2011.

'Guy Mollet's Third Way: National Renewal and the French Civilizing Mission in Algeria'. In *French History and Civilisation. Papers from the George Rudé Seminar.* Vol. 2. Ed. Vesna Drapac and André Lambelet (2009), pp. 169–180.

The Memory of Resistance. French Opposition to the Algerian War (1954–1962). Oxford and New York, 1997.

Faivre, Maurice. *Le Renseignement dans la guerre d'Algérie.* Panazol, 2006.

'Le renseignement dans la guerre d'Algérie'. In *Militaires et guérilla dans la guerre d'Algérie.* Eds. Jean-Charles Jauffret and Maurice Vaïsse. Bruxelles, 2001, pp. 291–309.

Faligot, Roger and Rémi Kauffer. *Le Croissant et la Croix gammée. Les secrets de l'alliance entre l'Islam et le Nazisme d'Hitler à nos jours.* Paris, 1990.

Faligot, Roger and Pascal Krop. *DST. Police Secrète.* Paris, 1999.

La Piscine. Les services secrets français, 1944–1985. Paris, 1985.

Faure, Claude. *Aux Services de la République. Du BCRA à la DGSE.* Paris, 2004.

Favrod, Charles-Henri. 'La Suisse des négociations secrètes'. In *La Guerre d'Algérie et français.* Ed. Jean-Pierre Rioux. Paris, 1990, pp. 397–401.

Fedorowich, Kent and Martin Thomas. Eds. *International Diplomacy and Colonial Retreat.* London, 2001.

Fleury, Georges. *Histoire secrète de l'O.A.S.* Paris, 2003.

Forcade, Olivier. 'Michel Debré et les fins politiques du renseignement'. In *Michel Debré. Premier Ministre, 1959–1962.* Eds. Serge Berstein, Pierre Milza and Jean-François Sirinelli. Paris, 2005, pp. 489–513.

Frank, Nikolaus. 'Weltweite Caritas'. In *Menschlichkeit als Spiritualität. Georg Hüssler zum 85. Geburtstag.* Ed. Deutscher Caritasverband. Freiburg, 2006, pp. 113–25.

Frank, Robert. 'Michel Debré et l'Europe'. In *Michel Debré. Premier Ministre, 1959–1962.* Eds. Serge Berstein, Pierre Milza and Jean-François Sirinelli. Paris, 2005, pp. 297–314.

Frémeaux, Jacques. *Le Monde arabe et la sécurité de la France depuis 1958.* Paris, 1995.

Feldman, Lily Gardner. *Germany's Foreign Policy of Reconciliation: From Enmity to Amity.* Lanham MD, 2012.

Fichter, Tilman and Siegward Lönnendonker. *Kleine Geschichte des SDS: der Sozialistische Deutsche Studentenbund von Helmut Schmidt bis Rudi Dutschke*, 4th edn. Essen, 2007.

Fickers, Andreas. 'Radio und Fernsehen als nationale Sozialisierungsinstanzen? Der Rundfunk im Rahmen der westdeutschen und französischen Wiederaufbaumodernisierung der 1950er Jahre'. In *Wandel und Integration. Deutsch-französische Annäherung der fünfziger Jahre*. Eds. Hélène Miard-Delacroix und Rainer Hudemann. Munich, 2005, pp. 291–308.

Fischer-Tiné, Harald. 'Indian Nationalism and the "World Forces": Transnational and Diasporic Dimensions of the Indian Freedom Movement on the Eve of the First World War'. *Journal of Global History* 2/3 (2007), pp. 325–44.

Follorou, Jacques and Vincent Nouzille. *Les Parrains Corses: leur histoire, leurs réseaux, leurs protections*. Paris, 2006.

Fontaine, Darcie. 'Treason or Charity? Christian Missions on Trial and the Decolonization of Algeria'. *International Journal of Middle East Studies* 44 (2012), pp. 733–53.

Forschungsstelle für Zeitgeschichte in Hamburg. Ed. *'Kampf dem Atomtod!': Die Protestbewegung 1957/58 in zeithistorischer und gegenwärtiger Perspektive*. Munich, 2009.

Fraleigh, Arnold. 'The Algerian Revolution as a Case Study in International Law'. In *The International Law of Civil War*. Ed. Richard Falk. Baltimore ML, 1971, pp. 179–243.

Fraser, Cary. 'An American Dilemma: Race and Realpolitik in the American Response to the Bandung Conference'. In *Window on Freedom: Race, Civil Rights, and Foreign Affairs, 1945–1988*. Ed. B.G. Plummer. Chapel Hill NC, 2003, pp. 115–140.

'Decolonization and the Cold War'. In *The Oxford Handbook of the Cold War*. Ed. R.H. Immerman and P. Goedde. Oxford, 2013, pp. 469–85.

Frey, Marc, R.W. Pruessen and T.T. Yong. Eds. *The Transformation of Southeast Asia: International Perspectives on Decolonization*. New York, 2003.

Friedrichsmeyer, Sara, Sara Lennox and Susanne Zantop. Eds. *The Imperialist Imagination: German Colonialism and its Legacy*. Ann Arbor, 1998.

Fuhrmann, Malte. *Der Traum vom deutschen Orient: zwei deutsche Kolonien im Osmanischen Reich 1851–1918*. Frankfurt/Main, 2006.

Gallarotti, Giulio. 'Soft Power: What is it, Why It's Important, and the Conditions Under Which it Can Be Effectively Used'. *Journal of Political Power* 4/1 (2011), pp. 25–47.

Gallisot, René. 'La décolonisation du Maghreb: de l'Afrique du Nord française au Maghreb en suspens'. In *La guerre d'Algérie 1954–2004. La fin de l'amnésie*. Ed. Mohammed Harbi and Benjamin Stora. Paris, 2004, pp. 63–106.

Gearson, John P.S. and Kori Schake. Eds. *The Berlin Wall Crisis: Perspectives on Cold War Alliances*. New York, 2002.

Geiger, Tim. *Atlantiker gegen Gaullisten: außenpolitischer Konflikt und innerparteilicher Machtkampf in der CDU/CSU 1958–1969*. Munich, 2008.

Genève, Pierre. *La Main Rouge*. Paris, 1960.

Gerwarth, Robert and Stephan Malinowski. 'Hannah Arendt's Ghosts: Reflections on the Disputable Path from Windhoek to Auschwitz'. *Central European History* 42/2 (2009), pp. 279–300.

Geyer, Michael. 'Cold War Angst: The Case of West-German Opposition to Rearmament and Nuclear Weapons'. In *The Miracle Years. A Cultural History of West Germany, 1949–1968*. Ed. Hanna Schissler. Princeton NJ, 2001, pp. 376–408.

Ginio, Ruth. *French Colonialism Unmasked. The Vichy Years in French West Africa*. Lincoln NB, 2008.

Girardet, Raoul. Ed. *La crise militaire française, 1942–1962: Aspects sociologiques et idéologiques*. Paris, 1964.

L'idée colonial en France de 1871 à 1962. Paris, 1972.

Girault, René. 'La France en accusation à l'ONU, ou les pouvoirs d'une organisation internationale'. *Relations Internationales* 76 (1993), pp. 411–22.

Gleditsch, Kristian S. 'Transnational Dimensions of Civil War'. *Journal of Peace Research* 44/3 (2007), pp. 293–309.

Glowczewski, Xavier de. 'La guerre d'Algérie au miroir de la presse allemande (1958–1962)'. *Revue d'Allemagne et de pays de langue allemande* 31/3–4 (1999), pp. 541–53.

Goldsmith, Christopher. 'The British Embassy in Paris and the Algerian War: An Uncomfortable Partner?' *Journal of Strategic Studies* 25/2 (2002), pp. 159–71.

Goscha, Christopher E. and Christian Ostermann. Eds. *Connecting Histories: Decolonization and the Cold War in Southeast Asia*. Stanford CA, 2009.

Goschler, Constantin. *Schuld und Schulden: Die Politik der Wiedergutmachung für NS-Verfolgte seit 1945*. Göttingen, 2005.

Göttsche, Dirk. *Remembering Africa: The Rediscovery of Colonialism in Contemporary German Literature*. Rochester NY and Woodbridge, 2013.

Gray, William G. *Germany's Cold War. The Global Campaign to Isolate East Germany, 1949–1969*. Chapel Hill and London, 2003.

Grosse, Pascal. *Kolonialismus, Eugenik und bürgerliche Gesellschaft in Deutschland, 1850–1914*. Frankfurt/Main, 2000.

Grosser, Alfred. 'La France en Occident et en Algérie'. In *La guerre d'Algérie et les français*. Ed. Jean-Pierre Rioux. Paris, 1990, pp. 382–88.

Großmann, Johannes. *Die Internationale der Konservativen. Transnationale Elitenzirkel und private Außenpolitik in Westeuropa seit 1945*. Munich, 2014.

'Vom 'christilichen Kominform' zur 'geistigen Nato'. Das Internationale Comité zur Verteidigung der Christlichen Kultur als transnationale antikommunistische Propagandaagentur'. *Jahrbuch für Historische Kommunismusforschung* (2011), pp. 139–54.

Guillon, Jacques. 'La contrabande des armes pendant la guerre d'Algérie'. *Revue Historique des Armées* 200 (1995), pp. 105–18.

Gunkel, Markus. *Der Kampf gegen die Remilitarisierung: Friedensbewegung in Hamburg 1950 bis 1955*. Frankfurt/Main, 2009.

Gupta, Amit Das. 'Ulbricht am Nil. Die deutsch-deutsche Rivalität in der Dritten Welt'. In *Das doppelte Deutschland. 40 Jahre Systemkonkurrenz*. Eds. Udo Wengst and Hermann Wentker. Bonn, 2008, pp. 111–33.

Haas, Eric J. 'Operations at the Border: Efforts to Disrupt Insurgent Safe-Havens'. *Art of War Papers*. Fort Leavenworth KA: US Army Command and General Staff College, 2011.

Haas, Gregor. *Die Auslieferung in Frankreich und Deutschland*. Berlin, 2000.

Hacke, Christian. 'Nationales Interesse als Handlungsmaxime für die Außenpolitik Deutschlands'. In *Deutschlands neue Außenpolitik. Bd. 3: Interessen und Strategien*. Ed. Karl Kaiser and Joachim Krause. Oldenbourg, 1996, pp. 3–13.

Weltmacht wider Willen: die Außenpolitik der Bundesrepublik Deutschland. Stuttgart, 1988.

Haddad-Fonda, Kyle. 'An Illusory Alliance: Revolutionary Legitimacy and Sino-Algerian Relations, 1958–1962'. *Journal of North African Studies* 19/3 (2014), pp. 338–57.

Häde, Ulrich. 'Die Auslieferung – Rechtsinstitut zwischen Völkerrecht und Grundrechten'. *Der Staat* 36/1 (1997), pp. 1–26.

Hadhri, Mohieddine. *L'URSS et le Maghreb: De la révolution d'octobre à l'indépendance de l'Algérie, 1917–1962*. Paris, 1985.

Haftendorn, Helga. *Deutsche Außenpolitik zwischen Selbstbeschränkung und Selbstbehauptung*. Stuttgart, 2001.

Sicherheit und Entspannung: zur Außenpolitik der Bundesrepublik Deutschland, 1955–1982. Baden-Baden, 1983.

Hagen, Gottfried. 'German Heralds of Holy War: Orientalists and Applied Oriental Studies'. *Comparative Studies of South Asia, Africa and the Middle East* 24/2 (2004), pp. 145–62.

Haleh Davis, Muriam. 'Restaging Mise en Valeur: "Postwar Imperialism" and the Plan de Constantine'. *Review of Middle East Studies* 44/2 (2010), pp. 176–86.

Haller, Oliver. 'German Industry, the Cold War, and the Bundeswehr'. In *Rearming Germany*. Ed. J.S. Corum. Leiden, 2011, pp. 145–75.

Hamon, Hervé and Patrick Rotman. *Les Porteurs de Valises: la résistance française à la guerre d'Algérie*. Paris, 1979.

Hannoum, Abdelmajid. 'The Historiographic State: How Algeria once Became French'. *History and Anthropology* 19/2 (2008), pp. 91–114.

Hanrieder, Wolfram F. *Deutschland, Europa, Amerika. Die Außenpolitik der Bundesrepublik Deutschland 1949–1994*, 2nd edn. Paderborn, 1995.

'The Foreign Policy of the Federal Republic of Germany, 1949–1989'. *German Studies Review* XII/2 (1989), pp. 311–32.

Hansen, Peo and Stefan Jonsson. 'Bringing Africa as a "Dowry to Europe"', *Interventions* 13/3 (2011), pp. 443–63.

Harbi, Mohammed. *Aux origines du FLN: Le populisme révolutionnaire en Algérie*. Paris, 1975.

1954. La guerre commence en Algérie. Brussels, 1984.

Le FLN, mirage ou réalité: des origines à la prise du pouvoir (1945–1962), 2nd edn. Paris, 1985.

and Stora Benjamin. 'La guerre d'Algérie: de la mémoire à l'Histoire'. In *La guerre d'Algérie 1954–2004. La fin de l'amnésie*. Ed. Mohammed Harbi and Stora Benjamin. Paris, 2004, pp. 9–16.

Harnden, Toby. *Bandit Country: The IRA and South Armagh*. London, 1999.

Harrison, Alexander. *Challenging de Gaulle: The O.A.S. and the Counterrevolution in Algeria, 1954–1962*. New York, 1989.

Harrison, Christopher. 'French Attitudes to Empire and the Algerian War'. *African Affairs* 326 (1983), pp. 75–95.

Harrison, Hope M. *Driving the Soviets up the Wall: Soviet-East German relations, 1953–1961*. Princeton NJ, 2003.

Harrison, Martin. 'Government and Press in France during the Algerian War'. *American Political Science Review* 58/2 (1964), pp. 273–85.

Hazen, Jennifer M. *What Rebels Want: Resources and Supply Networks in Wartime*. Ithaca NY, 2013.

Heggoy, Alf Andrew. *Insurgency and Counterinsurgency in Algeria*. Bloomington IN, 1972.

Hein, Bastian. *Die Westdeutschen und die Dritte Welt. Entwicklungspolitik und Entwicklungsdienste zwischen Reform und Revolte 1959–1974*. München, 2006).

Heine, Peter. 'Salih as-Sarif at-Tunisi, a North African Nationalist in Berlin during the First World War'. *Revue de l'Occident Musulman et de la Méditerranée* 33 (1982), pp. 89–95.

Heintzen, Markus. *Private Außenpolitik. Eine Typologie der grenzüberschreitenden Aktivitäten gesellschaftlicher Kräfte und ihres Verhältnisses zur staatlichen Außenpolitik*. Baden-Baden, 1988.

Henissart, Paul. *Wolves in the City: The Death of French Algeria*. New York, 1970.

Henker, Fritz. 'Algerische Arbeiter in der Bundesrepublik Deutschland'. *Zeitschrift für Kulturaustausch* 20/2 (1970), pp. 233–36.

Henssler, Vera. 'Für die Propaganda nach dem Orient ist bei weitem die wirksamste Waffe der Rundfunk: NS-Auslandspropaganda in den Nahen Osten und Nordafrika'. *Zeitschrift für Geschichtswissenschaft* 59/11 (2011), pp. 920–37.

Herbert, Ulrich. *Geschichte der Ausländerpolitik in Deutschland. Saisonarbeiter, Zwangsarbeiter, Gastarbeiter, Flüchtlinge*. 2nd edn. Bonn, 2003.

and Karin Hunn. 'Guest Workers and Policy on Guest Workers in the Federal Republic. From the Beginnings of Recruitment in 1955 until its Halt in 1973'. In *The Miracle Years. A Cultural History of West Germany, 1949–1968*. Ed. Hanna Schissler. Princeton NJ, 2001, pp. 187–218.

Herbst, Ludolf. *Option für den Westen: vom Marshallplan bis zum deutsch-französischen Vertrag*. München, 1989.

Herf, Jeffrey. *Nazi Propaganda in the Arab World*. New Haven CT, 2009.

Hervo, Monique. *Chroniques du bidonville: Nanterre en guerre d'Algérie 1959–1962*. Paris, 2001.

Hildebrand, Klaus. '"Atlantiker" versus "Gaullisten". Zur Außenpolitik der Bundesrepublik Deutschland während der sechziger Jahre'. *Revue d'Allemagne et des Pays de langue allemande* 23/4 (1990), pp. 583–92.

Integration und Souveränität: die Außenpolitik der Bundesrepublik Deutschland, 1949–1982. Bonn, 1991.

Hill, Christopher. 'World Opinion and the Empire of Circumstance'. *International Affairs* 72/1 (1996), pp. 109–131.

Hoffman, Bruce. *Inside Terrorism*. Rev. edn. New York, 2006.

Hong, Young-sun. '"The Benefits of Health Must Spread Among All": International Solidarity, Health and Race in the East German Encounter with the Third World'. In *Socialist Modern: East German Everyday Culture and Politics*. Ed. Katherine Pence and Paul Betts. Ann Arbor MI, 2008, pp. 183–210.

Cold War Germany, the Third World, and the Global Humanitarian Regime. Cambridge, 2015.

'Kalter Krieg in der Ferne. Dekolonisierung, Hygienediskurse und der Kampf der DDR und der USA um die Dritte Welt'. In *Umworbener Klassenfeind. Das Verhältnis der DDR zu den USA*. Ed. Uta A. Balbier and Christiane Rösch. Berlin, 2006, pp. 77–95.

Hopkirk, Peter. *On Secret Service East of Constantinople: The Plot to Bring Down the British Empire*. London, 1994.

Höpp, Gerhard. 'Frontenwechsel: Muslimische Deserteure im Ersten und Zweiten Weltkrieg und in der Zwischenkriegszeit'. In *Fremdeneinsätze. Afrikaner und Asiaten in europäischen Kriegen 1914–1945*. Eds. Gerhard Höpp and Brigitte Reinwald. Berlin, 2000, pp. 129–42.

Muslime an der Mark: als Kriegsgefangene und Internierte in Wünsdorf und Zossen 1914–1924. Berlin, 1997.

and Peter Wien, René Wildangel. Eds. *Blind für die Geschichte? Arabische Begegnungen mit dem Nationalsozialismus*. Berlin, 2004.

Horne, Alistair. *The French Army and Politics, 1870–1970*. London, 1984.

A Savage War of Peace: Algeria, 1954–1962, 4th edn. London, 2002.

Hough, Jerry F. *The Struggle for the Third World: Soviet Debates and American Options*. Washington, 1986.

House, Jim and Neil MacMaster, 'La Fédération de France du FLN et l'organisation du 17 Octobre 1961'. *Vingtième Siècle* 83 (2004), pp. 145–60.

Paris 1961: Algerians, State Terror and Post-Colonial Memories. Oxford, 2006.

Hudemann, Rainer. 'Französische Besatzungsmacht und deutsche Bevölkerung nach zwei Weltkriegen'. In *Politischer Wandel, organisierte Gewalt und nationale Sicherheit. Beiträge zur neueren Geschichte Deutschlands und Frankreichs. Festschrift für Klaus-Jürgen Müller*. Eds. Ernst Willi Hansen, Gerhard Schreiber und Bernd Wegner. Munich, 1995, pp. 427–45.

Hull, Isabel. *Absolute Destruction: Military Culture and the Practice of War in Imperial Germany*. Ithaca, 2005.

Hünseler, Peter. *Die außenpolitischen Beziehungen der Bundesrepublik Deutschland zu den arabischen Staaten von 1949–1980*. Frankfurt/Main, 1990.

Hyam, Ronald *Britain's Declining Empire: The Road to Decolonisation, 1918–1968*. Cambridge, 2007.

Imlay, Talbot. 'International Socialism and Decolonization during the 1950s: Competing Rights and the Postcolonial Order', *American Historical Review* 118/4 (2013), pp. 1105–1132.

'"The Policy of Social Democracy is Self-consciously Internationalist": The German Social Democratic Party's Internationalism after 1945'. *Journal of Modern History* 86/1 (2014), pp. 81–123.

Innes, Michael A. 'Deconstructing Political Orthodoxies on Insurgent and Terrorist Sanctuaries'. *Studies in Conflict & Terrorism* 31 (2008), pp. 251–67.

Ed. *Denial of Sanctuary: Understanding Terrorist Safe Havens.* Westport CT, 2007.

'Protected Status, Sacred Sites, Black Holes and Human Agents'. Special Issue of *Civil Wars* 10/1 (2008), pp. 1–6.

Jalali, Ali Ahmad and Lester Grau. *The Other Side of the Mountain: Mujahideen Tactics in the Soviet-Afghan War.* Fort Leavenworth KS, 1995.

Jarausch, Konrad H. and Michael Geyer, *Shattered Past: Reconstructing German Histories.* Princeton NJ, 2003.

Jauffret, Jean-Charles. 'L'Armée et l'Algérie en 1954'. *Revue Historique des Armées* 187 (1992), pp. 15–25.

Jeismann, Michael. *Das Vaterland der Feinde: Studien zum nationalen Feindbegriff und Selbstverständnis in Deutschland und Frankreich, 1792–1918.* Stuttgart, 1992.

Jennings, Eric. *Vichy in the Tropics. Pétain's National Revolution in Madagascar, Guadeloupe and Indochina, 1940–1944.* Stanford CA, 2001.

Joesten, Joachim. *The Red Hand: The Sinister Account of the Terrorist Arm of the French Right-Wing 'Ultras' in Algeria and on the Continent.* London & New York, 1962.

Johnson, Ian. *A Mosque in Munich: Nazis, the CIA, and the Rise of the Muslim Brotherhood.* Boston and New York, 2010.

Kaddache, Mahfoud. *Histoire du nationalisme algérien, 1919–1951*, 2 Vols. 2nd edn. Algiers, 1993.

'Itinéraire d'un militant nationaliste: Ouamara Mohammed, dit 'Rachid'. In *Militaires et guérilla dans la guerre d'Algérie.* Eds. Jean-Charles Jauffret and Maurice Vaïsse. Paris, 2001, pp. 503–15.

'Les tournants de la guerre de libération au niveau des masses populaires'. In *La guerre d'Algérie et les Algériens 1954–1962*, Ed. Charles-Robert Ageron. Paris, 1997, pp. 51–70.

Kahleyss, Margot. *Muslime in Brandenburg: Kriegsgefangene im 1. Weltkrieg: Ansichten und Absichten.* Berlin, 2000.

'Muslimische Kriegsgefangene in Deutschland im Ersten Weltkrieg – Ansichten und Absichten'. In *Fremdeneinsätze. Afrikaner und Asiaten in europäischen Kriegen 1914–1945.* Eds. Gerhard Höpp and Brigitte Reinwald. Berlin, 2000, pp. 79–118.

Kaiser, Daniel. 'Transnationale Dimensionen antikolonialen Widerstands in Mosambik'. *Forschungsjournal Soziale Bewegungen* 27/3 (2014), pp. 38–45.

Kaiser, Karl. 'Transnationale Politik. Zu einer Theorie der multinationalen Politik'. In *Die anachronistische Souveränität. Zum Verhältnis von Innen-*

und Außenpolitik. Ed. Ernst-Otto Czempiel. Köln/Opladen, 1969, pp. 80–109.

Kaldor, Mary. *New and Old Wars: Organized Violence in a Global Era*, 3rd edn. Stanford CA, 2012.

Kalter, Christoph. 'Das Eigene im Fremden: Der Algerienkrieg und die Anfänge der Neuen Linken in der Bundesrepublik'. *Zeitschrift für Geschichtswissenschaft* 55/2 (2007), pp. 142–61.

Karabell, Zachary. *Architects of Intervention: The United States, the Third World, and the Cold War, 1946–1962*. Baton Rouge LA, 1999.

Keck, Margaret E. and Kathryn Sikkink, *Activists beyond Borders: Advocacy Networks in International Politics*. Ithaca NY, 1998.

Keller, Fritz. *Gelebter Internationalismus: Österreichs Linke und der algerische Widerstand (1958–1963)*. Wien, 2010.

Kelly, George A. *Lost Soldiers. The French Army and Empire in Crisis, 1947–1962*. Cambridge MA, 1965.

Keohane, Robert O. and Joseph Nye. Eds. *Transnational Relations and World Politics*. Cambridge MA, 1971.

Kessler, Jean. 'La surveillance des frontières maritimes de l'Algérie 1954–1962'. *Revue Historique des Armées* 187 (1992), pp. 94–101.

Khalidi, Rashid. 'Consequences of the Suez Crisis in the Arab World'. In *Suez 1956: The Crisis and its Consequences*. Eds. Wm. Roger Louis and Roger Owen. Oxford, 1989, pp. 377–92.

Kilian, Werner. *Die Hallstein-Doktrin. Der diplomatische Krieg zwischen der BRD und der DDR 1955–1972*. Berlin, 2001.

Kilcullen, David. 'Countering Global Insurgency'. *Journal of Strategic Studies* 28/4 (2005), pp. 597–617.

'Counter-insurgency Redux'. *Survival: Global Politics and Strategy* 48/4 (2006), pp. 111–30.

Kitson, Simon. *The Hunt for Nazi Spies: Fighting Espionage in Vichy France*. Chicago, 2008.

Kittel, Manfred. 'Wider «die Kolonialmacht der französischen Großkapitalisten und die Rüstungsmillionäre des Nordatlantikpakts»: SED und Algerienkrieg 1954–1962'. *Revue d'Allemagne et des Pays de langue allemande* 31/3–4 (1999), pp. 405–22.

Klimke, Martin. *The Other Alliance: Student Protest in West Germany and the United States in the Global Sixties*. Princeton NJ, 2009.

Klose, Fabian. *Menschenrechte im Schatten kolonialer Gewalt. Die Dekolonisierungskriege in Kenia und Algerien 1945–1962*. München, 2009.

Klotzbach, Kurt. *Der Weg zur Staatspartei: Programmatik, praktische Politik und Organisation der deutschen Sozialdemokratie 1945–1965*. Bonn, 1996.

Knortz, Heike. *Diplomatische Tauschgeschäfte: 'Gastarbeiter' in der westdeutschen Diplomatie und Beschäftigungspolitik 1953–1973*. Köln, 2008.

Kohser-Spohn, Christiane and Frank Renken Eds. *Trauma Algerienkrieg. Zur Geschichte und Aufarbeitung eines tabuisierten Konflikts*. Frankfurt/Main, 2005.

Koller, Christian. '*Von Wilden aller Rassen niedergemetzelt': Die Diskussion um die Verwendung von Kolonialtruppen in Europa zwischen Rassismus, Kolonial- und Militärpolitik (1914–1930).* Stuttgart, 2001.

Kollmer, Dieter H. 'Reasons of State: A Military and Foreign Trade Necessity. The International Mix of Armaments in the Build-up Phase of the Bundeswehr 1953–1958'. In *Rearming Germany*. Ed. J.S. Corum. Leiden, 2011, pp. 177–201.

Kolton, Randy J. *Isolating the Theatre of War: Operational Implications of Border Sanctuaries in Limited War*. Fort Leavenworth KA, 2014.

Koopmann, Martin. *Das schwierige Bündnis. Die deutsch-französischen Beziehungen und die Außenpolitik der Bundesrepublik Deutschland 1958–1965*. Baden-Baden, 2000.

Korteweg, Rem. 'Black Holes: On Terrorist Sanctuaries and Governmental Weakness'. *Civil Wars* 10/1 (2008), pp. 60–71.

Kröger, Martin. 'Revolution als Programm. Ziele und Realität deutscher Orientpolitik im Ersten Weltkrieg'. In *Der Erste Weltkrieg: Wirkung, Wahrnehmung, Analyse*. Ed. Wolfgang Michalka. Munich, 1994, pp. 366–91.

Kuck, Dennis. '"Für den sozialistischen Aufbau ihrer Heimat?" Ausländische Vertragsarbeitskräfte in der DDR'. In *Fremde und Fremd-Sein in der DDR. Zu den historischen Ursachen der Fremdenfeindlichkeit in Ostdeuschland*. Ed. Jan C. Behrends, Thomas Lindenberger and Patrice Poutrus. Berlin, 2003), pp. 271–82.

Kuhn, Raymond. *The Media in France*. London, 1995.

Kusterer, Hermann. *Der Kanzler und der General*. Stuttgart, 1995.

Kyle, Keith. *Suez. Britain's End of Empire in the Middle East*. London, 1991.

van Laak, Dirk. *Imperiale Infrastruktur. Deutsche Planungen für eine Erschließung Afrikas 1880 bis 1960*. Paderborn, 2004.

Über alles in der Welt. Deutscher Imperialismus im 19. und 20. Jahrhundert. München, 2005.

Lacouture, Jean. *De Gaulle. Le souverain, 1959–1970*. Paris, 1986.

De Gaulle. Le politique. Paris, 1985.

Lake David A. and Donald Rothchild. Eds. *The International Spread of Ethnic Conflict: Fear, Diffusion, and Escalation*. Princeton NJ, 1998.

Lappenküper, Ulrich. 'Adenauer, de Gaulle und der Algerienkrieg 1958–1962'. *Revue d'Allemagne et des Pays de langue allemande* 31/3–4 (1999), pp. 603–15.

Die Außenpolitik der Bundesrepublik Deutschland 1949 bis 1990. Munich, 2008.

Die deutsch-französischen Beziehungen, 1949–1963. Von der 'Erbfeindschaft' zur 'Entente élémentaire', Bd. 1–2. Munich, 2001.

'Diplomatische Faktoren: die deutsch-französische Annäherung im europäischen und transatlantischen Zusammenhang 1950–1958'. In *Wandel und Integration. Deutsch-französische Annäherungen der fünfziger Jahre*. Ed. Hélène Miard-Delacroix and Rainer Hudemann. München, 2005, pp. 69–86.

Large, D.C. *Germans to the Front: West German Rearmament in the Adenauer Era*. Chapel Hill NC, 1996.

Larsdotter, Kersti. 'Fighting Transnational Insurgents: The South African Defense Force in Namibia, 1966–1989'. *Studies in Conflict and Terrorism* 37/12 (2014), pp. 1024–38.

Lawrence, M.A. and F. Logevall. Eds. *The First Vietnam War: Colonial Conflict and Cold War Crisis*. Cambridge MA, 2007.

Lazreg, Marnia. *Torture and the Twilight of Empire: From Algiers to Baghdad*. Princeton NJ, 2008.

Lebovics, Herman. *True France: The Wars over Cultural Identity, 1900–1945*. Ithaca NY, 1991.

Lee, C.J. Ed. *Making a World after Empire: The Bandung Movement and its Political Afterlives*. Athens OH, 2010.

Lefeuvre, Daniel. 'Les réactions algériennes à la propagande économique pendant la guerre d'Algérie'. In *La guerre d'Algérie et les Algériens, 1954–1962*. Ed. Charles-Robert Ageron. Paris, 1997, pp. 231–44.

Lefèvre, Sylvie. 'Associer l'Allemagne au développement économique de l'Afrique: un leitmotiv français avant la décolonisation (1950–1956)'. *Revue d'Allemagne et des Pays de langue allemande* 31/3–4 (1999), pp. 463–80.

Leggewie, Claus. *Kofferträger. Das Algerienprojekt der Linken im Adenauer-Deutschland*. Berlin, 1984.

'Kofferträger: Das Algerien-Projekt in den 50er und 60er Jahren und die Ursprünge des "Internationalismus" in der Bundesrepublik'. *Politische Vierteljahresschrift* 25/1 (1984), pp. 169–87.

LeSueur, James D. *Uncivil War: Intellectuals and Identity Politics during the Decolonization of Algeria*. Philadelphia PA, 2001.

Linsel, Knut. *Charles de Gaulle und Deutschland 1914–1969*. Sigmaringen, 1998.

Lischer, Sarah K. *Dangerous Sanctuaries: Refugee Camps, Civil War, and the Dilemmas of Humanitarian Aid*. Ithaca NY, 2005.

Lodge, Tom. 'State of Exile: The African National Congress of South Africa, 1976–86'. *Third World Quarterly* 9/1 (1987), pp. 1–27.

Lorenzen, Jan. 'Die Haltung der DDR zum Suez-Krieg. Das Jahr 1956 als Zäsur in der Nahost-Politik der DDR'. *Deutschland Archiv* 28/3 (1995), pp. 278–85.

Loth, Wilfried and Robert Picht. 'De Gaulle und die europäische Einigung'. In *De Gaulle, Deutschland und Europa*. Ed. Wilfried Loth and Robert Picht. Opladen, 1991, pp. 45–60.

De Gaulle, Deutschland und Europa. Opladen, 1991.

Louis, Wm. R. *Ends of British Imperialism: The Scramble for Empire, Suez, and Decolonization*. London, 2006.

and R. Robinson. 'The Imperialism of Decolonization'. *Journal of Imperial and Commonwealth History* 22 (1994), pp. 462–511.

Lux, Michel. *La guerre d'Indochine, au 3e escadron monté du Cambodge, 1949–1951*. Nantes, 2009.

Lyons, Amelia H. 'The Civilizing Mission in the Metropole: Algerian Immigrants in France and the Politics of Adaptation during Decolonization'. *Geschichte & Gesellschaft* 32 (2006), pp. 489–516.

MacMaster, Neil. 'Identifying "Terrorists" in Paris. A Police Experiment with IBM Machines during the Algerian War'. *French Politics, Culture & Society* 28/3 (2010), pp. 23–45.

Colonial Migrants and Racism: Algerians in France, 1900–1962. Basingstoke, 1997.

Macmillan, Hugh. *The Lusaka Years: The ANC in Exile in Zambia, 1963–1994*. Jacana Media, 2013.

Madureira, Luís. 'Kalashnikovs, Not Coca-Cola, Bring Self-Determination to Angola: The Two Germanys, Lusophone Africa, and the Rhetoric of Colonial Difference'. In *German Colonialism: Race, the Holocaust, and Postwar Germany*. Eds. Volker Langbehn and Mohammed Salama. New York, 2011, pp. 275–93.

Malinowski, Stephan. 'Modernisierungskriege: Militärische Gewalt und koloniale Modernisierung im Algerienkrieg (1954–1962)'. *Archiv für Sozialgeschichte* 48 (2008), pp. 213–48.

Mameri, Khalfa. *Les Nations Unies face à la question algérienne*. Alger, 1970.

Manela, Erez. *The Wilsonian Moment. Self-Determination and the International Origins of Anticolonial Nationalism*. Oxford, 2007.

Marchand, Suzanne L. *German Orientalism in the Age of Empire: Religion, Race and Scholarship*. Cambridge, 2009.

Marcowitz, Reiner. '"Die Kommunisten stecken dahiner": Unionsparteien und Algerienkrieg (1954–62)', *Revue d'Allemagne et des Pays de langue allemande* 31/3–4 (1999), pp. 555–66.

Option für Paris? Unionsparteien, SPD und Charles de Gaulle 1958–1969. Munich, 1996.

and Hélène Miard-Delacroix. Eds. *50 Ans de relations franco-allemandes*. Paris, 2012.

Marshall, Alex. 'Imperial Nostalgia, the Liberal Lie, and the Perils of Postmodern Counterinsurgency'. *Small Wars & Insurgencies* 21/2 (2010), pp. 233–58.

Marshall, James. 'Citizen Diplomacy'. *American Political Science Review* 43/1 (1949), pp. 83–90.

Maß, Sandra. *Weiße Helden, schwarze Krieger. Zur Geschichte kolonialer Männlichkeit in Deutschland, 1918–1964*. Cologne, 2006.

Masset, Dominique. *Une Affaire Intérieure Française? La Belgique et la guerre d'Algérie (1954–1956)*. Louvain-la-Neuve, 1988.

Mayer, Frank. 'Adenauer and Kennedy: An Era of Distrust in German-American Relations?' *German Studies Review* 17/1 (1994), pp. 83-104.

Mazower, Mark. *No Enchanted Palace: The End of Empire and the Ideological Origins of the United Nations*. Princeton NJ, 2009.

McCormack, Jo. *Collective Memory: France and the Algerian War*. Lanham MD, 2007.

McDougall, James. *History and the Culture of Nationalism in Algeria*. Cambridge, 2006.

McMeekin, Sean. *The Berlin-Baghdad Express: The Ottoman Empire and Germany's Bid for World Power*. Cambridge MA, 2010.

el-Mechat, Samya. 'Les Etats-Unis, l'Algérie et l'équilibre stratégique 1954–1962'. In *La Guerre d'Algérie au miroir des décolonisations françaises*. Ed. Charles-Robert Ageron. Paris, 2000, pp. 343–60.

'L'Improbable "Nation Arabe". La Ligue des états arabes et l'indépendance du Maghreb (1945–1956)'. *Vingtième Siècle* 82 (2004), pp. 57–68.

Tunisie. Les chemins vers l'indépendance (1945–1956). Paris, 1992.

Mélandri, Pierre. 'La France et le «double jeu» des États-Unis'. In *La guerre d'Algérie et les français*. Ed. Jean-Pierre Rioux. Paris, 1990, pp. 429–50.

de Meneses, Filipe Ribeiro and Robert McNamara. 'The Last Throw of the Dice: Portugal, Rhodesia and South Africa, 1970–74'. *Portuguese Studies* 28/2 (2012), pp. 201–15.

Merom, Gil. *How Democracies Lose Small Wars: State, Society, and the Failures of France in Algeria, Israel in Lebanon, and the United States in Vietnam*. Cambridge, 2003.

Metzger, Chantal. *L'Empire colonial français dans la stratégie du troisième Reich (1936–1945)*. Paris, 2002.

Meynier, Gilbert. *L'Algérie Révélée*. Paris, 1981.

Histoire intérieure du FLN, 1954–1962. Paris, 2002.

'Problématique historique de la nation algérienne'. *NAQD. Revue d'études et de critique sociale* 14/15 (2001), pp. 39–52.

Miard-Delacroix, Hélène. *Question nationale allemande et nationalisme. Perceptions françaises d'une problématique allemande au début des années cinquante*. Lille, 2004.

Michels, Eckard. 'Die Bundesrepublik und die Unabhängigkeit Tunesiens und Marokkos 1951–1962'. *Revue d'Allemagne et de Pays de langue allemande* 31/3–4 (1999), pp. 439–52.

Deutsche in der Fremdenlegion 1870–1965. Mythen und Realitäten, 5th edn. Paderborn, 2006.

Miller, Michael B. *Shanghai on the Metro: Spies, Intrigue, and the French between the Wars*. Berkeley CA, 1994.

Mohand-Amer, Amar. 'L'Union générale des travailleurs algériens (UGTA) dans le processus de transition'. In *Le Maghreb et l'indépendance de l'Algérie*. Eds. Amar Mohand-Amer and Belkacem Benzenine. Oran, 2012, pp. 39–49.

Monarch, Robert M. 'Denying Sanctuary: Rejecting Safe Havens in Counterinsurgency Operations'. *Strategy Research Project*. US Army War College, 2009.

Montarsolo, Yves *L'Eurafrique contrepoint de l'idée d'Europe. Le cas français de la fin de la deuxième guerre mondiale aux négociations des Traités de Rome*. Aix-en-Provence, 2010.

Moore, Clement and Arlie Hochschild. 'Student Unions in North African Politics'. *Daedalus* 97/1 (1968), pp. 21–50.

Morapedi, Washa G. 'The Dilemmas of Liberation in Southern Africa: The Case of Zimbabwean Liberation Movements and Botswana, 1960–1979'. *Journal of Southern African Studies* 38/1 (2012), pp. 73–90.

Moravcsik, Andrew *The Choice for Europe: Social Purpose and State Power from Messina to Maastricht*. Ithaca NY, 1998.

Morelle, Chantal. 'Debré et l'Algérie. Quelle Algérie française ?' In *Michel Debré. Premier Ministre, 1959–1962*. Eds. Serge Berstein, Pierre Milza and Jean-François Sirinelli. Paris, 2005, pp. 449–69.

Motadel, David. *Islam and Nazi Germany's War*. Cambridge MA, 2014.

Moser, Thomas. *Europäische Integration, Dekolonisation, Eurafrika: eine historische Analyse über Entstehungsbedingungen der Eurafrikanischen Gemeinschaft von der Weltwirtschaftskrise bis zum Jaundé-Vertrag, 1929–1963*. Baden-Baden, 2000.

Muelle, Raymond. *7 ans de guerre en France. Quand le FLN frappait en métropole*. Monaco, 1994.

Müller, Herbert L. *Islam, Gihad ('Heiliger Krieg') und Deutsches Reich: Ein Nachspiel zur Wilhelminischen Weltpolitik im Maghreb, 1914–1918*. Frankfurt/Main, 1991.

Müller, Klaus-Jürgen. 'Die Bundesrepublik Deutschland und der Algerienkrieg'. *Vierteljahrshefte für Zeitgeschichte* 38/4 (1990), pp. 609–41.

'La guerre d'Algérie vue par la presse ouest-allemande'. *Relations internationales* 58 (1989), pp. 177–85.

'Le réalisme de la République fédérale d'Allemagne'. In *La Guerre d'Algérie et les Français*. Ed. Jean-Pierre Rioux. Paris, 1990, pp. 409–28.

'Suez 1956: Die Bundesrepublik zwischen London, Paris und Washington'. In *Grossbritannien und Deutschland. Gesellschaftliche, kulturelle und politische Beziehungen im 19. und 20. Jahrhundert*. Ed. Frank Otto and Thilo Schulz. Rheinfelden, 1999, pp. 195–210.

Müller Peter F. and Michael Mueller. *Gegen Freund und Feind. Der BND: Geheime Politik und schmutzige Geschäfte*. Reinbek, 2002.

Mumford, Andrew. *Proxy Warfare*. Cambridge, 2013.

el-Mustafa, Azzou. 'Le nationalisme Marocain et les États-Unis 1945–1956'. *Guerres mondiales et conflits contemporains* 177 (1995), pp. 131–8.

Muth, Ingrid. *Die DDR-Außenpolitik 1949–1972. Inhalte, Strukturen, Mechanismen*. Berlin, 2000.

Nalty, Bernard. *The War against Trucks: Aerial Interdiction in Southern Laos, 1968–1972*. Washington DC, 2005.

Narr, Wolf-Dieter et al. Eds. *Das andere Deutschland nach 1945 – als Pazifist, Sozialist und radikaler Demokrat in der Bundesrepublik Deutschland – Klaus Vack*. Köln, 2005.

Ndumbe, Kum'a. *Was will Bonn in Afrika? Zur Afrikapolitik der Bundesrepublik Deutschland*. Pfaffenweiler, 1992.

Nehring, Holger. *Politics of Security. British and West German Protest Movements and the Early Cold War, 1945–1970*. Oxford, 2013.

Newman, Kitty. *Macmillan, Khrushchev and the Berlin Crisis: 1958–1960*. London, 2007.

Ninkovich, Frank A. *The United States and Imperialism.* Malden MA, 2001.

Noack, Paul. 'Er kam und ging als Fremder. Charles de Gaulle in der westdeutschen Einschätzung zwischen 1958 und 1970'. In *De Gaulle, Deutschland und Europa.* Ed. Wilfried Loth and Robert Picht. Opladen, 1991, pp. 83–94.

Nolan, Michael E. *The Inverted Mirror. Mythologizing the Enemy in France and Germany, 1898–1914.* Oxford & New York, 2005.

Nozière, André. *Algérie: les chrétiens dans la guerre.* Paris, 1979.

Nye, Joseph. *Soft Power: The Means to Success in World Politics.* Cambridge MA, 2004.

Obitchkina, Evguenia. 'La politique gaullienne vue de Moscou: les illusions perdues'. In *De Gaulle et l'Algérie, 1943–1969.* Ed. Maurice Vaïsse. Paris, 2012, pp. 110–23.

Olejniczak, Claudia. *Die Dritte-Welt-Bewegung in Deutschland: konzeptionelle und organisatorische Strukturmerkmale einer neuen sozialen Bewegung.* Wiesbaden, 1999.

Onyedum, Jennifer Johnson. '"Humanize the Conflict": Algerian Health Care Organizations and Propaganda Campaigns'. *International Journal of Middle East Studies* 44/4 (2012), pp. 713–31.

Osterhammel, Jürgen and Niels P. Petersson. *Geschichte der Globalisierung. Dimensionen, Prozesse, Epochen*, 4th edn. München, 2007.

Pahlavi, Pierre C. *La guerre révolutionnaire de l'armée française en Algérie 1954–1961. Entre esprit de conquête et conquête des esprits.* Paris, 2004.

Panzer, Michael G. 'Building a Revolutionary Constituency: Mozambican Refugees and the Development of the FRELIMO Proto-state, 1963–1968'. *Social Dynamics* 39/1 (2013), pp. 5–23.

Paret, Peter. *French Revolutionary Warfare from Indochina to Algeria: The Analysis of a Political and Military Doctrine.* New York, London, 1964.

Parker, J.C. 'Small Victory, Missed Chance: The Eisenhower Administration, the Bandung Conference, and the Turning of the Cold War'. In *The Eisenhower Administration, the Third World, and the Globalization of the Cold War.* Eds. K.C. Statler and A.L. Johns. Lanham MD, 2006, pp. 153–74.

Parsons, Craig. *A Certain Idea of Europe.* Ithaca NY, 2003.

Pas, Niek. *Aan de wieg van het nieuwe Nederland. Nederland en de Algerijnse oorlog, 1954–1962.* Amsterdam, 2008.

Patterson, Henry. *Ireland's Violent Frontier: The Border and Anglo-Irish Relations during the Troubles.* Basingstoke, 2013.

Pattieu, Sylvain. *Les Camarades des Frères. Trotskistes et libertaires dans la guerre d'Algérie.* Paris, 2002.

'Le 'camarade' Pablo, la IVe Internationale, et la guerre d'Algérie'. *Revue Historique* 303/3 (2001), pp. 695–729.

Péan, Pierre. *Le Mystérieux Docteur Martin (1895–1969).* Paris, 1993.

Perkins, Kenneth J. 'North African Propaganda and the United States, 1946–1956'. *African Studies Review* 19/3 (1976), pp. 65–77.

Perraudin, Michael and Jürgen Zimmerer. Eds. *German Colonialism and National Identity*. New York, 2011.

Perrenoud, Marc. 'La Suisse et les accords d'Évian: la politique de la Confédération à la fin de la guerre d'Algérie'. *Politorbis. Revue trimestrielle de la politique étrangère* 31/2 (2002), pp. 8–38.

Pervillé, Guy. 'Guerre étrangère et guerre civile en Algérie, 1954–1962'. *Relations Internationales* 14 (1978), pp. 171–96.

'L'insertion internationale du FLN algérien'. *Relations Internationales* 31 (1982), pp. 373–86.

Pfeiffer, Rolf. 'Ein erfolgreiches Kapitel bundesdeutscher Außenpolitik: Die Adenauer-Regierung und die Suez-Krise von 1956'. *Historische Mitteilungen* 13/1 (2000), pp. 213–32.

Pfeil, Ulrich. *Die 'anderen' deutsch-französischen Beziehungen: die DDR und Frankreich, 1949–1990*. Weimar, 2004.

Piazza, James A. 'Incubators of Terror: Do Failed and Failing States Promote Transnational Terrorism?' *International Studies Quarterly* 52 (2008), pp. 469–88.

Piazza, Pierre. *Histoire de la Carte Nationale d'Identité*. Paris, 2004.

Planche, Jean-Louis. *Sétif 1945: histoire d'un massacre annoncé*. Paris, 2006.

Plant, J.J. 'John Baird: A British MP Who Supported the Algerian Revolution'. *Revolutionary History* 10/4 (2012), pp. 197–202.

Plum, Werner. 'Algeriche Arbeiter in der Bundesrepublik'. *Gewerkschaftliche Monatshefte* 11/8 (1960), pp. 469–70.

Gewerkschaften im Maghreb. Hannover, 1962.

Plunka, Gene A. *The Rites of Passage of Jean Genet: The Art and Aesthetics of Risk Taking*. Cranbury NJ, 1992.

Poidevin, Raymond and Jacques Bariéty. *Les Relations franco-allemandes 1815–1975*. Paris, 1977.

Poiger, Uta G. 'Imperialism and Empire in Twentieth-Century Germany'. *History and Memory* 17/1–2 (2005), pp. 117–43.

Poley, Jared. *Decolonization in Germany: Weimar Narratives of Colonial Loss and Foreign Occupation*. Bern, 2005.

Polkehn, Klaus. 'Die Mission des Si Mustapha – ein Deutscher kämpft für Algerien'. *Comparativ* 16/2 (2006), pp. 30–45.

Poppinga, Anneliese. *Konrad Adenauer. Geschichtsverständnis, Weltanschauung und politische Praxis*. Stuttgart, 1975.

Porch, Douglas. *The French Foreign Legion: A Complete History*. London, 1993.

The French Secret Services: From the Dreyfus Affair to the Gulf War. Basingstoke, 1996.

Poutrus, Patrice G. 'An den Grenzen des proletarischen Internationalismus. Algerische Flüchtlinge in der DDR'. *Zeitschrift für Geschichtswissenschaft* 55/2 (2007), pp. 162–78.

Prados, John *The Blood Road: The Ho Chi Minh Trail and the Vietnam War*. New York, 1999.

Quandt, William B. *Revolution and Political Leadership: Algeria, 1954–1968*. Cambridge MA & London, 1969.

Ramscheid, Birgit. *Herbert Blankenhorn (1904–1991): Adenauers außenpolitischer Berater*. Düsseldorf, 2006.

Rash, Felicity J. *German Images of the Self and the Other: Nationalist, Colonialist and Anti-semitic Discourse, 1871–1918*. Basingstoke, 2012.

Record, Jeffrey. *Beating Goliath: Why Insurgencies Win*. Washington DC, 2007.

'External Assistance: Enabler of Insurgent Success'. *Parameters*. Autumn 2006, pp. 36–49.

Reider, Bruce J. 'External Support to Insurgencies'. *Small Wars Journal* 10/10 (2014), http://smallwarsjournal.com/jrnl/art/external-support-to-insurgencies (accessed 10 July 2015).

Remaoun, Hassan. 'L'intervention institutionnelle et son impact sur la pratique historiographique en Algérie: la politique "d'Écriture et de Réécriture de l'histoire". *Insaniyat. Revue algérienne d'anthropologie et de sciences sociales* 19/20 (2003), pp. 7–40.

Renken, Frank. *Frankreich im Schatten des Algerienkrieges. Die Fünfte Republik und die Erinnerung an den letzten großen Kolonialkonflikt*. Göttingen, 2006.

Rey-Goldzeiguer, Annie. *Aux origines de la guerre d'Algérie 1940–1945: de Mers-el-Kébir aux massacres du Nord-Constantinois*. Paris, 2002.

Richter, Jan Stefan. *Die Orientreise Kaiser Wilhelm II, 1898. Eine Studie zur deutschen Aussenpolitik an der Wende zum 20. Jahrhundert*. Hamburg, 1997.

Romo, Maria. 'Le gouvernement Mendès France et le maintien de l'ordre en Algérie en novembre 1954'. In *Militaires et guérilla dans la guerre d'Algérie*. Ed. Jean-Charles Jauffret and Maurice Vaïsse. Paris, 2001, pp. 421–46.

Rosenberg, Clifford. *Policing Paris: The Origins of Modern Immigration Control between the Wars*. Ithaca NY, 2006.

Rousso, Henry. *Le syndrome de Vichy: de 1944 à nos jours*. Paris, 1987.

Rubin, Barry and Wolfgang G. Schwanitz, *Nazis, Islamists, and the Making of the Modern Middle East*. New Haven CT, 2014.

Ruedy, John. *Modern Algeria: The Origins and Development of a Nation*. Bloomington IN, 1992.

Ryan, David and Victor Pungong. Eds. *The United States and Decolonization: Power and Freedom*. Basingstoke, 2000.

Sabot, Jean-Yves. *Le syndicalisme étudiant et la guerre d'Algérie*. Paris, 1995.

Sahli, Mohamed. *Décoloniser l'histoire*. Paris, 1965.

Salehyan, Idean. 'No Shelter Here: Rebel Sanctuaries and International Conflict'. *Journal of Politics* 70/1 (2008), pp. 54–66.

Rebels without Borders: Transnational Insurgencies in World Politics. Ithaca NY, 2009.

'Transnational Rebels: Neighboring States as Sanctuary for Rebel Groups'. *World Politics* 59/2 (2007), pp. 217–42.

Samuel, Patrick. *Michel Debré. L'Architecte du Général*. Suresnes, 1999.

Sangmuah, Egya N. 'Eisenhower and Containment in North Africa, 1956–1960'. *Middle East Journal* 44 (1990), pp. 76–91.

'Sultan Mohammed Ben Youssef's American Strategy and the Diplomacy of North African Liberation, 1943–61'. *Journal of Contemporary History* 27/1 (1992), pp. 129–48.

Sayer, Ghislain. 'Le Quai d'Orsay et la construction de la Petite Europe: l'avènement de la Communauté économique européenne (1955–1957)'. *Relations internationales* 101 (2000), pp. 89–105.

Schade, Burkhard. *Das Studium im Ausland als prychologischer Prozess. Orientierungsprobleme bei Studenten aus Entwicklungsländern an deutschen Hochschulen*. Bonn, 1968.

Scheck, Raffael. 'Nazi Propaganda toward French Muslim Prisoners of War'. *Holocaust and Genocide Studies* 26/3 (2012), pp. 447–77.

Scheffler, Thomas. *Die SPD und der Algerienkrieg (1954–1962)*. Berlin, 1995.

'Orientalisten und Orientkenner als Väter der deutschen Politikwissenschaft?' In *Annäherung an das Fremde. XXVI. deutscher Orientalistentag*. Ed. Holger Preissler and Heidi Stein. Stuttgart, 1998, pp. 63–70.

Scheu, Joseph. 'Auf Friedensmission. Algerien-Vietnam-Biafra-Polen'. In *Menschlichkeit als Spiritualität. Georg Hüssler zum 85. Geburtstag*. Ed. Deutscher Caritasverband. Freiburg, 2006, pp. 148–57.

Schildt, Axel. 'Der Beginn des Fernsehzeitalters: ein neues Massenmedium setzt sich durch'. In *Modernisierung im Wiederaufbau. Die westdeutsche Gesellschaft der 50er Jahre*. Ed. Axel Schildt and Arnold Sywottek. Bonn, 1993, pp. 477–92.

Moderne Zeiten. Freizeit, Massenmedien und 'Zeitgeist' in der Bundesrepublik der 50er Jahre. Hamburg, 1995.

Zwischen Abendland und Amerika. Studien zur westlichen Ideenlandschaft der 50er Jahre. München, 1999.

and Arnold Sywottek. '"Reconstruction" and "Modernization": West German Social History during the 1950s'. In *West Germany under Construction: Politics, Society, and Culture in the Adenauer Era*. Ed. Robert G. Moeller. Ann Arbor MI, 1997, pp. 413–43.

and Detlef Siegfried. *Deutsche Kulturgeschichte: die Bundesrepublik – 1945 bis zur Gegenwart*. Bonn, 2009.

Schilling, Britta. *Postcolonial Germany: Memories of Empire in a Decolonized Nation*. Oxford, 2014.

Schmidt, Gustav. '"Tying" (West) Germany into the West – But to What? NATO? WEU? The European Community?' In *Western Europe and Germany. The Beginnings of European Integration 1945–1960*. Ed. Clemens Wurm. Oxford and Washington, 1995, pp. 137–74.

Schmidt, Heide-Irene. 'Pushed to the Front: The Foreign Assistance Policy of the Federal Republic of Germany, 1958–1971'. *Contemporary European History* 12/4 (2003), pp. 473–507.

Schmidt-Eenboom, Erich. *Schnüffler ohne Nase. Der BND – die unheimliche Macht im Staate*. Düsseldorf, 1993.

Scholtyseck, Joachim. *Die Außenpolitik der DDR*. München, 2010.

Schönwälder, Karen. 'Why Germany's Guestworkers were Largely Europeans: The Selective Principles of Post-war Labour Recruitment'. *Ethnic and Racial Studies* 27/2 (2004), pp. 248–65.

Schüle, Annegret. '"Die ham se sozusagen aus dem Busch geholt": Die Wahrnehmung der Vertragsarbeitskräfte aus Schwarzafrika und Vietnam durch Deutsche im VEB Leipziger Baumwollspinnerei'. In *Fremde und Fremd-Sein in der DDR. Zu den historischen Ursachen der Fremdenfeindlichkeit in Ostdeuschland*. Eds. Jan C. Behrends, Thomas Lindenberger, and Patrice Poutrus. Berlin, 2003, pp. 283–98.

Schunck, Peter. 'De Gaulle und seine deutsche Nachbarn bis zur Begegnung mit Adenauer'. In *De Gaulle, Deutschland und Europa*. Eds. Wilfried Loth and Robert Picht. Opladen, 1991, pp. 21–43.

Schwanitz, Wolfgang. 'Djihad "Made in Germany": Der Streit um den Heiligen Krieg, 1914–1915'. *Soziale Geschichte* 18/2 (2003), pp. 7–34.

Schwarz, Hans-Peter. *Die Ära Adenauer. Epochenwechsel, 1957–1963*. Stuttgart, 1983.

Die Ära Adenauer. Gründerjahre der Republik, 1949–1957. Stuttgart, 1981.

Adenauer: Der Staatsmann, 1952–1967. Stuttgart, 1991.

Scioldo-Zürcher, Yann. *Devenir Métropolitain. Politique d'intégration et parcours de rapatriés d'Algérie en métropole (1954–2005)*. Paris, 2010.

Segers, Mathieu. *Deutschlands Ringen mit der Relance: Die Europapolitik der BRD während der Beratungen und Verhandlungen über die Römischen Verträge*. Bern, 2008.

Shawcross, William. *Sideshow: Kissinger, Nixon, and the Destruction of Cambodia*, 3rd edn. New York, 1987.

Shepard, Todd. *The Invention of Decolonization. The Algerian War and the Remaking of France*. Ithaca NY & London, 2006.

Sicking, Louis. 'A Colonial Echo: France and the Colonial Dimension of the European Economic Community'. *French Colonial History* 5 (2004), pp. 207–28.

Simon, Catherine. *Algérie, les années pieds-rouges. Des rêves de l'indépendance au désenchantement (1962–1969)*. Paris, 2009.

Simon, Jacques. *L'immigration algérienne en France des origines à l'indépendance*. Paris, 2000.

Slobodian, Quinn. 'Bandung in Divided Germany: Managing Non-Aligned Politics in East and West, 1955–63'. *Journal of Imperial and Commonwealth History* 41/4 (2013), pp. 644–62.

Foreign Front. Third World Politics in Sixties West Germany. Durham NC, 2012.

Smith, Tony. 'A Comparative Study of French and British Decolonization', *Comparative Studies in Society and History* 20/1 (1978), pp. 70–102.

Soutou, Georges-Henri. *L'Alliance incertaine: les rapports politico-stratégiques franco-allemands, 1954–1996*. Paris, 1996.

Spire, Alexis. *Étrangers à la carte: L'administration de l'immigration en France (1945–1975)*. Paris, 2005.

'Semblables et pourtant différents. La citoyenneté paradoxale des "Français Musulmans d'Algérie" en Métropole'. *Genèses* 53 (2003), pp. 48–68.

Staniland, Paul. 'Defeating Transnational Insurgencies: The Best Offense is a Good Fence'. *The Washington Quarterly* 29/1 (2005–6), pp. 21–40.

'Organizing Insurgency: Networks, Resources, and Rebellion in South Asia'. *International Security* 37/1 (2012), pp. 142–77.

Steinert, Johannes-Dieter. *Migration und Politik: Westdeutschland – Europa – Übersee, 1945–1961*. Osnabrück, 1995.

Steininger, Rolf. *Der Mauerbau. Die Westmächte und Adenauer in der Berlinkrise 1958–1963*. Munich, 2001.

Stevens, Richard L. *Mission on the Ho Chi Minh Trail: Nature, Myth, and War in Viet Nam*. Norman OK, 1995.

Stockwell, Sarah. *The British Empire: Themes and Perspectives*. Malden MA, 2008.

Stoler, Ann Laura. *Along the Archival Grain: Epistemic Anxieties and Colonial Common Sense*. Princeton NJ, 2010.

Stora, Benjamin. *Algeria, 1830–2000: A Short History*. Trans. Jane Mary Todd. Ithaca NY, 2001.

Ils venaient d'Algérie. L'immigration algérienne en France (1912–1992). Paris, 1992.

La gangrène et l'oubli. La mémoire de la guerre d'Algérie, 2nd edn. Paris, 1998.

'La gauche et les minorités anticoloniales françaises devant les divisions du nationalisme algérien (1954–1958)'. In *La guerre d'Algérie et français*. Ed. Jean-Pierre Rioux. Paris, 1990, pp. 63–78.

Le Mystère de Gaulle. Son choix pour l'Algérie. Paris, 2009.

Storkmann, Klaus. *Geheime Solidarität. Militärbeziehungen und Militärhilfen der DDR in die 'Dritte Welt'*. Berlin, 2010.

Streng, Marcel. '"Abrechnung unter Nordafrikanern?" Algerische Migranten im Alltag der französischen Gesellschaft während des Algerienkriegs (1954–1962)'. *Werkstattgeschichte* 35 (2003), pp. 57–80.

Sutton, Michael. *France and the Construction of Europe, 1944–2007. The Geopolitical Imperative*. New York, 2007.

Talbot, John. *The War Without a Name: France in Algeria 1954–1962*. New York, 1980.

Talbott, John. 'French Public Opinion and the Algerian War: A Research Note'. *French Historical Studies* 9/2 (1975), pp. 354–61.

Taubert, Fritz. *La guerre d'Algérie et la République Démocratique Allemande. Le rôle de l'« autre » Allemagne pendant les « événements » (1954 à 1962)*. Dijon, 2010.

'Ideologie oder Macchiavellismus? Die Algerienpolitik der DDR'. In *Trauma Algerienkrieg. Zur Geschichte und Aufarbeitung eines tabuisierten Konflikts*. Eds. Christiane Kohser-Spohn and Frank Renken. Frankfurt/Main, 2005. pp. 245–61.

Ther, Philipp. 'Imperial instead of National History: Positioning Modern German History on the Map of European Empires'. In *Imperial Rule*. Eds. Alexei Miller and Alfred J. Rieber. Budapest, 2004, pp. 47–66.

Thiemeyer, Guido. 'West German Perceptions of Africa and the Association of the Overseas Territories with the Common Market 1956–1957'. In *L'Europe Unie et l'Afrique. De l'idée d'Eurafrique à la convention de Lomé I*. Ed. Marie-Thérèse Bitsch and Gérard Bossuat. Bruxelles, 2005, pp. 269–86.

Thomas, Martin. 'Defending a Lost Cause? France and the United States Vision of Imperial Rule in French North Africa, 1945–1956'. *Diplomatic History* 26/2 (2002), pp. 215–47.

'The Dilemmas of an Ally of France: Britain's Policy towards the Algerian Rebellion, 1954–62'. *The Journal of Imperial and Commonwealth History* 23/1 (1995), pp. 129–54.

Empires of Intelligence. Security Services and Colonial Disorder after 1914. Berkeley CA, 2008.

Flight or Fight: Britain, France and Their Roads from Empire. Oxford, 2014.

'France Accused: French North Africa before the United Nations, 1952–1962'. *Contemporary European History* 10/1 (2001), pp. 91–121.

The French Empire at War, 1940–1945. Manchester, 1998.

The French North African Crisis: Colonial Breakdown and Anglo-French Relations, 1945–62. London, 2000.

'Policing Algeria's Borders, 1956–1960: Arms Supplies, Frontier Defences and the Sakiet Affair'. *War & Society* 13/1 (1995), pp. 81–99.

Thomas, Nick. *Protest Movements in 1960s West Germany. A Social History of Dissent and Democracy*. Oxford, 2003.

Thompson, Robert. 'Rear Bases and Sanctuaries'. In *The Lessons of Vietnam*. Ed. W. Scott Thompson and D. Frizzell. New York, 1977, pp. 73–85.

Tibi, Bassam. *Arab Nationalism: Between Islam and the Nation-State*, 3rd edn. Basingstoke, 1997.

Timm, Angelika. 'The Middle East Policy of East Germany'. In *Germany and the Middle East. Past, Present, and Future*. Ed. Haim Goren. Jerusalem, 2003, pp. 245–62.

Tomlinson, B.R. 'What is the Third World?' *Journal of Contemporary History* 38/2 (2003), pp. 309–311.

Trachtenberg, Marc. *A Constructed Peace. The Making of the European Settlement, 1945–1963*. Princeton NJ, 1999.

Treistman, Jeffrey. 'Home Away from Home: Dynamics of Counterinsurgency Warfare'. *Comparative Strategy* 31/3 (2012), pp. 235–52.

Trentin, Massimiliano. 'Modernization as State Building: The Two Germanies in Syria, 1963–1972'. *Diplomatic History* 33/3 (2009), pp. 487–505.

Treverton, Gregory F. *Covert Action. The Limits of Intervention in the Postwar World*. New York, 1987.

Triepel, Heinrich. 'Die auswärtige Politik der Privatperson'. *Zeitschrift für ausländisches öffentliches Recht und Völkerrecht* 9/1 (1939), pp. 1–30.

Tripier, Philippe. *Autopsie de la guerre d'Algérie*. Paris, 1972.

Troche, Alexander. *Ulbricht und die Dritte Welt: Ost-Berlins 'Kampf' gegen die Bonner 'Alleinvertretunganmaßung'*. Erlangen, 1996.

Tusa, Ann. *The Last Division: A History of Berlin, 1945–1989*. Reading MA, 1997.

Tyre, Stephen. 'From Algérie Française to France Musulmane: Jacques Soustelle and the Myths and Realities of "Integration", 1955–1962'. *French History* 20/3 (2006), pp. 276–96.

'The Gaullists, the French Army and Algeria before 1958: Common Cause or Marriage of Convenience?' *Journal of Strategic Studies* 25/2 (2002), pp. 97–117.

Ulloa, Marie-Pierre. *Francis Jeanson: A Dissident Intellectual from the French Resistance to the Algerian War* Trans. J.M. Todd. Stanford CA, 2008.

Unger, Corinna. 'Histories of Development and Modernization: Findings, Reflections, Future Research'. *H-Soz-u-Kult* (2010) 09 December 2010 (http://hsozkult.geschichte.hu-berlin.de/forum/2010–12-001).

'Modernization à la Mode: West German and American Development Plans for the Third World'. *GHI Bulletin* 40 (2007), pp. 143–59.

Vaïsse, Maurice. *Alger, le putsch (1961)*. Bruxelles, 1983.

'Aux origines du mémorandum de septembre 1958'. *Relations Internationales* 58 (1989), pp. 253–68.

Ed. *La France et l'opération de Suez de 1956*. Paris, 1997.

'France and the Suez Crisis'. In *Suez 1956: The Crisis and its Consequences*. Ed. Wm. Roger Louis and Roger Owen. Oxford, 1989, pp. 131–43.

La Grandeur. Politique étrangère du Général de Gaulle 1958–1969. Paris, 1995.

'La guerre perdue à l'ONU?' In *La Guerre d'Algérie et les Français*. Ed. Jean-Pierre Rioux. Paris, 1990, pp. 541–62.

'Michel Debré et la Défense ou la voie étroite d'un Premier ministre'. *Revue Historique des Armées* 236 (2004), pp. 49–62.

'Post-Suez France'. In *Suez 1956: The Crisis and its Consequences*. Eds. Wm. Roger Louis and Roger Owen. Oxford, 1989, pp. 335–40.

Vertovec, Steven. *Transnationalism*. London, 2009.

Vétillard, Roger. *Sétif, mai 1945: massacres en Algérie*. Paris, 2008.

Villatoux, Paul. 'L'Institutionnalisation de l'arme psychologique pendant la guerre d'Algérie au miroir de la guerre froide'. *Guerres mondiales et conflits contemporains* 4/208 (2002), pp. 35–44.

and Marie-Catherine Villatoux, *La République et son armée face au 'péril subversif': guerre et action psychologique 1945–1960*. Paris, 2005.

Violet, Bernard. *L'Affaire Ben Barka*. Paris, 1995.

Wall, Irwin M. *France, the United States and the Algerian War*. Berkeley CA, 2001.

'The United States, Algeria, and the Fall of the Fourth French Republic'. *Diplomatic History* 18/4 (1994), pp. 489–511.

Warner, Roger. *Back Fire: The CIA's Secret War in Laos and its Link to the War in Vietnam*. New York, 1995.

Weiss, François. *Doctrine et action syndicale en Algérie*. Paris, 1970.

Weitz, Eric D. 'The Ever-Present Other. Communism in the Making of West Germany'. In *The Miracle Years. A Cultural History of West Germany, 1949–1968*. Ed. Hanna Schissler. Princeton NJ, 2001, pp. 219–32.

Weitbrecht, Dorothee. *Aufbruch in die Dritte Welt. Der Internationalismus der Studentenbewegung von 1968 in der Bundesrepublik Deutschland*. Göttingen, 2012.

Wentker, Hermann. *Außenpolitik in engen Grenzen: Die DDR im Internationalen System 1949–1989*. Munich, 2007.

Werkentin, Falco. *Die Restauration der deutschen Polizei. Innere Rüsting von 1945 bis zur Notstandsgesetzgebung*. Frankfurt/M, 1984.

Westad, Odd Arne. *The Global Cold War: Third World Interventions and the Making of Our Times*. Cambridge, 2007.

Wettig, Gerhart. *Chruschtschows Berlin-Krise 1958 bis 1963: Drohpolitik und Mauerbau*. München, 2006.

Whelehan, Niall. *The Dynamiters: Irish Nationalism and Political Violence in the Wider World, 1867–1900*. Cambridge, 2012.

Wigger, Iris. *Die 'Schwarze Schmach am Rhein': rassistische Diskriminierung zwischen Geschlecht, Klasse, Nation und Rasse*. Münster, 2007.

Wildenthal, Lora. *German Women for Empire, 1884–1945* (Durham NC, 2002);

'Notes on a History of "Imperial Turns" in Modern Germany'. In *After the Imperial Turn*. Ed. Antoinette Burton. Durham NC, 2003, pp. 144–56.

Wilkens, Andreas. 'Vom Rhein bis zum Kongo. Französisch-deutsche Wirtschaftsprojekte und Politik in Afrika 1950–1959'. *Revue d'Allemagne et des Pays de langue allemande* 31/3–4 (1999), pp. 481–96.

Willetts, Peter. 'Transnational Actors and International Organizations in Global Politics'. In *The Globalization of World Politics*, 3rd edn., Eds. John Baylis and Steve Smith. Oxford & New York, 2005, pp. 425–47.

Williams, P.M. *French Politicians and Elections 1951–1969*. Cambridge, 1970.

Williamson, Richard D. *First Steps toward Détente: American Diplomacy in the Berlin Crisis, 1958–1963*. Lanham MD, 2012.

Winock, Michel. *L'Agonie de la IVe République: 13 mai 1958*. Paris, 2006.

Winrow, G.M. *The Foreign Policy of the GDR in Africa*. Cambridge, 1990.

Wokoeck, Ursula. *German Orienatalism: The Study of the Middle East and Islam from 1800 to 1945*. Abingdon, 2009.

Wolfrum, Edgar. 'Das Bild der »düsteren Franzosenzeit«. Alltagsnot, Meinungsklima und Demokratisierungspolitik in der französischen Besatzungszone nach 1945'. In *Vom »Erbfeind« zum »Erneuerer«. Aspekte und Motive der französischen Deutschlandpolitik nach dem Zweiten Weltkrieg*. Ed. Stefan Martens. Sigmaringen, 1993, pp. 87–113.

Wright, Vincent. *The Government and Politics of France*, 3rd edn. London, 1996.

Zantop, Susanne *Colonial Fantasies: Conquest, Family, and Nation in Precolonial Germany, 1770–1870*. Durham NC, 1997.

Zasloff, J.J. *The Role of the Sanctuary in Insurgency: Communist China's Support to the Vietminh, 1946–1954*. RAND Memorandum, May 1967.

Zatlin, Jonathan R. 'Scarcity and Resentment: Economic Sources of Xenophobia in the GDR, 1971–1989'. *Central European History* 40/4 (2007), pp. 683–720.

Zeller, Joachim. *Kolonialdenkmäler und Geschichtsbewußtsein. Eine Untersuchung der kolonialdeutschen Erinnerungskultur*. Berlin, 1999.

Ziebura, Gilbert. *Die deutsch-französischen Beziehungen seit 1945: Mythen und Realitäten*. Pfullingen, 1970.

Zimmerer, Jürgen. *Von Windhoek nach Auschwitz. Beiträge zum Verhältnis von Kolonialismus und Holocaust*. Münster, 2007.

Zoubir, Yahia H. 'The United States, the Soviet Union and Decolonization of the Maghreb, 1945–62'. *Middle Eastern Studies* 31/1 (1995), pp. 58–84.

'U.S. and Soviet Policies towards France's Struggle with Anticolonial Nationalism in North Africa'. *Canadian Journal of History* 30 (1995), pp. 439–66.

II Theses

Amiri, Linda. 'La Fédération de France du Front de Libération Nationale: 1954–1962. Organisation politico-administrative'. Thèse de doctorat. L'Institut d'Études Politiques de Paris, 2013.

Bernardot, Marc. 'Une politique de logement: la SONACOTRA (1956–1992)'. Thèse pour le doctorat. Université Paris 1-Panthéon-Sorbonne, 1997.

Carlson, Mark A. 'The Pakistan Safe Haven: Feeding the Fight in Afghanistan'. PhD Dissertation. Air University, 2008.

Cartwright, Hal V. 'Revolutionary Algeria and the UN: A Study in Agenda Politics'. PhD Dissertation. University of Maryland, 1974.

Fontaine, Darcie 'Decolonizing Christianity: Grassroots Ecumenism in France and Algeria, 1940–1965'. PhD Dissertation. Rutgers University, 2011.

Hagen, Katrina M. 'Internationalism in Cold War Germany'. PhD Dissertation. University of Washington, 2008.

Long, B.W. 'The Saar dispute in Franco-German Relations and European Integration: French Diplomacy, Cultural Policies and the Construction of European Identity in the Saar, 1944–1957'. PhD Dissertation. Indiana University, 2007.

Nieder, Heinrich. 'Die französische Fremdenlegion – Légion Étrangère und die Auswirkungen ihrer Anziehungskraft auf Deutsche. Eine sozialwissenschaftliche Studie'. Diss. phil. Universität Nürnberg-Erlangen, 1962.

Prakash, Amit. 'Empire on the Seine: Surveillance, Citizenship, and North African Migrants in Paris (1925–1975)'. PhD Dissertation. Columbia University, 2010.

Quemeneur, Tramor. 'Une guerre sans « non »? Insoumissions, refus d'obéissance et desertion de soldats français pendant la guerre d'Algérie (1954–1962)'. Thèse de doctorat. Université Paris VIII, 2007.

Rueger, Fabian. 'Kennedy, Adenauer and the Making of the Berlin Wall, 1958–1961', PhD Dissertation. Stanford University, 2011.

Schonauer, Karlheinz. 'Geschichte und Politik der Jungsozialisten und der SPD 1946–1973. Der Wandel der SPD-Jugendorganisation von der braven Parteijugend zur innerparteilichen Opposition'. Diss. phil. Freie Universität zu Berlin, 1980.

Schwanitz, Wolfgang G. 'Deutsche in Nahost 1946–1965: Sozialgeschichte nach Akten und Interviews'. Habilitationsschrift, Bd.1. Freien Universität Berlin/ Princeton University, 1995.

Verber, Jason. 'The Conundrum of Colonialism in Postwar Germany'. PhD Dissertation. University of Iowa, 2010.

III Websites

Archives Nationales, Algérie. www.archives-dgan.gov.dz/ (accessed April 2006, currently unavailable).

Friedrich Ebert Stiftung, Bonn. 'Nachlass Peter Blachstein. Biographische Informationen'. www.fes.de/archiv/adsd_neu/inhalt/nachlass/nachlass_b/blachstein-pe.htm (accessed 21 October 2013).

Bönnen, Ute and Gerald Endres. 'Der Algerienkrieg: Kampf an vielen Fronten'. Manuskript und Dokumentarfilm, Erstausstrahlung bei ARTE, 1998. http://home.snafu.de/endres/index.html (accessed April 2006, no longer available).

Brynen, Rex. *Sanctuary and Survival: the PLO in Lebanon*. Boulder CO, 1990. http://prrn.mcgill.ca/research/papers/brynen2_01.htm (accessed 25 November 2014).

Fehse, Erika. 'Si Mustapha Müller – kurze Zeit des Ruhms'. TV Reportage, Westdeutscher Rundfunk, 1992. www.erika-fehse.de/content/kritiken/k_mustapha.php (accessed 12 December 2014).

German Missions in the United States. Word of the Week: *Nibelungentreue*, 28 February 2014. www.germany.info/Vertretung/usa/en/__pr/GIC/TWIG__WoW/2014/08-Nibelungentreue.html (accessed 12 August 2014).

Schirmbeck, Samuel. 'Konspirativ: Wie der hessische Untergrund den algerischen Freiheitskampf unterstützte'. Fernsehreportage, *'Hauptsache Kultur!' Hessen Fernsehen*, 23 March 2002, 21h45. http://static.hr-online.de/fs/hauptsachekultur/themen/230302thema1.html (accessed May 2006, no longer available).

US Army Field Manual FM3–24. May 2014. http://armypubs.army.mil/doctrine/DR_pubs/dr_a/pdf/fm3_24.pdf (accessed 10 July 2015).

Index